Praise for

EINSTEIN IN BERLIN

"A frighteningly vivid picture of the political and cultural upheavals that shook Germany . . . One of history's most absorbing periods, refracted in the career of a key figure." —*Kirkus Reviews*

"An excellent account of both the human and the scientific sides of the scientist during the most crucial years of his life."
—*St. Petersburg Times*

"Meticulously researched, Levenson's work is a marvelous addition to extant Einstein biographies." —*Booklist*

"Of value to all who wish to comprehend modern science in its cultural context, Levenson's sensitive and considered book assays the creativity and chaos conjured up by two of the most provocative proper nouns—*Einstein* and *Berlin*—to have emerged from the dizzying heights and debasing horrors of the twentieth century."
—Timothy Ferris, author of *Coming of Age in the Milky Way* and *The Whole Shebang*

"Vividly portrays the scientist at work and provides a lively narrative of the era . . . excellent." —*Publishers Weekly*

"Told with insight and flourish." —*Library Journal*

"This extraordinarily well-crafted and deeply engrossing book smoothly combines physics, history, and a sympathetic portrait of Einstein's personal life. . . . . Altogether exemplary."
—National Public Radio, Boston (WBUR)

Also by Thomas Levenson

ICE TIME
Climate, Science, and Life on Earth

MEASURE FOR MEASURE
A Musical History of Science

EINSTEIN

in

BERLIN

THOMAS LEVENSON

BANTAM BOOKS

New York • Toronto • London • Sydney • Auckland

EINSTEIN IN BERLIN
A Bantam Book

PUBLISHING HISTORY
Bantam hardcover edition published April 2003
Bantam trade paperback edition / February 2004

Published by
Bantam Dell
A Division of Random House, Inc.
New York, New York

Book design by Glen Edelstein

Library of Congress Catalog Card Number: 2002038570

ISBN 0-553-37844-9

Manufactured in the United States of America
Published simultaneously in Canada

BVG 10 9 8 7 6 5 4 3 2 1

For
Henry and Katha

In memory of
Rosemary Montefiore Levenson
1927–1997

CONTENTS

EINSTEIN IN BERLIN

Prologue

THE ADORATION

IT BEGINS WITH A FAMILIAR STORY, THE TALE OF THE MAGI.

In the summer of 1913, two men came from the (north)east to Zurich, bearing gifts. In their own spheres, the two were kings. One of them, Walther Nernst, a small, round, funny, self-absorbed man, was a brilliant experimental chemist. The other, tall and lean, bespectacled, with a neat mustache and a precise elegance of manner, was Max Planck, inventor of the quantum theory and the most admired physicist in Germany.

They came from Berlin, the kaiser's capital, a boomtown, the center of the world, if one's world was theoretical science. Zurich was no backwater, with its universities and its wealth, but Berlin had the talent and the ambition. Yet Planck and Nernst boarded their train and made the journey, bringing tribute, coming as supplicants. They came to adore a thirty-four-year-old man of obscure origins whose work had burst upon the world of physics as a revelation. In 1913 Albert Einstein was barely eight years into his career as a physicist—a generation junior to the reigning giants of his field—yet he was already acknowledged as the first among equals, the dominant theoretical mind of his day. The two Germans went to Zurich; the magi traveled to the manger. They brought both gifts and praise. But this time, they sought something in return: Albert Einstein, in Berlin.

They did not stint on treasure. To snare Einstein, Planck and Nernst offered him election as the youngest member of the Prussian Academy of Sciences, the German Empire's elite scientific society. They promised him a faculty appointment at the University of Berlin under terms most professors can only dream of: no teaching obligations whatsoever, with the right to lecture as he pleased. They completed their homage with the gift of the directorship of his own physics institute, to be built soon under the umbrella of the Kaiser Wilhelm Institutes. And all this came with a specially funded salary of twelve thousand deutsche marks, the maximum payable to a Prussian professor.[1]

It was, on its face, an absurdly generous proposition—a position specifically tailored for Einstein, intended for him alone, offered him by two of the men he most admired. The subtext was clear: this was the promised land, a place not only of praise but of freedom, both intellectual and financial. Above all Planck and Nernst held out the lure of entry into the charmed circle, the community of the best and brightest that lay in wait in Berlin. Should he go? How could he not? And yet—not so fast. Dazzled but not blinded, Einstein told the two Germans they would have to wait. He needed a little more time, a night to sleep on it. Planck and Nernst acquiesced and left their quarry still uncaught.

In Switzerland on a summer night in 1913, two men, modern magi, waited upon the pleasure of the young prince. Planck and Nernst emerged from their night in limbo and then killed a few more hours on a sightseeing expedition by train. Einstein had promised to greet them on their return, holding a flower. If it were white, he was turning them down. If red, he would come to Berlin.[2]

Midday in Zurich. The city flows around each side of the long lake. The bridges span the river, flowing through the heart of town near the railway station. Einstein's university stands just up the hill to the north of the main station, a grand, vaguely classical building. A little funicular tram runs from its plaza down to the tangled intersection at the center of town. At the turn of classes, students and professors jam in for the two-minute ride into town. A train pulls in beneath the vault of the station. Two men in early middle age step out of a carriage. They look anxiously down the length of the train for a younger man. A photograph from that time shows him—dark, curly, close-cropped hair, deep-set eyes, cleft chin, a dark soft suit, arms crossed. The camera missed the edge of humor, but caught the confidence. The jokester appears on the platform. The older men look to his hands. They see the flower. It is red.

Albert Einstein celebrated his thirty-fifth birthday on March 14, 1914. The day passed without fanfare—there are no cards or letters in the record conveying either congratulations or thanks. He left Zurich one week later, detouring on the way to Berlin through Leyden and Haarlem in the Netherlands for physics talk with some of his favorite colleagues. He traveled alone. His wife, Mileva Maric, and his two young sons, Hans Albert and Eduard, had left before him on a vacation that he chose to avoid. He arrived in Berlin at the beginning of April.

Albert Einstein in Berlin! For all the inducements laid before him, there was still something absurd about the idea. Einstein, after all, had renounced his German citizenship two decades earlier, preferring statelessness to the prospect of mandatory service in the German army. From the other side, Planck and Nernst had, in essence, bought him to be an ornament for the kaiser's capital. As Einstein himself put it, the two men looked at him "as if I were a prize hen or a rare postage stamp."[3] Neither side ever made the mistake of seeing this as a love match. Each sought something from the other, and the story of that bargain, how it was kept and then broken illuminates one of the great mysteries of the twentieth century. The mystery is this: what happened to mutate the ostentatiously civilized imperial metropolis that Einstein entered in 1914 into the city perched on the edge of the abyss that he left for good at the end of 1932, just three weeks before Adolf Hitler became chancellor of Germany? It is no coincidence that Einstein's time in there tracks that transformation so precisely. Rather, his experience in Berlin can be seen as measure of the place. It was almost as if he were a kind of human Geiger counter tracing Berlin's state and fate at any moment for those eighteen crucial years—until that moment came when it was simply no longer possible for Einstein to survive there.

In 1913, of course, he did not have even a ghost of suspicion that events would turn out as disastrously as they did. In fact, for most of his time in Berlin, the man and his adopted home seemed to be compatible. Einstein would write as late as 1931 that Germany and the

Prussian Academy "have granted me enviable living and working conditions during the best years of my life."[4] Still, he was essentially unsurprised by Germany's collapse into barbarism—and it was at least in part his fear of the German *geist,* its spirit, that made him hesitate that one last night in the face of Planck and Nernst's temptations. Moreover, after the decision to go but before the move, he betrayed real fear at the specter of what he called "Berlinerization," by which he seems to have meant some combination of bourgeois affectation and an excessive reverence for authority, adding "God save and preserve me" from such a fate.[5] Yet while he readily accepted that danger in exchange for the promise of time, colleagues and cash, the entire exchange still begs a question. What was in it for Berlin? If this was a bargain entered into freely by two sides, what did the leaders of German science expect to get when they emptied their vaults for one man, that wandering Jew, Albert Einstein?

THERE IS NO DOUBT that whatever Einstein represented to those who sought him out, they wanted him very badly indeed. Planck and Nernst's mission carried with it an incredible array of official glory. The offer to Einstein involved the imperial government, which would appoint him to his governmental position as a professor at Berlin; Germany's leading capitalists, whose money would support both Einstein's salary and the Kaiser Wilhelm Institutes; and the German scientific elite, who would anoint him one of their own by approving his membership in the Prussian Academy. The meticulous organization of the effort to capture Einstein, the offer too good to refuse, the persistence displayed by the two scientists in Zurich, all testify to the extraordinary weight that the powers-that-were in Berlin placed on his presence. All that for a single scientist contemplating such abstruse mysteries as the weight of light and the bend of time. But why?

Einstein understood at least one of the reasons. His self-description as a prize hen acknowledged that he was a trophy to be collected, testament to the taste and glory of the collector. Trophies offer validation, gratification, a seal of victory, of competition conquered. It takes ambition to seek such prizes, and a certain kind of insecurity to require them. Berlin in 1913 was a city marked by enormous ambition and a deep, persistent ambivalence about itself.

The ambivalence had its roots in a fundamental line of tension. Berlin's competition to be what the Germans call a *Weltstadt*—a world-city—came from the other, far more established great capitals of Europe: Paris, Vienna, London. Just as the young German Empire, born only in 1871, entered the Great Power competition at a perceived disadvantage to the older, more practiced British, French, Austrians and Russians, so Berlin had to battle to gain the prestige, respect, even deference that its rulers believed were due.

Exactly what official or elite Germany really wanted to achieve is still not entirely clear. Colonies, respect, wealth, a smashing victory of any kind over the disdained French (defeated so swiftly in the Franco-Prussian War of 1870) or the even more loathed British with their giant empire—all those weighed in. Culturally, unquestioning veneration of German civilization served as a minor national religion, consolation for perceived slights: Germany may have been an infant nation politically, less than fifty years old in 1914, but German culture could claim Bach and Beethoven, Dürer, Kant and Hegel. And in the realm of science, Germany brooked no rivals. With the heritage of such giants as Newton's rival Leibniz, and such nineteenth-century heroes as Bunsen and Kirchhoff, Helmholtz and Roentgen and many others, German researchers in the early twentieth century saw themselves as the leaders in an intellectual and technological transformation without precedent—all to the greater glory of a Germany struggling for recognition on the international stage. "We Germans are the most industrious, the most earnest, the best-educated race in Europe," one German intellectual proclaimed to an American journalist in 1914. "Russia stands for reaction, England for selfishness and perfidy, France for decadence, Germany for progress."[6] While that was special pleading to a neutral at the outbreak of war, the belief it expressed was broadly shared and married to the deep desire to see Germany's glory acknowledged by the world at large.

With progress defined as the goal, the need to exalt German science took on a driven urgency. For an ambitious young nation, science was prime cultural territory to conquer. Support for scientific research served to absolve a multitude of other sins—bombast and vulgarity among them—as when, in 1908, the kaiser gave an ill-judged interview to the *London Daily Telegraph*. Wilhelm told the paper that he himself had prevented Russia from attacking Britain during the Boer

War, and that he had provided the plans with which the British Empire finally triumphed. In fact the kaiser had given veiled comfort to the Boer cause, and had had no influence at all on the British campaign. Missteps and outright, provable falsehoods like these annoyed the other powers involved and so embarrassed him at home that Wilhelm cast about for a way to rebuild his prestige. Adolf Harnack, an entrepreneurial theologian who had his ear, seized the moment to press his plan for new, independent research facilities, places where German scientists could defend what many perceived to be threats to Germany's preeminence in basic research. Each discovery, said Harnack, would shine a light on the benevolent prince who created them. The kaiser seized on the initiative, and gave his blessing to the Kaiser Wilhelm Institutes in Dahlem, a suburb of Berlin. Fund-raising started in 1910, and by October, 10 million marks had been pledged—4 million more than the minimum necessary.

This was German civilization in action. For the kaiser, patronage for scientific research showed him to be progressive, the leader of a modern state. For wealthy Germans, contributions demonstrated both loyalty to their emperor and a willingness to participate in the nurturing of "the best-educated race in Europe." Rich Jews in particular contributed heavily, sometimes seizing the chance to press complaints of official anti-Semitism. The Rothschilds, for example, gave 300,000 marks, while objecting to government failures to promote Jewish scholars to full professorships.[7]

Not all of the upper classes were so moved. The old Prussian aristocracy gave much less. They felt no need to curry court favor, nor were they looking for a path, such as scientific discovery, that would help any upstart group or class establish its position in society. (To make matters worse, the weight of Jewish money itself made the project suspect in some eyes. Science was already being seen as potentially too Semitic, not necessarily the thing a true German could love.)[8] But ample money did come in and the kaiser could claim the credit. Here in Europe's newest great capital, the sober pursuit of knowledge could be made to flourish, both for its own sake and for the good of the state. All that was needed to complete the picture were the individuals who could secure and amplify Germany's scientific dominance.

Hence Einstein. Berlin may have been the world's most notable scientific center—Nernst and Planck were there, of course, and Einstein's friend, Fritz Haber, one of the great chemists of the twentieth century, along with Heinrich Rubens and Emil Warburg and dozens of others. But something more was required, something that could propel the image of Berlin beyond such worthy epithets as "best educated," or "most industrious." To his suitors, Einstein could actually secure Germany's intellectual status both in fact and in the eyes of the world. In a letter to the Prussian Ministry of Education, Planck and his colleagues had written that Einstein had "a worldwide reputation at a young age"; that his relativity theory was "fundamental"; that his conception of time was "revolutionary," an idea that, in its mathematical form, "gives the whole system of physics a new unified character." Einstein was unique: "Among the great problems in which modern physics is so rich, there is hardly one to which Einstein has not brought some outstanding contribution." All true, but not the bottom line. "The interests of the Academy really require that the opportunity that now presents itself to obtain such an extraordinary person be taken advantage of as fully as possible . . . *the entire world of physics* will consider Einstein's joining the Berlin Academy of Sciences as an especially valuable gain for the Academy."[9] (Italics added.)

The ministry agreed, requiring only that the Academy make certain that Einstein would accept before extending its formal invitation. In due course, it dispatched Planck and Nernst to Zurich with their unprecedented offer. That prize pullet Einstein clearly understood what lay behind that offer. Hence the bargain. He would accept the necessity of living in Berlin, capital of a nation he had already abandoned once, in exchange for the freedom to think and to associate with the best of those who thought along with him. Berlin would welcome, even lionize, a man of many defects—a savant spouting incomprehensible ideas, of suspect religious background and dubious reverence for the state—the better to see itself and be seen as the center of civilized Europe. Both sides found the price acceptable.

Chapter One

"SUSPICION AGAINST EVERY KIND OF AUTHORITY"

THE BERLIN SUBURB OF DAHLEM REMAINS A PRETTY PLACE, QUIET, DOMINATED by its university and the science institutes renamed after the disasters of two World Wars in honor of Max Planck. In 1914 it was less than an hour by train on a good day from the heart of Berlin, and its houses were large and comfortable, ideal for a professor and his family. On his arrival, Einstein moved into an apartment in one such house, a flat that his wife, Mileva, had chosen on a visit the previous winter. She and their two sons, aged twelve and four, joined him in mid-April, two weeks later. That household was to survive less than four months.

Marriages end. People once consumed with love grow older, more distant. In this, Einstein and Mileva made a relentlessly ordinary couple. They married; they separated; eventually (despite Einstein's promise to the contrary) they divorced. At first glance, only the speed of the collapse surprises. In Zurich, the Einsteins had seemed to be a functioning family. In Berlin, within weeks, Einstein refused to remain in the same building as his wife. It was no coincidence that the break coincided with the move. A transition that had first appeared as a simple career boost became, or he used it, as the chance to forge a much deeper breach with his past. He had married Mileva at the tail end of a tumultuous adolescence. Moving to Berlin at the near edge of midlife,

Einstein found that he could—or would—no longer tolerate the consequences of that choice. Arrival in Berlin was not merely a beginning; it marked the dismal end of a drama in which Einstein had once been the hero.

ALBERT EINSTEIN WAS BORN in the south German city of Ulm in 1879, the first child of Hermann and Pauline Einstein. Hermann came from Buchau, a small town in Württemberg, one of the petty Germany states. He was one of what were known as the "meadow Jews," from long-established communities scattered through the small towns and farm villages of south Germany. There had been Einsteins, originally Ainsteins, in Buchau since 1665, but by the time of Hermann's birth in 1847, small-town routines had begun to crumble. The emancipation of Germany's Jews had begun in the wake of Napoleonic reforms, though it took until 1862 for the kingdom of Württemberg to grant its Jewish subjects full civil rights. For Hermann, the first step was to attend secondary school in a big city—Stuttgart. He did well there, showing a marked mathematical bent, but his family was large and his two sisters needed dowries, so university was out of the question. Faced with the need to make a living, he abandoned Buchau, this time for the old cathedral city of Ulm, where he sold feathers for mattress stuffing. There, in 1876, he married a young woman—a teenager—named Pauline Koch. They remained in Ulm until 1881, when the young family moved to Munich.

Hermann had married up. The Koch family had been small-town merchants, but they made their move sooner and more aggressively than had the Einsteins. Pauline's father and uncle had entered the wholesale grain trade in the 1850s, building a business near Stuttgart that ultimately became a government supplier. The Kochs educated their daughters. Pauline was thus relatively rich, raised to city customs, sophisticated and smart; eleven years younger than her husband, she nonetheless was the sparking center of her household. She became pregnant in 1878, and almost from the moment that Albert emerged, she fixed on him all the ambition a bright, ambitious young mother could bring to bear.

Einstein inspired some worry early on: his grandmother complained that baby Albert was "fat, much too fat," and he was slow to speak. Family legend had it that he remained silent until his third year, when he finally came out with complete sentences. His first recorded utterance came when he was two. Pauline was pregnant with her second child and Einstein was promised a toy when mother and baby came home from the hospital. On seeing his sister, Maja, for the first time, he is supposed to have asked "But where are its wheels?" He could be a willful child, prone to tantrums that could extend to the point of real violence. He struck out at his sister, once trying to drive a hole in her skull with a toy hoe, and he valiantly resisted the first imposition of formal education, finally striking his tutor with a chair. The woman fled in horror, never to be seen at the Einstein house again. But Albert was Pauline's prize, and she would persuade, flatter, labor as necessary to nurture him. Maja remembered her mother sitting for hours at the piano coaxing, cajoling and ultimately compelling the cantankerous six- and seven-year-old Albert through his violin practice, until finally the boy discovered his genuine love of the instrument. Behavior like this did not go over well at school. At the start, Maja recalled, he was "considered only moderately talented, because he needed time to mull things over, and he wasn't even good at arithmetic, in the sense of being quick and accurate."[1] Unfortunately, in Einstein's first encounter with modern German methods of instruction, his teacher held his pupils' attention by rapping the knuckles of any child who did not answer fast or precisely enough to please him. Einstein suffered.

But not too much. Despite Maja's claim, Einstein was always capable of fine performance, to his mother's immense satisfaction. In his first year of elementary school, when he was seven, she wrote to a relative that "Albert got his grades yesterday. He was ranked first again."[2] The myths that Einstein did poorly at school or that he failed mathematics are only that—myths. With a few exceptions, his marks ranged from good to excellent from primary school into university—and that included creditable work in fields far removed from those he truly cared for. He performed acceptably in the required Greek and Latin lessons at gymnasium, and at university he followed his father's wishes that he gain at least a sliver of useful knowledge by taking—and passing—business classes like Banking and the Stock Exchange and the Mathematical Foundations of Statistics and Personal Insurance. There is no evidence that he ever made any significant use of what he learned in those courses, but the image of Einstein on Wall Street has its charms.

But while Pauline could boast of his ability there was always cause for concern. Even as a small child, Einstein could not hide his contempt for whatever seemed to him arbitrary, coercive or simply stupid in school. For example, Bavaria required all students to take religious instruction, so despite his parents' lack of interest in Judaism, the nine-and-a-half-year-old dutifully began to study with a more pious relative.[3] Almost immediately, he found himself entranced by Jewish tradition, a devotion that lasted about two years. He refused to eat pork, composed religious songs to sing on his way to school, and pondered the biblical stories of creation and miracles. But when he turned eleven he received as a gift Aaron Bernstein's series of popular science books—brightly illustrated introductions to the big ideas of the day. The shock was enormous and immediate. More than half a century later, Einstein recalled that he read the Bernstein series "with breathless attention,"[4] and that "through the reading of popular scientific books I soon reached the conviction that much in the stories of the Bible could not be true. The consequence was a positively fanatic orgy of free-thinking, coupled with the impression that youth is intentionally being deceived by the state through lies."[5]

Einstein went on to write that this loss of faith was "crushing," and that "suspicion against every kind of authority grew out of this experience, a skeptical attitude towards the convictions which were alive in any specific social environment—an attitude which has never again left me . . ."[6] The immediate consequence of this revelation came in secondary school, where he found himself virtually at war with the faculty at Munich's prestigious Luitpold Gymnasium. As he remembered it decades later, the school had been a maelstrom of arrogance and stupidity, its acts of intellectual violence directed at his independence of mind and will, committed not only by the school but by the state of which it was an arm.

One almost pities his teachers. As Maja recalled, one of his instructors lost patience one day and snapped that nothing would ever become of him. When Einstein complained that he had done nothing wrong, the teacher replied that it was impossible to lead a class with him in the room because his attitude lacked the required respect.[7] He hated being treated like this. "The style of teaching in most subjects was repugnant to him," Maja wrote, adding that "the military tone of the school, the systematic training in the worship of authority that was supposed to accustom pupils at an early age to military discipline was also particularly unpleasant for the boy."[8]

The crisis came in 1894, when his parents, uncle and sister moved first to Milan, then to Pavia, in northern Italy, so that Hermann Einstein and his brother could establish a new business there. Einstein remained behind with distant relatives to complete his schooling at the gymnasium. He fought yet again with one of his instructors, and using the incident as a pretext, he persuaded his family doctor to write a note saying he was suffering from an unspecified nervous ailment that prevented him from attending school. He left Munich, made his way to Italy, arrived at his parents' house without warning, and announced his decision to them: he was going to renounce his German citizenship. Statelessness was preferable to allegiance to a Germany he already disdained.

There was a little more to the story, of course. Einstein had a very practical motive for escape. If he remained in Munich past his sixteenth birthday he was subject to conscription into the imperial army. Should he fail to appear when summoned, the law would consider him a deserter. It is hard now to even imagine him as a soldier. As the historian Fritz Stern put it, "The image of Einstein in a field-gray uniform does boggle the mind"[9]—and pity the poor sergeant who would have had to try to turn the young Einstein into any sort of trooper. But the issue was more than just a simple desire to avoid military service. When Einstein became a Swiss citizen in 1901 (after Zurich's municipal police had concluded that he was "a very eager, industrious and extremely solid man"),[10] he did so knowing that the privileges of citizenship brought with them the obligation to enter the Swiss army. As required, he presented himself to the military medical examiners on March 13, 1901, but they found that he had varicose veins and flat and sweaty feet and concluded that he was unfit for duty.[11] There is no suggestion that he minded the snub. At this moment in his life he did not hate all uniforms, just the kaiser's.

Einstein did take minimal precautions before abandoning Munich. He used the doctor's note that declared he was unfit to attend classes to get his formal release from gymnasium, thus avoiding the stigma of school failure. When he reached his parents' new home in Pavia, he promised them he would study on his own for the entrance examination to Zurich's Polytechnic, which was not only a leading technical university but happily did not require candidates who passed the requisite examinations to have completed secondary school. Even so, Maja wrote, his parents were "alarmed by his high-handed behavior," and apparently tried to nudge him back on course; but he "adamantly declared that he would not return to Munich" under any circumstances. Of necessity, Pauline and Hermann "resigned themselves to the new situation with grave misgivings."[12]

Einstein delivered. Maja reported that he worked systematically through the necessary textbooks, though she did admit that "his work habits were rather odd: even in a large, quite noisy group, he would withdraw to the sofa, take pen and paper in hand, set the inkstand precariously on the armrest, and lose himself so completely in a problem that the buzz of voices stimulated rather than disturbed him."[13] The work was not only play for him, it was devotion, almost prayer. The religious metaphor is his. He dated the discovery of his vocation back to a gift he received when he was twelve: "A wonder . . . a little book dealing with Euclidean plane geometry." It was revelation: "Here were assertions," he was to write, "as, for example, that the intersection of the three altitudes of a triangle in one point, which—though by no means evident—could nevertheless be proved with such certainty that any doubt appeared to be out of the question. This lucidity certainly made an indescribable impression on me."[14]

That book was a German version of Euclid, given to Einstein by Max Talmud, a medical student who was a friend of the family and tutored Albert on the side. Responding to the boy's hunger, Talmud followed with more advanced texts, which he also devoured, until, before long, the teacher could no longer keep up with his student.

The examination for the Polytechnic came in October 1895, ten months after Einstein had left Munich. As he had expected—and promised his parents—he did well on the math and physics tests. But his humanities papers were another matter, and Einstein admitted that although his examiners were perfectly kind to him, "that they failed me seemed . . . entirely just."[15] Chastened just enough, Einstein enrolled at the cantonal secondary school at Aarau, a small town near Zurich, with the promise that after graduation, he would be guaranteed a place at the Polytechnic.

Aarau gave him an academic experience unlike anything he had yet encountered. He lodged with Jost Winteler, the classics teacher at the cantonal school, and the Winteler family became a surrogate for his own. Winteler was liberal in his politics and contemptuous of what both he and his lodger saw as the German love of guns and bluster. In the evenings, the Wintelers would sit around the supper table, reading to one another and debating, and Einstein was welcomed into the circle and expected to speak his mind. The Aarau school was similarly progressive, with a new laboratory facility that could have been purpose-built as Einstein's playground. Even his musical talent drew praise. The contrast with the Luitpold Gymnasium could not have been more stark. Aarau became "an oasis of civilization within that European oasis, Switzerland."[16]

Einstein responded exuberantly to the change in circumstances, and delivered on his side of the bargain. Final exams came in September 1896, and he ranked first in his class. Again, the math and natural science tests posed no difficulties, but a hint of what his year in Aarau meant for him came in his French examination. His thoroughly mediocre grade of 3 out of a possible 6 was entirely deserved, given his cavalier approach to the language's grammar and syntax. But he titled his essay "My Plans for the Future" *(Mes Projets d'Avenir),* and brief as it is, only three paragraphs, it conveys confidence, ambition, and a ready sense of irony: ". . . young people especially like to contemplate bold projects," he wrote, and "it is natural for a serious young man to envision his desired goals with the greatest possible precision." Since no one could be more serious than he, he detailed his prospects. Assuming he passed his exams, he expected to study mathematics and physics at the Zurich Polytechnic, with his objective a teaching job focused on "the theoretical part of these sciences." What drove him to this plan? "Most of all, my individual inclination for abstract and mathematical thinking"—though he also acknowledged that his "lack of imagination and practical sense" might have something to do with his choices. He saved the most telling statement for last. He would become a theoretician and a teacher because, in the end, he was "much attracted by a certain independence offered by the scientific profession."[17]

This is the first time—or the first that survives—that Einstein committed his basic credo to paper. The essential catechism never changed. He delighted in thinking and he treasured autonomy, ranking them above all else. He said so here, aged seventeen. He would say the same until his death.

* * *

THE YEAR IN AARAU HAD OFFERED HIM a glimpse of an intellectual utopia. His next stage, at the Polytechnic in Zurich, was supposed to grant him the keys to the kingdom. He enrolled in October 1896, joining what was primarily an engineering school and enrolling in Section VI A, which covered the fundamental sciences: mathematics, physics and astronomy. The class entering with Einstein included just ten others.

At first, university life seemed perfectly congenial. The curriculum was flexible; Einstein could complete his core requirements in just three terms, leaving more than half his time free to pursue whatever interested him. He confessed to some errors in his choices: "I had excellent teachers," he was to write later, "for example [Adolf] Hurwitz and [Hermann] Minkowski, so that I really could have gotten a sound mathematical education." Instead, he haunted the physical laboratory, "fascinated by the direct contact with experience." The choice had its costs: "It was not clear to me as a student that the approach to a more profound knowledge of the basic principles of physics is tied up with the most intricate mathematical methods."[18] He would pay for his error into his Berlin years, as he scrambled to grasp the mathematical ideas he needed to complete his greatest single achievement, the general theory of relativity.

At the time, however, Einstein was incorrigible, and he let his mathematics slide. He responded more readily to the physics curriculum, praising one instructor for his clarity in the introductory course, while writing that Heinrich Friedrich Weber's mastery of thermodynamics was so good that "I am looking forward from one of his lectures to the next."[19] Such passion paid off. In his second-year examinations, he scored a 5.7 out of a possible 6, again the top in his class. But he soon fell off that pinnacle. He later admitted that the Polytechnic made him "suffer much less under such coercion . . . than is the case in many another locality,"[20] for which, read "any German university." Still, by his third year he was cutting classes regularly, reading physics texts on his own. He failed a laboratory class, received an official reprimand for sloth, and angered Weber, his department head, who in frustration burst out, "You are a smart boy, Einstein, a very smart boy. But you have one fault. You do not let yourself be told anything."[21]

Einstein ignored Weber. He followed his own lead almost until the end, taking advantage of "a friend . . . who attended the lectures regularly and who worked over their content conscientiously." With these notes in hand, Einstein gained "freedom in the choice of pursuits until a few months before the examination, a freedom which I enjoyed to a great extent and have gladly taken into the bargain the bad conscience connected with it as by far the lesser evil."[22] He got away with this, but only just. He slumped badly from his midcourse triumph, falling to last among the four students who passed their final examination in 1900.

He could point to distractions beyond physics to explain his performance—and one above all: the lone woman in his class, Mileva Maric, a Serb whose family lived in Novi Sad, a village in what was then the Austro-Hungarian Empire. Einstein had arrived at the Polytechnic as something of a lady's man. He had the looks for the role; he was a gorgeous youth, and even into his forties a family friend would write that "he had the kind of male beauty that, especially at the beginning of the century, caused such havoc."[23] One anecdote has him passing an open window while he was still living in Munich. He saw a young woman practicing the piano. He ran home, according to this perhaps apocryphal story, seized his violin, and ran back to accompany her with brio. He had left behind at least one girlfriend when he fled Munich for Pavia, and in Aarau he had fallen in love with his landlord's daughter, Marie Winteler.

His letters to Marie betrayed a deadly gift for romance. A note from her "made me endlessly happy." His mother laughed at him because "I am no longer attracted to the girls who were supposed to have enchanted me so much in the past." He dropped Marie, though, and very soon: in his first year at the Polytechnic, passing on the news through her mother in a letter that maintained the high gloss of romance. "I cannot come to visit you," he told Pauline Winteler. "It would be more unworthy of me to buy a few days of bliss at the cost of new pain . . . to the dear child." He sorrowed too, he confessed. "I myself have to taste some of the pain that I brought upon the dear girl through my thoughtlessness and ignorance of her delicate nature."[24] Some pain, perhaps—but not much and not for long. In his classmate Mileva, he had someone close at hand to ease any remaining suffering.

He was eighteen then and she was four years older. Some connection existed between them early in their time at the Polytechnic, but the relationship developed real substance in their third and fourth years—the same time that Einstein's academic performance began to slip. In the summer of 1899 he wrote her a remarkable letter, at once callow, the words of an excessively young man, and in some sense desperate, as if grappling with a loss he feels but cannot prevent. "It is interesting how gradually life changes us in the very subtleties of our soul," he told her, "so that even the closest of family ties dwindle into habitual friendship. Deep inside we no longer understand one another and are incapable of empathizing with the other, or knowing what emotion moves the other."[25] This was a love letter.

But Einstein could also be much more ardent, and in the early years he told Mileva often how much he longed for her. As late as 1899, he was still corresponding with at least two other women in language that kept his options wide open, but by 1900, as the end of the Polytechnic curriculum approached, he zeroed in on his "Dollie." His letters overflowed with his unique blend of soft words and physics. In the summer of 1900, they were forced to separate, geographically at least. He had graduated on time from the Polytechnic but Mileva had failed her finals. He had returned to his family in Italy while seeking a job, while she was forced home to present-day Serbia to prepare for a second attempt. On August 1 he wrote, "I just realized that I haven't been able to kiss you for an entire month, and I long for you so terribly much"—and "I long terribly for a letter from my beloved witch . . . only now do I see how madly in love with you I am!" adding with equal verve, "I've been studying a good deal, mainly Kirchhoff's notorious investigations of the motion of the rigid body. I can't stop marveling at this great work."[26] A week later it was "Have courage, little witch! I can hardly wait to be able to hug you and squeeze you and live with you again. . . ."[27] and then again, "Oh how happy I'll be to hold you close to my heart again!"[28]

There were discordant notes. Einstein's mother was adamantly opposed to the relationship, and he let Mileva know in excruciating detail just how much his parents hated her. In one extraordinarily blunt letter he told her that his mother had "shifted to a desperate attack. 'You are ruining your future' . . . 'No decent family will have her. If she gets pregnant you'll really be in a mess.' " He told Mileva with pride how he had scolded his mother for even suggesting the two of them might forget themselves so—but he also wrote that his mother was confident that "ways and means might be found" to break the pair up. That was a challenge, and he seems to have enjoyed taunting his parents. One short poem he sent to Mileva read, "To my folks all this/Does seem a stupid thing,/But they never say a single word/For fear of Albert's sting."[29]

The relationship changed decisively in the spring of 1901 when the two finally saw each other again at the northern Italian resort of Lake Como. There Pauline Einstein's nightmare came true: Mileva became pregnant. The two did not marry. Einstein took on a series of short-term teaching and tutoring jobs in Switzerland and Mileva ultimately went home to her parents in Novi Sad to have the baby. His initial reactions to the news of the birth were those of any young father. "Is she healthy, and does she cry properly?" he asked. "What are her eyes like? Which one of us does she more resemble? Who is giving her milk? Is she hungry? She must be completely bald. I love her so much and don't even know her yet!"[30] Still, despite these claims of affection, the baby, named Liesl and immediately nicknamed Lieserl (little Liesl), swiftly disappeared from Einstein's correspondence. He never saw her. In the autumn of 1903, Einstein asked about Lieserl's bout with scarlet fever in a letter to Mileva—but that is the last time the baby appears in any of his writings. It seems almost certain that she died young either of that illness or within a few years of some other childhood disease.[31] Lieserl was gone, and by all the evidence that has survived, he never expressed any feeling about the loss.

No record remains of Mileva's feelings either, not about her pregnancy, her daughter, or her absent lover. While pregnant, she failed her university exams a second time, ending her chances of completing her degree and starting a career of her own. For Einstein, the Lieserl episode left his relationship with her formally unchanged. As far as he was concerned, they were still engaged, and they would actually marry when he finally landed a job. But that was proving to be a formidable hurdle. He had been unemployed since graduation—and with the passage of time, his prospects seemed to grow only worse. He had expected to get a research assistant post, either at the Polytechnic itself or at any other physics-literate university. But rejection followed rejection from every professor who bothered to respond to his flood of letters and postcards, until, as he told Mileva, "soon I will have honored all physicists from the North Sea to the southern tip of Italy with my offer."[32] He blamed the Polytechnic's Weber, suspecting him of secret character assassination. He grew so bitter that when his former professor died in 1912, the nicest thing he could say was that "Weber's death is a good thing for the ETH"[33]—the name the university had been changed to.

He may have been right about Weber's role in his plight; his academic decline in his last years there certainly left Weber with little reason to help him. But as Einstein came to grasp that he might actually be barred from an academic career altogether, he and his family grew more desperate. In a gesture that would probably have horrified Albert had he known, Hermann Einstein injected himself into the struggle in the spring of 1901, after his son had been jobless for almost a year. He wrote a letter to Wilhelm Ostwald, Leipzig's professor of physical chemistry, that reveals both genuine paternal pride and sorrow at his inability to help him. "Please forgive a father who is so bold as to turn to you, esteemed Herr Professor, in the interests of his son. . . . All those in a position to judge the matter can assure you that he is extraordinarily studious and diligent and clings with great love to his science. . . . He is oppressed by the thought that he is a burden on us, people of modest means." Hermann asked Ostwald to write his son some words of encouragement, "so that he might recover his joy in living and working," and added that if Ostwald could help Albert find a job, "my gratitude would know no bounds."[34]

The request was polite, humble, modest in its hopes, and ineffective. Ostwald did not reply. Einstein never seems to have learned of his father's action. Rather, he simply gave up, forgoing for the time being any hope of reentering the Academy. Instead, he tried to get a job as a secondary school teacher. All he was able to find were short-term substitute positions, and he was finally reduced to tutoring two students in mathematics. He applied for a job with an insurance company—and was rejected. In the end, he abandoned any hope he may have had about remaining even on the periphery of science and turned instead to a classmate from the Polytechnic. Marcel Grossmann used family connections to line up Einstein's famous job at the Swiss Patent Office in Bern. Einstein would later collaborate with Grossmann on some of the most important work of his career, but it was this early gesture that he valued above all. Decades later he wrote to his widow that "without

Grossmann's help I would not actually have died, but I would have suffered a spiritual death."[35]

EINSTEIN LEARNED OF THE PATENT OFFICE post in March or April of 1901. The deadly waiting continued, however; the job was not advertised until December, and it was not until June 1902 that he finally began work as a patent examiner, third class. He moved to Bern by himself early in February. Even with a job in hand, one more obstacle to marriage remained, one that may have surprised the patient Mileva. Einstein could not bring himself to marry without some kind of assent from his parents, acquiescence if not approval. In October 1902, he learned that his father had fallen dangerously ill. He rushed to Italy, arriving just before the end. The two men spoke. Hermann had been quieter than his wife about his son's choice in lovers, but he too had never approved of Mileva. At the last, however, he gave in and consented to the match. Then he asked his family to let him be and turned toward the wall. Albert left the room. On the tenth of October, Einstein's father died, alone.

The sense of rejection was palpable, overwhelming. Einstein, according to his longtime secretary, Helen Dukas, "never recalled [his father's death] without feelings of guilt."[36] He left Italy, returned to Switzerland, and married Mileva Maric in a civil ceremony on January 6, 1903. After the wedding, Einstein had to wake up his landlord to let them in. He had forgotten his key.

That was a bad omen and an accurate one. After all that had passed, the ardent lover of the early letters had already retreated. Just a year earlier he had promised Mileva the moon and stars, his entire devotion: "When you are my dear little wife, we'll work hard on science together so as not to become old philistines—right? . . . Everyone but you seems alien to me, as if held back by an invisible wall."[37] But now, with the reality of marriage and a life together at hand, Einstein had his doubts. His friend and biographer, Abraham Pais, reports that near the end of his life, Einstein told him that he had entered into that marriage with his fingers crossed behind his back, never telling Mileva of his reservations.[38]

She sensed the change from the beginning. She had received the same training he had, attended the same university, but she seems, at best, to have served him as a sounding board, an audience who listened while she did her chores. There was nothing left of the notion that the two of them might work, publish and rise together, as had Pierre and Marie Curie. Einstein did pursue serious scientific investigation almost as soon as he settled in to his job, working on his own research at night, on the weekends, and even in slow times at the patent office. He produced four papers from 1902 to 1904, none of them remarkable but all competent enough to be published in the professional literature. But Mileva played no role in the work. Instead, Einstein sought out the conversation of men, especially two aspiring young physicists, Maurice Solovine and Conrad Habicht, who with him comprised a trio he dubbed the "Olympia Academy," and seeing much of his Polytechnic classmate and now patent office colleague, Michele Besso. Mileva took care of the house, of her husband, and then of their son, Hans Albert, who was born in 1904.

From Mileva's perspective, her situation grew worse in the year after Hans Albert's birth. Nothing in Einstein's prior work hinted at the outpouring of discovery that came in 1905, still called his *annus mirabilis*—his miracle year. Apparently completely out of the blue, he made one of the founding discoveries of quantum physics, the study of the fundamental constituents of matter and energy; he used statistical mechanics to establish the reality and sizes of atoms and molecules; he produced an account of Brownian motion, a mystery more than a century old; and finally, he created the special theory of relativity—all this in a span of just six months. (Einstein's major ideas from this period are discussed in detail below.)

With the possible exception of Isaac Newton in the plague summer of 1666, no one had ever produced such an explosive burst of new ideas; certainly no one has since. There were, of course, ten years of work that went into the creation of an overnight success; Einstein had thought about what became special relativity a decade before, while the issue of the quantum began to press in on him in 1901. Still, he dated his sudden awareness of the solution for relativity to April 1905. Six weeks later, the work was done. The paper was complete, ready for publication.[39] He thanked just one person, Michele Besso, who "stood by me in my work on this problem," adding, "I am indebted to him for many a valuable suggestion. . . ."[40] He acknowledged no debt to Mileva.

Some writers have argued that Einstein did worse than snub her, actually stealing the credit for what was truly a combined effort.[41] He did mention such joint work in early letters, once writing of "our work on relative motion."[42] But there is no record that she significantly contributed to the ideas or the final form that made up the special theory, and the circumstantial evidence strongly suggests that she did not. She herself never claimed to have done so, before or after her break with Einstein. That was beside the point. The real issue was that she wanted genuine involvement in her husband's professional life, and she did not get it.

EINSTEIN, THOUGH, began to enjoy the rewards of his accomplishment almost immediately. The most important early notice came in the form of a letter from none other than Max Planck, even then a great man. Planck asked for clarification of some of the subtleties of relativity—and Einstein rejoiced. From that moment Planck inspired affection bordering on love precisely because that first letter treated the very young man as a colleague.[43]

Other tributes arrived in due course. The Einstein biographer Albrecht Fölsing has traced the widening circle of notice and acceptance—and contrary to Einstein's perception of neglect, enthusiastic responses came strikingly swiftly. The first published notice of the new theory appeared in November 1905 in the proceedings of the Prussian Academy, a bare two months after the September publication of his paper—essentially instantly, allowing for the time lag imposed by journal publication cycles. Those who wrote directly to him about the work make up an all-star list of the great names in German physics. Fölsing's research turned up exchanges with Philipp Lenard, then merely a Nobel Prize–winning experimenter and not the anti-Semitic Nazi collaborator he would become. Lenard may have anticipated Planck (the date of Planck's first letter is unknown) when he sent a reprint of one of his own papers to a delighted Einstein. The legendary Wilhelm Roentgen, of X-ray fame, wrote to the patent clerk to ask him for a relativity reprint. Paul Drude, a physicist whose work Einstein had read and praised at the Polytechnic, cited the paper in two influential books in 1906, this despite an earlier incident in which Einstein, then completely unknown, had written to Drude to correct what he saw as an error in a paper—only to be infuriated by the brush-off he received. The list goes on, with correspondence and reprints flowing from and to everyone, from senior men like Arnold Sommerfeld in Munich to graduate students like Max Born, then in Breslau.[44] And it was only a matter of months before Germany's physicists sent out emissaries to meet the prodigy face-to-face. The first to arrive was Max von Laue, Planck's assistant, dispatched by the great man himself. Legend has it that Laue asked a neatly dressed young man to lead him to the author of relativity theory. The young man, of course, was Einstein, then just twenty-six years old. Much later, Einstein told a friend that Laue was the first real physicist he had ever seen. The friend thought, "Didn't you ever look in a mirror?"

These were the colossi of the German scientific elite; everyone named above had either already received or would win a Nobel Prize for physics. They were the leading powers in German academic science, heads of institutes and departments. The discoveries they made defined the cutting edge of physical knowledge. Most significant, these men offered Einstein a glimpse of an undiscovered country, a Germany wholly unlike the state he had disdained a decade before. Theirs was no parade-ground empire peopled by the pedants and petty autocrats of his Munich school days. Rather, Einstein found himself engaged with a German-speaking, Germany-based elite of talent, one that seemed completely comfortable welcoming a total outsider, an amateur of science, a Jew, a mere patent clerk. The real German Empire was no more attractive to him than it had been ten years before, but this was, it appeared, an alternate Germany, a community of intellect independent of that or any other state. The seduction of a willing Albert Einstein had begun.

Einstein's scientific career in the years immediately following the triumphs of 1905 reinforced his vision of and passion for this borderless commonwealth. He remained at the patent office for a surprisingly long time. The reason had less to do with lack of academic opportunity—though the rigidity of the central European university system did mean that substantive offers were slow to come—and much more with the simplest of reasons. The Swiss government paid its patent examiners better than Swiss universities did their junior faculty. His break came in 1908, when the University of Zurich sought to fill a newly created position in theoretical physics. Money remained the problem.

Its initial offer came in almost 25 percent less than his patent office salary, but Einstein held out and forced the university to match the 4,500-franc total. With that last detail in place, in the spring of 1909 he finally quit the Swiss civil service, and became a full-time member of the professoriat—or, as he wrote to his friend and fellow physicist Johann Jakob Laub, "So now I too am an official member of the guild of whores."[45]

Einstein's rise did not give much pleasure to his wife. As he began to travel in ever more elevated circles, Mileva found herself left farther and farther behind. The move to Zurich pleased her—she loved the city and would ultimately live there until her death—but she bitterly resented the growing distance success put between her and her husband. "With such fame," Mileva wrote that same year, "not much time remains for his wife." She blamed a rival: "I am so starved for love . . . that I almost believe wicked science is guilty."[46]

Almost certainly, Einstein would have agreed. He suggested as much in his frequent declarations of love for science as a refuge from "the merely personal."[47] But at the same time, in a warning of worse to come, Mileva faced more tangible rivals. Einstein's old habit of juggling more than one flirtation continued. He seems to have settled down in the first years of his marriage, but by no later than 1909 he had started to rove. He entered into a correspondence with an old girlfriend, Anna Meyer-Schmid, by then herself married. Mileva discovered the exchange, exploded with jealousy, and wrote to the woman's husband, to whom Einstein then had to write a humiliating letter of apology.[48]

Nothing more seems to have come of that dalliance. Einstein was very slow to forgive Mileva for what he saw as unwarranted intrusion into his private affairs, but the birth of their second son, Eduard, in 1910, helped to ease the tension for a while. Then came a professional move. In 1911, the German University in Prague was able to extract him from Zurich—and temptation—with the offer of a full professorship and more money.

It was in Prague that Einstein truly broke through to the first rank of world science. A Belgian businessman named Ernest Solvay funded the first of a series of invitation-only meetings devoted to the most pressing problems in the physical sciences. Just twenty-three men and one woman were invited to Brussels. The attendees included such stars as Marie Curie; Britain's Ernest Rutherford, the pioneer of atomic physics; Planck; Hendrik Lorentz, one of Einstein's most important predecessors in the development of what became relativity; France's Henri Poincaré, another key figure from relativity's prehistory; and many more. At thirty-two, Einstein was the youngest there. Even so, he was already recognized as first among equals, asked to deliver the concluding lecture. He reveled in the attention. His twenty-year friendship with Curie began then, and his affection for Holland's Lorentz would deepen to the point of filial love. Immediately after the congress, Einstein called Lorentz "a living work of art," and at his funeral in 1928, Einstein spoke with longing of a man whom "everyone followed gladly . . . for they felt that he never set out to dominate, but only to be of use."[49]

Einstein in Belgium in the autumn of 1911 experienced in the flesh the ideal he had first begun to recognize in the reception given to special relativity. For a few days in the fall of 1911, Brussels's Grand Hotel Metropole became home to his dreamed-of stateless nation, a community led by grace and talent, an international village that overlay the real world of brick and stone, of cities and borders. But once again, his triumph fostered Mileva's sorrow. In one of the saddest exchanges in their entire correspondence, written in the context of the Solvay Conference, Mileva told Einstein that "I would have loved only too much to have listened a little and to have seen all those fine people. . . . It has been an eternity since we have seen each other. Will you still recognize me?"[50] Einstein's response was to thank her for a ham he discovered in the hamper she had packed for him on his journey, and to reassure her that "the apples also did an extraordinary amount of good."[51]

Two people talking straight past each other. Mileva wanted a companion and grew bitterly jealous of anyone or anything that kept her husband from her. Einstein sought comfort, and freedom from distraction. Demands from within his home were unacceptable. Every attempt that Mileva made to force her husband to pay attention to her heightened his sense of the fetter, of trespass into his time, thoughts and actions. He withdrew. She pushed herself forward, more and more plaintively. He recoiled.

THE END GAME IN THEIR MARRIAGE coincided with the final sequence of moves that would culminate in Berlin. Prague hung on to him for just sixteen months. Then Zurich struck back, luring Einstein home to Switzerland in July 1912 with an offer that contained within it an element of truly sweet revenge. Twelve years after he had been deemed unqualified as a research assistant there, he returned to his former university, the ETH, as full professor of physics—a position that became available on the death of his old nemesis, Weber. And there matters stood until the next temptation came, in the persons of Planck and Nernst and the looming, awesome presence of Berlin behind them.

Zurich should have been able to hold him. It was the leading city in the country he loved best. Einstein never gave up his Swiss citizenship, even after becoming a U.S. national in 1940. Every day, walking the halls of the ETH where those who had scolded him once ruled was a satisfying reminder of how far he had come. He had colleagues he valued, including his former classmate Marcel Grossmann, the most important collaborator on the work that would become his crowning triumph, the general theory of relativity. He had enough money, a comfortable home, companions with whom to play his violin, familiar hills on which to walk—truly all his worldly desires. He had already demonstrated that he could make himself at home almost anywhere, so another move remained a possibility. But clearly, it needed an extraordinary lure to budge him, one that almost of necessity would have to be a ridiculous offer, far and away the best deal any European thinker could hope for.

That is, of course, what Einstein got in the promised package of Academy membership, directorship of a new physics institute, a generous salary and a professorship without teaching responsibilities. But at the same time there was another temptation, one that Mileva had both anticipated and feared since the Meyer-Schmid fiasco. He had traveled to Berlin in the spring of 1912 to see his mother, who had moved there after Hermann Einstein's death. During this visit he renewed contact with another relative, Elsa Einstein Löwenthal. Elsa, then thirty-six, three years his senior, divorced with two daughters, was both first and second cousin to Einstein—the daughter of his mother's sister and of his father's first cousin. They had known each other since childhood, had played together at the Einstein home in Munich, and had even attended their first opera together.[52] Einstein remembered her as a lively, witty girl, but they had dropped out of touch during his Swiss years.

That brief encounter just after Easter, however, rapidly escalated beyond familial affection.

An exchange of letters followed, at first perhaps merely too warm, then positively scalding. "I must love somebody . . . and this somebody is you,"[53] he wrote Elsa in that same year, before retreating and breaking off the affair. But his restraint lasted less than a year, and his letters resumed where they left off: "I now have someone . . . I can live for," he wrote in late 1913, adding that "both of us will have each other, something we were missing so badly, and give each other equilibrium and a happy view of the world."[54] Einstein's attitude toward his wife shifted from distant toleration to stunning brutality. He dismissed her as "an unfriendly humorless creature who . . . undermines others' joy of living through her mere presence," adding that she "gets nothing out of life" and is "the most sour of sourpusses."[55] He told Elsa not to worry that Mileva was going to join him in Berlin. She did not count, he reassured his cousin, and his marriage was no more than a convenient fiction: "I treat my wife as an employee I cannot fire."[56]

The final phase of the breakup turned truly ugly. The family briefly lived together in Berlin, moving into the apartment in Dahlem that Mileva had found for them. But for her, the situation proved to be even worse than she had imagined. The reality of life with an almost wholly hostile husband was intolerable. She was famous within her family for her capacity for catastrophic sorrow. From the beginning, in the happiest days, Einstein referred to "our dark souls,"[57] a hint at the bleakness of mood to which Mileva, at least, was prone. In that same early period, she described her capacity for despair. Hearing news that threatened their relationship, she told Einstein, "robs me of all desire, not only for having a good time but for life itself . . ." and that "it seems that I cannot have anything . . . without punishment."[58] For her, the life she was asked to lead in Berlin was the ultimate sanction, a disaster, doom.

So, only three months after arriving in Berlin, she and the boys left. While waiting for Michele Besso to come from Zurich to escort them back there to live, they lodged with Fritz Haber and Clara Immerwahr, both distinguished chemists who had been Mileva's hosts on her earlier house-hunting expedition. Haber served as a kind of liaison between the sundering couple, shepherding the last, futile attempts at reconciliation. Einstein wrote out the terms under which he would continue the marriage in a sad and bitter document. He told Mileva that she would have to give up on a personal relationship with him, unless outside circumstances demand they keep up appearances. She must promise to keep his study neat, launder his clothes, and provide him with three meals a day in his room. They would not travel together. And, Einstein wrote, she must commit herself explicitly to three points: She is "neither to expect intimacy from me nor reproach me in any way." She "must desist immediately from speaking" to him at his command. She must leave his office or bedroom "immediately, without protest, if I so request."[59]

At the last moment, Mileva told Einstein through Haber that she would accept even these terms. He wrote back, saying in effect that he did not believe her. He repeated that what he proposed was a "business relationship, in which the personal aspects must be reduced to a tiny remnant." He would behave properly toward her, just as he would toward any stranger. But that was all, take it or leave it. "If it is impossible for you to continue living together on this basis, I shall resign myself to the necessity of a separation."[60] A final meeting on July 29 went badly. That day she left with their two sons.

Einstein accompanied Besso and his departing family to the train station, and Haber came along too. Even then, Mileva hoped for a miracle. Hans Albert later said that she took the break very hard, and that the whole family suffered most during the first months back in Zurich.[61] They lived a vagabond existence, renting rooms in a lodging house while Mileva waited to see if the marriage could somehow be revived. It could not—and from the beginning of their separation Einstein was clear on where he stood. "I don't expect to ask you for a divorce," he wrote her, "but only desire that you stay in Switzerland with the children."[62] He wrote to Elsa that they had parted bitterly, and that "she sees my conduct as a crime against her and the children." In a letter to Elsa he said that he had "sobbed like a little boy" on their departure,[63] but his sorrow did not last out the day. In a second letter that night he told her, "My good fortune is slowly beginning to dawn on me. . . . Surely the pain of separation from my children will ease soon, and I'll be so content that I shall want to envy myself."[64]

Elsa herself quickly felt the sting of this newfound complacency. He had won his heart's desire: a life clear of domestic entanglements, of too close a connection to either his family or his mistress. When his wife and sons boarded their train, he returned not to Elsa's comfortable flat but to the Dahlem apartment.[65] Elsa remained a few minutes away, available to cook or keep him company as needed. But she did not become a constant presence, someone with the right to expect him to answer her when she spoke. Einstein dried his tears, settled himself in his chair, and in the welcome quiet of an empty apartment, began to work.

Chapter Two

"CONSISTENCY AND SIMPLICITY"

TO WORK, THEN, WITH GREAT PLEASURE, TEMPERED ONLY SLIGHTLY BY the Germanness of the experience. "Life is better here than I anticipated," Einstein wrote after a month in Berlin, "except for a certain discipline with regard to clothes and so on, that I have to submit to on the orders of a few old gents so as not to be counted among the local rejects. . . ."[1] Those disapproving elders were his fellow members of the Prussian Academy, worthies who addressed each other by title and dressed for dinner. Einstein, just turned thirty-five, termed his colleagues "peacocklike" in their grandeur. To follow the line of his own metaphor, he seems to have burst in on them with the swiftness and scruffy cheek of a town sparrow, chattering loud enough to disturb the ancient fowl in their roosts.

What constraints there were did not chafe much. There is a photograph from this period, taken shortly after Einstein's arrival. He stands with another man, Fritz Haber, already becoming one of his closest friends, in an empty hall. They are both dressed appropriately in three-piece suits, wing collars and dark ties with wide, heavy knots. Haber leans in a little. Older and much more important officially, he still seems to defer slightly, cocking his head as he turns to face the camera. Einstein stands as he usually does in such pictures, square to the lens, looking intently directly through the photographer to the viewer. He is comfortable, at home.

That image captures the essence of Einstein's Berlin in those first few months. Berlin was delightful, he assured his close friend Paul Ehrenfest, with all that he needed at hand: "A pretty room and an interesting colleague in Haber"[2]—and not just Haber. It was not only the established talents who made for Einstein's satisfaction, men like Planck and Nernst, but the concentration of younger, ambitious researchers who had come to Berlin for many of the same reasons that he was there. These were people like the relativity enthusiast Max Born; Lise Meitner, a chemist who had survived the extraordinarily rigid male hierarchy of the Kaiser Wilhelm Institutes; his astronomer friend Erwin Freundlich; and many others.

It was in the midst of this collection of vivid talents that Einstein came to praise Berlin itself, albeit with an obligatory barb. "I now comprehend the Berliners' smugness," he wrote, "for there is so much happening around them that their inner emptiness does not pain them as it would in a quieter place."[3] Einstein only occasionally collided with that city Berlin, but it was there, and it formed the backdrop to a life spent amidst the largest group of like-minded people he would ever knew.

He quickly settled into a congenial pattern. Most often he worked at home in a large study. He would walk as necessary to the Kaiser Wilhelm Institutes, pleasant buildings set on graceful grounds. His own theoretical physics establishment, promised in the deal that brought him to Berlin, would not open its doors until 1917, but Haber's chemistry facility was up and running, and the two men soon came to spend considerable time together.

The Prussian Academy's weekly meetings brought Einstein downtown, to the heart of official Berlin. The Academy stood on Unter den Linden, the grand, bombastic avenue that runs from the Brandenburg Gate to Alexanderplatz, lined with great state buildings, the university and the library, all guarded by the equestrian statute of Frederick the Great. To get there, he could take the S-bahn, the fast commuter link into the heart of town, thus bringing himself into his most direct contact with ordinary Berliners. Once inside the Academy, however, the surge of the crowd vanished. There, elderly scholars would listen respectfully to presentations ranging from Babylonian inscriptions to the four-dimensional structure of the universe. It was not unknown for a fair proportion of the membership to doze through the sessions. Einstein gave his first lecture to the Academy in early July 1914, discussing his attempt to go beyond his original great discovery, the special theory of relativity, to something still more encompassing, a theory that would include a description of gravity.

This was a project that Einstein had pursued off and on for seven years. He had begun in 1907, when he first focused on what his original theory of relativity could *not* explain. That theory, completed in the miracle year of 1905, describes only uniform motion—essentially what happens to time and space for anyone or anything traveling in a straight line and at a constant speed. That meant that, breakthrough though it was, this "special" theory of relativity was obviously incomplete. In 1907, he began to think about a broader version of the theory, one that would encompass nonuniform motion, anything changing speed or direction. Gravity produces such motion, and its effects were captured in the most famous idea in science: Sir Isaac Newton's law of gravity. But as Einstein examined Newton's law, he found what appeared to be a contradiction between it and relativity—one based on the completely different approach to the role of time within each theory.

That realization that relativity and Newtonian gravitation were incompatible led Einstein to realize that something altogether new was needed—a relativistic understanding of the nature of gravity that would replace that of the great Newton. By 1913, he believed he had succeeded, with a theory that made one clear prediction that could be tested against observations in the real world. One consequence of Einstein's first theory of relativity was the recognition that light has mass. In the new theory he carried the argument one step further. Anything with mass (or energy, for the two categories are interchangeable) must be subject to the effect that produced the phenomenon of gravity. Thus, a ray of light, traveling across the universe, could be bent from its path by the presence of a big enough mass, one generating a large gravitational effect—like our own sun. So Einstein used his new theory to calculate how much a ray of light coming from a distant star should bend as it grazed the edge of the solar disk. The value he found was just large enough to observe—but only at the one moment that stars appear in the daytime sky during a total eclipse of the sun.

The next available eclipse was to occur on August 21, 1914, visible from the Crimean Peninsula in the south of Russia. Erwin Freundlich, a young astronomer based in Berlin, had pursued Einstein since 1911, looking for ways to validate the physicist's emerging theory of gravity. Now he was prepared to lead a team of three equipped with four astronomical cameras, to photograph throughout the two-minute window of totality during which stars close to the sun could be seen.

Einstein did not have much to do with the detailed planning for the observations. He had little practical knowledge of astronomy, and Freundlich was on hand to handle the technical problems of photographing an eclipse. Einstein's task was to secure the cash needed for the trip, five thousand marks. Two thousand came from the Prussian Academy, to cover the cost of the instruments and technical supplies. The balance was found by Emil Fischer, a Nobel laureate chemist and a force behind the creation of the Kaiser Wilhelm Institutes. Fischer was a fund-raiser of genius, able to extract the large sums he needed from German industry. This time, it was Krupp's turn, and a foundation established by the steel and arms giant handed over the three thousand marks necessary to cover Freundlich's travel and living expenses.

With that, the German scientific establishment killed two birds with a single grant. They petted and soothed their latest acquisition, giving Einstein the satisfying sensation of seeing his work properly, even lavishly, supported. At the same time, they backed the bet that had made them seek him out in the first place. The stakes were, in fact, enormous. The theory being tested was as ambitious as it gets. A theory of gravity is a theory of the structure of the universe as a whole. Only one man had found such a construct so far: Sir Isaac Newton. But if Einstein were right, then bravo for him—and for Germany too, glowing in the reflected prestige of the man who surpassed the greatest name in the history of science, the irreducibly English Newton.

This was a prize worth a gamble, but for all of Einstein's confidence, most of his colleagues believed that it was beyond his or anybody's grasp. Planck had tried again and again to warn Einstein off. On his recruiting trip to Zurich in 1913, he said, "As an older friend, I must advise against it. . . . In the first place, you won't succeed, and even if you do, no one will believe you."[4] Most scientific peers in Berlin agreed, neither understanding Einstein's methods nor seeing much value in his results to date. The issue boiled over at a lecture in Vienna in the fall of 1913, when Einstein confronted an audience that challenged him on each component of his theory. His antagonists concerned themselves with this new idea "only with," in his words, "the intention of killing it dead."[5] The discussion grew heated, occasionally almost insulting, but he waited out the storm. Finally, he responded to the hubbub by saying mildly that he and they would have to wait for, and abide by, the observations to come.[6]

To Einstein, the matter was simple: if you believed special relativity, then Newton's theory of gravity could not be true. The reason why emerges from the essential structure of the special theory, which is almost shockingly simple. Einstein's great accomplishment in 1905 had been to take just two concepts, both known to all physicists of his day, think about them deeply, and from them derive the entire conceptual apparatus of special relativity.

The first of those two ideas was the "relativity principle," originally formulated by Galileo, which held that the laws of physics behave in exactly the same way for anyone standing still and for anyone else moving at a constant speed. The second principle on which Einstein based his reasoning was the discovery, first suggested by the work of James Clerk Maxwell in the 1850s, that the speed of light in a vacuum is a constant, identical for all observers throughout the universe whether moving or not. The problem was that the two statements were, or seemed to be, incompatible.

The conflict revealed itself in a very simple issue, the question of the addition of velocities. In its most basic form, the problem goes like this: If a person walks along a railway car within a train traveling in a straight line at a constant speed of ten miles per hour, how fast is she moving? To the woman on the train, her speed is her walking pace of three miles an hour. To someone standing on the embankment, the woman on the train is moving at her own pace plus the speed of the train, for a total of thirteen miles per hour. Both observations, of course, are right, and it was Galileo who first worked out the mathematical rules to show that both accurately describe the same event. Those rules are called the Galilean transformations. In the formal language in which Einstein first learned all this, Galileo's principle of relativity holds that the laws of mechanics are invariant under the Galilean transformations. Put more simply, Galilean relativity states that both observers can use the same laws to make the same kinds of measurements, and that both their observations can be shown to be equivalent accounts of the identical physical situation.

What all this meant was that if light obeyed Galileo and Newton, its speed too should change for different observers. If one of them stands still next to a beam of light while another runs alongside it, then, using classical (that is, Newtonian) reasoning, the person standing still should measure one speed for light, the 186,000 miles per second predicted by Maxwell, but the person running alongside the beam should find a different value. He ought to measure a velocity of light of 186,000 miles per second, less the speed at which he runs, perhaps twelve miles an hour. Remember the image of the train: if you run alongside the train, then the train will move more slowly away from you than if you simply stand still and let it pass. And so this should be for light, if you believe Newton.[7]

To most of Einstein's contemporaries, this is the way a well-behaved universe would behave. The same reasoning holds, no matter how complicated the setup. Under Newton's laws, different observers moving in different directions and speeds should measure different values for the velocity of a given ray of light, values that could be reconciled by Galileo's principle of relativity. Yet no one ever did. Relentlessly, stubbornly, throughout the last years of the nineteenth century, the speed of light never varied, no matter how precise the experiment, no matter what the motion of the experimental apparatus. Maxwell was right and Newton was wrong—*had* to be wrong—at least where light was concerned. It was a scandal.[8]

It was an obvious scandal, too, one that many others besides Einstein recognized as a fundamental issue. The most sophisticated looked for the simplest assumptions they could find about physical reality that would allow them to preserve both Newton and Maxwell essentially intact. The person who probably came closest to that kind of solution was the Dutch theorist Hendrik Lorentz. Along with the Irish physicist George Fitzgerald, he suggested that objects could actually change their shape as they sped up, becoming shorter along the direction of their travel. Then, with the aid of some complex mathematical manipulations, Lorentz demonstrated that this shrinking would produce the paradoxical effect that both the observer standing still (who does not change his shape) and the one running as fast as she could, shrinking appropriately as she went, would now both be able to measure exactly the same speed for a beam of light racing past both of them.

In one sense all this was an accounting trick—a fudge to make the numbers come out right. Even its inventors accepted the fact that the physical picture behind the math was very odd indeed: it seemed to fly in the face of logic to accept the notion that objects actually changed their shape, their physical form, with every change in their motion. But even that leap was acceptable, given that the new theory preserved Newton's laws, with the addition of this one concept that came to be called the Lorentz-Fitzgerald contraction. And in fact, the idea does work. The rules Lorentz discovered (called the Lorentz transformations, superseding Galileo's) are still used to relate measurements by different observers. But the underlying idea remained no more than a wild guess about the way nature actually works, a gambit aimed at preserving the cherished ideas of generations of physicists.

Einstein's approach turned on one of his unique gifts—his ability to transform an apparently impenetrable thicket of physical ideas into the simplest possible image with what were known as "thought experiments." These were flights of the imagination in which it was possible to analyze events in ways that simply couldn't be done in the real world. By framing his ideas in pictures Einstein found himself able to strip a physical system or problem down to its pure essence, the simplest form possible. He could then ask questions—run the movie—to see how different events would play out in his abstract, imagined version of physical reality. His very first thought experiment had come to him in 1895, when he was just sixteen, and it contained the germ of the idea that ultimately became the special theory of relativity. What would it be like, he asked, to ride a beam of light, moving with it at precisely its speed of travel?

His answer then was inconclusive, disappointing. If you could ride the beam of light, as he knew, the conventional Newtonian worldview would tell you that the waves of light traveling with you would appear to you to be standing still. He already knew that Maxwell's theory declared that this couldn't happen: in formal language, it said that a stationary electromagnetic wave field could not exist. It was a significant insight. Such a contradiction meant that this was a real problem, a fissure in the structure of physical knowledge. At sixteen he lacked the knowledge he needed to tackle relativity itself. But the image stayed with him, and he continued to contemplate the scandal of relative motion for the next ten years, through the polytechnic, unemployment, and into his tenure at the patent office.

When he finally arrived at his solution to the problem of relative motion, the answer emerged astoundingly quickly. Einstein finally grasped that if the speed of light were truly a constant, something else had to give. All that had to be sacrificed was the belief that time is absolute, that there is one clock that ticks for the entire universe, beating out seconds that are the same for all. More formally, his crucial insight came when he realized that "time cannot be absolutely defined." Observers in motion with respect to each other will perceive time passing at different rates, as measured by the clocks each observer holds.

To work out what that meant in practice—how measurements of time and distance vary depending on one's motion—Einstein analyzed the concept of simultaneity: what it means to say that two events happen at the same time. Once again, the solution turned on one of his trademark thought experiments. This time he imagined two observers, one standing at the midpoint of a moving train and one on the embankment next to the tracks. Then he pictured two bolts of lightning striking each end of the train at the instant that the watcher on the train passed the luckless soul standing by the tracks amid the storm. The question Einstein asked himself was: Do both observers agree that the two bolts of lightning hit the train at the same time?

The pivotal moment came when he understood that the answer has to be no. The man on the embankment sees the strikes as simultaneous, but the one on the train does not. How can this be, given that both of them are describing the same events? Einstein's answer is, in effect, Take what you know seriously. Light has a fixed speed. The signal that carries the image of the lightning bolt from the end of the train to the observer's eye, the beam of light that you or I would see and recognize as a lightning strike, has to cover some distance to get from where the bolt hits to where the two weather-watchers happen to be. To reach the observer on the embankment, standing still relative to the train, the signal—the light from each bolt—has to cover the same distance: half the length of the train. Each signal will take the same amount of time (the speed of light is a constant, fixed for both bolts) to cover an identical distance—and both signals will reach the observer at the same instant: the precise time that he says both bolts hit the train.

But for the watcher on the train, the situation is different. She is moving as the bolts hit. In the time it takes for the light to travel from the strikes to where she stands, she and the train will have traveled some small distance. The light from the forward strike will have a slightly shorter distance to travel before it reaches the eye of the traveling observer than the light from the rear, chasing the advancing motion of the train. This observer will see first the flash from the forward bolt, and then, an instant later, the flash from the trailing one. In other words, the two strikes occur at different times for this observer, one slightly before her counterpart standing next to the train sees his "simultaneous" flashes, and one slightly after. These two people in two different states of motion cannot agree on the timing of the identical events. Thus, Einstein concluded, simultaneity has only relative significance.

That was the key idea that underlies the special theory. The issue for physics, Einstein argued in the completed work, did not lie with imagined processes like Lorentz's contraction. Rather, what was needed was a whole new way of thinking: a new way of understanding—and measuring—the concepts of both space and time.

It was a huge ambition, and Einstein masked it—but only a little. Sometime during the five weeks it took him to work out the finished theory, he wrote with deliberate lack of fanfare to his friend Conrad Habicht. The work was "only a rough draft at this point . . . which employs a modification of the theory of space and time," he said, but not to worry: "The kinematic part [on motion] will surely interest you."[9] When the paper was complete, Einstein let his feelings show more readily, telling another friend that his "joy is indescribable."[10] He submitted the paper to the *Annelen der Physik* in June 1905, and on September 28 the work appeared under the modest title "On the electrodynamics of moving bodies."

In this paper, Einstein fleshed out his new thinking with an analysis of simultaneity, formalizing the reasoning outlined above with a clear definition of what it means to say that some event has occurred at a particular time. Time, he argued, is measured by clocks; in a crucial sense, time *is* the ticking of a clock, the measurement itself. To assert that an event occurs at a particular moment simply means that the observer notes that a given event occurs as his clock reads one particular number. If, as he wrote, someone in a railway station asserts that a train arrives at seven, "that means, more or less, 'the pointing of the small hand of my clock and the arrival of the train' are simultaneous."[11] This in turn means that all measurements of time are records of simultaneous events—and all such measurements are subject to the same problem experienced by the two observers trying to measure the lightning flashes. Because no two observers in motion relative to each other can agree on simultaneity, they cannot agree on *any* measurement of time.

Next, he went on to prove that measurements of both time *and* distance vary systematically, depending on the motion of observer and/or the object to be measured. Again, he emphasized the importance of the measuring apparatus, in this case a standard length rod, a measuring stick. Using reasoning similar to that of the example with the lightning bolts, he showed that an observer standing still, for example, will come up with one measurement for a measuring rod held in the hand of an observer moving past her. Meanwhile the moving observer will record a different number for its length. The difference turns on the fact that both observers have to time the moment at which they measure the position of the front and the back of the object. Because observers' measurements of time will vary, so will their accounts of distances. The faster the motion, the greater the effect. Again, as with time, two observers in motion relative to each other cannot agree on their measurement of space.

With that, Einstein was finally able to show how the speed of light remains constant for all observers. Speed is simply a measurement of the distance traveled divided by the time it takes to get there (sixty-five miles, traveled in one hour, works out to the speed limit on U.S. interstate highways). That ratio—distance/time—can remain constant for different observers if their measurements of distance and time vary consistently—which is exactly what Einstein argued. This arithmetical argument yields a set of equations, a restatement of Lorentz's transformations, which uses one constant, the velocity of light, to reconcile any two observers' view of events.

Relativity as cosmic bookkeeping: Einstein's theory, at bottom, is simply a tool to reconcile different descriptions of the same reality. But the implications of the way he balances his books were stunning. For example, in that first paper he noted that a clock at the North Pole must run just slightly faster than an identical clock at the equator. Beyond that result, Einstein came up with one argument to show how the speed of light acts as a speed limit. (A simplified version of his answer comes from calculating what happens to the equations of special relativity as speeds approach that of light: time slows to a stop, masses reach infinity, and distances shrink to nothing. As the joke runs, 186,000 miles per second is not just a good idea, it's the law.)[12] And finally, in a three-page paper submitted in September 1905, Einstein used relativistic reasoning to analyze the formal concepts of kinetic energy (the energy of a body in motion) and mass. Using special relativity, he was able to derive a simple formula that asserted that the two, mass and energy, are equivalent, different forms of the same stuff, bound together in an extraordinarily simple relationship. The equation he found states that the amount of energy represented by a given amount of mass is equal to that mass multiplied by the speed of light squared, which yields an enormous number.[13] Einstein originally wrote the mathematical expression of that statement this way: $K_0 - K_1 = L/V^2 * v^2/2$. Its more familiar form is $E = mc^2$. It was not just commonsense notions about time and space that Einstein overturned; plain "facts" about the nature of the material world were also under siege.[14]

This was not only good news, it was great news, for strange as relativity might have seemed, it made sense of the nonsensical. His version of relativity expanded Galileo's, bridging the gap between the new science of electricity with the older mechanics. The fixed speed of light, far from being the problem that had to be explained away, became the solution, the single constant that made it possible to interpret each observer's different view of the universe. But the bad news for older ways of thought—and for many older thinkers—came with relativity's repeated assaults on basic notions and principles. Most important, the relativistic view banished the comforting notion of some absolute referent in the universe. God's clock and God's ruler do not trace out the span of the cosmos. Rather, Einstein showed, statements about time and space make sense only within each observer's frame of reference. All measurement, all perspective, is local.

Nearly a century later, it is almost impossible to convey the shattering power of this idea, the way that one simple argument recast the whole worldview of physics. The theory compelled those for whom the problem mattered to alter their fundamental picture of how nature worked—and many, perhaps most, people do not like that kind of experience. Einstein himself tried from the start to downplay the untoward quality of his new theory. He always resisted calling the work revolutionary. He even tried to avoid the name *relativity* at all, arguing that the chief point of his work was invariance, the demonstration that the laws of physics, including electromagnetism, do not change no matter how one moves through the universe. But Max Planck knew better. As one of the editors of the *Annelen,* he saw the paper early, and apparently grasped its significance almost immediately. He understood that the flexible character of time and space was both the intellectual and emotional core of the idea—and he used the term *relativity* years before Einstein did. But even though Einstein finally surrendered on the name, he continued to resist the suggestion that his work was recklessly new. Relativity itself, he argued, was simply the logical development of ideas already in the making, and if he had not come up with it when he did, there were others who were on the brink of doing so.[15]

That was true, as far as it went. Special relativity does represent the culmination of classical physics, the final, corrected version of work pursued across three centuries, rather than one of the radical departures that were to be completed over the next twenty-five years. But the heart of the matter is that the special theory compelled physicists to alter not just details but basic approaches. Unsurprisingly, Einstein himself realized first that the truly revolutionary impact of relativity lay not simply in what it said but in what it forced him to do next.

The problem emerged innocently just two years after his initial discovery. In 1907 he had been invited to prepare a review article summarizing the state of relativity. But in the course of analyzing its applications across physics, he began to confront the fact that gravity presented relativity with a real challenge. He knew, of course, that gravitation highlighted what the special theory left out—anything to do with nonuniform motion, including the acceleration produced by the pull of gravity. But the deeper problem lay with a direct clash between Newton's gravity and relativity, even limited as it then was. Once again, time lay at the heart of the matter. Time plays no role in Newton's theory. Gravity is always there, to be felt immediately whenever two objects appear. The theorist Michio Kaku illustrates this with a striking example. What would happen, he asks, if the sun were suddenly to disappear? How quickly would we on earth cease to feel the tug of its gravitational attraction, and fly off inexorably into cold, dead space? According to Newton's description of gravity, the catastrophe would be felt instantly, the effect of the sun's gravity vanishing before any other hint of disaster could reach us.

But that cannot happen in a cosmos governed by relativity. Nothing, no signals, no events, not even information about events, can travel faster than the speed of light. Light takes eight minutes to travel from the sun to the earth. In any theory of gravity compatible with relativity, the effect of a change in the sun has to take at least that long to be felt. We would neither see the image of the sun vanish, nor feel any consequences, until eight minutes after the calamity that destroyed our star had occurred.

There it was, a flat disagreement between Newton's gravity and Einstein's relativity. Only one of the two theories could be correct—and Einstein bet on relativity. Never mind that there was nothing obviously wrong with Newton's theory as a description of nature. In plain language the classical law of gravity describes a force that acts between any two bodies, pulling them toward each other. That gravitational attraction is equal to the product of the two masses divided by the square of the distance between them, all multiplied by a constant. (The formula expressing this thought reads $F = gMm/d^2$). When Newton published this law in his *Principia Mathematica,* that one formula generated one of the most remarkable findings of the scientific era, the discovery of the planet Uranus. It linked events on earth—the fall of the apple—with dynamics that spanned the universe, from the constancy of the moon's orbit to the behavior of the most distant stars in the sky. And except for one seemingly minor observational anomaly—an unexplained wobble in the orbit of Mercury—the theory worked astonishingly well. Einstein did not care. As he saw it, gravity should bend to the basic rules that govern the relativistic universe. If it did not—if Newton's theory failed the test of special relativity—then it had to be replaced with something else, an idea that was compatible with the special theory.[16]

So Einstein set out to develop a theory of gravity of his own. He outlined the beginnings of the work in the 1907 review paper, and proceeded to develop his thinking over the next year. He then put the question aside, for the most part, until 1911. He switched his focus back to the mysterious problem of the quantum, the bizarre new theory about the behavior of energy (and matter too, after 1912) on the very smallest scales, to which he had made a fundamental contribution in that miracle year of 1905. He paused briefly to complete some work on statistical physics. (In 1910 he published what is now accepted as the definitive physical answer to the question "Why is the sky blue?" in a paper on a phenomenon called critical opalescence.) But at last he returned to the gravitation problem, working in collaboration with two old friends, Marcel Grossmann, his colleague at the ETH, and Besso, still a patent officer in Bern. Finally, in 1913 he published what he believed was the final form of the new, more general relativistic theory. It contained specific predictions, including the amount of the deflection of light around the sun—the number he hoped to confirm with Freundlich's eclipse expedition.

As it turned out, the theory itself was still unfinished, and its history is set out below in Chapters Five and Six. It would require another two years of hard thinking to bring Einstein to his ultimate conclusion. In all, it took him more than ten years from the completion of special relativity, eight years from his first formal statement of the problem, to reach his final answer. He stuck it out because he had to. The idea that gravity might escape relativity seemed messy, unnecessary, ultimately unacceptable. "The simpler our picture of the external world and the more facts it embraces," he wrote in a kind of physicist's credo, "the stronger it reflects in our minds the harmony of the universe."[17]

Thus Einstein's faith. But even among those who accepted the special theory swiftly and eagerly, few followed its logic all the way through. Special relativity was right, it worked, it closed the terrifying sinkhole that had opened up in the midst of the old physics, and that was sufficient. But Einstein's approach to gravity pushed relativity beyond itself into parts of physics that had seemed just fine, so why bother? As Planck had said, even success would not matter because no one would believe him.

Against that wall of indifference, Einstein countered in words that still sound strange coming from a scientist. "I am now completely satisfied," he wrote of his theory to Besso in 1913, "and no longer doubt the correctness of the whole system, no matter whether the solar eclipse observation succeeds or not."[18] Observations did not matter, Einstein seemed to be saying; the pure elegance of the thinking was what counted. He explicitly applied the idea of beauty as an arbiter of scientific truth. This was more than confidence. The traditional measure of discovery was nature. Either a theory agreed with observation and was held to be valid or it did not and it failed. In the end, Einstein did not claim that his ideas could stand repeated failure. But he believed, both in 1913 and thereafter, that a theory needed to be beautiful, formally graceful, if it was to capture a glimpse of nature in action.

This explains in part why Einstein in his first months in Berlin found himself facing resistance. To overturn Newton because, in effect, his new theory was more elegant, more complete, was simply not good enough for his colleagues. Even his patron, Max Planck, described him as one who "runs the risk of losing himself occasionally in dark regions and encountering unexpected hard contradiction."[19] Logical virtuosity was fine for mathematicians, but physicists examine the material world, and from that alone (as Einstein certainly agreed) could come final sanction for any new claim of principle. His prestige was enough to secure him a hearing and the funds needed to check the theory. But that was all. His word was not good enough; what was needed were data, Freundlich's photographs of starlight bent by the sun.

Freundlich and his two companions set out for the Crimea, leaving Berlin on July 19, 1914, reaching their destination the following week. The four cameras arrived safely and preparations seemed on target for the August 21 deadline. There had been a hint of a possible difficulty a few weeks earlier, but by the middle of July the problems seemed under control. Barring clouds over the sun during the critical two minutes of totality, from a scientific point of view there was every hope of success.

Chapter Three

"THIS 'GREAT EPOCH' "

JUNE 28 MARKS THE ANNIVERSARY OF A FAMOUS VICTORY AND A DEVASTATING defeat, the triumph of the Turks over the Serbs at Kosovo in 1389. That battle and its legacy shaped the ethnic divisions of the Balkans, securing the westward expansion of Islam into Bosnia-Herzegovina and leaving the Orthodox Christian Serbs with a memory of oppression and defeat that goads nationalistic passion to this day. The Ottoman Empire held Bosnia for almost five centuries, until the Hapsburg monarchs of the Austro-Hungarian Empire—the Ottomans' ancestral rivals—finally managed to wrest control of the province in 1908. The Serbs were again denied, this time on the more subtle battlefield of big power politics, and in patriotic circles hatred of Austro-Hungarian imperialism deepened with the fear that Serbia itself might be annexed next.

Humiliation compounds itself. By 1914, Serb nationalists were gripped by recent memory compounding ancient rage. It was a posture of perpetual grievance, and it is a measure of their capacity for self-immolation that the Serbs chose June 28 for their national day. To pick that date for an Austrian state visit to Bosnia's capital city of Sarajevo was thoughtless at best, a deadly insult at worst.

On the morning of June 28, 1914, Archduke Franz Ferdinand, heir to the Austro-Hungarian throne, entered an open car accompanied by his wife. They were a handsome middle-aged couple, he in uniform wearing the trademark feathered cap of the Austrian infantry, she a model of haut-bourgeois elegance, carrying roses and wearing a veil beneath her broad-brimmed hat. They began the day cordially, smiling at those who approached their car, gracefully adapting to the ritual of official ceremony. Across the continent on the Baltic seashore, another potentate was enjoying a less constrained day. Kaiser Wilhelm II of Germany, a recent guest at the archduke's palace, was aboard his yacht *Meteor* in the midst of the fleet gathered for the annual Elbe regatta. Kiel week was the height of the German yachting season, and there was an international audience, including a squadron from Britain's Royal Navy.

The archduke and his wife began their drive through the streets of Sarajevo toward the governor's mansion. Along the route, a Serbian man—one of six conspirators—stepped through the crowd to throw a bomb at the royal car. It bounced off the side of the vehicle and exploded next to the following car, injuring eleven men, three in the royal party. The archduke chose to continue his visit, though he complained harshly to the mayor of Sarajevo of his welcome.

At Kiel, the starting gun sounded, with the racers cheered on by both the German High Seas Fleet and the Royal Navy's four battleships and three cruisers. In Sarajevo, the injured men had been taken to a hospital, and after his meeting with the mayor, Franz Ferdinand decided to visit them. His driver got lost, and turned in to a side street at about eleven in the morning. Nineteen-year-old Gavrilo Princip was walking down that same road, regretting the lost opportunity that his bomb-throwing coconspirator had botched. Discovering his error, the archduke's driver slowed. Princip recognized the car coming toward him and drew a pistol. He stepped out into the roadway and fired twice. The car leaped forward, with two figures in the backseat slumped and bleeding. With no Turks for the Serbs to vanquish, Austrians had to suffice. June 28: remember Kosovo.

At Kiel, a motorboat sped out toward *Meteor* shortly after 2:00 P.M., and a sailor tossed a telegram over the rail. The archduke's driver had found the road to the hospital, but too late. Franz Ferdinand and his wife bled to death before reaching care. Kaiser Wilhelm read the telegram with the news. *Meteor* put about. The regatta was canceled.

Wilhelm left the coast for Potsdam and Berlin, where his ministers could consider the German response to the outrage. It was June 28, 1914: remember Sarajevo.[1]

AND THEN . . . for the moment, not much. The murder of the Austrian heir was seen as a heinous crime, but initially the crisis seemed local, an issue only for Austro-Hungary and Serbia. In Berlin, Albert Einstein took little note of it, proceeding with his talk at the Prussian Academy five days afterward, seeing Freundlich off toward the eastern heart of the conflict later in the month. Throughout the last week of June, Europe actually seemed somewhat more stable than it had over the preceding months. In March a war scare had swept through Germany. Officials "encouraged" the newspapers to publish dire articles on military production and preparedness in Russia and France, so as to condition the public for a new round of German military expenditures on top of the record 1913 bill of 1.3 billion DM. On March 11, *Die Post,* one of the leading right-wing papers, had sounded the trumpet: "Michel [Germany], wake up! Dark clouds are rising on the east and west. . . . Michel, wake up, so that nobody can overpower you while you're sleeping. . . . A war is dawning before us, a war like none history has seen before. . . . They can come! The *furor teutonicus* once destroyed even the Roman Empire."[2]

But the crisis passed. Intellectuals and other cultural leaders tilted against the threat. Thomas Mann and twenty-nine other artists decried censorship. Almost four hundred clergymen called on political leaders to "take the Sermon on the Mount more seriously." A new Organization for International Understanding was formed to fend off a drift to war.[3] And the public danced. "In those times, when the smell of sulfur never left the air, the Berlin public discovered a new passion," wrote Theodore Wolff in a memoir written ten years later titled *Der Krieg der Pontius Pilatus—Pontius Pilate's War.* "After the one-step and the two-step had done their duty, the new miracle was called Tango. . . . To make the new steps easier for women, bizarre and very inelegant dresses emerged, long and heavy and wrapped around the legs as a cloth is wrapped around the altar. Then, one day, they were slashed in the middle, like trousers, and cut up the side as well, so that with every movement of the body or the air, the dresses opened for glimpses of what was hidden." It was suddenly a grand and giddy time, except for the hint Wolff sensed of "the society of Boccaccio, which devoted itself to pleasure in order to forget the plague."[4]

The plague loomed. Each new volley of war talk and each newly approved, ever-larger budget for arms felt almost seductive, promising danger and adventure all in one. But in the spring of 1914 this had the air of old news, just another round of the endless grumble, posturing and bombast that characterized European diplomacy. Life in Berlin persisted pretty much as normal. The French were still welcome at an exhibition featuring works by Delacroix and Cezanne. Throughout June *Frankfurter Zeitung,* the leading serious newspaper in Germany, had carried advertisements for real estate in Russia. Expressions of civic pride—calls for support for the arts and to beautify Berlin, for example—still spurred the newspaper's editorial coverage, along with a kind of sports-page view of the competition of cultures between Germany and the other great states.

Even on the 29th of June, although *Frankfurter Zeitung*'s first edition reported on the assassination of the Austrian heir, its second edition returned to its usual boosterish tone. An article on the 1916 Olympic games, scheduled for Berlin, urged all Berliners and Germans to support the games as a chance for international contact. The paper did report the news as it flowed in, of course. There were accounts of anti-Serb demonstrations in several cities, and the staid, left-of-center broadsheet warned that anti-Serb propaganda would be used more widely and recklessly than before. France was said to hope for a new crown prince who could stabilize the Austro-Hungarian monarchy. Russia decried the oppression of the Slavs, while Britain, Russia's ally, saw Slavic conspiracies loose across Europe. It was all normal, the great power game, told in a tone of reporting that suggested this was no more than an ordinarily important story. Diplomats rather than soldiers were making the news, and if the pattern of years past held, there would be a huff and a puff and Europe would tiptoe on, nervously, but at peace.

So, as June turned into July of 1914, the summer shaped up splendidly. As late as July 21, the down-market *Berliner Volksblatt* instructed its readers on how to get a tan, and rather coquettishly decried the possibly immoral costumes that produced the best results. "We didn't realize what was coming up," Heinrich Eduard Jacob wrote in his memoir of life before the war. "On the contrary, one could say that the closer we came to August 1914, the deeper we would throw ourselves in the completely restless turbulence of Berlin life. . . . The books, the writers, the actors! Berlin had been the great attraction for all of them. . . . Everything was filled with a throbbing life and the idea of death was unimaginable to us."[5]

Unimaginable, and yet the rush toward war was sudden, swift, hidden behind the sunlit foreground of the summer, ludicrous and implacable. Even now, with all the advantages of hindsight, it seems preposterous that a pair of murders carried out by a gang of six young, patriotically obsessed zealots should lead to the mobilization of millions, and battle across all Europe. The study of why the war came has filled libraries almost since the first shots were fired. The question actually breaks into two: why did Europe go to war at all, and why then?

THE FIRST HALF of that puzzle centers on Germany's recent history as the newest of the Great Power states. German unification came through a series of victorious wars fought between 1864 and 1871 with Denmark, Austro-Hungary, and France. These wars were waged at first just by Prussia, with Austro-Hungary as an ally against Denmark, and then by the coalescing German union. Each triumph brought with it new territory, until in 1871 the disparate German states, along with pieces of each of the three defeated nations, were bound together under the rule of the new German emperor, Kaiser Wilhelm I of Prussia. The Prussian chief minister, Otto von Bismarck, forged this new union while dominating German politics for almost thirty years.

Bismarck's governing philosophy was simple. All power ultimately resided in the person of the monarch himself, which in practical terms meant the kaiser's government—that is, in himself as its leader. The people were subjects, not citizens, no matter how many parliamentary delegates they might elect. Bismarck was astonishingly and consistently successful in maintaining that view, beating back each attempt to assert parliamentary control over his administration. The rigged voting system within Prussia itself helped. There, in what was by far Germany's largest state, the electorate was divided into three classes based on the amount of taxes they paid, with equal representation given to each class. This meant that traditional, exceptionally conservative Junker landowners could maintain their near-monopoly of military power and their hold on the key levers of governmental power under the rule of a kaiser who was both king of Prussia and emperor of Germany. Under the system that had been formed at the time of unification, the Imperial German Reichstag was a weak legislature, able to vote on matters brought before it by the government but with very little authority to originate legislation. Early in Bismarck's tenure as chancellor of Germany, the Reichstag was divided between three main factions—the right wing, led by the Conservative party, associated with the Junker aristocracy; a centrist grouping; and a liberal wing associated with the urban middle class. The so-called Iron Chancellor was a master at playing them off against each other, ensuring that the legislature was never in a position to demand a greater share of state power. He loathed and feared the emerging specter of socialism, represented politically by a new party, the Social Democrats, or SPD. The SPD, explicitly the party of the working class, gained seats with every election, its growing power within the Imperial Reichstag frightening Bismarck to the point where he was willing to risk civil war in 1890—"to smash the crockery," as he called it—to suppress rising socialist support.[6] Above all, he believed in the absolute prerogative of royal command, demanding that his king never yield to the temptation of governing by consensus, or fall prey to any soft-headed and misguided benevolence. Rather, he wanted a ruler "who in critical times would rather fall with sword in hand on the steps of his throne, fighting for his right, than surrender."[7]

There was one almost liberal ideal that Bismarck defended, however: the supremacy of civil authority over the military, at least in the realm of politics. In this he was opposed by the Army General Staff, sometimes explicitly and always by subterfuge. The conflict had been present since before the birth of the German Empire, with the Prussian army demanding complete independence of action, subject only to the direct orders of the kaiser. The real argument lay in what the generals thought military prerogatives included. At different times the high command demanded power over the decisions about whom to fight, when to fight, what the war aims were and even what domestic decisions needed to be made to secure the army's ability to fight. Despite bitter feuds, Bismarck was able to hang on to control of foreign policy throughout his long career, but he never resolved the underlying tension, nor did he come close to subordinating the military to civil authority.

Both Bismarck and the generals did share an abiding fear: the threat of a two-front war, a simultaneous confrontation with both Russia and France, ever hungry for revenge after the defeat of 1871. Most of Bismarck's famed maneuvering on the European stage was driven by his attempt to secure Germany against that threat. His aim from 1871 until he lost power in 1890 was to keep Germany on the majority side of the Great Power system that had dominated Europe since the end of the Napoleonic wars. At first, Bismarck pursued what seemed the most natural combination with Austro-Hungary and Russia—but tensions between Vienna and St. Petersburg grew over disputes in the Balkans until Russia ultimately pulled away, to be replaced by Italy in what came to be called the Triple Alliance. He maneuvered around the greatest power of all, Britain, gaining British aid in resolving a series of Balkan crises, while pressuring London to concede some ground to German colonial ambitions in Africa and in the Pacific. France was browbeaten, periodically threatened with another "prophylactic" war whenever revanchist sentiment there grew too bold.

But the system of alliances that Bismarck created carried with it a hierarchy of unacknowledged risk. First, his treaties called for mutual defense and mutual response to an attack on any one member of an alliance. This ensured that any conflict would be a wide one, potentially involving all the major European powers. Worse, he pioneered the use of secret and partly secret treaties. Those against whom alliances were aimed could not know exactly what was being proposed to threaten them—and hence had to assume the worst. Finally, the system was incredibly fragile. Germany could feel secure only as long as the Triple Alliance dominated Central Europe. But such domination could only increase the insecurity of its rivals, motivating nations like France and Russia to form competing alliances of their own. While Bismarck was in power, he had the skill to prevent any overwhelmingly dangerous combinations from coalescing. But the single greatest flaw in his policy was that it was his, and did not survive him. Bismarck was merely a chief minister—effectively, but not in fact, the ruler of Germany. He had been appointed by a king, and was retained in power by that same ruler, Wilhelm I, kaiser of Germany, until Wilhelm's death in 1888.

Wilhelm's oldest son, Frederick, reigned for just three months before throat cancer killed him, and was followed by his younger brother, Wilhelm II, young, ambitious, anxious to be both admired and loved, and deeply resentful of anyone who challenged his amour propre. The young monarch and the old, choleric, authoritarian minister were bound to clash. They coexisted nervously for two years, but in 1890 Wilhelm forced Bismarck out over a purely domestic matter, a labor bill before the Reichstag, and the Iron Chancellor was finished.

And as Bismarck went, so went his Germany. He left behind him an unbroken socialist SPD. By 1914, it would be the single largest party in the Reichstag, maintaining a state of near permanent confrontation with a kaiser and a ruling class that had no intention of surrendering any power to a popular government. The old Prussian elite mobilized their forces against the rising power of the socialist parties. Groups like the Prussian Bund and the Pan-German Bund confronted the workers' organizations. The Prussian Bund declared that "radical, godless, revolutionary democracy" must be countered by "a lot of Prussian steel."[8]

More dangerous, with Bismarck gone, there was no overwhelming personality to keep the generals' ambition in check. The General Staff's assertion of primacy in all things military was left unchallenged, ultimately leading to the point where it abandoned Bismarck's aim of avoiding a two-front war and began to plan for just such a conflict. Worst of all, Bismarck's reverence for the German Empire's form of monarchy worked only so long as its chancellor served a ruler more or less amenable to good sense. Kaiser Wilhelm II was a disaster.

Wilhelm II remains a poster child for all that is wrong with hereditary government. Vainglorious, desperately insecure, hugely ambitious, quick to take offense, ill-educated, boorish, narrow in his interests, knowledge and associations, the young kaiser was both a patsy for those in his government and in his army who were gripped by the lust for power. He was a menace in his own right, as he dreamed of the glory that could be his as lord of a world-dominating state. In a policy shift flowing directly from the kaiser downward, Germany's government began to view Britain as its chief rival from the 1890s forward. Britain and the German states had been national friends and occasionally official allies for centuries. Prussia and Britain had combined to challenge Napoleon, and the armies of both nations met at Waterloo to assure the final defeat of the odious French Empire. Close ties had persisted throughout the nineteenth century, made stronger by bonds of royal marriages. Queen Empress Victoria was Wilhelm II's grandmother, and her son, Albert, was his uncle. In any military calculus, the British Empire was not the primary threat, for both France and Russia presented much more obvious direct military dangers.

Yet despite all this, Britain obsessed the kaiser. It was the barrier that, in his mind, prevented the German Reich from assuming its rightful place at the very top of the world's hierarchy. Worse yet, it kept him, personally, from finally trumping the arrogant ease of command wielded by his own family, the British royal clan. From the very start of his reign, Wilhelm was more than touchy about his English relatives, and especially his uncle Bertie, Albert, Prince of Wales. On his first trip outside Germany after becoming kaiser, he compelled his Austrian hosts to bar Albert from Vienna for the length of his visit for fear that his uncle would fail to give him the respect due an emperor. His grandmother Queen Victoria was deeply offended on Bertie's behalf, writing, "This is really too vulgar and too absurd. . . ." But she eventually overlooked the insult, restoring the peace by offering the kaiser an honorary Admiral of the Fleet commission in the Royal Navy.[9] The truce did not hold. The historian Alexandra Richie ties at least part of the kaiser's and Germany's subsequent breach with Britain to the next clash between Wilhelm and Bertie at the annual Cowes regatta held in the Solent off the south of England in 1895. There, Wilhelm alienated British society with his bombast ashore, claiming protocol priority over his English hosts, and his poor sportsmanship afloat, challenging the results of a race he lost. Albert ultimately shunned his nephew, refusing to race against him again, and the kaiser retreated to his own regatta at Kiel, where he played host to the B list of European society, along with the occasional American parvenu.[10] In fact, the loss of such playground privileges would not have mattered much but for the kaiser's subsequent broadsides leveled at British official policy and actions. The real breach with Britain opened in earnest in 1901, when Wilhelm injected himself into the Boer War, the great crisis of British imperial rule. In a telegram to Paul Kruger, the leader of the Boers and president of the New Republic of South Africa, Wilhelm called British troops "armed bands" and congratulated Kruger on his new state's (short-lived) independence.

Well before that, soon after Bismarck's fall, his successors began to undo the Iron Chancellor's multiple balancing acts. One of the first acts of the new government was to refuse to extend its treaty with Russia, which led directly to a French-Russian thaw that virtually forced Russia and France to combine—exactly what Bismarck had worked so carefully to avoid. Preparations for what eventually came to be seen as the inevitable war began in earnest in 1891, when the leadership of the General Staff passed from the hero of the Franco-Prussian War of 1870, Helmuth von Moltke, into the hands of Alfred von Schlieffen. Schlieffen was a master tactician, and by 1905 he had completed his blueprint for continental conquest. In his scheme, the enemy to be knocked out first was France, while a blocking force neutralized Russia and the British were to be persuaded or compelled to hang back on their island where they belonged.

It was a bold vision, one that accepted great risk against the prospect of enormous reward. It was also a measure of the final failure of Bismarck's vision for Germany in Europe. By accepting the Schlieffen plan, the German leadership simply assumed what it had once sought to forestall: Germany's encirclement by powers hostile to it, who could be dealt with only by conquest. And if the preparations for the land campaign left any doubt about Germany's ultimate aims, the naval competition the German government launched with Britain provided the smoking gun. Creating German sea power was Kaiser Wilhelm's pet project, for it represented a direct thrust at Uncle Albert's pride and joy, the British navy. Pushed by Germany's most brilliant sailor, Admiral Alfred von Tirpitz, his government in 1897 decided to build a fleet of nineteen new battleships with the explicit purpose of defeating the British Channel Fleet in the seas between Heligoland and the River Thames.

Britain rose to the challenge, building new battleships of its own and reorganizing the distribution of the fleet so that more of its capital ships were stationed close to home, able to confront the growing German threat. And then, in 1906, a single new British vessel rendered all of Tirpitz's fleet obsolete. In that year the Admiralty, led by Britain's own charismatic admiral, Jackie Fisher, launched the ship of Fisher's dreams: H.M.S. *Dreadnought.* It was the first all-big-gun battleship, carrying ten twelve-inch cannon, and it was the first capital ship to be powered by turbines. It was faster, better armored, and could fire more weight of shell farther than any ship at sea. It was designed to be death on water for any opposing force, and Fisher bragged that "three twelve-inch shells bursting on board every minute would be *hell.*"[11] The *Dreadnought* was the future—so much so that its name became synonymous with "battleship"—and every serious sailor in the world recognized this, including Admiral Tirpitz. In 1907, work began on a German battle fleet centered on the new dreadnought design.

As before, the challenge was clear; Germany intended to match or surpass Britain's power at sea. To British observers the implication was obvious. While Britain possessed only a small standing army—a negligible threat by the standards of the continental powers—the Royal Navy was the defense of the entire empire. By trying to build a force that could threaten that fleet in its home waters, Germany appeared to be planning a direct assault on the essential bulwark of British power everywhere—and in particular to ensure that Britain could not intervene in a continental conflict. This no British government could accept, and the resulting race to build ever greater numbers of ever more powerful battleships became a competition that many in both countries saw as having only one end: a final battle to determine who would rule the world.

Ultimately, the naval race demonstrated the harm inherent in the twin devils of the German military's defiance of civilian power and of the kaiser's inept rule. By the last years before the outbreak of the Great War, Germany's Foreign Service and its navy were actually warring over which would control negotiations with Britain. The sailors won. The naval attaché in Britain, Captain Wilhelm Widenmann, had a deep and long-nurtured hatred of the British and an absolute commitment to the competition that was supposed to end in effective German dominance at sea. As his nominal boss in London, Ambassador Count Wolff-Metternich sought to negotiate an agreement to ease naval tensions, but Widenmann poisoned the well both in London and at home—in London by reaffirming German intentions to build up as powerful a fleet as needed to counter British force in the home waters, and in Berlin by provoking the kaiser into reaffirming that "he—Widenmann—is an officer and can be disapproved only by the Supreme War Lord [sic], not by his civilian superior."[12] Widenmann's successor as attaché, Captain E. von Müller, was, if anything, worse, decrying an offer of a naval holiday—a break in the building programs of both nations—from the First Lord of the Admiralty, Winston Churchill. Müller reviled "the inky diplomats" and framed Churchill's offer as a devious plot by the perfidious British to trip up the expansion of German naval power. As Gordon Craig, one of the most influential postwar historians of Germany, put it, "In this plain distortion of the very purpose of diplomatic reporting, we can detect the bland assumption of military and naval leaders that they alone had the right to determine the foreign policy of the empire."[13]

That dynamic lies behind what is perhaps the best summary analysis of the prelude to August 1914, an argument laid out by Donald Kagan in his masterful book on the broader question of the origins of war. In his view Germany was unequivocally the prime mover whose actions for more than two decades had aimed at conflict. "From the 1890s," he writes, "Germany was fundamentally a dissatisfied power, eager to disrupt the status quo and to achieve its expansive goals, by bullying if possible, by war if necessary."[14] The response of the other Great Powers was a perfect mirror image of Bismarck's vision for Germany's place in Europe. France and Russia made common cause; after the debacle of German encouragement of the Boers, France and Britain launched an entente aimed at ending their centuries of hostility; and finally the three nations formed a formal alliance, aimed directly at bumptious, belligerent, power-hungry Germany. With that, the full evil of the interlocking alliance structure could make itself felt. The Triple Entente confronted the Triple Alliance of Germany, Austro-Hungary, and Italy—and the minor states aligned with one side or the other, until flare-ups between even minor players routinely raised the specter of continental war.

The first real threat of such a war came in 1905, when Germany attempted to block the spread of French power in Morocco. German bungling led to a humiliating climb-down, leaving the French firmly in place, while strengthening the ties between Britain and France. Next came a crisis in the Balkans in 1908 and 1909 that threatened to explode into a Great Powers confrontation. Morocco prompted another stare-down between Germany and France in 1911; again, Germany was forced to back down. The next year brought yet another Balkan confrontation. Each time the diplomats talked their way out of the threat, but every round of saber rattling set the adrenaline running in Berlin. In 1913, in the context of renewed Balkan troubles, the kaiser said to the king of Belgium that if war was inevitable, let war come. That statement had a fatalistic ring to it, but the apparent unconcern mocked the underlying fact. A European war probably was inevitable.

Too many guns and soldiers were at hand, and Germany itself had accumulated too many grievances and slights, trivial or even imaginary though they might have been. On the German side, in fact, the General Staff had been preparing for its great opportunity, the climactic continental battle, for more than two decades.

And finally, there came Sarajevo, and yet one more Balkan mess. All the preconditions for war were there: the grievance, the hunger for revenge, the delicately balanced alliances and the pressure of mobilizations that put more and more armed men in close proximity. Yet a bit of mystery still remains. Why, after so many approaches to the brink, couldn't Europe have talked itself out of disaster one more time? The dispute between Austria and Serbia was hardly more significant than any of the previous crises. There was nothing obvious for anyone besides those two to fight over, no territory in dispute or privileges to be won or defended. Europe's foreign ministers had talked their way out of worse before. So why did all the Great Powers decide, as if agreeing with Kaiser Wilhelm, that since war was inevitable, let it happen now?

There is no certain answer. Peter Gay has termed this moment "war psychosis . . . a release from boredom, an invitation to heroism, a remedy for decadence."[15] His is as persuasive a diagnosis as any: the outbreak of war resulted from a catastrophic combination of ennui and naïveté. From the moment the archduke bled to death in his car, events seemed simply to follow one after the other, as if in automatic sequence. Beneath the usual rhythm of daily life, behind all the costume balls and abstruse lectures at learned academies, the series of increasingly dangerous moves followed one after the other. On July 5, 1914, Germany promised Austria its support in the event of a war with Serbia—or with Russia. On July 13, Austria received a report that there was no link to be found between the assassination in Sarajevo and any actions by the Serbian government. Nonetheless, on July 14, the Austrians began to draft an ultimatum for the Serbs, a move intended to invite rejection. The document was delivered on the 23rd, with an answer demanded within two days. On the 24th, Russia began to mobilize.

And within a day or two, a German scientific expedition to the Crimea in Russia reached its destination. Without evident nervousness its members set about their work. Freundlich and his colleagues made contact with an Argentine expedition seeking to photograph the elusive planet Vulcan during the eclipse. Freundlich had arranged to collaborate with this group to measure the deflection of light. All the pieces were in place; nothing remained but to inspect their gear and wait.

The collective rush to war continued, virtually in lockstep. On July 28, the kaiser wavered just a little in his enthusiasm for war, but it was too late. Austrian forces, secure in the promise of German support, moved on Serbia. Russia's mobilization advanced, and in their turn the Germans and Austrians began to counter the Russian preparations. On the 30th, the czar committed Russia to the full mobilization of all the empire's military resources. Germany called on France to remain neutral but France refused, starting its own mobilization on the 31st. In the evening of August 1, the German ambassador to Russia delivered a document to the Foreign Ministry in St. Petersburg, a declaration of war. In a photograph of the vast crowd in the Odeonsplatz in Munich cheering the news of impending war, a young man is clearly visible, lifting his hat as if to cheer. It is a portrait of an impoverished Austrian watercolorist, already sporting that trademark trimmed mustache: Adolf Hitler.

That night, a small force of German soldiers entered Belgium, to be followed by the full invasion force two days later. Germany declared war on France on August 3, having sent patrols across the border the day before. Italy abstained from the conflict, for the time being, so the final gladiator entered the arena at 11:00 P.M. on August 4, when the British Empire formally declared that a state of war existed with the German Reich. The conflict now embraced almost all of Europe.

And at the far edge of the continent, on the Crimean Peninsula, three German scientists suddenly became enemies to their hosts. Freundlich and his team were arrested and held in internment camps as prisoners of war. The Russians seized their cameras, which left the neutral Argentine scientists unable to complete their observations. In the end, though, this small failure among all the disasters of that August did not matter much. The eclipse was a tease. Clouds gathered at totality, just as the sun was about to vanish completely, and then cleared beautifully soon after the moment passed. Freundlich and his two companions did not languish very long after his lost chance. They were held briefly and then swapped for Russian officers in one of the first prisoner exchanges of the war. To Einstein's relief, the three men got back to Berlin at the end of September. No further attempt to test his prediction would take place until the war ended.

It mattered little to him. He would use the time thus gained to return to his thinking about gravity and repair what had turned out to be a significantly flawed theory. The immediate crisis overwhelmed any disappointment that he might have felt. Life had been better than anticipated in Berlin back in those ancient days of May, but that Berlin had already disappeared. One war "poet" sang of the official mood: "Powerful, with honor and solidarity/Germany protects what was given from God. . . . When criminals unite/to burn down my peaceful house/Out sword! War and Blood!"[16]

EINSTEIN NEVER RECONCILED HIMSELF to the shock of 1914—not merely the fact of battle but the naked joy that everyone, it seemed, took in the good fight. "That a man can take pleasure in marching in fours to the strains of a band is enough to make me despise him," he wrote years later, looking back on the war. Such a man "has only been given his big brain by mistake; unprotected spinal marrow was all he needed."[17] Much more quickly than most, he focused on the war's disastrous impact, not simply the devastation and loss of life it threatened but the loss of sensibility, of a way of thinking. In August he wrote to his friend Ehrenfest that Europe was gripped by madness, and that humankind was "a sorry species" to rejoice at the outbreak of such collective insanity.[18] These feelings never abated. In war he saw the destruction of what he most prized: the collapse of reason, the loss of the ability to think as individuals. "Heroism on command, senseless violence and all the loathsome nonsense that goes by the name of patriotism—how passionately I hate them." In the end, as at the beginning, there was only revulsion. "How vile and despicable seems war to me!"[19]

This state of mind was thoroughly at odds with that of those closest to him, the men who had brought him to Berlin in the first place. Walther Nernst provided a kind of deadly comic relief. With the outbreak of hostilities Nernst, bespectacled, plump, fifty years old, and a professional chemist of the first rank, took it on himself to leave his laboratory and volunteer for active duty. He drove well and owned his own car, so he set himself up as a military courier. His wife drilled him in the proper military bearing and then he launched himself toward the German Second Army on the march through northern France.

Haber responded more soberly but with greater effect. As early as 1909 he had begun weighing the importance of chemistry to war, and in 1912 he approached the Prussian War Ministry with an offer to coordinate the work of his physical chemistry institute with the needs of the military.[20] At the time, the General Staff ignored him, but in 1914 Haber tried again. His staff at the Kaiser Wilhelm Institutes dwindled to five as call-ups took their toll, but he reorganized the remaining few on military lines and sought official rank for himself. He hoped for an officer's commission, but that was too ambitious for a mere scientist and a converted Jew, so he had to settle for a sergeant's slot. Nonetheless, though he continued to hunger for the seal of Germanness that a commission in the kaiser's army would bring, he began to turn his group into probably the most bellicose of all the German research establishments.

Such behavior by men he considered friends did not surprise Einstein or greatly put him off his stride. Fairly quickly he recovered much of his equilibrium, explaining to Zangger that he had found out how to get by. "I am now beginning to feel well amidst the current mad turmoil," he claimed, by the simple expedient of isolating himself "from all things with which the crazy public busies itself."[21] But even Einstein's walls could be breached if the shock was great enough. What finally struck home was the way Planck greeted the war—Planck of all people, the man whom Einstein would eventually eulogize in a letter to his widow, saying, "How different and how much better it would be for mankind if there were more like him."[22] Yet even Planck eagerly sent his students into the army. Germany was the victim, Germany was a peace-loving nation, but Germany could not show patience forever, Planck told the young men before him, so now, "Germany has drawn its sword against the breeding ground of perfidy."[23]

That is to say, against neutral Belgium. The Germans had hoped that the Belgian army would stand aside, allowing their army to proceed to France without interruption. That hope was quickly dashed; on the first night of the war German soldiers came under fire from *francs-tireurs,* snipers, who struck at the invading forces from what cover they could find. The sniping evoked the response that became a centerpiece in the argument over right and wrong in the war. In the first of a series of reprisals for continued Belgian resistance, German soldiers leveled the small town of Hervé, holding its inhabitants collectively responsible for what they regarded as cowardly civilian attacks on military targets.

But affairs like this seemed mere distractions. The first major obstacle was the city of Liège, surrounded by a network of elaborate fortresses. The initial attack failed, and the Germans even showed some signs of panic, but General Erich von Ludendorff rallied his forces and led them into the city, where all resistance ceased by August 15. The German advance continued, little affected either by the ongoing efforts of the snipers or by encounters with the regular forces of France and Belgium. (A top German diplomat in Brussels complained of Belgium's continued intransigence with a mixture of sympathy and disdain: "Oh, the poor fools! Why don't they get out of the way of the steamroller? We don't want to hurt them, but if they stand in our way they will be ground into the dirt.")[24]

Continuing Belgian resistance led to an ongoing and escalating series of reprisals, with German soldiers obeying orders to murder over a thousand civilians. The punishment culminated in the destruction of about a fifth of the town of Louvain. A German officer told a visiting American diplomat that when the work there was done "not one stone will stand upon another! Not one, I tell you. We will teach them to respect Germany. For generations people will come here to see what we have done!"[25] Actions like these and the very public announcements that confirmed that the German command knew of and approved reprisal killings combined to fix in Allied opinion an image that would remain in place until the time came to assign blame for the war: the essential German was a barbarian who bathed in the blood of innocents.

That was an image that deeply offended German men of culture, and in the early autumn, Germany's intellectuals had enough of what they took as almost personal slanders. Their response demonstrated how wide a gap separated the cultural elites of the warring nations, and defined the chasm that had opened between Einstein and men he counted among his closest friends. On October 4, the major newspapers published an "Appeal to the Cultured World," a manifesto defending Germany against charges of aggression and brutality. It stated that Germany bore no responsibility for the war; Germany had not violated the neutrality of Belgium; no atrocities had been committed there—in fact, it was the western powers, Britain and France, who were at fault, for "having allied with Russians and Serbs" to produce "the shameful sight of Mongols and Negroes driven against the white race." Germany was a land of impeccably civilized sensibilities, whose actions throughout the war would be conducted as befits "a cultured nation to whom the legacy of Goethe, Beethoven and Kant is fully as sacred as its hearths and plots of land."[26] The manifesto was presented as a message from Germany's intellectual leaders and was signed by ninety-three of the most famous German artists, writers, scholars and scientists. Among them were Philipp Lenard, the conservative but not yet rabid Nobel laureate in physics; Emil Fischer, founder of the Kaiser Wilhelm Institutes; Nernst, safely back from his French adventure; Haber; and, worst of all, Max Planck. Einstein had passed over the enthusiasms of his colleagues in midsummer with only private disdain. This appeal, though, was too much to bear in silence.

The Manifesto of Ninety-three had shocked at least one other person besides Einstein, a physician named Georg Friedrich Nicolai, an adjunct professor at Berlin University and a close friend of Elsa Einstein. He drafted a countermanifesto titled "An Appeal to Europeans" and brought it to Einstein for editing and signature. It asserted that there could be no victors in the war, and called on the educated men from each nation to work together after its end to ensure that the terms of any peace agreement did not set the stage for future conflicts. It rejected the idea of annexing territories, and called for a kind of European unity that would eliminate the possibility of war. It urged the best from both sides to reestablish international connections, and to avoid the impulse to blame one side or another for the conflict. Above all, it rejected the naked, ugly nationalism of the manifesto: that document was "unworthy of what until now the whole world has understood by the term culture, and it would be a disaster if it were to become the common property of educated people."[27]

All in all, this countermanifesto was—or seems now—relatively benign, blaming no one, urging restraint, calling for a fair and permanent peace only after the war had run its course. The document was written to offend as little as possible. It was a complete failure. Einstein and Nicolai gained only two signatures besides their own. One was from the octogenarian astronomer Wilhelm Förster, a signatory to the first manifesto who presumably had come to his senses. The other was from a friend of Nicolai's. Esteemed though he was, Einstein lacked the kind of all-eclipsing prestige he was to gain in the 1920s, which would have made his name alone enough to carry the document, so he and Nicolai abandoned the effort. Their "appeal" was eventually published in Switzerland as part of a book in which Nicolai argued more generally against war. But in Germany in 1914, even a tepid expression of regret at the conflict was anathema. It was not treason; rather, and worse, it was irrelevant.

For Einstein, that was the real tragedy, the fact that the community of science and intellect that he believed he had joined in Berlin had collapsed so swiftly and so completely. What truly galled him was that the men he considered his peers were so eager to prostrate themselves in a paroxysm of nation worship, sacrificing their intellectual honesty to do so. At a minimum, they could have read the widely published reports in German newspapers on the assault on Antwerp, for example, with its inevitable destruction of civilian property, and long before October, the chancellor of Germany himself, Theobald von Bethmann-Hollweg, admitted in public that Germany's invasion of Belgium was a clear breach of the rights of a neutral state. "The wrong that we are committing," he said, praising himself for his honesty, "we will endeavor to make good as soon as our military goal is reached."[28]

In other words, the signers of the Manifesto of Ninety-three—Einstein's friends—had no excuse. They knew or should have known that what they signed was false in at least some of its particulars, bombastic and defensive and ultimately absurd as a broader claim of moral stature. In Einstein's view, lending support to such tripe was disgraceful. Indeed, it was itself a kind of treason, a betrayal of the polity of ideas that he believed superseded any mere national allegiance. The sense of hurt, the rage at such desertion, stayed with him. In 1918 he wrote, recalling the original insult, "Innumerably often, in these gloomy years of general nationalistic blindness, men of science and the arts have made public declarations which have already unmeasurably damaged feelings of solidarity among those who are devoting themselves to higher and freer goals. This solidarity," he remembered, "had been well-developed before the war." But that halcyon time, that community of the best and best-intentioned, had now been shattered, perhaps irreparably. "The clamor of narrow-minded priests and slaves of the leaden principle of power has become so noisy that the better-minded, feeling so completely isolated, dare not lift their voices."[29]

Language like this captures Einstein's capacity for contempt, especially for what he saw as the essence of the German character. He pulled no punches. It took him less than a year of war to conclude that the Germans were a people motivated by fear and the love of force.[30] He always understood that the Germans had no monopoly on folly, that others besides his nearest neighbors could thrill to the adventure of war. But soon after the war began, he diagnosed a special pathology in Germany, a disease of culture and society that propelled it into war. The masses were "immensely submissive, 'domesticated,'" he told the French author and committed pacifist Romain Rolland in a conversation that took place in neutral Switzerland in 1915. The elites were worse. They were hungry, Einstein told Rolland, driven by their urge for power, their love of force, and the dream of conquest.[31]

Einstein's worst forebodings of the move to Germany had never stretched to this. The war was madness, he wrote to a friend, and as the battles pressed on into autumn he added, "In living through this 'great epoch' it is difficult to accept the fact that one belongs to that species that boasts of its freedom of will." He dreamed of "an island for those who are wise and magnanimous," where even he could be a patriot.[32] There was no such place. Instead, he remained in his flat in Dahlem, alone but for the company of men who thrilled to the sound of the guns.

Chapter Four

"ALL THE LOATHSOME NONSENSE"

EINSTEIN RARELY MINCED WORDS. THE WAR REVEALED THAT THE GERmans were sheep, as he told Rolland, the elites as well as the masses, all of them a strange, violent, murderous breed, but still sheep. Rolland had a larger view. He told Einstein that the French were not much better, just as committed to a fight to the bloody end. Einstein was unforgiving. How could *his friends* behave so badly? How dare they abandon their vocation as scientists? What caused those few whom he knew best to fall in love with war?

Einstein generalized from there, asking the larger question: were men like Planck and Haber and the rest just like everyone everywhere, ordinary victims of a madness that knew no borders? Or were they and Germany exceptional, the distinctive products of a psychology and a culture peculiarly devoted to state violence and pathological nationalism? The issue still provokes bitter controversy, especially within Germany. In that first autumn of the war Einstein quickly came to his own conclusion. He told Ehrenfest that all Europe seemed mad to him, without distinction. But even a collective derangement sweeping across the continent did not fully account for the stands taken by most German intellectuals. For Einstein, the first months of the war provided an object lesson in what it might mean to be a good German, a willing subject of the reich. As he watched both his friends and what he could grasp of the broader German experience, he came to his conclusion. A Germany that could transform even such wise men as Planck into unthinking agents of the state had to be truly different among the warring nations.

Was he right, or perhaps the better question—was this judgment reasonable? Can we say now, almost a century removed from Berlin in August of 1914, that Germany's eager belligerence was genuinely different in kind from that of Britain or France or anywhere else? There is a drawing from the British magazine *Punch* in 1916 that shows how Germany's enemies argued the point. Though it reflects all the bitterness of a nation two years into a wretched war, it provides a snapshot of the "German problem" as seen west of the line. The cartoon depicts the essence of all things German. A helmeted, mustachioed ogre vaguely resembling the kaiser wears the skins and sandals of a Hun. He carries a mace and blood drips from his hands. Standing in front of the door to a fortress, he peers over a ruined landscape, bodies strewn at the base of the parapet. Tacked to the door is a sign in formal German script: "*Weltmacht oder Niedergang*"—"World Power or Decline." The eternal German, according to *Punch:* bluster, brutality, cynicism, and moral oblivion, all tied up into one frighteningly effective package.

The slogan is the key to the image, for it comes not from *Punch*'s editorialists but from General Friedrich von Bernhardi, one of the leaders of the *Deutsche Wehrverein* (The German National Defense League) and one of the foremost German war enthusiasts. Bernhardi's central tenet held that the Germans had both the right and the need to fight wars of aggression. He published his most influential work, *Deutschland und der nächste Krieg—Germany and the Next War*—in 1912. "War is a biological necessity of the first importance," he wrote, "a regulative element in the life of mankind which cannot be dispensed with. . . . The struggle is not merely the destructive, but the life-giving principle. 'To supplant or to be supplanted is the essence of life,' says Goethe, and the strong life gains the upper hand. . . . The weaker succumb."[1] As for single men, so for nations: "Strong, healthy, and flourishing nations . . . require a continual expansion of their frontiers . . . since almost every part of the globe is inhabited, new territory must, as a rule, be obtained at the cost of its possessors—that is to say, by conquest, which thus becomes a law of necessity."[2]

This was not mere bluster. Similar aspirations found concrete expression in the specific plans that had been drawn up to provide for Germany's necessary conquests. In the late nineteenth century General Bronsart von Schellendorff dreamed of a greater German Reich that would reach from the Baltic to the Mediterranean. The enlarged Germany would incorporate Denmark, Holland, Belgium, northern France as far as the Loire, part of Switzerland, Trieste, and Venice. Such an empire, wrote Schellendorff, would not be "the work of a madman. . . . We have at hand the means of founding it, and no coalition in the world can stop us."[3] Behind the bravado lay genuine belief. Einstein himself located the seat of such faith in the Franco-Prussian War of 1870 and 1871, the Prussian victory that completed the creation of the Prussia-dominated modern German state. Ever since, "virtually all men of education have been captivated," as he told Rolland, by what he called Germany's "religion of power."[4] That peculiarly German cult had its prophet. Bernhardi, with his choice of domination or decay, had simply distilled the teaching of his mentor, Berlin University's professor of history, Heinrich von Treitschke.

Treitschke's career turned on the newness of the German state. Created out of the forced union of older territories like Prussia, Saxony and Bavaria, the new Germany was unquestionably a Great Power, but the new empire faced the task of persuading its own people that they were, in fact, Germans first, with a common heritage and destiny, and not some polymorphous agglomeration of Prussians, Saxons, Bavarians and all the rest. To argue Germany's case to its population of putative Germans, a small but highly vocal group of academic writers and speakers created a doctrine of state power and a passionate account of Germany's special mission. Treitschke was the most influential of them all.

Treitschke was an ardent apologist for the power structure of the new empire. He wrote that "millions must till the soil and forge and plane, that a few thousand can research, paint and rule."[5] He was a determined and influential anti-Semite, writing in one instance that Heinrich Heine, despite all his popularity, had to be rejected as fundamentally anti-German: "Of all our lyric poets, he was the only one who never wrote a drinking song; to him, heaven seemed full of almond cakes, purses of gold, and street wenches, for the oriental was incompetent to carouse after the German manner."[6] And above all, he was a defender of the prerogative of authority, of rule centered on the kaiser and his designated government. He rejected any democratic impulse, for that would allow "the uneducated, immature, and unreliable man to have as much influence as someone who is wise, industrious and patriotic."[7] Rather, what came first had to be "the moral sanctity of the State."[8]

Treitschke's influence lasted long enough for Einstein to remind Rolland of the damage the historian had done. What made the historian so dangerous, Einstein suggested, was the emotional power of his formula linking Germany's national identity with its right—and even its obligation—to fight.[9] "War," Treitschke wrote, "must be taken as part of the divinely appointed order . . . war is both justifiable and moral, and . . . the ideal of perpetual peace is not only impossible but immoral as well."[10] For him it was simple: Germany had become a Great Power, and Great Powers have certain needs and certain duties. Such a nation "cannot allow even its symbols to be contested. If the flag is insulted the state must claim reparation; should this not be forthcoming, war must follow, however small the occasion may seem; for the state has never any choice but to maintain the respect in which it is held among its fellows."

Treitschke was absolutely certain of one point. More than any of the other Great Powers, Germany in particular had to fight. In a view that became increasingly prevalent, Treitschke painted a portrait of a Germany hemmed in on the Continent, surrounded by hostile powers, France to the west, Russia to the east. Even worse, Germany had been shortchanged in the quest for colonies overseas. That was unacceptable, given Germany's rise to Great Power status. "Up to the present," Treitschke told his students, "Germany always had too small a share of the spoils in the partition of non-European territories."[11] The solution was straightforward: "We must and will, take our share in the domination of the world by the white race."[12]

The depth of Treitschke's conviction remains astounding, reverberating through page after page of dense and muddy prose. He had his critics, and in the 1890s an increasing number of academic colleagues began to separate themselves from him as his lectures grew more and more extreme. But even skeptics could be swayed. The historian Hans Delbrück was far more moderate in his politics than Treitschke, yet still he argued, "We want to be a world power and pursue colonial policy in the grand manner. . . . Here there can be no step backward. The entire future of our people among the great nations depends upon it. We can pursue this policy with England or without England. With England means in peace; against England means—through war."[13]

No subtletly there, but the question remains: even if Germany's academics were all fire-breathers, did what they say matter? In 1914 the issue had a practical edge. Did the war parties carry the people with them? Did the Germans simply have the misfortune to be led by a handful of vicious men (which could happen to any nation), or were they, as Einstein came to believe, a people eager to follow such leaders, slavish, bloodthirsty and brutal? The existence of war fever alone hardly proves the case. The rush to volunteer and extravagant expressions of self-sacrifice struck other capitals too. The volunteers lined up in Paris and London. David Lloyd George, whom the war would propel to the prime ministership, remembered "a crowd of young men . . . pushing their way through to give their names for enlistment. . . . For days I heard, from the windows of Downing Street and the Treasury, the movement of myraid feet towards the stands and the shouting of names of eager volunteers by the recruiting sergeants."[14] In England as much as in Germany, the war was understood to be a test of national character. *The Times* led its issue of the 5th of August by asserting, "We must suffer much, but we shall suffer for the great name of England and for all her high ideals, as our fathers did before us."[15] Some in Britain went further, echoing the argument in Germany in favor of the cleansing joy of war. A. L. Smith, master of Oxford's Balliol College, told one lecture audience, "War is indeed a mighty creator. It is an intellectual awakener and a moral tonic. . . . It purges away old strifes and sectional aims, and raises us for a while into higher and purer air. . . . It reveals to us what constitutes a modern nation, the partnership between the living, the dead and the yet unborn."[16]

Nonetheless, the allies of the Entente, Britain, France and Russia, had no doubt that the Germans were different, qualitatively, absolutely other—and morally crippled to boot. One writer in 1915 put it that "perhaps the worst nightmare of this war has been that it has . . . revealed to us the existence of an extraordinary gulf yawning between the nations, between Germany on the one hand and the Allies on the other. The standards of judgment, the ideas of right and wrong, entertained by the two sides in this war are so wide asunder that each is totally incapable of understanding the point of view of the other."[17] The

French psychologist Gustave Le Bon in his book *The Psychology of the Great War* declared that "Prussia transformed the mental orientation of the German people in less than fifty years. Her historians persuaded them of their superiority over all the other nations in the world; her philosophers taught them that right was a feeble illusion when confronted by might; her politicians caused visions of universal domination to glitter before their eyes; and her harsh barrack system [of education] enslaved their wills."[18]

The bias there is obvious, as is Le Bon's anger. There is plenty of evidence that Germany was never the monolithic nation of bloody automatons that its enemies derided. Nor was it true, despite what Einstein told Rolland, that all of Germany's people were beasts or fools. Many publicly opposed the coming war. As many as 100,000 Social Democrats had demonstrated against the threat of war as late as the evening of July 28, and at least some observers noted that the rush to enlist was greatly exaggerated. The press reported the vast numbers who volunteered: 1 million, 1.5 million, even more, were supposed to have swarmed the recruiting offices. Yet the official records show that only about 300,000 men actually enlisted in the first months of the war.[19]

Firsthand accounts also confirm the existence of significant ambivalence. Reichstag member Hans Peter Hanssen was in his home district during the summer crisis and did not reach Berlin until August 2. "On the way," he noted in his diary, "I read high-sounding newspaper accounts describing the jubilation and enthusiasm in Berlin. The opposite is evidently the truth." Instead of the boisterous crowd the press had reported, Hanssen saw that "there was no rejoicing, no enthusiasm; over all hung that same heavy, sad, and depressed atmosphere."[20]

In the end, though, the existence of dissent does not alter the larger story. Support for the war in Germany was broad, deep and real. German public opinion, however greatly manipulated, celebrated the German rush to war. The young, disaffected and impoverished Adolf Hitler had a fairly typical reaction to its outbreak. He felt a "release from the painful feelings of youth. I am not ashamed to admit . . . gripped by wild enthusiasm, I fell to my knees and thanked Heaven from an overflowing heart for granting me the good fortune to be allowed to live at this time."[21]

Far more distinguished men agreed. In an eerie echo of Hitler's words, Thomas Mann asked, "How could the artist, the soldier in the artist, not praise God for the collapse of a peaceful world with which he was fed up, so exceedingly fed up!"[22] Rainer Maria Rilke's "Five Songs," written in August of 1914, cried out in joy: "At last a God . . . The Battle-God suddenly grasps us, flings the firebrand."[23] Mann again: the war brought with it "purification, liberation . . . and an enormous hope."[24]

That was the dominant impression of the war transmitted to the German public: it was to be a great, transformative struggle, political and class divisions forgotten, as the kaiser himself proclaimed: "In time of war, all parties are overcome. Now we are all only German brothers."[25] The *Vossische Zeitung* reported on August 3 that "the first war enthusiasm displayed by young people has subsided. . . . In its place has come a deep seriousness, one free from doubts and questions."

However much this may have been propaganda, an attempt to invoke national unity by proclaiming its existence, great numbers of Germans truly felt the thrill of the moment. Certain Berliners were conspicuously demonstrative. *Vorwärts,* the newspaper of the Social Democratic party, gave special play to the fact that on the 5th of August, "in all of their synagogues, the Jewish community of Berlin celebrated a day of war-prayers. . . . Only the purest and most holy enthusiasm could be seen on all faces. . . . After the celebration, the community marched out of the synagogues singing *'Die Wacht am Rhein'* "—"The Watch on the Rhine," the archetypal German patriotic song.[26]

The celebrations had their practical effect. The new soldiers saw themselves in grand terms, as fully committed to the nation as a Treitschke or a Bernhardi could have hoped. "Dear Mother," wrote Walter Limmer, a twenty-four-year-old law student, "if at this time we think of ourselves and those who belong to us, we shall be petty and weak. We must have a broad outlook and think of our nation, our Fatherland, of God—and then we shall be strong."[27] The news that Britain had declared war galvanized him, along with his fellow recruits, and he told his parents on August 7 that "it is a joy to go to the front with such comrades. We are bound to be victorious! Nothing else is possible in the face of such determination to win. My dear ones, be proud that you . . . too have the privilege of sending several of those you love into this struggle."[28]

Only with hindsight does such romantic bravado become pitiable.

Limmer's own awakening was quick enough. After his first brush with the enemy he wrote of his disillusion to his parents. Battle was "ghastly." He told his parents that he was waiting it out in "a sort of grave-like hole which I dug for myself in the firing line." One did not find glory in such a circumstance; one simply prayed for "the special mercy of God if one is to come out of it alive."[29] He died within days.

Only the speed with which he lost his faith distinguishes Limmer. Before the war, he had been an ordinary young man, well educated, with good prospects, a family he cared for, at least one young woman important enough to mention in letters. He was someone with a life before him, and no obvious need of combat. Yet like thousands of his fellows, he had embraced the faith that battle itself was a cleansing, spiritually renewing force, a value in itself and essential for the nation. Germany was engaged: the Social Democratic party approved funding for the war effort; university professors and rectors (Max Planck among them) preached of the glory of duty to the fatherland; the kaiser bellowed "The sword is being pressed into our hands! Now I commend you to God!" to the throng beneath his balcony; the crowd roared, and went to war.

And that was only August. What happened next was perhaps the worst of all possible outcomes. Any doubts, any significant opposition to the war foundered on the stunning successes won by Germany and Austria in the earliest campaigns. Battle was, it appeared, just as magnificent as promised—especially for those, unlike poor Limmer, who remained safely distant from the artillery. To the soldiers on the march, to the lasting delusion of the generals in command, and above all to the ordinary German and the elite back home that included virtually all of Einstein's closest scientific friends, the first campaign of the Great War was a grand and glorious time to be alive.

The conquests came almost too swiftly to report. The fortress town of Namur came under siege on the 19th. Brussels fell the next day, while the Germans launched the artillery barrage against the Allied front that marked the next phase of the battle: a rapid advance through Belgium and then down south and east toward Paris. At the same time, an outnumbered German army met the French forces advancing to within ten miles of the Rhine through then-German Lorraine. The Germans won a clear victory, forcing the French back through their own territory into their prewar defensive positions.

Farther to the east, the Germans faced enormous Russian armies advancing past the East Prussian border. Initial panic at the German headquarters ended with the appointment of a new commander-in-chief, General Paul von Hindenburg, and a new deputy, General Erich von Ludendorff, fresh from his victory at Liège. Ludendorff faltered at the point of the Russian advance into East Prussia, but bold leadership from subordinates turned what might have been a debacle into one of the great victories of the war, the Battle of the Masurian Lakes. The Russian army collapsed, losing 30,000 men, and its commander, General Samsonov, killed himself. The survivors retreated chaotically, leaving behind over 100,000 prisoners. Within a month, no Russian soldiers remained in German territory.

All this was prelude to the campaign supposed to end the war, the rapid thrust toward Paris. By late August, over half a million German soldiers held positions across the center of Belgium, facing fewer than 350,000 French, Belgian, and a handful of British troops. The Battle of Mons began on August 23. The hugely outnumbered British were thrown back; the Belgians began their withdrawal from Namur; and the French forces, by far the largest in the alliance, were pushed steadily rearward across the border into France.

Mons was the first defining moment for the conflict on the western front. On the German side, the victory was intoxicating. The British forces were a joke, and the German soldiers knew how to defeat the French as a matter of routine. It was obvious that a clear and decisive triumph was within reach. At the same time, a remarkably unfiltered report on the battle that appeared in *The Times* of London stunned a British government and public almost completely starved of news and accustomed only to reports of imperial triumph. The dispatch, by Arthur Moore, told of a "terrible defeat" and "the broken bits of many regiments" in flight before the enemy. With that, the British began to get a sense of the urgency already felt by the Belgians and the French, coming to grips with the idea that this was no soon-to-be-settled squabble among the powers. The war had become a fight for national survival.

But while Mons seemed to hold out the possibility of a decisive German triumph, there was still plenty of work left for the victors. So far, everything had worked according to plan—*the* plan, the evolution of the original vision Count Alfred von Schlieffen had laid down in

1905. Schlieffen, Germany's most influential prewar chief of the General Staff, had argued that the key to a two-front war in Europe turned on victory in the west. In his original scheme, a relatively small force in the east would hold the giant Russian army at bay—as his successors were doing—while a thin covering shield along France's northeastern border with Germany would serve as a decoy to disguise the main attack: a massive force charged with swinging behind the enemy defenses around the French left. It was a classic campaign of indirection, a tactic praised by the seminal strategic thinker B. H. Liddell Hart.[30]

It was a gambler's plan, but the military skill it embodied is clear. Schlieffen and his staff proposed deployments of Germany's forces in ways that might well have achieved the promised victory. His successors modified those plans, shifting more troops to the eastern front to counter the terrifying numbers that Russia could bring to bear. Many observers, including Liddell Hart, have argued that the changes were ultimately disastrous. And yet, even in its original form, the Schlieffen plan relied on raw hope, almost fantasy. German generals knew as well as anyone that Germany was so outnumbered by its potential enemies that it could not win a war of attrition. Therefore their vision of the campaign to come had to assume that a single lightning victory could completely drive the opposing armies from the field. Because anything less almost guaranteed defeat, the possibility of prolonged resistance was simply wished away. Win or lose, everyone had to be home by Christmas.

After Mons, it seemed as if Schlieffen's gamble would pay off. The German armies continued to advance, though they ran into some opposition—a surprisingly tenacious moving defense by the British, the successful destruction of crucial bridges by the Belgians, and most important, by a series of counterattacks by the French. On August 29, a French force stung the German First Army advancing through Belgium. This alone was threat enough to shake the German high command into altering the course of its Second Army, which was supposed to sweep south and west in a wide arc all the way around Paris. Instead, that force was ordered to shorten the axis of its turn to pass in front of Paris and trap the French.

The Germans advanced, twin pincers pivoting. The French forces defending Belgium and the northern frontier retreated. The Belgian army struggled to hold on to a tiny swath of coast and countryside. The small British expeditionary force seemed to vanish in headlong retreat; and the defeated French armies along the eastern border were forgotten. The Germans marched forward, past Château Thierry on the Marne River, past the mouth of the Ourca, past Compiègne and far down the Oise. By September 3, patrols advanced to within eight miles of Paris. At night, the glow from the city's lights was clearly visible. Somewhere in the midst of the advance, a middle-aged chemist turned dispatch driver named Walther Nernst could almost smell victory. It would have—it should have—taken just a few days more to take those last few steps and swing into parade down the Champs-Élysées.

Should have . . . But the Germans lay at the far end of a supply line that was in complete disarray, more than a hundred miles beyond the last railhead. Their 1.2 million men had marched hard and far, and had become hungry, exhausted, and dangerously undisciplined. They faced a combined Allied force just slightly smaller than their own. What kept them going was the lack of any sign that the French and British would do anything but retreat ever farther back. September 4 passed with little change along the front. That night there was no sign of anything untoward across the line. The first hint came at dawn. On September 5, the big guns fired and the Battle of the Marne began. French forces blasted a thirty-mile-wide gap through the exhausted and disoriented Germans. The British reversed their flight and marched through that enormous hole. By September 11, the entire German force was falling back, ultimately coming to rest along a line northeast of Compiègne, Rheims, and Verdun. What followed was a grim version of a three-legged race, each army tied to the other, each trying and failing to leapfrog past the enemy along a track west and north, both sides attempting to turn the corner and outflank the other in what became known as the race to the sea. By October 15, the Germans reached Ostend on the Belgian North Sea coast, but the French and British held the line at Nieuport, just to the south. British forces advanced back into Belgium, forcing the Germans out of a little tongue of ground that included the town called Ypres. Sir John French, the British commander in Belgium, telegraphed back to London on October 21 that "the enemy are vigorously playing their last card, and I am confident that they will fail."

French was right, up to a point. The battle that followed, First Ypres, was a bloody, grinding affair, with none of the grand balletic maneuvers imagined by planners before and through the first weeks of the war. The Germans struggled to achieve by brute force the victory they had failed to win with grand strategy. They were now fielding new regiments made up of idealistic volunteers moved by love of country and the sheer exuberance of a release from peacetime strictures and conventions. These regiments had been thrown together with what in retrospect seems to have been impossible haste. Hitler was at the front, in battle, less than three months after signing up. To say that these forces were barely trained is to do them a kindness; they were shoved up to the front line as fast as trains could carry them. Even after the bloody debacle of the Marne, the conviction that this was to be a short war was so strong in Berlin (and London and Paris) that none of the powers had planned for the needs of a longer one. In Germany in particular, the memory of two races to Paris—the successful campaign of 1870, and the almost-there experience of battle just past—reinforced the belief that victory must come from one last determined push. But there were no regulars or trained reserves left; the prewar German plan had not provided for the contingency of battle *after* the first crushing blows had landed. There appeared to be no choice but to use whatever—whomever—came to hand. Any warm bodies had to fill the gap.

The result was what the Germans came to call the *Kindermord*—the children's slaughter. The name was perfect. Forty thousand men—boys—were killed or wounded in twenty days of fighting, between one-third and one-half of the troops committed to the battle for Ypres. As usual, it was the exuberantly eager who died first and most. The archetypal action came in October, when a detachment mostly drawn from the *Wandervögel* volunteers—members of a youth organization dedicated to outdoor adventure—charged a strong point. They died almost to the last man, and as "the heroes of Langemarck" became an emblem of the compleat German: selfless and brave, marching to battle with a song, dying joyfully for the sake of country and kin.

Throughout the fall, on either side of the line, newly raised regiments were thrown into attacks on prepared positions. The pattern of the war to come began to make itself felt. Men would rush forward. Machine-gun fire would kill many, often most. The remnants would be blown back by devastating artillery fire and counterattacks launched before the attackers could dig in. Adolf Hitler's List Regiment arrived at Liège on October 23, and then made its way to Lille in the evening of the following day, struggling through a hopelessly clogged and chaotic transport system. On October 29 it mustered out toward the front. In an early letter Hitler offered a romantic, heroic vision of the war: "For four days we were engaged in the fiercest battle, and I can proudly say that our regiment fought like heroes," he wrote in a letter in December to his landlord in Munich. The casualties, though, were horrific. Hitler claimed his regiment lost about 3,000 out of 3,600 men (probably an exaggeration) and that his own company was down to just forty-two unwounded effectives. His own conduct was apparently exemplary; he received his first Iron Cross (second class) for his actions in the battle. That was, he wrote, "the happiest day of my life." There was just one flaw: "Most of my comrades who had earned it just as much were dead."[31]

But an idealized gloss like this could not last, even for Hitler. In February he wrote another letter with a different description of the same battle, one that would have been familiar to virtually any veteran of the western front. The affair had begun with the confusion of a night march: "No one knew precisely what was happening, but we all believed it was a kind of drill." That illusion was swiftly shattered. As night wore into morning, "the roar of the guns had gradually grown stronger. . . . At 9:00 A.M. we rested for two hours in a park and then on again until 8:00 P.M. At 9:00 P.M. we were handed our rations. I couldn't sleep, alas." Hitler's column had now reached the edge of the battlefield. As he prepared to rest, he found "a dead horse four paces in front of my palliasse. It looked as if it had been dead for two weeks at least. The beast was half-decomposed." If the smell didn't keep the young soldiers awake, the noise would. A battery just behind the bivouacked company fired two shells with monotonous regularity, four times an hour. "They kept screaming and whistling through the air, followed by two dull thuds in the far distance. Every one of us listened out for them. We had never heard anything like it before."

What came next was worse. As one historian put it, the main job of the infantryman in the First World War was to be shelled. Hitler's first taste of the experience was typical: "While we lay pressed one against the other whispering and looking up into the starry sky, the distant noise grew closer and closer, and the individual thuds of the guns came faster and faster until finally they merged into one continuous roar. Each one of us could feel his blood pound in his veins. . . . Unsure of what was really going on, we all waited anxiously for the next move. Then everything died down until finally the hellish din stopped completely, except for our own battery, which kept spitting its iron salutes into the night every fifteen minutes." The only good news was that the shellfire had created a large crater just in front of the bivouac into which Hitler and a few others tipped the stinking horse. The attack warning sounded three times over the next day and night. They broke camp at three that next morning, and then at seven Hitler wrote, "The fun started in earnest." His company moved forward to a staging ground prepared with foxholes. It came under shellfire again, the shrapnel "bursting on the edge of the wood, and cutting down trees like wisps of straw. We looked on curiously. We didn't yet sense the danger, and so none of us was afraid." Then came the order to attack. "We fanned out and raced across a field towards a small farm. To either side of us shells kept bursting and English bullets kept whistling by. But we paid no heed . . . then we were ordered forward once more. I was right out in front, way ahead of most of the platoon. Suddenly I heard that file-leader Stöwer had been wounded. O dear, I thought, that's a fine start! . . . Our captain was in the lead now. Then men started to fall all around me. The English had turned their machine guns on us."

Caught in the open, Hitler's platoon dived into a gully, but could not find adequate cover. Men were being wounded, and when the platoon regrouped in a little wood, it looked, Hitler wrote, as if they had been pared down. Next, led by a junior sergeant, they kept going. The pressure on them grew steadily: "Shells burst into the wood once again and threw up showers of stone, earth and sand, tore up the heaviest tree by their roots and smothered everything in a horrible, greeny-yellow, stinking vapor." They clung to the edge of the wood until an officer appeared, and then they ran on. They found their way to a position another regiment had captured from the British, and waited while yet another artillery duel took place. Finally, they managed to reach the British lines, and began to fight men instead of invisible machine guns and cannon. The Germans got the better of it initially, capturing a number of British soldiers, while "those who did not surrender were mowed down." But the inevitable counterattacks came, along with yet more shells. It was a bloody mess; Hitler came upon his major "lying on the ground with his chest torn wide open, and a heap of bodies all around him." They attacked again, but the small group of men with whom Hitler found himself was torn apart, until all but he were killed or wounded.

And so the battle wore on—a local success here and there, a daily diet of deaths and wounds, a slow grind, army against army. Hitler remained a true believer, committed to the war. The Germany to which he hoped to return at war's end was to be "a purer place, less riddled with foreign influences." He had begun well, as he saw it, fighting bravely enough to earn the first of his prized medals for his conduct in the field. And yet, while he may have loved the possibilities of warfare more than most, he ended one letter with an apology that hints at the facts of life on the western front: "I . . . beg you, dear Herr Assessor, to forgive my poor hand. I am very nervous right now. Day after day we are under heavy artillery fire from 8:00 A.M. to 5:00 P.M., and that is bound to ruin even the strongest of nerves."[32]

That marked an ordinary *Frontkämpfer*'s—frontline soldier's—recognition of a new, harsh truth. Despite local successes, the Germans had failed to break the new Allied line in Belgium. At the same time, the British and French were unable to crush the Germans. The battle at Ypres became a battle *for* Ypres, a struggle over a little bulge of ground stretching eastward from the town. By November, one German cavalry officer admitted to his diary that "as matters stand now, not only here but all along the line, both we and the enemy have so crippled ourselves by infighting that we cannot get in a blow properly."[33] The appalling weight of artillery fire held both armies in check. In response, out came the shovels. By year's end the rows of trenches begun in Belgium would stretch from the North Sea to the Swiss border. For the next four years, with minor ebb and flow, the western front would remain fixed along that scratch in the earth: fifteen hundred miles of muddy ditches, home and abattoir for men counted in millions.

Chapter Five

"UNNECESSARY ERUDITION"

BACK HOME IN BERLIN IN THAT FIRST AUTUMN OF THE WAR, THE DEVILish pressure of stalemate was hard to see, much less understand. The average man in the street did not realize it, but the failure to capture Paris meant that Berlin—and all of Germany—were under siege. That battle was taking place at a distance, out of sight, but to the most acute observers it was clear that the contest that could decide the war had begun not on the 1st of August but on the 12th, the day the British imposed a naval blockade on Germany.

In fact, the Germans had already drawn blood at sea on August 6, 1914, just two days after Britain entered the war, when the H.M.S. *Amphion,* a British light cruiser, sank after colliding with a German mine. The British response to Germany's scattering of mines through international waters was to declare the North Sea a restricted area, and to sow it with mines of their own. Ships crossed those waters at their peril—unless they first entered British harbors for inspection and confiscation of anything of potential military value to the Germans, after which they would be escorted through the complex minefields.

The German fleet tried to strike back. On September 3, 1914, H.M.S. *Pathfinder,* a British cruiser, was on patrol in the North Sea, steaming through waters apparently empty of enemies. It was struck and sunk by a torpedo fired by the German submarine *U-21*. Two hundred fifty-nine men drowned. That victory and other strikes against warships proved the effectiveness of the U-boat weapon, and the next move was probably inevitable. On February 4, 1915, Germany declared a blockade of its own against all ships, British or neutral, carrying war matériel or food to the Allied powers. The United States immediately protested, threatening to hold Germany to "strict accountability" for any loss of American lives or property. That threat was put to the test with the sinking of the British liner *Lusitania* on May 7, 1915. More than 1,100 people drowned, 128 of them American. Public opinion was outraged, but for the time being, the United States remained aloof from the conflict.

German opinion rejoiced, of course. One centrist newspaper declared: "With joyful pride we contemplate this latest deed of our Navy. It will not be the last."[1] It wasn't, but despite a campaign that ultimately sank over two thousand British vessels, German U-boats never broke the Royal Navy's stranglehold on Germany's harbors. Over time, as at least a few on both sides understood, that siege would be devastating, potentially decisive.

In Berlin, however, even military planners did not at first grasp the full danger. They saw the issue in simple terms: France, Britain and Russia could all purchase the arms, ammunition and raw materials they wanted on the open market, especially from America. As a neutral, the United States would in theory sell to either side. In practice, British control of the oceans meant that only the western Allies could access America's enormous industrial plant. As early as the campaigns of 1915, the impact of American supplies struck home, most terribly in the form of ammunition cased in steel. In contrast to the more common cast-iron munitions, steel-cased shells were vicious. They were designed to shatter into an exceptionally fine rain of shrapnel, thousands of pieces exploding outward at high speed. There was no defense against such shells except to endure them, to build better trenches, and to hope for the best. Given that for much of the time, the western front represented little more than a thousand-mile-long artillery duel, the logistical advantages of Germany's enemies became a waking nightmare for the General Staff.

But despite such direct operational concerns, the slower and ultimately greater danger from the blockade came from the fact that Germany on its own produced only about two-thirds of its food. Given enough time the blockade could literally starve Germany into submission. A wave of panicked grocery buying in early August 1914 reflected fear grounded in hard fact. The solution, of course, was a quick victory—and that had slipped from grasp at the Battle of the Marne.

Worse, the six weeks or so of unbroken successes at the outset of the war had enlarged German appetites for the spoils that had seemed within their grasp. With total triumph so nearly won, and with a mounting butcher's bill of the dead, pressure mounted from within and outside the German government to hold fast to a set of war aims that could be gained only by total military victory: the absorption of Belgium; territory seized from France; huge reparations payments; more colonies; land in the East; the displacement of Britain as the dominant global power. There could be no real negotiation on such demands. They could only be decided by total victory or defeat on the battlefield. If the stalemate persisted, there was no political path to a negotiated settlement.

All this left Albert Einstein in a peculiar position. He knew far earlier than most that the war was going to be a long one. Among his friends were a few who recognized that Germany had missed its chance in the west. Einstein's complicated colleague Fritz Haber was one of them; so was a more distant acquaintance, Walther Rathenau. Rathenau, Jewish, rich, technologically sophisticated, was the chairman of AEG, the giant German electrical firm. As recently as July 31, 1914, he had protested in print in one of Berlin's leading daily newspapers that a Serb-Austrian conflict should not be allowed to provoke wider war.[2] But just a week later, he called on the War Department in Berlin to offer his expertise in organizing Germany's raw materials and industrial production for a war that would last for at least several months.

Rathenau was a strange man even to those who knew him well—vain, very proud, exceptionally intelligent, at once self-consciously rational and a romantic. He had a keen, if overwrought, sense of the consequences of his actions in the war. Two days after his first visit to the War Department, he returned and was offered the job of heading the new department of war raw materials. The day after that, he wrote to a friend that he was aiding the "overthrow of the gods to whom, before August 1914, the world prayed." Now, abruptly, he found himself part of a process of destruction, and "Paradise will not come in the world which is now being formed." Instead, what was emerging would, he wrote, "seem to many [to mark] the decline of Europe."[3]

These elegantly fraught sentiments were luxuries now. He knew better than almost anyone else that the British blockade could on its own condemn Germany to defeat. In his tenure at the War Department, he led the successful effort to organize Germany into a military-industrial state that would survive four years of ferocious and logistically costly warfare. And Einstein knew what Rathenau was doing, knew that his efforts were aimed at keeping Germany in the fight as long as necessary.

That was where Haber came in. Haber, perhaps first among leading scientists, understood the danger of a stalemate. He did not lose his head like Nernst and rush off to play soldier. Instead, he dedicated himself and his institute to the task of inventing a new, more thoroughly devastating weapon that could break the static bloodletting of trench warfare. Accordingly, in November 1914, he began to focus on the chemistry of chlorine. Chlorine compounds are intensely poisonous: exposure to chlorine gas can produce burning throats, scarring of the lungs, choking and suffocation. Haber set himself the task of finding the right formulation that could poison entire sections of the enemy line. Einstein had his office at Haber's institute, spoke to him regularly, relished his company, found himself becoming an ever closer friend. So by the end of 1914 at the latest, he had to have known what Haber was doing. To Einstein, the chemist's zealotry for his task was clear evidence of a kind of madness. He would widen his indictment as the war went on. "Our whole, highly praised technological progress," he wrote later to his longtime friend Heinrich Zangger, a professor of forensic medicine in Zurich, "and civilization in general, can be likened to an ax in the hand of a pathological criminal."[4] If so, it was his friends who forged that ax while he watched, fully aware of what was happening around him.

Yet Einstein remained in Berlin, kept his office in Haber's institute, attended the meetings of the thoroughly prowar Prussian Academy. He shrugged off the complete ineffectiveness of his own protests against the war and continued as much as possible with the routine he had established in the brief period during which he had known Berlin at peace. He had choices, more than almost any other senior man in any of the combatant nations. He retained his Swiss passport and could have returned to Zurich, which would have brought him close to the sons he swore he missed terribly. Holland remained a possibility—another neutral country. He was on almost filial terms with Hendrik Lorentz, and his old job offers could conceivably have been revived. He could have fled Berlin. He did not. By all accounts he never even seems to have contemplated such a move. Why not?

Perhaps most simply because Einstein had an almost unbounded capacity to narrow his focus. If he had work that interested him and was given the freedom to think as he pleased, he could block out almost anything. "The lack of real companions . . . is perhaps even greater than you experience in Zurich,"[5] he wrote to Zangger in the spring of 1915, but "why should not one, like a servant in an asylum, be able to live cheerfully? . . . Up to a point one can choose one's madhouse—but the difference between them is less than one might have thought."[6] He continued along familiar lines, trying (and failing) to interest his colleagues in what he saw as a critical problem. On October 19, 1914, and again on October 29, the same day that Adolf Hitler and his List Regiment marched forward into the cauldron of First Ypres, Einstein lectured to the Prussian Academy. His topic was the current state of his attempt to produce a conception of gravity by generalizing the special theory of relativity. Gravity remained a hard sell. At best he was greeted by polite doubt, and as usual many in the room would have found the ideas he presented beyond them. This was no surprise. In this, as in his antiwar work, he accepted the notion that his concerns were irrelevant to most of those surrounding him.

He gave his audience fair warning that something big was brewing. He was beginning to break loose from the certainty he had felt the year before. Then, fresh from the labor of working out the unfamiliar and complicated mathematics of his latest conception of gravity, he had boasted that his theory was complete. But now, although he retained his basic faith in that formulation, he sensed that the ideas he had developed were not quite sound. Still, he told his audience, the answer lay near at hand. The academicians were unmoved. Einstein affected an air of distracted unconcern; if not encouraged, he was at least left undisturbed, which was, of course, the prospect that had brought him to Berlin in the first place.

It took him a while to put that freedom to use. He passed the first autumn of the war with little significant research to report. As Christmas approached he sent presents to his sons in Zurich but spent the holiday with Nernst in Berlin, safely back home from his jaunt toward Paris. In the trenches Christmas Eve brought an impromptu, unofficial truce. An explosion had torn through Haber's institute a week before the holiday, killing one of his collaborators on the chemical warfare project, but Einstein's office was untouched and he remained undisturbed.

In the new year, he resumed his work on gravity. He stuck with the problem for the next eleven months, until in a sudden flurry of thought, the final, correct form of his theory took shape. The story of that discovery, from its roots in 1907 to its ultimate, sudden conclusion in 1915, is an instance of a genuine scientific epic, a hero's journey. Einstein himself remembered times of "intense desire" and "alternations of confidence and misgiving until one breaks through to clarity and understanding. . . ." The effort to comprehend gravity, he said much later, took "years of searching in the dark for a truth one feels but cannot express."[7] Feeling and desire, hope and doubt, the years of darkness and the faith required to imagine an unseen truth—all these are elements of the quest that culminated in a revelation: a wholly new vision of what shapes the universe.

FOR EINSTEIN, the birth of that vision turned on a single critical clue, an insight gained from a simple image. It was another thought experiment, one that seemingly had spontaneously floated through his mind, and then stuck. It had come to him in 1907 on an ordinary working day. He was at his desk at the patent office, daydreaming. Whatever patents lay before him drifted out of mind as he pondered the state of special relativity two years after its creation. He was working on a review article on the application of the special theory to different branches of physics, but the question of gravity was holding him up.

He remained at his desk. He thought; as he remembered much later, his mind and eye wandered until he found himself staring out the window. A workman was fixing something on a rooftop across the way. The sight of a man precariously balancing at such a height led inevitably to the thought of falling, and anyone could imagine what came next: the man losing his footing, slipping, then tumbling over the edge, twisting and turning as he went.

So far most of us, fellow physicists included, could follow Einstein, tracking the roofer's fall in our imaginations. But there we would stop, hopefully before the inevitable outcome, until our minds moved on to the next thought. Einstein did not. Something about the image of the man in midcourse held his attention until it became what he called "the happiest thought of my life." In an unpublished manuscript written around 1921, he restated his insight in more formal language: *"For an observer falling freely from the roof of a house there exists*—at least in his immediate surroundings—*no gravitational field"* (italics in the original). He put it more simply a year later, telling his audience that his first glimpse of a breakthrough on gravitation came that day in 1907 when he suddenly realized that "if a man falls freely he will not feel his own weight."[8]

One of Einstein's most famous aphorisms is that "the whole of science is nothing more than the refinement of everyday thinking,"[9] and this is one example of what he meant: the creation of a simple mental picture, a scene anyone could imagine and comprehend, that leads toward a fundamental new idea. Yet this is also one of those "only Einstein" moments. Fine—so one feels no weight in free fall. What of it? Virtually any physicist of Einstein's day or after would have enjoyed the idea for a moment and then moved on, possibly distracted by the thought of the instant when the man catastrophically experiences his weight once more.[10] (As the old joke goes, it's not falling that kills you, it's trying to stop.)

And what was so happy about this thought anyway? Einstein's thinking had an aesthetic tinge, a hunger for what could be called beautiful in the realm of ideas. He was ready to recognize what mattered in that stray image of a fall because it could help make a clumsy line of reasoning take on grace. "It was deeply dissatisfying to me," he said, that "although the relation between inertia and energy is so beautifully derived [in the equation $E = mc^2$], there is no relation between inertia and weight"[11]—that is, between special relativity and gravity. (Inertia is a property of mass—the *m* in Einstein's equation. It is, to use the relativist Kip Thorne's version of the definition, the resistance a body has to being accelerated by forces acting on it.[12] Weight is the property of mass that experiences the tug toward the floor caused by the earth's gravitational attraction.)

Einstein's unfortunate roofer for the first time linked the experience of gravity with motion, and relative motion at that. Einstein dubbed that connection "the equivalence principle"—a concept as important to him as his original relativity principle. The equivalence principle states that a person in free fall, like that imaginary roofer, cannot determine whether he is actually falling under the influence of gravity or is simply floating in a gravity-free region of space where only uniform motion, *inertial* motion, takes place. (It is called inertial motion because no forces are acting to overcome the inertia of a body and change its motion. Acceleration, by contrast, is exactly that change in motion, speeding up, slowing down, that inertia resists.)

In other words, never mind that as Einstein sees the situation sitting at the window, the roofer is accelerating, speeding up as he plummets. The roofer himself feels no change; as long as he falls he feels only weightlessness, no push or tug of any sort—which is the signature of inertial motion. The two states—motion under the influence of gravity, and motion only under the influence of inertia—thus had to be seen as equivalent, both of them accurate descriptions of the same phenomenon.

The idea of equivalence does not stop there. Another thought experiment derived from his original epiphany brings the equivalence principle to life. In a variant of Einstein's original picture, imagine a person standing in an elevator, stopped on the top floor of a tall building. She feels all the effects of gravity. Her feet are firmly planted on the floor; she feels the weight of her body. If she drops a set of keys, it will fall to the floor, and she may reasonably conclude that she is standing still within a constant gravitational field.

If the elevator's cable should snap, however, the scene changes abruptly. As the elevator car plummets in free fall, the sensation of weight disappears. Keys let loose from a hand simply stay there, suspended in midair. If the woman were to push off with her toes, she would fly upward toward the ceiling, as if actually flying. For the time being, as far as she can tell, any gravitational field has disappeared. By all the evidence available to her, she could be floating in the midst of empty space, far removed from the slightest influence of the earth's gravity. Her central realization so far is the same as that of the roofer; free fall with a gravitational field and motionlessness in a gravity-free tract of space feel exactly the same. They are *equivalent* descriptions of the same experience and they are indistinguishable from each other.

Now switch the scene. Imagine that an observer is actually locked within the closed cabin of a rocket ship, deep in space, far from any gravitational tug. Decades of images of space travel set the stage for us: such an astronaut would float weightless, able to perform elegant, slow-motion space gymnastics.[13] But if the rocket motor were then to ignite, everything would change once again. Seen from outside the spaceship, the front of the cabin (the one opposite the direction of the motor's thrust) would rise as the ship began its journey. To the astronaut within, however, the sensation would be exactly that of falling down, meeting the rising floor with a thud. She would once again feel the sensation of weight. Anything she dropped would fall to the floor. According to any test that she could run within the closed cabin, the rocket has been gripped by a uniform gravitational field—no different, as far as she can tell, from the rocket's being fixed in place on the surface of the earth. Her conclusion: the sensation of acceleration produces exactly the same effects as the tug of gravity. The two phenomena are effectively identical, which meant, Einstein declared in his review article of 1907, that the physicist could "assume the complete physical equivalence of a gravitational field and the corresponding acceleration of the reference frame." (The term *reference frame* provides a rigorous definition of what it means to be an observer. As Kip Thorne explains the concept in his excellent book *Black Holes and Time Warps,* "A reference frame is a laboratory that contains all the measuring apparatus one might need for whatever measurements one wishes to make." Crucially, a reference frame travels as a single unit; the lab and all that it contains "must move through the universe together; they must all undergo the same motion.")[14]

Thus, in formal terms, the conclusion that Einstein drew from his equivalence principle is that all physical laws remain the same both in reference frames freely falling under the influence of gravity and in inertial reference frames in some completely gravity-free region of space. Epiphany! This was what made Einstein's original image of the roofer such a special thought. The equivalence principle led him directly to the essential connection lacking in special relativity, the idea that linked inertia and weight. Weight, he now understood, is just the perception of a change in the inertial motion of any object, no matter what causes the change, acceleration or gravity. Free fall produces the same experience as inertial motion; acceleration produces the identical perception—that of weight—as does standing still on the surface of the earth, fixed within a gravitational field.

Einstein pursued other ideas in the 1907 paper, notably two dealing with more technical issues of the interaction between gravity and light. This was where he first suggested that gravity could bend light.[15] He also analyzed an effect known as the gravitational red shift of light. In this account, the wavelength and hence the color of light changes, depending on the mass of the source from which that light comes: the bigger the mass, the stronger the tug of gravity, which yields a greater shift toward redder—longer—wavelengths. (In the rainbow spectrum of visible light, violet and blue have the shortest wavelengths, and red has the longest.)[16]

Both of these ideas were correct in essence, though as it turned out, Einstein's first attempts to calculate the details of light bending produced the wrong numbers. Nonetheless, each was a useful stepping stone toward a deeper understanding of the way gravity must behave in a relativistic universe. At this stage, all that he felt he knew for certain was the equivalence principle, and that this principle should drive all his subsequent thinking about gravity. The new theory, he recognized, would have to be fundamentally different from Newton's, with its description of gravity as a force reaching out instantly over any distance. Rather, the fact that a change in speed produces the same observable effects as the tug of a gravitational field meant to Einstein that his theory had to be able to describe gravity as a property of mass *in motion*.

From the beginning, in other words, he recognized that the way objects travel through space under the influence of what we call gravity lay at the heart of his still-unformed theory. What the final description of gravitation would be, he had no idea, not yet. But he was certain that it could be found. Abraham Pais, Einstein's biographer and friend, captured the essence of the moment as well as anyone could. Pais wrote of the 1907 paper that "I admire this article at least as much as the perfect relativity paper of 1905, not so much for its details as for its courage. . . . With total lack of fear he starts on the new road. For the next eight years he has no choice. He has to go on."[17]

* * *

THE NEXT MAJOR STEP in the project turned on a discovery made not by Einstein but by Hermann Minkowski, who had been his math professor at the Polytechnic and was now a professor at Göttingen. After a promising start, they had not gotten along, Minkowski calling him a lazy dog. Thus, the discovery of special relativity caught Minkowski by surprise, to the point where he confided to Max Born that "I really wouldn't have thought Einstein capable" of such work.[18]

At the same time, he recognized an opportunity in Einstein's version of relativity. Einstein had couched his new theory in very simple, unsophisticated mathematics, not much more complicated than high school algebra. Minkowski saw something deeper in relativity, and in 1907, he began to work on a restatement of the idea in more graceful mathematical language. The results, announced in 1908, were too abstruse for his inattentive former student. On first reading, Einstein dismissed the work with the same sort of disdain that must have infuriated his erstwhile teacher. "Now that the mathematicians have seized on relativity theory," he said, "I no longer understand it myself."[19]

Minkowski, however, had a gift for the telling phrase at least equal to Einstein's. As he saw it, his results fundamentally transformed how humankind must understand the nature of existence in the material world. "Gentleman," he began his first lecture on the new mathematics in 1908, "the concepts of space and time that I wish to present to you have sprung from an experimental physical soil. Therein lies their strength. Their tendency is radical. Henceforward space by itself and time by itself must dwindle into mere shadows, and only a form of union between the two will preserve its independence."[20] Minkowski was the first to recognize clearly that Einstein's relativity condemned the old view, in which space occupied three dimensions—our familiar height, width and depth—and time ticked on regardless, completely unconcerned with what happened in space. To replace it, he proposed a world that exists in four dimensions, three of space, one of time, all inextricably intertwined. And most important, Minkowski came up with the mathematics that could describe what happens within what has come to be called spacetime.

The critical value of this work was that it tamed the most troubling idea in Einstein's relativity. At first glance, the special theory seems to state simply that any of us in motion relative to any other will come up with accurate but different measurements of distance and duration. We simply have to live with the fact that each of us sees the world a little bit differently. In Einstein's version, the map of space and the flow of time are distinct for each of us, with their precise metrics determined by the speed at which we travel. Relativity theory as Einstein left it then provides the tools for reconciling those different views. But they remain distinct, "relative" to each other, each uniquely associated with the individual frame of reference within which each observer stands.

Minkowski's breakthrough was to find the way to express each such observation in a single, absolute form, one that all observers could accept. He did so by showing that time as a geometrical idea can be treated exactly like space as a number, a coordinate. Just as three coordinates define any location in three-dimensional space, Minkowski demonstrated, it is possible to give any event a unique location in his new, four-dimensional spacetime—defined by the three numbers that fix its position in space, and the one that marks it off in time.

In practice, the spacetime coordinates of the start of Minkowski's working day could read like this: Minkowski sits in his chair, three feet from the back wall, six feet from the window, twelve feet up from street level at 8:37 A.M. on September 16, 1907. (To make the concept more abstract and easier to manipulate, a mathematician would lay out a coordinate system, a grid, and fix Minkowski's position as a point, M_0, defined by four numbers, X_0, Y_0, Z_0, and T_0. The idea, though, remains the same—four numbers uniquely locate Minkowski within the experience of his life.)

While that's simple enough, and not much different from what Einstein imagined, Minkowski went on to consider what happens when another event occurs. Back to that morning: Minkowski sits, lost in thought in his room. He gets up, thinking still, and wanders over to the window, looking toward but not seeing the lamppost outside, the couple on the sidewalk, the play of light across the street. His position in space is now five feet from the back wall, leaning against the windowframe, still twelve feet above ground level. As his attention finally shifts to the scene in front of him, his watch marks the time: forty-two minutes and seven seconds past eight in the morning. Four more numbers define Minkowski's location as another point in spacetime—the new locations listed above, ones that a mathematician could write X_1, Y_1, Z_1, and T_1, which uniquely define the point M_1.

The next step was the key. Minkowski showed how to use the geometry of four dimensions to fix those two points, those two events—Minkowski sitting, Minkowski standing—into a single, absolute picture, one that any number of observers could accept as the true description of their different, relative measurements. The detailed geometrical argument is somewhat complex, but Minkowski reworked Pythagoras's formula, the one that relates the three sides of a right triangle in the equation $a^2 + b^2 = c^2$, into an equation that defines the shortest distance between two points in ordinary three-dimensional space. Minkowski revised his new formula to define the single path that marks out the smallest distance between any two points in four-dimensional spacetime. That path is called the absolute interval, a single measurement that combines the intervals in both space and time that separate two events. It is a map that does not change.[21]

In essence, the concept of the absolute interval tamed the inherent strangeness of Einstein's original scheme. Einstein had demonstrated that two people moving with respect to each other cannot agree when and where each event they both observe has occurred. Minkowski's work now showed that despite such relativistic disagreements, both observers would still measure the same combined totals of space and time that separated each event. By framing such measurements into the new, unified concept of spacetime, Minkowski was able to identify the unique relationship between one event and the next. While Einstein had always affirmed that while the two observers' measurements would differ, there was only one sequence of underlying phenomena, Minkowski's accomplishment was to make that sequence explicit—plain for anyone to see. His absolute interval was the device, the concept, that marked out the precise relationship between one place and time in the cosmos and any other.[22]

That was what Minkowski boasted of in his lecture, as he condemned space and time to their place in the shadows of memory. The picture seemed strange at first—after all, it took Einstein himself about four years to come to grips with it. But Minkowski was speaking the truth when he proclaimed the power of his idea. He caught its force in one of his most striking phrases, the concept of the "world-line" of a particle or a person, the continuous track through spacetime each of us marks out as we exist, move, interact with others, and continue on.

Imagined this way, there is a unique line in spacetime that describes any person, including you sitting and reading these words. You hold more or less still in space—but are moving nonetheless, traveling incredibly fast. (To make manipulating spacetime a little easier, physicists have developed a trick to express measurements of space and measurements of time in the same way, using the same units. The speed of light provides the ultimate yardstick. How long does a meter last in time? Just so long as light takes to cross that distance—3.3 billionths of a second. How far is a second? It is the distance light travels in one tick of the clock, 186,000 miles, or 300 *million* meters.)[23]

Another second ticks off, your hand turns the page, and all of us who have lived that second have traveled that same immense distance of time. Every life can be seen as such a world-line tracing this way and that through our four-dimensional universe. Lines cross, we meet, perhaps join, and then separate. Some world-lines end before others, and it becomes possible to look back on such journeys as fixed and finished forms. Great art trades in spacetime. A work like Michelangelo's *David* contains in its column of marble the whole story, if you choose to view it that way. There is the boy, the young shepherd, Jonathan's friend, Saul's harpist, and all the rest trailing behind the perfect young man, poised, sling at the ready, at the edge of that next instant when Goliath roars. As for stone, so for us: when we view it from a four-dimensional perspective, a life lived in sequence becomes sculpture, a trace through Minkowski's spacetime, a figure that we can now recognize as a single whole. The planet earth itself travels its elegant, elongated spiral, one full turn around its orbit for every year it moves along the axis of time, a dance to continue until a dying sun swallows us up and turns motion into the frozen memory of spacetime.

Beyond such images, Minkowski's new spacetime contained within it a radical notion of the methods available to the physical sciences, a sea change in the way physicists could think about how the world works. Minkowski's work injected geometry, the description of shapes, their properties and their interaction, back into the heart of physics from which it had been banished since the time of Descartes. His spacetime geometry was dynamic, concerned with things that move and change, offering tools with which to analyze events, not just static relations between drawings on a grid. Awareness of the power of such tools was nascent in Minkowski's work, but not yet fully developed. That would take Einstein, and the effort to come between 1912 and 1915. Ultimately, though, Einstein realized that understanding such geometry could produce fundamental new physical insight—an idea that is one of the great conceptual leaps of twentieth-century science.

At the time of Minkowski's announcement, however, Einstein showed an almost reckless disregard for what seemed to him a mathematician's parlor game. Minkowski's work was "unnecessary erudition," he said, and proceeded to ignore it. For several years, from 1907 to 1911, he veered away from the problems of gravity and relativity. Instead, he concentrated most of his attention on an issue that would continue to engage him throughout the rest of his career: the problem of the quantum, the behavior of matter and energy in the realm of the very small. He had proposed his quantum theory of light back in 1905: the concept that light traveled in discrete particles—quanta—and not in a continuous wave; and he had spent much of the four years up to 1911 trying to comprehend the key questions raised by that theory. Late in 1911, speaking at the first Solvay Conference, Einstein asked his colleagues to join him in what he regarded as the fundamental issue facing them all, the "supremely important but unfortunately still essentially unanswered question"[24] of the quantum theory of light and heat. There were no answers yet—none from Einstein, and none that he could evoke from his colleagues. The meeting resembled, he said, "a lamentation on the ruins of Jerusalem."[25]

Chapter Six

"MY GRANDEST DREAMS HAVE COME TRUE"

EINSTEIN HAD TRAVELED TO BRUSSELS FOR THE SOLVAY CONFERENCE FROM his new home in Prague. The move from Zurich to Prague in April 1911 to take up an appointment as full professor of physics had been in some ways a wrenching one. More than any other city they had lived in so far, Zurich was home for both him and Mileva. It was the place where their friends were old ones. He and Friedrich Adler had been fellow students at the Polytechnic, and he now lived downstairs from the Einsteins. Einstein had enormous affection for Adler, who was now in the physics department at Zurich University—along with a kind of debt, though he did not know of it. Adler had originally been the first choice for the Polytechnic professorship, but he had vacillated long enough to scare off his suitors. Adler himself felt that Einstein deserved the post—on the day he learned that he was out of the running, he wrote his father that there was "a man who on principle and from the point of view of the people involved, should certainly get it rather than myself . . . it is felt to be a scandal, not only here but in Germany, that a man like that should sit in the Patent Office."[1] There was also Heinrich Zangger, a true polymath, and an expert in mining disasters (he was famous for orchestrating the rescue of some one hundred trapped French miners after an underground explosion in 1905), who had an amateur's love for science. Brownian motion fascinated him, and after Einstein published his explanation of the physics behind the phenomenon in the third of his "miracle year" papers in 1905, Zangger had gone to Bern from Zurich to seek him out. It was one of the first visits that acknowledged Einstein as an authority, a scientific mentor, and he treasured Zangger for the accolade. Now, living in the same city for the first time, the two had become very close—and would remain so through the years to come when Zangger was pressed into service as an intermediary between the estranged Albert and Mileva.

More famous figures came to call as well. In a classic case of mutual incomprehension, Einstein met the psychoanalyst Carl Gustav Jung after attending one of Jung's lectures. He never had much interest or confidence in the alleged "science" of the mind that Jung and his former mentor Sigmund Freud were developing. His later friendship with Freud would emerge more from the shared experience of fame and some politics in common than from any interest in Freud's theories. But Einstein made a good-faith attempt to explain his work, if not himself, to Jung and his circle, and although Jung admitted that he understood very little of what was said, the conversations were satisfying enough to sustain a sporadic series of visits.[2] More significant, it was in Zurich that the Berlin chemist Walther Nernst came to quiz Einstein for the first time. Nernst was then working on a problem in thermodynamics, the same issues that had stimulated his colleague Max Planck to formulate the first quantum theory in 1900. His new measurements matched predictions derived from Einstein's version of quantum theory, and Einstein was elated to hear the news.

Nernst was impressed too. He reported on his encounter to colleagues at home, including Emil Fischer, chemistry professor at the University of Berlin and a man whose self-imposed duties included the defense of German science. Fischer then wrote to Einstein, "Your great theoretical papers in thermodynamics created a sensation in the world of the natural sciences, and are often discussed in our circle, especially since Mr. Nernst became engaged in the experimental test of your conclusions." He added a surprise: "It so happened that I related this to an acquaintance of mine from the chemical industry [Franz Oppenheim, one of the founders of Agfa]. He was very pleased that German [sic] researchers like you, Mr. Planck, and Mr. Nernst have taken over the leadership in this fundamental area, and he believes it the duty of the well-to-do in Germany to promote these splendid endeavors a bit by providing financial support."[3]

Financial support meant a no-strings-attached grant of fifteen thousand marks, paid over three years, enough money so that Einstein did not feel the need to correct Fischer's labeling him a German. There was no offer here, no hint of a job behind the grant. But a sum like that was a lovely carrot to offer anyone who just might become a suitable ornament for German science. At a minimum, the encounter turned Nernst into a valued friend rather than a professional colleague—a transformation the Germans were to use to good effect, of course, when the time came, three years later, to pursue Albert Einstein in earnest.

In 1911, though, the German University in Prague beckoned, with its lure of both more money and the prestige that came with a full professorship. It proved to be something of a fool's bargain. He and Mileva found the dislocation from their beloved Zurich unsettling. "The people are haughty, shabby-genteel, or subservient, depending on their lot in life," he wrote to Zangger shortly after his arrival in April. "Houses and things are somewhat dirty and run-down," he added, and "the animosity between Germans and Czechs seems to be quite strong."[4] There was none of the ease he felt in Switzerland, the sense of being immersed in ways of life he shared. "The people are so alien to me," he told Besso a month later. They lacked "natural sentiments; unfeeling and a peculiar mixture of class-based condescension and servility, without any kind of goodwill to their fellow man." Prague itself was a city of "ostentatious luxury side by side with creeping misery on the streets. Barrenness of thought without faith."[5]

Still, despite these grim impressions, Einstein managed to re-create a version of his Zurich rhythm. A memoir written by Dmitri Marianoff, a future husband of Einstein's stepdaughter, recorded that "he loved sitting under the trees in the gardens of the cafés on the Moldau River with his confreres, drinking their white coffee and beer." By contrast, Marianoff wrote, Mileva loathed her new home. "She wanted to join in these talks, but she was left at home with the children and she became more and more discontented every day." Tension had actually been brewing since before the move. The couple's last year in Bern, 1909, had been marked by that bitter battle over Albert's overly friendly correspondence with his former girlfriend, Anna Meyer-Schmid. The fray had left scars, imposing a chill on the marriage that lasted for months. Though this eased when she became pregnant with their second son, Eduard's birth in July 1910 meant that Mileva was largely confined to home. In Prague, she felt herself even more trapped—abandoned, as she saw it, by her husband's indifference. Her "fiery disposition resented the fact that she was never taken into Einstein's full confidence in the working out of his problems," Marianoff wrote.[6]

Albert made no move to relieve her sense of isolation, although he did not entirely neglect his family. Paul Ehrenfest visited during the winter of 1912, and said that Einstein was a weekend family man, pushing Eduard's pram while the rest of the family and their guest strolled along. He is reported to have worn his court uniform—a kind of Gilbert and Sullivan admiral's rig required for his investiture in the august office of professor in the Austro-Hungarian Empire—in a public park, purely to amuse Hans Albert. But there is no doubt that when he felt the need for like-minded company, he sought it outside of home. There was something of a salon life among the German-speaking Jewish elite, and he was a frequent guest at the Tuesday evening sessions at Berta Fanta's home. Her family owned a well-known pharmacy in the heart of the old town, and Fanta, a musician and an intellectual, played host to a loose network of the local intelligentsia who would come together to make music and argue philosophy. The novelist Max Brod was one of the regulars. Brod, an amateur pianist, would accompany Einstein on the violin, and from time to time Brod's friend, Franz Kafka, would show up, spending the evenings in silence on the edge of the crowd. He and Einstein almost certainly coincided at one of the Fanta soirees, though there is no evidence that they ever spoke.

Brod, however, was fascinated by the physicist, and observed him closely enough to draw a striking portrait of him, thinly disguised as the character Johannes Kepler in his novel *Tycho Brahe's Path to God*. To Brahe, Einstein/Kepler was a terrifying and admirable enigma. The character he saw was single-minded, virtually fanatical in the pursuit of the truth and fully willing to pay the consequent price: "He had no heart and therefore had nothing to fear from the world. He was not capable of emotion or love."[7] When the book appeared in 1915, Nernst is said to have told Einstein, "This Kepler is you."[8]

Einstein did not disavow Brod's portrait. He read the book, praised his grasp of "the cliffs of the human soul," and let it go at that.[9] Bluntly,

Brod was right. Einstein's family and Prague's social life, its comfortable cafés, its distressing dirt and petty hatreds—all these were ultimately incidental, diversions or distractions. They had little hold on Einstein's imagination, especially when, in the spring of 1911, he began to glimpse a major advance in his theory of gravity.

EINSTEIN'S OFFICE in the physics building at the university overlooked one of Prague's main insane asylums (it is still in operation today), and he said of his neighbors that they were "the madmen who do not study physics." The gibe suited his next discovery about gravity, for he now began to analyze the interaction between gravity and time. His latest thoughts, he acknowledged, were shocking. Absurd though it may have seemed, clocks in different gravitational fields behave differently. The result, he said, was "of fundamental significance."[10]

The chain of reasoning that revealed that gravity warps time began via the study of the suggestion that gravity bends light. Einstein had known this earlier, but in Prague he worked out the detailed analysis of the phenomenon. The thought experiment that illustrates it picks up from where the equivalence principle left off. Imagine Einstein's rocket once again, this time with a window in the crew compartment. If the rocket is at rest relative to a flashlight being held outside the window, then the beam from that light will travel straight across the rocket to the far side of the cabin. But if the rocket's motors ignite and the craft begins to accelerate, the picture will change. The rocket rises just a little in the time it takes for the flashlight's beam to travel from one side of the compartment to the other. The beam will strike the far wall just a little lower down than the point at which it entered through the window. To an observer within the rocket, the light bends, actually curving downward a little. Accelerate more, and the light bends more. Given the equivalence principle, if acceleration bends light, then gravity must as well.[11]

The connection to time followed directly. Again, the analysis hinges on a thought experiment, a picture, that centers on the question of how to measure time. Einstein's version of this thought experiment relied on an extension of his earlier thinking about the gravitational red shift of light, the fact that a beam of light stretches as it encounters a gravitational field, changing its frequency or wavelength. The argument he developed out of that idea is valid but complex, so the thought experiment he used then has been recast in simpler terms. Return once more to Einstein's rocket, fitting a clock to the nose of the ship while placing another one on the bottom bulkhead, back by the engines. At rest, the clocks remain synchronized by a flash of light that the clock at the top emits at each second. But then the engines start, and the ship begins to accelerate.

Now, between each flash of the clock at the nose, the rocket has moved, accelerating to ever faster speeds. Each flash thus has to travel a shorter and shorter distance to the clock at the tail, which has been rising to meet the signal with the motion of the rocket as a whole. Thus each signal takes less time to reach the second clock than it did when the rocket was at rest. The same will be true for the next flash, and the flash after that. Anyone checking will see that each flash from the first clock arrives in just a little less than a second, as ticked off by that second clock. Given that, there can be only one conclusion. The clock at the nose is running faster than the clock at the tail of the rocket. Once again, the equivalence principle states that there is no difference detectable between acceleration and gravity, which means that clocks in a gravitational field must behave in exactly the same way that the accelerating clocks on board the rocket do. A clock placed where gravity tugs more strongly, closer to the center of the earth, must run more slowly than one perched a little farther from the earth's center. The tick of time runs more slowly on the flat north German plain around Berlin than it does on top of one of the mountains near Zurich that the young Einstein might have climbed.[12]

Thus Einstein fought through to the last step in the chain of reasoning. The invention of special relativity had already altered the definition of time. No longer an absolute, time became simply that which any given clock actually measures, given its relative motion. Minkowski had demonstrated how the mathematics of spacetime connected one observer's findings to any other's. But here Einstein pushed even further, demonstrating that *all* measurements of time are strictly local. If gravity affects clocks, that means that time varies from place to place. It must bow to circumstance, the chance of whether one finds oneself at the Dead Sea or on Everest, or even merely in the basement or on the third floor.[13] That each place, any place, could have its own unique flow of time was a new vision, and not a comfortable one—not then, and not now. But by no later than the middle of 1911, Einstein saw where any extension of relativity theory must lead. Gravity bends time.

The insight was tremendous, with a deep significance that became clear to him within a couple of years, and there was more that he uncovered during his time in Prague. Special relativity had told him that mass and energy are equivalent, functionally simply different forms of the same thing. That meant, he now realized, that *any* form of energy would exert gravitational influence just as mass would, including the energy contained within the gravitational field itself. Thus every change in the strength of a gravitational field would produce a little extra variation as the increase or decrease in the energy within the field fed back into the system as a whole. For example, when the earth moves a little bit farther away from the sun on its elliptical orbit, the increase in distance reduces the sun's tug on the earth just a little. What Einstein had just grasped was that such a drop in the strength of gravity would amplify itself a little, because of the decrease in energy represented by the weakening of gravity as felt on earth. The change feeds on itself in what is formally called a nonlinear process. That seemed to be bad news for him, because equations that describe nonlinear phenomena are hard to understand and notoriously difficult to solve. But the discovery turned out to be one of the critical milestones in the development of the final theory.[14] Even so, as he finished this phase of the work, in March of 1912, he complained to his usual confidant, Besso, that though "I have been working furiously on the gravitation problem . . . every step is fiendishly difficult."[15]

Frustration clung to him for several months more. Later that spring he wrote to another friend that "the further development of gravitation theory" was running into enormous obstacles.[16] But he knew the hint was there, hidden somewhere in his recognition that gravity alters the path of both light and time, even if he did not know yet where the thought would lead. By late summer, his persistence found its reward. In part, he benefited from another change of scene. In August 1912, after less than two years in Prague, he left the university to take up the professorship of theoretical physics at Zurich's ETH. Crucially, the move reunited him with his old classmate, Marcel Grossmann, who had become professor of mathematics at the ETH. Einstein now needed his help.

The issue that prompted this request concerned the seemingly arcane question of what happens to different measurements on a rotating disk. It was a question that seems at first to be almost completely irrelevant to gravity, or, for that matter, to the real world in general. Yet within it lay a paradox, which, when combined with what he already knew, held the essence of the radical theory Einstein had been seeking. The paradox arose out of a question of special relativity that had already been studied by several researchers, most notably Max Born. They wanted to understand what happens to the circumference of a disk, the distance around the edge of the circle, when, LP-recordlike, it begins to rotate. More than two thousand years ago, Euclid had shown how to calculate the length of any circle's circumference. It is an equation known to every schoolchild: multiply the length of the disk's radius—the distance from the circle's center to its rim—by two and then again by pi (written π), $C = 2 \pi r$. However, if a disk begins to rotate, its edge must move too. This is where special relativity takes over. That theory states that objects in motion will shrink in the direction of their travel when measured from a point at rest, such as the center of the disk. Out on the edge, very short segments of the circumference can be imagined as tiny moving straight lines. According to special relativity, they must shrink as they speed by a stationary observer. Extrapolate the measurement of each segment to the circumference as a whole and the entire rim shrinks. But the radius does not move relative to any observer at the center, so it remains the same length whether the disk is rotating or standing still. This means that Euclid's formula cannot hold in all cases. The circumference of the rotating disk is shorter than that of the same disk standing still. In motion, it measures less than $2 \pi r$, deviating ever further from that number as it spins faster and faster.

Born, who was Minkowski's former assistant, had spoken on this question at a conference in Austria in 1909. Einstein was present. The two met and are known to have spoken privately, and they almost certainly compared notes on the conundrum of the rotating disk. But Einstein seems to have missed the critical message. Perhaps his old disdain for mathematics, for "useless erudition," distracted him, obscuring the sting in the tail of this apparently minor corner of relativity theory. Born's results really meant that if one constructs the conditions carefully enough, Euclid's geometry fails within a relativistic universe.

Euclid wrong? Even as late as the first decade of the twentieth century, such a challenge to Euclid still seemed improbable. His *Elements* is almost certainly the most influential scientific text ever written. As the mathematician Robert Osserman has pointed out, in more than two thousand years no one has ever found an error in its analysis of the geometry of planes, surfaces and solids. All its conclusions follow logically from clearly stated premises, without a single lapse of reasoning. For most of history Euclid's system was understood to generate facts, not just methods for analyzing reality. Nature itself has seemed content to follow the rules Euclid laid bare, and scientists from Ptolemy to Galileo and Newton recognized in his geometry the scaffolding of the cosmos. The shortest distance between two points is a straight line, parallel lines never intersect, the angles of a triangle add up to 180 degrees; all this and more, not only in the *Elements* but out here in the real world. Almost all human artifacts seem to embody Euclid's eternal verities, all his straight lines, angles, and embracing curves. (Look to the Vatican, with its wide welcoming plaza, its facade and columns lifting straight upward to the elegant circles that shrink to a point on the dome of St. Peter's—or better, for pure geometrical power, gaze on the Great Pyramid at Giza.) Nothing else in the history of science—not the concept of the atom, not the ancient model of the cosmos—comes close to this kind of influence on human thought. What started as an assumption became an article of faith. In Euclidean geometry humankind possessed a piece of the truth, or, in Einstein's terms, that geometry offered a glimpse of the way that God *had* to make the universe.

But now, suddenly, an attack—one that emerged not from the logic chopping of mathematicians (as Einstein would have seen it) but from something physical, something to be found in the real world. That fractious disk, spinning away with its shrinking circumference, did not conform to the rules laid down in classical mathematics. It was not so much that the old geometry was wrong; rather, it had become irrelevant, it did not apply. Its logic still held firm, but it was no longer absolutely, necessarily, connected to nature. It is a tribute to the strength of Euclid's hold on the imagination that as late as 1909, Einstein himself missed the significance of the breach. Even then (even now, for most of us), it was hard to shake the sense that the world of experience follows Euclid's design. Perhaps that is why it took Einstein three more years to register that the old system, for all its elegance, could not describe the universe of relativity. When that realization came, it was liberation. The old map had to be thrown away and a new one had to be found.

Einstein's return to Zurich brought him that epiphany, the realization that "the foundations of geometry have physical significance."[17] If Euclidean geometry failed the test of nature, there must be another geometry, one that could encompass relativistic phenomena and contain key insights about properties of the universe that it described. The difficulty was finding such a geometry. He dimly recalled one of his university courses in the mathematical theory of curved surfaces. That was what triggered his question to Grossmann. In the polite version of the story he asked Grossmann if he knew of any geometries that differed from Euclid's. Grossmann retreated to the library and returned with his answer the next day. There was indeed such a geometry, Grossmann told his friend. The great Bernhard Riemann had developed his non-Euclidean system to analyze the properties of curved space sixty years before.[18]

Another version is less genteel but perhaps more accurate. Einstein returned to Zurich, beset. He knew he didn't know enough math to solve his problem, so he begged: "Grossmann, you must help me, or else I'll go crazy."[19] Grossmann already knew the answer: Einstein had to look at Riemann's work. The only problem, Grossmann warned, was that Riemann's geometry was far too difficult for mere physicists. Worst of all, he said, its equations were nonlinear, a level of complexity that physicists traditionally shunned. Einstein, of course, knew this already: his Prague work had shown him that any relativistic theory of gravity had to be nonlinear. Einstein immediately conscripted his friend to guide him through. When the search for a new theory of gravity was finally over, Einstein revealingly praised Grossmann as the man "who by his aid . . . saved me the study of the relevant mathematical literature." Little had changed since their undergraduate days, when Grossmann had lent the young Einstein the notes that enabled him to avoid the necessity of actually attending something so dreary as a mathematics class.

Einstein's debt to his friend now was greater by far. Riemann's geometry describes what is called positively curved space, a cosmos in which the circumference of a circle is always less than the Euclidean value of twice pi times the radius. Crucially, Riemann's ideas allowed Grossmann and Einstein to measure the precise amount of curvature at any point in space. Riemann had even extended his work to propose models of the universe with different types of curvature. Those ideas anticipate not just Einstein's work but much of modern cosmology as well. All Riemann lacked was one crucial piece: the physics behind the mathematics, the mechanism in the real world that could produce such curvature. He did not know how the universe we actually inhabit might flex and bend. That was the step that Einstein could now supply.

At the center of the breakthrough lay two interwoven concepts. The first derived directly from Minkowski's mathematical recasting of relativity in the guise of four-dimensional spacetime. Minkowski's chief motive in creating this concept lay with his desire to simplify the relativistic worldview. But the scheme that emerged from that work retained one vital characteristic held over from earlier ideas of the space-and-time vision that preceded it. Minkowski's spacetime formed a flat, four-dimensional map, a background against which to view the tapestry of events that took place *within* it. This new vision of the universe was still the vessel of history, unmoved and unmoving, isolated from any of the drama of action, interaction, and motion within it.

But with the discovery that gravity bends time, that static conception became untenable. If one dimension of spacetime can flex or curve—as it must, because of gravity's effects on time—then spacetime itself must warp. With that realization, Einstein's thinking took on the elegant sweep of his best work. First, what he now knew: gravity is a property of matter and energy. Gravity bends time. Riemann's geometry, the mathematics of positively curved surfaces and spaces, can measure and analyze such bending. To all this Einstein now added the last, new piece: the total amount of mass and energy determines the strength of the gravitational field in any particular location, and hence the amount any given region of spacetime will bend.

And in this picture, what is gravity? It is that local curvature of spacetime, the particular shape given to spacetime by mass and energy. Large masses like the earth or the sun deform the spacetime around them. Think of that deformation as a dent in space, a well with the massive object at its center. The geometrical description of such dents reveals the rules that govern how the distribution of matter and energy determine the shape of space and time. Those rules are laws of nature, the laws that describe the behavior of gravity everywhere throughout the universe.

This was a sudden insight that entranced Einstein from the moment he first glimpsed the correct train of thought. He wrote to his fellow physicist Ludwig Hopf at the beginning of his work with Grossmann, "It is all going marvelously with gravitation. If it isn't all a trick, I have found the most general equations."[20]

Einstein was ever an enthusiast, entranced by the glory of every alluring new idea that he encountered long before he worked through its implications. This time he was almost but not quite right. Within a few months, by the fall of 1912, he found himself completely entangled in the complexity of his new way of thinking. Some of the difficulties were simply technical, products of the gaps in his knowledge. Despite Grossmann's help, he still had to struggle to master a significant body of intricate and abstract mathematics. As he admitted to Sommerfeld, "I have become filled with a great respect for mathematics, the more subtle parts of which I used to regard as sheer ostentation."[21] But beyond the issue of mastering new tools, the great challenge lay with the meaning of his new conception. It is all well enough to say that gravity is somehow connected to the shape of spacetime, but then what? Such a claim flies in the face of experience, of common sense, of the feeling of weight with which each of us greets the earth's gravitational field as we rise in the morning.

So the next question that Einstein had to resolve was how the geometry of spacetime could produce the effect we feel so clearly as a force. What is it that produces the tug that we feel every moment of our existence on earth? In his new scheme, that question became: How do three-dimensional creatures like ourselves perceive things that affect us in four dimensions? The answer turns on the idea of the shortest path between two points. On a perfectly flat surface, as Euclid's geometry states, that shortest distance must be what common sense tells us it should be: a straight line (Minkowski's absolute interval). But in regions of spacetime affected by gravity, like those near a star, there are no straight lines. The shortest distance between two points now traces out a curve, a path that bends around the local dent in spacetime created by something like the sun's great mass. What we perceive as gravity, Einstein concluded, is the shortest possible path through such curves and bends. (Such paths are equivalent to great-circle routes on earth, called geodesics, lines that trace out the shortest distance between two points on the curved surface of our planet.)

But the difficulty is still there: those of us who live and perceive in three spatial dimensions can't see curves in four dimensions. We still feel gravity as a force, as weight. Another famous thought experiment provides a hint of how such sensations could emerge out of the experience of living in more dimensions than we can perceive directly. In a modified version, that experiment begins with an image of a vast, seemingly featureless plain. Someone living on such a plain finds his surroundings so flat that he can only perceive two dimensions, length and width, and cannot detect any changes in altitude. One day, he sets out for a walk on the most direct track between his home and a distant village. After a mile or so his steps come harder. It takes a little more effort to keep going. He begins to puff and labor. Our walker clearly senses that he is being tugged by something—a force he could call gravity—that has made itself felt as he walks on what he thinks is a straight line. To anyone able to see all three dimensions, there is a simpler explanation. What our hiker feels as a mysterious force is simply the consequence of having traveled the shortest path up a hill. The "gravity" felt by the hiker is nothing more than the measure of the curvature of his space, the rise of a slope he could not see himself. The analogy is not perfect, of course, as it deals only in space, not time. But the essence of the picture is true: we cannot see curves in four dimensions, even though they are there. We exist in a locally curved region of space and time created by the mass of the earth. The tug we feel downward as we stand by our beds in the morning is the sensation of our daily slide down that well in spacetime, a slope heading inward toward the center of the earth. It is a sensation born of the geometry of experience, an exercise in spacetime dynamics that, in practice, holds our feet to the floor.

Einstein understood all this by the spring of 1913, exhausting himself in the process. He and Grossmann published their collaboration in mid-1913, dividing the responsibility and the credit. (Grossmann had insisted that he wanted no connection to the physics.) Einstein was almost sure that it was the last word. He told Ehrenfest that "the gravitation problem has been solved to my complete satisfaction."[22] He was wrong.

The critical flaw was that the new theory actually violated the special theory of relativity. Recall that the relativity principle asserted that there were no special observers whose measurements of time or distance could be more "true" than anyone else's. That idea's extension into the equivalence principle stated that no reference frames existed in which an observer could distinguish between acceleration and gravity without some external clue, like the sight of a rocket engine starting up. But in this version of Einstein's gravity theory, observers in certain reference frames could distinguish between the two phenomena. Given that the equivalence principle was the assumption from which the whole theory had emerged, this contradiction made Einstein nervous. In August, shortly after publishing his claims, Einstein confessed to his friend and mentor Hendrik Lorentz that "my faith in the theory still wavers." A failure to preserve the equivalence of acceleration and gravity, he admitted, meant that "the theory contradicts its own starting point," leaving "everything up in the air."[23]

Characteristically confident, Einstein did not believe that the difficulties he confronted genuinely undermined the theory. He seems never to have wavered in his conviction in the core idea that gravity was simply curved spacetime. He believed, and he staked his name and fame on that faith. There is a reason that Einstein remains, by broad consensus, the greatest scientist of the twentieth century, and it is intimately intertwined with this, his flawed theory of gravity. That he could think himself this far was remarkable enough. That he could recognize its flaws, however slowly, was essential. That he never lost his conviction that the theory held within it the heart of a great truth illuminates what his biographer Pais accurately called his extraordinary courage. There is a famous line of Einstein's, written in a letter to a friend in the spring of 1914, at a time when he had begun to lose just a bit of his certainty about the work of the previous year. No matter, he told Zangger, "Nature shows us only the tail of the lion. But I do not doubt that the lion belongs to it, even though he cannot reveal himself whole because of his great size."[24]

THERE EINSTEIN RESTED for a time. He was right when he told Ehrenfest that his new theory would make his colleagues uncomfortable. Planck's old warning—that he could not succeed with gravity and that even if he did, no one would believe him—seemed to be coming true on both counts. Between the middle of 1914 and the early months of 1915, he worked a bit more on the theory and produced a brief paper, written with a Dutch physicist named Adriaan Fokker, that addressed some of the problems he had already identified. But there he stopped. After Freundlich's eclipse expedition collapsed, he could find little to do. There were no other specific observations on hand that could confirm or deny the theory. 1914 stumbled out with its momentary Christmas truce, and the new year began, with the war reasserting its hold on all of Europe.

Einstein concentrated. In January came his private complaint that his colleagues were ignoring "the depth and necessity" of general relativity. Briefly, he occupied himself with what was essentially busywork, including an interlude in which he dabbled at the laboratory bench. He enjoyed himself thoroughly, boasting of the "wonderful experiment" he and his collaborator, Wander Johannes de Haas, had performed. They were trying to demonstrate an old hypothesis that magnetism was produced by the motion of electrical charges. They tested the specific case of iron, looking for evidence that electrons tracing out closed orbits around the iron nuclei would produce both "hidden" currents creating magnetism and angular momentum—torque. Einstein had come up with a theory that made a specific prediction for the amount of torque in a given magnet, but the results he and de Haas arrived at were embarrassing. One out of two sets of measurements they made contained the "correct" answer, so they threw away the less promising numbers, declared victory, and walked away. Unfortunately, they were off by a factor of two. Their experimental design had been complex, cantankerous and ultimately incapable of the precision the measurement demanded. Eventually, de Haas retracted their joint paper, blaming the error on the bad habit (common to theoreticians) of calculating rather than measuring critical values within the experimental apparatus. Einstein let the episode pass in silence.

Still, it passed the weeks while doing little harm. That summer Einstein returned to theoretical matters. He went to Göttingen, home to David Hilbert, Germany's leading mathematician, to deliver a series of talks on what he still claimed was the "already quite clarified theory of gravitation." That version still contained the fundamental problem of privileged observers, but the underlying concept caught Hilbert's attention, and Hilbert began to retrace Einstein's steps, bringing to bear even more sophisticated mathematical tools of non-Euclidean geometry as part of his attempt to create a relativistic theory of gravity.

Einstein returned home. The summer passed with little progress on the gravitation problem. In September he left for a vacation in Switzerland. He visited Mileva, who continued to dream of reconciliation, but he spent most of his free time with his sons, walking in the hills with his older boy, Hans Albert. On the 16th, he met Rolland at Lake Geneva and the two of them mourned the cause of peace. And then, at last, something broke. Early in October, shortly after his return to Berlin, within days or weeks, Einstein finally understood that his theory of gravity, as worked out in 1913 and elaborated since, was in fact seriously flawed. There are no notes left from this period, so the exact timing, and even the precise question that roused him, remains unknown. But the revelation was unequivocal. He confessed his errors: that while he had "believed that I had discovered the only law of gravitation" possible, now, at long last, he had "completely lost faith in the field equations"[25]—the same ones he had once praised so highly.

It was the denial of the equivalence principle that troubled him. Einstein now accepted the judgment that any general theory of relativity had to be truly general. Its description of reality, its laws, had to work the same way for all observers. Anything less was simply unacceptable. Another apparently minor difficulty emerged when he tried to analyze the behavior of rotating gravitational fields, for example those surrounding a spinning planet or a star. The problem had seemed simple enough, but the field equations of the 1913 theory could not describe the situation accurately. Einstein admitted later that this alone could have falsified his earlier effort.

One last hint took on great importance: the problem of Mercury's skittish orbit. Einstein had long since dismissed the existence of any mythical planet Vulcan as the cause for Mercury's tiny wobble. Instead, he wanted to show that it was the particular shape of spacetime near the sun that caused Mercury's orbit to deviate from Newton's predicted path. But his 1913 equations could only account for about one-third of the observed orbital variation. Taken together with a crisis of the equivalence principle and the theory's inability to describe the specific case of gravity and rotation, the inability to find one good solid confirmation in nature was decisive. The 1913 theory could not be saved. There remained some last, large idea to be found.

The answer finally emerged when he found a mathematical solution that made the theory truly consistent for all observers. He wrestled with the very complicated equations of his revised theory for much of October. On November 4, 1915, he presented his results to the Prussian Academy meeting that day, proclaiming victory. His haste showed. There were still some errors, and while most observers lost their privileges, not all did. But still, Einstein had made a major step forward: his new description of gravity contained Newton's old *almost* true law as an approximation describing weak gravitational fields—those we feel on earth, in contrast to those much stronger fields very near stars, for example. By showing how his theory contained and extended Newton's, he was able to bolster his claim that a relativistic theory of gravity was truly an advance, a new, more general, more powerful description of nature.

He spoke again at the Academy meeting on November 11, eliminating a few of the errors he found in his November 4 paper. The breakthrough came when he linked the new mathematics with his final, critical understanding of what curves in curved spacetime. Up until these last few weeks, despite his acceptance of Minkowski's four-dimensional picture, Einstein still found it difficult (as most still do) to abandon older conceptions of space and time as distinct categories. He had proved to his satisfaction that gravity warps time, but he still assumed that space remained flat, unmoved by gravity. But a close reading of his latest equations revealed that gravity distorts not just time but three spatial dimensions of spacetime as well.

With that Einstein had what he had sought. As he reported to the Academy on November 18, the theory was virtually complete, and it was producing hard numbers. His earlier calculation of the deflection of light near the sun yielded a prediction of .83 arc seconds—the same number that emerges from Newton's equations. Now the addition of warped space to warped time doubled that number, to 1.7 arc seconds. This meant that the next eclipse would provide an unequivocal test of his theory, a single number that could distinguish it from the competition. Was the curvature of space and time a physicist's fantasy, an obvious violation of common sense, or was it the real thing, a glimpse of nature as nature is? Look, measure, and see.

The other finding Einstein reported in the same talk was even better. In the last several days, he had also recalculated his theory's prediction for the orbit of Mercury. The new equations yielded an orbit that wobbles forty-three arc seconds per century—exactly the observed number. Most important, as Einstein announced with a justified air of triumph, the result accounts for Mercury's travels "without the need for any special hypothesis"—no mythical planets, no weird, unobserved phenomena of nature. The equations themselves simply cranked out the correct orbit as if by magic. Even Einstein was stunned by the result. When the right values appeared before him, he said, he became "beside himself with joy." He confessed to palpitations of the heart, and, as he told his experimental partner de Haas, he felt as if something had snapped within him. He even admitted that the Mercury result left him so excited that he could not work for days.[26]

He was not quite done. The November 18 paper retained a handful of unnecessary assumptions, and still contained the possibility that some observers could distinguish between acceleration and gravity, thus violating the equivalence principle. One more week of intense work followed, until on November 25, 1915, Einstein returned to the Prussian Academy to present his final theory of gravity. No holes remained, no unnecessary assumptions, no special observers.

Much later, Einstein tried to explain how he felt when he finally reached the end of his long road. It was impossible to express, he said, because the emotions of such moments can be "known only to him who has himself experienced them." But Einstein reveled in the pure joy of those weeks as he circulated the news. Study the equations well, he told Sommerfeld, for "they are the most valuable discovery of my life."[27]

In its most concentrated form, that discovery boils down to just one formula, still called the Einstein equation, a single line of symbols from which all else flows. In the formal symbolism of mathematics, it reads like this: $G_{\mu\nu} = 8\pi\ T_{\mu\nu}$. On one side of the formula lies spacetime; on the other lies matter-energy: together, the two halves of the universe. The equation defines their relationship—most simply, as the great physicist John Wheeler put it, it describes how matter and energy tell spacetime (the universe) what shape to be, while for its part, spacetime tells matter-energy (all that the universe contains) how to move. Objects within a gravitational field, with no other forces acting upon them, must travel along the shortest possible paths through the four-dimensional curvature of spacetime. Put the two sides of the equation together and the result is a universal theory, an account of the shape of the cosmos, its evolution, and even, potentially, its ultimate fate. The last such theory was Newton's, and it had been said that humankind lived in Newton's universe.

November 25, 1915. For the fourth week in a row Einstein makes his way from his apartment near the Kurfürstendamm to the center of Berlin. At the Academy, a group of men gather, all middle-aged or older. Some of them would have followed his thoughts over the previous lectures. A few may even have grasped the scale and ambition of the idea unfolding before them. Einstein stands to speak once more. It does not take long; this last statement fills just three pages. There are no errors, nothing left to add. The work is finished. He comes to a close, makes conversation as necessary, and goes home. The glow is still there a few days later. He writes to his friend Besso that he is "content, but a little worn out."[28] Where Newton's theory was, his now stands. We live still in Einstein's universe.

Chapter Seven

"IS THE OLD JEHOVAH STILL ALIVE?"

Back in the spring of 1915 in Berlin, in the Plaza just in front of the Brandenburg Gate, workers maneuvered through a growing web of scaffolding. Over several weeks the construction within rose and its outlines became clear. It was a figure of a man almost twenty feet high, the likeness of General Paul von Hindenburg, the "victor of Tannenberg," the first great triumph on the eastern front. The statue was made from Russian wood, and aside from being an appropriate use of war booty, the timber construction had another virtue. Patriotic Berliners could purchase nails of iron, silver or gold for one, five or a hundred marks apiece, and then hammer them home into the hide of the conquering hero. For a time in that still hopeful year of 1915, the project was a considerable success. People would come, buy their nails, and clamber up a tall ladder to smash their contributions home—sharing the glory of one battle while being seen to help fight the next one.

This was war as a grand and common crusade, the workingman's one-mark iron nail setting just as proudly as the rich man's gleam of gold. The effort echoed other eruptions of civic duty. Copper was valuable to the war effort, and over the course of 1915, homeowners donated the copper sheathing from their roofs. Pots, pans, and window hardware followed. If in time such gifts became an official duty, compelled by the

Ministry of Defense's powers of requisition, still, some spirit of common enterprise had operated from the start.

Even so, the popular mood in Berlin in 1915 was greatly changed from the happy days of the summer of 1914. As the year ground on, it became clear to the broad Berlin public, not just the militarily or politically well informed, that the war would not end soon. On May 23 Italy belatedly declared war against Germany and Austria-Hungary—its former partners in the Triple Alliance—and crushed any lingering fantasies of a rapid victory. In the midst of the growing gloom, Einstein tried once more to move German opinion. A civic organization called the Berlin Goethe League announced plans to publish a *Patriotic Album* intended to ease the public's mind about the rightness of the cause. Perhaps naively, the league sought a contribution from Einstein. In October in the midst of the final dash to general relativity, he wrote a three-page credo titled "My Opinion of the War." The organizers, taken aback, sought his permission to cut two paragraphs that ridiculed the German love of the state. On November 11, the day of his second gravitation lecture to the Academy, he paused to tell them that he wanted to keep the offending paragraphs. "All genuine friends of human progress," he wrote, should combat "the glorification of war. . . . This, in my opinion, includes everything that goes by the name of patriotism."[1] In the end, though, he surrendered, agreeing to publish his article in its truncated version.

What remained was still strong medicine. Where the conventionally patriotic German saw the world's fate bound up in Germany's victory, Einstein saw the war as a deadly fracas between little boys. "I will never forget," he wrote, "the sincere hatred my schoolmates felt for the first-graders of a school in the neighboring street." As a result, "innumerable fistfights occurred, with many a hole in the head the result." As for children, so for nations. War was essentially mindless. Violence, he argued, was the result of instinctive male aggression, the human species's animal nature. "We 'jewels of creation' are not the only ones who can boast of this distinction," he wrote, noting that "the bull and the rooster" outdo us. The belligerents' aims and reasons were irrelevant since pretexts "can always be found when passion requires them."

To combat this inherent human passion for war, Einstein told his readers, all that could be done was to treat "the hunger for power and greed . . . as despicable vices." That was all he had to offer: a pious wish that human beings would behave better than they had to date. Time and history may color our reading of his words, but it still seems obvious from the plain language of his text that any such hope was overwhelmed by the expectation of hope denied. The war would wear on, until, with luck, the full weight of catastrophe might ultimately persuade human hearts to alter. Einstein's best guess of the odds of that happening? Not good. "Why so many words," he asked, "when I can say it in one sentence, one very appropriate for a Jew: Honor your master Jesus Christ not only in words and songs but rather, foremost, by your deeds."[2]

His disdain is clear. The document as a whole reads as if he anticipated its irrelevance and chose to fire off his best, most surgical invective while he had the chance. Nowhere in it does he display any illusion about his power to move opinion about the war. He was asked for his opinion; he gave it. If his readers were not yet prepared to heed him, he would wait.

Such patience was essential, for the critical fact of the war between 1915 through 1917 was its endless sameness—the agonizingly slow bleed that official Berlin worked hard to disguise. For a while, even after the events of late 1914 and early 1915 set in motion the bloody calculus of attrition, the carnival atmosphere of the first weeks of the conflict remained, evolving to adapt to the new situation. The first significant casualty lists had come as a shock when they appeared in Berlin newspapers on August 10, 1914, but the surprise and horror soon wore off. On August 22, when the first groups of wounded soldiers were brought back to the capital, they were "welcomed by crowds paralyzed at the sight," as Berlin chronicler Paul Weiglin wrote. But the convoys quickly became routine, and "Berlin's inhabitants soon got used to the fact that the names of the dead soldiers grew too many to be published."[3] Rather than dwelling on the hard facts of the human cost of war, Berliners now sought and found a kind of entertainment in the spectacle. As a matter of conscious effort, even of public policy, artists, writers, and the government itself began to institutionalize the romantic enthusiasm of the first weeks, creating an experience of the war as carnival, something to obliterate the emotional dullness of everyday life.

Berlin's nightlife did its part. Movie theaters had banished foreign films within weeks of the start of the conflict, French productions first of all. In their place came grimly predictable patriotic movies with familiar titles like *Die Wacht am Rhein*. Vaudeville acts and legitimate theaters alike leaped into the breach as well, offering uplifting fare like *My Life for My Fatherland* and *Nun woll'n wir sie verdreschen!—C'mon Let's Beat Them!* One long-running show proclaimed: "As a Neanderthal in the trenches/I'm living through a lovely time/I'm sitting here in silent solitude/. . . with nothing to do but shoot/as soon as the enemy shows his head."[4]

It was supposed to be funny—the singer swaying in time to the music, happy in the midst of a set mocked up to hint at the battlefield. Stage guns are light and they point easily, and in the spirit of pantomime the enemy could fall acrobatically to cheers whenever a member of the chorus with clown's training died pathetically enough. The drinks would circulate, the hours passing in the glow of imagined victories. It was possible to laugh, and to believe in the dream of glory.

By day, much the same message was hammered home. In the spring of 1915, the once left-leaning newspaper *Vorwärts* loyally described Berlin's newest tourist attraction: a life-size replica of a front-line trench. It was complete in every detail, the newspaper assured its readers: "The full length of the war-trench is fenced with thin wooden branches tied together with wires. . . . Every few meters, the trench is protected by shoulder works that prevent exploding grenades from scattering fragments too widely. Observation posts . . . interrupt the continuous line of the trench every twenty or thirty meters." Best of all, the trench showed the comfortable circumstances in which German boys fought their war. "The most interesting [sights] are the soldiers' quarters . . . equipped with every comfort of modern times except a roof garden . . . as in the cabin of a boat, the smallest place offers enough room for the peaceful, sleeping soldiers."[5] That, of course, was the reason the exhibition was built. From the start, this was something more than a simple tourist destination. Rather, these clean and well-finished trenches served to domesticate the war, transforming it into the familiar rhythms of civilian life. The soldiers on the line clearly had all that was required for modern existence. Why long for peace when war was so well organized and so comfortable?

Such idealized mockeries of the real thing were not unique to Germany, of course. The other combatants also faced the problem of

Albert Einstein with his son Hans Albert in 1904 or 1905.

Mileva Maric in 1899, when still enrolled at the ETH.

The bustle of prewar Berlin. The clatter of street life is what made such observers as Walther Rathenau mourn the lost tranquillity of their Athens on the Spree.

The religion of speed: Berlin's rush to "world city" status was carried on the rails of an ever-expanding transit system. Its stations became monuments.

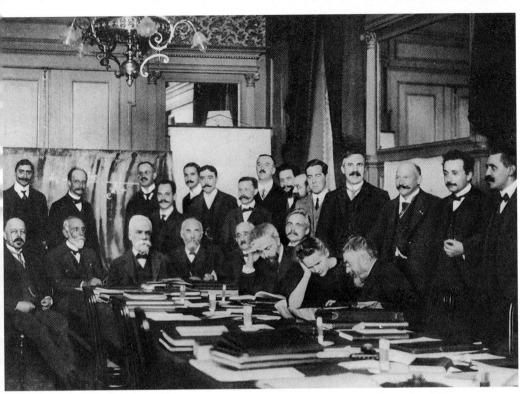

The First Solvay Conference, Brussels, 1911. Einstein stands second from the right.

Fritz Haber with Einstein shortly after the move to Berlin.

Among the crowd gathered to celebrate the start of the war in Munich's Odeonsplatz was the young Adolf Hitler.

The poster child for the ills of hereditary monarchy: Kaiser Wilhelm II.

Glory days: a young woman pins a flower on the tunic of a new German recruit.

Crowds gather around one of the first casualty lists posted in Berlin.

With horses vital to the war effort, circus elephants haul coal in wintertime Berlin.

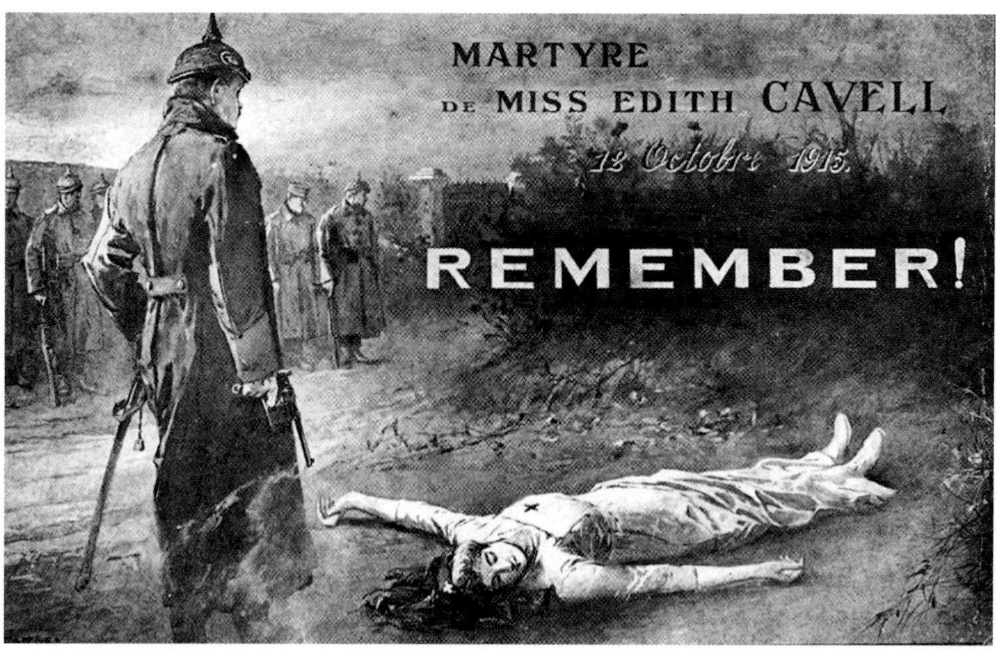

French propaganda, decrying the barbarity of the German murder of the British nurse Edith Cavell.

German propaganda aimed at its own home front, showing the glorious charge to victory that never quite happened.

Adolf Hitler, on the right, with two other dispatch carriers.

This giant statue of Hindenburg, built early in the Great War, was used both as a rallying symbol and as a fund-raising device.

Illusion: a model trench in a Berlin park.

Reality: British soldier stares at a destroyed German machine-gun nest in a trench at the Somme.

Winston Churchill's "placeless names and sterile ridges": here an utterly destroyed section of the Passchendaele battlefield.

Victims of gas.

Spartacist fighters using rolls of newsprint for cover in a clash with Freikorps forces in 1919.

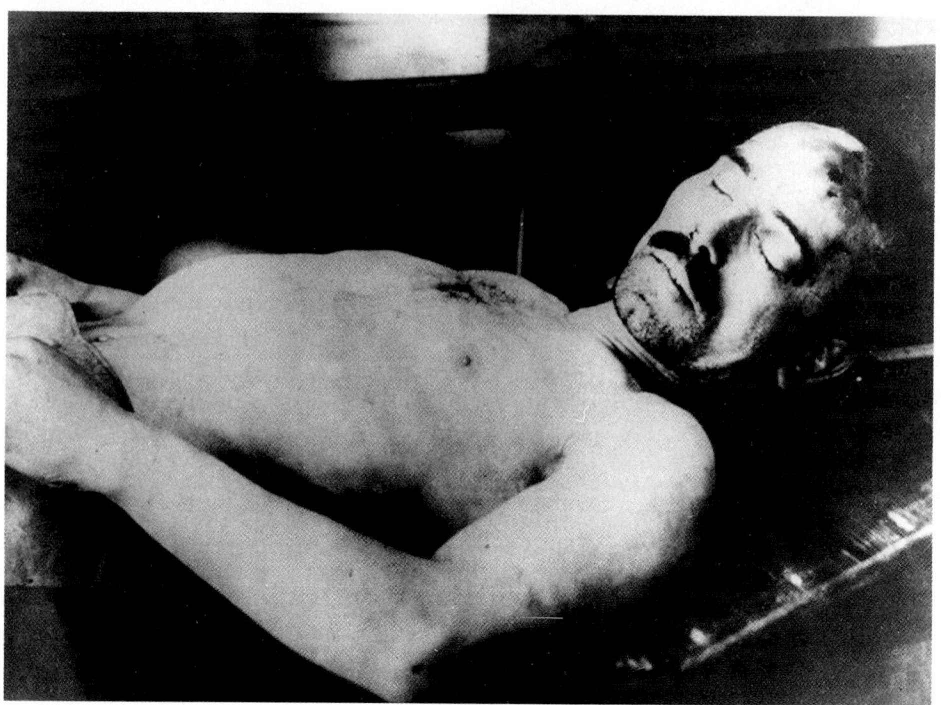

Spartacus Week's aftermath: Karl Liebknecht's battered corpse.

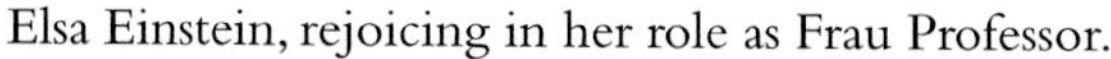

Elsa Einstein, rejoicing in her role as Frau Professor.

Zürich. 14.X.13.

Hoch geehrter Herr Kollege!

Eine einfache theoretische Überlegung macht die Annahme plausibel, dass Lichtstrahlen in einem Gravitationsfelde eine Deviation erfahren.

Grav. Feld

Lichtstrahl

MOUNT WILSON OBSERVATORY ARCHIVES

Am Sonnenrande müsste diese Ablenkung 0,84" betragen und wie $\frac{1}{R}$ abnehmen (R = ~~Sonnenradius~~ Entfernung vom Sonnen-Mittelpunkt).

0,84"

Stern

Sonne

Es wäre deshalb von grösstem Interesse, bis zu wie grosser Sonnennähe ~~grosse~~ helle Fixsterne bei Anwendung der stärksten Vergrösserungen bei Tage (ohne Sonnenfinsternis) gesehen werden können.

Einstein drew this diagram of starlight bent by the sun's gravity in a 1913 letter to the American solar astronomer George Ellery Hale. He still had not arrived at the correct figure for the amount of deflection, but he already knew that gravity had to bend light.

The University of California's Lick Observatory used the eclipse of 1922 to reconfirm Einstein's prediction of the bending of light. In conditions superior to those of the 1919 eclipse, general relativity again passed the test.

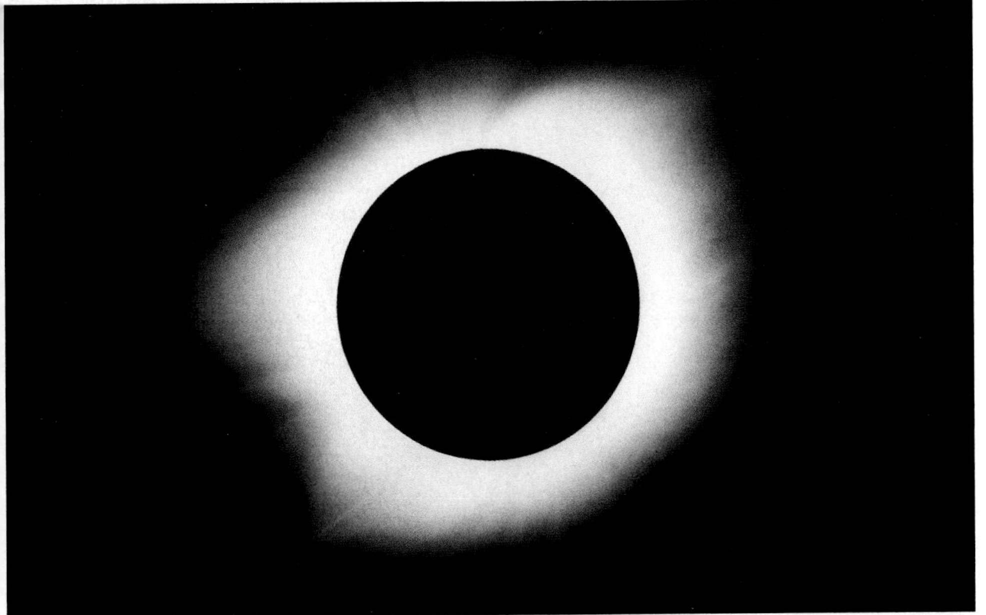

14. Dezember
1 9 1 9
Nr. 50
28. Jahrgang

Berliner

Einzelpreis
des Heftes
25 Pfg.

Illustrirte Zeitung

Verlag Ullstein & Co, Berlin SW 68

Eine neue Größe der Weltgeschichte: Albert Einstein,
dessen Forschungen eine völlige Umwälzung unserer Naturbetrachtung bedeuten
und den Erkenntnissen eines Kopernikus, Kepler und Newton gleichwertig sind.

The cover of the magazine Berliner Illustrirte Zeitung, dated 14 December 1919. The headline reads, "A New Giant in World History."

Erich Mendelsohn's Einstein Tower, a building that Einstein somewhat ambiguously described as "organic."

The shock of celebrity: Einstein on parade in New York City in 1921.

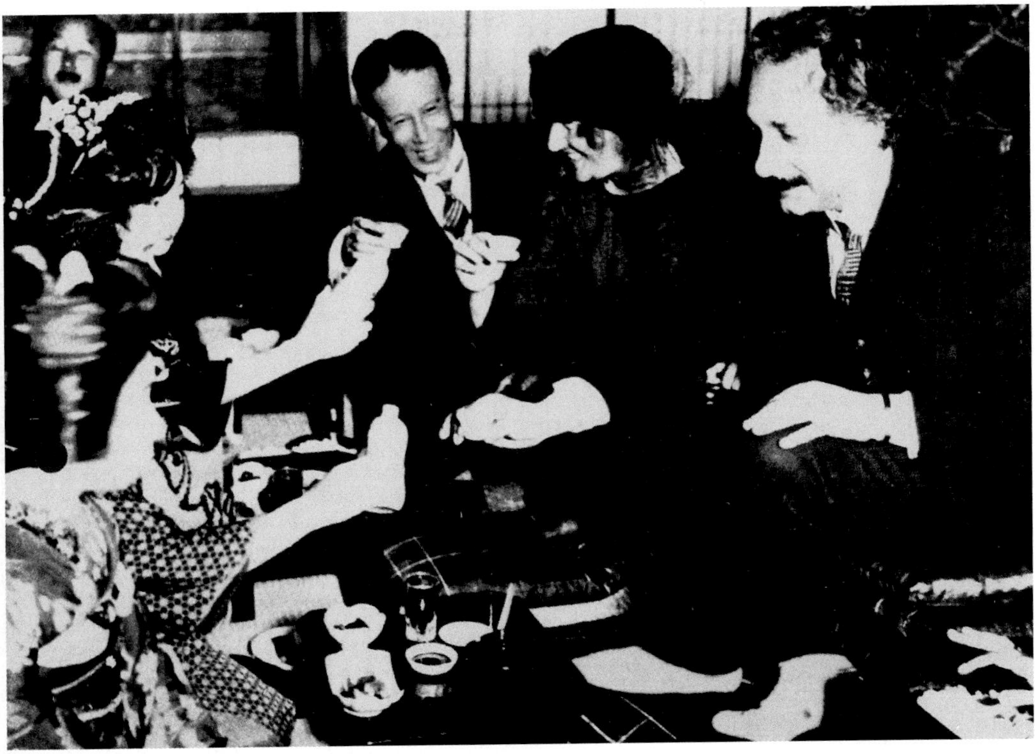

Einstein and Elsa in Japan in 1922.

The omnipresent Count Harry Kessler, in a portrait by Edvard Munch.

Einstein lecturing in Paris in 1922.

making the war palatable to the civilian population, and they found similar solutions. In London, troops built exhibition trenches in Kensington Gardens—a display that, like its Berlin counterpart, was surreal in its perfection. It had straight, almost precision-engineered walls, and sandbags stacked in exquisite order. The display was popular and may have been a comfort to those who imagined that it resembled the real thing. Official descriptions from the front were equally sanitized and equally unreal. A report from 1916 uncovered by the historian Paul Fussell brings the war fully into the embrace of the familiar: "The firing trench is our place of business—our office in the city, so to speak. The supporting trench is our suburban residence, whither the weary toiler may betake himself periodically (or, more correctly, in relays) for purposes of refreshment and repose."[6]

Tripe like this was the sort of home-front fodder that reduced fighting soldiers on either side of the line to fits of laughter and/or rage—although by and large, letters from both sides' trenches glossed over unacceptable details. Diaries, though, were a different matter. The Englishman Thomas Hulme, a literary critic and occasional poet, wrote a typical private description of trench life in his diary entry for January 17, 1915: "I had to crawl along my hands and knees through the mud in pitch darkness, and every now and then seemed to get stuck altogether. You feel shut in and hopeless. I wished I was about four feet. This war isn't for tall men. I got in a part too narrow and too low to stand or sit and had to sit sideways on a sack of coke to keep out of the water. . . . You can't sleep and you sit as it were at the bottom of a drain with nothing to look at but the top of the ditch, slowly freezing. It's unutterably boring. . . . I feel utterly depressed at the idea of having to do this for forty-eight hours every four days."[7] Even less suitable for home-front consumption was the brute fact that men died badly in the trenches. In June 1915, the writer Robert Graves came upon a soldier, still alive, whose brains were spilling out of his head into the mud at the bottom of a trench. The sight shocked the usually sardonic Graves: "I had never seen brains before; I was someone who regarded them as a poetical figment. One can joke with a badly wounded man. . . . One can disregard a dead man. But even a miner can't make a joke over a man who takes three hours to die after the top part of his head has been taken off by a bullet fired at twenty yards range."[8]

That kind of misery was found in German trenches as well as in those opposing them, of course; but shared hardships masked the fact that there were distinct styles of trenches, national variations that reflected specific strategic intentions. The British built the least comfortable trenches: sloppy, seemingly hastily dug ditches, prone to damp and worse, lacking almost all the amenities that could make life in them slightly less miserable. Dugouts, sleeping quarters, parapets, good sentry positions, sufficient lumber—none of these existed in the appropriate numbers or quality to lift the British trench experience above squalor. The deliberately cultivated message was that the trench in which a British soldier happened to find himself was a temporary expedient, a staging ground for the real business of the war: attack, the "big push" that would lead to a breakthrough and the end of the war. French trenches were usually better, but they too retained the provisional sense of the British version.

German trenches, by contrast, displayed at least a distant kinship to the public display in Berlin. Proper sleeping dugouts did exist, with staircases, kitchens and even electric lights and doorbells. German trenches tended to be strongly built, with the appropriate number of sentry posts and machine-gun nests. They made much greater use of lumber and real building materials than British defenses. They were built to last, and some effort was made to render them comfortable. The implication was clear. The people who occupied such fortifications intended to remain where they stood.

And so they did through the middle years of the war. The record of battle on the western front from late 1914 through 1917 was one of variations on a theme, bloody repetitions of familiar mistakes, mostly made on the British and French side of the line. Both Allies suffered acutely from one of the governing pathologies of the war, a plague of generals with disastrous judgment, little imagination, and supreme self-confidence. The Germans had their own share of dreadful officers, but the record of awful military performance by the western Allies beggars belief even today. From the beginning of the 1915 campaign, the British began as they were to go on, in an escalating repetition of blunders. In March 1915, British forces under General Douglas Haig attacked a German line at Neuve-Chapelle in northern France, near the Belgian border. After the introductory artillery barrage ended, British and Indian formations went over the top along a two-and-a-half-mile front, directly into preprepared machine-gun fields of fire. A few stretches of the German forward trenches were overrun, but in certain sections, the slaughter was unbelievable. On one four-hundred-yard line about one thousand soldiers advanced toward the German wire. Every one of them died. None even reached the trench line beyond. In all, the British Empire lost more than eleven thousand casualties for the gain of a swatch of ground two thousand yards wide by twelve hundred deep.

At that, Neuve-Chapelle was a cheap disaster by the evolving experience of the war, and both sides thought that there might be some way to force a speedy resolution. On the German side, the generals began to pay attention to the work of their scientists, especially that emerging from Fritz Haber's laboratory. Haber's fellow chemists Carl Duisberg and Walther Nernst had originally taken the lead in gas weapon research, trying to mate tear gas and other irritating but not deadly compounds with artillery shells and grenades. The hope was to come up with something that would overwhelm the enemy long enough for their attackers to swarm past the trench line and force a breach. These early gas weapons had the virtue of being probably legal under the terms of prewar agreements, and both sides experimented with their use. Neither of the opposing forces developed nonlethal systems that worked, however, and even though deadly gas weapons *were* clearly forbidden under international law, Field Marshal Erich von Falkenhayn, chief of the German General Staff, made the decision himself. Germany would develop poison gas technology for use on the front.

With that, Haber's chlorine research took the lead. After the 1914 explosion that killed one member of his laboratory working on a more volatile compound, he turned to the problem of how to release clouds of chlorine gas that could simply drift across no-man's-land to the unprotected trenches of the enemy. The idea was good enough to earn Haber what he seems to have valued beyond all else: a commission as a captain in the German army, a nearly unprecedented reward for a once-Jewish civilian scientist.

There were naysayers. Haber's boss, Emil Fischer, a fellow chemist and director of the institutes, "wished him failure from the bottom of my patriotic heart,"[9] for he foresaw that once Germany used lethal gas, everyone else would do the same. Worse, on the western front, where the depth and the strength of the trench system made gas such a potentially valuable weapon, the advantage lay chiefly with Germany's enemies, for the winds mostly blew from west to east, from the British and French lines toward Germany's. But Haber still saw gas as a potential war winner, and the German General Staff agreed. They asked the chemists how long they had before their enemies could retaliate. Duisberg guessed that it would take five to six months for anyone else to catch up—and the generals chose to go ahead.

The Ypres salient offered a tempting first target. The salient formed a little tongue of land in Belgium, jutting a few miles west into the German line. German planners believed that its elimination would lead to a breakthrough to the sea and the potential destruction of the entire British and French line. So early in the spring, several thousand chlorine canisters were shipped west to a staging area near the town of Langemark. On their arrival, though, the winds refused to cooperate. For weeks the gas did produce casualties, but they were all Germans, wrestling with the balky and unfamiliar weapon. Finally, in one of the classic blunders of the war, Falkenhayn lost patience with the delay. On April 17, he ordered reserve troops who were earmarked for the exploitation of a successful gas attack to head out instead to the east, to support the German spring offensive against the Russians. Five days later, the wind turned at last, blowing east to west. The Germans chose to go forward with a test of the new weapon, and the order was given for an attack on April 22. As dusk approached, German soldiers released 168 tons of chlorine along a four-mile front.[10]

That first April evening, there would have been almost no warning and no sense of anticipation. Compared to the usual terrors of the battlefield, the puffy clouds of smoke may have seemed almost benign. In its path stood three divisions: one Algerian, one territorial (the equivalent of a national guard unit), both under French colors, and one Canadian. The gas cloud advanced, drifting, rolling, stretching across the muddy wreck of no-man's-land. The Germans waited and watched until the billowing mass of chlorine reached the Allied line.

The effect was dreadful, as General Sir John French reported to his superiors. Hundreds of soldiers "were thrown into a comatose or dying position."[11] Chlorine killed slowly enough to enable its victims to experience all the details of their dying. To onlookers, gassed soldiers lying in rows seemed as if they were drowning on dry land. They gasped for air, their lungs filling with fluid. Their doctors could do nothing but watch. Later in the war, gas attacks using different compounds produced the signature aftermath captured brilliantly in John Singer Sargent's painting: lines of blinded men walking with tiny, halting steps, each soldier with a hand on the shoulder of the man in front of him, painfully seeking the way back to an aid station and whatever comfort could be found.[12] In that first gas battle, the Algerians broke, leaving a hole in the line a half-mile wide. The Germans, wearing primitive respirators, advanced into the gap. They captured two thousand prisoners and a number of cannon. But by now their reserves were long gone, eastward bound for Galicia. The Germans had had the benefit of complete surprise, and the advantage of a weapon for which their enemy had no defense and no response—but they lacked the warm bodies required to press beyond the front lines into the western Allies' rear. The net result of this first use of lethal gas in battle was no change at all in the stasis along the front.

It wasn't supposed to be this way. Haber had told his colleagues that gas was actually humane because it held out the real prospect of ending the war swiftly—and he may in fact have believed the claim, at least in those early days of 1915. But Fischer had been right, and within five months, the western Allies retaliated, though with no greater tactical success than the Germans. Haber was a true believer, however, and he persisted. Gas compounds and gas masks improved—by 1917 Haber himself would lead a staff of well over a thousand pursuing yet newer and deadlier compounds and delivery systems. The effort was systematic and highly organized. He developed quantitative methods to compare the lethality of different compounds, and his assistants, as the historian Jeffrey Johnson put it, "must have sacrificed thousands of hapless cats" as they tested each new potential weapon.

Ultimately, gas warfare was a complete failure, doomed by its lack of precision, the development of defenses, and the ease of retaliation. It made the war more grotesque, but it had no impact on its outcome. Haber himself did not waver, but even he was not immune to the suffering that flowed from his work. Shortly after the first Ypres attacks he traveled east to test the new weapon on the Russians. He left behind in Berlin his wife, Clara Immerwahr, who had long since ceased to pursue her own chemical research. Her despondency and growing alienation from her husband deepened as she learned of his commitment to chemical warfare. As Haber studied how to kill Russians more effectively, Immerwahr found the service revolver he had left behind. She shot herself. Her reasons remain unknown. But the horror of gas was in her mind that spring.

GIVEN THE FAILURE of such miracle weapons, the essential stasis remained in place in the west, enforced by simpler, older weapons: artillery and the machine gun. The Germans were the acknowledged masters of the art of defensive machine-gun fire, and they found the perfect foil in their British enemies, especially the disastrous Douglas Haig, soon to be commander of all British forces on the western front. Haig assured the British War Council in April 1915 that the machine gun was—in his famous and characteristically obtuse phrase—"an overrated weapon."[13] If brave British troops failed to overcome a given weight of fire, then what was needed were more troops and the grit to use them: a doctrine the British army was to put to the test time and again, with identical results and escalating casualty lists. The climax of the 1915 campaign came on the 25th of September at the Battle of Loos, when almost ten thousand soldiers went over the top along six and a half miles of the line. To the Germans, Loos became known as the field of corpses. A German regimental record reported that the British advanced "as if carrying out a field-day drill in peacetime. Our artillery and machine guns riddled their ranks . . . the machine guns caught them in the flank and whole battalions were annihilated."[14] Official British accounts tried to put a brave face on it, but Robert Graves told a different story. An officer had led his platoon over the top and a few yards forward. His men dropped, and the officer whistled the advance. No one moved, and so, wrote Graves, "he jumped up from his shell-hole and waved and signaled Forward. Nobody stirred. He shouted: 'You bloody cowards, are you leaving me to go alone?' His platoon sergeant, groaning with a broken shoulder, gasped out: 'Not cowards, sir. Willing enough. But they're all f——g dead.' "[15]

Such successes reinforced the midwar evolution of German strategy: hold the line in the west, triumph in the east, and then use the resources in men and matériel from the Russian front to bring the British and French to bay. All that had to be done was to kill those foolish enough to charge prepared defenses, and eventually the attackers would lose both the will and the ability to force the issue. It was a brute force approach, lacking any subtlety or sophistication. Worse, it condemned everyone to an almost infinitely prolonged war. As the strategist B. H. Liddell Hart wrote in an extreme instance of British understatement, "A method [attrition] which requires four years to produce a decision is not to be regarded as a model for imitation."[16]

The dynamic of trench warfare did have one clear virtue from the German point of view: it took place on French soil; but even so, as the stalemate ground on, even the most insulated civilians had to grapple with the ghastly butchery of trench warfare itself. At home in Berlin, the rising toll sharpened the debate about what Germany hoped to gain from the fight—what all its blood and treasure was supposed to buy.

The ultimate goal remained that of the prewar ultranationalists: Germany was to gain power enough to equal, or better yet overcome, Great Britain itself. In the first weeks of the war, when it appeared as if Germany might sweep to a swift, total triumph, the different factions in the ruling elite presented competing visions for the vastly enlarged Germany that victory would bring. Details of their motivation differed. Walter Rathenau, for all his pride in his liberal sensitivity and his status as a lover of European civilization, presented the big-businessman's goal of an economic empire: a German-dominated *Mitteleuropa*. Austria-Hungary would be incorporated into a pan-German economic union that could ultimately overwhelm or absorb the Low Countries and Scandinavia. France would then be forced to accept an accommodation. Britain would increasingly be barred from any role on the Continent, while Russia would simply be frozen out. Matthias Erzberger, a Catholic Center party politician who like Rathenau had close ties to German industry, set three basic goals with the highest priority as always being Germany's triumph over what it perceived as its greatest global rival: "1.) The elimination of the intolerable tutelage exercised by Britain over Germany in all questions of world politics. 2.) Shattering the Russian colossus. 3.) Elimination of weak 'allegedly neutral' states on Germany's frontiers."[17] Others, especially those who like the kaiser measured power by the amount of real estate to which one could lay claim, went much further, calling for the direct annexation east and west of Belgium, perhaps the Netherlands, swaths of Poland and more, along with the establishment of German hegemony over the continent of Europe.

To make German ambitions yet more clear, Wilhelm himself had weighed in with a proposal just one month after his "no lust for conquest" speech. He suggested that Germany should annex territory in the west from Belgium through northern France, which should then be "cleared of human beings." In their place would come "deserving N.C.O.s and men" from Germany's victorious army. The kaiser's chancellor, Bethmann-Hollweg, felt this idea might "encounter many practical difficulties," but he did add that "one might consider whether a formula might not be found in the preliminary peace imposing such an expropriation, up to a certain point, on the conquered state."[18] No one used the term *lebensraum*—living space—here. That term, originally Bernhardi's, would reenter the national vocabulary thanks to Adolf Hitler's malevolent gift for the telling phrase. But it was a familiar idea, and most important, these leaps of ambition that were commonplace after the early victories of the war hardened into dogma over the next two years. In the summer of 1915 Bethmann-Hollweg proclaimed, "A new circumstance must come! If Europe is ever to achieve peace, this can only come through Germany's occupying a strong and unassailable position. Germany must so extend her position, so fortify and reinforce it, that the other powers lose the taste for any more policies of encirclement."[19]

Other voices weighed in: military leaders seeking particular tactical or strategic advantages; industrialists looking to gain natural resources and to undermine Britain's colonial empire; politicians and academics advocating the expansion of German territory for the sake of imperial glory and an edge in the naked competition among the surviving Great Powers. Each plan varied in its details, or in the sophistication with which it framed its demands, but the basic story remained the same. Any acceptable peace had to yield a Greater Germany. This would be its reward for the sacrifices of war and the guarantor of future power and national glory. As the war ground on and the butcher's bill lengthened, the more vital such total victory became. Bethmann-Hollweg again, speaking to the Reichstag on May 28, 1915: "The greater the danger which we have to face . . . the more necessary it is to hold out," until, he argued, German forces could achieve a victory sweeping enough to compel their adversaries to do as the Germans dictated. There could be no negotiated settlement to the war.

TO THE ACUTE OBSERVER this was obvious from late 1915, if not before. Einstein got the message, certainly, and the shock of the essential unreason inherent in the religion of triumph overcame his prewar disdain and ignorance of politics. He was no fool, of course. In public, he retained the essential caution of the first statements to which he had put his name in 1914. But the war-aims debate confirmed what he told Romain Rolland in 1915. The victories in the east had revived the "hunger and the appetite of the Germans." Einstein also virtually predicted that Germany would lose the war. This was not the common view, he noted, for "everyone is convinced of victory, and one hears officially that the war will continue only for another six months or even less." But the real situation was far more grave (and Einstein's loose tongue here might have caused him real trouble, given that he was passing the private views of knowledgeable officials on to an enemy national). "Those who know," Einstein told Rolland, then living in self-imposed exile in neutral Switzerland, "realize the situation is grave and that it will become worse if the war goes on." Shortages of critical military matériel threatened to cripple the German war effort, he said, even though virtually all of his colleagues were working to invent synthetic substitutes.

Even so, Einstein recognized that any German collapse was a long way off, and in the meantime, as he told Rolland, the war was unstoppable. Rolland wrote that he hoped for an Allied victory to "ruin the power of Prussia and of the dynasty"—but not because he loved the Allies. He had no particular sympathy for England, but said he still preferred "that England win rather than Germany because England will know better how to bring the world back to life."[20]

Shortly after the war, Einstein was to write with longing of a time that he placed in an impossibly distant past, when "the savants and artists of all Europe were so closely united by the bond of a common ideal that cooperation between them was scarcely affected by political events." It was "a lost paradise," an Eden from which the burning sword had banished thinking humankind.[21] He blamed Germany first, always, for the current situation, but over time he acknowledged the reality of a common tragedy. The war, he told Ehrenfest in 1917, "slays the innocent along with the guilty."[22] This was the true evil.

It was a fresh thought. Until then, his opposition had had a formal tinge. He was aware of the human cost, the burden of the common soldier, but it remained an abstraction, an impersonal category of experience, until as the war progressed he began to confront human suffering with an immediacy new to him. People he knew were losing those they loved. For all that he boasted of his "pronounced lack of need for direct contact with other human beings," those deaths mattered.[23] Most physics students and the younger graduates were in uniform, as were the sons of his nearest professional colleagues. His beloved Max Planck lost one of his sons, while the other was a prisoner of war. The news was still worse for Walther Nernst. Nernst, whose love of military maneuvers seemed almost harmlessly silly in September of 1914, had sent both of his boys off to the front. Both were killed. With that, Einstein's carefully cultivated autonomy clearly began to lapse. "Nernst lost his two sons in the war," he told his old friend Besso. "Is the old Jehovah still alive?"[24] Joining almost all his fellow Berliners, he too could animate the names that rolled down the black-bordered columns of newsprint with faces, memory and loss.

Chapter Eight

"I HAVE BECOME FAR MORE TOLERANT"

ONE OF THE PERSISTENT THEMES OF EINSTEIN'S LIFE WAS HIS ABILITY TO maintain extraordinary concentration in almost any conceivable circumstance. Throughout 1916 and 1917, in near-total political and scholarly isolation, he continued to produce an astonishing, sustained outburst of genuinely important ideas. For the most part, he spent 1916 focusing on the radical possibilities inherent in general relativity. He was stimulated in part by the strange, almost unbelievable ideas developed by one of his former Berlin colleagues, Karl Schwarzschild. In peacetime Schwarzschild had been the director of the Astrophysical Observatory in Potsdam. When the war began, he volunteered and served in the eastern theater. His great mathematical talent earned him the job of solving ballistics problems for German artillery batteries. The task was simple for a man of his gifts, and it left him with enough time to keep abreast of scientific developments back in Berlin. He learned of Einstein's breakthrough by early December 1915, and he set out to rework the problem of Mercury's orbit using a more sophisticated mathematical technique than Einstein had. Einstein himself read the resulting paper to the Academy on January 13, 1916. Schwarzschild continued to work on general relativity, but as the winter wore on, he began to feel more and more poorly. In March, he was evacuated to Berlin. He remained in hospital in the capital for the next two months, diagnosed with a skin disease, pemphigus, for which no treatment existed. He died on May 11. He was forty-two.

Einstein was genuinely affected by his passing. That June, he rose again at the Academy to eulogize Schwarzschild, a man he had barely known before the war. The speech praised his accomplishments and predicted accurately that his work would have a lasting impact on science; and he told Hilbert that he found "Schwarzschild's death distressing" because "among the living there remain probably only a few who know how to apply mathematics with such virtuosity as he did."[1] Privately, though, he spoke more sharply of the dead man, deploring Schwarzschild's contribution to the task of killing more efficiently, and on the day of the funeral, he wrote to Besso that "Schwarzschild . . . is a real loss. He would have been a gem, had he been as decent as he was clever."[2] Einstein was apparently willing to ignore similar, and much more deadly, war work by close friends like Haber, but Schwarzschild was a distant acquaintance, and hence fair game.

Most notably, Schwarzschild beat Einstein to one of the first major discoveries lurking within the detailed structure of general relativity. This finding emerged from the study of a simplified model of a star. Schwarzschild's reading of the situation produced something even Einstein found unbelievable, the first clues that would ultimately lead to the identification of what we now call black holes. A black hole is an object whose gravitational field is so strong that while anything can fall into the hole, nothing, not even light, can escape out again.

Schwarzschild himself was investigating what would happen if the mass of a fluid sphere—an idealized star—were squeezed into a smaller and smaller sphere. He found that as his model star shrank, there was a specific circumference at which its mass would reach a critical density. At that point, the star's gravitational field would be strong enough to bend spacetime so severely that it would close in on itself, creating a sealed loop. As physicists later came to understand, when that happened, nothing, not even light, could escape from within that now-isolated island of spacetime. Instead, because light, like all else in the universe, must travel along the curve of spacetime, anything within that sealed loop must remain inside it, cut off forever from the universe beyond. Physicists now use the term "horizon" to describe the point at which spacetime becomes so strongly warped that nothing that falls within that horizon can reemerge. There is no returning across the boundary that Schwarzschild was the first to recognize—no exit and no escape.

Ultimately, the interpretation and extension of Schwarzschild's work demonstrated that the equations of general relativity could yield cases in which the curvature of spacetime becomes infinite. Such infinities are called singularities, and they provide the formal mathematical description of black holes. Perhaps most strange, the concept of a singularity is now understood as an account of a physical reality where the laws of physics break down. In other words, the conventional framework of general relativity works perfectly up to a black hole horizon. It even allows a physicist to describe the conditions that can produce a black hole. But, rather like Moses glimpsing the promised land while being forbidden to enter it, general relativity cannot fully penetrate a black hole. It fails as a detailed description of the events that take place within the incredibly contorted spacetime that lies inside what is now called a Schwarzschild singularity.

It would be some decades before this concept was fully understood—Einstein himself always thought of Schwarzschild's solutions to general relativity as mathematical pathologies rather than descriptions of real physical objects. He was wrong. While it is impossible to see a black hole itself—after all, no light can escape its grasp—black holes have been detected indirectly, by observing the effect of their gravitational fields on nearby objects and by identifying the radiation released as objects cross an event horizon. As Schwarzschild's work implied, and as J. Robert Oppenheimer and George Volkoff showed in 1938, black holes can form when stars collapse. Under certain conditions at the end of a star's life, such a collapse continues until the remains of the star reach a density high enough to produce a black hole horizon. Beginning in the late 1950s, the study of black holes has extended to the point where they have been implicated in some of the most dramatic events in the universe. Black holes can form through other processes than the collapse of single stars. In the gas- and star-rich conditions in which whole galaxies are thought to form, giant black holes can emerge when the dense, closely packed collections of matter at the center of such nascent galaxies begin to fall inward, pulled by the mutual gravity of everything in the neighborhood. Such giant, galactic black holes have been implicated as the engines that drive the furious energies found in the mysterious objects called quasars, associated with the early stages of galactic evolution.[3]

In the event, Einstein swallowed his disbelief and presented Schwarzschild's new work to the Academy in February 1916. Even if he doubted its ultimate significance, the work dovetailed neatly into his own attempts to comprehend general relativity. Most important, the overarching structure of the theory allowed him to seek specific solutions to its system of equations. Sometimes, as with Schwarzschild, a solution itself suggested the existence of a phenomenon that no one had previously imagined could exist. If a particular mathematical solution to Einstein's equations could be found, that meant general relativity had made another prediction, a concrete claim about the real world. And because at bottom, relativity theory describes how matter and energy shape space and time, its power to create new ideas extends over the entire universe and all that it contains.

Some of those ideas were genuinely weird, so far beyond prior experience that even Einstein sometimes found them hard to swallow. Schwarzschild's singularities were strange enough, but Einstein's first forays into the universe of general relativity were no better. To start out, he explored a hitherto unsuspected phenomenon called gravity waves. Such waves, he argued, would move through a gravitational field, in a direct analogy to the way electromagnetic waves—light, radio, microwaves and everything else up and down the spectrum—move through an electromagnetic field. Electromagnetic waves form when electrically charged masses accelerate relative to each other—which is the formal, abstract description of the basic process that produces every radio and television signal, among much else. Similarly, Einstein showed that two gravitational masses accelerating relative to each other—two stars colliding, for example—should produce gravitational waves, fluctuations in the intensity of the gravitational field that travel at the speed of light.

Einstein did not get his picture of these waves quite right at first. The version he announced in June 1916 contained a mathematical error that he corrected in 1918. But even with that correction, the notion that event after event in the universe sends its ripples crashing throughout spacetime proved hard to take. There was literally no evidence that such waves did exist. The predicted effect was so small that for decades before and after Einstein's death, it was possible to regard the whole idea of gravity waves as yet another mathematical anomaly within the labyrinthine corridors of general relativity. That rejection has crumbled, and the modern consensus is that Einstein's waves are real. But this is a recent judgment, born of a series of astronomical observations in the late 1970s that provided strong indirect evidence that gravity waves do form. Even now, although very large and delicate detectors are being built, no such wave has yet been observed directly.[4]

Einstein himself had a moment of doubt in 1936, but once he found the mathematical mistake that had tripped him up, he never again lost faith in the idea. He did not spend much time on the problem, however, for even in 1916, gravity waves were simply a warm-up, almost an intellectual sketch that he used to gain a sense of familiarity with his new theory. The headline performance got under way in the summer of 1916 when he first started to question the structure of the universe as a whole. When he was done in February of 1917, he had founded an entire discipline: the modern science of cosmology.

Einstein began in his usual way, by thinking about flaws in Newton's theory of the universe. He argued that when extended into infinite space, Newton's conception led directly to the conclusion that the density of mass in the universe as a whole must approach zero. Over time, he said, the random motion of stars traveling through that universe would produce a billiard ball effect: one star after another would ricochet in a bounce "great enough to send that star on its journey to infinity, whence it never can return." Over enough time, chance event piled on chance event would leave the universe empty: "A vanishing of the density at infinity . . . implies a vanishing of the density at the center."[5]

But the universe does exist, and as we can see for ourselves, it is dense, rich, packed with stuff—our sun, the planets, millions of stars, the braided weave of the Milky Way. Newton's version (or rather, the description of universe-scale behavior developed by his successors using his physics) clearly could not describe what was actually to be seen out there in the cosmos. Having thus cleared the ground, Einstein set out to create his own universe to replace Newton's. He made two critical assumptions. First, the universe contains an average density of matter that "is everywhere the same and different from zero." Second, it is static, with no change in its structure over time. Expressing those two articles of faith mathematically, Einstein then derived a solution to the equations of general relativity that would describe the behavior of such a model of the entire cosmos.

The universe that emerges from that solution has no limits, but is finite. It exists as a kind of four-dimensional ball, a "hypersphere"—the same shape, as the mathematician Robert Osserman has pointed out, that Dante imagined in *Paradiso,* when Beatrice led the poet from the surface of the earth upward to the Prime Mover. There they looked beyond into the country of the angels who danced on the spheres of the realm of the empyrean.[6] The essence of both the scientist's concept and the poet's image is that the surface of a sphere (in either three dimensions or four) has no border, no end, but does have a finite area or volume. One can go around and around on the surface of the earth and never fall off; but there is only so much ground to cover and no more. So it is for Einstein's universe. It has no end, but it encompasses a finite volume of spacetime. Within that volume lies all the matter and energy in the universe, so the cosmos also has a finite, positive mass (or mass-energy) density, meeting the first of Einstein's conditions. The total sum of matter and energy created a universe-wide gravitational field, which determined the shape of spacetime for the entire system: a cosmos that formed into a curved four-dimensional surface.

As far as it went, Einstein's conception was correct. It remains the basic picture of the structure of the universe that we hold today. But, unfortunately, he retained one flawed critical assumption. Left alone, his universe could not stand still. Assuming no outside forces existed, the total gravity of the system would lead it to collapse in on itself. Alternatively, some initial outward push or an evolutionary change in the curvature of spacetime could drive an expansion of the universe over time. But one thing was certain. Unmodified, the equations of general relativity do not permit our universe to remain fixed in place, unaltered throughout time.

But the idea of a dynamic universe, one in constant flux, was anathema to Einstein. More deeply, as of 1917, very few physicists grasped how big the universe is. Our own galaxy, the Milky Way, was still generally seen to be all there was, and it appeared to be essentially static. His fix for the problem was to add a new term to his gravity equations, a number he called the cosmological constant. The cosmological constant served as the expression for a kind of antigravity, a force that pushed out between masses whose gravitational fields tug inward. (Or, more accurately in the language of general relativity, the cosmological constant reverses the curvature of spacetime produced by a gravitational field.) The correction was small, and it did not appear to alter any of general relativity's conclusions about the orbit of Mercury and so on. But it had no basis in any actual physical idea or observation in the real world. The constant was, Einstein acknowledged, "at present unknown . . . [and] is not justified by our actual knowledge of gravitation."[7] Still, it did the job. By adding the cosmological constant to the general theory, Einstein's universe became nicely disciplined, standing still, unchanging throughout eternity.

The first hint that he might be wrong came from theory, when two men independently came up with dynamic descriptions of the universe. In February 1917 Willem De Sitter, professor of astronomy at the University of Leyden in the Netherlands, responded to Einstein's theory almost as soon as it appeared by proposing a model of an expanding universe. Einstein looked for some flaw in De Sitter's work that could rule out so unsettling a notion, but he soon gave up and admitted that there was nothing formally wrong with the idea.[8] More dangerous, in 1922 a Russian mathematician, physicist and meteorologist named Aleksandr Friedmann worked out a relativistic cosmology that explicitly predicted that the universe must either be contracting or expanding.

Friedmann had a very hard time making his case known. First, he sent his paper to Einstein, who ignored it. He went in person to Berlin, but Einstein was out of town. Finally, another physicist put the work in front of Einstein. His initial reaction was that the idea was simply wrong. Then, when he realized that Friedmann had done the work correctly, he returned to his rebuff of Schwarzschild's singularities—Friedmann's results were mathematically interesting but possessed "no physical significance." But within the year, he realized that there was no fundamental objection to what Friedmann proposed, and for the first time, began to retreat from the cosmological constant.

Friedmann did not live to enjoy a full vindication. He died in 1925, probably of typhoid fever complicated by the accumulated strains of hard living during the Russian Revolution and the subsequent civil war. But even then astronomers were beginning to make progress in settling the issue of the dynamic universe, first with Edwin Hubble's discovery in 1924 that the Andromeda Nebula was in fact the Andromeda *Galaxy,* an island "universe" of stars the equal of our own Milky Way. Next, in 1929, Hubble used his own and others' results to show that twenty-five such newly identified galaxies were receding, rushing away from us in every direction. Crucially, Hubble also showed that the farther a galaxy is from earth, the faster it recedes, a systematic relationship of distance and velocity that is now known as Hubble's law. That law describes a dynamic, expanding universe—like the one formed in an initial explosion, now known as the big bang. In 1931 Einstein traveled to Hubble's home institution, the Mount Wilson Observatory above Pasadena, California. He looked through the big telescope, discussed what had been seen there, and almost immediately retracted the cosmological constant.

Actually, he may have been premature. The cosmological constant has enjoyed a revival of late. The problem is that the amount of mass and energy believed to exist in the universe should produce a large enough gravitational field to slow down the big bang–driven expansion of the universe by a certain amount. However, several recent observations suggest that this expansion is actually accelerating—that not only is the total gravitational energy of the cosmos failing to slow down the big bang explosion, something out there is actually speeding up the rate at which the universe is flying apart. These observations are still somewhat controversial, but even so, some theorists have proposed "dark energy"—a mysterious phenomenon that repels objects—to account for the apparent acceleration of cosmic expansion. The concept of dark energy does fit into certain versions of modern quantum theory, so a factor to account for it has been introduced to a number of cosmological theories. That factor is being called the cosmological constant. Contrary to most published accounts of these developments, however, the new constant is *not* Einstein's. Even though it plays essentially the same role in modern theories that it did in Einstein's original one (it is a measure of whatever might push back against gravity), the new constant has both some direct observational and some theoretical underpinnings. By contrast, Einstein's version was simply bookkeeping, a fudge factor introduced to force his theory to conform to what he thought ought to exist in nature.[9]

This is where his frustration came in. He had come so close. Without the constant, Einstein would have made one of the boldest predictions in the history of science: his new theory required (had he only the gumption to stick with it) that the universe alter constantly, despite all experience and settled judgment. All he had to do was say so, and wait. For once in his career the comparison was not with Newton, who completed a revolutionary transformation of the understanding of the cosmos, but rather with Copernicus, who launched that revolution with an idea that was wrong in detail, however right it might have been in essence.

This was cold comfort. Einstein no more relished admitting to error than anyone else. Still, Copernicus is surely good company. Einstein's first static-universe paper, submitted to the Prussian Academy in February of 1917, launched the entire field of what has become big bang cosmology—the study of the origins and evolution of the cosmos. As further developed by Friedmann and his successors to accommodate the reality of the expanding universe, general relativity remains the core of our understanding of the evolution and large-scale structure of the universe. The grand thought at the heart of the enterprise was Einstein's. He was the first to possess the breadth of both insight and ambition to treat the entire universe as an object for scientific scrutiny. In creating cosmology, he began the task we are still striving to complete—to capture all of material reality within a single idea.

AND AT THAT, he still wasn't finished. The miracle year of 1905 still astounds people, as it should; but few realize just how much he achieved in the eighteen months from October 1915 to the late winter of 1917. There were, of course, the series of discoveries in general relativity—its correct formulation, the gravity wave analysis, his foray into cosmology. At the same time, he wrote the first popular account of special and general relativity, a book finished in December 1916. Titled *Relativity,* it is still in print, and it remains one of the best plain-language introductions to the two theories.

And that was not all. There were some minor efforts during this period, including a couple of oblique contributions to war-related research. In one case, a brief paper on the behavior of airplane wings, Einstein seems to have forgotten entirely the actual hard fact of the war. What motivated him, he wrote, was simply curiosity. How could it be that both flying machines and birds manage to keep "soaring through the air in their flight?" To his chagrin, he had been unable to find "even the simplest answer" anywhere in the professional literature of aerodynamics. So his goal, he said, was merely "to give some readers pleasure when I try to remedy this deficiency."[10] What followed was a not very technical discussion of issues raised by fluid dynamics, wave motion, and the behavior of wings. His wing does look a little strange—it is a flat surface with a little hump in it—which has led some writers to treat the image as a design suggestion, an attempt to advance a specific military technology. Dennis Overbye in his recent work has documented the fact that Einstein's wing was actually built and fitted to an airplane, with near-disastrous results. (The plane flipped in the air soon after takeoff, and the test pilot was barely able to land safely.)[11] But while this incident has led some to suggest that Einstein might have been a touch hypocritical in his pacifism, he claimed to be motivated by pure scientific curiosity.

He could not make the same excuse in his other major foray into work with military significance. In 1914, before the war began, Einstein had been hired by the Anschütz Company to serve as an expert witness in a legal dispute with the American firm Sperry. The case involved a patent dispute over an instrument called a gyrocompass, a mechanical device that keeps a constant orientation to the earth's axis even in the far north, where ordinary magnetic compasses cease to function. Einstein's initial review of the patent papers interested him enough to stimulate his love of precision gadgetry, and he continued to consult with Anschütz throughout the war, offering advice as late as July 1918. During the war the gyrocompass had essentially only one significant use: helping German submarines to navigate to their targets. Germany's submarines had attacked unarmed and neutral merchant ships with great effect ever since the imposition of a blockade of Britain in February 1915.

This was widely known, yet against that backdrop, Einstein never discussed or explained his work on the gyrocompass. He seems initially to have been motivated at least in part by the prewar expert witness's fee of one thousand marks (one month's salary), and later, during the war, by the technical fascination of the problem. He was an inveterate tinkerer, and had relished playing with instrument design since his patent office days. After the war he even came up with an improved version of the gyrocompass that he patented in his own name. He would eventually hold more than two dozen patents, alone or jointly, including one for a refrigerator developed with the Hungarian physicist Leo Szilard that was later licensed by General Electric. (Perhaps fortunately, the Einstein fridge never made it past the prototype stage, thus saving all of us from having to contend with yet one more kitchen appliance smarter than its owners.) The gyrocompass offered him one more puzzle to solve, and he was no more immune to the lure of a pleasing problem than any other physicist has ever been.

Still, Einstein does seem to have been embarrassed by the episode. He denounced the moral bankruptcy of unrestricted submarine warfare to Romain Rolland in a letter in 1917, though he did not protest publicly during the war. Understandably if not admirably, he kept quiet after 1918 about what he had done during the conflict that could have aided Germany's military. He never returned to aerodynamics after his one foray into the field, and he scrupulously avoided any public notice of his gyrocompass work—though he continued to bank the royalties he received on his postwar patents.

Even so, Einstein's war-related work was a minor component of his output in 1916 and 1917. Beyond it and beyond his astounding contributions in general relativity and cosmology, he still found the energy to return to an old problem, the question of the quantum—the study of the simplest, smallest building blocks of both matter and energy. His role in the creation of quantum physics will be discussed below, but three crucial facts about this work should be noted here. First, the work, developed in two significant papers in 1916 and 1917, was genuinely important, not mere tinkering with ideas he had put aside years before. Next, no later than the summer of 1916, almost a decade before the revolutionary ideas of quantum mechanics were to compel a probabilistic worldview, he was the first to notice that chance must play a role in quantum processes. No one among those who developed the original quantum theory from 1900 on had previously suspected that randomness might form an inherent part of the theory. He did not like the fact that it did, not then and not ever. The notion that chance could undermine the strict predictability of traditional cause and effect was, he said, a "weakness of the theory." But, he added, "I fully trust in the reliability of the road taken."[12] Einstein would later be ridiculed by younger physicists for his hatred of the role of probability in the quantum revolution. In 1935 Oppenheimer, for one, called him "absolutely cuckoo." But such critics forgot that Einstein was there before all others, the first to recognize the central role of randomness within the subatomic world.

And that leads directly to the third, perhaps most astonishing, fact. Einstein retained, almost alone among his colleagues, the belief in the crisis represented by the quantum. He was confident that general relativity had settled the basic question of the organization of the universe on the large scale. On the smallest scales, though, those within the atom, the situation cried out for similar clarity. He now set out to crack that question too. He did not get there in his two wartime papers, but by 1917 he had managed both to restate and advance the quantum issue in ways that would lead more or less directly to the renewed assault that came after the war's end.

It was, in sum, an unparalleled effort. In the space of eighteen months Einstein sustained an almost continuous production of important and sometimes revolutionary thought. He produced fifteen significant scientific papers, and he wrote for popular audiences as well. He lectured, he tinkered, he corresponded avidly with colleagues, and at the end of the period he was still trying to extend the reach of his own science into every corner of modern physics—all this in the midst of a World War that he on occasion took the time and some personal risk to oppose. Abraham Pais once asked, rhetorically, "Does the man never stop?"[13] Well, no—not really, not of his own volition.

Chapter Nine

"SLAVERY MADE TO APPEAR CIVILIZED"

NO ONE'S WILL IS ABSOLUTE. EINSTEIN'S FEVERISH PACE CRASHED TO A halt in February 1917, when he fell ill with what was first identified rather vaguely as a liver ailment. It was serious and for a time seemed actually life-threatening; he lost over fifty pounds in two months. Characteristically, he kept working from his sickbed long enough to finish the cosmology paper, though he had to cancel a longed-for trip to his consoling friends in neutral Holland, Lorentz and Ehrenfest. In March, the diagnosis shifted to gallstones, and Einstein reported to Besso that the doctor had ordered "spa treatment, strict diet," and that in consequence, "I am feeling very significantly better; no more pain, better appearance."[1]

The reality was less promising. He was still sick and he collapsed periodically; he would not recover fully for four years. Each new diagnosis told only part of the story. The deeper problem was exhaustion, brought on by overwork and disastrously compounded by the harsh conditions of life within an increasingly famished Berlin. The British blockade had its desired effect: slowly, steadily across the years of war, Germany was starving, unable to replace the food it used to buy from abroad—over 30 percent of the total consumed. The pressure had been there from the start, especially in the big cities. As early as December 1914, just before Christmas, Berlin's newspapers had begun to publish housekeeping tips: how to feed three people for two weeks on less than two marks. Try potato soup (twice); potato pancakes; baked potatoes; potatoes with onions; potatoes and fat—with a bit of cabbage, rice and a frightening concoction called wheat soup thrown in for variety's sake. Rationing followed in February, after the military gave up on using market prices to control supplies. Each Berliner was restricted to half a pound of bread per day, and ration cards for meat, eggs, and fat. Potatoes came under rationing soon afterward. The black market erupted almost instantly. Black-market prices rapidly exceeded the average Berliner's budget, and fears of a complete collapse in the supply of the most basic staples led to the first significant wartime protests, the so-called *Kartoffelkrawalle*—the potato revolt, in which housewives denouncing rising potato prices took to the streets.

Soon, a threatened shortage of potatoes led to the infamous *Schweinemord*—the government-mandated slaughter of pigs intended to save for people the potato-based fodder that swine would have consumed. The cull was handled with impressive efficiency, the goals for slaughter escalating as estimates of the potato supply crashed. In all, 9 million pigs were killed in nine months—which briefly improved local meat supplies. Berlin was also briefly overwhelmed with potatoes well in excess of needs for either food or seed; and then faced a predictable, devastating meat shortage once the millions of carcasses had been consumed. By the autumn, the government had introduced meatless and fatless days: Tuesdays and Fridays to begin with, extending to Sundays for bars and restaurants. *Ersatz*—imitation, or substitute—entered the German culinary vocabulary late that year, with one attempt to use dried and ground straw instead of wheat in bread, along with a meatlike offering made of dried and milled plant husks mixed with animal hides. Eventually, coffee, jam, butter, even "pepper" made from fire ashes, all appeared in ersatz form, with the originals available only sporadically for those who could bear the cost.

The winter of 1915–1916 marked the start of truly life-threatening hunger on a wide scale. In what became known as the turnip winter, turnips took pride of place on Berlin's tables. The fresh variety was used in bread, jam, soup and cakes. There was ersatz coffee made from dried turnips. Perhaps most dispiriting of all, someone managed to brew a mildly alcoholic concoction from turnip scraps and called it beer. At the same time, as rudimentary price controls began to take hold, Berlin wholesalers evolved a system called the chain trade, in which one merchant would sell food to the next distributor, taking the allowed markup, and the erstwhile buyer would then sell his goods to the next wholesaler, and so on until the original price had legally doubled or more. Increasingly, though, price was not the problem; absolute scarcity ruled. Meat markets closed outright for three weeks in the spring of 1916, and Berlin housewives became adept at what became known as the butter polonaise—the relentless dance from one shop queue to the next, chasing each sudden appearance of a little stock of food. In 1915, the death toll attributed to blockade-induced malnutrition was over 88,000. In 1916, the number topped 120,000.

Such numbers were minor, within the gruesome accounting of the war, and Germany was, of course, trying to impose the same hardship on its enemies by expanding its submarine blockade of the British Isles. But it faced the same problem it had encountered from the start of the war: despite the submarine successes, no U-boat victory could break the British surface fleet's absolute grip on the sea lanes into Germany's northern ports. The German navy tried to cut through once, on May 31, 1916, off Jutland, on the remote tip of the Danish peninsula. There the German High Seas Fleet met the British in the one major surface naval battle of the war. The fight itself was inconclusive. In two separate engagements over two days the Germans sank fourteen British ships for the loss of ten of their own.

Given that tally, the German press (and even some British observers) declared Jutland a German victory, with the kaiser proclaiming that "the spell of Trafalgar is broken." But it was the German ships that retreated back to their home ports, where they were to stay for the rest of the war, while the British remained on station. This was the final verdict on the prewar dreadnought race: the Royal Navy still ruled the sea. It continued to bar the shipping lanes into the Baltic ports, and Germany slowly strangled.

In the big cities, and especially in Berlin, there was simply not enough food to keep everyone alive. The actress Asta Nielsen, on a visit to Berlin from neutral Denmark, witnessed a typical scene. One morning, she saw a horse collapse dead in the street. "Within less than a second, women rushed towards the cadaver as if they had been poised for this moment, knives in their hands." The death of a carthorse was almost enough to set off a riot on its own. "Everybody was shouting," Nielsen observed, "fighting for the best pieces. Blood spattered their faces and their clothes." Others rushed up, struggling to sop up some of the blood if they could not lay their hands on any flesh, until finally, she wrote, "when nothing more was left of the horse beyond a bare skeleton, the people vanished, carefully guarding their pieces of bloody meat tight against their chests."[2]

The incident was not unique. There were food riots in thirty cities across Germany in 1916. The turnip winter had been bad enough, but that of 1916–1917 was even worse, with temperatures plunging to an *average* of -1 degree Fahrenheit in February. The potato crop failed again and the coming of summer brought no respite. Berlin police headquarters reported on July 3, 1917, that even given the near disaster of the previous winter, "food provision has reached its worst level since the war began. The majority of the population is suffering severe famine conditions," and "children are suffering the most." In one incident covered by the police, one hundred fifty people attacked a market warehouse, injuring several grocers and police officers, but the riot fizzled when it became clear that there was no food to loot. On July 14 the police record sounded a stronger warning: "The situation has nearly gone out of control." Most families in Berlin were desperate, crossing over into true starvation territory. One week later, the police made their case yet more starkly. "The Berlin population is completely focused on the food questions. All other problems, especially military ones, have become secondary."[3]

Deprivation like this was political dynamite. There had been few mass protests during the previous three years; the potato revolt had been an exception. But in the face of famine and with no sign of any breakthrough on the western front, the city finally began to rouse itself. Karl Liebknecht was the focal figure in the resistance. He had a long history with the ruling regime, having been arrested for the first time in 1907 for antimilitary agitation. A member of the SPD, he bitterly objected to its passive acquiescence in the war effort. In 1916 he reinvigorated the faction he had helped found years earlier, renaming it the Spartacus League. He was its leader, though his colleague Rosa Luxemburg, a Polish exile, was the brains of the outfit. For Liebknecht and Luxemburg, the war was yet one more instance of workers suffering to protect capitalists. Opposition to the war was both in the interest of the working class, who were being used as cannon fodder, and the obvious first step in the overthrow of the corrupt ruling regime. The Spartacus League was minuscule compared to the SPD, but by early 1917 conditions had become so bad that Berlin's workers began to follow its red banner. Liebknecht was arrested for antiwar agitation on May 1, after a demonstration in Potsdamer Platz in the heart of Berlin. Thousands rallied in Liebknecht's support at his trial. He was convicted and imprisoned, but Berlin's working men and women—now augmented by returning and disabled veterans—began to take to the streets in what were to the police and their masters increasingly frightening numbers.

EINSTEIN HIMSELF REMAINED mostly insulated from the evolving chaos in Berlin. He did not face the same risk of outright famine that overtook many of the poorest Berliners; while he did go short, back channels saved him as they did most of the wealthy or well connected. His friends in Switzerland sent him food parcels, and more help came from relatives still living in the farming districts of southern Germany where both his parents had grown up. Not all the packages got through—he complained of thievery in the post office—but the supply line was sufficient to keep him well above the margin of subsistence. Still, he remained frail throughout 1917. In April he turned thirty-eight, but whatever the calendar said, his body felt different—old. He began to call himself names: "a creaking corpse; an old wreck; a hatched egg."[4] The war had already given him cause to think of death, of course, and at least in the abstract, it held no terrors for him. In 1916, while still hale and energetic, he had written to Hedwig Born, the wife of his good friend and fellow relativist Max Born, to say he had no fear of what could come. "I feel myself so much a part of everything living," he wrote in that terrible summer, "that I am not in the least concerned with the beginning or ending of the material existence of any one person in this eternal flow."[5]

But as his illness dragged on, his tone shifted. Exhausted and in pain, he concerned himself more with the latest news from his gut than with grand thoughts of man's fate. "The operating instructions for my stomach are being honored conscientiously," he reassured Besso in the summer of 1917, though a letter two weeks later told of a renewed attack and he continued to issue bulletins from that front from time to time.[6] But as much as possible, he continued to ignore his condition, writing to his close friends about science and administrative matters, along with the occasional dark and passive meditation on the war. Despite the occasional food riot or strike, the will to fight—the German delusion—remained. Einstein declared that it felt as if the age of martyrdom had returned, complete with its crusades and its witchcraft trials. Little had truly altered in Berlin during the war years, he told Zangger, safe in neutral Switzerland. Living in the imperial capital, he remained alone, "on my own, isolated by mentality and outlook."[7]

He was not completely solitary, though. There was someone whose significance he had refused to admit for many months. Finally, in early December 1917 after ten months as an invalid, he let drop one precious bit of gossip. It was so offhand a remark to so old and important a friend that it has the air of ultimate calculation. The letter was to Zangger, Mileva's friend as much as his, who now served as an intermediary between the two of them. He was feeling much better, he wrote. "I have gained about four pounds since the summer." How? It was entirely due to his cousin Elsa's meticulous nursing. She had taken him thoroughly in hand, he reported, cooking all his meals. And—by the way—to take full advantage of Elsa's convalescent care, he had moved. It was only temporary, he told Zangger, but "I now live in the apartment next door to hers."[8]

Einstein and Elsa, Elsa and Einstein—this was Mileva's worst nightmare coming true. For all practical purposes Einstein's marriage had ended long before. But for years after the break in 1914, Mileva continued to hold out some hope, a fantasy of reconciliation. To Einstein such a thought was preposterous, even though he had agreed not to divorce her, thus enabling her to retain her unchallenged title as Mrs. Einstein. Apparently she clung to that scrap of status, and the thought that as long as they remained legally bound, there was some slim chance that their marriage might recover. But Einstein still saw her at best as an obstacle, another problem that lay between him and his various desires; at worst she was explicitly an enemy, someone to hound and hobble him—and he often told her so. Within six weeks of her departure he had written to her that nothing she might do would surprise him, that he expected her to villainize him to his children, to estrange him from his friends, to seek "to spoil in every way whatever remains of my pleasure in life." There was justice in that, he had conceded rather cruelly, the appropriate reward for his own stupidity: whatever Mileva did "was proper punishment for my weakness in shackling my life to yours."[9]

By early 1915 matters between them had more or less settled down. In time, Einstein softened his tone slightly, conceding that she remained "officially my wife, the same as before." He continued to grumble fairly regularly about money matters, although as the war progressed he did have some real cause for concern because the value of his salary declined with Germany's eroding mark; still, he made quarterly payments to her and reveled in his bachelor estate. His memory of his time with his wife could still prompt eruptions of bile—"Life without my wife is a veritable rebirth for me personally," he wrote Zangger, adding that "it feels as if I had left ten years of prison behind me."[10] But for a time he seemed capable of letting most of his vitriol go, the rank hatred of the period when they had split.

This lull in hostilities ended in February 1916, when he wrote to Mileva and formally asked her for a divorce "so that we can each arrange the rest of our lives independently, as far as the situation allows."[11] Tactlessly, characteristically, he told her that he was seeking a divorce only so that he might ease the way for Elsa's now marriageable elder daughter, who otherwise "must suffer from the rumors that are circulating with regard to my relationship with her mother."[12] He arrived in Zurich in April for Easter holidays, perhaps anticipating a momentary awkwardness before completing the necessary formalities. After all, he had laid out in detail a comprehensive financial plan, and he had assured Mileva that he still loved his boys, that he still wished to be as much of a father as possible to them.

He didn't have a clue. All of this could only be devastating to her—the idea of divorce; his unrelenting, unfeeling tone; and above all his casual, who-cares excuse for breaking his old promise to let her be a wife in name at least. Elsa's reputation was at stake? Let the strumpet roast, and her daughters too! When Einstein finally came face-to-face with Mileva and his sons in Zurich, the truce collapsed. She objected bitterly when he came to take Hans Albert for a second outing. The boy took his mother's side, and ceased to write to his father for several months thereafter. Einstein stalked out in fury and, holding on to his anger after his return to Berlin, wrote from that safe distance to Besso (like Zangger, a friend to both sides of the sundering couple) that he now had an "irrevocable resolve" not to see or speak to her again. She was a harridan, a shrew, possessed of "natural craftiness . . . unafraid to use all means when she wants to achieve something." She was the Medea he had always feared she would become, and he would have nothing more to do with her. A divorce was essential.

The problem—and the proximate cause of Einstein's outburst to Besso—was that after Einstein's visit in the spring, Mileva had collapsed. Her condition defied diagnosis, though it may have begun with a series of heart attacks. Whatever her illness, it was serious enough for Zangger and Besso to fear for her life. Einstein's first reaction was that this was old news, a familiar tactic. She abhorred the thought of divorce, so, as in the past, she was prepared to throw a fit to get her way. "Dear Michele," he chided Besso, "I understand your remark about the effect of emotional tension as the cause of the present circumstances . . . but I personally have the suspicion that the woman is leading both of you kindhearted men down the garden path." In any event, there was no going back. "I would have been mentally and physically broken if I had not finally found the strength to keep her at arm's length, out of sight and out of earshot."[13]

Besso replied, warm, polite, but firm: "A deception is not at issue here." Zangger had examined her and Mileva was truly ill. Besso had no thought of blame. "We are sinners one and all," he wrote, adding that if one's good deeds were not weighed against one's wrongs, "then surely we all belong in hell." But the truth was the truth, and "the woman's sufferings had left their mark clearly on her appearance." He resolutely refused to take sides. "All this does not mean to say, though, that any pair of horses could be used in a single team," that is, that Einstein and Mileva should remain married, while conceding "that *she* does not quite understand this I can grasp better than that you cannot."[14]

Einstein, chastened, answered that he was sure, if Besso said so, that Mileva was truly suffering. Compounding matters, his younger son, Eduard, also fell ill in mid-1916 with what was diagnosed as an ear infection. The condition grew into something more serious until by the spring of 1917, just as Einstein's health was at its worst, Zangger recommended sending the boy to a sanatorium. Einstein agreed, but held out little hope: "It's impossible," he wrote to Besso, "that he will ever be wholly fit," and, in an astonishing addendum, "who knows whether it wouldn't be better for him if he could depart from us before he really came to know life! *I am to blame for his being and reproach myself, for the first time in my life.*"[15] (Italics added.)

In time Eduard did recover, but with Mileva also ill, Hans Albert was essentially left alone. The Zangger family took him in temporarily, but Einstein saw the accumulating crises as yet one more opportunity. Perhaps, at last, this was the time to bring his older son to Berlin, never mind Mileva's desires. He still did not get it. He had no gift for empathy, no ability to imagine himself into the emotional life of anyone else. His behavior was of a piece, a symptom of that same deep gap in his understanding of people. He could reason himself to a powerful moral position and then rely on his strength of mind and will to hold to it. He did oppose the war; he did defend his fellow Jews; he longed for justice and was willing to put himself to great pains and occasional real risk to uphold his beliefs. But to grasp what someone else felt, to understand the impact of his personal desires and deeds on the minds and hearts of the individual human beings around him—that was vastly more difficult. In a perfect expression of his unvarnished obtuseness, he wrote to Besso that at bottom, he simply did not understand Mileva's complaint. After all, "she has a worry-free life, has her two fine boys with her, lives in a lovely area, can use her time freely, and basks in the aura of abandoned innocence. The only thing she lacks is someone to dominate her!"[16]

Besso apparently let the nastiest edge of this letter pass, and as he became more aware of the seriousness of her condition, Einstein apologized to his friend and calmed the flow of invective about Mileva. She, from having been "the woman" who tormented him, became again "my wife." It was still a queasy subject, though, and he never handled it with grace. In a letter to Besso in which he thanked his friend for news of Mileva's improving health, he expressed the same chilling thought that had come to him during Eduard's illness. If her disease were cerebral tuberculosis, he wrote, "as seems probable, a quick end would be better than long suffering." A pious hope for a kind death has a chilling ring to it when the mercy sought is for an estranged spouse who is obstinately blocking the way forward.

Mileva didn't die, but neither did she recover swiftly. A renewed collapse in December, possibly triggered by a letter from Einstein to Hans Albert that the boy refused to show to his mother, finally persuaded him to drop talk of divorce. While all this was going on, he still struggled to retain some tie to Hans Albert himself. Unsurprisingly, the relationship became ever more fraught. The boy's distrust of his father had emerged very early in his parents' separation, which Einstein seems to have sensed. A letter written in late 1915 from him to his son, then just thirteen, illustrates the gap that had opened between them. He wrote, "Yesterday I received your dear little letter. I was already afraid you didn't want to write to me at all anymore." He floundered on: "In any case, I shall press for our being together every year for a month so that you see that you have a father who is attached to you and loves you." If that were not sufficient, he reminded Hans Albert (and perhaps himself) that there were special advantages to being Albert Einstein's son. "You can learn a lot of fine and good things from me as well that no one else can offer you so easily," he wrote. "What I have gained from so much strenuous labor should not be there only for strangers but especially for my own boys."

There is something pleading in this letter, as it seeks both to placate his son and to bind him within a web of affection and cajoling. The weakness in Einstein's position was also clear in his plea that the work that kept him from his boys was somehow "for" them. Not true—as he admitted in the rest of the letter—and in any event, even if valid, the claim did not matter. There is no question that he sought a real connection to his son. But he had scant resources to offer. The lasting message was that physics did outrank family for Einstein. The physical distance between them was a barrier, but Einstein's lack of empathy was the greater obstacle; the notion that Hans Albert should be satisfied with his work and fame as evidence of his father's love betrays the poverty of his offer.

The rest of his note contains some good advice: do the work that gives you pleasure; play the pieces you enjoy on the piano "even if your teacher doesn't assign them to you"; improve your dexterity in games of ring-toss with Eduard. But however well intentioned, it all reads like a man flailing to connect with a stranger. And ultimately, Einstein did not try terribly hard. Only twenty-six letters exist from Einstein to his son during the fifty-two months of the war. He stayed in touch, but that was it. Family matters were essentially distractions.

But then came his collapse in February 1917. Elsa cooked for him: the surest path to his heart, or at least to his gratitude. He recovered enough to travel by July, first to Zurich to pick up Hans Albert and take him to visit Eduard, convalescing at a sanatorium in the Swiss village of Arosa. Next he made his way to Lucerne, where he could be cosseted by his sister, Maja. It was on his return to Berlin that he finally took the fateful step that he had resisted since the summer of 1914: moving from an apartment a safe ten-minute walk from Elsa's to a flat across the hall. At that distance she could and did take exquisite care of her cousin. There was, as Einstein knew, a price to be paid. If he received the attention of a wife, then he owed his benefactor something: recognition, status. Elsa had always known what she wanted. Marriage, the life of Frau Professor, would be a vast improvement on life as a divorcée. For Einstein's part, he seems to have come to a decision composed in equal measure of his love of comfort—Elsa treated him very well indeed—and of a sense of fairness, rendering payment for faithful and devoted service. Or perhaps it was simpler still. In his illness he had needed her; as he recovered he found he could tolerate her company. The formality of marriage mattered to her, so why not?

EINSTEIN'S WILLINGNESS TO MARRY—actually, his acquiescence to it—was Elsa's long-sought goal, the culmination of a project that took seven years, end to end. Recently, as biographers have turned their attention to Mileva and the damage done to her by her relationship with Einstein, Elsa has often suffered by comparison. In caricature, she was the archetypal other woman. She embarked on an affair with a married man, strove for years to defeat her rival, and finally glowed in her triumph. But while there is some truth in this, given her iron resolve to rope Einstein into wedlock, Elsa was as much an object of pity as she was anyone's idea of a vulpine female. She was an adult who chose to act as she did—and this time Einstein made his conditions plain before they took any irrevocable step. But he remained a man in whose company one could become extraordinarily lonely. While Elsa may have persuaded herself that she understood her cousin, life with him could be extraordinarily painful, and so it was almost from the moment when it appeared that the two of them might form a life together.

At first, it had all seemed wonderful. Throughout 1912 and 1913, the years of their clandestine affair, as noted earlier, Einstein boiled over with both passion and affection. "I would give something to spend a few days with you . . ." he had written in the spring of 1913, and then, after he received his Berlin offer, that "one of the main things that I want to do is to see you often."[17] Elsa basked in the glow of such love; she kept the letters from this period until she died, when they were found tied with a ribbon and bound with a note that read "especially beautiful letters from the best years."[18] As his relations with Mileva deteriorated beyond repair through the rest of that year and into the next, the letters reflected the impending breakup. If she had chosen to notice, they could have given Elsa some advance warning about the man she wanted to marry; this was the period when he described his wife as "an employee I cannot fire."[19]

On arrival in Berlin and even briefly after Mileva left for Zurich, his ardor for his cousin continued to shine. His letters revel in the prospect of the happiness each would create for the other, and leaping ahead—he couldn't wait—when the two would be safely and sweetly married. "How much I look forward to the quiet evenings we shall be able to spend chatting alone, and to all the tranquil experiences that lie ahead," he had burbled on the day after Mileva's departure. "Now after all my thought and work, I shall come home to find a dear little wife who will receive me cheerfully and contentedly."[20]

A dear little wife . . . It was a role Elsa was perfectly happy to assume and one that Einstein seems to have promised from the start. But almost immediately clouds appeared. On August 3, he hinted at a holdup but told her not to worry: "I assure you that I love you and will never part from you. Have patience, and be content!"[21] Within days, though, the sweet prospect of marriage evaporated. Mileva's hopes and fears probably had some impact on this, but from the tone of his rather abject letter to Elsa, his own inclinations had played an equal part. "It's brutal that I had to disappoint you so," he began, and one can almost hear the soothing, slightly embarrassed tone. He swore the issue wasn't love; "it is not a lack of true affection that scares me away from marriage again and again." Well then, what was the problem? Einstein floundered: "Is it the fear of a comfortable life, of nice furniture . . . of becoming some kind of a contented bourgeois? I myself don't know. . . ." But still, he added, don't worry, for his feelings would endure, even better for the absence of marriage: "You have someone you can lean on just as much as a wedded husband," he assured her, and what's more, "the little bit of distance in our external life will be sufficient to protect what has made life so wonderful for us now from becoming banal and dull."[22]

Strip away the fluttering attempts to ease the blow and the message is clear. Einstein, so recently escaped from one marriage, had no desire to enter another. He liked his life, with Elsa available but unable to lay any real claim on him. As he had told Besso, "The agreeable, really fine relationship with my cousin does me tremendous good, the permanent nature of which is guaranteed by a renunciation of marriage."[23] There was nothing new in this, and nothing that would change later. He really hated what he saw as the core of marriage, the fact that it gave someone else an undeniable hold upon oneself. "Marriage makes people treat each other as property, and no longer as free human beings," he said once, and then, more directly, "Marriage is but slavery made to appear civilized," and yet again, even more nastily, "Marriage is the unsuccessful attempt to make something lasting out of an incident."[24]

And so from 1914 to 1917, it suited Einstein to keep relations with his cousin incidental. That Elsa was bitterly disappointed seems highly likely, but she had little choice in the matter. Their affair certainly continued: Einstein's concern for Elsa's reputation in 1916 in the context of his first attempt to gain Mileva's consent to a divorce confirms that they were spending enough time under the same roof to threaten her good name. But he remained obstinately independent, unwilling to push Mileva too hard, and evidently content to go on as before.

His collapse in 1917 forced his hand, but by now no hint of any grand passion remained. He acknowledged her care and her cooking—but that was all. Elsa herself had changed in the five years since they met. She was no longer the plump, attractive, energetic young divorcée of his first fantasies. She was now definitively middle-aged, beaten down by wartime deprivation, her relationship to Albert as much that of a caregiver as of a potential wife and bedmate. His summertime move to the apartment next to hers proved to be a preview for the marriage. He ate her food three times a day, while she learned his requirements: peace and quiet, no interruptions while working, separate bedrooms—the same list, phrased more graciously, that he had presented to Mileva. By early 1918 at the latest, he managed to persuade himself that he might just be able to tolerate actual marriage to her, and he made the final move across the hall into her apartment.

In the end, he treated the whole affair as a matter of convenience. In a letter to Besso's wife, Anna, he reprised the issue of Elsa's marriageable daughters who still needed the cover of respectability. He added that if he didn't go through with the marriage this time, "think of the difficulties" that would arise because "owing to my illness I am compelled to live in the same flat as Elsa."[25] Anna Besso suffered fools poorly; she wrote back that Elsa deserved no such consideration, she should suffer whatever difficulties might arise, for she had known what she was doing when she chased a married man. She added in barely veiled language that Einstein was showing himself to be weak, illogical, and close kin to a hypocrite.[26] Einstein felt the force of her argument only too well, but it was too late, or perhaps he could see no reasonable way out. Elsa was waiting.

Mileva remained the obstacle, because her formal complaint of Einstein's adultery was needed to set the legal process in motion. But after four years, Einstein's friends in Zurich, the long-suffering duo of Besso and Zangger, managed to convince her that there truly was no hope for the marriage. Her surrender came in a terribly sad document. She would file her complaint if Einstein truly demanded it of her, but she said that she was too ill to grasp all the details. Couldn't he just wait till the war was over?[27] No, she was told, he couldn't. Besso stepped into the breach, advising her, while in Berlin Fritz Haber served as Einstein's intermediary, reprising the go-between role he had played when Mileva escaped to his home prior to returning to Switzerland. Between them, they shaped the deal that would secure her financial future. The arrangement had one neat twist. Einstein pledged to her the award money from his Nobel Prize. Such a sum would provide for her indefinitely, but he had not yet won the prize. Still, all parties were confident enough to agree to the provision—and she would indeed reap the benefit in 1922.[28]

With Mileva's acquiescence, the way finally seemed clear. There was, though, a last sudden crisis, one Einstein created himself, the event that in this whole miserable story transcends the ordinary cruelty inherent in bad endings to bad marriages. Einstein was thirty-nine in 1918, and Elsa was forty-two. Her older daughter, Ilse, was twenty—of marriageable age, as Einstein had pointed out more than once. The theoretical physics institute promised him in Planck and Nernst's initial seduction of 1913 had finally been opened in October 1917, and he took the opportunity to employ Ilse there as a clerk. At the institute, they were thrown together frequently. He saw a young woman, slim, attractive, and above all new and hence alluring as no old lover like her mother could be. It is not clear what exactly happened between them. Einstein in one letter to Ilse spoke of an action "usually confined to my head" that "strayed down to my fingertips"—which sounds as if it could have been an unwelcome grope on the job. Ilse herself denied that sex itself was involved, and an affair was not really the core of the issue. What distressed Ilse, the reason she sought outside advice in May 1918, was that suddenly "the question was raised whether A. wished to marry Mama or me."

Dropping that bombshell, Ilse begged Georg Nicolai for help. Nicolai was intimately familiar with each side of this triangle: he was at once her mother's old, dear friend, Einstein's pacifist conscience, and just to tangle matters as much as possible, also Ilse's former lover in a brief affair early in the war.[29] Ilse, still very much his admirer, begged for his help in a long letter that she told him to destroy after reading. The whole matter had begun as a joke, Ilse said, but it soon became serious. "Albert is refusing to take any decision. He is prepared to marry either me or Mama." She had no interest in marriage, she said, and less still in sex with Albert: while she loved him very much, "I never wished nor felt the least desire to be close to him physically. This is otherwise in his case—recently at least." Still, "I know that A. loves me very much, perhaps more than any other man ever will, as he also told me so himself yesterday." There were other considerations too. "The third person to be mentioned in this odd and certainly highly comical affair would be Mother." Perhaps it was true, as Ilse said, that "if she saw that I could really be happy only with A., she surely would step aside out of love for me." But, she added more realistically, "it would certainly be bitterly hard for her. And I do not know whether it would really be fair if, after all her years of struggle, I were to compete with her for her place, now that she is finally at the goal." And besides that, Ilse added, the "philistines"—one of Einstein's favorite words—would surely have a field day.[30] What to do?

Such a revealing letter, and such a mess. The worst of it was Einstein's aloof disinterest: he would wed either one, mother or daughter, as they chose. He sought comfort in his living situation. Sex was separate, with no necessary connection to marriage (though Ilse clearly excited him as Elsa no longer could). Marriage to one woman or another weighed little in the equation. Einstein had already made it clear to Elsa that their wedding would not change their basic living arrangement, with their separate bedrooms, her duties as a hausfrau, and the absolute priority of his work and his pleasures. Now there was the chance that the best she could hope for was the housekeeping, without even the reward of the public status as the wife of a great man. Einstein's own inclinations here are hard to judge, whether in fact he deeply preferred the idea of marriage to Ilse over Elsa. Indeed, he may truly not have cared very much, reasoning that both would be part of his household, "his small harem," as he termed Elsa and her two daughters in a letter to Besso.

Ilse herself seems to be the one who finally acted, complaining, with some cause that it was unfair to ask a "twenty-year-old . . . to make the decision on such a serious matter." She told Nicolai that she found Einstein physically uninteresting—she emphasized that she had no desire to have a child by him—and she feared that she would find being Einstein's wife a fetter, adding that "marriage is really a devilishly silly affair." Ultimately, she wrote, the question was: "What is the best for the happiness of the three of us, and especially Albert?" Her answer was to step aside, and the episode became a closely guarded family secret, revealed only in 1998 with the publication of Einstein's wartime correspondence.

Einstein has no defense here. Anna Besso was right. He was a hypocrite, as well as, on some level, an emotional imbecile. Appallingly, Ilse is believable when she said that Einstein did not care which woman he married. Given that, one can imagine how he construed his leaving the choice to mother and daughter as the right moral action. If he did not value marriage and did not care who claimed the title of wife, then why not let those who did prize such things work it out as they saw fit? That getting into the position of having to choose in the first place might have been a "mistake," or more accurately, a viciously cruel demand to place on those closest to him, seems not to have occurred to him.

Einstein did eventually acknowledge, in a way, that he might have done better. As he told Besso's children just after Michele Besso's death, he admired his oldest, dearest friend most for one great accomplishment: he "managed to live for so many years not only in peace but also in lasting harmony with a woman—an undertaking in which I twice failed rather disgracefully."[31] There is some level of recognition, perhaps even a little self-knowledge here: an admission, but no real regret.

It is also true that even in the midst of his worst dealings with his wives Einstein sought to act as an honest man. Honest he may have been—in science and his political life he was in fact scrupulously so. But in the realm of what he dismissed as the "merely personal," whatever truthfulness he possessed he wielded in self-defense. He was perfectly willing to cause both Mileva and Elsa real pain in the context of his "honest" statement of his desires or expectations. At the time, there was one clear result. If Elsa had any doubts about the kind of man she was marrying, the tussle with Ilse must have laid them to rest.

Elsa, so close to her goal, chose to proceed. By the summer of 1918, the two of them settled into a routine, waiting out the legal formalities. Einstein paid little attention to the war, planning a vacation on the seaside with Elsa and her daughters, cosseting his stomach, eating a special diet that she dutifully prepared three times a day. For a few weeks, he simply enjoyed his reclusive idyll. Writing to Zangger from the German coast, he said, "That's the nice thing about my current situation, that unperturbed, I can occupy myself with thinking, without any worries about professional duties." Einstein was speaking as much about his position in Berlin as he was about his holiday, but his sense of ease and pleasure shone through. "Thinking for its own sake is like music!" he crowed.[32] The war raged; Berlin starved; Mileva and Elsa both had wounds to heal; Einstein's body was still treacherous. The mystery of the quantum lurked, tantalizingly, he wrote, just beyond his reach. Life after the war was still to come, at once longed for and unimaginable. But for a brief moment there was a calm, a moment's lull, and Einstein reveled in his delight, the pure pleasure of his mind at play.

Chapter Ten

"A NEGATION OF SUPERSTITION"

THE BEACH WAS BUT AN INTERLUDE. THE REALITY WAS BERLIN, AND almost everything Einstein saw there in the last full year of the war was disheartening. "I could not imagine such people existed if I did not see them before me," he had confided to Besso in March 1917. Even worse, he said, thinking about his colleagues, it was most often those who "in private are perfectly selfless and responsible that are the most rabid." Despite this, he told Besso that he retained a kind of hope in the prospect of "salvation from an external force"[1]—meaning through Germany's defeat. He had to mask such sentiments most of the time, for the censors routinely inspected his letters, but his meaning was plain, and in his writings and his conversations in Switzerland during the war, he made his hope for a German catastrophe absolutely clear. He believed that a German collapse was a safe bet, given the British blockade and the unrelenting pressure of attrition. From his perspective, if collapse were to come, the sooner the better, for only then could the moral order—not the political system but the kind of relations between individuals he had known before the war—have a chance to emerge.

Here, however, both knowledge and imagination failed Einstein, as they did uncounted others. Only those who had actually fought understood as no one could on the home front how bankrupt the old webs of social relations had become. The artist George Grosz, for example, had been drafted into the army early in the war. He returned home to Berlin in 1916 to recover from what was termed brain fever. He was a leftist, but he shared with front-line soldiers of all persuasions an utter disdain for the home front's illusions. To him, the city of Berlin, untouched by war, was a swamp of utter corruption. During his convalescence he created a series of works, beginning with a lithograph titled *Metropolis.* In his climactic image, *Widmung an Oskar Panizza*, the city glows deep red, shining through the windows of the buildings. It is a city lit from within by hellfire and lust. A mob overruns the streets, while a triumphal parade cuts through the chaos. A demented general leads a charge, with his chest full of medals, a sword upraised, a trumpet to his lips, while Death presides at the heart of the crowd, riding a black coffin and drinking from a bloodred flask. The threat of destruction is everywhere, and all those present stampede in a headlong race to outrun death.

"I am totally convinced that this epoch is sailing on down to its own destruction," Grosz wrote to a friend while working on the canvas. There was no hope, he believed, no possibility of recovering any lost civilization, and he left a clear visual clue to make the painting's meaning plain: "On the right a young man is throwing up, vomiting on the canvas all the beautiful illusions of youth."[2] Of the war itself, he wrote that "what I saw [on the western front] filled me with disgust and aversion for mankind." There, swiftly, war "came to mean nothing but filth, lice, idiocy, disease and deformity."

Grosz's paintings and drawings from 1916 and 1918 all home in on this raw open sore. Berlin in 1917, was, as Grosz wrote, "cold and gray," punctuated by a feverishly gay nightlife—"Heaven and Hell side by side, right here on earth." But, as he argued in the work he created during his convalescence, Berlin and Germany could not ignore forever what was happening, day in and day out, in the trenches to the west.

It is something of a cliché to see the western front as the crucible of all that came after the war in Germany, France and England. But the cliché contains an essential truth. The accumulation of misery on both sides of the trenches—all fifteen hundred miles of them—had long since created a broadly shared awareness of the endless, monotonous, inescapable banality of the slaughter, its sheer, bloody, stupid sameness. The scale of the battles grew, the death tolls lengthened, and the astounding repetition of failed tactics raised the cost of failure ever higher. Liddell Hart asserted that nothing actually changed meaningfully on the entire western front from 1915 through 1917, and in purely military terms he was right. The story of the war was not one damn thing after another. It was the *same* damn thing, the same horror, over and over again.

Nonetheless this judgment, though accurate, is not the whole truth. There was evolution across the war, a kind of education that each army endured. The major combatants on the western front responded to the stalemate with a series of efforts to break the deadlock. Eventually, at different times, the forces of each nation achieved a kind of epiphany, a moment of clarity when the ultimate futility of the effort became obvious to the mass of soldiers on the front lines.

In part, what drove men on the front to reject any return to prewar "normality" was the experience of the unbridgeable gulf that separated the true front-line soldier from the generals and their staffs who presided over debacle after debacle. Doctrine formed well before the war held that the commanders of armies in the field should wield control from behind the lines, as much as fifty miles removed from the fighting. Reports were leapfrogged in stages back from the front. Messengers (like Adolf Hitler) would run on foot to carry dispatches to company headquarters, where an abbreviated version of that information could be transmitted farther back to battalion and regimental commands. From there officers would carry edited versions still farther back to divisional headquarters, and, finally on to some elegant and peaceful château housing the top command. Critical data could arrive hours or even days after the fact, assuming it made it through the chain at all. By the time a message reached the "château generals" in command of whole battlefields, the mud of the trenches and smell of decaying bodies had long since been wiped clean.

To those in the trenches, the staff were cowards, trading on unjust privilege to run the war. The sense of alienation, of a basic divide between the cowardly rear echelons (and civilians) and the fighting man, was absolute. It was the same story on both sides of the line. Both the German and the Allied commanders almost literally had no conception of the reality their orders evoked. Front-line soldiers hardly ever saw an officer over the rank of lieutenant colonel at the trenches. When high-ranking officers did make a rare journey toward the zone of combat, they reacted with a kind of stunned disbelief. On the British side, Haig's chief of staff, Lieutenant General Launcelot Kiggel, moved up toward the battleground at Passchendaele in the Ypres salient in 1917. The historian Paul Fussell notes that the anecdote is a little too perfect to be wholly believable, but one witness recorded the general's reaction, and Fussell argues that the account is essentially true. As his car carried him through devastated swamps closer and closer to the battle, General Kiggel "became more and more agitated. Finally, he burst into tears and muttered, 'Good God. Did we really send men to fight in that?' "[3]

"That" was the ground that British troops had contested for more than three years. Kiggel's commanding officer, Haig himself, deliberately avoided even that much contact with the war, because, his son explained, he saw it as "his duty to refrain from visiting casualty clearing stations because these visits made him physically ill." The French commander-in-chief, Marshal Joseph Joffre, ordered his staff to stop bringing him maimed soldiers to decorate, for the sight would rob him "of the courage to give the order to attack."[4] The ultimate château general was, of course, Kaiser Wilhelm II, "the supreme War-Lord." When he came forward far enough in 1916 to view a presumptive German victory, he is said to have vomited. Thus affected, the kaiser passed almost all the rest of the war at the palace in Potsdam, or at his even more isolated country retreat, entertained at table by fictitious tales of the trenches told by young, genteel, unbloodied officers.

Thus untroubled by direct contact with the outcome of their decisions, generals on both sides pursued their theories of war, reproducing failed tactics on larger and larger scales. Throughout the campaigns of 1916 and 1917 the British and the French continued to fight as they had in 1915, merely increasing the numbers of men in the persistent belief that all they had lacked before was enough effort, enough pressure. The Somme battle, begun on July 1, 1916, reiterated the disaster of Loos on a grand scale. The memoirist Henry Williamson recorded the results of the initial assault. "I see men arising and walking forward, and I go forward with them, in a glassy delirium wherein some seem to pause, with bowed heads, and sink carefully to their knees and roll slowly over, and lie still. Others roll and roll, and scream and grip my legs in uttermost fear, and I have to struggle to break away while the dust and earth on my tunic changes from gray to red."[5] In that initial assault, the British lost about 21,000 killed and another 25,000 badly wounded—more men lost in that single day than on any other of the war.[6]

And from that catastrophic beginning, the French and British pressed the Battle of the Somme for four and a half months. It cost an official total of 146,404 British Empire and French dead. It was reckoned an Allied "victory" in the accounting of attrition, for by some highly disputed accounts the Germans lost slightly more: 164,055 killed. This was the balance sheet of the western front, a measure in which each soldier was simply an interchangeable digit, a coin to be spent until one side or the other went bankrupt.

On the German side 1916 was the year of Verdun. On February 5, 1916, the German commander-in-chief, Field Marshal Erich von Falkenhayn, launched his assault on a key French fortress in the hope of actually speeding up the meat grinder of attrition. No breakthrough was desired or even really sought. The measure of triumph was the same as at the Somme: more of theirs than of ours. As a war-making philosophy it had the sole virtue of clarity. It was also the bloodiest strategic decision yet, the epitome of the Great War.[7]

The battle for Verdun lasted ten months. The best estimates suggest that about 377,000 French soldiers were killed or wounded, against just under 340,000 Germans. But despite that nominal advantage, Verdun cost the Germans their best hope of forcing a victory on the western front. Once they failed to break the French defense, the logic of attrition became inexorable. They had far fewer men under arms than the Allies, and they, even less than their enemies, could not tolerate such triumphs.

Despite the growing danger at the front, the Verdun fiasco actually strengthened the position of the General Staff in Berlin. Falkenhayn was personally discredited by the failure, and was dismissed as the leader of the army on August 28. The next day Field Marshal Hindenburg, the triumphant commander of Germany's eastern campaign, was installed in his place, bringing his deputy Ludendorff with him. The two generals shared a deep distrust of Chancellor Bethmann-Hollweg, and when the chancellor began tentatively to explore the possibility of a negotiated peace, they moved to undermine his and the civilian government's control over any aspect whatsoever of the war effort. Bethmann-Hollweg survived in office until the summer of 1917, but long before then, no later than the turn of the year, the two generals had consolidated their hold on power. For the last two years of the war, Hindenburg and Ludendorff were the de facto dictators of Germany, more powerful than the kaiser himself. Their rise killed the last, admittedly feeble flickers of hope for a negotiated end to the war.

For a while, it even looked as if they might pull it off. Victory on the eastern front would leave Germany free to pour its entire military strength into the western campaign. But despite an unbroken string of defeats, the Russians fought on. However, the same harsh winter that had spawned Germany's first major protests brought riot to the streets of St. Petersburg. As the czar's government imposed cuts in food and fuel, the strikes and demonstrations grew increasingly violent as the cold deepened, until the ill-disciplined and hungry St. Petersburg garrison mutinied. On February 27, 1917, the czarist government fell. (This date is according to the Julian calendar, then in use in Russia.) Hunger and cold were, however, only the sparks of revolution. The ever-lengthening casualty lists had already undermined the Russian stomach for war. Russia's total wartime dead totaled approximately 1.7 million, second only to Germany's losses, and in contrast to the Germans, those deaths came in the course of a series of unequivocal defeats. Without even the veneer of military competence to shield the czarist government, it could only rely on the habit of obedience—and when that collapsed, so did the regime.

To the enormous frustration of Germany's generals, however, Czar Nicholas II's abdication did not lead to an immediate end to the war in the east, because Russia's new, moderately leftist provisional government promised the western Allies on June 18 that it would continue to fight. In response, the German military looked for ways to push the situation in St. Petersburg over the edge and into total disarray. It had long been part of the German strategy to foment revolution in Russia. As early as 1915, political radicals captured as prisoners of war had been identified, funded, and sent back to Russia to sow such seeds. But when the czar's fall failed to bring an end to the conflict, it was time for stronger measures. German political intelligence had identified an exile then living in Switzerland as a suitably vicious revolutionary, one who could accomplish Germany's real goal: "to create the utmost chaos in Russia."[8] To the German military, Vladimir Ilyich Lenin was the decisive weapon that could destroy Russia as a military power. They organized his safe passage back home, and Lenin, traveling with his wife and thirty comrades, all technically enemy nationals, arrived at Berlin's central train station on April 11, 1917. The next day the group was escorted to another train that would take them on to Petrograd, as the revolutionists had renamed St. Petersburg.[9] Lenin's deputy, the propaganda expert Leon Trotsky, soon followed, as did nine tons of German gold—50 million deutsch marks—all to be directed to the sole end of destroying Russia as a military power in the Great War.[10]

Lenin performed exactly as desired. Kerensky's government had been hobbled from the start by its commitment to continue in a war that neither the army nor the Russian people wanted to fight. The Bolsheviks, with their platform of "Peace, Land, Bread," used any means necessary to create the impression that the provisional government was edging ever closer to collapse. It worked. Lenin's campaign culminated in a swift decapitating coup in October that drove Kerensky's moderates out of the Winter Palace; in essence, a handful of men simply walked into the building and ordered its occupants out of their way. This was a triumph for German policy, made concrete when Lenin announced his Peace Decree on November 8, 1917. On December 15, an armistice was proclaimed between Russia and Germany.

It was a glorious victory, hailed especially by the pan-German annexationists, still dreaming of the vast empire to the east that now lay open for the taking. With such riches in prospect, the idea that Lenin's example might inspire a homegrown revolutionary threat in Germany seemed remote. But hints of danger were present, and not everyone was moved by the glow of victory—certainly not as long as the meat grinder in the western trenches remained in working order. George Grosz captured the loathing that some of the rank and file felt for their masters in his most famous wartime drawing, titled *The Faith Healer,* a work even more explicit than his *Metropolis* paintings. Around the edges of the drawing is a group of bored, contemptuous officers. They gossip, doodle, smoke cigars, ignoring the action in the center of the room. There, a fat and comfortable doctor, complete with pince-nez and a Prussian mustache, holds an ear trumpet up to the belly of a corpse in the late stages of rot. Bits of skin and hair, the remnants of genitals and guts, hang off the almost completely exposed but still bespectacled skeleton. The doctor listens, and renders his verdict: *KV*—*"Kriegsverwendungsfähig"*—"fit for active duty." The bitter punch line is that the phrase also evoked a bit of wartime jargon: *"Kadavergehorsam"*—"the obedience of a corpse."[11]

It was no joke; the truth was too close for satire. When the playwright Carl Zuckmayer suffered a head wound, he was evacuated to an army hospital. But in only one week, still barely able to stand, he was sent back to the front. He was well enough to die, Zuckmayer was told, "and that's all we need young officers for now."[12] Grosz himself, when ordered to return to duty in 1917, tried to drown himself in a latrine. He was to be executed for what his officers termed an attempted desertion, but Count Harry Kessler, a well-connected art lover and man-about-town, intervened to secure his provisional release back to the hospital. Thus rescued three times—from the front, his own hand, and his commanders—Grosz poured out his rage in the paintings and drawings that rendered the fighting man's judgment on the war. But he had already made his point. Better dead in a pool of shit than face the trenches once more.

THERE WAS, HOWEVER, one group of fighting men for whom the disillusion of the war went deeper even than despair in the face of its unending pointlessness. Germany's Jews had seized on the 1914 crisis as their chance to prove their true loyalty to the German fatherland. The German-Jewish community, most of it, went cheerfully into the army, to the tune of *"Wacht am Rhein"* just like all the other hopeful naïfs. On the first Saturday of the war, many of Berlin's synagogues started their services with a prayer that had been published in the Jewish press. The faithful proclaimed that "we Jews want to show that the ancient blood of heroes lives in us . . . Until now we stood in our land protected and secure. Now, because our fatherland must be secured and protected, it should rely upon us." And with firmness in the right as they were given to see the right, the Jews of Berlin concluded that in their aims,

"Almighty God awards us his blessing and support."[13] The major organizations of German Jewry, the *Central-Verein* and the *Verband der deutschen Juden,* joined in, calling for Jews to offer up their *Gut und Mut,* their wealth and their courage, for Germany: "Brothers in faith! We call on you to devote your faith and bravery to the fatherland above and beyond the call of duty! Volunteer! Rush to the flag!"[14]

Perhaps the most grotesque expression of such dedication came from Ernst Lissauer, proudly claimed as a Jew by the community and the press, in his famous *"Hassgesang gegen England"*—the "Hymn of Hate Against England." It is a ghastly poem, mostly remembered as a nearly perfect expression of German bloodlust. But what most readers miss is the fact that the piece was propaganda aimed not just at Germany's enemies but at the Germans themselves; the poem's Jewish author laid claim to full membership in a pan-German bond of animus and violence. The key to that message lies in these lines: "You we will hate with a lasting hate,/We will never forgo our hate,/Hate by water and hate by land,/Hate of the head and hate of the hand,/Hate of the hammer and hate of the Crown,/Hate of seventy millions, choking down./We love as one, we hate as one,/We have one foe and one alone—England!"[15]

That was one version of the German-Jewish dream: the assertion, presented as fact, that Jewish Germans could love and hate as one with the Gentile majority. More temperate voices made the same point more gracefully. Rabbi Leo Baeck, a leading liberal Jew, sermonized that "we understand each other because we understand duty." This war would "decide the culture and morality of Europe. Fate now lies in the hands of Germany and in the hands of those who are on its side."[16] A few Jewish thinkers, more pragmatic than most, identified a specific Jewish interest in a German victory. A Russian defeat at the hands of Germany just might end the reign of terror, of pogroms and casual oppression that the vast population of eastern Jewry had endured for centuries.[17] (In Poland, two young men, Isaac Bashevis Singer and his more radical brother, Israel Joshua, wondered whether the German advance might mean release from Russian tyranny.) For the most part, though, the response was simple and uncalculating. Jewish leaders proclaimed Germany's campaign "a holy war," fought for the "purity of the fatherland."[18]

Berlin's Jews, Germany's Jews, heard the call. In all about 100,000 Jews joined up out of a total population of 550,000, and about 12,000 died in action or as a direct result of wounds received at the front—both numbers proportionate to the casualty figures for Germany as a whole.[19] At first, their experience seemed to match their hopes: that Germany had at last become a place that, in the words of the kaiser, "knew no parties, only Germans." Officially, the new Jewish soldiers were shown every consideration. Orders under the kaiser's name laid out precise arrangements for Jews at the front to observe the Day of Atonement on September 30, 1914. Special food was provided for the end of the fast, and on the eastern front those who could were permitted to attend services in local synagogues. Publicly, German leaders emphasized the valor of the Jews. The German ambassador to the United States, Johann Heinrich Graf von Bernstorff, told a German newspaper in New York that "our Jewish soldiers are excellent fighters. They are brave, faithful, and intelligent, and our government knows how to value such virtues." Hatred of the Jews was a thing of the past: "Because of the war, any harassment is being eliminated . . . now that the German people have been convinced of the faith and loyalty of our Jewish citizens." It was to be a permanent change, Bernstorff said. "Anti-Semitism can be considered finished in Germany. *As soon as the war ends* [italics added], full equality will become the norm."[20]

And for a while, mere weeks for some, months for others, the first half of the war for many, Jewish experience in the field appears to have been tolerable. Petty harassment took place, but by and large Jewish soldiers seemed to blend in fairly well. Alfred Zweig, a rabbi serving at the front, wrote of a gathering at Christmas 1915. "I was able to explain why I as a Jew could participate at this 'family celebration' this year," he said. The war had abolished differences between Germans. "The shared experiences of battles, fighting, danger, fear and misery that unite all of us make it impossible for me to stand apart from my comrades on Christmas Eve." The speech was a success, according to Zweig, and at the front itself his point that "a hostile bullet does not care if it hits a Jew or a non-Jew" seems to have been broadly accepted.[21] Soldier-Jews seized on each act of bravery and official acknowledgment to make the case for full membership within the German nation. Infantryman Alfred Weil wrote home in late 1914 that "my dear cousin has already been promoted. I cannot tell you how happy I am. Finally the Jews receive the justice due them." Writing from Ypres in the midst of the *Kindermord,* a Jewish doctor exulted, "Yesterday a major told me that a young rabbi from Strasbourg received the first Iron Cross of the battalion." It was a glorious moment: "Nobody will be able to defame the Jews as cowards in this hard fighting. Nobody will be able to call us draft dodgers!"

Almost a century later, this desperate blend of braggadocio and passionate yearning seems both impossibly hopeful and utterly heartbreaking. In memoir after memoir, letter after letter, Jewish soldiers implicitly acknowledged the basic truth: Germans were disposed to call Jews cowards, and worse. Yet these soldiers still expressed the transcendent faith that the Jews would overcome; that the mere fact of Jews demonstrating courage under fire and uncomplaining stamina in the face of common misery would at long last persuade their fellow Germans to welcome them home. The bubble burst for Jewish soldiers at different times, prompted by particular, specific shocks—just as each man from the army at large who lost his faith in the conduct of the war could point to the exact moment when the madness revealed itself plain. Julius Marx enlisted in the earliest days of the war and served till the end. His memoir described his trench experience in extensive, even exhausting, detail; part of his aim was to show simply that Jews experienced the same wretchedness as all other German soldiers. The key passages, however, describe the special circumstances a Jew faced as he fought alongside his supposed comrades. Marx began the war with a clear and heart-lifting sense of the common purpose he shared with his fellow soldiers, but the reality of his situation made itself apparent early. In his diary entry for September 7, 1914, he tells of overhearing members of his company as he dozed: " 'Man, but still, he's brave.'

" 'It would be better if he were not.'

" 'Really? Yesterday you said he was a coward Jew!'

" 'Coward Jew? Already?' "[22]

By October, Marx observes that "it is so obvious that I am handled as the company's Jew," and that "one has to listen to the old hated sayings again." The unity of the first days of the war has evaporated, and Marx finds himself "surrounded by comrades with whom one has shared all suffering . . . and suddenly one feels desperately lonely."[23]

Outright discrimination, as opposed to slights and gibes, came significantly later, in 1916 and 1917, when Marx had a field promotion blocked by officers in his own regiment who did not wish to share their mess with a Jew.

That was a broadly typical reaction. Back at headquarters in Berlin the old order reigned almost completely unchanged, no matter what happened at the front. Max Rothmann, a well-connected professor of medicine in Berlin, lost his older son in October of 1914. Throughout that first fall of the war, he tried to enroll his second son, then just fifteen, in the Prussian cadet academy. For the next five months, Rothmann was given an elaborate, quintessentially correct display of Prussian bureaucratic rejection. Finally, in December, at the end of his patience, Rothmann wrote that he considered himself "proudly, a pure German." With his oldest son dead, he sought a personal meeting with the kaiser to press "my deepest wish that my second and now only son can devote himself to duty for his country by serving as an officer." An official in the War Ministry replied in January with the irritation of one who was not heeded the first time out. Don't bother the kaiser, for "the Ministry of War is strictly bound to its principles," he wrote, those "already expressed in our earlier correspondence. It will not change its point of view."[24] At that, Rothmann gave up and volunteered for service in field hospitals. He died in 1915, ostensibly of exhaustion.

To Germany's Jews, especially those in service, these survivals of the familiar forms of rejection were depressing, if unsurprising. Julius Marx's initial reactions were weariness and sorrow, not shock. But as the war progressed and Germany's fortunes wavered, routine anti-Semitism began to take on a different flavor. Marx described a gathering of Jewish soldiers for the Jewish High Holidays in September 1916. The soldiers met in a barn somewhere in France after prayers. Marx's friend, Sergeant Nathan, burst out first: "We are fighting two fronts at the same time"—against the French and British, and against their fellow Germans. "*Why,* for God's sake? We are sitting in the same shit as the others. There we are good comrades, buddies, but otherwise we are just the 'Jew!'" Marx said that the Jews were fighting both for Germany and for Jewish equality in Germany. Not so, a soldier named Wolff replied. There was no hope for a victory over German prejudice, no chance at all. "If we win this war, no one will promote German-Jewish soldiers anymore." A return to the status quo would be bad enough, but worse, said Wolff, "If we lose the war, I tell you, the Jews will be blamed. We will be blamed for the defeat."[25]

He was right. In October 1916, the order came from Berlin to perform a census of Jews in the military. Anti-Semitic organizations in Germany had launched a campaign asserting that Jews were shirking, avoiding call-up, and then, if unlucky enough to get swept up in the draft, scrabbling for jobs safely in the rear. The Ministry of War was sufficiently persuaded to require a count, noting in their order that the purpose was to check whether or not "Jews were able to complete their military service in the safety of the reserve." The implication was obvious, and the abuses followed as if by clockwork. The better unit commanders tried to mask the significance of the questions, but others tried to transfer Jews out of front-line duties to the rear to help confirm the slander. When despite this the census yielded a picture of Jewish service equivalent to that of the country as a whole, the result was kept secret.

The data, though, were irrelevant, for the point had been made. Those who led Germany into war needed cover should the conflict end in disaster. The Jews were handy. On their side, the Jews also understood the Ministry of War's census. Marx's lieutenant called him in, and with some embarrassment asked him the required questions. Marx couldn't understand the purpose at first. Then the light dawned. The ministry, he said, was making them "second-grade soldiers, a joke for the whole military." The lieutenant agreed, but continued on, asking Marx's date of birth. "And is it for this," Marx asked him, "that we are willing to die for our country?"[26]

Once the official census took place, Jews in the army knew they had lost their private battle. No amount of heroism in battle would secure their place in peacetime, especially in a defeated Germany. As the war progressed, the combination of extreme economic hardship at home and the endless bloodletting at the front prompted the search for scapegoats. The usual suspects were available. A leading Jewish cultural journal had earlier trumpeted the success of the Jewish soldiers' campaign against prejudice, but in its review of the year 1917 it reported that the situation had changed decisively for the worse: "The more the services of our German-Jewish soldiers become familiar, the worse the anti-Semitic propaganda seems to become. With growing effort the anti-Semites are preparing their ground. . . . They are getting their weapons ready—denunciation, defamation, prejudice—to be used in the war against us that will begin when this war ends."[27] And on the other side, those involved made their purposes plain. That year, Heinrich Class, the leader of the intensely militaristic Pan-German League, one of the leading groups that had promoted Germany's colonial ambitions in the pre-1914 era, told his executive committee that it was their job to "whip up for national political ends the already burgeoning anti-Semitic mood."[28] If the war ended badly enough, Class said bluntly, it will become imperative to wage "the most ruthless battle against Jewry to divert the all too justified indignation of our good and deceived people."[29]

Such plans would have come as no surprise to Albert Einstein. As he had told Rolland, if Germany should lose or even suffer beyond some unacceptable threshold, the Germans would transform themselves into "a country of savages." He always thought that the attempt to assimilate was both impossible and immoral, an act of cowardice. He himself had never felt the temptation. If the choice was to be either Jew or German, there was no contest. But he acknowledged his connection to the community that wanted to call itself by both names, not just Jews in Germany but German Jews. Most important, the fate of the Jews in the last years of the war was to confirm his ultimate sense of himself: whatever else he might be, however much he rubbed shoulders with the elite in Berlin and beyond, he remained in Germany irreducibly the alien, a Jew.

This is not to say that Einstein's relationship to Judaism was simple or angst-free. After his childhood extremes of intense devotion followed by radical disillusion, his stance toward religion of any kind had become largely that of mildly amused contempt. Religion, including his own heritage of Judaism, was superstition, ancient tribal cant, not to be taken seriously by serious thinkers. Thus, when he was appointed to his professorship in Prague in 1910 and had had to fill out an official form declaring his faith, he wrote "without religious affiliation." That was not good enough, at least not for the Austro-Hungarian emperor in Catholic Vienna. It did not matter what he professed, but he had to admit to something. So Einstein said that for such purposes he was a Jew, and his official papers were amended to reflect his "Mosaic" commitment.

The declaration meant as little to him as the "most picturesque uniform" he had had to wear for his official induction as a civil servant of the monarchy. It was, he told his friend Zangger, "a comical scene," in which he "took the solemn oath of office in front of the viceroy of Bohemia . . . putting to use my Jewish 'faith,' which I put on again for this purpose."[30] Einstein showed the precise value he set on his official claim of Jewishness when he moved back to Zurich in 1912. The man he had hoped would succeed him in Prague, Paul Ehrenfest, refused to compromise his true atheist's principles. Einstein scolded him. "Your refusal to acknowledge a religious affiliation" was just this side of "willful stupidity," he assured him, with the benefit of recent experience. Once he became a professor Ehrenfest could revert to unbelief.[31]

This episode has often been misread to suggest that Einstein's later declaration of his Jewish allegiance in Berlin was something new, born entirely of his experience after coming to Germany. Einstein in Prague knew other Jews with backgrounds similar to his own—the same combination of German language and little interest in the content of the religion itself. But it was also in Prague that he encountered for the first time examples of much more traditional Eastern European Jews, with their special garb and rituals. The religiosity of these Jews had no discernible effect on his beliefs, but they did give him his first exposure to a Jewish community that had a culture, a daily round of life that was clearly distinct from the ruling order around them. Prague showed him that there existed, however strange or even comical some of that people's practices may have seemed, Jewish people who were utterly unlike the amalgams he himself knew: German- or Swiss- or Italian-Jews.

By the time he reached Germany, three years after Prague, Einstein had come to view any attempt to deny Jewish otherness as risible. He alternately laughed at and decried what he saw as the pathetic attempts by Jews seeking to "pass" as Germans, craving an acceptance he felt they would neither get nor should desire. Soon after he came to Berlin, Haber had urged him to convert, "so that you belong to us wholly and totally."[32] The delusions embodied in that plea are astounding, especially for one as brilliant as Haber. As Einstein dismissively told him, the "us" to which Haber thought he belonged was a fantasy. And the idea that Einstein would want to belong to such a club, even if it existed! He was always brutal about Haber's pretensions despite their bond of friendship. Haber was "that pathetic creature, the baptized Jewish *Geheimrat* [privy councilor]." A gibe sent to another convert in 1925 could have been meant for Haber as well. "A pity you had yourself baptized," he said. "As a rule it reflects a preponderance of self-interest over a sense of community."[33]

Pure Einstein: he never lost that ruthless, swift gift of scorn, nor ever learned (or chose) to self-censor. If you were Einstein's enemy, or perhaps even worse, his friend, you knew exactly how your actions measured up; there is a subgenre of his correspondence of belated apologies to those closest to him.[34] But behind the cutting skill with which he expressed himself lay a much more serious and considered reaction to the lure of Germanness. Einstein condemned any "inner dependence on the surrounding Gentile world," which produced an acute "moral danger of the Jew who has lost touch with his own people and is regarded as a foreigner by the people of his adoption."[35] And more personally, in an essay he later wrote on Zionism, "I have always been annoyed by the undignified assimilationist cravings . . . which I have observed in so many of my [Jewish] friends."

Certainly, his experience of the majority culture in Germany made the choice of allegiance easy. The impact of immersion in the genteel anti-Semitism of Berlin just before the war seems to have been enough for him. "When I came to Germany," he was to write some years later as part of an explanation for his conversion to Zionism, "I discovered for the first time that I was a Jew, and I owe this discovery more to Gentiles than to Jews."[36] Einstein's nose for slights was unsurpassed, and the routine, commonplace bigotry of the German academic elite (especially the nonscientists) gave him a good whiff of the odium attached to the Jew.

And if the assimilationist strategy in the face of such opprobrium was to attempt to disappear, to transform oneself as Haber had into a simulacrum of a "true" German, Einstein saw all this as a provocation to declare himself ever more unequivocally. It was no accident that he emphasized his Jewishness in 1915 when he told the German people to "honor your master Jesus Christ in deeds and not merely in words and song."[37] If Germany wished to rub his nose in its distaste for its Jews, he was perfectly ready to return the favor, contrasting the barbarism of Prussia with the millennia of Jewish civilization. But any such claim, any identification with Judaism, begged a question posed to him throughout his life. If he was a Jew, just what sort of a Jew did he aim to be?

Einstein never had any doubt about the kind of Jew he wasn't. For all his explicit, often courageous stands with his fellow Jews, including his devout, incomprehensible eastern kin, the actual practice of the religion filled him with a mixture of amusement and somewhat bewildered derision. Judaism for him was not defined solely by faith, nor by the attenuated standard of heritage, of family history. Faith first. Snails can be defined, he once wrote, as creatures with shells, and Jews can be defined as those with Jewish faith. But just as "a snail can shed its shell without thereby ceasing to be a snail, the Jew who abandons his faith . . . is in a similar position. He remains a Jew."[38] That almost sounds as though he was saying that a Jew is a Jew by inheritance, by blood—which had just enough truth to it to make him profoundly uncomfortable, given his loathing of the racialist rhetoric of the German ultranationalists. But if the actual content of the religion was an embarrassing relic and blood was the trait your enemies used to define you, then what was left? For Einstein, it was fairly simple. Faith was not required, but culture, an ethos, was. Judaism supplied a framework for life here and now. "The Jewish God is simply a negation of superstition," he said—a claim that would surely have startled the rabbis, though the next step in his catechism would not: in the Jewish tradition "it is clear that 'serving God' was equated with serving the living." Einstein's was a Judaism of the Prophets, of men like Micah who said that the essence of the Law could be reduced to a single command: "Only to do justice, and to love goodness, and to walk modestly with your God."[39] Einstein's credo came to much the same conclusion. For him, Judaism was "the democratic ideal of social justice, coupled with the ideal of mutual aid and tolerance among all men" and a passion for "every form of intellectual aspiration and spiritual effort."

Note God's absence. Like Spinoza, Einstein pledged his faith in the divine presence immanent in the harmony of nature. But he had no patience for what he saw as the childish fantasy of a personal God, some white-bearded old man on a throne, watching from up there and from time to time meddling in the daily minutiae of human existence. If his rejection of the Bible as a twelve-year-old had not been enough, the war would have convinced him. His "old Jehovah" was a nice rhetorical touch, but given the news from the front, such a personal deity could only be malicious, mocking his creation or absent altogether. "I see with great dismay that God punishes so many of His children for their ample folly, for which obviously only He himself can be held responsible," he told one too-patriotic correspondent. "Only His nonexistence can excuse him."[40] Einstein would play Jacob's role throughout his life, wrestling with something he called God to determine the shape of nature. For him, that old-time religion consisted simply of the love of knowledge, justice, and the independence of the individual—"the features of the Jewish tradition that make me thank my stars that I belong to it."

That was a definition of Judaism and the Jewish God that could wean Einstein from his earlier disdain for religion. As far as he was concerned, he need not argue with the Bible about God. "There has never been a conflict between our religious outlook and the world outlook of science," he wrote, which is true enough for those whose Judaism is a doctrine of action rather than faith, a religion of this world. Not all Jews would agree, though Einstein's formulation is one shared by many in the liberal Jewish community. But the key is that Einstein believed it, and gained solace in the thought—especially four years into a war, in a city where he was surrounded by those who pledged a very different creed.

Chapter Eleven

"I PREFER TO STRING ALONG WITH MY COUNTRYMAN, JESUS CHRIST"

THE SPRING OF 1918 WAS BLEAK, DIRE IN BERLIN, EQUALLY SO IN THE Allied capitals, as each waited for the stalemate to break. In response to this war-weariness Einstein made one last attempt to influence opinion. He approached David Hilbert, who was not only Germany's greatest mathematician but also perhaps its most prominent non-Jewish intellectual opposed to the war. He proposed to Hilbert that they and a handful of others write short essays in support of the concept of moral progress, an ethical idea opposed to what Einstein called the "grim principle of power."[1] It was a vague proposal, and reading it now is a reminder of how much has changed since the days when extremely intelligent people could hope to improve their world simply by saying that it could be a better place. In any event, it was much too late for such piety, and Hilbert turned Einstein down. Anything said in the midst of the war would be taken as an expression of guilt, Hilbert argued. It would be better to wait until the war's end, and then try to coax their fellow German academics back to some semblance of reason.

So Einstein remained silent, waiting. Official Berlin waited with him, watching, for while Einstein may have curtailed his explicit public opposition to the war, he remained on the books as a potential troublemaker. On January 31, 1918, the Berlin police had forwarded to the Minister of Interior Affairs the names of thirty-one known pacifists in the capital who, because of their internationalist sympathies, were to be given permission to travel only with the explicit approval of the military high command. Einstein showed up at number nine on that list. The decree had little practical effect, for with the contentiousness of his divorce negotiations he had already abandoned any plans for his usual summer trip to Switzerland.

But if such attention had little impact on Einstein, the police did recognize the emphasis in his thinking that many others missed. From its beginning he had found the war to be variously foolish, immoral, and reprehensible. As far as his private judgments went, he could fairly be called a pacifist, in that he could imagine no justification for choosing war as a legitimate means of settling international disputes. As he put it to a nationalist German academic in February 1918, "I prefer to string along with my countryman, Jesus Christ, whose doctrines you and your kind consider to be obsolete. Suffering is indeed more acceptable to me than resorting to violence."[2]

But throughout the Great War, Einstein's views remained much more narrowly focused. In what turned out to be the war's last year, he still concentrated on the same issue he had recognized at its beginning: how to rebuild the links within an international community of science that were dissolving in the acid rhetoric of nationalism. The project he proposed to Hilbert aimed at restoring the connections between like-minded men of culture in Europe. He wanted to make sure that those committed to the life of science would be able to speak to one another when the barrage finally lifted. That was the implication of Einstein's police dossier. He may have been a pacifist of sorts, but he was an internationalist through and through, a person for whom the entire idea of wars fought in the name of the state was absurd.

So Einstein resumed his vigil, waiting for the peace—any peace. War news in Berlin remained highly unreliable to the last, but even the casual newspaper reader would have been able to recognize the fact that the stalemate that had lasted for more than three years seemed finally to be ending. Germany had launched a new offensive in March, and for the first time since August 1914, the war in the west broke free of the trenches.

* * *

AND, IT SEEMED, toward a German triumph. For the western powers, the situation in early 1918 was one of enormous danger. Most dangerous, they faced a reinforced German army. The armistice with revolutionary Soviet Russia reached at the end of 1917 had freed up some 900,000 men for battle in France and Belgium. For the first time since 1914, Germany outnumbered its opponents on the western front. There was a seemingly minor hiccup: Hindenburg's and Ludendorff's rise to absolute power had so invigorated the pan-German hunger for new territory that the General Staff lost sight of the immediate strategic goal. German negotiators sought control of Russian Poland, Belorussia, the Ukraine, Finland, the Baltic states and more—territory stretching all the way to the Caucasus, more land than that of the entire Austro-Hungarian Empire. These German demands proved too rapacious even for a Bolshevik government desperate for an end to hostilities. Rather than simply seize the peace and move their eastern army to France in time for the first battles in the spring campaign, however, Hindenburg's military-dominated government chose to renew its assault on an obstinate Russia. Three more weeks of fighting followed. German forces advanced to within eighty miles of Petrograd, and in their second surrender the Soviet regime handed over all the territory demanded by the Germans in the treaty of Brest-Litovsk, including ground added to the earlier proposal, in what Berlin celebrated as the first half of its long-delayed triumph.

It was a fool's victory and Germany's most prominent fools celebrated accordingly. The kaiser designed a new coat of arms, complete with aurochs, the fanciful beasts he thought inhabited his new fiefdom. Lesser aristocrats scrambled to stake their own claims, and the military command began to plan how to use all the oil, iron, wheat and treasure suddenly at their command.[3] In fact, it was not possible for any of that wealth to flow swiftly enough to affect the course of the war, and Hindenburg's military government had wasted precious time on Russia when it should have been shipping troops west. Worse, this vast new colony required an enormous garrison, which meant that hundreds of thousands of soldiers who could have been marching off to fight Germany's remaining enemies were stuck, spread out from Vilna to Sebastopol. Nonetheless, the disaster of a two-front campaign was over for the Germans, and though it took until March of 1918 to get them moving, fifty German divisions could at last head west, where the battle that would decide the war was about to start.

At that moment, the virtually exhausted British and French confronted the futility of all their previous attempts to defeat the German forces. The British prime minister, Lloyd George, acknowledged the failure, commenting on the bloody waste of the Battle of Passchendaele in August 1917 (part of the larger battle of Third Ypres), with its gain of less than five miles at a cost of nearly a quarter of a million casualties. "We have won great victories," he wrote—but added, "I sometimes wish it had not been necessary to win so many."[4] His minister of munitions agreed. That usually happy warrior, Winston Churchill, wrote that "thank God our offensives are at an end. Let them traipse across the crater fields. Let them rejoice in the occasional capture of placeless names and sterile ridges."[5]

But even though their enemies were exhausted, the Germans still had to race against a new threat, one created by their greatest wartime gamble. On February 1, 1917, the German navy had initiated unrestricted submarine warfare in an effort to strangle Britain. That meant that American ships now became legitimate targets. Chancellor Bethmann-Hollweg had opposed the move, believing that U-boat attacks on U.S. ships would inevitably bring America into the war. He was overruled by the military, who were convinced both that the Americans would not fight and that even if they did, Germany's blow to Britain would be so severe that the war would be over before American power could be brought to bear.

Their judgment was very nearly right. The first three months of the campaign saw the Germans claiming to have sunk 3 million tons of shipping, compared with just 300,000 tons sunk in January, the last month of restricted submarine warfare. Although British records suggest the true number was nearer half that total, even so, the destruction proceeded at a terrifying rate. Two months after the armistice Winston Churchill wrote that it had been "neck and neck to the very end," and "the more one knows about the struggle, the more one realizes on what small, narrow, perilous margins our success turned."[6] But the inevitable countermeasures of convoys, improved antisubmarine weaponry, and an unanticipated leap in new-ship construction blunted the German attack. As the American author William Seaver Woods put it in his marvelously titled book *Colossal Blunders of the War,* the what-ifs of the submarine campaign—what if the Germans had built more U-boats, what if they had been just a bit more successful through the summer of 1917, what if America had behaved as the German generals had dreamed it would?—were all instances of "those fatal 'ifs' that paved the Kaiser's path to defeat."[7] Most significant, the order to attack at will on the high seas led directly to the U.S. declaration of war on Germany on April 6, 1917, two months later. Bethmann-Hollweg had been right. The General Staff had guessed wrong on one premise: America would fight. The outcome of the war would turn on the military's second leap of faith, that the German army could force a decision on the field before the Americans arrived in strength.

This dictated German strategy for 1918. Against the American influx German forces could count on just the one-time boost of the troops released from the eastern front. At the same time, deteriorating morale at home had to be overcome. The demonstrations that had begun in Berlin in 1917 after the bread ration had been cut continued despite attempts at repression, and mass strikes were sweeping the capital by the turn of the year. In January, 400,000 workers downed their tools and more than a million people turned out to protest both the war and the desperate hunger they were suffering during its fourth winter. The military government declared martial law, called out the troops garrisoning Berlin, forced workers back to their jobs at gunpoint, and sent many straight to the trenches. But even with armed calm in the capital, the trend was clear. It was no longer only the radical supporters of Karl Liebknecht's Spartacus League who took to the streets. Now even the rank and file who remained loyal to the larger, traditionally socialist wing of the SPD were mobilizing in ever greater numbers.

Most threatening of all to the military autocrats running Germany, the strikers were demanding more than an end to the war. Popular demands now included replacing Prussia's traditional three-class voting system with universal suffrage, an end to the monarchy, and the establishment of a genuinely democratic republic. The generals ruling Germany understood what was at stake. This was a call to revolution—suddenly and frighteningly familiar in the wake of Russia's swift descent into insurrection and chaos. Ludendorff wrote in a private letter after a renewed series of strikes in the spring that he was simply fighting a rearguard action. His goal was to maintain the old order against demands for popular sovereignty; if he could not prevent that, he declared, the war was not worth fighting, and "I would favor the conclusion of any kind of peace."[8] The leisurely pace of attrition could no longer be tolerated.

Thus, the German General Staff launched its final gamble, an offensive designed to achieve what neither side had managed since September 1914: a decisive breakthrough and the complete defeat of its enemies on the field. The date was set for the first day of spring, March 21. The primary thrust was at the point where the British and the French armies joined at the battlefields of the Somme and the Aisne, familiar, long-contested ground. The aim of the attack was to split the two armies and race to the sea, cutting the British off from their supplies while bursting the French line to complete the encirclement of Paris left unfinished in the first months of the war. It was a last throw of the dice. Cavalry officer Rudolf Binding, writing the day before the assault, felt something much grander than his customary weariness: "It is a tremendous thing for every one of us. . . . It will be a drama like a Greek tragedy, with a fate hanging over it, shaped and created by man alone, and ready to descend on the head of him who is responsible."

From the first, fate beamed on Germany. After a deceptively brief artillery barrage German troops roared forward, overwhelming the British and French. They gained four and a half miles in some sectors, a triumph—overrunning a total of one hundred forty square miles at a cost of just under forty thousand casualties. The year before, on the same Somme battleground, one hundred forty days of fighting had gained the British and French just ninety-eight square miles at a cost of half a million killed and wounded. The Allies trembled, and the Germans exulted: Kaiser Wilhelm crowed that "the battle [was] won, the British utterly defeated."[9]

It was a stunning, apparently irreversible swing of fortune. For the first time in four years German soldiers in the west advanced as they had been taught, overwhelming their enemy with tactical innovation, skill, tenacity, weight of metal and seemingly brilliant generalship. The strange, almost forgotten sensation of victory hit the German forces like a drug. Infantry Lieutenant Ernst Jünger declared that his company found their "spirit of attack kindled by success to a white heat of recklessness in every single man." As the English before them ran and fell, "it seemed as though death itself feared to cross our path." In such moments, victory goes to those "whom the thrill of action intoxicates and hurls forward with an impetus not to be resisted."[10] Drunk on triumph, the Germans pushed on—for a week, and a few days more.

Then, on March 30, the assault that had leaped forward so easily petered out. Analyses after the war reveal that the campaign was deeply flawed from the start. Different historians have pointed to a variety of weaknesses in the German plan. At the most basic level, military analysts point to a structural flaw in the essential conception of the attack, one reminiscent of the failure of the German dash for Paris back in 1914. It is a cardinal sin among soldiers to outrun one's lines of supply, but the plans for the spring offensive made no provision for reequipping the advancing troops, especially those moving through the devastated, roadless, railless ground of the Somme battlefield. For a brief time, Ludendorff's armies strung themselves out over meaninglessly conquered territory, far from their depots of food, ammunition, guns, replacements. And with each passing day, those victorious soldiers were mutating into targets for the converging reserves of their enemies.[11]

Binding's experience was typical. His men advanced against some resistance—he described his capture of a British general who held them up with the last machine gun in his brigade—but mostly he wrote of a bizarre odyssey through the unique landscape of the western front. "We have now spent two nights in the crater field of the old Somme battle. No desert of salt is more desolate," he wrote.[12] It took four days rather than one to burst clear of the devastation. The Somme battlefield was twenty-five miles wide, and so thoroughly wrecked that swift movement was impossible. The delay was threatening in itself, but the undamaged lands beyond the battlefield contained another danger. On March 28, the day his men breached the Somme devastated zone, Binding felt the advance slow down. He made for Albert, the nearest town, and on its outskirts "I began to see curious sights. Strange figures, which looked very little like soldiers, and certainly showed no sign of advancing. . . ."

This was the triumphant German army: "Men driving cows before them on a line; others who carried a hen under one arm and a box of notepaper under the other. Men carrying a bottle of wine under their arm and another one open in their hand. Men who had torn a silk drawing room curtain off its rod. . . . More men with writing paper and colored notebooks. Evidently they had found it desirable to sack a stationer's shop. Men dressed up in comic disguise. Men with top hats on their heads. Men staggering. Men who could hardly walk."[13]

Men of normally exemplary discipline, men trained to the highest pitch of military skill, but starving men, tired men, men who had spent four years ankle-deep in mud and worse—men who could not, would not, give up their chance to loot. Meanwhile, the British and the French were on the move. On March 29 the gap between the two Allied armies was nine miles wide, but by the first of April they made contact again, and the entire offensive was effectively at an end.

On April 4, two weeks after the whole enterprise began, Binding felt the return of his customary fatalism. The familiar shelling of the western front had resumed, and his quarters stank of "blood, sweat, urine, excrement, iodoform and wet clothes." At the end, his men simply halted in place, so exhausted, he wrote, "They were just like used-up horses which stand fast in the shafts and dumbly take the blows of the whip. . . . They could not advance; they could not shoot; they could not even get out of the way of the fire; they just stuck there." The enemy was probably in much the same state, he guessed, but no matter: "When two opposing forces are entirely exhausted it is a matter of indifference whether the generalship on one side is abler than on the other. They are equally ineffective; both weapons are equally blunt."[14] Binding anticipated the order that came on April 5. Ludendorff halted his assault.

The battle was over, and the Germans had lost, though they held on to their territorial gains for a while. They had been beaten not so much by their enemies as by the western front itself, the devastation of the battlefield, the impossibility of maintaining a coherent chain of men and matériel across that battleground, and the failing morale and physical strength of each individual soldier. The sum of the German accomplishment was as Churchill had hoped: merely the conquest of placeless names. The war was not quite over yet; the German army made four more attempts to seize the initiative. On July 15, 1918, they tried for the last time, an assault aimed directly at Paris. But here at last the western Allies met the Germans with a surprise of their own. Their frontline trenches were thinly held decoys. The German barrage rained down on empty holes and its infantry charge was obliterated by a vicious field of fire from untouched, fully armed defensive trenches to the rear.

In these four months of combat, almost a million British, French and newly arrived American soldiers had been killed or wounded. German casualties were virtually the same—but as always they had fewer men to spare, and the Americans were now arriving in strength. On July 18, the Allied forces launched their counterblow. The German forces managed a fighting retreat, painfully surrendering ground so recently conquered. In a typical action, German forces battling the French near Soissons were finally forced to fall back, leaving behind 35,000 prisoners and 700 guns. Among the individuals honored for their courage was Corporal Adolf Hitler, who earned the Iron Cross First Class for "personal bravery and general merit."[15] But individual acts of courage could not alter the course of the war, and Germany's army never returned to the attack. It is a measure of the capacity for self-delusion that as late as July 15, the German chancellor, Georg von Hertling, Bethmann-Hollweg's replacement, wrote that his government had expected to receive peace feelers from their enemies. But even such blinkered optimism could not hold indefinitely. By the 18th, with the German line shattering as it never had throughout the war, von Hertling said, "even the most optimistic among us knew that all was lost. The history of the world was played out in three days."[16]

EVEN THEN, the General Staff and the top civilian leaders told no one of the disaster. Much of the bitter history that came after Germany's defeat turns on the persistence of the grand illusion of victory, the sense, maintained till almost the last gasp, that Germany would be able to impose its peace on its enemies. The newspapers continued to work under censorship, so no sense of the true fate of the spring offensive made it into print. As far as ordinary Berliners could discern, Germany was in the midst of consolidating one more victory throughout the summer. It was a plausible belief; campaign maps still showed sweeping moves forward. Even if the papers had been free to publish as they wished, it would have taken a very sophisticated war reporter to recognize that the lack of a breakthrough was a distant forewarning of disaster. Ordinary people had no chance to discern the truth. From their perspective, they knew that Germany had completed a total victory in the east, and that the war in the west persisted but German generalship and the daring and pluck of German soldiers had done very well indeed over the spring. Even if absolute triumph remained out of reach, surely Germany held a commanding position.

The newspapers also published bad news, of course, but only stories their readers already knew. In August, for example, readers of *Vossische Zeitung* could learn of rumors that factories were making paper out of sugar and vice versa. There was news that potatoes would entirely replace the paltry meat allowance in the weekly ration after August 18. On the 26th, the paper suggested that Berliners experiment with "long forgotten fruits" like the berry of the mountain ash, a common tree around Berlin. Such berries were supposedly easy to pick, good for both juice and jam, and "even though their taste seems strange and a little too bitter at first," the paper loyally added that "one will easily get used to it."[17] But while hardship in Berlin was obvious and hence had to be covered, there was no suggestion that the war was going worse than usual.

The very acute and the exceptionally well connected may have been able to piece together a bit more, weighing the effects of hunger visible on the streets of Berlin with the bits and pieces of stories gleaned from wounded soldiers home on leave. But Einstein, who in Haber and others continued to possess a conduit to war news, still had no clue. His correspondence through the summer and the early autumn reveals no hint that he knew how close was Germany's collapse.

That ignorance ran deeper still among those whom Einstein most loathed. The appearance of victory in March and early April had led the ultranationalist right wing to reassert the same annexationist ambitions that had dangerously delayed peace on the eastern front. Now, with the advances in the west, the vision of a Greater Germany expanded yet again. The annexationists, including Ludendorff himself, continued to lay claim to Belgium, the bulwark by which Germany could protect "the seas from English tyranny." Alsace-Lorraine, too, would remain German. The French iron mines of Briey and Longwy represented a matter of "life and death for the German iron industry," as both the industrialists and the labor unions agreed. Cash—as much as 190 billion marks—would be needed to pay back Germany's war loans, and that too should come from the conquered. All these demands were being made in public, in the Reichstag and in the press, in August and even September of 1918. "We have no use for a peace of understanding," proclaimed General Eduard von Liebert, one of the leaders of the pan-German movement. "That would mean our ruin"—a Germany again unable to exert its will beyond its borders.[18] No use, perhaps, but staggering bluster. This was Germany's religion of power in full cry, bellowing from within the dreamworld of the right in an apparently willed determination to ignore the reality of the battlefield. It would take something overt, literally a smoking gun, to force a change. As Einstein had said a year earlier, such illusions "can only be cured by harsh lesson of reality."[19]

That lesson was coming fast now. The Allied advance in July pressed the Germans back with unprecedented ease, miles a day. By no later than August 9, with the continued success of the offensive, the General Staff at last understood the implications. Crown Prince Wilhelm wrote to his father and his commanding officers, urging them to offer an immediate return to prewar borders in exchange for peace. Ludendorff refused to consider the idea, and fought on for three more months, all in the hope of persuading the Allies to permit Germany to hang on to some prize to dangle before the German people as compensation for the suffering of the last four years. It was a final instance of the fatal General Staff habit of hope, the dream that one's enemies will act as one wants them to.

The Allies pressed on, breaching the last prepared German defensive position on September 29. The western powers still could not quite believe in their impending victory—at the end of September Britain's leaders were working out the manpower allocations that would free up enough soldiers for their 1919 offensive. But those at the top in Germany knew beyond doubt. On October 1, with the Allied advances continuing, Ludendorff finally lost his nerve. He urged the latest chancellor, Prince Max of Baden, to make an immediate peace offer, stating that "every day lost costs thousands of brave soldiers' lives." But Max still could not quite believe in the complete failure of German hopes, and he refused at first to ask for an armistice, instead seeking some formula that would allow Germany to retain something:

Alsace-Lorraine, for example, and incorporating Polish-speaking regions into East Prussia.

And while this newest chancellor maneuvered, the last weeks of the war offered yet more waste and pain. Berlin was still being told that the war could be won. Newsreels depicted German victories, soldiers taking enemy positions and marching their captives back toward the east. Patriotic plays and uplifting movies played to full houses throughout the fall.[20] One gauge of the success of the General Staff's control of information came on September 30, when political leaders were called to the Reichstag for a briefing on the state of the war. Many arrived apparently expecting to hear of the long-promised victory. When they learned the true situation the reaction was one of utter shock. The Social Democratic party's leader, Friedrich Ebert, blanched, and a conservative member is reported to have said, ominously, "We have been deceived and cheated, deceived and cheated."[21] By whom was not yet known.

The delusion crumbled further across October. Cholera had already broken out in Berlin, but it was quickly overshadowed by something worse. The epidemic outbreak of influenza that had begun in Britain and India in June reached the German trenches in July. By autumn, the disease, dubbed the Spanish flu, was showing signs of pandemic spread. In Berlin in October, the newspapers reported over thirty thousand cases and fifteen hundred deaths. The newspapers had tried to make light of the cholera threat—*Vossische Zeitung* blithely reported that "the fact that several people in Berlin were infected with cholera is no surprise to medicine and doctors"—but no one could talk away fear of the flu. *Berliner Morgenpost* reported that it was the worst wave of infection in years, and in an unintentionally ironic cultural note, printed an announcement of the new show at the Apollo Theater: *The World Is Coming to an End*.

Still, the war continued. Ludendorff and Hindenburg had finally persuaded Prince Max to request an armistice on October 4 in a telegram to President Wilson. Max offered a truce with no preconditions and not a surrender, but the move was interpreted both by Germany's enemies and by her military leadership in the field as an admission of defeat. Wilson rejected the proposal on October 8, but by then the two German commanders had regretted their weakness, and began to plan for a new defensive stand at the German frontier. They sent a telegram to their front ordering the army to prepare to fight to the last. Some of the formations in the field might have obeyed the order; although by then German soldiers were surrendering in unprecedented numbers. Left-wing and revolutionary agitation at home had begun to influence front-line troops as well, with Spartacist and Russian-funded organizers finding at least some willing ears in the army throughout the summer and fall of 1918. The army remained intact, however, and most units retained their discipline virtually till the end.

The high command's failure of nerve proved fatal. Protests from at least one of the field commanders forced Ludendorff and Hindenburg to withdraw their order for a fight to the death, and Ludendorff resigned, thus positioning himself to dodge any blame for the imminent catastrophe. Next, the military handed over political power to a civilian administration headed by Prince Max. This was Germany's first truly parliamentary government, holding power at the pleasure of the legislature, not the monarchy, but the move failed to calm the crisis. On October 29 the sailors of the German High Seas Fleet at Kiel mutinied, refusing to move when orders came for a suicide sortie. By November 6, the mutiny had spread to the rest of the navy. The mutineers had established sailors' councils—echoes of the sailors' and soldiers' soviets in Russia that formed during the revolution there—and some of the mutineers raised the red flag, the symbol both of the Soviet Union and of Liebknecht's Spartacists. In the Reichstag, opposition members called for the kaiser's abdication and then resigned en masse. On November 7, the Allied commander-in-chief, the French marshal Foch, received a message from German headquarters requesting talks. The two sides met at the Compiègne Forest early in the morning of the 9th. That same day, hundreds of thousands rioted in the streets of Berlin, many of them armed, many wearing red armbands or waving red banners. In the forest, Foch forced the Germans to request an armistice before he would reveal his exact terms: immediate evacuation of all occupied territory in the west, including Alsace-Lorraine, and the surrender of the German artillery, machine guns, and airplanes. In addition the Germans would have to hand over their submarines, their surface fleet, thousands of railway engines, and tens of thousands of trucks and railway cars. They would have to withdraw from their conquests in the east, and Germany would have to pay reparations to Belgium and France.

The government that had to consider those terms was not the one that had dispatched the delegation. On November 9, the kaiser received a telegram from the commander of the Berlin garrison informing his emperor that all his troops had deserted. Prince Max, recognizing the inevitable, announced Wilhelm's abdication to the Reichstag that day (before Wilhelm had actually agreed to go) and then resigned himself, handing power over to the largest political party represented in the Reichstag, the moderate-left Social Democrats, led by Friedrich Ebert. That afternoon, Ebert's deputy Philipp Scheidemann declared the formation of the German Republic in a speech to a vast audience in the plaza in front of the Reichstag. The next morning Wilhelm II fled to exile in Holland.

THE SPD HAD HELD the most seats of any party in the Reichstag before the war, and back then, a series of electoral gains had raised the prospect of a government in which the kaiser would have been forced to include them. The start of the war had frozen those ambitions, while the decision to vote for war credits had split the party. But the Social Democrats could still claim more popular support than any other party, and Ebert and his colleagues hoped that such support, combined with war-weariness, would produce a smooth transition. Ebert himself was a career Socialist, a party bureaucrat who had been selected for the leadership in 1913 because he was a competent administrator. Two of his sons had died in the war, and he had retained enough loyalty to the old regime to hope privately for a constitutional monarchy.

Any hope for so modest a transformation never had a chance, doomed by the enormous mass rage on the streets and in particular by the intervention of Karl Liebknecht and his Spartacus League. The League had powerful allies. Lenin had returned the favor Germany's generals had done him by sending his own agitators and funds to Berlin to foment Germany's revolution. His ambassador had arrived in Berlin in April, along with 12 million marks with which to finance revolt and several hundred Russian "diplomats" whose mandate was to organize the coming triumph of Germany's proletariat. That help flowed directly to the Spartacists, and in November, Liebknecht sought to emulate his hero, Lenin, by using the cover of chaos in the streets to seize power before the opposition could organize against him.

Liebknecht did in fact have some claim on popular support. The growing numbers of soldiers' and sailors' councils supported radical change, and he could point to the red flags and symbols now seen everywhere throughout Berlin. So on November 9, immediately after the declaration of the founding of the German Republic, Liebknecht countered by heading over to the Imperial Palace, festooned with a new flag—a red blanket—that was hastily raised up to the roof. There he declared the foundation of a German *Socialist* Republic, founded to "complete the World Revolution." The crowd, many of whom had just cheered Scheidermann, shouted again.

Ebert and his fellow Social Democrats had one advantage. They held the formal titles and offices of power. For the time being, they chose to pay no attention to Liebknecht's proclamation and after the two declarations, Berlin's streets froze in a kind of unnatural calm, a pause before the clash. Meanwhile, the nominal government faced an even more pressing problem; it took Ebert's new administration until well into the night to authorize the German delegation at armistice talks to agree to whatever it took to end the war. The armistice document was signed at 5:10 A.M. on November 11, 1918. The cease-fire would begin at 11:00 A.M.—the eleventh hour of the eleventh day of the eleventh month of the year.

Those final six hours of the war were surreal. The news of the cease-fire order passed swiftly down the line, but the fighting did not stop. U.S. Army captain Harry Truman, commanding an artillery battery, fired under orders until 10:45 A.M. British troops were ordered forward, with instructions to achieve their objectives by 11:00. German fire persisted too. Among those killed were British soldiers wearing the Mons star, veterans of the first battle of the war. Within the German lines, troops waited for news of the negotiations in the midst of preparations for a last battle. Early that morning Georg Bucher went to his company commander to beg for more machine-gun ammunition. At 7:15, an attack came; Bucher's machine guns broke it up before the Americans facing him reached his barbed wire. His company's casualties were light. One new recruit went down with a chemical burn. Bucher comforted him by telling him how much worse it could have been, how he could have lost his leg. "The youngster seemed, God knew why, to find comfort in my words," Bucher wrote. At that moment, Bucher's company commander returned, leaping along like a madman, shouting, "Cease fire at eleven A.M.! Pass the word along, cease fire at eleven."

Hearing that, Bucher wrote, "all we could think of was how to survive the next three hours." But within minutes, the neighboring section of the line came under artillery fire, though Bucher knew the Americans across no-man's-land must have heard the news too. Soldiers of proven courage began to waver, gathering their gear for flight. At 10:30, the wounded newcomer cheered up, calling out the time left. As he spoke, the Allied artillery shifted aim, and began to shell Bucher's position. Gas came next, and "everyone cowered in the shelters with clenched hands. The thought that death might overtake them a hundred times in that last half hour had completely unnerved them." The shelling died down, and the gas lifted. Bucher and his company returned to the forward trench, grenades and rifles at the ready to repel any last charge. At ten minutes to the hour, he stared over the parapet, watching the shell smoke drift in the breeze. There was still just time for something to happen. Time ticked on. He stared at his watch. The hand moved. It was over.

Bucher's experience was representative, but he did not experience the ultimate evil the war had to offer in those last hours and minutes. There was one last incident that captured the essence of war on the western front, the distillation of its arbitrary violence. At two minutes to 11:00 in the vicinity of Mons a Canadian private named George Price was hit by a sniper's bullet. He died instantly. The man who killed him remains unknown. That man made a choice. He was a marksman, a skilled soldier. He had just moments remaining in which it was legal for him to kill. There was no need to fire, no purpose, and some risk, at least to himself and any comrades near him. If he waited until 11:00, and then put his gun down, the only consequence would be that a young stranger would go home. Instead, the shot rang out. Two minutes ticked past. The war ended. George Price lay dead.

This was the western front, four years of struggle captured in a single instant, one bullet fired by one faceless man that killed one last enemy. Here was the archetypal act of a war of attrition. George Price's death was meaningless, a waste, a bloody horror—just like those of all the millions who had died before him.[22]

The dreadful tally of the dead accompanied the lines of German soldiers marching home across France, prodded by Allied guards and serenaded by the victors' regimental bands. The journey left plenty of time for the defeated army to dwell on its losses—and consider whom to blame.

Chapter Twelve

"SOME KIND OF HIGH-PLACED RED"

WHO LOST THE WAR? WASN'T IT OBVIOUS? ACTUALLY, NO—AND ACUTE observers knew it. The American commander, General John Pershing, believed that the Allies had missed their chance to hammer home to the Germans the one critical lesson they should have learned. On November 11, 1918, the German army on the western front still stood on conquered land in France and Belgium. To Pershing that was a terribly dangerous fact. "What an enormous difference a few more days would have made," he said. "What I dread is that Germany doesn't know that she was licked. Had they given us another week, we'd have taught them."[1]

Pershing knew his enemy. The army and the German people had never confronted the full reality of their fate. They had never been forced, as the French and Belgians were, to suffer under the heels of triumphant invaders. Instead, for them, the war just stopped. That laid the groundwork for the great lie of November 1918. To those who could not stand the fact of defeat, there was only one possible explanation for Germany's surrender. The German army and its dead had to have been the victims of treachery and deceit. Germany would have won—it should have won—but for the stab in the back.

To a certain extent, the myth of the stab in the back was a calculated falsehood, an exercise in disinformation that had been anticipated well before the ultimate defeat. As noted in Chapter Ten, in 1917 pan-German forces had begun to libel Germany's Jews as the scapegoats for failure in war. The next year, Ludendorff covered his resignation by proclaiming that if the home front would only support the army, "the war could be maintained for some months."[2] A German surrender, therefore, could only be due to the cowardice, or treason, of those lurking safely behind in Berlin. The story made it back to the trenches. Georg Bucher wrote of a conversation he had in early November with a soldier named Dengler who complained of the politicians negotiating with the French. "Who actually gave *them* the right to make terms for an armistice?" Dengler asked him. "The people, Dengler!" Dengler persisted: "We've carried on for four years for the sake of the people, and now when they've got empty bellies they want to shut up shop?"[3] It was the same at the top. On November 1, as the kaiser rejected a call for his abdication, he began to focus on those he saw as the true villains. "I would not dream of abandoning the throne," he swore, in the face of the threat "of a few hundred Jews and a thousand workers."[4]

Loud words and lying ones—it was his cousin, Prince Max, who finally bundled the kaiser off to Holland, shoving him along before he could be thrown bodily out of his palace. But if Wilhelm II showed little tactical sense, those around him managed to orchestrate what was probably the most skillful military maneuver of the war: shifting the blame for their failure onto the Social Democrats, the apparent victors in what was misnamed a revolution. As the German historian Arthur Rosenberg would argue, "This government had not won all these changes by fighting for them, but had received them as a gift from above."[5] Thus, it was the new parliamentary leaders who had to orchestrate Germany's surrender, not the generals or their unbeaten army. Any betrayal needs a betrayer. Someone must hold the knife that stabs from behind.

Ludendorff, who knew that Germany had actually lost the war on the battlefield, saw the armistice as an act of moral cowardice, and his argument established the foundation for the more virulent charges to come. He had conceded that the defeat was inevitable in a memorandum on October 31, 1918: "of that there could be no doubt." Nevertheless Germany should not have asked its enemies for peace. "The garrison of a fortress that capitulates before it is utterly exhausted lies under the stigma of dishonor," he declared. "A nation which accepts humiliation and allows conditions to be forced upon it which destroy its existence without having fought to the uttermost is on the downgrade. If the same things happen to it after it has made every possible effort, it will survive."[6]

In these early days, Ludendorff did not follow his line of thought to its obvious conclusion. Others did. General Friedrich von der Schulenburg said the key code words as early as November 9, declaring that his soldiers would say that they had been "stabbed in the back by their comrades at arms, the navy, together with Jewish war profiteers and shirkers."[7] That thought had an eager echo in the mind of one enlisted man, a wounded soldier from Bavaria's List Regiment, the victim of a gas attack on October 13 that had left him temporarily blind—a recently decorated corporal named Adolf Hitler.

According to his prison memoir, *Mein Kampf* (*My Struggle*), the armies at the front began to take notice of antiwar protests back home in the summer of 1918. He found the clamor for democracy absurd. "What did we care about universal suffrage? Had we fought four years for that?" The soldiers' war aim had been clear from the first. "The young regiments had not gone to their death in Flanders crying 'long live universal suffrage and the secret ballot' "—and he should know, because he had served in one of them—"but crying *'Deutschland über Alles in der Welt,'* " Germany above all others in the world. This was, he noted, "a small but not insignificant difference." If soldiers did not seek the vote, then who did? It was the "political party rabble" never seen at the front, except for those very few who joined "all decent Germans with sound limbs."[8]

Nonetheless, despite corruption back home, Hitler wrote, the sharp end of the German army, its *Frontkämpfers,* the trench fighters, did not truly begin to waver until October, when political dissent erupted even in his own regiment. Then came the gas attack, and the weeks in hospital where he hungered for information, chasing rumors of impending crises until he heard "disgraceful news from the front": the army itself actually wanted to surrender. On November 10, a minister visited the hospital and spoke of the kaiser's resignation, of the new republic and of the defeat. Hitler crumbled. "It had all been in vain. In vain all the sacrifices and privations; in vain the hunger and thirst of months which were often endless; in vain the hours in which, with mortal fear clutching at our hearts, we nevertheless did our duty; and in vain the death of two millions who died." And worse than the hard fact of defeat, of being beaten on an honorable battlefield by a superior force, Hitler said, was that Germany's sons had died "so that a gang of wretched criminals could lay hands on the fatherland. . . ."[9]

It was not only men as extreme as Hitler who felt this way. At the front, the architect Walter Gropius also warned of the rot. He felt some joy at the thought that his fellow soldiers had begun to oppose the war and doubt the kaiser, but even though he was desperate for it to end, Gropius's immediate reaction to defeat was still a sense of betrayal. "For four years I have given my all for this insane war and have lost, lost, lost, while a lot of those at home fatten themselves on our backs," he wrote. "What a gloomy fate to have to sacrifice everything that makes life worthwhile for an ever more doubtful patriotic ideal."[10]

There was a world of difference between Gropius and Hitler, of course. Gropius was worn out and mournful. Hitler felt angry, betrayed, and ready for revenge. As well as any ordinary soldier, he knew that the German army had been beaten on the battlefield, but he absolved both the army and its leaders from any connection with that failure. Rather, "miserable and degenerate criminals" had betrayed the army and their country. That was a delusion, of course, one repeatedly exposed throughout the 1920s. But the unhappy truth could not match the power and comfort of such a fantasy. Absent the overwhelming pounding that Pershing had wanted to inflict on the Germans, it remained possible to dream that Germany could still have won the war but for cowardice and base treason at home.

Men like Hitler certainly knew who had done this to them. It had to have been the Jews, the capitalist Jews, and those other Jews who dominated the left-wing parties. They were a minority to be sure, but one of ineradicable duplicity and with an implacable hatred for Germany. They had set out to dishonor the nation, and the sudden collapse of the German military effort and the acceptance of the harshest terms for peace were evidence of their success, a stab in the back that could not be tolerated and must be avenged. "There is no making pacts with Jews," as Hitler would later write in perhaps his most famous declaration on the subject. "There can only be the hard: either—or."[11]

Not all those who believed in the stab in the back shared Hitler's obsession, of course. But even if there were many who could not name the specific criminals who had betrayed Germany, the historical "truth" of such treachery remained terribly easy to believe. Hence that popular certainty that the nation had been deceived and cheated of the victory that was its due, a belief that only became stronger the more time passed. Looking beyond Hitler's hatred of the Jews, there were plenty of individuals tied to the disaster. It was not a general who had signed the hated armistice agreement: not Ludendorff, or Ludendorff's last-minute replacement, Wilhelm von Gröner, or the actual commander-in-chief and dictator of Germany for the last two years of the war, Field Marshal Paul von Hindenburg. Rather, it was the parliamentarian Matthias Erzberger who led the German delegation. The lines of responsibility were clear. The old government and the army had fought to the last; the new one had failed at the very start. It was the latter whom Hitler four years later termed "the November criminals of 1918," and it was they who would ultimately be called to account.[12]

HINDSIGHT MAKES THE DANGER OBVIOUS, the risk inherent in leaving one's enemies such wonderful cover and such tempting targets. But in that November, at the instant of what Germany's Social Democrats saw as the ultimate victory in their fifty-year struggle, the idea that the "November Revolution" could ever be reversed seemed ludicrous. The real problem now appeared to be controlling the pace of change. On November 11, a fellow parliamentarian told the left-wing Reichstag member Hans Peter Hanssen that he "had not expected that it would go so fast and so easily." It was this speed that seemed most amazing. "The fact that the old order has crumbled without offering any appreciable opposition shows how thoroughly rotten it was."[13] By implication, there could be nothing left to fear from that old relic, for it was utterly decayed. Albert Einstein, also writing on the 11th, was even more sanguine. In a letter to his sister, Maja, and her husband he virtually crowed with joy. "The great event has taken place! . . . And the funniest thing of all is: people are adjusting themselves remarkably well to it." There was the hope of redemption even for Germans, and this was the moment, at long last. "That I could live to see this! . . . Where we are, militarism and the privy-councilor stupor have been thoroughly obliterated."[14]

Einstein himself was a recognized figure in revolutionary Berlin—or at least his university colleagues hoped he was. He told his mother that his colleagues saw him as "some kind of a high-placed Red," which, in the suddenly dawning new day, made him an intermediary between the professoriat and the government. In fact, there were few who could fill that role, given that the new government was filled with the kind of man the extremely conservative Academy had long disdained, starting at the top with Ebert, the son of a tailor. So when the student council of the University of Berlin (which was modeled on the sailors' and soldiers' councils that had themselves been modeled on Russia's early soviets) jailed the rector and his deans, Einstein was asked to try to get them out. Accompanied by Max Born and one other scholar, he went first to the Reichstag, where the delegation was admitted after a journalist at the building recognized him. They listened while the student council debated new academic regulations, and then Einstein was asked his opinion of them. He replied that the rules as proposed would replace academic freedom with specific regulations, and rather carefully put it that "I would be very sorry if the old freedom were to come to an end."[15] After an awkward moment, the three academics were referred to the chancellery, where, again, Einstein's name and face sped their way through to the new chancellor. Ebert himself paused in the midst of the chaos to handle the release of the university administrators.

Significantly, it was not just Einstein's "redness" that helped here. His fame extended beyond the Academy, well into popular culture. There was even a joke going around that December: "Do you know what wise man gets mentioned the most in Berlin?" asks one. "No, no idea," replies the straight man. "It's Professor Einstein, of course!" "Why him?" "Well—everywhere you go, on the trains and trams and buses, you always hear *Ein steien!* [Step in]"[16] While life must have felt grim indeed for that quip to seem funny, Einstein was happy to use whatever notoriety he possessed for his own ends. He told Besso that he enjoyed "the reputation of an irreproachable Socialist . . . yesterday's heroes are fawning over me in the hope that I can break their fall into the void."[17] It was a strange world, as he said, but perhaps he could improve it. Later that winter he was to propose going to Paris to seek food aid for a Germany facing yet another winter of privation. He knew that the French might not acknowledge the extent of the danger after so many wartime lies, but he felt "they will believe me if I give my word of honor."[18]

In the end Einstein did not go, but he retained his basic optimism, even glee, throughout that late autumn and winter. On November 14, he wrote that "for me, as an old, convinced democrat, republican and a person almost fanatically devoted to rights, joy drowns out all other reactions of anxiety."[19] Still, while he was hopeful, he was not blind. He knew there were reasons to be anxious. He confided to Besso a month later that the new government was still a shell, "dependent on the common herd . . . struggling assiduously but with minimal success against the economic crisis" of inflation that was just beginning to accelerate. But for the most part, he viewed the victory of his cause as certain, and the vanquished as objects of benign pity. "The Academy meetings are amusing now"—one can almost hear him gloating—and "the old folks are mostly completely dazed and disoriented." There were dangers, to be sure, but the risk came from excesses on the left, not a revival on the right. Berlin was the flash point for what seemed to be a looming Soviet-style eruption. "Here the Russian example is disquietingly prevalent," Einstein wrote, describing the Spartacus League's campaign against Ebert's administration as that of "runaway slaves without a true sense of solidarity and a broad overview."[20]

That is, the battle for Berlin (and hence Germany) was fought at first not between the right and the left but between the precarious coalition of the moderate parties of the left and a genuinely radical movement bent on establishing a Germany modeled on Lenin's model of a one-party dictatorship. From that moment on November 9 at the Imperial Palace when Liebknecht had placed Germany at the vanguard of world revolution, his Spartacists set out to create chaos on the streets, just as Lenin's Bolsheviks had done to undermine Kerensky's moderate coalition. Machine-gun fire rang across Berlin as early as November 10, and skirmishes erupted almost at random on the streets of the city. Einstein's family had its own brush with revolution. He reported to his sister that "Ilse, who is as red as they come, got into a little shoot-out and took to her heels."[21]

The conflict intensified as the German army evaporated in the first month of the peace. Two million men returned from the field and dispersed into the streets. They sought jobs, food, shelter and heat—and none of those were to be found in Berlin as winter came. *Vossische Zeitung* reported that unemployment was growing not only because former soldiers came looking for work but because in the context of the city's turmoil and uncertainty, factories were laying off the workers they had, not hiring new ones. On December 7, the Spartacists declared a general strike. Machine guns set up on the Siegesallee opened fire as the striking workers marched into view. Twenty died in what *Vossische Zeitung* called the heaviest fighting of recent days.

The bulk of the news chronicled life within a Berlin that was becoming ever more schizophrenic. It was in part a city desperate to establish some kind of peacetime life, in part a battleground. On December 23, the Berlin Philharmonic hosted what *Vossische Zeitung* claimed was the first public ball since war broke out, its hundreds of guests eager to mark the coming of peace by dancing into the night as none had done since 1914. Peacetime crime reporting returned to horrify and amuse Berliners. The New Year's Eve murder of a money courier in the Hotel Adlon had everything needed to gratify them, including a missing man with a false identity and the hint of a homosexual liaison. But despite such signs of normalcy—culture both high and low reasserting itself in the pages of Berlin's newspapers—the threat on the streets remained.

Einstein had witnessed one break in the tension, the parade on December 10 to honor soldiers home from the front. He wrote to his sons that "everyone was up and about in order to welcome the men who had had to endure such terribly long and harsh ordeals and dangers." It was a cheerful day, Einstein said, though he cautioned that "Tete [Eduard] should not go in for vile soldier games. I don't like that at all."[22] But whether or not his son picked up a toy rifle, Einstein remained convinced that Germany itself was done with its games of war. He told Besso that the "military religion has vanished" and he thought it would never return.[23] He rarely let such dreams obscure his judgment, and it is remarkable that he missed the note Ebert had struck in his comment to the returning soldiers: "I salute you," he told the troops passing before him, "who return unvanquished from the field of battle."

"Unvanquished," and hence heroic still, to be honored, perhaps worshiped. Einstein had diagnosed the problem—he had recognized from the start the new government's powerlessness, its failure to find some other faith with which to replace the theology of the gun. But he did not seem to recognize the solution available to an administration desperate for support. Ebert had. On the very first day of his administration, hours before the armistice was signed, General Wilhelm

Gröner, the General Staff's new chief, telephoned him. Ebert asked where the army stood, and Gröner told him that the officer corps would serve the new government, at least long enough to suppress any revolution coming from the farther left. But there was a price to be paid for this support: the government would have to guarantee the military's autonomy—that is, grant it the same independence from political control it had enjoyed under the kaiser.

The Faust legend is particularly German, and it has always been easy to see this devil's bargain as its echo. It is possible to believe that the fate of the German Republic was sealed at its birth, fatally compromised by its accommodation with the old evil of German militarism. In fact, there were plenty of opportunities both seized and missed over the next fourteen years; the republic did not fail simply because Ebert and Gröner came to their understanding. And at the time, Ebert acted, as he thought, under the pressure of necessity. But his choice revealed one crucial truth about the new Germany. Even if its new civilian government needed some kind of an army, its fraught alliance with the old military elite meant that the priests of the old religion of power lived on. The bargain began to go bad almost immediately.

A hint of what was to occur came in late December in the tragic farce of the battle for the Imperial Palace. Except for the shelling, the affair would have been comic. A detachment of about three thousand armed former navy recruits called the Peoples' Naval Division had occupied the palace since the armistice. In mid-December, they began to demand money from the government. On December 23, when they failed to get all they wanted, they stormed Ebert's chancellery, cutting the phone lines and taking hostages. Ebert, using a secret line, called military headquarters and Gröner agreed to send a detachment of the Imperial Horse Guards; but while these nominally loyal troops were still on the march, Ebert persuaded the invaders to leave the chancellery and return to their bivouac at the palace. Then he tried to call off the approaching force, and Gröner refused. He and his officers were "at the end of our patience," he told Ebert. Civilian methods did not suit, and the army would act as it saw fit. They were "determined to hold to the plan of the liquidation of the Naval Division and we shall see to it that it is carried out."[24]

The Horse Guards attacked the palace at dawn on December 24. Their artillery blew the palace gates open, and the hugely outgunned

Naval Division retreated to the stables. There they came under renewed fire, and with thirty dead and over one hundred wounded, were ready to give up. But as the two sides waited through a twenty-minute truce, the balance of power shifted. As soon as the Spartacists had learned that the Horse Guards were marching on the palace, they hit the streets in search of people to stand in front of it and protect it from what they accurately called the counterrevolution. Thus, when the firing ceased, at around 9:30 in the morning, thousands of Berliners moved in: men and women, many of them old enough to be the parents of the soldiers on both sides. They surrounded the Imperial Guards, scolding them, urging them to relent, to retreat. Slowly, the guards began to waver, falling back, until their officers despaired and marched them away from the palace.

It was a victory of a sort for Liebknecht and his party, though no one seems to have noticed how much firepower the regular troops were able to bring to bear. It was Christmas Eve, and Berlin's almost surreal ability to juxtapose slaughter with a party showed itself once again. Count Harry Kessler was a wealthy supporter of the arts, a liberal and a bon vivant, as well as one of Albert Einstein's friends. He was a relentless diarist, and his journal contains an extraordinary portrait of life as a member of the left-wing elite lived it during the German republic. Of the battle at the palace, he wrote that "throughout the bloodletting, hurdy-gurdies played in the Friedrichstrasse . . . jewelers' shops remained unconcernedly open, windows brightly lit and glittering. In Leipzigstrasse the usual Christmas crowds thronged. . . ."[25] The dead still lay scattered about the kaiser's old stables, but the next day would be Christmas with its promise of renewal and the wealth of kings.

Despite this setback, the revival of the military's fortunes began almost immediately. On Christmas Day, Liebknecht's Spartacist movement mounted a huge street demonstration, damning Ebert's rule. Liebknecht, unlike Rosa Luxemburg, his smarter, more cautious and more systematic partner, was an ambitious and excitable man, intoxicated by his apparent strength in Berlin. He set what was supposed to be the second and final phase of Berlin's Marxist transformation for the first days of January, despite the fact that he had neither organized armed forces nor a clear revolutionary program. His so-called Spartacus week began on January 5, when he and a coalition of left-wing leaders called a demonstration in defense of the left wing chief of police. Spartacist supporters seized key buildings, including that of the Police Headquarters. Factions set up machine guns wherever they gained a foot. In Kessler's record of that week, rifle fire and bursts from automatic weapons become a kind of constant counterpoint, just one more note of Berlin's street music: "At nine o'clock, at home," he wrote on January 7, "I could hear machine gun fire in front of the door. Towards one in the morning, a hot exchange of shots in the street. At two, more rifle fire."[26]

Throughout, though, Berlin retained its split rhythm of insurrection and pleasure. Kessler was attending a cabaret during Spartacus week when someone fired off a gun; the performance continued undisturbed. He wrote that "the Babylonian, immeasurable depth of chaos and violence in Berlin has only now become clear to me through the revolution. . . . It's as if Berlin were an elephant, and the revolution were a penknife. It sticks into the elephant, which shakes itself but then strides on, as if nothing in the world had happened."[27] Kessler reported that he got good service at the Kaiserhof Hotel on January 6. On the 8th, he wrote that there was still traffic on the streets, and that barrel organs could still be heard. On January 14, after heavy, bitter fighting, he went to hear a band performing opera, standing on the broken glass that littered the street in front of the battered headquarters of Berlin's police. "A large crowd collected in the street," he wrote, "partly to see the damage, and partly to hear *Lohengrin*"[28]—even as the shooting continued.

By then, though, the main battle was all but over. Among Liebknecht's many errors, the worst was his failure to grasp that he lacked the raw strength to hold out against well-armed troops, provided that those soldiers possessed the will to keep on killing until resistance collapsed. Conscript troops, the vast bulk of the then vanishing German army, posed no threat, but among Germany's unvanquished warriors remained many for whom the war could not end until the enemy at home was destroyed. In December and January, such men had begun to join what became known as Freikorps—irregular units whose soldiers signed month-to-month contracts. At their core were the elite of Germany's wartime shock troops, those used in the usually catastrophic first wave of attacks against enemy trenches. These were the men that Hermann Göring would praise as those who could not be "debrutalized," soldiers who could be relied upon to kill as ordered. Ebert and his defense minister, Gustav Noske, craved that reliability, and Noske entered into a deal with Freikorps leaders: official recognition in return for an essentially free hand in dealing with the Spartacist insurrection.

Whether the republic could have avoided the use of such means is an open question. But even if the Freikorps were an inevitable byproduct of the German defeat and its creation of a sudden surplus of violent, angry men, the decision to use Freikorps troops was desperately risky. Once dependent on the Freikorps, the republic lost its chance to create a military arm that was uniquely committed to the new democratic state. The Freikorps were in effect hired by their commanders, who themselves came from the right wing of the already conservative Prussian officer corps. Their troops usually bore a personal loyalty to such officers. They formed private armies, reminiscent of the bands of condottiere that roamed Renaissance Italy—those companies of mercenaries that were, in Jacob Burkhardt's marvelous description, "full of contempt for all sacred things, cruel and treacherous to their fellows."[29] These were soldiers who were as happy to overthrow their employers as their employer's enemies.

Noske seems to have ignored such dangers. On January 6, he escaped the Spartacus-threatened chancellery and moved to his temporary military headquarters in Dahlem. On the 9th, he sent in the first Freikorps elements the capital had seen, a twelve-hundred-man force from the Potsdam Regiment that received and obeyed orders to shoot anyone who came within ten feet of their column. The first target to be attacked was the *Vorwärts* building. Some of the few hundred Spartacist supporters fought bravely, aiming from behind the cover of vast rolls of newsprint, but they were a rabble armed with pistols and rifles matched against a trained unit that possessed cannon and tanks. The artillery continued to fire even after the defenders waved the white flag, and the Potsdam soldiers retained sufficient reserves of brutality to execute at least seven Spartacists who had already surrendered.

Following this success, Noske himself joined the Freikorps sweep through the city on the 11th. On the 14th, Liebknecht and Luxemburg fled the center of Berlin and hid in a western suburb. They were betrayed almost immediately, and arrested the next evening. After an interrogation at the regimental headquarters that was mostly a beating, the two leaders were led out, ostensibly to be transported to Moabit Prison. As first Liebknecht and then Luxemburg passed through the doorway, a waiting private named Otto Runge clubbed them down with his rifle butt. Liebknecht was then taken to the Tiergarten, shot, and dumped at a morgue as an unknown corpse. Luxemburg, with the marks of her beating too obvious even for this charade, was shot and then dropped into a canal. Her decayed and unrecognizable corpse was found four months later. The long-running campaign of right-wing political assassination had begun.

Noske did not apologize, and though a horrified Ebert ordered an inquiry into the murders, only two people were convicted. Neither served any jail time. The majority of Berlin's population did not seem to mind; the level of brutality apparently fell within acceptable bounds. When the Freikorps first marched into Berlin, they had been met by cheers from those who, in the words of one partisan of the right, rejoiced that "the criminals have not won their criminal game," that "the beautiful metropolis on the Spree has not become the spoil of this human dross."[30]

Applause like this translated directly into political power, and Ebert and his government went ahead with the elections scheduled for January 19. The Social Democratic party won a plurality of the delegates elected to create a new constitution for the German Republic. Despite such tenuous shows of strength, however, Berlin was still deemed too dangerous for the new assembly, so the country's first freely elected government met in Goethe's hometown of Weimar, a small university city a hundred fifty miles from the capital. The constitution that emerged from this provincial isolation bore the marks of the avoidance of risk that had led the delegates to Weimar in the first place. It expressed the belief—actually a pious hope—that Germany and its people were now committed democrats, as if saying it was so could create democratic behavior. It failed to curb the power of the states within Germany, which meant that extremists with strength in a single region—Bavaria, say, or Prussia—could climb to power locale by locale. Worst of all, it allowed the civil service, university faculties, and the judiciary to remain intact, carrying over to the republic a body of men raised in, trained by, and almost monolithically loyal to the old imperial regime.

It was, of course, the easy choice; Ebert and his Social Democrats quailed at the task of creating a new administrative apparatus from scratch, and he certainly felt some need to co-opt the old order.[31] But he had fair warning of the consequences. The battle for the streets of Berlin was being fought even as the delegates drafted the constitution, and the General Staff had already showed what it would do with power. What had been seen as a reasonably contained response to insurrection now became a full-fledged terror campaign, its pretext a renewed uprising and general strike in March. Noske used the false rumor that Spartacists had murdered dozens of police officers to send 42,000 Freikorps troops into Berlin, including those under the command of the man who had ordered the Luxemburg and Liebknecht assassinations. Seventy Freikorps soldiers died. Their comrades killed over twelve hundred Spartacists, real and alleged. This was true civil war, not the comic-opera version in which bullets cannot faze the cabaret dancers. Noske declared a state of siege in Berlin on March 6, and Kessler's diary entries lack their usual irony. "Executions have begun. A batch of thirty for a start. Noske is ensconced in the Ministry of War behind barbed wire," and this good democrat, wrote Kessler, had become just another "tyrant Dionysus." Those accused of sympathy with the left had to lie low or pay the consequences. George Grosz told Kessler that even Einstein had gone into hiding. It was not true, but the existence of the rumor suggests the level of fear Noske's terror produced. In the morgues the bodies were laid out naked, tagged by numbers, their clothes piled in heaps on their chests. As the artist Käthe Kollwitz reported, women would file in to view the corpses. "I heard loud wailing from that room," she wrote. "Oh what a dismal, dismal place the morgue is."[32]

The far left never again came so close to overthrowing by force what was now called the Weimar Republic. But the republic's open support for and clear dependence on the Freikorps highlighted the threat from the right. The *Manchester Guardian*'s correspondent in Berlin wrote as early as the end of the January uprising that "the formidable military machine, which seemed to be crushed forever, has risen again with astounding rapidity. Prussian officers are stalking the streets of Berlin, soldiers marching, shouting and shooting at their command."[33] This resurgence was ratified when Ludendorff returned to Berlin from his self-imposed exile, astounded at the amateurism of those he saw as his inevitable enemies: "It would be the greatest stupidity" he told his wife, if the government "were to allow us all to remain alive." He would never make such a mistake. If he regained power, "I would have Ebert, Scheidemann [who succeeded to the chancellorship when Ebert became president] and company hanged and watch them dangle."[34]

This was the dilemma of Weimar, present from the moment its leaders chose their allies. Its traditional enemies, especially those who led the Freikorps, could not be appeased, no matter how freely they were permitted to arm and fight. And for those who were or wished to be its friends, the republic's embrace of armed terror was evidence of fundamental failure, a surrender to the very forces the revolution was supposed to sweep aside. Kessler put the contradiction bluntly: "The paradox of a republican-social-democratic government allowing itself and the capitalists' safes to be defended by hired unemployed soldiers and by royalist officers is simply too insane."[35]

Chapter Thirteen

"A STATE OF MIND . . . AKIN TO THAT OF A . . . LOVER"

ALBERT EINSTEIN HAD OTHER THINGS ON HIS MIND BESIDES POLITICS IN the spring of 1919, however. Overwhelming as Berlin's troubles became, it is also true that even during revolutions most people spend their time trying to do what they had planned to before the shooting started. Even with his hopes for the revolution, the actual daily course of the struggle was simply less important than his daily life. On the personal side, the signal event of the year was his divorce. On February 14, a district court in Zurich formally ended Einstein's marriage to Mileva Maric. In court papers, he admitted his liaison with Elsa, and he acknowledged that Mileva "has made her displeasure known to me"—a remark that has to stand as one of jurisprudence's all-time understatements. Mileva got custody of the children with visitation rights for Einstein. He, as punishment for his adultery, was ordered not to marry for another two years. He turned forty on March 14—an event he allowed to pass without notice, avoiding anything like the press attention that had marked Haber's sixtieth birthday celebration the previous year. And then, on June 2, 1919, ignoring the Swiss court's order, Einstein and Elsa made their way to the Registry Office in Berlin and quietly, finally, married.

There is a striking photograph of the two of them, walking along a

Berlin street a year or two after their marriage. Elsa's influence on her husband (how sweet it must have been for her to say that word, after all her struggles!) can be seen directly: he is well dressed, even dapper, the picture of a comfortable bourgeois. His long coat appears tailored and trim, and his walking stick hangs on his forearm. He stares directly at the camera, with just the hint of a smile. Elsa too is elegantly dressed down to her fur-trimmed coat; she is clearly a well-off woman in the midst of handsome middle age. Unlike Einstein, she does not simply smile; she grins hugely, her whole face a map of satisfaction and pleasure. And perhaps most significant, she does not look at the camera. She walks behind Einstein—not much, a pace or two, but behind—and her eyes gaze to the side, toward him. She is happy, she keeps watch over him, she knows her place as he proceeds, comfortable and undisturbed.

In fact, the reality of remarriage institutionalized some of what Elsa had sought for and from Einstein. His biographer and good friend Philipp Frank painted him as a tourist in his new life. He now "lived in the midst of beautiful furniture, carpets, and pictures," Frank wrote. "His meals were prepared and eaten at regular times. Guests were invited. But when one entered this home, one found that Einstein still remained a 'foreigner' in such a surrounding—a bohemian guest in a middle-class home."[1] His visitors, those who could get past Elsa's conscientious gatekeeping, regularly remarked on his simplicity, his lack of pretense, and often on his shabby costume, too. Einstein at home dressed very differently from the Einstein whom Elsa would permit to be seen in public, slacks and a sweater being about the limit of his tolerance for fashion. That was unremarkable, except for his willingness to receive strangers in such clothes—something that a proper German professor like Planck or Haber would never have dreamed of doing.

But for all of Einstein's seeming obliviousness to his surroundings, he arranged his household as he told Mileva he wanted it all those years ago. Elsa could not enter his study without permission, and that attic room was not even to be cleaned, lest his papers be disturbed. She may have prepared his meals at regular intervals, but if he were working, the food had to wait. He kept his separate bedroom, and as he chose, his silence. Elsa and her daughters learned to tiptoe around him when the veil of concentration came down. As Frank put it, they both faced the issue of whether "she could create tolerable living conditions for Einstein in which he could carry on his work." Frank believed that by and large she had, and that Einstein knew it. "There is no ideal solution to this problem, and since Einstein believed less than most men in the possibility of an ideal solution, he did not feel hurt when his wife did not completely represent this ideal."[2]

Elsa herself at least half acknowledged that marriage to Einstein was perhaps not quite as much fun as she had imagined. Her often-photographed smile was genuine enough, for she took great pleasure in being married to a famous man, but a letter unearthed by the biographer Albrecht Fölsing reveals some pain as well. "One must not dissect him, otherwise one discovers deficits," she wrote, and then, bravely, "I find him wonderful, even though life at his side is enervating and difficult . . . in every respect."[3] Frank describes her husband coming to virtually the same conclusion, writing that his lack of "any illusion about the possibility of happiness in life has saved Einstein from the mistake made by many a husband who looks upon all the defects that are characteristic of life itself as defects in his wife." Still, it is likely that Einstein did not suffer Elsa's perceived flaws entirely in silence. He left the details to his correspondents' imagination, but he acknowledged that there were battles, describing himself once as a man "so vulgar as to oppose every war, except the inevitable one with his own wife."[4]

It was not as bad as all that, of course. At least as far as friends could tell, he and Elsa were capable of getting along perfectly well. Harry Kessler dined at their apartment after enough time had passed for any immediate bloom of marriage to have faded, and he saw a happy couple. They were a little too purely bourgeois for his taste—"rather too much food in a grand style"—but still, "this really lovable, almost still childlike couple lent an air of naïveté to the proceedings." The other guests included some of Germany's establishment figures, but, said Kessler, with more than a hint of hero worship, "An emanation of goodness and simplicity on the part of host and hostess saved even such a typical Berlin dinner-party from being conventional and transfigured it with an almost patriarchal and fairy tale quality."[5] However much the two may have clashed privately, Einstein enjoyed his comfort and a pleasant home, while Elsa relished the pleasures of a life far more interesting than she had known as a suburban divorcée.

* * *

IN ANY EVENT, marriage was only one of Einstein's concerns in the spring of 1919. Since November 1915 he had had no doubt that the general theory of relativity was correct. Its conceptual elegance, together with its accurate description of the orbit of Mercury, were sufficient to persuade him of the truth of the work. In the years that followed, his general-relativity papers had spread widely as he and others passed the word through neutral Holland and Switzerland. Some more theoretically inclined scientists regarded those papers themselves as proof enough. Men like Arthur Eddington simply accepted the theory on the strength of what one reviewer called "one of the most beautiful examples of the power of general mathematical reasoning."[6] But other than the Mercury prediction, and a not-quite-reliable measurement of one other quantity, there was no real-world evidence to support his picture of gravity.

A clear test did exist. In 1915 Einstein had made one straightforward prediction. His theory required that the path of a beam of light passing near a massive object must bend by a specific amount—about 1.75 seconds of arc for a beam of light tracing a trajectory that grazes the surface of the sun.[7] To make the prediction still more precise, Eddington, perhaps the most theoretically gifted astronomer of his day, calculated the amount gravity should bend light under Newton's system. He found that Newtonian gravity would bend a ray of light passing close to the sun just .87 seconds of arc—half the general relativity number, and, coincidentally, the same number Einstein had derived in the earlier version of his theory published in 1913. (Einstein had, of course, tried to test that prediction by sending his astronomer friend Erwin Freundlich to observe the Crimean eclipse of 1914—an expedition that, considered all in all, ended in a fortunate failure.)

Now, with the new claim, the same observation presented itself, and the British Astronomer Royal, Sir Frank Dyson, pointed out that the total eclipse that would take place on May 29, 1919, presented a perfect opportunity to check Einstein's new law of gravity. The path of totality mostly crossed the open South Atlantic, but it would make a few landfalls. Dyson suggested that the Royal Observatory at Greenwich send two expeditions to measure the effect, one to Sobral on the

Brazilian mainland and the other to the tiny island of Principe, off the West African coast. The Principe team was to be led, Dyson decided, by Einstein's leading British partisan, Arthur Eddington.

The choice of Eddington emphasized perhaps the most remarkable feature of the whole endeavor. Dyson had set his plans in motion and raised the substantial amount of money required in 1917, with the intention of confirming a German—that is to say, an enemy—scientist's work in the midst of the disasters of the Third Ypres. And this was not just any idea: Einstein's theory of gravity explicitly challenged that of Newton, the patron saint of British science. The nationalism of intellectual life, and the absorption of most researchers into the military or war work in Germany, would have made such a choice almost inconceivable in Berlin had the situation somehow been reversed. At the same time, in 1917, many Britons would have regarded lifting a finger to aid anything German as the next door to treason. Yet the British scientific establishment chose not only to go ahead but to fend off its own military as it did so. Eddington was a Quaker, opposed to war under any circumstances. With the start of conscription in Britain in 1916, he had been ready to declare himself a conscientious objector, but Cambridge University officials were able to head off a confrontation by persuading the army that Eddington's scientific work was too valuable to risk at the front. The exemption held until late spring 1918, when the German advance led Haig to tell his men that "each one of us must fight to the end."[8] The age limit for the call-up was raised to thirty-five, and the Ministry for National Service, desperate for fresh bodies, sought to revoke Eddington's noncombatant status.

But Eddington simply refused to contemplate going to war. He told the hearing officers that "I cannot believe that God is calling me to go out to slaughter men," and added with great bravery under the circumstances that he would continue to refuse "even if the abstention of conscientious objectors were to make the difference between victory and defeat." This was a man after Einstein's heart (and the two became good friends after the war), but his stand was one that could very well have landed him in prison. But Dyson intervened, mixing a defense of the intellect with a canny appeal to nationalism. Eddington's work was fully the equal of his Cambridge predecessors, Darwin, Ball and Adams, he said. It was vital that Eddington be allowed to continue, for his efforts "maintain the tradition of British science . . . particularly in view of the widely spread but erroneous notion that the most important scientific researches are carried out in Germany." And by the way, Dyson mentioned, he had just received a grant to observe the eclipse of 1919, an event of "exceptional importance." He added, truthfully, that "Professor Eddington is peculiarly qualified to make these observations."[9] He somehow forgot to tell the tribunal that the reason the expedition was so crucial was so that a British team could confirm the most significant scientific theory of the age, one produced in Berlin by a Prussian academician, Albert Einstein.

Dyson's ruse succeeded. The draft board let Eddington loose, provided that when the time came he went south and actually observed his eclipse. Even Einstein understood the exceptional nature of the British actions, writing in *The Times* of London in November 1919, "It is thoroughly in keeping with the great and proud traditions of scientific work in your country that eminent scientists should have spent much time and trouble, and your scientific institutions have spared no expense, to test the implications of a theory which was perfected and published during the war in the land of your enemies."[10] To Eddington himself, Einstein wrote a somewhat backhanded compliment: "I am amazed at the interest my English colleagues have taken in the theory in spite of its difficulty"—its complex mathematics, certainly, and its still more complex tangle of emotions.[11]

The eclipse observations turned on the comparison of two photographs, one taken of the stars that would be seen close to the sun during the few minutes of darkness during the total phase of the eclipse, and another of the same star field taken at night before or after the eclipse, when the mass of the sun could not disturb any of the beams of light that traveled through space to earth. If gravity bent light, as both Newton and Einstein said it must, then the positions of those stars would change between the two photographs. The light from the stars closest to the disk of the sun would be tugged more than the light of those farther away. The ultimate goal of comparing the eclipse images with the nighttime photographs was to prove whether or not gravity bends light, and if it did, by how much.

There were thus three possibilities. Both Newton and Einstein could be wrong and light might be unaffected by gravity, in which case the two photographs would show no change in the position of the stars. The stars could move a little, just enough to confirm the

Newtonian number. Or, as Eddington deeply believed, the deflection in the path of the starlight passing closest to the sun would show a deviation of 1.7 seconds of arc, exactly as Einstein proposed. Three months before the eclipse, on the night before the Principe and Sobral teams were to sail south, the four eclipse observers met for a last time in Dyson's study in Greenwich. Eddington laid out the calculations that produced the Newtonian and relativistic numbers, making no secret of his faith in Einstein. Eddington's assistant, E. T. Cottingham, apparently could not resist the opening, and asked Dyson what it would mean if they measured something different altogether, say twice Einstein's value. Dyson answered, "Then Eddington will go mad and you will have to come home alone!"

The two teams sailed in March, with Eddington and Cottingham reaching Principe on April 23. For the next several weeks the two scientists set up housekeeping and prepared their equipment, and Eddington incautiously noted that the team was in clover. Having tempted fate, he woke on May 29, the day of the eclipse, to a torrential rainstorm. The rain stopped at noon and by 1:30, already well into the partial phase of the eclipse, the two men got their first sight of the sun. The clouds thickened and cleared over the face of the darkening sun, and Eddington recalled that "we had to carry out our program of photographs in faith." They worked as fast as they could—as he wrote, "I did not see the eclipse, being too busy changing plates, except for one glance to make sure it had begun and another halfway through to see how much cloud there was." The clouds were worst at the start of totality, but broke just enough as the period of total darkness was coming to the end. The team took sixteen photographs, but only the last six held out much promise. Four of those six could only be developed back in England, and of the remaining two, just one was clear enough to permit a preliminary field analysis. It took Eddington five days to reach the point where he could measure his best plate. On June 3, he took it and compared the positions of its stars with those on the test images. He looked up, turned to Cottingham, and told him, "You won't have to go home alone."[12]

What Eddington saw was a deflection ultimately measured at 1.61 seconds of arc, plus or minus .3—close enough to the predicted value of 1.75 arc seconds to claim confirmation of Einstein's theory. He later recalled the moment when he derived that value from the blurred stars on that plate as the greatest of his life. In public he was more circumspect. His first telegram back to England from Principe read simply, "Through cloud. Hopeful. Eddington." The Sobral team had better weather and made several useful photographs, but on analysis, their images seemed to confirm a deflection only half Einstein's value: Newton's number. Eddington was convinced there had to be an error, but by September, he was willing to say to the British Association meeting only that the observed deflection lay between the two predicted values. Results had been expected from the British expeditions within six weeks of the eclipse, but the news was now seriously overdue. Finally, in October, Eddington and his colleagues concluded that the primary Sobral instrument had an optical defect that systematically produced errors in its results. Fortunately, four images taken by a second instrument at Sobral consistently showed the Einstein value, confirming the best data from Principe. That was sufficient, at least for the committed Eddington. He discarded the contradicting images with their distortions produced by clouds or bad glass, and prepared to report his results.[13]

Einstein knew of the problematic Sobral results, but seems never to have lost his confidence. Two friends were visiting one day that summer, Paul Oppenheim and his wife, Gabriella Oppenheim-Errara. Einstein was feeling ill, so he greeted them from his bed. As they talked, a telegram arrived from Lorentz with promising news, though not final confirmation. Gabriella remembered the scene more than seventy-five years later. Einstein was in his pajamas. She could see his socks. The telegram was brought in; Einstein opened it, and said, "I knew I was right." Not, she insisted, that he felt, or believed he was right. "He said, 'I knew it.' "[14]

Then, in late October, Einstein heard the good word directly from England. On November 6, the Royal Society met at its headquarters on Piccadilly, in the heart of London's West End, Joseph John Thomson presiding. The philosopher Alfred North Whitehead made a special journey down from Cambridge to attend. He wrote that "the whole atmosphere of tense interest was exactly that of the Greek drama: we were the chorus commenting on the decree of destiny as disclosed in the development of a supreme incident. There was a dramatic quality in the very staging: the traditional ceremonial, and in the background the picture of Newton to remind us that the greatest of scientific generalizations was now, after more than two centuries, to receive its first modification. Nor was the personal interest wanting: a great adventure in thought had at length come safe to shore."[15] To Whitehead, what made the event so grand was its inevitability, the ultimate certainty that comes when some human being discovers a piece of the truth. He had come from Cambridge to hear revelation. "The laws of physics," he wrote, "are the decrees of fate."

Fate rose to speak in the person of Sir Frank Dyson, who presented the results of the eclipse observations. He outlined the work Eddington and his colleagues had done to date, emphasizing the meticulous and difficult measurement procedures and analysis required to understand the story the eclipse photographs could actually tell. In the end, he told the society that the answer was clear: "After a careful study of the plates I am prepared to say that they confirm Einstein's prediction. A very definite result has been obtained that light is deflected in accordance with Einstein's law of gravitation." It was all true for nature had said so: space and time curve; matter and energy bend around its contours; light traces out the geometry of spacetime; Einstein's universe, strange as it may seem, is the one we inhabit.

Dyson's announcement and subsequent remarks from Eddington and the chief Sobral observer Andrew Crommelin did not pass completely unchallenged. One member, Ludwick Silberstein, raised an objection, based on the lack of any additional confirming tests of Einstein's theory, and gesturing toward Newton's portrait, declared, "We owe it to that great man to proceed very carefully in modifying or retouching his law of gravitation." But the great physicist J. J. Thomson, discoverer of the electron, and like Newton before him, president of the Royal Society, spoke last. "This is the most important result obtained in connection with the theory of gravitation since Newton's day, and it is fitting that it should be announced at a meeting of the Society so closely connected with him." Einstein's theory, confirmed by the British eclipse observers, was, Thomson said, "one of the highest achievements of human thought."[16]

Einstein was thoroughly unprepared for what came immediately after this grand ritual. But even in the midst of all the furor that was to follow, both he and Eddington recognized the extraordinary power of a radical theory joined to its unequivocal observational confirmation. Eddington put it whimsically, in a lengthy parody of the *Rubaiyat* of Omar Khayyám that concluded: "Oh leave the Wise our measures to collate/One thing at least is certain, LIGHT has WEIGHT/One thing is certain, and the rest debate—/Light-rays when near the Sun DO NOT GO STRAIGHT."[17]

Einstein, typically, spoke of this more grandly. Before the results came in, a student had asked him what he would feel if the English failed to confirm the deflection of light. Einstein's faith was unshakable. If the eclipse proved the theory wrong, "then I would feel sorry for the dear Lord. The theory is correct."[18] He was neither bragging nor blasphemous. He had hinted at what he meant, or rather what he hoped, in a speech given in 1918 to honor Max Planck on his birthday. "The longing to behold . . . pre-existing harmony," he said, drove both Planck and (by implication) himself. Glimpsing such beauty, Einstein said, turns on a peculiar form of devotion: "The state of mind which enables a man to do work of this kind is akin to that of the religious worshiper or the lover; the daily effort does not originate from a deliberate intention or program, but straight from the heart."[19] A year later, Eddington could tell Einstein that his beloved returned his passion.

Chapter Fourteen

"ST. FRANCIS EINSTEIN"

ON NOVEMBER 6, 1919, ALBERT EINSTEIN STILL POSSESSED THE LIFE HE had known since he arrived in Germany five years before. He was a famous professor, perhaps more outspoken than some, but just one among many luminaries of the Berlin intellectual scene.

On November 7, *The Times* of London published an issue largely concerned with the detritus of the recent war—negotiations between the powers; Allied demands on Germany; accusations of war crimes; reconstruction. But on page 12, tucked in among those tales of misery, came this headline: "Revolution in Science/New Theory of the Universe/Newtonian Ideas Overthrown." *The Times* correspondent noted that "the greatest possible interest had been aroused in scientific circles" at a meeting of the Royal Society.

The reporter admitted that he was somewhat at sea in the discussion. "No speaker succeeded in giving a clear non-mathematical statement of the theoretical question," he wrote, perhaps to reassure himself as much as his readership. But no matter. For all the quibbles of some members of the society, *The Times* declared, the president had confirmed that "our conceptions of the fabric of the universe must be fundamentally altered." The qualities of our cosmos, the newspaper duly informed its readers, "hitherto believed absolute, are relative to their circumstances." What circumstances? Relative to what? It did not matter. These were words to mystify and provoke.

That was just the first hint of what was coming. On November 9, with headlines even more exuberant than those of its London namesake, *The New York Times* blared, "Lights All Askew in the Heavens." Scientists were "more or less agog over results of eclipse observation," the paper then declared, as well they should be, given that "stars [were] not where they seem or were calculated to be." Fortunately, New York's *Times* was swift to reassure its readers that "nobody need worry," or, for that matter, think that much about it, for "just twelve wise men" were capable of comprehending the new work.[1]

Over subsequent days, the paper reconsidered, concluding that Einstein's work was perhaps a bit more subversive than it had originally seemed. In an editorial on November 11, it complained of the absurdity of the notion that light has weight. There was worse: it decried the arrogance of those incomprehensible experts who required that sensible men (meaning *New York Times* reporters) accept such nonsense on the authority of their impractical, unreal mathematics.[2] Before long, of course, *The New York Times* did come around, updating the story each week in November and sending a reporter to interview Einstein in Berlin in December. It was clear that he had ushered in a new order, one that was, like it or not, a mysterious realm, at once glorious and horrifying. "The raising of blasphemous voices against time and space," the paper pronounced, inspired "a state of terror where they seemed to feel, for some days at least, that the foundations of all human thought had been undermined."[3]

The German press and people took slightly longer to recognize the celebrity in their midst. The two best serious newspapers both waited until the middle of November to publish their accounts of the Royal Society's deliberations. The German coverage began with a much more sober cast than that in the United States, but by December, it began to dawn on at least some Germans that there was more to the story beyond just another success of German physics. By then Einstein was becoming a worldwide celebrity. The first truly iconic image appeared in Germany, on December 14, 1919, when the newest issue of the *Berliner Illustrirte Zeitung* hit the streets.

That issue's cover is a classic, an anticipation of dozens (perhaps hundreds) of images made over the rest of Einstein's life. His face is still that of a fairly young man, though he looks wearied and careworn. Unlike the bravura, postwedding images with Elsa, he does not engage the camera. Rather he looks down and away, his eyes focused beyond the reader's gaze; it is a portrait of a man who goes where ordinary mortals cannot follow. He rests his chin on his hand—the pose of the thinker—and if there is an air of wistfulness about him, the overwhelming impression is of a man transcending the woes of the everyday. The caption hammered the point home, proclaiming that Berlin could now lay claim to "a new great figure in world history: Albert Einstein, whose investigations require a complete transformation of our understanding of nature, and are equal to the insights of Copernicus, Kepler and Newton." This was Einstein the seer, a prophet who had gone to the mountain and come back to tell the world of the wonders he had witnessed there.

Einstein himself did not quite understand what this early burst of celebrity might mean—or even why he was so singled out for attention from the media. In the article in *The Times* in which he thanked the British for their willingness to confirm the work of an enemy in time of war, he added a postscript that expressed his view of fame: "Here is yet another application of the principle of relativity for the delectation of the reader: today I am described in Germany as a 'German savant,' and in England as a 'Swiss Jew.' Should it ever be my fate to be represented as a *bête noire,* I should, on the contrary, become a 'Swiss Jew' for the Germans and a 'German savant' for the English."[4]

The Times sniffed at this attempt at humor, observing that "Dr. Einstein does not apply any absolute description of himself." But the joke (which he used on other occasions, altering the nationalities as necessary) had a particular resonance for him. An Einstein who could be Jewish, German, or Swiss could also be right or wrong. That Einstein was no oracle but a man trying to understand certain difficult ideas that had little to do with most people's usual concerns. Einstein felt the effects of the posteclipse hysteria as a kind of din that crowded out his attempts to string one thought after another; as he wrote to Zangger in December of 1919, "With fame I become more and more stupid, which of course is a very common phenomenon."[5] But as he also told Zangger in a subsequent note, he fully expected that the cult that was springing up around him would evaporate before long.

It was already too late for that. Once the British had anointed him the greatest scientist since Newton, Einstein was stuck. He was now a symbol, the personification of scientific vision and wisdom. His initial response to his apotheosis was like that of many overnight celebrities since: he both reveled in the attention and failed to grasp the voraciousness of the cult of fame. The ridiculousness of his situation came home to him over the next decade in incidents large and small. In 1921, on a visit to England, Einstein stayed with the former cabinet minister, Lord Haldane—a visit that began with Haldane's daughter fainting dead away when the mythical physicist walked through the door. The newspapers covered minor and even fictitious mishaps, publishing reports that Einstein had lost his luggage (an item *The New York Times* thought fit to print in 1926), or that Elsa had grown worried when he lost himself in thought in his bath (of interest to readers in Vienna in 1927).[6] Throughout the '20s and into the '30s, he was a reliable public draw, attracting a crowd simply by showing up. Perhaps the most surreal of such encounters was to come in 1931, when he arrived by ship in Los Angeles to take up a visiting post at Caltech. There was a horde at the pier, including the by-then usual pack of reporters and photographers. There was also a gaggle of cheerleaders, a line of girls in blue-and-white dresses, chanting "Einstein, Einstein, rah, rah, rah" as he and Elsa stepped off the gangway. They then walked along the line, a royal couple reviewing their honor guard, while Elsa beamed and said, "Nice, very nice."[7]

Exposure like this left people, or at least the media, hungry for words direct from the icon's mouth. His opinion was sought and published on almost any subject imaginable. Newspapermen in America asked him what he thought about Prohibition; he answered that since he did not drink, he had no opinion on the subject, a banal remark that nonetheless earned a roar of laughter from the crowd surrounding him.[8] (He was more responsive later, arguing against it on the grounds that "nothing is more destructive of respect for the government and the law of the land than passing laws that cannot be enforced.")[9] A newspaper in Britain wondered if he thought there were creatures living on Mars, and published the sober report that "Professor Einstein believes that Mars and other planets are uninhabited."[10] Activists of all stripes had sought his endorsement for their causes; Einstein, a man rarely at a loss for judgments and opinions, was usually prepared to respond, and anything he said could and almost always did end up in print. He found himself weighing in publicly on the death penalty (against, given its "(1) irreparability in the event of an error of justice; (2) detrimental moral influence on those who . . . have to carry out the procedure.")[11]; on homosexuality (in favor of decriminalization); on abortion rights (for, unequivocally: "a woman should be able to choose to have an abortion up to a certain point in her pregnancy.")[12]; on the trappings of wealth (derision); on radio (a good thing for bringing people together); on George Bernard Shaw (though Einstein was "no judge of art," Shaw's sense of humor was a good thing).

The list goes on and on, and if Einstein enjoyed the attention up to a point, the dangers in such public exposure became obvious fairly quickly. In 1921 he told a Dutch interviewer that "it strikes me as unfair, and even in bad taste, to select a few individuals for boundless admiration, attributing superhuman powers of mind and character to them." The public's delusion, the error inherent in such hero worship, was bad enough, he implied, but it was worse from the target's point of view. "This has been my fate, and the contrast between the popular estimate of my powers and achievements and the reality is simply grotesque."[13]

It was a touchy point. To Einstein's colleagues any hint of personal aggrandizement was scandalous, evidence of a betrayal of the scientist's code. Max Born published a book on relativity in 1920 intended for a fairly advanced general audience, and in the original edition made the radical decision to include a brief biography and a photograph of Einstein.[14] Frivolity like this horrified respectable physicists, so much so that Max von Laue, a friend of both men, wrote to Born that he "and many colleagues would take umbrage at the photograph and the biography."[15] Such emphasis on the man behind the science was unacceptable, a pandering to the public cult of personality that had no business in the serious work of science. Born, conscientious to a fault, overcame his publisher's objections and removed the offending passages from subsequent editions.

Einstein himself came under direct attack over a book being prepared by an impoverished Jewish journalist named Alexander Moszkowski. The work was intended to explain his theories through a series of conversations with Einstein himself. Born's wife, Hedwig, weighed in first. She had found a list of Moszkowski's earlier works, which included joke books and speculations on the occult. Hedwig could imagine the type of book that would issue from such a writer: something "at a very low level. The ink shitters (the gutter press) will get hold of it . . . and afterwards you will be quoted all over the place, and your own jokes will be . . . thrown back at you. . . . Verses will be composed in your honor; a completely new and far worse wave of persecution [publicity] will be unleashed not only in Germany but *everywhere* until the whole thing will make you sick with disgust."

That would be bad enough, but worse yet was the fact that Einstein's cooperation with Moszkowski would be, as Hedwig put it, "your moral death sentence for all but four or five of your friends." No one but those closest to him would believe, she said, that Einstein had not sought out the publicity. "The *fact is simply that a man in his early forties, a comparatively early age, gave permission to an author to record his conversations.* If I did not know *you* well . . . I would put it down to vanity." In sum, Hedwig thundered, "we, your friends, are deeply shocked at this prospect. This book, if published *anywhere at all,* would be the end of your peace everywhere and for all time."[16] A week later, Max Born seconded his wife's condemnation, urging, almost begging Einstein to withdraw permission for publication. "I *implore* you, do as I say. If not: Farewell to Einstein!" Acting as a friend, Born volunteered to go to any lengths, "even to the North Pole," to kill the publication. But he was convinced that Einstein had no idea of the risk he ran by appearing to court the masses. "Forgive the officiousness of my letter, but it concerns everything dear to me (and Planck and Laue, etc.)," Born wrote. "You do not understand this, in these matters you are a little child." [This to a man three years his senior, and his mentor!] "We all love you, and you must obey judicious people (not your wife)."[17] [All emphases are in the originals.]

Einstein bowed to the pressure and withdrew his permission for the book. Moszkowski published anyway, but the work made little impact, appearing "without any earth tremors (so far)," as Einstein told Born. Half a century later, while editing his correspondence with Einstein, Born felt compelled to explain why feelings had run so high back then, given that by the 1960s "the publicity we fought against is commonplace, and spares no one. Every one of us is interviewed and paraded before the general public in the papers, on radio and television . . . no one thinks anything of it." But for Born in 1920, the principle still held that the object of public scrutiny ought to be able to control his encounter with public acclaim. Principle or no, however, the times had already changed, as Einstein's experience was demonstrating with each passing wave of adulation. Something new was emerging, the creation of the modern idea of a celebrity, a person ultimately famous for being famous.

This was, of course, a status that brought with it its own problems. Einstein was one of the first to confront the apparatus of the twentieth century's star-making machine. Despite his proud boast that his independence of public opinion meant that "therefore, nothing can happen to me" as a result of such scrutiny, he was simply wrong. He had a fast mouth, and given the speed with which the modern press could transmit his every word, he could find himself in all kinds of trouble. His attitude toward women, for example, embroiled him in controversies that he never dreamed might exist. After his first visit to the United States, *The New York Times* published a shocking report on July 8, 1921. The headlines shouted that the great man had concluded, "Women Rule Here/Scientist Says He Found American Men Toy Dogs of the Other Sex/People Colossally Bored." The article was based on an interview with a Dutch journalist in which Einstein had speculated about the experience of fame—a conversation that was perfectly innocuous until he started talking about specific cases. *The New York Times* quoted him as saying that "the excessive enthusiasm for me in America appears to be typically American. And if I grasp it correctly, the reason is that people in America are so colossally bored, very much more than is the case with us." Amid their ennui, such people seek excitement, something "over which they can enthuse. And that they do, then, with monstrous intensity." Worse yet, having ridiculed his audiences as rubes, gaping and cheering for no good reason, Einstein added his suddenly famous insult, that American men, for all their good, solid qualities, were "the toy dogs of the women," who cashed in on their husband's hard work to cloak themselves in luxury.[18]

Predictably, *The New York Times*—and American opinion—were outraged by such stuff, with the newspaper's editorialist thundering that "Dr. Einstein will not be and should not be forgiven for the boorish ridicule of hospitable hosts who honored him. . . ."[19] Equally predictably, Einstein moved swiftly to patch up the quarrel, claiming that he had been misquoted and assuring the papers in Berlin that "I was shocked when I read that newspaper." Really, truly, he had loved his brief tour of the United States. What he remembered best was "the warm and welcoming reception I experienced from colleagues, authorities, institutions, and private persons." And pointedly, aimed as much at his German audience as the American one, he added, "Even though you might find more individual thinkers in Germany, the uncomplicated American way and their moderate political attitudes are refreshing."[20]

It was a graceful and mostly successful recovery. Einstein continued to enjoy enthusiastic welcomes on subsequent trips to America. And as much as his gaffe embarrassed him, it reinforced a lesson that took some learning: his circumstances were truly altered. Almost certainly, in those early years of his celebrity, he had no idea that off-the-cuff remarks printed in Rotterdam would quickly turn up in news columns an ocean away. The weirdness was not just that what Einstein might say could be seen as news but that the news business, the public's eyes and ears, could seek its prey so greedily.

That must have been the hardest part of all: the realization that he was no longer quite his own property. He had always fired quickly, and often from the hip: his mouth and pen could and did carry him across the border of the cruel and the crude from time to time. But until now he had been able to repair whatever damage he might cause, retracting any mistakes in his science, and passing off the more personal gaffes with a smile, an apology, and the excuse that he always spoke without rancor. He would be forgiven and he would move on. Not any longer. His burst of recognition, bestowed as if from heaven, carried with it the burden of public appetite, a hunger that could neither be evaded nor fought. His face was recognized in the same way that only a handful of others were known—Mary Pickford, for example, or Charlie Chaplin. Eventually, Einstein and Chaplin got a chance to compare notes on what it meant to become a kind of public property. While Einstein was visiting Caltech in 1931, Chaplin invited him to the premiere of *City Lights.* As the two men entered the theater, the crowd behind the ropes cheered wildly. Einstein asked Chaplin, "What does it all mean?" "Nothing," Chaplin replied, which (as he surely knew) was not quite true.[21] It was simply that Chaplin had little love for the claim being laid on him, the demand that he share his life with those cheering him.

And if Chaplin allowed himself a touch of sarcasm, Einstein too was being a little coy. By the time the two men spoke, Einstein had had more than a decade of experience with the roar of the crowd. To the end of his life he complained often of the cost of fame. "To be called to account for everything one has said, even in jest, in an excess of high spirits or momentary anger" was almost reasonable, he said. But "to account for what others have said in one's name, when one cannot defend oneself"—that was unfair.[22] Nevertheless, he was always complicit in his celebrity, available as needed to reporters, and willing throughout his life to address popular audiences on a seemingly endless range of subjects. He posed patiently for picture after picture, ready to respond to almost any request for a shot—happy to be seen riding a bicycle or tossing his hat in the air (a particularly nice trick for the newsreel boys). Once asked what he did for a living by someone who had not recognized him, Einstein said that he was a photographer's model. That was the bargain: people might celebrate him for all the wrong reasons, or for no reason at all, but in exchange, he gained a pulpit. The toy-dog fiasco was an illustration, if a painful one: people now listened when Einstein spoke. But the underlying question remains: why? Why was it Albert Einstein, uniquely among his colleagues, who became *the* transcendent emblem of science, the one icon recognized around the world?

Partly, the answer lies with pure chance: the fact that Einstein happened to photograph well. He had always been handsome, even overtly sexy in his younger days. (Consider the challenging eyes and sensitive face on display in many of the early pictures.) And by 1919, he had become much more than just another pretty face; he was someone whom the camera clearly loved. Einstein joked about it, describing himself for an eight-year-old cousin as a fellow with a "pale face, long hair, and a tiny beginning of a paunch. In addition an awkward gait, and a cigar in the mouth. . . . But crooked legs and warts he does not have and so is quite handsome. . . ."[23] The photographers' lenses caught the wit as well as the gravitas. Einstein came across as a man composed of equal parts impenetrable wisdom, humor, moral strength and a bit of an edgy challenge to established authority. He had that hallmark of celebrity, the gift of seeming to be almost anything his audience wanted him to be.

But if luck played its part, so did Einstein himself. He had both the personality and the will to create a public persona. Others simply did not. Marie Curie was the one other scientist of their day as well-known worldwide as Einstein—and she had been famous for much longer. Yet she never earned the cult status that Einstein gained almost immediately. Media attention always burdened her, at times becoming a vicious assault, as in 1911, when the Paris newspapers vilified her for her affair with the married physicist Paul Langevin. Einstein met her at the first Solvay Conference, just as she was enduring the worst of her drubbing by the press. He commiserated with her, writing that he had become "quite enchanted" with Curie, and that "the horror story peddled in the newspapers is nonsense." He found the whole notion of Curie as a femme fatale a little ridiculous—"despite her passionate nature, she is not attractive enough to represent a danger to anyone."[24]

Here, Einstein was mistaken. She and Langevin had been involved, at least until the weight of public vitriol overcame them.[25] But still, he had recognized the tenor of Curie's personal style. As he rather cruelly put it, "Madame Curie is very intelligent, but has the soul of a herring." According to Einstein, she displayed what emotions she had by "railing at things she does not like," hardly a congenial public style.[26] After the Langevin witch hunt and other, equally brutal snubs, Curie withdrew as much as possible from the public stage. Her devoted volunteer work for France during the Great War restored her reputation, but she did not respond to the admiration that came her way. After the war she traveled to the U.S. and the American crowds turned out, donating the money needed to buy her a precious gram of radium. But they failed to love her, and she in her turn had little to offer them but thanks. She appeared on that tour as a rather grim woman in black, shielded by her acknowledged and almost feared greatness. In the dichotomy of being and doing, Curie simply was—in contrast to Einstein, who was happy to perform on his own behalf.

Einstein joked, expressed grand thoughts, mused about the universe or war and peace or progress or almost anything else. He was gregarious, visibly capable of enjoying himself in the company of others, whatever he might say about solitude. He wrote well, with an eye to the common reader. There is a role that cultural heroes have always had to play to reach and hold their audience, a tricky balancing act between grandeur and an engaging welcome. Only Einstein among his fellow scientists in this first epoch of twentieth-century celebrity truly grasped the need to greet his public. As he wrote in an introduction to one of his most popular works, he sought a "simple chat between you and us." He warned that the reader might find the work hard going, but said that he would be satisfied "if these pages give you some idea of the eternal struggle of the inventive human mind" to grasp the laws of nature.[27] Heady, powerful stuff—inviting the reader to participate, or at least watch, as the most inventive mind of the age revealed its secrets.

Beyond his own acts and gifts, however, there was another aspect to his sudden fame. He arrived on the scene at exactly the right time: the moment when the technology that enabled him to reach his audience was just beginning to mature. It may have surprised him to see his Rotterdam interview so swiftly transmitted to New York, but over the years of war reporting, the media had begun to create its modern global reach. At the same time, the immediate postwar years saw the explosive growth of the movie industry. Einstein played to the newsreel camera. Even better, and usefully in the silent-film era, he was not expected to be intelligible. These newsreels, so popular in those years, presented him more as a persona than a person, a readily recognizable collection of attributes. That funny hair, the smile, the eyes marked him as surely as the mustache and cane identified the Little Tramp. He was the first scientist (and in many ways the last as well) to achieve truly iconic status, at least in part because for the first time the means existed to create such idols.

Nevertheless, Einstein's apotheosis was not simply a matter of technological destiny, or the accident of possessing the talent for the job. Rather, Einstein's biographer Abraham Pais has argued, the mystery that he embodied generated the veneration he enjoyed, not in spite of but because his worshipers were unsullied by anything like real comprehension of his ideas.[28] Einstein himself made the same point in his Rotterdam interview. Why was it, he asked, that so many people all around the world showed such excitement for "my theories, of which they cannot understand a word?" The answer, he said, was simple: "I am sure that it is the mystery of non-understanding that appeals to them."[29]

Put that together with the fact that Einstein appeared on the international stage just after a catastrophic war. There he was, a German scientist and a pacifist, his genius celebrated by his country's recent enemies, rising to say that in the midst of all the misery, sorrow, and terrifying pressure of change, there are truths in the world. It was like Moses coming down the mountain, Pais said. Here was yet one more Jewish prophet bringing word to the world of order in the cosmos.

This was the stuff of civilized hope. Einstein promised not merely that truth still survived but rather that even in the midst of the numbing disaster of the war it could yet be sought and found. In the immediate aftermath of the war, he was the living expression of the best that human beings could be. William Carlos Williams celebrated that man in his poem "St. Francis Einstein of the Daffodils," written in response to Einstein's first visit to America in 1921: ". . . At the time in fashion/Einstein has come/bringing April in his head/up from the sea/in Thomas March Jefferson's/black boat bringing/freedom under the dead/Statue of Liberty/to free the daffodils. . . ." Williams's Einstein came "shouting/that flowers and men/were created/relatively equal." It did not matter to Williams that he could not say what Einstein meant; what counted is that he recognized what his Einstein could become: "It is Einstein/out of complicated mathematics/among the daffodils . . ." the scientist who speaks the truth, who merges into nature, Einstein transformed into "spring winds blowing four ways, hot and cold,/shaking the flowers."[30] St. Francis Einstein, Professor Albert Einstein—all-knowing and unknowable—bless all here.

WILLIAMS, OF COURSE, rhapsodized from the safe distance of New Jersey. Sainthood was in short supply in Berlin in the years immediately following the war, however. The central tension of Weimar between utopian or revolutionary hope and violent despair was present in the culture of Berlin from its start. You could read it in the penny dreadfuls, pulp novels of unparalleled gore. There were books that featured page after page of killings, sexual longing, rape and torture. Murder had become recreation and spectacle; literary killers took pleasure in watching their victims die, while real Berliners grew coarse and immune to cruelty. As the historian Alexandra Richie notes, there were documented cases of repeat killers who made serious money by selling the butchered carcasses of their victims as pork on the black market. Nothing that even the most inventive pulp writer might dream up could exceed the everyday viciousness to be found in Berlin.[31]

Serious artists responded to the same horrors. Visions of violence, random destruction, and a morally unhinged society could be found in work that ranged from Grosz's and Dix's canvases of despair (many dating from before the end of the war), to fiction, the legitimate stage and its slumming cousin, the cabaret, and even that newest medium, the movies. But at the same time, there was a movement—or rather, perhaps, an aspiration—to find in the fact of the revolution some real hope for a German spiritual and moral transformation. For those who felt so, "St." Einstein's aura and often vague impressions of his work became talismans, potent symbols of a possible better future. Einstein offered a cloak of legitimacy to that dream, not by any particular word or act of his own but through the uses true believers made of him. The very strangeness of his message made him the perfect messenger: an uncorrupted man, not of this place, come to sanctify the overthrow of the old world.

It was thus no accident that one of the first and most dramatic products of the avant-garde in Berlin after the war was Erich Mendelsohn's *Einsteinturm,* the Einstein Tower at Potsdam, commissioned to house an observatory that could confirm and extend general relativity. Mendelsohn told his wife that he wanted to erect a building that would capture "the mystique around Einstein's universe."[32] To do so, Mendelsohn, then a relatively unknown young architect, came up with a marvelously whimsical structure that is one of the masterpieces of Expressionist architecture. The original Expressionists were painters, working before the war. Paul Klee, a fellow traveler in the prewar movement, said that they sought "to make things visible"—to reveal inner truths as opposed to the focus on outward appearances they saw in Impressionist works. The war interrupted the movement in its first years, but the need to depict its horrors as powerfully as possible revived the style. It emphasized a surprising sense of shape and line and the use of powerful, symbolic colors in a wide range of media. It was an enormously varied movement, encompassing works that ranged from those of Klee before and after the war to the violent distortions of artists like George Grosz. In architects' hands, Expressionism could produce buildings that were truly startling, wholly unlike classical forms; and Mendelsohn's translation of an impression of Einstein into masonry is a whimsical gem. It rose, gleaming white, curved and streamlined, a futuristic ship ready for its maiden voyage, set at any moment to launch itself into space. Think Buck Rogers and Hollywood's early visions of cities of the future—and remember that Mendelsohn's real structure anticipated such fantasies by a decade and more. The tower opened in 1921, and Einstein's reaction was ambiguous. It was, he said, "organic," a judgment onlookers took as more of a compliment than may have been intended.

But his lack of enthusiasm for modern architecture was hardly the point. Einstein's existence was enough to justify almost any ecstatic vision of a new order. To Mendelsohn and like-minded artists, the belief that they and he were engaged in the same task was what counted. Mendelsohn saw Einstein's work as a blend of the comprehensible and the irreducibly strange. He sought the same in his own work, writing that "between these two poles—the rational and the irrational, reason and unreason—move my nature, life and work."[33] More broadly, Berlin's architects consciously sought what Einstein seemed to embody: an explosion of new creation that could sweep away the accumulated grime of old, outmoded ideas. In the years immediately after the war Berlin was in fact the center of an extraordinary explosion of creativity in all the arts. For artists on the hopeful left, their best work was intended to advance a utopian revolution. They pursued wild ambition and a kind of ecstatic hope, even amid the wretchedness of Berlin in 1919. The goal was nothing less than to remake their city and the lives of all those living there. In Ludwig Mies van der Rohe's words, "Architecture is always the will of the age conceived as space, nothing else."

The "will of the age"—it was such a grand, grandiose claim, yet on the scene, at that moment, it seemed a statement of fact. "It is a hopeless endeavor to make the form and content of earlier architectural epochs usable for our time," Mies wrote. "One cannot make forward strides looking to the rear, nor can one be the bearer of the will of an age while living in the past."[34] Walter Gropius had been a leader of prewar Germany's architectural innovators. A war veteran and head of the new Bauhaus, the architectural institute that he established in Weimar in 1919, said the same, decrying the mind-numbing effect of "the exhausted and dying practice of a derivative decorative architecture."[35]

Gropius's most famous prewar building before he started the Bauhaus had been the Fagus Factory in the town of Alfeld, an all-steel-and-glass structure completed in 1911. That building had been a radical step forward, not just in its use of materials but because of Gropius's explicit attempt to create a work space that would make the work within that space easier and more pleasant. Now he felt the need to argue his case again, recognizing that it was not obvious to everyone that modern architecture critically shaped modern life. Behind his analysis lay the fact that the material basis of existence, the actual daily reality of life in cities like Berlin, had already been transformed by steel, glass, trains, numbers, news and haste. Mendelsohn, more playful by far than either of his two more famous colleagues, made the same case in a surprisingly sweet poem titled *"Warum diese Architektur?"*—"Why This Architecture?":

Think back just one hundred years:
Crinoline and wigs
Tallow light and spinning wheels
General stores and craftsmen's guilds
Then think of us, now, think of what
surrounds you:
Bare knees and a sporty 'do
Radio and film
Automobile and airplane
Specialty shops and department stores.
Don't think they're superficialities—
the deeper meaning is in them.
*(*Die literarische Welt, *9 March 1928)*

Mendelsohn, with considerable courtesy to those shocked by the new architecture, tried to explain what such meaning might be: "And so you ask, what is this architecture for?" He answered that it was simply what the times required, what each person needed to truly live now. "Certainly man remains man and the heavens are broad as ever/But the world around you is enormously alive, cities of millions, skyscrapers, eight-hour flights from Moscow to Berlin." The old was irredeemably past, so Mendelsohn demanded sincerity, the clarity to see the world as it was. "Only one who has no rhythm in the body—

do not think of jazz, be serious—does not understand the metallic swing of the machine, the humming of propellers, the enormous new vitality that stimulates, blesses, and makes us creative." In such a new reality, modern human beings had just one choice: live now or rot.

> To disavow our life is self-deception, is miserable and cowardly. . . . Therefore be brave, be smart. Grab life by the hair, right where its best heart beats, in the middle of life, the middle of technology, traffic and trade. Accept it just as it is. . . .[36]

Be brave, follow one's heart, be blessed. The religious note was no accident. The modern urge in art in Germany was deeply entwined with a felt need for salvation, for transformation. Gropius had the same essential impulse as Mendelsohn, though his buildings, with their sharp angles and extreme clarity of form, were strikingly different from the younger man's "organic" structures. Humankind had fallen. It was the duty and power of art, of modern art, to raise all up again. In 1918, writing from the western front, Gropius had found himself "livid with rage sitting in chains through this mad war, which kills any meaning of life."[37] For creative men and women emerging from that madness, their duty was clear: they had to find or invent reasons for living. Above all, whatever was sought or made had to be truly new, for the old was doubly damned: once just for being old, and then again for having killed so many that it killed meaning itself. The past had to be abandoned, Gropius urged his fellow Germans, and in its place, he said, "let us desire, conceive, and create the new structure of the future," one that would "one day rise toward heaven from the hands of a million workers like the crystal symbol of a new faith."[38]

That impulse inspired many beyond the ranks of architects and painters. Berlin's *Novembergruppe*—the November Group—came together in 1918, dedicated to the twin goals of art and social transformation—more precisely, to using art to foster social change. The group pledged loyalty to a manifesto that grandly declared, "We regard it as our highest duty to devote our best energies to the moral cultivation of a young, free Germany." Painters, sculptors, playwrights, actors, composers and art dealers all joined. Erich Mendelsohn was the leading architectural figure in the early days of the group, sharing with the rest in their commitment to the proposition that "all of us revolutionaries of the spirit (Expressionists, Cubists, Futurists)" could join together in a "broadly conceived program [that] . . . should achieve the closest possible relationship between the people and art." How revolutionary the group actually might be was open to question—the original circular calling for members assured potential signatories that the artistic program of the group would be in the hands of the proper authorities: "to be carried out in the various art centers by trusted associates."[39] But if the November Group enthusiasts retained their stereotypical German love of the proper channels, they and the other "revolutionary" artists' organizations that formed in the months immediately after the war expressed the pious hope that art could make a difference to the fate of the new and free German Republic. The marriage of art and politics could generate very bad art, of course, didactic, preachy, self-indulgent and self-satisfied; and some of the most radical expressions were explicitly antipolitical and antiaesthetic. Dada, for example, with its slogan "Down with Art," generated performances like the famous race between a sewing machine and a typewriter. (The typewriter lost, and its jockey, Berlin Dada's spokesman Richard Huelsenbeck, smashed his machine on the stage.) With such acts, the Berlin Dadaists took the evisceration of what art was supposed to be to its logical extreme, but the initial impulse was the same as those of less flamboyant movements. The shock of Dada served to compel its audience to recognize the utter worthlessness of the old order.

But alongside such statements of radical revulsion came desperately sincere attempts to assert new meaning and a new conscience in the wake of the moral scorched earth left behind by the war. Max Beckmann, for example, painted without compromise. Beckmann avoided the inadvertent condescension of proclaiming his art's close relationship to the people, but he did possess the same sense of mission as the November Group's members. The idea of redemption and the possibility of salvation appear even in the most terrifying of his works, like the painting *Die Nacht,* or *Night.* In it, a grotesquely contorted man dressed in a white gown—a shroud—dominates the canvas, struggling against the hangman's rope. As he convulses at the moment of death, a wholly proper gentleman in vest and tie grips his arm. A woman, probably a prostitute, occupies the foreground. She shows her back to the viewer, red-stockinged legs splayed, buttocks exposed, her hands bound above her in a position of supplication. The painting is bleak, pale, drained of color but for the few sudden splashes of red. The tableau seems to offer no hope at all—yet Beckmann hints at another meaning. The woman, raising her bound hands before the tableau of the hanged man, might be pleading, but she could be praying too, Magdalene at Calvary.

Beckmann was not alone in his vision of the dystopic city, the ruined place in which Berliners dwelt. George Grosz outdid him in grotesquerie; Ludwig Meidner's postwar paintings depicted a hateful, heartless city; Otto Dix's works featured dismembered bodies, with the subtext of the debauchery of the rich. All this was the art that the Nazis later called degenerate. But *Die Nacht* was hardly arousing. Beckmann painted what he perceived, a world radically unhinged. For Beckmann, bearing witness in this way formed the essential first step to transcending that chaos. "Now we have looked horror square in the face every day for four years," he wrote in a creative manifesto published in 1920. Retreat was untenable. "Complete withdrawal to achieve personal purification and that famous immersion in God remains for now too bloodless and also too loveless for me." Better to sweep away the wreckage of the world that had brought such horror on itself, and to create new reasons to live in the present, in this place. "That is my crazy hope," he declared, "to build a tower in which people can scream out all of their rage and despair, all of their poor hopes, joys and wild desires. A new church."[40]

Beckmann had the gift to combine his disparate visions. He could merge his painted perception of the disorder, the memory of the war in all its ghastliness, the chaos of daily life in the violent early years of Weimar, and his longed-for prospect of some new church, a new sense of meaning in the world. That search for meaning is what brought Einstein into the mix. At least some of the intellectuals and artists on the left asserted that their inspiration came from the strange revelations of modern science, especially Einstein's, with its mysterious language and counterintuitive claims. Maurice Raynal described the general nature of the interaction between artists and scientists in the ferment immediately after the war. Raynal, a friend of Picasso, wrote that "one heard talk about the fourth dimension, non-Euclidean geometry, the theory of numbers and so forth." But no one really knew what such talk meant, he said, what the actual content of the new discoveries might be. Rather, "these conceptions seemed to sponsor ventures on the artists' part to strange lands beyond the frontiers of conventional art."[41]

One of the most striking instances of such confluence came in a movie, the R. Weine masterpiece *The Cabinet of Dr. Caligari,* which opened in Berlin on February 27, 1920. Perhaps the greatest Expressionist film, *Caligari* told the story of two students who visit a carnival and encounter a somnambulist, Cesare, controlled by his strange master, Dr. Caligari. As the movie progresses, Cesare is revealed to be a zombie who murders to Caligari's orders, and Caligari himself turns out to be the director of an insane asylum. There are chase scenes (at one point, Cesare, having killed one of the two young heroes, absconds with the other's girlfriend); sudden inexplicable deaths; and Caligari's own fate to relish when at the end of the film he howls, strapped inside a straitjacket, prisoner in the realm he once ruled.

That was a story with an obvious message. The sleeping Cesare leaping to murder at the command of a madman was a transparent reference to that ordinary German doing the will of the state. Caligari represented the essence of insanity: authority unchecked by any constraint. But the film's significance extended far beyond its overt message. *Caligari* was shot entirely in the studio. Every set was created, painted. The city of the film possessed no straight lines. Size and shape contorted; darkness dominated, with just enough light cutting through the blackness to half illuminate the distorted frame. Time seemed discontinuous; events collided rather than following the conventional logic of linear narrative and cause and effect. The order that the audience thought they understood vanished in the world of the film. The evaporation of moral truth took place in a setting that defied the material truths that should have been unassailable. A rooftop tilts crazily; the moment hangs; an almost human monster lives and dies; time and space shift before the eyes of the viewer. *Caligari,* wrote the critic Kurt Tucholsky, "is something completely new."[42]

Of course, radical innovation like this existed alongside much more prosaic work—films intended to make money, from the quasi-pornographic *Hyenas of Lust* to the purely frothy entertainments turned out by the dominant German studio, UFA. *Caligari* ran in Berlin for just four weeks, and out of about one thousand German silent films produced by the year 1925, only about forty aimed at something other than the mass market.[43] Most Berliners spent far more time with movies that demanded little from them, or in cabarets that featured the arrays of nude dancers for which the city was famous, or with the tabloids and ever grim versions of the new genre of the crime novel that specialized in graphic, anatomically precise descriptions of human butchery.

Still, Berlin in 1920 was home to a community of men and women desperate to find new ways of seeing, whose work created the perception that here the reality of modern life was being sought and found. The ambitions of the avant-garde, Beckmann's vision of creating a new church, the dream that one could overturn the old and find new truths—all this seemed extraordinarily important, unstoppable, to those creating the work. *Caligari* was the catalyst for a burst of Expressionist filmmaking that produced several true classics of the silent film era—*Nosferatu,* for one, still the ultimate vampire movie, and the marvelously ominous *Dr. Mabuse the Gambler* among many others. These were dark films, literally and emotionally, works that emphasized danger, fear, and the random cruelty of human existence. There was little of reason in them, and less of science. But Albert Einstein's influence is detectable here too, as a kind of whiff in the air that the artists breathed. In those early years of Weimar, the one scientific notion that everyone had heard was that the universe is radically unlike what it appeared to be. Reality was not what it seemed; the stars themselves are not where they were thought to be. In this context, art that bends time and fractures space becomes a little easier to imagine. The artist who cared for such things had that much more room in which to move. Berlin was creating its own legend, its own myth. As the playwright Carl Zuckmayer said, it was a place that "ravenously devoured people's talents and energies, masticated them, digested them—and spit them out again." But, given what German art's new masters were creating—the radical reimagining of the built world, images of striking power, revolutionary cinema, new music, experimental theater, a design revolution, and on and on through all the forms available to an artist—Berlin represented an irresistible challenge, a Mecca to which a certain kind of pilgrim was compelled to come. As Zuckmayer said, "Once you had Berlin, you had the world."[44]

Chapter Fifteen

"GROW[ING] ANGRY WITH MY FELLOW MEN"

BUT IN ALL THAT TUMULT, WHO DID POSSESS BERLIN? WEIMAR'S CULtural adventurers could take aim at the sacred cattle of the old regime. From the end of 1919 on, they could and did seize upon Einstein (among much else) as an emblem of the irreversible triumph of radically new ways of comprehending the world. But one man's revolution is another's treason. In Berlin in 1920, the fact of Germany's defeat suffused every public act and thought. For the rising right, the cult of the new was the enemy of the real Germany. As the ever dyspeptic George Grosz warned, Berlin was "all frothy on top." Underneath, its "so-called freedom of expression" was a bitter battle between those who embraced the hope of change and those who rejected the new with all the passion and violence they could command.

That loathing existed almost from the moment of armistice, but the culture wars began in earnest after the initial chaos of the revolution gave way to a revival on the right during the early months of 1919. The catalyst for many came with the announcement of the terms offered to Germany by its enemies in the Treaty of Versailles. The Allies, dominated by the bitter and vengeful massif that was France's president, Georges Clemenceau, presented a draft treaty to the Weimar government's representatives on May 7. Official and ordinary Berliners received the news the following day. The territorial demands were bad enough: Germany would have to surrender the provinces of Alsace and Lorraine, captured from the French in 1871; France would hold Germany's own soil west of the Rhine River for fifteen years, along with coalfields elsewhere. Poland was to gain Upper Silesia, and worse still, it would fold what was called the Danzig Corridor into its borders. That was truly a knife in the heart of Prussian dreams of European domination. The corridor was a strip of land east of Berlin that stretched from the main, landlocked body of Poland to the Baltic Sea at the port of Danzig (modern Gdansk), and it would be administered by the League of Nations as a "free city." (The League itself derived from a covenant written into the Versailles Treaty.) The ostensible goal was to give Poland access to the sea. The real point of the provision was to split Prussia in two, severing the East Prussian homeland of the most militaristic, land-hungry and conservative Junker aristocrats from West Prussia and Berlin.

The list went on. Denmark and Belgium would receive back territory Germany had seized in previous wars, along with land that had been part of Germany proper. All its overseas colonies would have to go. The net loss to Germany was about 13 percent of its home territory, 10 percent of its population, and disproportionate amounts of its natural resources, including a full three-quarters of iron ore reserves. Piled on top of such demands came the predictable disarmament clauses. Germany's army was restricted to one hundred thousand men, and the armed forces were forbidden most of the significant weapons of modern war, including airplanes, tanks and capital ships. The western Allies would give up nothing.

Given Germany's own territorial ambitions during the war, this massive assault on the homeland itself was bitter indeed, the more so given that on the field of battle the victorious Allies had never actually captured any German soil. But the ultimate horror of the Versailles Treaty for the German polity came with the "war guilt" clause, and its corollary demand for reparations. The draft treaty presented in May stated that "Germany accepts the responsibility of Germany and her allies for causing all the loss and damage to which the Allied and Associated Governments and their nationals have been subjected as a consequence of the war imposed upon them by the aggression of Germany and her allies."[1] Germany was to blame, wholly and solely, for all the horror of the war. To expiate this guilt, the Allies insisted that

Germany would have to pay. The treaty conceded that "the resources of Germany are not adequate . . . to make complete reparation" for all the losses its enemies suffered. Nonetheless, the document set no limit on the amount ultimately due, and Germany was compelled to offer its most important economic resources, coal, chemicals, shipping and the like, to meet any shortfall in the final bill. To the victors, Germany remained a criminal country. Its guilt survived despite any superficial change in its government. It could not be trusted. It was to be disarmed, partially dismembered, partly occupied, and rendered so poor that it could never rise again to threaten Europe.

German reaction to this humiliation was immediate and predictable. General Gröner almost welcomed the treaty's harshness, believing that "the proposals will be contested all the easier because they are so laughable."[2] But Clemenceau was unamused and unbending. When the Germans received revised peace terms six weeks later, the changes were so minor that they were simply handwritten on the original text. German war guilt was reemphasized as "the greatest crime against humanity ever committed," as Kessler noted in his diary. To Kessler, the atmosphere had the terrifying feel of July 1914: the stifling sense of an unavoidable disaster bearing down upon the world. It was, he wrote, "as if the entire sap of life has dried up in me."[3] Farther to the right, the reaction was both more chaotic and more choleric. No one knew how the army would react, though it was clear that at least part of the officer corps favored outright rejection of the treaty. Gröner had already asked Field Marshal Hindenburg—still regarded as the true leader of the German military by most officers—whether Germany should fight. Hindenburg at first suggested that the army must resist, if only to save German honor. Gröner pointed out that "the significance of the gesture would escape the German people." On consideration, Hindenburg admitted that armed opposition was futile, but in his letter to the government, he added that for his part, "as a soldier, I cannot help feeling that it were better to perish honorably than accept a disgraceful peace."[4]

In other words, Hindenburg, as ever, was keeping his hands more or less clean. His letter gave him the cover to claim that it was the civilian government that chose to sign the Versailles Treaty, and not the General Staff. As in the fall of 1918, Hindenburg, and by extension the German officer corps, managed to go on record as the sole honorable party in the whole ugly affair. Those less adroit soon paid up. Matthias Erzberger, the man who had led the treaty delegation, was assassinated while walking in the Black Forest in 1921—a crime Kessler had predicted within days after he signed the Versailles document. (As an indication of the depth of German loathing for the peace treaty, even Kessler could not muster any sympathy for the unfortunate politician, writing that Erzberger had got what he deserved, a fate "self-incurred on account of his pernicious activity.")[5] More broadly, the war guilt clause framed a set of grievances that regardless of their merits fueled right-wing rage. In November 1919, Hindenburg gave voice to the anger the right felt against its enemies, foreign and domestic. Asked why he thought Germany had lost the war, he answered with words deployed as weapons, loaded and deadly. He repeated the legend of the stab in the back, attributing the original quote to an unnamed English general, and then said, "No guilt applies to the core of the army. Its achievements are just as admirable as those of the officer corps. Where the guilt lies has clearly been demonstrated."[6] Picking up on this theme, a still-obscure ex-corporal named Adolf Hitler, in one of his earliest speeches on record, delivered in April 1922, made the connection between the treaty, Germany's plight, and the appropriate response still more explicit. Because of the war guilt clause and its consequent reparations, Hitler said, "we are already a colony of the outside world."[7] Later that year, he added, *"We must demand great enlightenment on the subject of the Peace Treaty. With thoughts of love? No! but in holy hatred against those who have ruined us"*[8] (italics in the original). Germany, as ever, remained a victim, sacrificed to an unjust fate. Someone would have to pay.

To many observers, of course, the danger in providing Germany with such a ready-made grievance was obvious. The British prime minister, David Lloyd George, had failed to moderate the French hunger for revenge. Quietly and uselessly, he concluded, "You may strip Germany of her colonies, reduce her armaments to a mere police force and her navy to that of a fifth-rate power; all the same, in the end, if she feels that she has been unjustly treated in the peace of 1919, she will find means of exacting retribution from her conquerors."[9]

In fairness, however, it is a mistake to blame the debacle at Versailles for all the sorrow that followed. The treaty did become a potent symbol to the right of Germany's betrayal from within and without.

But it is also true that the German ultranationalist right always aimed for a return to power (and for revenge), no matter what the treaty said. And while the war guilt clause was inflammatory, on the practical level the treaty terms that mattered to ordinary Germans were the economic ones. Einstein, generally something of a cynic in matters of practical politics, was almost dismissive of Versailles. On June 4, 1919, in the midst of the treaty conference, he wrote to Max Born that "I do not see the political situation as pessimistically as you. Conditions are hard, but they will never be enforced." It was all a matter of propaganda and face, Einstein reassured his younger colleague. "The French are motivated by fear. . . . Eventually, Germany's dangerousness will go up in smoke, together with the unity of her opponents."[10]

Einstein had little patience for the grasping demands of the victors; he told Born in December that "the behavior of the Allies is beginning to appear disgusting even by my standards." The economic consequences of meeting reparations demands were beginning to bite, and even he felt a touch of the resentment of the losing side. "Here all fixed and movable property is being bought up by foreigners, to the point of our becoming an Anglo-American colony." Fortunately, he and Born were safe: "Just as well that we do not have to sell our brains or make an emergency sacrifice of them to the state."[11]

Beyond such feeble attempts at humor, Einstein was starting to consider what political role he could or should play in the new German and European order. The overarching problem was simple: the winter of 1919–1920 brought with it ferocious hunger. Einstein wondered if he should speak out internationally, but concluded that he would have little effect, for while the English and the Americans were already sending food aid, "little can be done in the face of this mass suffering." But Versailles was hardly to blame for the crisis, he continued to argue. "To rise against the treaty would only make sense if one believed in its significance, which I do not." The settlement "certainly goes too far, but since its fulfillment is quite impossible, it is better that its demands are objectively impossible to fulfill, rather than just intolerable." And in any event, the real threat to Germany came, according to Einstein, from the internal dynamics of German politics. He thought that the forces of Russian-inspired communism were on the rise, but the present danger, as he gauged it, was that whatever bloody-mindedness existed on the left, "the forces of reaction are also growing more violent all the time."[12]

Alongside such public turmoil, personal sorrow bore down on Einstein in the winter of 1919–1920. Most pressing, his mother, Pauline, entered the final stages of her battle with abdominal cancer, by then metastasizing throughout her body. Einstein's relationship with her had been complicated, to put it politely, ever since the battles over his affair with and marriage to Mileva, twenty years before. Back then, he had complained to Mileva that his mother and sister both "seemed somewhat petty and philistine to me, despite the sympathy I feel for them." Still, life moves on, the twenty-year-old Einstein had mused, and some people cannot move with it. It was nothing to fret about, it was just a fact that over time "even the closest family ties dwindle into habitual friendship."[13] In the years after the marriage, that judgment held true. Very few letters survive between Einstein and his mother, less than ten between 1902 and 1918, and those that do exist are brief, cordial, a little gossipy, and almost completely devoid of emotion. He had let some feeling show in a postcard he sent telling her of the preliminary results from the British eclipse expeditions, beginning, "Dear Mother, Joyous news today . . ." He was happy enough to feed what he called "Mama's anyhow already considerable mother's pride."[14] But from what he committed to paper before his mother's final illness, it would be hard to suggest that he recognized a significant bond of feeling between them.

But Einstein's emotional life was always something of a mystery to himself until the real world put the core of his feelings to the test. Pauline had fallen ill while living with her daughter, Maja, in Lucerne, and after a period of hospitalization, she announced that she wished to be with her son. She and Maja came to Berlin in December 1919. The cancer had spread uncontrollably and painfully. She was given morphine, which clouded her thoughts, but initially Einstein expected her to live for several months. In fact, she failed rapidly, and died at his home near the end of February 1920. At that point, he finally seemed able to gauge the weight of his loss. On the heels of her funeral at the Schönberg Cemetery in Berlin, Einstein wrote to Zangger to tell him of his mother's death. "We are all completely exhausted," he said first, in what seems an oblique reference to the extraordinary emotional weariness that comes at the end of a deathbed vigil. And then, explicitly, "One feels in one's bones the significance of blood ties."[15]

Blood ties. These were not words that Einstein often used, nor welcomed when said by others. But Pauline's death did not permit him to ignore the fact of kinship. When Hedwig Born's mother died a few months later, he wrote to her, "I know what it means to see one's mother suffer the agony of death and be unable to help. There is no consolation."[16] As he told the Borns, his mother's death left him even more than usually rootless, unconnected to wherever it was that he found himself. "My father's ashes lie in Milan," he wrote. "I buried my mother here only a few days ago. I myself have journeyed to and fro continuously—a stranger everywhere."[17]

And increasingly so in Berlin itself. While he had been occupied with his personal affairs, the threat from the right in Berlin had deepened. The crisis Einstein had anticipated ultimately broke in March 1920. The government had ordered several Freikorps battalions to disband, as required by the Versailles Treaty. In almost immediate response, Freikorps troops in support of a coup led by an obscure East Prussian politician named Wolfgang Kapp marched on Berlin on March 12. At first, Kapp appeared to have an open road to power. General Hans von Seeckt, the army chief of staff, betrayed his nominal civilian superiors, and refused to order the Berlin garrison to defend the city against the advancing troops, a move that fatally undermined Defense Minister Noske's residual authority over the military. At 7:00 A.M. on March 13, Kapp's troops marched through the Brandenburg Gate. Germany's elected leadership made a rapid getaway to Dresden. Kapp's forces occupied the empty buildings and he declared himself chancellor, named an obscure general to be minister of defense, and appointed a handful of other nonentities to the cabinet.

Almost immediately the putsch became farce. One civil servant loyal to the republic (or at least to the outward forms of state administration) had somehow mislaid the official seals. This being a proper German coup, no actual state action could be taken without the right stamp. Another gave his clerical staff time off, and a considerable haze of confusion descended on Germany's would-be strongmen. To greater effect, the government in absentia called a general strike in Berlin.

Kapp lost the use of his phones. His offices lacked gas and water. The streetcars ceased running; offices were shuttered; factories lay still. A couple of adventurers from Munich, Adolf Hitler and his mentor, the anti-Semitic writer Dietrich Eckart, flew up to Berlin to join the putsch, but they were too late. On March 17, the army withdrew its implied support for the putsch and some soldiers even arrested their officers to move the process along. Kapp fled to the airport, and the Freikorps bullyboys stumbled out of town. As they were leaving, the last detachments lingered long enough to fire into a crowd of Berliners cheering their defeat.

This fiasco was nominally a victory for democratic rule—but only barely. Kessler recorded a prediction that not one of the conspirators would suffer as a result of their treason, and he was right. Within weeks, units that had taken part in the putsch were deployed for action against Spartacist uprisings in central Germany. The treacherous Seeckt remained at the head of an increasingly autonomous army, and a parallel coup against the state government in Bavaria survived, unscathed by the strike in Berlin. The capital remained more democratic than not, more to the left than the right, but the country as a whole did seem to be slouching rightward, a perception ratified by the Reichstag elections on June 6. The Weimar coalition lost its majority for the first time, with its member parties substantially associated with the working class losing more than a third of their previous support. In their place, a new coalition composed of center-right parties of the middle class took power. Kapp lingered on in justified obscurity in Sweden, but his brief emergence had widened the breach in Germany into which the forces of the nationalistic, authoritarian, militaristic right could flow. The impact of that shift extended well beyond politics and culture, as those who saw modernity as poison gained greater and greater power. And most prominent among the targets of reaction were the work and person of that suddenly too-famous man, a so-called scientist, the Jew Einstein.

THE FIRST INSTANCE of a campaign directed specifically against Einstein was, like Kapp's episode, both farce and a botched anticipation of subsequent, far more serious attacks. The Kapp putsch shook Einstein, eroding his faith in Germany's ultimate deliverance from its militarist psychosis. The country now seemed to him "like one who badly upset his stomach but has not yet vomited enough."[18] In that context, he was a hugely tempting target, a symbol that a wide range of different sensibilities on the right could loathe. Fame, of course, had opened the gate, for before the eclipse results, he was not prominent enough to be worth significant public vituperation. But once international celebrity descended upon him, his defects became obvious. For some, it was more than enough that he was a man of the left, openly and defiantly critical of Germany during the war. His Judaism was also an obvious goad, clear evidence that whatever his goals were, they would not serve to strengthen a resurgent Germany.

Still, while anti-Semitism certainly motivated some of Einstein's early opponents, it was only one source of the rage and confusion evoked on the right by the claims of relativity theory. For them, he represented intellect—mind, not heart. More broadly, he was the embodiment of reason as opposed to authority, reason that could compel changes in fundamental beliefs. That was subversive enough, especially when there were German orators who argued in the 1920s that "we suffer today from an excess of culture. Only knowledge is valued. . . . What we need is instinct and will."[19]

This was Adolf Hitler speaking in the spring of 1923. For all the obvious reasons his are the speeches we now remember, but this should not overshadow the wider implication of what he was saying at the time. His underlying claim of authority, of the power of the will to create objective facts, was widely shared across the more mystically minded right. Stripped of the emotional charge of Hitler's name, a deeply and broadly felt need remained, a desperate desire to force the world to be something other than what it was becoming. The protofascist literary critic Adolf Bartels wrote in January 1920 that "we want back the Germany of Bismarck." He decried the "Jewish disfigurement" of the arts, and called for a wholly different approach to the understanding and representation of German life. The Jew's original sin, according to Bartels, was to venerate the human mind at the expense of a much greater impulse. It was the Jew, he said, who "elevates the puny individual to the measure of all things, while that role can, of course, be played only by national character, something large."[20]

"National character," of course, allows no room for the single independent mind. What counted, or ought to, was the concept of a national spirit, a uniquely German essence that could overcome any constraints, whether human laws or those of nature. Einstein spoke for the opposition. In his birthday speech in praise of Planck delivered in the last year of the war, he had argued that individuals using their reason had both the responsibility and the power to extract truth from nature. "The supreme task of the physicist"—an individual, a solitary thinker—"is to arrive at those universal laws from which the cosmos can be built up by pure deduction."[21] He admitted that in that search the irrational had some role to play; intuition and the facts of nature itself guide the thinker toward the laws he seeks. But the nub of the argument was clear enough to encourage all those who, like Mendelsohn and Williams, saw Einstein as a hero of the autonomy of the human mind. It was, of course, just as clear to those enraged by their own and Germany's fate.

The first assault aimed directly at Einstein came in the summer of 1920. Special relativity had faced its skeptics since 1905. Even the great Lorentz, sincerely and completely without political bias, did not fully acquiesce in some of its basic tenets.[22] But even early on, some of the opposition was more sinister. In 1911, a German experimental physicist named Ernst Gehrcke wrote the first of a series of articles denouncing the theory of relativity, claiming in one paper that the acquiescence of his fellow scientists in Einstein's work was "an interesting case of mass suggestion in physics."[23] After Einstein published his general theory of relativity, with its solution to the problem of Mercury's orbit, Gehrcke tried again, this time claiming that the orbital question had been answered years before by someone else, a real German, without the use of relativistic ideas. In both incidents Gehrcke's claims were refuted, in the latter case by Einstein himself, but the halo of fame that enfolded him in 1920 inspired Gehrcke and others of like mind to try again.

It began with a group of nationalist and increasingly overtly anti-Semitic figures who actually formed an official, properly registered organization. The society had a resonant name: *Arbeitsgemeinschaft deutscher Naturforscher zur Erhaltung reiner Wissenschaft*—the Working Group of German Scientists for the Preservation of Pure Science. On August 24, 1920, they held a public meeting. One speaker termed relativity the scientific equivalent of Dada, while Gehrcke gave his presentation at a quite technical level, most likely mystifying most of an audience unfamiliar with the language of physics. Einstein was in the audience, but said nothing. Three days later he delivered his broadside in the newspapers. "I have good reason to believe that other motives besides a search for truth underlie this enterprise," he wrote, and it was clear what they were: there would have been no problem "had I been a German national with or without swastika instead of a Jew with liberal international opinions. . . ."[24] He could not have been more blunt. The swastika, a common symbol for the sun in ancient and medieval cultures, had been seized upon as an emblem of the ultranationalist and the "pure German" and anti-Semitic *völkisch* movements in Germany as early as the 1870s. It was touted as an expression of pure Aryan culture, deriving from its supposed origins in the Aryan conquest of the Indian subcontinent thousands of years earlier. After the First World War several Freikorps units adopted the broken cross for their flags. By the time of Einstein's comments—well before Hitler seized it for his own purposes—the swastika had become a clearly recognized badge of irredentist rightist and anti-Jewish politics.

Einstein's diagnosis of his opponents' motives was essentially correct, but his colleagues thought that his language was a mistake—a howitzer aimed at what virtually all of them saw as a mosquito. Einstein swiftly agreed, regretting his tone, telling the Borns that "everyone has to sacrifice at the altar of stupidity from time to time." Among all else, the furor reminded Einstein of the cost of fame; he also told the Borns that "like the man in the fairy tale who turned everything he touched into gold—so with me everything turns into a fuss in the newspapers."[25]

Still, throughout the furor Einstein gained ample public support from his fellow physicists, most of whom regarded what became known as the Antirelativity Society as a trivial embarrassment. (That support went beyond the scientific community; he also received votes of confidence from such prominent figures as the writer Stefan Zweig and Minister of Culture Konrad Haenisch, among others.) But the controversy did not end there. The autumn meeting of the Society of German Scientists and Physicians pitted Einstein against Philipp Lenard, a Nobel laureate whose work, ironically, had led to Einstein's early breakthrough on the quantum theory of light. Lenard's role in the ongoing reaction to Einstein was a critical feature of the debate, for at first—here—he ignored the anti-Semitism of some of his allies and spoke simply as one who objected to the corrosive consequences of

Einstein's approach to physics. Relativity theory, with its reckless assault on space, time and motion, "offended the common sense of a scientist."[26] That is, relativity, being counterintuitive, ought to be false; it would be more comfortable if it were not true, less troubling to the soul. Put that way, Lenard's was a pathetic argument but not actually a malicious one. But Lenard did not rest there. By 1922, the grounds of his objection changed. Now he denounced Einstein as a false German, decried Jewish habits of disputation, and called for the reassertion of a "sound German spirit" in science, whose revival would ensure the destruction of "the alien spirit . . . which is so clearly seen in anything that relates to the 'relativity theory.' "[27]

Lenard's justification for this claim went like this. Step 1: Einstein's science made no sense. Step 2: therefore, it had to have been produced out of a malign desire to undermine the clarity of science and the certainty of its conclusions. Finally, the ultimate step in this syllogism, Einstein's evil impulse here was born of the inherent Jewishness of relativity's author. It was not the first time Einstein's Judaism had been implicated in his work. Arnold Sommerfeld, one of Germany's genuinely great physicists and actually both an early partisan of relativity and later a friend, had written in 1907 that the younger man's ideas troubled him: "Works of genius though they are, this unconstruable and unvisualizable dogmatism seems to contain something almost unhealthy . . . perhaps [this theory] reflects . . . the abstract-conceptual character of the Semite."[28] The fact that even a figure like Sommerfeld could use such categories illustrates the pervasiveness of race thinking in German intellectual culture. To many there, the whole enterprise of modern physical thought was just another instance of what Hitler in *Mein Kampf* in 1924 was to decry as a fixed fact of Jewish cultural life: that the Jew's "intellect will never have a constructive effect, but will be destructive."[29]

At the same time, it is crucial not to leap too far ahead, to see in the antirelativity crusade of the early 1920s a broad German readiness to abandon reason, decry all Jews, and leap into the arms of the man on the white horse. Lenard was ridiculed for his objections and rendered virtually irrelevant to German science throughout the '20s. His allies received even less notice after their initial flurry of activity. As with the Kapp fiasco, the antirelativity tempest was folly compounded by stupidity, although it did serve as a warning for those with the wit to judge, who certainly included Einstein. After his momentary fit of bile appeared in the newspapers, he relaxed—but the thought that Germany might not be a fit place to live did occur to him, and to others as well. As the newspaper *Vossische Zeitung* warned its readers in September 1920, there was a plot afoot to lure Einstein to one of the top British universities. The British, the article said, recognized that "nothing could be regarded as a greater contribution to the restoration of Germany's prestige than the theory of relativity, Albert Einstein's latest scientific achievement." But, as the newspaper went on, the British had noted that "German national pride obviously cannot accept the fact that the world's best mathematician is a Jew, not just a pure and simple German." Thus the rumored British offer of a university position (which did not materialize) that, as the newspaper argued, "could be the chance for England to gain some prestige itself."[30]

The thought of leaving did cross his mind. The year before the supposed British gambit, Einstein told his friend Ehrenfest that the issue had come up with Planck, who had sought his promise "not to leave Berlin unless conditions deteriorated to the point where he would regard such a step as natural and popular." He resisted the temptation for now, however, and whatever impulse to leave he may have felt soon passed. He told the Borns that a cottage near a lake and a sailing dinghy would probably keep him content enough to remain a Berliner. Still the question lingered long enough to force him to consider just what held him to a city and a country that now, in peacetime, he could abandon for any destination he chose. He had already concluded that Berlin still gave him what he needed most, and he refused to be driven out by the likes of Lenard. Though he told a reporter that "I feel like a man in a good bed but plagued by bedbugs,"[31] it remained "the place to which I am bound by the closest human and scientific ties."[32] He had reassured Planck back then, acknowledging that if he left, his friends would suffer: "My departure would be doubly painful at this time of supposed humiliation."[33] Planck and Born, Haber and von Laue and the rest—these were the ties that mattered, and they were strong enough to hold him, for all but the most unforeseen of circumstances.

NOT THAT THERE WASN'T PLENTY of provocation beyond mere personal attacks. Einstein could defend himself well enough, but he was acutely aware that other Jews could not. And while his awareness of German hostility to Jews dated at the least back to his move to Berlin, if not to boyhood, he, along with virtually all of Germany's Jews, was unprepared for the new and more obviously virulent anti-Semitism that appeared as the war ended. He was too insulated to feel physically at risk, but he heard the news and understood the implications of incidents large and small. A diarist named Heinrich Buxbaum captured one typical experience, endured on a train journey in 1919 or 1920. In a crowded car one man began to complain that the Jews were to blame for his personal troubles and others chimed in, blaming the Jews for an incredible range of malfeasance, until Buxbaum, an assimilated, quiet, ordinary man, could not keep listening. "I am Jewish . . ." he began, but could say no more before the crowd in the train turned on him, shouting and beginning to strike. "A man sitting next to me suggested throwing me off the train," Buxbaum wrote. "With some difficulty I freed myself, running to the restaurant car." He stayed there until he reached his station. As he got off, he saw one of his attackers leaving the train, and realized that he knew the man—they played in the same soccer club. Hindsight renders Buxbaum's conclusion almost grotesque in its unconscious anticipation. "I never realized," he wrote, "that such an ordinary, normal man could be such a horribly threatening anti-Semite."

Buxbaum's experience was frightening, but the Jews who truly suffered during the early Weimar years were those who could not "pass" under any circumstances, as Buxbaum had until he opened his mouth. Eastern European Jews began to flow into Germany as soon as the war ended, driven west by the waves of pogroms and persecution that had intensified in the chaos of the Russian Revolution and civil war. That exodus helped to boost the Jewish population of Berlin from 44,000 in 1910 to 173,000 by 1925. These *Ostjuden,* eastern Jews, formed a sudden, alien presence in the capital, a magnet, a target. Many of the refugees settled in the crowded, poor, tenement neighborhoods of the eastern part of Berlin, and as their community grew, it took on an exotic, almost fantastic aura—or a disgusting one, depending on one's presumption. Walter Mehring's play *Der Kaufmann von Berlin (The Merchant of Berlin),* first produced in 1929, was to provide a bitter, sharp account of how the immigrants had been seen by established Berliners. Denounced variously as Jewish, communist, bourgeois, reactionary and anti-Semitic, Mehring's tale of an impoverished *Ostjude* who grew wealthy as a black marketeer described the refugee neighborhood as a place of stinking courtyards, dark streets and claustrophobic alleys. It was a neighborhood of tenements "covered from the roof to the ground with Hebrew letters like dead tropical plants." And, inhabiting this place out of time, "a bizarre group dressed in long black caftans traveled back and forth, moving unsteadily through the confined ghetto."[34]

In such neighborhoods Berliners found themselves confronted by the unassimilable stranger. Mehring, as suggested by the varied critical reactions to his play, kept his feelings about his own encounters cleverly masked, but for many others these strange-looking, strange-smelling interlopers were the nightmare incarnate. The purest expression of this came, unsurprisingly, in Adolf Hitler's *Mein Kampf,* written during his prison term between November 1923 and December 1924. He told of his "conversion" to anti-Semitism, a revelation that turned on an encounter on the streets of Vienna with what he claimed was the first traditional, eastern Jew he had ever seen. Lucy Dawidowicz in her landmark work *The War Against the Jews* has cast considerable doubt on the trustworthiness of Hitler's account of this epiphany, but even if his account of the event was false, it does reveal how an anti-Semite in the early 1920s sought to depict the Jewish menace.[35] In one of the sharpest passages of his book, Hitler wrote of arriving in the Austrian capital from his home in the small town of Linz. Slowly, he grew accustomed to the strange look and pace of the metropolis until at last, "with open eyes, I saw not only buildings but also the people." One day, thus restored to sight, Hitler came face-to-face with "an apparition in a black caftan and black hairlocks. Is this a Jew? was my first thought." This was not what he was used to from his life in the provinces: "I observed this man furtively and cautiously, but the longer I stared at this foreign face, scrutinizing feature for feature, the more my first question assumed a new form: Is this a German?" Soon, Hitler wrote, "wherever I went, I began to see Jews, and the more I saw the more sharply they became distinguished in my eyes from the rest of humanity." The center city, in fact, "swarmed with a people which even outwardly had lost all resemblance to Germans."[36]

As Hitler described it, when he looked deeper and deeper into the world of Vienna's Jews, all the other ills that these aliens carried with them became obvious. He presented his discoveries in *Mein Kampf* as original research, based on meticulous, almost sociological investigation, but in fact his litany was wholly conventional—and at first, simply a reiteration of prewar anti-Semitism that emphasized ideas of racial purity and cleanliness. He grew "sick to his stomach at the smell of these caftan-wearers." They had "unclean dress" and affronted him with "their generally unheroic appearance." These were criminals, masters of the trade in prostitution and white slaving, represented in every "form of filth or profligacy." Their prominence in the press enabled the Jew to act as "pestilence, spiritual pestilence, worse than the Black Death." And critically, Jewish moral degeneracy was inherent, apparently "chosen by Nature for this shameful calling."[37]

This was all vile stuff, but it was not uniquely Hitler's vision. His polemic merely parroted charges that dated back at least forty years. The term "anti-Semitism" itself appeared first in 1873 in a pamphlet by Wilhelm Marr, titled *Der Sieg des Judentums über das Germanentum—The Victory of Jewry over Germandom*.[38] (By convention, that year and that pamphlet mark the emergence of "modern" anti-Semitism, as distinct from the older, simpler oppression of a community that had rejected Jesus.) Central to the development of this new movement was the fear and suffering created by the rapid spread of urban and anonymous modes of life—the big city with all its rumored and lived evils. In Marr's writing and that of those who followed him, the formula fell into place long before Hitler wrote his screeds. German and Austrian anti-Semites proclaimed that the Jews were a distinct, biologically alien group—"there must be no question here of parading religious prejudices," Marr wrote in his foundational text, "when it is a question of race and when the difference lies in the 'blood.'"[39] In the next step of the argument, such irretrievably alien infiltrators could be seen to be by their nature a threat to those of other races, of other blood. Finally, it followed that the people of the city, the Jews, were the implacable enemies of the simpler, purer people of the land. As one Austrian newspaper put it in the 1880s, the battle was between the "rural population of primitive peoples against the free spoilers of the world in the cities." There could be no quarter, for this was "a struggle for existence, a struggle by Nature against the enemies of the rights of Nature," a battle ultimately to be fought against "men of book learning, our German Jew-scribes and insulters of peasants and burghers."[40]

For all the shock value of such writing, though, it is easy to overrate prewar anti-Semitism, and it is certainly too facile to say that the Germans after the war simply picked up where their predecessors had left off. The early movement was actually a haphazard and fundamentally weak affair. By the 1890s it became obvious that the major German anti-Semitic figures, from Adolf Stoecker to Otto Böckel, were divided on a whole host of issues, ranging from peasants' rights to problems of social reform. More serious, as Kaiser Wilhelm II and his government increasingly expanded Germany's imperialist ambition, anti-Semitism lost its special demagogic focus on the one true enemy. It might be France that barred the way, or Russia, or ever-treacherous England, as crisis followed crisis from Beijing to Aden, from wrangling over colonial railway concessions to the escalating naval arms race. With so many adversaries to choose from, a few Jews at home came to seem trivial. Thus, by the turn of the century, if not before, Germany's Jewish community could persuade itself that Germany at least acquiesced in its presence, whatever casual bigotry might linger. Even better, the situation held out the hope that German Jewry could cement its bonds to its non-Jewish fellow citizens by joining in the adventure of creating a truly world-spanning reich. That dream had reached its climax in August 1914, as Jews in their thousands rushed to enlist.

The depths of this delusion were plumbed well before the war ended, of course, as Germany's Jewish soldiers had discovered. Anti-Semitism had not died during the run-up to imperial glory; when the reich suffered, the Jew still served as a convenient repository of all ills and hurt. But the new hate was not the same as the old. Hitler expressed, though he did not invent, the transformation. Anti-Semitism ceased to be simply a political movement that pitted city against farm, nor did it remain a kind of deranged social Darwinism that feared alien stock crossbreeding with the pure species. Now, with the collapse of German arms, the Jew could be tagged with specific, rather than general, crimes. This new conflict pitted Jewish traitors against German patriots, the November criminals against the real German, the trench fighter. The ultimate target of Germany's revanchist anti-Semites was, of course, the Weimar state, seen as dominated by Jews and as the proximate cause of Germany's defeat. As Hitler put it, "The Jewish Revolution of 1918 was made by a small determined group" who had to be fought and ultimately overthrown.[41] That was a claim easily and powerfully articulated, at least in certain circles, as demonstrated by the extraordinary credence given to the Russian forgery *The Protocols of the Elders of Zion,* with its account of an alleged plot to assure Jewish world dominance, published in Germany in January 1920, along with the growing popularity of a new genre of anti-Semitic novels. A characteristic example was probably N. Jünger's *Volk in Gefahr (People in Danger).* Jünger hit all the familiar tropes: the citified Jew outwitted the poor, honest "true" German; both Orthodox and assimilated Jews conspired in treachery; above all, Jünger's Jews actively sought to stab the nation and its brave *Volk* in the back.[42]

To a certain extent, such vitriol had its impact. Between 1919 and 1921 the presence of the truly foreign, those apparitions in caftans who had supposedly so shocked the young Hitler, served as a ready target of German scorn and fear, creating a climate of opinion in which attacks on the *Ostjuden* achieved virtually official sanction. Eastern Jews could be imprisoned almost without cause. Being unemployed was enough to land a Jew in a holding camp. So was suspicion of subversive acts or intent, an alleged failure to pay taxes, or practically anything else a policeman could dream up. Once jailed, the *Ostjude* was purely a victim, unable through any act or official challenge to alter the course of events. Predictably, the camps became hellholes. The first independent review of conditions within them came after a fire swept through the holding prison at Stargard in May 1921. A Jewish newspaper reported that when the fire broke out, guards left the barracks doors locked and barred prisoners attempting to escape through the window. As one sergeant explained, it was only prudent to do so; that way no Jews would try to escape through the windows the next time a camp caught fire. The newspaper quoted the guard as saying, "Let them burn. That is the best thing that could happen."[43]

Worse yet, in some ways, was that the strangeness of these new Berliners was sufficient to unsettle even many who should have known better within the established German Jewish community itself. Some joined the new Union of National German Jews, set up in 1921 to battle "all forces among German Jewry which sought to strengthen a non-German Jewish identity." At the first public meeting of the new organization, the keynote speaker "stressed the fundamental differences between the Eastern Jews . . . and the assimilated Western Jews." Given such differences, the speaker said that "as a German . . . [he] would favor stricter immigration rules." Even worse, Philipp Frank, a physicist and early Einstein biographer, told of an extreme case: a German-Jewish professor who said *after* the Nazis seized power and had begun the official persecution of the Jews, "One cannot blame Hitler for his views about the Jews." Why not? Hitler was an Austrian, and exposure to the Austro-Hungarian Empire's motley collection of *Ostjuden* would naturally tend to arouse revulsion and disdain. The issue was simple, said the professor. "If he had known the German Jews well, he would never have acquired such a poor opinion of us."[44]

Smug stupidity like this was of course not the universal response within the Berlin Jewish community. The filmmaker and diarist Erwin Leiser's initial response to contact with eastern Jewry was almost that of revulsion. On his way to school, he recalled, he passed through one of the most densely crowded of immigrant neighborhoods, "and every morning I had to smell all those smells I feared and despised." But Leiser, like many assimilated Berlin Jews, altered his initial reaction on closer contact. He met one of the most prominent of the eastern rabbis, and in his home discovered what Leiser felt as the "miraculous force" in the spiritual life of religious Jews.[45] For others, especially such writers as Franz Rosenzweig, Arnold Zweig, and Martin Buber, contact with eastern Jews during and after the war shaped their powerful responses to traditional forms of Jewish observance; the *Ostjuden* acted as a catalyst for a modest religious revival in Berlin and Germany.

That revival did not extend as far as Einstein, though. His commitment to the *Ostjuden* refugees in Germany was political, an argument against their forced removal to the holding camps. He felt kinship, a tie of identity, but the religion itself remained alien to him, at least in its overtly traditional form. When he was to visit Palestine in 1923 and saw Jews praying at the Wailing Wall, he felt scorn for these "dull-witted clansmen of our tribe." They made such spectacles of themselves, "praying aloud, their faces turned to the wall, their bodies swaying to and fro." He found it "a pathetic sight of men with a past but without a present."[46] Put slightly differently, and coming from a less squeaky-clean source, such a judgment expressed at that time could sound highly suspect, just this side of overt bigotry. In Einstein's mouth, the impact is a little different. Given his life's work, such religiosity could only have seemed foolish, a kind of superstition. Nevertheless, his disdain for what he saw as credulousness could not blind him to the raw facts at home: anti-Semitism in Germany was on the rise; it was virulent and newly violent; and Berlin's eastern Jews—the indigestible other—had become the obvious first target for the worst abuses.

Einstein did not suffer this in silence. At first he merely spoke, denouncing a plan announced in 1919 to deport the eastern Jews. As attacks against them—the weakest and most vulnerable of Germany's Jews—became more obvious and more frequent, he made the decision to go one step farther. In 1917, Britain's Balfour Declaration had called for the creation of a Jewish homeland in Palestine, providing the first Great Power sanction for the nationalist ambitions of the Zionist movement. In 1921 Einstein publicly allied himself with the Zionists and their leader, the English chemist Chaim Weizmann, by announcing his support for the creation of an independent Jewish state. "Incitement against these unfortunate fugitives," he said, "who have only just saved themselves from the hell which Eastern Europe means for them today, has become an effective political weapon, employed with success by every demagogue." The assault on those Jews "awakened in me the Jewish national sentiment," which led him to "demand the preservation of the Jewish nationality as of every other."[47]

Those were remarkable words to come from as committed an internationalist as Einstein. His willingness to speak in the language of nationalism illustrates just how threatening the circumstances of German Jews had come to appear in the early 1920s. In its baldest form, Zionism sought exactly what Einstein abhorred in Germany: it divided rather than linked; it asserted the need to create or seize power for one ethnically defined group; it valued the institutions of a state, with all the rights and privileges that Einstein ridiculed when they were asserted by his German colleagues. He knew this and it set his teeth on edge; as late as 1938 and in the face of the obvious brutalities of the Nazi regime, he was still voicing his sorrow that those he called his "tribal kin" might need a state. "My awareness of the essential nature of Judaism resists the idea of a Jewish state with borders, an army, and a measure of temporal power," he said in a speech to a Zionist audience in New York. "I am afraid of the inner damage Judaism will sustain—especially from the development of a narrow nationalism within our ranks."[48]

Others felt that same tension. Neither Einstein nor the early Zionists wanted to sacrifice the transcendental role of Jews as a people defined by a relationship with some concept of God, whether conceived as a supernatural being or an ethical system. The philosopher Martin Buber, one of the most prominent religious German Jews, produced this apologia for Zionism: "This national concept was named after a place and not, like the others, after a people, which indicates that it is not so much a question of a particular people as such but of its association with a particular land, its native land."[49] Whether or not that strikes us today as a distinction without a difference, the point is that Buber used this formula to disassociate the newer Jewish nationalism from the dangers and failures of the nationalism he knew best, the German veneration of the state.

Einstein would have understood Buber's reasoning, though he never expressed much faith that Zionism could avoid the fate of any movement that sought state authority. The best he could hope for, as he wrote in 1921 to Maurice Solovine, his friend from the earliest days in Bern and the patent office, was that "the Jews, considering the smallness and dependency of their colony in Palestine, are not threatened by the folly of power."[50] Nevertheless, the daily experience of Jews in Germany left him ripe for enlistment in the Zionist cause. In March of that year Weizmann dispatched the prominent German Zionist Kurt Blumenfeld on a recruiting mission. Weizmann wanted Einstein to tour America with him to raise money for the creation of the Hebrew University in Jerusalem. At first he refused, arguing correctly that Zionists had little interest in what he might have to say, hoping instead merely to capitalize on his name. By his own account Blumenfeld had no good counterargument, but in the end he simply told Einstein that he had very little choice in the matter. Weizmann had said he needed the physicist's help, and, as head of the Zionist movement, Weizmann outranked both of them. To Blumenfeld's considerable surprise, Einstein agreed. Even then, though, Blumenfeld was under no illusion as to the nature of this commitment. Blumenfeld warned Weizmann, "please be careful with Einstein. . . . As you know [he] is no Zionist." Einstein never did formally join any Zionist organization, and he quarreled publicly on more than one occasion with his purported allies. As he later told Abraham Pais, "As Freud would say, my relations with Weizmann were ambivalent."[51]

But on that first journey Weizmann and Einstein got along well. Arrival in New York brought with it the beginnings of America's passion for Einsteiniana described above—that overt press of fame that simply never made much sense to its object. Still, he was in good form and good humor throughout most of his visit. The second-best line of the trip belonged to Weizmann. When Weizmann, a chemist before he was a Zionist, was asked what he thought of relativity, he replied, "Einstein explained his theory to me every day, and on my arrival [in the U.S.] I was fully convinced that he understood it." The very best line of the trip was Einstein's. On being told that a physicist in California claimed to have found evidence that the special theory of relativity was false, Einstein dismissed the difficulty by saying, *"Raffiniert ist der Herrgott aber boshaft ist er nicht"*—"Subtle is the Lord, but malicious He is not."[52]

But throughout the round of public speeches, fund-raisers and lectures, Einstein's perception of his role proved mostly true. His speeches were spectacles rather than actual exchanges of ideas, and as he told Besso, "I had to let myself be exhibited like a prize ox."[53] The humiliation was just barely acceptable, only because, as Einstein confided to Solovine, he felt he had no option: "I am really doing whatever I can for the brothers of my race who are so badly treated everywhere."[54] In that aim he was successful, though less than Weizmann had hoped; his speaking tour raised about $750,000, significantly below the target for the trip.

But for Einstein himself, the experience of speaking to an international audience on an issue that had nothing to do with his science marked a clear turning point. He had now taken on the role of an actor on the world stage, a person who sought and sometimes had the power to influence events. Others were swift to recognize and capitalize on his peculiar political status, his ability to serve as a kind of intermediary between institutions that did not connect through normal channels. His return from America included a detour via England. Eddington had arranged this to celebrate the Royal Astronomical Society's award of its Gold Medal to Einstein. But when a nationalist clique on the board of the society blocked the proposed honor for a former enemy,

Lord Haldane offered to host him anyway, in the service of Anglo-German reconciliation. Einstein's private visit to the Royal Astronomical Society was cordial, but the real test of his political skill and value came with his public lecture at King's College, London. To prepare for the ordeal, Einstein and Haldane, formerly Britain's war minister, went first to Westminster Abbey, where Einstein laid flowers on the grave of Sir Isaac Newton. Unmoved, the audience at King's greeted Newton's German successor—usurper—with silence. Einstein's attempt to mollify his listeners began with his first sentence, flattering them by saying, "It is a particular pleasure to me to have the privilege of speaking in the capital of the country from which the most important fundamental notions of theoretical physics have issued."[55] He went on to praise Newton and Faraday and Maxwell by name, and then to honor the intelligence of his audience by giving them a clear and lucid overview of the general theory. By the end of his account his audience relented. When he finished, they rose in a standing ovation.

Such persuasiveness in a potentially hostile arena made Einstein an asset for the Weimar government. Here was a man who could present the human face of a Germany desperately trying to restore ordinary relations with its former enemies. Britain, in fact, had been a fairly easy trial run; after all, by confirming Einstein's theory the British could most easily share his glory. The real test of his willingness and ability to play the role of roving ambassador came the following year, in March of 1922. The French physicist Paul Langevin formally invited Einstein to lecture at the Collège de France. In considering the offer, Einstein weighed both German and French responses to the invitation. In Germany Einstein had already lost one colleague to bitterness over matters French. He had been quoted in *Figaro* early in 1922 as claiming that Germany shared the blame (at a minimum) for creating the misery of the war, and that as a consequence, it had earned the hardships that followed its defeat. Arnold Sommerfeld wrote asking him to disavow the quotes, but Einstein replied that he would not, despite the fact that *Figaro* apparently had published what was in essence a private conversation. With that, Sommerfeld virtually ceased to speak to his erstwhile friend.

Thus burned, Einstein felt at first that the visit Langevin proposed could only exacerbate such wounds. Many French had no desire to hear from a representative of the enemy. The French Academy of Sciences split over even the simple mechanics of an Einstein lecture, with at least thirty members swearing to walk out should a German ever enter the room. Such persistent resistance to the idea of reconciliation left Einstein in a kind of frustrated despair. He expected better of his fellows. "The common herd can be led by mass suggestion," as he was to tell Marie Curie during a later outburst of France's hyperpatriotism, but "if this world is so contrived on this side and that, then I prefer to remain in my lair rather than to go outside and grow angry with my fellow men."[56]

So Einstein at first refused to go to Paris, writing to Langevin that whatever he said in Paris about politics "would not win me sympathy either on this or the other side of the Rhine."[57] But within a week he changed his mind. He had spoken with Walther Rathenau, Germany's foreign minister, and the most prominent Jew in politics. "Rathenau told me it was my duty to accept" the invitation, Einstein wrote Langevin, "so I accept."[58] Germany needed France's friendship, or at least a reduction in its overt hostility. Einstein could help; therefore he must go.

The trip was at best only a partial success. He gave a series of lectures to invitation-only audiences at the Collège de France, but he failed to overcome the Academy's resistance. The newspaper accounts of his visit were mostly warm—as one newspaper told a perhaps bemused readership, Einstein's visit was "the victory of the Archangel over the Demon of the Abyss." He was received cordially by a wide range of French scientists, and he seems to have reckoned the trip more useful than not. He thanked Solovine for his help in Paris, days that were "unforgettable, but devilishly tiring." Best of all, from his point of view, Germany received reports of the beginnings of reconciliation: "I am told the newspapers did a good job, with the result that the aim of the operation was fully realized."[59]

Einstein hoped so, the more strongly after what he saw on his last day in France. He had asked to see tangible effects of the war, so his hosts arranged a car to take him on a tour of the ruined battlefields near Paris. Joined by Langevin and Solovine, the party made its way along a northeasterly course to San Quentin, and then beyond, to the wrecked land around Rheims. The moonscape quality of the battleground remained, four years after the cease-fire. Einstein saw a countryside flattened and pitted by shellfire, buildings leveled, wreckage strewn about, the traces of gas barrages marked by stands of withered trees. At one point, he got out of the car and told the three Frenchmen with him that "all the students in Germany must be brought here . . . all the students in the world." He never knew, they could not know, the devastation of the war. "How necessary it is that they come and see."[60]

He was right. With each passing year increasing numbers of Germans saw war more as glorious fiction than bloody fact. Some might have sobered up if confronted with the impact of the real thing. But as always, he was overestimating the power of reason to move unreasoning minds. In the spring of 1922, despite increasing overt German anti-Semitism, Einstein was as famous as any man in Berlin. He had influence, perhaps even power. He dined with counts and cabinet ministers. After his day viewing the trenches and the desolation of no-man's-land, he promised his hosts that in Berlin "I will describe all I have seen to the people back there."[61] But he could not be heard where none would listen. A few weeks after his return, he went to the Prussian Academy of Sciences, attending the regular meeting scheduled for April 20. He entered the room and took his seat. He waited. His fellow academicians gathered. No one joined him. The professors took their seats, keeping their distance. The meeting began. He sat. The meeting ended. He rose. He made his way out, passing through the knots of scholars, Germany's most learned men. There is no record that he spoke.

Chapter Sixteen

"THAT BUSINESS ABOUT CAUSALITY"

AT ABOUT 10:40 A.M. ON JUNE 24, 1922, WALTHER RATHENAU LEFT HIS house in the countrified suburbs of Berlin. He settled into the backseat of his jaunty open car. His chauffeur got behind the wheel. There was no need for conversation between the two. Rathenau, appointed Germany's foreign minister less than three months before, drove to work each day along the same route at much the same time. The driver put the car in gear and set out as usual up the Königsallee. Germans are often parodied as creatures of order, and there was never a man who more aspired to be the perfect German than Rathenau. By mid-1922 in Berlin, however, his precision had become not so much a routine as an invitation.

Rathenau's driver drove on sedately, hugging the middle of the road. About three blocks from the house he slowed to cross a set of streetcar tracks. As he did so, a six-seater open touring car drew level with Rathenau's automobile. There were a driver and a young man in the front and two more young men in the back, all wearing leather coats and driving caps. A witness said that Rathenau looked over, as if worried the cars might crash. At that moment, Erwin Kern, twenty-five years old, a former navy officer, leaned from the window of the overtaking car. He rested the butt of his automatic pistol on his other arm and aimed at Rathenau. The range was no more than a few feet.

Rathenau was looking at his killer as the man fired. Kern shot rapidly, five times—the witness said it sounded like a machine gun—and Rathenau slumped over. As he fell, one of Kern's accomplices stood up and pitched a hand grenade into Rathenau's car.

Rathenau's driver pulled over, then sped on to the nearest police station. As he drove, the grenade went off, jolting the car forward. The driver kept the car moving, though, and a young woman walking by, a nurse named Helene Kaiser, leaped into the passenger compartment. "Rathenau, who was bleeding hard, was still alive," she said. "He looked up at me, but seemed to be already unconscious."[1] The chauffeur turned the car around and raced back to Rathenau's house. His bleeding body was carried inside and set down in the study. By the time the doctor arrived, Walther Rathenau was dead.

Einstein's friendship with Rathenau dated back to the war. It was a unique relationship, perhaps the only one in which the arrogant and exceptionally successful Rathenau acknowledged someone else's intellectual superiority. In their initial encounters, Rathenau emerges as a kind of academically ambitious puppy attempting to attract the notice and approval of the scientist. In mid-1917, for example, he sent off a truly extraordinary letter commenting on Einstein's physics in a series of brief queries, including a rather grim (and prescient) reinterpretation of the simultaneity thought experiment. Instead of Einstein's two lightning bolts striking a moving train, Rathenau imagined a scene in which an assassin tosses two sticks of dynamite onto a train carrying the czar of all the Russias. "What startles the czar twice," he wrote, "is only a *single* matter for the assassin." But while he seemed to understand that part of Einstein's physics, he struggled much more when it came to the deeper thickets of time and motion. "The smaller insects are, the faster they move," as he confidently told Einstein. "It is customary to feel sorry for dayflies. I told myself sometimes: maybe it is not so bad; in the end, time diminishes with mass." But through all the nonsense he was careful to praise his surely bewildered correspondent: "Enough of this. Instead of cheerful thanks I have given you a *pathologia mentalis,* which must have appalled you." He was going to send it anyway, he wrote, to demonstrate "the forceful effect of your ideas on a poorly shielded brain."[2] Einstein, charitably, merely noted that "Rathenau's real interests did not lie in the field of theoretical scientific thought."

Still, he liked Rathenau a great deal, praising him to his mother as an "eloquent and sparkling spirit."[3] Thus, shortly after his return from Paris in March 1922, it was only natural for Einstein to spend an evening with his friend, briefing him on the results of the trip Rathenau had urged Einstein to make. But that was not the only reason for the visit. The Zionist leader Kurt Blumenfeld had actually drafted Einstein into this session. Blumenfeld cared little if at all about German-French relations. Rather, he thought that Rathenau's decision to accept the appointment to the Foreign Ministry was a disaster, both for Rathenau personally and for Germany's Jews as well. He brought Einstein along to help him cudgel Rathenau into withdrawing from the government.

So, early that month, Einstein and Blumenfeld went to Rathenau's home at about 8:00 P.M. They stayed until 1:00 in the morning, trying to answer one question: should Rathenau resign? To Blumenfeld, it was simple. However Rathenau conceived of himself, to the German public he was a Jew and a capitalist. (Rathenau had given up his post as head of the giant AEG conglomerate when he entered the cabinet.) He was not—or at best he was just barely—a German. The individual risk he faced as foreign minister was bad enough. The German right's assassination campaign that began in earnest with the murders of Karl Liebknecht and Rosa Luxemburg in 1919 had already claimed over three hundred victims by 1922. Adding to the danger, any Jew so thoroughly in the public eye as Rathenau would inevitably be a target for anti-Semitic attacks.[4] But what worried Blumenfeld more was that Rathenau as foreign minister had become the symbol of Jewish—not German—governance. Blumenfeld argued that "you are focused only on yourself, and you are not willing to see that every Jew, not only the Jews living in Germany but every Jew in the world, is made responsible for what you do and what you decide not to do." Thus the question he posed to his host: Does any Jew possess "the right under any conditions to represent the policy of any people but his own?" No, of course not, and for the reason Rathenau least wanted to acknowledge. "You refuse to be identified with the Jewish people," Blumenfeld said, but "the truth is you are not one with the people [the

Germans] you seek to represent."[5] Resign, begged Blumenfeld. Save yourself and us.

Not a chance. To Einstein's annoyance, Rathenau played devil's advocate throughout the night, arguing either side as it pleased him. Einstein tried to referee, according to Blumenfeld, occasionally interjecting some remark to keep the conversation on track. But in the main, he had less to say than the other two. He had little interest in the question of Rathenau's relationship to the Jews or in his response to Blumenfeld's Zionist cause. For Einstein, the issue boiled down to his belief that Rathenau was well on his way to getting himself killed—and he very much wanted his friend to live. He had already concluded that it was madness for a Jew in Germany then to take on so public a role. He said so again after Rathenau's assassination: "I regretted the fact that he became a minister," adding that he believed that "the natural conduct in public" of Germany's Jews "should be one of proud reserve."[6]

That was what Rathenau, famously proud, notoriously aloof, could not accept. He was one of the most conspicuously complicated men of his generation. He possessed fantastic riches derived from one of the most technologically advanced industrial companies in the world, and yet, in a series of writings, he denounced the mechanization of life and the disproportionate power and wealth of Germany's and capitalism's elites. He was an internationalist whose personal efforts in organizing Germany's war production had enabled the German military to keep fighting for one and perhaps two extra years. During that time, he used his influence to advocate a negotiated settlement, yet when Ludendorff sought an armistice in October 1918, Rathenau called for a mass draft of Germany's citizenry to defend the fatherland to the last gasp. He counted the defiantly antinationalist Albert Einstein as a friend, yet declared his own faith: "I am a German of Jewish descent. . . . My people is the German people, my fatherland is Germany, my religion is that Germanic faith that is above all religions."[7] So much for Blumenfeld's attempt to claim him for the Jews—or rather, as Blumenfeld saw it, his attempt to restore Rathenau to his senses, to the point where he could recognize the reality that lay behind his desperate desire to be the most German German of them all.

Strikingly and creditably, though, despite all his faith in Germany Rathenau never seems to have toyed with the idea of conversion, the obvious step taken by ambitious assimilationist Jews. His Judaism was a private fact but he never denied its existence. Early in his career he had written one article in which he scolded Jews for their overt difference, their separation from modern European society. But as early as 1911 he published a series of articles that criticized those Jews who converted to gain a material or a social edge. He argued that Germany's Jews were not "different in character" from the mass of Germans, and that the Jew was worth fully as much as what he called his "autochthonic fellow countryman." Taking the argument one step farther, he condemned "-pseudo-Germanic exclusiveness" and "the injustice that [occurs] in Germany."[8] Pride again: Rathenau refused to accept any necessity to declare himself exclusively for either Germany or Jewry. *He* knew the depth of his allegiance to the fatherland; who then should presume to doubt it?

But as Einstein wrote after Rathenau's death, his friend's "avowed allegiances were contradictory. He felt himself to be a Jew and thought along international lines, but at the same time, like many talented Jewish intellectuals, he was in love with Prussianism, its Junker mentality and its militarism."[9] The war, as his sister Edith told the ubiquitous Harry Kessler, wrecked Rathenau's dream of a marriage between his two sides. In part he suffered simply because of the blunt fact of Germany's defeat, but as much or more pain had come when he found that his passion for Germany was so completely unrequited. "It really hurt when, in the war, he longed to help his 'beloved,'" Edith said, "and his Jewishness hung like a millstone round his neck."[10] The pangs of rejected love grew worse in the first months of the November revolution. Someone suggested that he be named the first president of the new republic, but the delegates to the provisional assembly literally laughed aloud at the thought. To Rathenau, blinded by unfulfilled desire, such derision was merely "their way of greeting a German whose intellectual achievement they either did or did not know . . . it made me think of the sardonic laughter in the halls of Ithaca."[11] Thus spoke a modern Odysseus, dreaming of his moment of triumph and the slaughter of Penelope's rapacious suitors. Even so, he could not stop seeking some mark of favor from Germany, a chance to prove that he was uniquely able to serve his country in its growing need. As Kessler recalled, when the chance came at last to join the Weimar cabinet in 1921 as minister for reconstruction, "the instinct which really dominated the whole of his complex personality, his longing for activity and power, made it a foregone conclusion."[12]

Einstein agreed. Late in the evening of that last conversation, Rathenau told Einstein and Blumenfeld, "I am the right man for the position. I am fulfilling my duty for Germany." And, he added, rhetorically, "Why should I not repeat what Disraeli did?" As Einstein told Blumenfeld, Rathenau would be happy to take on the job of being pope—and, he added, he would do the job very well if it came his way. But it was obvious to Einstein, Blumenfeld, and almost certainly Rathenau too, that the foreign minister was marching straight toward his death. Early in his term he had brandished a pistol in his office, complaining to a visitor that the situation had deteriorated to the point where he had to carry his own gun to work. Beyond such theatrics, though, he took almost no real precautions. He ignored police warnings that they could not protect him as long as he followed his clockwork routine. Near 1:00 in the morning, as their conversation wound down, Einstein and Blumenfeld gave up their attempt to dent Rathenau's almost Christ-like fatalism. He told his guests that he sought to "break down the boundaries erected by anti-Semites to isolate the Jews," and, said Blumenfeld, "Rathenau interpreted the death that awaited him as a fulfillment of his German mission. He played with the idea of a sacrificial death." Above all, Blumenfeld recalled, "he knew that his nickname *Jesus im Frack* (Jesus in tails) was not used only by his enemies."[13]

And so he refused to resign. Not long after that inconclusive talk, Erwin Kern and his band of four disaffected students and veterans found one another and began to plot to assassinate some Jew prominent enough to matter. They settled quickly on Rathenau—he was the most obvious target, as made clear by the doggerel rhyme that had become a Freikorps marching song: *"Knallt ab den Walther Rathenau/die gottverdammte Judensau."* ("Shoot down Walther Rathenau/the goddamned Jewish sow.") The conspirators shadowed their intended victim, learning his habits and his routes. Meanwhile, Rathenau continued to represent his country, doing so with considerable skill. In his brief tenure as foreign minister he forged a new relationship with Russia, and briefly made progress in negotiations with France on reducing Germany's reparations burden (though this advance did not survive a change in the French leadership). But such defenses of German interests were of no import to the conspirators. A test run on June 20 convinced Kern that a revolver would not do; he would need an automatic to be sure of hitting his target. He picked one up that evening, no great feat in the gun-ridden Berlin of 1922. On the morning of June 24, car trouble almost sidelined the murderers, inviting unhappy comparison with the Serb gang that by blind luck had managed to kill the archduke Ferdinand in that distant Sarajevo of June 1914. But the car revived just in time. They pulled out of an alley behind Rathenau's car. Within minutes, he lay bleeding to death.

YET EVEN THOUGH the assassination was almost expected by those in the know, a crime committed on a schedule, the news stunned Berlin. Rathenau's chief conservative antagonist in the Reichstag was met the next day with cries of "Murderer! Murderer!" Chancellor Joseph Wirth told the Reichstag that the assassination proved that "Our fatherland . . . is being threatened . . . by a . . . murderous campaign. First they shout that we commit crimes against our people . . . and then they wonder when misled boys murder."[14] Einstein, in an obituary notice, laid the blame more explicitly on those he knew best, the rabid right German intellectual elite. "I would not have believed that hate, delusion, and ingratitude could have gone this far," Einstein wrote. "But to those who have led the moral education of the German people during the last fifty years I want to say: One shall recognize them by their sad achievements!"[15] The labor unions across the country called for a day of mourning, and millions of men and women marched to honor one of Germany's wealthiest industrialists.

On the right, the first impulse was to duck the initial wave of outrage. Ludendorff, characteristically, argued that Rathenau's killing had been a put-up job, a communist trick, for no true German would stoop so low as to shoot a man down on the street. But the facts made a mockery of such clumsy slander. Rathenau's assassination confirmed what had been a growing perception. Murder in Germany now served as a more or less ordinary tool of politics, wielded, especially on the right, with increasing success. Emil Gumbel's dismal report, "Four Years of Political Murder," demonstrated the depth of the danger faced by the republic and by those on the left. "The right is inclined to hope that it could annihilate the left opposition . . . by defeating its leaders. And the right has done it," he wrote. "All of the leaders of the left who openly opposed the war and whom the workers trusted . . . are dead." Add to that tally the moderate leftists, most recently Rathenau, murdered by right-wing assassins, and, Gumbel concluded, "the effectiveness of this technique is for the moment indisputable."[16] Worst of all, the killers could act with impunity. In the cases of twenty-two murders by leftists, seventeen of the murderers were punished harshly, with ten receiving the death penalty; while only one rightist implicated in the more than three hundred assassinations between 1918 and 1923 suffered any significant consequences.[17]

Such conclusions begged the obvious question: who would be next? Albert Einstein, perhaps. Two weeks after the murder he told Planck, "A number of people who deserve to be taken seriously have independently warned me not to stay in Berlin for the time being, and, especially, to avoid all public appearances in Germany. I am said to be among those whom the nationalists have marked for assassination." In response, he canceled his scheduled keynote address in September at Germany's leading scientific meeting, a long-planned hero's progress. He let the rumor circulate that he had left Berlin for destinations unknown; as he told Solovine, it had been "nerve-wracking since the shameful assassination of Rathenau. I am always on the alert; I have stopped my lectures and am officially absent, though I am actually here all the time."[18] This was fame with a vengeance: "The trouble is that the newspapers have mentioned my name too often, thus mobilizing the rabble against me. I have no alternative but to be patient—and to leave the city."[19]

In fact, Einstein did not rush to flee Germany. He remained in semiseclusion through the summer and fall, though he did appear very much in the open at a peace demonstration in August. But despite that bravado, the truth remained that Berlin was increasingly inhospitable. Early in 1922, before Rathenau's murder, he had accepted an invitation to lecture in Japan in November and December. He had promised his friends the year before that he would leave Germany only under extreme duress. He did not think the threat he faced personally after Rathenau's death met that standard, but given the opportunity, he was ready to give Berlin a rest for six months. So, in October, he and Elsa traveled to Marseilles and boarded the *Kitano Maru* bound for Kobe.

Japan loved Einstein. He was greeted by crowds at each stop on the tour, and his public lecture series, despite the extremely high ticket price, garnered eager audiences along the entire route. Two thousand paid to hear him in Tokyo alone. The tour turned into a redoubled version of what he had already experienced the year before: enormous crowds hungered for the sight and sound of a man who had become an icon. As the German diplomats monitoring his progress reported, "All eyes were turned on Einstein, everyone wanted at least to shake hands with the most famous man of the present day."[20]

He loved Japan. It was wonderful there, he told Solovine. "Genteel manners, a lively interest in everything, an artistic sense, intellectual honesty combined with common sense."[21] A photograph from that visit conveys his pleasure, and suggests something more. He and Elsa sit, smiling, holding tiny, delicate porcelain cups. Even seated they tower over the elegant kimono-clad women serving them. The traditional implements of Japanese hospitality form a still life on the low tables, and a spare, angular flower arrangement can be seen behind the couple. The aesthetic was Japanese, but the virtues expressed were Einstein's as well: simplicity, precision and grace. And hence, perhaps, Einstein's celebration of Japan. One picture is not proof of anything, but the contrast with the ragged streets and bitter wounds of Berlin could not have been more complete. At the instant the photographer shot, Einstein leaned gently forward. A woman held out a flask. In the next moment, she would have poured out a sip, brief, pure, intense. No bullets, no vitriol aimed at the Jews, no learned bigotry. It was just a quiet moment, and the taste of something strange and new.

STILL, JAPAN WAS JUST AN INTERLUDE, a temporary escape. Einstein treated the journey as his Grand Tour, with tourist side trips to Colombo in Ceylon, Singapore, Hong Kong and Shanghai. The two most significant events of the trip actually occurred on the voyages out and back. One was his first visit to Palestine, a stopover on the journey home. He gave the inaugural lecture in a temporary hall to mark the founding of the Hebrew University in Jerusalem—the project that had been the object of his fund-raising exercise in the United States the year before. (He gave his talk in French, not German. French was then, as now, an international language, and German was not. Einstein's internationalism ran very deep.) He accepted what ever after he considered one of his greatest accolades, honorary citizenship in the new

Jewish town of Tel Aviv. Most significant, he saw in Palestine Jews doing all the work of a modern civil society, from cultivating farms to digging ditches to running cities. He told Solovine that "the brothers of our race charmed me as farmers, as workers, and as citizens."[22] As noted earlier, he was contemptuous of the traditional Jews he saw there, ridiculing the rows of the mystics and true believers swaying before the shrines of the Holy Land. But seeing Jews moving dirt, directing traffic and building universities—that vision of Jewish nation building anchored Einstein's lasting commitment to his idiosyncratic version of Zionism.

But even Einstein's sojourn in the city on a hill took second place to something that happened earlier, on the outbound leg of the journey. On November 10, 1922, a telegram reached Einstein's house in Berlin that read "Nobel Prize for physics awarded to you more by letter signed Aurivillius."[23] (Christopher Aurivillius was the secretary of the Royal Swedish Academy of Sciences.) The *Kitano Maru* was still at sea, somewhere north of Hong Kong, and there is no record of when the ship received word. But before Einstein reached Japan, he knew that the Nobel committee had chosen him, and he knew why.

Einstein's tangled history with the Nobel Prize constitutes one of the minor mysteries of twentieth-century science. Obviously, he had earned his Nobel long before—no one capable of judging the matter had any real doubt of that. He had received his first prize nomination in 1910, when he was just thirty-one. Everyone understood it was only a matter of time, so much so that Mileva Maric and her advisors had thought it prudent to accept as alimony the potential prize money offered by Einstein. So why did it take so long? After all, by 1922 he had completed work that, as we look back on it, could have earned at least three separate prizes and perhaps four (and as it happened, he still had work at or near Nobel levels left in him).[24] Put another way, what was it in the whole body of Einstein's work that finally pushed the Nobel committee over the edge?

It was not relativity. The committee was very clear about what it did and did not like about Einstein's work. Aurivillius's promised letter explained that the prize had been given "without taking into account the value which will be accorded your relativity and gravitation theories after these are confirmed in the future."[25] The special and general theories were too radical for what was then a hidebound and not very well informed prize committee. Instead, the Nobel grandees picked something they thought a little more manageable, a little safer. Avoiding any funny business about misbehaving clocks or space that bends, the official citation simply said that Einstein had earned his prize "for his services to theoretical physics and especially for the photoelectric effect."

The photoelectric effect? That result, published seventeen years before, in Einstein's miracle year of 1905, contained what he himself believed was the only truly radical idea he ever had. His inquiry into the photoelectric effect turned on the concept of the light quantum—light imagined as a machine-gun stream of individual particles, or quanta.[26] From its birth the quantum theory was one of the strangest, least anticipated physical ideas of the twentieth century; even now, the peculiarity of the quantum world puts any hint of weirdness in relativity in the shade. For the hidebound and traditionalist Nobel committee to give Einstein the prize for the photoelectric effect and not for relativity was, as Abraham Pais put it, "a touching twist of history." It may have been an accident of the committee's lack of deep knowledge of physics, but whatever the reason, Pais wrote, it was only fitting that the committee's members, "conservative by nature, would honor Einstein for the most revolutionary contribution he ever made to physics."[27]

Einstein agreed. Late in life, he confided to a friend that "I have thought a hundred times as much about the quantum problems as I have about general relativity theory."[28] He did so because he recognized almost from that very early Nobel Prize–winning work that the idea of the quantum created a huge problem—ultimately several problems. From the first, it was clear that the quantum realm and the cosmos described by relativity looked very different indeed. Relativity explored the behavior of the universe on the large scale, while the quantum theory explored what happened on the smallest of scales. Relativity saw spacetime and matter and energy as continuous phenomena, with no breaks, no gaps. Quantum theory's core concept was that energy and matter exist as tiny, independent, discrete packets at the finest, smallest, most fundamental levels. To Einstein, it seemed inexplicable and ultimately unacceptable that there could be two such separate descriptions of reality. From the very beginning of quantum theory, several deep problems appeared that ranged from the nature of quanta themselves to the issues of cause and effect—questions that would vex him in later life. Behind and beneath the specific mysteries, the qualitative differences that divided the relativistic and the quantum worldview always seemed to Einstein to demand a resolution that would encompass both views in a single, coherent idea. It all began, as the Nobel committee correctly intuited, with that first attempt to understand the quantum nature of light, his account of the photoelectric effect.

IT IS ONE OF THE RIDICULOUS COINCIDENCES of history that Einstein's invention of the quantum theory of light was so intimately linked to the photoelectric effect and to Philipp Lenard, the man who had studied it most deeply. Lenard would become the anti-Semite whose own Nobel Prize lent authority to his attacks on Einstein from 1920 forward. In 1905, of course, there was nothing of such nonsense. Lenard was simply trying to understand a phenomenon first noticed in the mid-nineteenth century: the fact that light shining on a metal surface could produce a spark, a discharge of electrical energy. The problem had begun as something of a curiosity, but as the mystery persisted it took on greater importance. By the time Lenard attacked the problem he wanted to understand precisely how the intensity of light—its brightness—affected the electrical emission sparking off the metal surface.

To find out, Lenard used a light source that he could adjust precisely from its dimmest setting up to a brightness one thousand times greater. As he worked through the lamp's full range, he uncovered an almost shocking fact. Brighter light would dislodge more electrons, which would increase the amount of electric charge produced—but the *speed* with which each electron took off from the metal surface remained the same. If light were a wave, as everyone believed, this result made no sense. More light, a more powerful wave, ought to pound the metal target harder, and produce a more violent, more energetic result. Something was deeply wrong, something was happening that did not tally with classical, Newtonian ideas about motion and energy.

For Einstein a mystery like this was almost absurdly delightful. In one of the most revealing of his early love letters to Mileva Maric, he told her that he had "just read a marvelous paper by Lenard on the production of cathode rays by ultraviolet light [the photoelectric effect]. Under the influence of this beautiful piece of work, I am filled with such happiness and joy that you must certainly share in some of it." Mileva, then pregnant with Lieserl, may have had other matters on her mind, as Einstein noted two paragraphs farther on, asking (before the gender of what ultimately turned out to be a daughter was known), "How [is] our little son?"[29]—the first mention in the surviving correspondence of her out-of-wedlock pregnancy. There is no hint that Einstein was trying to be cruel here. The letter simply expresses his habits of mind, his priorities. The flash of a spark that begged explanation held him in much greater thrall than a lover or a child.

It took him until 1905 to come up with the answer. To do so, he had, in effect, to emulate Alice's White Queen, and believe in six impossible things before breakfast. His key step was to pick up on a concept first developed by Max Planck in 1900 to solve a problem in the science of thermodynamics—heat—and apply it to the phenomenon of light. Planck had been searching for the correct form of the law that would describe the production of what was called the blackbody spectrum. That spectrum was simply a map of the distribution and intensity of the colors of light found in the glow produced when a certain kind of object gets heated up through the entire temperature range. Planck discovered the equation that predicted the precise shape of that spectrum, but to do so, he had to treat the radiant energy emitted by the system as if it came packaged in discrete bundles, tiny units that he dubbed quanta. These quanta formed amounts of energy of a fixed size that could be added or subtracted, but never divided. To Planck's surprise, and ultimately somewhat to his horror, the quantum concept worked, and when manipulated with a number we now call Planck's constant, his theory provided the first precise description of the behavior of energy at its finest level of detail.

Despite that success, neither Planck nor anyone else actually welcomed the idea of quanta. At bottom, the concept seemed bizarre. Einstein's description of the utter strangeness of the idea highlighted the gap between everyday experience and the quantum world. Imagine, he said, that you are thirsty. You go to the store, where you can buy only one or more bottles of beer. In that context, each bottle is an indivisible unit, the minimum quantity available to you, the quantum of beer. But, he said, "even though beer is always sold in pint bottles, it does not follow that beer consists of indivisible pint portions."[30] Buying a keg, instead of individual bottles, ought to solve the problem. Just turn the tap, and draw whatever you want—pints, quarts, ounces, whatever. Just so, the older idea that energy propagates in waves and fields (gospel to physicists since James Clerk Maxwell created electromagnetic field theory, if not before) held that energy is a continuous phenomenon, a flowing river, out of which one can extract any amount one desired. But in the brave new quantum world, a strange thing happens. Every time you turn the tap, beer—energy—flows only in particular quantities, a pint at a time, or else in whole-number multiples of that amount: two pints, three pints, and so on. The idea contradicts ordinary experience. It simply isn't true on the macroscopic level of the neighborhood saloon. But Planck had shown that at the level of the molecule, the atom, and the electron, the quantum picture held. Energy does only come in "bottles," in quanta. The quanta made no sense, but they fit the facts.

But at what price! Planck himself recoiled from the implications of his greatest discovery. He regarded the invention of the quantum of energy almost as a moral failure, born of his emotional need "to obtain a positive result . . . at whatever cost."[31] Einstein too recoiled at his first encounter with the quantum. He wrote that "it was as if the ground had been pulled out from under one, with no firm foundation to be seen anywhere upon which one could have built."[32] And other than Einstein, no one else seems to have taken Planck's desperate act all that seriously. It was almost as if everyone had decided politely to ignore the fact that a close friend had briefly gone bonkers. Between Planck's paper in 1900 and Einstein's in 1905, there were no meaningful contributions to the quantum theory. Even Planck beat a hasty retreat. He spent years trying to prove that his quanta were merely fictions, tools useful for certain calculations, rather than real phenomena in nature, the stuff of which the world was actually made. That left Einstein essentially alone, almost the only person thinking hard about the quantum between 1900 and 1905. In mid-1901, he seems to have put the question aside for a time, switching his attention to statistical physics and the nagging question of relative motion. But he learned of Lenard's discoveries about the photoelectric effect in 1902, and after that began to look more deeply into the nature of the quantum.

When he did so, he realized that he had to go beyond Planck's initial conclusion. Planck had treated energy as a quantum phenomenon, but he still thought of light traveling in waves, just as Maxwell's theory said, and just as all physicists of the day believed with near absolute certainty. (With good reason. A century of experiment had demonstrated that light behaves like a wave in a wide range of circumstances.) But for Einstein, then just twenty-six, the photoelectric effect provided the clue that allowed him to break with that established wisdom. The fact that Lenard's electrons all leaped off the metal surface with the same energy made sense only if every electron in the photoelectric spark had been dislodged from the metal by something that struck each individual atom with the identical impetus. What was there in nature that could deliver such precise, measured blows? Nothing—unless light behaved like Planck's energy quanta, traveling not as a continuous wave but in packets, in particles. It would be useful, Einstein said, "a heuristic view," to think of light as "localized at points in space [that] move without dividing and can be absorbed or generated only as a whole."[33] He was modest in his language, using the formalities of scientific writing to mask the almost reckless novelty of the idea, but in private he knew how far out on the quantum limb he stood, writing to a friend that his new ideas about light were "very revolutionary."[34]

And now to storm the Bastille. His next step described the properties of his newly invented light quanta. If light did exist as a stream of individual particles, then, in his quantum picture, each individual quantum would have a precise amount of energy associated with it. In technical terms, he proposed an equation that linked each quantum's energy to its frequency (its color) multiplied by Planck's constant—here making its first appearance as one of the fundamental constants of the universe, one of the numbers that order the cosmos at large. Einstein's equation made it clear that each light quantum of a particular frequency possessed exactly the same amount of energy as any other. Higher frequency light—the blue end of the rainbow—would pack more energy than lower frequency, redder quanta, but each individual color was associated with a unique amount of energy per unit of light.

Einstein's first claim, then, was that light consists of distinct, discontinuous particles. His second was that the energy carried by each such particle was directly related to the frequency or color of the light in question. Bold ideas both, but were they true? Certainly, he said. Look to the photoelectric effect, and those mysteriously synchronized electrons, all sparking off Lenard's metal plate with exactly the same kinetic energy. It takes a metaphoric leap, but using the concept of the light quantum, the photoelectric effect could be understood as a game of billiards at the subatomic level. Each quantum of light could be seen as a cue ball striking a single electron. Since by Einstein's new principle, every quantum of a given frequency had the same energy as every other, each electron would receive a blow of exactly the same strength as every other hit by a given color of light. A brighter light would contain more light particles, more quanta available to strike a greater number of electrons. But electron by electron, the target balls in this quantized game of pool would all receive exactly the same amount of kinetic energy from the individual quanta that struck them, and hence would all fly off the photoelectric surface at exactly the same speed—just as Lenard had observed. Crucially, this picture was more than an attractive mental cartoon. Applying his new law for the energy of quantized light to Lenard's law of the photoelectric effect, Einstein was able to predict what Lenard had actually observed with a satisfying tight fit. For Einstein, that was sufficient: light quanta were real. Their existence could be deduced directly from the evidence of nature, illuminated by the sudden, sharp leap of a charge sparking off a plate of metal.

OR SO EINSTEIN BELIEVED—and for years, Einstein alone. For all of his confidence, others recognized an obvious, almost appalling lapse of logic that struck at the heart of the concept of the light quantum. Einstein's central equation asserted that the energy of each of his particles of light was equal to Planck's constant, multiplied by the wavelength of the light being measured. Wavelength? That was, as Einstein certainly knew, a property of light *waves.* As such, on its face, it had nothing to do with the behavior of *particles,* little balls whizzing about. Rather, it seemed obvious that light could be either a wave or a particle, but not both. Einstein recognized—none better—that this wave-particle duality was truly strange, a fundamental challenge to any claim that physics and physicists truly understood the nature of light. In 1911, speaking to the best minds in the physical sciences at the first Solvay Conference, he argued two points. First, the quantum problem remained the most important one facing them all; physicists simply did not understand what happened at the smallest scales, the finest subdivisions of nature. Second, his own attempts to solve at least part of that problem foundered still on the conflict between the wave and particle pictures. "I insist on the provisional nature" of this concept, he said, because it does not "seem to be reconcilable with the experimentally verified consequences of the wave theory."[35]

Privately, Einstein put the issue more starkly. At one point, he even seemed to concede the essential falseness of his idea: "One cannot believe in the existence of countable quanta," he told Wilhelm Wien in 1912, "since the interference [wavelike] properties of light . . . are not compatible with it." And yet, almost despite himself, he said, "I still prefer the 'honest' theory of quanta to the . . . compromises found so far to replace it."[36] Writing at the same time of his attempt to apply quantum ideas to a problem in the science of heat, Einstein came up with one of his most famous aphorisms about the quantum. "Theory," he told Zangger, "is too pretentious a word" for what he called "a sort of groping without proper foundations." And then, the cry from the heart: "The more successes the quantum theory enjoys, the sillier it looks."[37]

For Einstein, there were two problems. First, it was obvious that the quantum theory was utterly unfinished. But there was an even more basic issue. He was the first to grapple with the damage the quantum perspective did to conventional, classical conceptions of the nature of reality. The dual images of light as wave *and* particle served as his point of entry. As early as 1909, he began to merge those two pictures. Extending his study of light quanta, he now refused to offer the coded apology of calling this view of light heuristic. Rather, he declared that "the current [i.e., old] theory of radiation is incompatible with this result"—that is, it was wrong.[38] In its place, he said, "it is my opinion that the next phase in the development of theoretical physics will bring us a theory of light that can be interpreted as a fusion of the wave and the emission theory."[39] Or, as he wrote later for a popular readership, there were "two contradictory pictures of reality; separately neither of them fully explains the phenomena of light, but together they do!"[40] For the first time, Einstein suggested that phenomena in nature could partake of both the wave and the particle, that light was at once both continuous and discrete.

That was yet one more remarkable—and solitary—leap of faith. Virtually all of his colleagues refused to accept this duality for another fifteen years. In the meantime, however, worse (or perhaps merely stranger) was just about to appear. Again, it was Einstein himself who first scented the danger. Immediately after he completed the general theory of relativity, he returned to quantum problems in an attempt to merge his work on the light quantum with Niels Bohr's work on the quantum nature of matter. In 1913, Bohr had shown that certain properties of the hydrogen atom—how it emits and absorbs particular colors of light—followed the logic of a quantized universe. In Bohr's description, the one electron in each hydrogen atom could occupy certain energy states but not others: the same discrete, granular concept Planck had developed for energy and Einstein for light. With his return to the problem of the quantum in 1916, Einstein was able to show that when one of Bohr's atoms emitted a quantum, or, as it would be renamed, a *photon* of light, it reacted like a cannon firing a shell: the atom involved recoiled from the shock. Proving this experimentally took another five years, but from 1917, as Einstein told Besso, "I do not doubt anymore the *reality* [emphasis in the original] of radiation quanta, though I still stand quite alone in this."[41]

But with that renewed conviction came a hint of great difficulties to come. In his work on the quantum behavior of atoms, Einstein began to recognize that quantum processes, some of them at least, appeared to turn on chance. Atoms, as Einstein knew, could emit photons spontaneously. In Bohr's model of the atom, electrons occupied particular orbits around the nucleus, and they could just jump from one orbit to the next—the famous quantum leap. With each such leap, they would emit or absorb a photon. But Einstein could find no way to predict when such leaps might occur, nor in what direction a photon would travel when the moment came. If there was one thing that Einstein believed in, along with every other physicist of his day, it was that effects follow causes, absolutely, without fail. But here in the flashing beacon of the hydrogen atom came the first hint that cause and effect might break down. If photons and electrons truly behaved like billiard balls, it should have been possible to identify the shove that set them in motion—the cause. Similarly, billiard balls go where they are aimed—the effect. But as Einstein understood the logic that he and Bohr together had forged, he had to conclude that sometimes events happen for no discernible reason. Similarly, he could not link the consequent events, the "effects"—the timing and trajectory of a flash of light—to any cause that would allow him to predict what would happen next. He could imagine producing statistics about the behavior of a lot of atoms, predictions based on probabilities that some number of quantum events will occur in any given amount of time. But for Einstein such a probabilistic description of nature fell far short of what he considered appropriate: the deterministic picture that would allow him to say that a particular event triggered a precisely defined consequence. It was, he noted at the time, "a weakness of the theory."

He was to call it worse than that. The quantum theory with all its snares became for him a joke played on humankind—on him—by "the eternal inventor of enigmas." For all his brave talk about God's subtlety, he did concede once to a close friend that after all, "maybe God *is* malicious."[42] But whatever his dislike for the notion of a probabilistic view of reality, Einstein pursued what he increasingly understood to be an essential crisis within quantum theory. In 1920, he complained to Max Born that "that business about causality causes me a great deal of trouble." As he told Born, "I must admit that there I lack the courage of my convictions"—that is, that causality could survive without some recourse to random processes, chance and statistics. But still, "I would be very unhappy to renounce *complete* causality."[43] (The emphasis is Einstein's.)

That unhappiness hardened into outright opposition, the start of a campaign to rid physics of the insidious cancer of randomness and probabilities, the disjunction between cause and effect. From the start, though, as Einstein conceded, his efforts went nowhere. Throughout the early 1920s, the quantum remained an intractable riddle. As he wrote in a popular article for a Berlin newspaper in the spring of 1924, there were two competing, fundamental ideas about the deepest nature of the material world. Both were indispensable, he said, but "as one must admit today despite twenty years of tremendous effort on the part of theoretical physicists," the two theories lacked "any logical connection" that would make sense of their competing visions of reality.[44]

Ultimately, Einstein would make two separate assaults on what he saw as the absurdity of the quantum picture. With his return to Berlin from the last leg of his Grand Tour, in March of 1923, he focused on the problem that occupied him the longest, his search for what he called unified field theory. Just as Maxwell had managed to unify electricity and magnetism in a single concept, Einstein hoped to link electromagnetism with his theory of gravity. Both of those existing theories were what are known as field theories—the phenomena being described were continuous, extending through space in unbroken fields of waves. So his aim in creating a new, unified wave or field theory was to find a way to incorporate the fundamental discontinuities of the quantum particles (like electrons) that form matter into a broader field concept. As he put it, he wanted to see matter, the apparently hard, discrete chunks of reality, as simply places within some kind of continuum where the field was exceptionally strong. He suggested an analogy, moving from the tiny realm of the quantum up to everyday experience. If his unified field concept were correct, that would mean that "a thrown stone is . . . a changing field where the states of greatest field intensity travel through space with the velocity of the stone." This mirrored, at least conceptually, what Einstein had already proved in gravitation. There, what we experience as a force is merely a consequence of a bend in the path of a four-dimensional spacetime field. Now, he proposed, not just forces but matter itself, the solid stuff of everyday experience, might be an illusion—our perception of the behavior of another, still more complicated field that is even farther beyond the reach of our senses. If Einstein were right, if his statement of "field being the only reality" were true, then continuous, unbroken systems of waves—not grains of cosmic dust—would be the stuff of which our universe was made. As usual, the stakes were colossally high. If his idea could be made to work, then, he said, he would have gained knowledge traditionally given only to divine beings. Such a theory would, he wrote, explain "all events in nature by laws valid always and everywhere."[45]

Einstein never achieved that goal. He never came close. He never stopped trying. He first wrote about unified theories in 1922, when he began his study of the idea that the universe might actually possess five dimensions: four spatial dimensions and one of time. The idea of five-dimensional spacetime was first developed by Theodor Kaluza in 1919 and then extended by Oskar Klein in 1926. Kaluza suggested that we live in a world in which there is one additional spatial dimension beyond the three with which we are familiar, height, width, and depth. Klein then went on to explain why no one had noticed this extra feature of space. He argued that there could be two kinds of dimensions—the three we are familiar with, which define space at large scales—and another kind that exists in the realm of the very, very small. Such a compressed dimension could curl around on itself, forming a looplike shape that could not be detected directly. To convey this counterintuitive idea, the theorist Brian Greene has proposed a simple thought experiment. Imagine a hose seen from a great distance. It looks like a line, a one-dimensional object. One number is enough to fix the position of anything on the hose, which is simply the definition of one-dimensionality. But examine the hose through binoculars and its tube shape becomes visible. Now it takes two numbers to fix a position: one for location along the length of the hose, and another for position around its cylindrical body. Look at the hose more closely, argues Greene, and the two-dimensional nature of its surface becomes obvious. That second dimension is much smaller than the first and it curls around on itself. It was invisible until the right technique could be found to discover it (the binoculars), but it was there all along. Similarly, in Kaluza-Klein theory the fourth spatial dimension lurked alongside the three with which we are familiar, curled up at every point in space, too small for it to be detected.[46]

But why bother invoking such an added dimension? Kaluza got excited about the idea because he found that by adding a spatial dimension to relativity's spacetime, he could express both Einstein's gravitational equations and Maxwell's electromagnetism within the same mathematical structure. In other words, the two theories could be unified into one. Kaluza wrote to Einstein about his five-dimensional universe in 1919, and at first Einstein responded with praise: "The formal unity of your theory is startling."[47] But as he and others investigated its details with more care, the work failed the critical test: its equations failed to produce the right numbers for such basic and well-known quantities as the mass and electrical charge of the electron. Such lapses meant that however elegant it might be, the new theory did not describe the universe—or at least, not our universe—and hence unified nothing.

Einstein's first attempt to produce a unification theory of his own came in 1925. It possessed few of the virtues of his best work. It was arcane, mathematically dense, and in part clearly arbitrary. (Such ad hoc expedients serve the scientist as a convenient deus ex machina, and they occasionally work wonders, as one did for Planck and his original quantum concept. But special pleading is usually a signal that the books are being cooked.) Ominously, the tendency toward mathematical intricacy marked a distinct departure from Einstein's clear, often visual epiphanies that had grounded both special and general relativity. In this new theory a system of eighty different independent fields had to be tamed to produce the familiar sights of gravitation and electromagnetic theory emerging somehow from the rubble. Einstein's hopes rose briefly. He claimed on publishing this result that "I now believe I have the true solution" for unification. But within weeks he was writing to friends that his new idea was "beautiful, but dubious," and then, baldly, that "my work of last summer is no good."[48]

Subsequent efforts went even farther down the same road. His colleagues noted with a mixture of awe and exasperation his habit of generating a new version of the theory every year, always with great expectations, only to withdraw the erstwhile breakthrough soon thereafter. Most troubling to those who loved him best was his willingness to pursue what seemed to them to be merely mathematical sleight of hand, hoping to trick one set of equations into revealing something that resembled physics—and this from the Einstein who had once said that "physics is essentially an intuitive and a concrete science. Mathematics is only a means for expressing the laws that govern phenomena."[49] His descent into apostasy (as it would appear to the younger generation of physicists, men like Wolfgang Pauli and J. Robert Oppenheimer) may have had its roots in the epiphany of general relativity itself. The experience of seeing such beautiful physics—the perfect solution to Mercury's orbit, for example—emerge as if by magic out of the mathematics of non-Euclidean geometry certainly shook him. The hunt through the thickets of seemingly arbitrary equations may have baffled his colleagues, but the truth had miraculously appeared there once. Why not once more?

That search continued to the end of Einstein's life. By then, however, he fully understood the difficulty, perhaps the impossibility, of his task. In 1948, a few months shy of his seventieth birthday, he wrote to Solovine that "in my scientific activity, I am always hampered by the same mathematical difficulties, which make it impossible for me to confirm or refute my general relativistic field theory [unified field theory]." After almost thirty years of effort, he could see no way out. "I shall never solve it; it will fall into oblivion and be discovered anew later."[50]

That was about as close as he ever came to admitting either failure or despair. But neither ever stopped him. In a pleasingly cantankerous letter he admitted his own frailty: "I am not convinced of the certainty of a single concept, and I am uncertain as to whether I am even on the right track." But no matter. For all such feelings of inadequacy—his own word—he chose to keep on plugging. Never mind that "in me, my contemporaries see both a heretic and reactionary who has, so to speak, survived himself."[51] His final paper, published posthumously, was yet one more progress report, another set of field equations that seemed, in passing, to hint at unification. In one of his last letters he crowed to Solovine that he had "finally managed to introduce another noteworthy improvement" to unified field theory, though he admitted that his theory could still not be confirmed because the mathematics was too complex.[52] On the last day of his life he called for paper and a pencil and the notebook with his latest calculations. Knowing he was perhaps hours from death, he kept on going, not in the expectation of reaching a solution, but because the question mattered and he still cared.

Einstein's faith has been vindicated in part. The unification of the different forces that govern the behavior of matter and energy in the universe remains the central goal of much of physics. Major progress toward that goal came in the 1960s and early 1970s, with the invention of what was dubbed the "electroweak" theory. That work, performed, mostly independently, by three men, Abdus Salam, Steven Weinberg, and Sheldon Glashow, unified the laws that govern electromagnetism with those that described one of the forces that govern behavior within the atomic nucleus, the so-called "weak force." More recent efforts have produced the forbidding structures of string theory. These ideas are the distant descendants of the approach taken early on by Einstein, following Kaluza and Klein. They do differ in critical respects from Einstein's approach. Instead of a mere five dimensions, string theories operate in as many as ten spatial dimensions. Most of those additional dimensions, their inventors say, have been compacted into such small balls as to leave our ordinary world of physical experience unaffected. (Small here means really tiny; the "extra" dimensions in many string theories exist at a scale of 10^{-33} centimeters and smaller. Some recent versions of string theory, including the latest "brane-world" idea, propose much larger "extra" dimensions, but no confirming evidence has yet been found.) More generally, Einstein had sought a purely geometrical account of unification, in an extension of the geometrical description of spacetime that led him to general relativity. String theories do employ some very recherché geometrical ideas, but in general they use a mathematical approach quite different from Einstein's. Still, in theme and ambition, modern string theory and unified field theory are kin, cousins at several removes. And as Einstein claimed for his earlier attempts, the new theories are seen to be elegant—to those who can judge, they are actually beautiful—though as yet they remain unblemished by any direct connection to the hard ground of nature. Still, a growing number of Einstein's heirs see themselves as Galahad to his Lancelot, with the grail he glimpsed within their grasp.

However, Einstein himself never had a chance of succeeding. He said once that his success turned on the fact that "God gave me the stubbornness of a mule and he gave me my nose."[53] His pursuit of unified field theory put that mulishness on full display, but in this instance, his nose for the right problem failed him. When he began, the only two forces known in nature were electromagnetism and gravitation, the two he tried to unify. But, critically, he did not know what he did not know. The forces that govern behavior within atomic nuclei, the so-called weak and strong forces, had yet to be identified. Lacking that information, Einstein did not even know what there was in nature that needed to be unified, and thus was certain to fail. Modern unification attempts have achieved their partial successes by accepting Einstein's themes, his belief that multiple forces, multiple worldviews, mask the existence of the one, true "final theory," to use Steven Weinberg's term. But they have rejected the approach that led Einstein down a thirty-year dead end.

He did pursue one other line of thought in his confrontation with the quantum and its corrosive consequences. Throughout 1923 and 1924 he continued to seek some remedy for the damage his early triumphs had done. Out of that effort he would produce two more critical ideas, each of which contributed to the ultimate quantum breakthrough, and for him the ultimate debacle. There was a gap between each result, a natural pause, as Einstein explained one night to Count Harry Kessler when both were bored at a banker's dinner party. Between discoveries, Einstein told Kessler, all he could do was think, secure in the conviction that enough thought "almost invariably brought progress with it." The difficulty and the opportunity in his line of work came from the fact that "without exception, every scientific proposition was wrong." That was "due to human inadequacy of thought and inability to comprehend nature, so that every abstract formulation of it was inconsistent somewhere." All one could do, he said, was to test each idea to destruction, replace it, and repeat the process, and so on, thought without end.[54]

Einstein traveled to Stockholm in the spring of 1923 to collect his Nobel medal. He spoke then on progress in relativity, on his theory of gravity. But that was the problem already solved; the quantum remained intractable, its denial of causality a continuing peril. He returned to Berlin and continued to think, to no apparent conclusion.

Chapter Seventeen

"A REICH GERMAN"

THE BERLIN TO WHICH EINSTEIN RETURNED FROM HIS GRAND TOUR WAS wholly transformed from the one he had left behind. Then merely a difficult and sometimes dangerous place in which to live, it had become almost an impossible city, a metropolis of desperation. Photographs capture the disaster. In one, a gaunt man pushes a wheelbarrow heaped to overflowing with money: cash, big bills. He is hurrying, urgent, desperate. In Germany at the height of the hyperinflationary period, a delay of an hour or two between being paid millions of marks and spending them could have dire consequences—the difference between bread for dinner or hunger. No prior experience could have prepared anyone for what happened from the latter half of 1922 through 1923. German currency almost literally exploded. The term itself, hyperinflation, had to be coined to describe the catastrophic increase in prices, the effective disintegration of the deutsche mark. Those who lived through the worst of it never fully recovered from the experience. That people starved as everything they owned vanished was horrifying enough. But more troubling yet was the thought that nothing made sense anymore, that the basic, supposedly indestructible fabric of national existence could unravel, apparently at a moment's whim.

The perception of a sudden crisis, though, was something of an illusion. The German government had courted inflation since 1914, as a matter of unstated official policy. Germany, poorer by far than its enemies, funded its war effort by printing money in the form of war bonds—80 billion marks' worth, sold mostly to the deeply loyal middle class. With the pressure of both war scarcity and the growth in the amount of paper money floating around, German prices tracked upward throughout the war, doubling in four years—an annual inflation rate of 18 percent. That was bad enough, especially for those on a fixed income or a salary from the state. But as prices shot upward during the immediate postwar period, the weaknesses hidden within German wartime economic policy were revealed. Goods cost almost twice as much in 1919 as the year before, an inflation rate of 100 percent, and prices tripled in 1920. The level of uncertainty rose with each boost in prices. In the fall of 1921, for example, with prices on the move again, Max Born wrote to "the mighty director of the Institute of Physics of the Kaiser Wilhelm Society"—Albert Einstein—to beg for rapid action on a grant application for the purchase of some X-ray equipment. If he could order the equipment at once, Born wrote, he could get what he needed for 100,000 marks. In ten days' time, though, he told Einstein, "we would be subject to the full price increase caused by the currency devaluation, which would amount to about 50 percent."[1]

Still, as Born later recalled, inflation at that moment still felt basically manageable. In late 1921, the mark dropped in value by half over a period of months, but slowly enough so that a leisurely exchange of letters between gentlemen was still sufficiently swift to dodge the worst of the damage. The weakness of the mark contributed to a sense of fragility, the feeling that Germans and Germany were anything but the masters of their fate, but for about a year the system seemed to be holding together (and Born did in fact get his X-ray apparatus out of Einstein). But any such sense of relative stability collapsed in the aftermath of Rathenau's murder. At the start of the war the mark had traded at 4.2 to the dollar. By mid-1921, the exchange rate stood at seventy-five to one and it topped a hundred to one before the end of the year, continuing its run to June 24, 1922—the day of Rathenau's murder—when one dollar could buy three hundred marks. From that day forward, the process moved into a higher gear.

Over the next four weeks, the mark lost more than half its value, trading at 493 to the dollar at the end of July. In August, it dropped to

1,134 to the dollar, breaking into unheard-of four-digit territory. September gave a momentary respite—it fell only another 25 percent for the month—but the hideous drop started up once again in October, its value halved that month and again in November. Even so, the plunge through 1922 was just the prelude to the real disaster. In January 1923, convinced (with reason) that the German government was using the racing inflation as a pretext to dodge reparations payments, French and Belgian forces occupied the Ruhr, Germany's industrial center and the source of most of its coal. The government was wholly unprepared for this, lacking both coal reserves for the winter and any means to dislodge the occupiers. The chosen policy of "passive resistance"—strikes and other work stoppages and slowdowns in the Ruhr—merely hastened economic collapse in the region and evoked overt brutality on the part of the French and Belgian armies.

In unoccupied Germany, the invasion of the Ruhr exploded the inflation bomb. By the end of January, one dollar bought more than 17,000 marks. By August, that same dollar could purchase 4,620,455 marks.[2] Upward of two thousand printing presses worked three shifts a day to produce the needed bills, which in August included the first *billion*-mark note, in itself the ultimate evidence of the utter absurdity of the time. Still, given the relentless determination of the Reichsbank to keep pace with inflation, the 100-billion-mark bill that appeared in October was the inevitable sequel. Printing such paper was a futile gesture, of course, formal acknowledgment that the mark had essentially ceased to exist. And as the nation's currency dissolved, the possessions of generations, the habits and customs and daily actions that make up a life, evaporated in a cauldron of meaningless numbers.

There were winners throughout the debacle. Anyone with a bit of hard currency could buy German products, sell them abroad, purchase essentials, including food, and resell them in Germany for literally inflated profit margins. Foreigners loved Berlin in the midst of the inflation, and so did those new rich who managed to accumulate vast property or industrial empires bought with ever cheaper marks. The most famous of these instant plutocrats was Hugo Stinnes. Stinnes had been well-off before the inflation, with interests in mining and electrical power generation. The inflation, however, launched him on an unprecedented shopping spree. If it could be bought, he grabbed it. By the time he died in 1924, he had managed to acquire the largest coal mine in Europe among his fifty-nine mining properties, along with a commercial and industrial empire that included over a hundred fifty magazines and newspapers, more than fifty banks, well over two hundred factories and heavy industrial works, and dozens of apparently randomly assembled companies. For the ordinary man or woman, the obvious unfairness of such stunningly sudden riches was compounded by the grotesquely conspicuous consumption that the new rich enjoyed. Glorious hotel rooms, fine drink, the best cabarets in Europe, and above all, plentiful, cheap women or men were there for the taking for anyone with dollars, francs or pounds. Russian émigrés who had managed to hang on to a little gold or family jewelry after the revolution found themselves wealthy again. One could hire the Berlin Philharmonic for the night for a hundred dollars, or procure thirteen- or fourteen-year-old prostitutes for far less, as long as one had the patience to wait until these formerly middle-class children had finished school for the day. Anything not bolted down—and much that was—was at risk; desperate men and women stole window latches, doorknobs, decorations on public statues, roofing materials—literally whatever could be pried loose and sold. Above all, the winners included anyone who had loans in marks to repay—and there lay the roots of the deepest grievance the German people had with their government.

It is a truism that debtors love inflation for a good and simple reason: the money owed becomes cheaper and cheaper. After the war there was no greater or more vulnerable debtor than the German state, overburdened by obligations to its own people and to its conquerors. The racing inflation of 1922–1923 allowed the government to dodge the greater part of its war debt, paying back the millions of ordinary Germans who had bought war bonds in money that was worth ever less and ultimately nothing. Conservative judges, holdovers from the previous imperial regime, ratified the government's argument that any debts denominated in marks could be paid back in marks. The judges ignored the fact that because of the inflation the real economic value of the repaid sum—the goods and services it could buy—was a tiny fraction of the value of the original loan. To the economically illiterate judiciary, a mark was a mark, no matter how many zeroes had begun to appear on banknotes. Cheap credit also helped German businesses revive, after a fashion, especially those that could borrow cheaper and cheaper German marks to support exports or any other foreign-exchange-earning activities.[3]

But, as John Maynard Keynes pointed out, the cost of manipulating money in this way was far greater than any strictly financial gain that the state or big business could claim from such transactions. The essential result of the inflation was a society-transforming transfer of assets from vast numbers of Germans to a handful of adventurers, big businesses, and ultimately (in the form of debts eliminated) to the government itself. Such economic recovery as followed came, as he wrote, "at the cost of a ruinous disorganization, present and still to come. [Germany] has confiscated most of the means of livelihood of her educated middle class, the source of her intellectual strength; and the industrial chaos and unemployment [likely to occur] may disorder the minds of her working class, the source of her political stability. The money of bankers and servant girls, which would have been nearly enough to restore Europe if applied with prudence and wisdom, has been wasted and thrown away."[4]

As Keynes suggested, the worst hit were those who had trusted the idea of Germany the most. All those bourgeois, middle-class patriots who bought their war bonds almost to the very end saw their holdings—in many cases virtually the whole of a family's savings, backed by the faith and credit of the German government—turned into confetti. The bonds were paid as they came due in marks that were worth nothing. Civil servants, teachers and professors earned fixed salaries. To the stunned horror of that entire class, the inflation pauperized them, and the response of the state to their plight cost them whatever faith they had in the new republican government. One professor told the British consul in Frankfurt am Main, "As things are today, professors, teachers, and men of science are not given the right to live; many of them indeed will probably die in the coming winter for lack of food, clothing and warmth." In this observer's view, the inflation had already fundamentally transformed Germany. Now, he said, "there is no demand for brains; that is, today brains have no longer a marketable value." Presciently (as we can say now, with perfect hindsight), he added: "The result can only be a catastrophe for Germany and the downfall of civilization in Central Europe, if not, indeed, the whole world."[5]

The professor was correct about the cost in lives, though the worst sufferers came from the working class, Keynes's "source of political stability." With only their labor to sell, lacking even the limited cushion of saleable possessions or accumulated savings, this group fell fastest into real danger. The situation was worse than the worst months of the blockade during the war. The grim statistics are clearest for children, though all ages and especially the elderly suffered terribly. In 1923 in Berlin, almost one-quarter of all elementary school children were below normal in height and weight. In one poor neighborhood, reported cases of tuberculosis leaped sixfold; in another, schools reported a 1,000 percent increase in children suffering from rickets.

Suicides, starvation deaths, and all the ailments and mortal threats of poverty that had spiked in the last years of the war reasserted themselves. Erich Maria Remarque, who would become most famous for his 1928 novel of trench warfare, *All Quiet on the Western Front,* wrote an inflation novel, *The Black Obelisk,* in which he described the abyss of despair that swallowed up so many Germans. In his story, a new widow tells how her husband had placed their daughter's dowry in a five-year savings account. The bank refused to allow him an early withdrawal. When the term finally ended, the money was worthless and his daughter's fiancé broke off the engagement. The young woman would not stop weeping, and her father, blaming himself, committed suicide. From realistic fiction to real life: the acme of the tragedy, as the head of the health department told the Reichstag in February 1923, was that even when someone was "released from his suffering by death, the misery is not yet at an end . . . because the unreachably high costs of burial make it impossible . . . to fulfill even the duties of the most basic piety towards the dead."[6]

The images that survive from the depths of the hyperinflation express something of the almost intolerable combination of absurdity and desperation that shot through the inflationary period. The streets of Berlin routinely saw carts and wagons traveling from the bank to a workshop, hauling a single day's wages by the sack and bushel basket. (At the worst of the galloping price increases, some companies paid the workers twice a day, so that their employees could shop during lunch and beat the afternoon inflation.) Subtler, more insidious pictures also convey something of the madness. Notoriously, paper dealers gathered the notes printed each week to sell as scrap paper the following week.

Even when drowning one's sorrows, it was impossible to escape: during 1923, German vintners began to sell wine in bottles sporting thousand-mark bills as labels.

But for all the shock value of such images, no picture can convey what the hyperinflation did to the feelings and courage of the German people. The newspapers had a better grasp of the situation. In a typical essay, Friedrich Kroner captured the emotional cost of the time. The deadening, relentless advance of the inflation "pounds daily on the nerves: the insanity of numbers, the uncertain future today, and tomorrow becomes uncertain again." He described the lines of desperate shoppers racing to buy something, anything, before it disappeared or streaked out of range. "Rice 80,000 marks a pound yesterday, costs 160,000 marks today, and tomorrow, perhaps twice as much; the day after, the man behind the counter will shrug his shoulders, 'No more rice.'" It was almost possible to laugh, but it was black humor indeed. One shop poster read "Cheaper butter! Instead of 1,600,000 marks, just 1,400,000 marks." But for all the seeming irony, Kroner added, "This is no joke; this is reality written seriously with a pencil, hung in the shop window, and seriously read." Some people simply could not take the strain. In the queue at the dairy store, a clerk taunts a desperate customer, he wrote, "and then comes the umbrella handle, a response crashing through the glass cover on the cream cheese. And the cop standing watch outside pulls a sobbing woman from the store. And there is an uproar. And charges are filed."[7]

Kroner witnessed this in August 1923, near but not at the peak of the madness. In the week that began on November 16, prices reached the ultimate level. A postcard stamp cost 40,000 marks; it took 100,000 marks to make a phone call. The cost of a sack of coal almost reached 2 billion. Official estimates of the cost of living for a family of four for a month topped 15 *trillion* marks. Worst of all, there still seemed to be no end in sight. Early in November, the mark had crossed the trillion-to-one threshold against the dollar, and by November 20 it had climbed yet farther, reaching what turned out to be a magic number: 4.2 trillion marks to the dollar. At that level, there was no hope. Anyone bound to a fixed salary, all those who had run out of heirlooms to sell, would not survive the winter. Every sign pointed to complete collapse.

And then it ended, just like that. In August the stunningly unsuccessful chancellorship of Wilhelm Cuno had crumbled, and the moderately conservative Gustav Stresemann rose to the top almost by default. A wave of political crises in several of Germany's states—miniputsches by both left and right—occupied the new government through September and October, as did the persistent threat of a Kapp-like coup involving at least a part of the high command. Over the course of the autumn, however, Stresemann and his economic advisors had pushed through a measure to create a new official bank with the right to issue currency that could replace the nonsensical paper spinning off the Reichsbank's presses. On November 15, the new bank began to issue what were called rentenmarks, bills backed by what was called a mortgage on Germany's gold reserves. The new currency traded against the old at a rate of a trillion to one, miraculously restoring the old 1914 rate for the German currency. Nine zeroes simply evaporated, and suddenly one dollar bought 4.2 rentenmarks in a civilized, well-behaved transaction.

The entire thing was a fiction, of course. Germany's gold reserves were worth no more on November 21 than they had been the day before. But the new government made it stick, partly by shutting down the printing presses, in part by drastically tightening credit, and in part because everyone was exhausted. It took some time for the reforms to take full effect—there was, after all, an understandable lack of trust in any currency coming out of Berlin. But over the next several months it became clear that the new mark would hold.

THE VICTORY CAME far too late. The inflation completed what the Versailles Treaty and the legend of the stab in the back had begun. It provided the hard right in Germany with a cause, an enemy, and above all, a rich field of real grievance from which to harvest support. In particular, one Bavarian rabble-rouser seized on the moment to thrust himself and his National Socialist party onto the national scene. The hyperinflation was a gift to Adolf Hitler, the lever with which he believed he could move all Germany.

Hitler sought to trade on the obvious question. The inflation had been the ruin of so many—the uncounted many thousands who died of the complications of a diseased currency; the millions who had been simultaneously robbed of their property and stripped of their status as "the traditional backbone of the country"—as Stresemann, echoing Keynes, called the middle class. Devastation like this demanded explanation. Whose fault was the inflation? Who was responsible for it? A Swedish commentator, bemoaning Sweden's huge losses from German transactions, equivalent to six months of the national budget, put the matter in its simplest terms. Was the entire episode a "monstrous swindle carried out intentionally, or was it an avalanche which no one could stop?"[8] But the idea of an avalanche, a merely random catastrophe, was almost too cruel and too frightening to accept. If there were truly no clear chain of cause-and-effect that could account for such disasters, who could say that they would not come again? Better by far that there should be someone to blame. This meant, of course, that even before the end of the inflation, the hunt began for the guilty.

As always, there were the usual suspects. The state, specifically the new and unloved republic, had failed at crucial junctures throughout the inflation year. Even such ultimately sympathetic observers as Konrad Heiden, one of the first and most determined opponents of Nazism, wrote bitterly in his account of Hitler's rise that "the state wiped out property, livelihood, personality, squeezed and pared down the individual [and] destroyed his faith." The net result was obvious and disastrous. "Minds were ripe for the great destruction. The state broke the economic man, beginning with the weakest."[9] Other witnesses and modern economic historians have argued that the government may have been incompetent but in general was not overtly malicious. While it acquiesced to, and may even have encouraged, the relatively mild inflation of the immediate postwar years, hyperinflation overwhelmed the official capacity to cope just as it did that of so many ordinary folk.

Balanced judgments like these offered cold comfort. To many (and not just those on the right), it did not matter whether Germany's leaders were merely feckless or truly evil. For Hitler, the search for those to blame went much deeper. His list of the guilty began with the inept national state, but as a rhetorical flourish, among the first of the culprits he named were his listeners themselves. "The German people," he said, were "made up of children, for only a childish people would accept million-mark bills." It was a demagogue's trick and an effective one, for ultimately children must be blameless. The fault lies with the grown-ups who allow them to come to harm. Hitler's Germans were fools, but good fools, done in by specific individuals willing to take advantage of the witlessness of their patsies. It was clear enough who they were:

first, those who passively stood by—"the bookworms" who were, he said, the "enemies of action." But ultimately, they too were dupes, educated out of the traditional German strengths of "instinct and will" by the ultimate usual suspect, the Jew, who should "never have made his way into our nation."[10]

There was nothing new in any of this, to be sure. Hitler's rhetoric did not alter much across the 1920s, and neither did his basic constellation of villains: democrats, socialists and Jews. But the inflation made the paranoia of the *völkisch* right much more plausible, almost respectable. In the midst of the hyperinflationary period, an eastern Jewish immigrant neighborhood in Berlin was struck by a riot—a pogrom—inspired by charges that Jewish interests were promoting the disaster. The inflation, in fact, seemed to shatter what remained of any residual willingness to accept Germany's Jews as Germans of the Jewish faith. It became easier than ever before to blame the alien Jew for almost any perceived ill, no matter how tenuous or bizarre the link might be. Nudism, for example, became something of a fad in the '20s. The habit drew both the youth groups that emphasized a return to nature, and those influenced by the health claims for what the Germans called *Freikörperkultur,* free body culture. Photographs of German youth acting out myths in the buff or playing nude leapfrog in a meadow convey the bathetic innocence of the movement, while its leaders ponderously defended its chaste virtutes. Magnus Hirschfeld, the famous (and/or scandalous) director of Berlin's Institute for Sex Research, testified at the trial of a physical education teacher who conducted gym classes in the nude that "the exercises were an indication of Mr. Koch's high ethical sense, which was shared by the participants."[11]

But especially after the inflationary episode, such high-minded (and desire-deadening) worthiness could not obscure the deeper truth obvious to those convinced of the hidden conspiracy seeking to unhinge all things German. A rightist city council member in Berlin was not deceived by the assurances of Dr. Hirschfeld: "If we look at the cause of this movement, we see the puppetmaster lurking in the background. . . . Yes, it is not the German spirit which envelops our German people. The puppetmasters are always the Jews." To Councilman Kunze, any hint of German decay could have only one cause. It was "the result of the Jewish infection of our people. It is the product of a pigsty, a Jewish pigsty."[12]

The most striking note was not the deadly seriousness with which part of the Berlin city council viewed the essentially feckless nudist movement—no one era or governing body has a monopoly on legislatorial foolishness. It was the shift in language. Jews here are not simply the enemy. Instead they can now be seen to form a subhuman element within Germany, disease vectors, a herd of filth-encrusted swine. Hatefulness itself was hardly new; but after the inflation it became newly acceptable to utter such swill. If the Jew were to blame for the inflation, the ready logic went, then there could be no act of wanton destruction that this alien plague could not achieve. The inflation made respectable what had before lurked on the fringes of German society and politics. Before the inflation, Hitler's political base was confined to Bavaria. In the first national election after the crisis ended, gained two million votes.

Hitler himself played no direct role in that campaign. His use of the inflation crisis culminated in the farce of his Beer Hall Putsch. Hitler himself often spoke in beer halls, a traditional venue for Bavarian political meetings. By 1923, he had achieved local notoriety as a fantastically mesmerizing speaker. The writer Carl Zuckmayer attended several of his speeches that year, once getting so close to the platform that he could "see the spittle spraying from under his mustache." To Zuckmayer, he was "a howling dervish," but he wrote that for those who believed Hitler dominated "not by the arguments but by the fanaticism of his manner, the roaring and the screeching . . . and especially by the hypnotic power of his repetitions, delivered in a certain infectious rhythm." Hitler had come up with his style on his own, and "it had a frightening, primitive force."[13]

That undeniable power as an orator had already propelled him with remarkable swiftness through the ranks of Bavarian right-wing politics. In the postwar turmoil, he had taken a job in an army intelligence unit, which was charged with preventing the spread of suspect ideas in the ranks—socialist or democratic notions in particular. On September 12, 1919, he went to a meeting of a tiny organization he thought could be useful to him in that task. That night, the group, grandly named the German Workers' party, discussed the idea that Bavaria should secede from Germany, and Hitler was moved to speak, violently, against the suggestion. His eloquence impressed the party's leader, Anton Drexler, to the point that he invited Hitler to join the party with membership card number seven.

Hitler moved aggressively to seize power within the party, expanding its search for members and publicity, taking over all party propaganda by the beginning of 1920. In March he left his army job to work full time for the party, now renamed the Nationalsozialistische Deutsche Arbeiterpartei—the National Socialist Worker's party, the Nazis. One of his earliest close allies was crucial to him: Ernst Röhm, an army officer who founded the bullyboy squads that would mature into the Sturmabteilung—storm detachments—called SA for short. These were the Storm Troopers, or Brownshirts, and in the autumn of 1921, Hitler began to use them in the earliest instances of what became a standard tactic of intimidation and calculated violence. The goal was not simply to hurt individual opponents but to create a highly public spectacle of chaos beyond the reach of established authority.

Over the next two years, Hitler continued to build his regional base, attracting a core of supporters devoted to him personally. Rudolf Hess signed up, a stolid ex-army man who became his nearest aide, his secretary, and then his deputy. Hermann Göring joined in the fall of 1922 after hearing Hitler speak. Some of those who found their way to the inner circle were true believers (like Hess himself); others were thugs who enjoyed the license to brawl and fornicate under the cover of saving Germany. But whatever the individual motivations, the numbers under Hitler's command grew from the fifty-five or so whom he encountered at his first meeting to the five thousand SA troopers who demonstrated against the occupation of the Ruhr and the German government's response in January 1923. Initially, Hitler's attacks had little effect because there was popular support for the government's policy of passive resistance to the occupation. But in September, the new chancellor, Gustav Stresemann, married his triumph over hyperinflation with an end to that policy. Protest strikes in Berlin and the other major cities had accompanied work stoppages, slowdowns and general obstruction in the Ruhr itself, and were popular across the political spectrum. But they came at a huge cost to Germany and its government, both because of the loss of industrial output and because of the money needed to support the strikers. Stresemann recognized that Germany would never recover economically as long as it continued to hobble itself, and seeing that passive resistance had no effect on the French, he called off the campaign. He was right to do so: Germany's boom of the mid-1920s derived in part from his determination to get the country back to work.

But the decision was hugely unpopular, seen as one more example of the Weimar Republic leadership's lack of spine, their willingness to surrender to their enemies. In September, even before Stresemann announced the policy shift but after rumors of it had become public, Hitler spoke at a mass rally of right-wing groups at Nuremberg, denouncing the republic with General Ludendorff standing beside him. He could now count on at least fifteen thousand SA members, and the next step seemed obvious. He would use that force and the public's outrage over the Ruhr to complete the putsch Kapp had so ineptly attempted three years before.

To do so, he had to persuade or compel Bavaria's right-wing, pro-monarchist leadership to support him. The revolution was supposed to begin on November 8, 1923. A Bavarian state official, Gustav Kahr, was scheduled to speak that night at a rally in the Munich Bürgerbräukeller, a giant basement tavern that could accommodate as many as three thousand drinkers at once. Hitler surrounded the building with a detachment of some six hundred armed SA men and then stormed into the hall with a few followers, Göring among them. Inside, among the packed rows of raucous drinkers, he panicked, for a moment becoming tongue-tied. Still, he had sufficient presence of mind to play his trump card, announcing that the legendary Ludendorff stood with him. This was news to the general, who had not been informed of any plans for insurrection, and was furious when Hitler's driver finally brought him to the beer hall. He chose to go along with what seemed to be a done deal, however; and seeing the great general standing by the former corporal, the beer-hall crowd acquiesced to the apparent coup.

But that was as good as it got. Neither local Bavarian commanders nor the high command in Berlin would accept the pathetic strutting of some unknown Bavarian adventurer, with or without Ludendorff's support. The next morning, the rebels—now numbering about three thousand—attempted one last show of force. They marched into the center of the city, where they were met by a small group of armed policemen barring the way. The police opened fire, killing sixteen Nazis against a loss of three of their own. The man standing next to Hitler in the front row was killed in the first volley. Hitler himself dived to the pavement. Then, according to witnesses, he was among the first to run away, fleeing to a nearby car. He was found two days later, hiding in a wardrobe in a suburban house.

By the time he came to trial for treason in February 1924, Hitler had regained much of the confidence he lost when the bullets actually flew. The court was inclined in his favor in any event. As Gumbel had already documented, many charges of murder failed even to reach the courts, quashed by prosecutors linked to the right by bonds of class, political beliefs, or both.[14] Hitler and his coconspirators were in an even more than usually privileged position, for the key leaders of the Bavarian state were compromised by their temporary acquiescence in the putsch. Ludendorff himself was acquitted, two of Hitler's associates were convicted but set free, and Göring fled into what turned out to be an entirely unnecessary exile. Hitler himself used the trial as a bully pulpit to great national propaganda effect, thus giving a boost to what would become the stunning election results for the far right two months later. He was found guilty—but for leading an armed and deadly revolt he received a slap on the wrist. He avoided the deportation that was his due as an Austrian national, and was sentenced to five years in Landsberg prison. He served just over thirteen months, including his four-month pretrial detention.

Hitler spent that time in considerable comfort, working on a draft of his manifesto, *Mein Kampf.* But despite his sudden rise to national notice, the Beer Hall melodrama looked as if it were the high-water mark for the bombastic, if magnetic, former corporal. With the inflation ending only two weeks after his failed grab for power, the opportunity that crisis had offered him faded away. In the reckless follies that passed for democratic party politics over the next several years, his National Socialists and other nationalist parties on the right looked for opportunities to make inroads, but the opening for a single swift blow appeared to have vanished. They failed to consolidate their election gains, and at least at the surface, politics in general seemed to diminish in importance. With the reemergence of stability, however precarious, life in Germany took a turn for the ordinary, a quality of suddenly enormous value. The change in mood happened quickly, and manifested itself in the most prosaic of gestures. As the American composer and occasional Berliner George Antheil noticed, "People had their brass doorknobs out again, whereas in 1923 you couldn't find a brass doorknob in all Berlin: people would steal it in the night."[15]

As LIFE RETURNED to a simulation of normal, any tally of the lucky ones would have to include Einstein himself. He and his family had been little touched by the inflation or the attendant economic chaos. In part, as Born had noted before the worst began, Einstein was insulated by his position at the physics institute. He was also, all his life, an admirably cautious man with his money. His German savings and Elsa's more substantial fortune suffered the same fate as the rest of Germany's bourgeois fortunes: they largely vanished. But he had been earning foreign currency, hard cash, ever since the eclipse news had created a worldwide market for his lectures and articles. Sizable amounts of that money lay safely in uninflated accounts in Leyden and London, which meant that the Einstein household's standard of living did not suffer. And, being both lucky and clever, he and Elsa managed to avoid much of the chaos on the streets by the simple expedient of being elsewhere. His tour to the Orient had kept them out of Berlin from November 1922 to March 1923, the months in which the hyperinflationary spiral took off. In July it was off to Sweden to deliver the lecture required of Nobel Prize winners. The Berlin newspapers announced that Einstein first planned and then had actually made a trip to the Soviet Union in the early autumn, but that was an anti-Semitic fraud, a plant intended to tar Germany's most prominent Jew with the stain of the Jewish pathology, communism. In fact, he remained in Berlin, mostly without interruption, until early in November.

Sometime in the first days of that month, Einstein received warnings that he was once again a target. The presumed Russian trip, with Einstein allegedly receiving "an imposing welcome" at the hands of the Bolsheviks, brought letters that threatened him with Rathenau's fate.[16] The danger seemed real enough for him to send Planck a note on November 7 that he was leaving town, and that his friend should not come to dinner on the 9th. As the Beer Hall Putsch was unfolding, Einstein had already made it to Leyden, in the Netherlands, home of Lorentz, his scientific paterfamilias. Planck wrote to him there, urging him not to abandon Berlin permanently, and to resist any temptations the Dutch physics community might offer him. Planck need not have worried. Einstein remained in Holland only long enough to see whether the turmoil in Bavaria might spread, returning to Berlin after Hitler's power grab failed.[17]

The irony in this renewed attack on Einstein as a political symbol is that during the inflationary period, he had emerged as a defender of Germany. In 1922, he had been asked to join the new League of Nations' Committee on Intellectual Cooperation, but the invitation had come to him as an individual, not as a representative of Germany. He was concerned at the time about the consequences of joining a body created by and for Germany's conquerors, though after some negotiations, he agreed to bring his name and fame to the committee. But when the French and Belgians occupied the Ruhr, he loudly resigned. In language any proper German nationalist would have echoed, he stated that "the activities of the League of Nations had convinced me that there appeared to be no action, no matter how brutal, committed by the present power groups against which the League was willing to take a stand."[18] Einstein, while still proudly declaring himself to be both an internationalist and a pacifist, extended his protest even to private scientific meetings if his presence could be interpreted as giving aid and comfort to Germany's oppressors. He told Lorentz that he would not come to a Solvay Conference in Belgium because, he felt, "were I to take part in the Congress, I would, by implication, become an accomplice to an action which I strongly consider to be painfully unjust. This feeling becomes all the stronger when I think of the French and Belgians who have, of recent years, committed too many sins to continue to pose as the injured innocents."[19] He rejoined the League committee in 1924, only after the stabilization had taken hold and it had become clear that the occupation of the Ruhr was going to be made subject to an international process of negotiation.

But more generally, it is a measure of the emotional turmoil of the inflationary period that Einstein, never much of a joiner, found himself declaring his allegiance to a variety of causes and commitments. For one, thanks to the Nobel Prize committee, he finally became an official German, despite the fact that he had retained his Swiss citizenship and passport since his move to Berlin. The actual prize ceremony (as distinct from the prize lectures, which are delivered whenever the laureate can make it to Stockholm) occurred while he was still on his world tour. By tradition, when a laureate cannot attend the Nobel Prize ceremony, the award is handed over to the victorious scientist's ambassador to Sweden. Both the Swiss and the German envoys claimed the honor, but after the firm declaration from the Prussian Academy that Einstein was truly "a Reich German," the German ambassador took precedence. This came as news to Einstein, who had asked that the Nobel Prize medal and certificate be sent to him through the Swiss embassy in Berlin. When the controversy arose, the Academy sought to bolster the case for his Germanness. They found (or asserted—it is not clear which) that he had taken an oath as a state official as a member of the Academy. Since only citizens could serve in such offices, Einstein had to be as German as they come. When presented with this finding, he decided it would be easier to acquiesce than fight, provided that it was accepted on all sides that he also retained his Swiss citizenship. He seems to have been more amused than moved by this minor uproar. He noted that the officials doing the research had formed "the decided opinion" that he was German. Faced with such strong feelings, he wrote, and given the lack of any evidence to the contrary, he "had no objections to this view."[20]

With much more decisiveness (and possibly in response to his acquired German identity), Einstein took on another mantle. Early in 1924 he formally joined Berlin's Jewish community. He continued to be impatient with the ritual content of the religion and with many of the organizations that dominated Germany's Jewish life. But especially after his visit to Palestine, he felt that he could not avoid the public acknowledgment of the commitment implicit in "my activity in Jewish causes, and more generally, my Jewish nationality."[21] By the mid-1920s, that new consciousness had led him to see Judaism and Zionism together as the foundations of what he called a "moral homeland." This was probably the only kind of state to which he could feel truly committed, and he now believed that a conscious, organized Jewish minority could make such a homeland real. In another of the strange bonds forged in Germany in the 1920s, Einstein even found support from Nietzsche, so soon to become a darling of the more educated German fanatics. The philosopher of the superman had discovered, Einstein wrote, that "one of the peculiarities of the Jewish people consists of their knowing how to realize the 'subtle utilization of misfortune.'" Einstein's hope was that Jews would come to "know themselves less poorly and to become brave."[22] If his joining a religious community whose declared faith he did not share would help, he would do so proudly.

But the whole whirlwind—the travel, the prizes, the unintended comedy of German officials conscripting him for Germany's greater glory, the pride of the Jews in the fame of the most famous of their own—all this was a distraction. In the spring of 1924 he told Besso that he thanked God that "the multitude doesn't worry themselves too much about me any longer, so that my life has become calm and undisturbed."[23] Buoyed by that release, Einstein reported that life was in fact becoming truly pleasant. He and his family were all well. On his last visit to Switzerland, he'd had a satisfactory holiday with his sons. The Nobel Prize was a real satisfaction, as was the malicious pleasure he gained from turning over the prize money to Mileva, a transfer that, he piously hoped, would not prove fatal to her. Above all, it was a joy to him that he had at last returned to the problem of quanta, "without interruption" and, he believed, "truly on the right path." He continued to follow what was indeed a valid course through the summer and fall of 1924. The cataclysms to come remained unforeseen, unimaginable.

Chapter Eighteen

"A SINGULAR TENSION"

REVOLUTION, CATACLYSM, AND YET MORE CHAOS TO COME? EINSTEIN WAS hardly alone in the middle of 1924 in dreaming of precisely the opposite. After the relentless tumult of Berlin in the early 1920s, he and his city both seemed to have found a kind of equilibrium, a dearly valued moment in which to catch a collective breath. He returned to his physics and pronounced himself satisfied with his progress. Berlin's working world revived, imbued with the calm that comes from knowing that today's wages will buy the same amount of stuff tomorrow morning as tonight. The death threats he had faced in the previous winter faded into inconsequence. The government of the republic daily showed up for work at the center of Berlin free from fear of yet another coup. No one counted on anything yet, but increasingly it seemed as if daily life could be trusted to be reliably the same from one day to the next.

To be sure, throughout the chaos of the previous years the conventional forms of family life had managed to persist. As many did, even at the worst of times, Ilse Einstein met someone, a writer named Rudolph Kayser. In 1924, in the midst of the sudden calm that had overtaken Germany, the couple married. But for all the conventionality of such an act, there was an edge to this particular wedding. It was Ilse herself, after all, who had proclaimed that marriage was "a devilishly silly affair"[1]—and then there were the feelings of her mother and stepfather to consider. Elsa may have felt a kind of relief to see Ilse wed, for the same reason that Einstein could well have had mixed emotions. The memories of five years earlier were surely still vivid.

Of course, Einstein's love life had been fraught from the beginning, back to his relationship with Mileva that had briefly seemed all-in-all to him when he was twenty-one. Age and time may have brought with it certain complexities, but in essence his ideas about sex and marriage had changed little, especially after his liaison with Elsa evolved into a proper bourgeois ménage. When Ilse slipped away, Einstein hired a young woman named Betty Neumann to take over his stepdaughter's role as secretary to the Physics Institute. As he had with Ilse, Einstein conceived a passion for Neumann. The affair between them lasted several months, perhaps longer, in 1923 and 1924. It ended, apparently abruptly, when Einstein wrote to Neumann toward the end of 1924 that he had to "seek in the stars what was denied him here on earth."[2] The language is that of the old Einstein falling in and out of love, grandiloquent and a touch absurd. Beyond the image of a saddened Einstein peering heavenward to seek his heart's desire looms the shadow of Elsa's strong hand coming down, severing a liaison that threatened to leap the bounds of mere indiscretion. It could not have been easy for her to do this—Mileva had long ago learned that Einstein acted as he pleased—and Elsa's task would only grow harder across the 1920s.

Part of her problem was that Einstein had become a catch. Dmitri Marianoff was briefly married to Elsa's younger daughter, Margot, and from his vantage as a stepson-in-law, he composed an intimate portrait of Einstein. In it, he described a man beset by camp followers: "Along with fame comes that unavoidable appendage of all great men—women." Marianoff noted that the women pursuing Einstein had a problem that those chasing other famous men did not. With a great musician, a celebrated painter or a writer, most women could find something to speak about, inserting a reference to Monet into their chat with an artist, for example, or of Ravel's *Bolero* to a composer. "But with Einstein," he wrote, "they were at a loss how to cross the bridge to him, and in some confusion they would hesitate and falter, and finally in desperation would invariably end by saying 'Please, Professor Einstein, can you explain to me your theory?'" Einstein would sometimes respond to such questions seriously, taking slightly malicious pleasure in seeing how long it took for his suitors to give up. But even so, the assaults continued, and Elsa was forced to put up with a fairly constant provocation. "Many of them were beautiful, and nearly all of them wanted more from Einstein than was indicated in their very formal approach," Marianoff wrote, and Elsa and Einstein regularly conspired to humor the tigresses stalking their prey. When women sought audiences alone with him, Elsa would agree, smiling knowingly, and he would smile back, "because both of them understood the motive behind the request." Elsa was clearly the hero of the drama; Marianoff praised "her tact and delicate instinct." But he was careful to assert that she felt no real danger, for everyone in the household understood that Einstein's suitors were merely "the worthless emphases of fame."[3]

Antonina Vallentin, another literary family friend, also painted a picture of a couple completely satisfied with each other, unruffled by either fame or its side effects. Vallentin's Elsa comes across as a saintly acolyte to her majestic husband: "She was fully conscious of having been favored by destiny in being allowed to share Albert Einstein's life; but she did not draw any personal pride from the fact. . . . She had surrendered herself to him completely and had no other care but her children and her well-being." Einstein in his turn "deliberately gave himself a lot of trouble to make his family as happy as possible."

In both of these more or less authorized biographies, the writers described an idyllic family, one in which each partner contributed to their joint happiness and both knew their roles: his to be great and yet provide for her happiness, hers to serve. But even these highly sympathetic witnesses revealed some of the cracks in this veneer of domestic bliss. Vallentin wrote that Elsa "knew better than anyone else some of the great man's weaknesses and certain dark sides of his great qualities."[4] Strikingly, Vallentin characterized Elsa herself as someone who "had allowed herself to age prematurely, either through laziness or resignation, as though she had deliberately wanted to put an end to her life as a woman."[5] Marianoff, meanwhile, provided fairly sharp hints that Einstein had no desire to cease living as a man. He told of a conversation with him about "an incident that had been bothering Elsa to the extent of involving her health." Marianoff wrote that "it was a delicate matter, one that should have been sent into pure oblivion for all concerned."

On that occasion, Marianoff urged Einstein not to discuss the issue with Elsa again, and he agreed. But as soon as the two men met up with Elsa, Einstein burst out with the whole story, to her evident anguish. Marianoff was "stunned and speechless at this moment." The two men walked in the garden after dinner, and Marianoff asked Einstein why he had told Elsa something he knew would hurt her. Einstein did not answer immediately, walking on. Then, slowly, he said, "We do things but we do not know why we do them." And that, Marianoff said, was what truly troubled Einstein: "He was not embarrassed at what he had done, but he suffered much embarrassment because he could not fathom the cause of *why* he did it"[6] (emphasis in the original).

Why he spoke troubled him, that is, but not what lay behind the hurt in the first place. Despite hagiographic attempts to deny the obvious—Marianoff's assertion that there were "no dark fires in his blood," for one—Einstein followed the Neumann imbroglio with a series of affairs throughout his remaining years in Berlin. Several of those were documented in a memoir left by the Einstein's live-in maid, Herta Waldow, who told of an arrangement between Einstein and an Austrian-born actress named Margarethe Lebach that illuminates the delicate balancing act each member of the household undertook. In the early 1930s, Einstein and Lebach met each other regularly at Einstein's summer house in Caputh on an arm of Lake Havel, near Potsdam. On the days when Lebach was scheduled to arrive, Elsa would leave for the city early in the morning, carefully remaining out of the way until well into the evening. The whole thing was conducted openly, and Einstein and Lebach made a recognized couple within the holiday community.

Elsa demonstrated her capacity for patience along with her willingness to take second place, but her tolerance was not infinite. When public humiliation became too much to bear she would retreat into a frozen silence that would last until Einstein lashed out. Marianoff reported one incident when the two of them fought. As the couple walked into the room where Marianoff sat, Einstein "was aroused and roaring like a lion." Einstein enraged was a memorable figure. "Let me tell you," Marianoff wrote, "when Albert's voice was raised in anger, one heard it in every corner of the house."[7]

That is not the image of an icon of otherworldly wisdom and calm. Anyone could have heard, a neighbor or a friend knocking on their door, as Einstein bellowed at his wife. To Einstein the whole incident was absurd, for he had broken no real promise, explicit or implied. He had been faithful to neither wife. He had always enjoyed the company of women, and he clearly enjoyed having sex with them. Equally clearly, he saw no particular reason why his home and his sexual lives needed to coincide. Above all, he rejected almost viciously any attempt to judge or mold his behavior. He expected Elsa simply to live with it. As Vallentin put it, "She knew his subconscious [sic!] fear of all that might interfere with his need of absolute independence."[8] Elsa's children put it much more simply. Elsa once complained bitterly to Margot and Ilse about the loathed Austrian woman. Her daughters told her that she had a clear choice: either leave Einstein, or put up with the affair, for, as one of her daughters reminded her, Elsa had known what she was getting into when she married him.[9]

Lebach continued to visit. Elsa remained Frau Einstein. Einstein did as he pleased. And as ever, such revelations beg the question: excepting the pleasures of historical gossip, why should we care? Einstein the skirt chaser may be less lovable than Einstein the sexless wise man, but neither caricature captures the essential man. Ultimately, he was merely a conventional philanderer, one who, like countless others before and since, pursued affairs outside his marriages more or less as he pleased.

BERLIN, BY CONTRAST, was famous for its public sexual frenzy throughout those mythically wicked years. It was notoriously home to lust's carnival—the place to come for any variety of sensual pleasure. That reputation was exaggerated in the telling; the transformation of sexual mores that did take place was only one fragment of the ferment of these years, and affected only a vocal, visible minority. Still, the sense of license in sex and so much else lay at the heart of both the myth of the grand cabaret of Berlin and of the far more tangled facts of that fraught and potent time.

The boulevardier Count Harry Kessler was there; he seems to have been everywhere in Berlin throughout the 1920s, a man in constant motion, witness to all the city had to offer. In one typical week in 1926, he held two dinner parties and went to a new play by Carl Zuckmayer. (Kessler dismissed it as "ribald farce with political highlights and lots of sturdy sex stuff . . . no more than an entertaining brawl.")[10] He lunched with an English diplomat to discuss Germany's entrance into the League of Nations, and followed it up that evening at a revue featuring Josephine Baker, whose nude dancing made her the toast of a mildly shocked Berlin. One night, Kessler's guests included Albert and Elsa Einstein. Elsa spoke proudly of Einstein's honors and his habit of ignoring them. He had failed even to open the package containing the latest two until she had prompted him, she said—his long-delayed gold medals from Britain's Royal Society and the Royal Astronomical Society. Kessler set a cultivated, intellectual table, however, so the conversation soon shifted to the latest news of the discovery of an object orbiting the star Sirius. Einstein explained how the unseen "moon"—actually a companion star—was detected through the effect of its gravity on its visible twin, and how the newly identified double star might illuminate a portion of his own general theory of relativity. That night he was clearly the center of attention, and Kessler produced a vivid snapshot of his famous friend. Einstein was "sublimely dignified, despite his excessive modesty and his wearing laced boots with a dinner jacket. He has become a little stouter, but his eyes still sparkle with almost childlike radiance and twinkling mischief."[11]

Later that week, after another equally proper, equally dignified dinner party, Kessler got a phone call at 1:00 A.M. summoning him to a party at the home of the playwright Karl Volmöller. Josephine Baker had appeared, and the party was beginning to warm up. So Kessler drove to what he called Volmöller's harem and found his friends "surrounded by a half dozen naked girls." Baker too was unclothed, wearing only a pink muslin apron. She had made her first reputation dancing in Paris, but achieved true notoriety in Berlin, where her performances served as a symbol for all the possibility and danger of the age. Baker was black—exotic in itself—and she danced in the nude but for her famous banana skirt. Kessler judged her Negro Revue "a mixture of jungle and skyscraper elements" and the jazz that came with it "ultramodern and ultraprimitive." Good, wholesome German entertainments failed miserably in comparison, dangling, Kessler wrote, "like a limp bow string, lacking inner tension and therefore style, with far too much of a 'cozy parlor' origin about them."[12]

The scene at Volmöller's displayed a trifle less art and rather more of the Berlin of legend, the capital of forbidden pleasure. Kessler tried to argue to himself that there was nothing much of sex in the air. He described Baker's dancing in the most pristine of terms, praising her "brilliant artistic mimicry and purity of style." She performed as "their dancers must have danced for Solomon and Tutankhamen"—that safe veneer of ancient history. She was "a child, a happy child, at play . . . a bewitching creature, but almost completely unerotic." She left him cold, he said: "Watching her inspires as little sexual excitement as does the sight of a beautiful beast of prey."

Well, maybe. For all of Kessler's enthusiasm for the divine Miss Baker, the party that swirled around them was taking on a less elevated tone. The naked girls "lay or skipped about among the four or five men in dinner jackets," while Volmöller's cross-dressing mistress, a Miss Landshoff, "looking like a dazzlingly handsome boy, jazzed with Miss Baker to gramophone tunes." The men stood around, watching. Volmöller began to talk of his next project, a ballet, while Baker and Landshoff fell into each other's arms "like a rosy pair of lovers." The conversation continued, Kessler proposing a pantomime for Baker and Landshoff to perform on the theme of *The Song of Solomon,* with Baker as the Shulamite (dark, but comely), and Landshoff in and out of her dinner jacket, as Solomon or the lover. The night grew later still. The nude bodies of the girls punctuated the proper formal wear of the men, clothed and in command, vulnerable only at the moment they acknowledged their desire.

Kessler never did. He retained his observer's distance throughout the 1920s. He skewered Volmöller mercilessly ten days after the scene with Baker in a diary entry that could pass for judgment on a much broader slice of Berlin's art world. It was at another of the playwright's parties. Plenty of women were there, and as usual they were "in every state of undress . . . it was impossible to tell whether they were lovers, tarts or ladies." Baker was present but did not dance, and other promised notables failed to appear at all. It was, Kessler concluded "a cheerless, almost tragic atmosphere for a man like Volmöller, who really has talent, to steep himself in." Kessler panned Volmöller's latest work in language that seems to reach past one single play. Its content was shallow, he wrote, "and it is difficult to see why he chose it. Beneath its classical surface it is evilly lascivious and there is some confusion of thought, an effort to combine disparate elements."[13]

Kessler here seems to be stumbling around one of the fissures in the Berlin legend. Berlin during the mid-1920s notoriously became Europe's Sodom, a place where the entire range of sexual appetites could be fed. Its famous cabarets and revue theaters themselves sold what by the mid-'20s was dubbed *Girlkultur.* The ideal Girl was supposedly the model for a new German woman, independent and self-assured. In practice, celebrations of such impressive creatures turned out to be an opportunity to view the young female form in as near complete undress as promoters could get away with. *Girlkultur* reached its apex in the array of enormous revues, especially the Tiller Girls. The Tiller Girls, actually an English troupe, set the standard for the higher-class (or more bourgeois) productions, performing as a kick line and precision drill team in revealing but not actionable attire. The Tillers were supposed to be beyond sex, untouchable, and while more acute contemporary observers noted that the presentation of a mass of attractive, young, scantily clad women might have some erotic significance, the Girl revues were the sanitized version of sexual fantasy in Berlin.

The competition offered a much rawer product. The notorious Ballet Celly de Rheidt rose and fell early on, but it set the basic tone: women—girls as young as twelve—dancing nude to themes that included a misreading of the legend of St. Elizabeth of Hungary, in which a dancer posing as a nun stripped bare to embrace first a statue of the Virgin Mary (another dancer) and then a crucifix. Tickets in 1920 went for one hundred marks and even higher, but "women of the demi-monde," as police reports termed them, got in for a token charge.

A court case against the Ballet Celly generated the regulations that would govern public displays of nakedness throughout Weimar: static nudity was fine, but heaven and the local police protect society from a naked woman in motion. The effect, as the historian Peter Jelavich has pointed out, was that the women standing passively, stock-still—the most vulnerable, the most readily available to the stranger's gaze—were those who could be seen completely naked. Those in motion were required by law to have a minimal costume that emphasized only their breasts and groins, precisely those body parts that most occupied the concerns of the police. Naturally, nude and near-nude cabarets packed them in.

The reaction by the police to the profusion of such performances provides a good stand-in for what the shows conveyed to the broader audience. Their reports reveal a weird stew of frustrated desire and an almost dismembering conception of the whole idea of sex, evident in the curious style of the police descriptions of the more arousing displays. Reporting on a dance by Anita Berber, one of the few performers who genuinely trod the boundary line between modern dance and nudie shows, one officer wrote, "The sexual parts, around which the pubic hairs seem to have been shaved off, are clearly visible and are so imperfectly covered by the band between the thighs that the labia bulge out to the left and right of the band. The posterior is uncovered."[14] *Are* clearly visible, *is* uncovered—the vice squad does not look, it is shown, and helpless, it succumbs to the lure of bulging labia or a naughty bum. Whatever the performer may have intended (and Berber, classically trained as a ballerina, could claim that her work was art), the message received was of sex abstracted and depersonified.

Which is precisely what drew many to Berlin's night world. Christopher Isherwood, one of the most important literary sources in the English-speaking world for the image of decadent Berlin, made his own interest in the city perfectly clear, though circumspectly and safely long after the fact. In his semiautobiographical novel *Down There on a Visit,* Isherwood's narrator, also Christopher, asks an older friend if Berlin were really so bad. His advisor replies, "Christopher, in the whole of the *Thousand and One Nights,* in the most shameless rituals of the Tantras, in the carvings of the Black Pagoda, in the Japanese brothel pictures, in the vilest perversions of the Oriental mind, you couldn't find anything more nauseating than what goes on there, quite openly, every day." Worse yet, such degeneracy had become absolutely commonplace, too ordinary to notice. "Those people don't even realize how low they have sunk," Christopher's guide warns him, playing Virgil to Isherwood's Dante about to enter the inferno. "Evil doesn't know itself there." Christopher, he said, was lucky, safe from even imagining the depravities that had become so routine in Europe's most wicked city. The younger man's response was immediate, predictable, and private: "Then and there I made a decision—one that was to have a very important effect on the rest of my life. I decided that, no matter how, I would get to Berlin just as soon as ever I could and that I would stay there for a long, long time."[15]

As he did, ultimately to compile a portrait of what the city offered someone moved chiefly by desire. Isherwood's own choice ran to men, but his experience and that of his contemporaries and friends captures the general atmosphere of Berlin in its guise as a pleasure palace. One of the first things to be noticed was how orderly a den of iniquity it was. For his friend, the poet W. H. Auden, Berlin was simply "a bugger's daydream." But the dream was properly organized, with the appropriate statistics on hand for easy reference. In a letter to a friend, Auden wrote with apparent approval, "There are 170 male brothels under police control"—a convenient system indeed. Auden ignored the implications of such official interest, and his letter veered immediately to his own triumphs: "I could say a lot of my boy, a cross between a rugger hearty and Josephine Baker."[16] Baker, popping up here as she seems to in every recollection of Weimar Berlin, emphasizes the heart of the issue. Berlin at night trafficked in the emblems of sex, in the idea of gratified desire—gay, straight or whatever. Baker was simply a convenient symbol, banana skirt and all, of Berlin's ability to produce the commodity that could fulfill whatever needs might present themselves.

All this sexual athleticism could be tiring, of course. Kessler complained of melancholy fatigue at the end of his evenings at Volmöller's. Isherwood fled the purely commercial experience of Berlin's West End sexual bazaar, retreating to a working-class neighborhood where his night life could continue unchecked, but among people he liked much more. For most, though, sex was simply there, merely a commodity, ultimately corrosively accessible. Walter Benjamin caught the boredom inherent in Berlin's sexual fantasy in a critique of the Girl revues. "Ever since it undressed the female form to the point of total nudity," he sniffed, "its only available mode of variation was quantity." Another observer took the ubiquity of sexual promise in Berlin personally, writing that it "destroyed for many of us younger men all the illusions about sex that some people retain throughout their whole lives."[17]

MORE BROADLY, for all of its wild parties, liberating or silly theatrical displays, even its broken illusions, the city's partly mythical sexual free-for-all was merely one small piece of the extraordinary hothouse that was Berlin between 1924 and 1929. The period from the end of the hyperinflation to the great crash marked what came to be known as Weimar's golden years—and certainly, in economic terms, it was the only stable period the republic experienced. The taming of the inflationary maelstrom allowed German industrial and commercial life to gain breathing space in which to revive; and that boost was followed in 1924 by the Dawes plan, created under pressure from the American government, which reduced Germany's annual "war guilt" payments to the Allies. With the new plan came loans from its former enemies. An extraordinary borrowing spree followed, with Germany receiving more than 30 billion marks in foreign loans between 1924 and the crash of 1929. Most of the loans originated in America, and most were short-term debts—an extraordinary and risky concentration of financial dependence.

In the mid-1920s, however, that seemingly bottomless well of cash funded both the German economy and Berlin's astonishing cultural explosion. Even so, despite its radically improved international and economic situation from 1924 forward, those within Germany who had opposed the republic from the start conceded it no virtues, and too many of its putative friends made sure that every failing was clearly documented. The right took everything from sex to strange new forms of painting, from cabaret jokes to the twisted sounds some Berliners seemed to relish as music, as yet more evidence of the moral madness of the new. At the same time, many of those creating this new art put forward their own critiques, attacking Weimar for its bourgeois complacency, its crassness, its ordinariness.

Almost any issue could start another battle over Germany's aesthetic and moral soul. For example, closely tied to the perception of Berlin as Sodom was the German public's fascination with the theme of *Lustmord,* sexual murder. Whole genres emerged, potboiler novels, cheap films, true-crime tales, to celebrate the horror and the seductive terror evoked by the collision between sex and violent death. Most famously, there was the true-crime case of Peter Kürten. Kürten was ordinary-looking, a married man, conventional, heterosexual—one of us, not one of them. After his arrest in 1931, he confessed to the murder of thirty-five victims, mostly women and children in Dusseldorf. His tale would inspire Fritz Lang's classic noir film *M.*[18] Kürten was deliberate in his crimes, a man who delighted in the terror he brought to his city. He followed Jack the Ripper (and anticipated celebrity-killers since) in the letters he sent to the press describing burial locations and hinting of crimes to come. In custody, Kürten himself emphasized the ties that bound him to the allegedly wholesome world beyond, lauding the scandal rags for creating "the man who stands before you today."[19] By implication: You helped me. You who wallowed in the terror of my killing spree were complicit in it. You gained by it and you share the credit.

There was an uncomfortable amount of truth in Kürten's charge. *Lustmord* supplied the sensational press with an inexhaustible source of material.[20] But while the old tale of the beauty murdered by the beast was always an easy sell, the theme of the sexual murder, of the violence at the heart of relations between individuals within society, also yielded striking, shocking, deeply troubling art. Otto Dix was consumed with images of murdered women. After the war, Dix, a combat veteran, produced an unsettling number of paintings that showed an intimate, almost obsessive knowledge of the damage a human body could sustain. Several of those works actually shared the title *Lustmord.* In an early version, he painted himself as the murderer, dressed in a garish suit, grinning hugely, swinging a severed leg while the other body parts fly around the death chamber. Later images remove the killer, leaving only the corpse. *Lustmord* from 1922 shows a partly dressed prostitute in a narrow room, stabbed in the belly and the throat, so freshly slaughtered that the blood still runs from the gash in her neck to a puddle on the floor. A work from the same year with the same title pushes the violence yet further: a naked woman lies on a bed, stabbed again and again, with blood trailing from her mouth, her side, her splayed legs. In the foreground a pair of dogs mate—a concession to the title of the cycle of etchings: *Death and Resurrection.*

Deliberately grotesque—but Dix claimed more than shock value. While he painted his women as victims, he also left hints of their complicity in their own deaths. Overtly sexual, draped over their beds, they lay brazenly in positions of physical welcome. The growing sexual autonomy of women in Germany in the 1920s clearly terrified some, perhaps many, men, Dix possibly among them. His paintings of living women tend toward the fleshy, with oversized, jutting breasts, nipples aimed like cannon at men overwhelmed by the force of the female body. His female corpses retain some of that menace amid their powerlessness, their literal loss of humanity. Given the artistic force of this almost pornographically rendered brutality, Dix can be seen as an aestheticized version of the monstrous Kürten, murdering those who needed killing, the loose woman ready to trap any man, all men.

But for all Dix's fascination and terror with the female body, his

Lustmord pictures were neither simply the record of a sublimated killing spree nor a bloody critique of sexual freedom. His *Two Victims of Capitalism* provides counterpoint. A soldier, his face disfigured by an open wound, stares over the shoulder of an aging prostitute. She is emaciated, grimacing, with syphilitic lesions visible on her face. She exudes menace—obviously diseased, a human plague rat. But she is wasting away, as clearly ruined as the soldier beside her; both are hungry, each suffering within a system that will soon kill them both. Her living death colors the images of Dix's murdered women. Their bodies—their weapons—may have so threatened and overawed their killers as to evoke a murderous rage. Dix's paintings chronicle violence; they wallow in it; and they play on the pity, horror and love of sensation that made *Lustmord* such a potent theme in Weimar Germany. But his images also depict the desperation, the loss and poverty that led his victims to their deaths.

George Grosz agreed, pushing the argument further still. He was less completely absorbed than Dix was in the actual depiction of murder, though he did execute several works that portrayed sex crimes. But his most pointed commentary came in his depiction of Berlin's war of all against all. In these drawings and paintings, older men, wealthy and assured of their power, confront women in some stage of undress. In most, Grosz suggests that power is slipping to the woman—a turnabout the man seems not to notice—as she calculates how best to use her body to deal with her client. In perhaps the most powerful of these images, the painting *Circe,* a beautiful young woman, dressed only in high heels, red garters, and a red flapper's hat, leans across a café table to kiss the pig's snout that emerges from the body of an expensively dressed rich man. "Men are swine," Grosz wrote to a friend, all animal lust and hunger for power. But here it is the woman who acts, who moves, whose tongue stretches to initiate the kiss—and Circe, after all, was the goddess who turned Odysseus's men into pigs.

There is more hope than fact in this image. Grosz wanted to believe that the swinish icon of a rich German man could be so readily brought low. As Kessler wrote after an afternoon at Grosz's studio, "The devotion of his art [is] exclusively to the depiction of the repulsiveness of bourgeois philistinism."[21] Grosz himself could hardly object to the excesses of Berlin's night life, to drinking parties that could last till dawn, to the idea of sex between any willing parties. His own wedding would have been enough to deny him any right to moralize. The "ceremony" occurred at the height of Grosz's Dada period. To create the right atmosphere, he printed up a handbill soliciting "well-built society girls with film talents" to come to a party at "studio Grosz." A surprising number actually showed up—over fifty, in one account—and one of Grosz's artist friends had located a healthy quantity of wine. Between the women and the booze, the result was what one of Grosz's friends bluntly called an orgy. The women stripped, but not the men, as usual. The night wore on into morning, and one guest woke up two days later in the bathtub to discover his clothes had been stolen.[22]

But for Grosz that was just good clean fun—and after all, the girls showed up on their own, willing enough to play. What outraged him was the transformation of sex into a commodity to be traded in a buyer's market. When the German bourgeois lamented the depths to which Berlin had fallen, all the while reaching for his teenage prostitute—that was the real moral crime. Critics on the right saw sexual license as a pathology of infection that produced sexual murderers. Surely good Germans could not behave so, not unless they had been infected by something not German at all—perhaps the very "degenerate" art that emerged to document and interpret the new sexual life of Berlin. That art in its turn declared that sex crimes—the venal sins of exploitation, the mortal ones of violence—derived ultimately not from an alien parasite but from corruption within. The mythical good German, confronted with desire and need, was revealed to be a pig, the beast in Everyman capable of almost any act.

MOST OF GROSZ'S COLLEAGUES did not follow him that far, though many agreed with his basic portrait of the German philistine. By the mid-1920s, after the exhausting roller coaster of revolution, civil war, economic collapse and continuous political upheaval, the emphasis for many artists shifted. Weimar Berlin remained the center of the avant-garde, not just in Germany but for Europe as a whole. The former enemies of the establishment were the new elite. Perhaps in consequence, by mid decade many of them, including Grosz, Dix and Beckmann, pursued a new artistic movement called Neue Sachlichkeit—the New Objectivity—that deemphasized polemics, the use of art as an explicit political tool.[23] It was a stance that stressed description: an attempt to paint what was really there in the world, as opposed to the overtly political edge of the Expressionists' attempt to convey the inner meanings of the scenes within their work. Despite the radical modernity of some of its most famous practitioners, the movement was in some sense a return to older artistic ideas. It emphasized painterly skill, nineteenth-century techniques of rendering realistic images, and a coolness of approach intended to let the subject speak for itself, undistorted by the artists' ego. The results included works of great elegance and beauty, but the shift from Expressionist confrontation to Objective description could also be seen as a retreat from the idea that art could change the world beyond art. The critic Siegfried Kracauer argued that "New Objectivity marks a state of paralysis. Cynicism, resignation, disillusionment: these tendencies point to a mentality disinclined to commit itself in any direction."[24]

But even if the political agenda was muted, or expressed in code, the works that emerged across the middle years of the Weimar Republic remain an astounding accomplishment, at once one of the truly remarkable outpourings of human expression in the twentieth century, and an enduring, terribly sad monument to what might have been, what Weimar had to offer itself and the world. Perhaps the landmark of the age of objectivity was Thomas Mann's masterpiece, *The Magic Mountain,* published in 1924. The book was enormous, its bulk filled out with the detailed representation of a world inhabited by a young man with tuberculosis who is confined to a sanitarium for seven years. Mann's ambition, of course, extended far beyond mere documentation. The novel is a portrait of Europe, especially prewar Europe, captured in the fevered environment of a sanitarium. The book culminates in a muted defense of Weimar, with its hero choosing life against the tyranny and romantic seductiveness of death. Mann had long since lost the bloodlust with which he welcomed the outbreak of war in 1914. By now, he had had enough of Germany's destructive impulses, and in his hands, objectivity produced the claim that for all the lovely drama of death, love and freedom have far greater value.

Mann's triumph with *The Magic Mountain* was not his alone. The book's publication served as evidence that Berlin had revived to become dominant as a cultural center. During the Weimar period, the city held the same lure for German speakers that Paris in the '20s dangled before Americans: it was the indispensable center of the imagination. Willy Haas, an editor and critic, found the exhilaration available to those who felt that they could and would produce in Berlin almost any invention (including self-invention). He loved it all: "the quick-witted reply of the Berlin woman," but also "the keen clear reaction of the Berlin audience . . . that taking-nothing-solemnly yet taking-seriously of things." The energy overwhelmed him. Haas celebrated "the indescribable dynamic, the love for work, the enterprise, the readiness to take hard blows and to go on living."[25]

Berlin became home to Bertolt Brecht, for example, who moved there from Munich in 1924 to try to make it at the center of Germany's theater world. His greatest hit, the *Threepenny Opera,* premiered in 1928. Again, like works that were more explicitly part of the New Objectivity movement, the play was attacked as a retreat—"a delight, more than a platform," as one critic complained.[26] But the show was a success precisely because of its ability to convey what Brecht saw. Its emotionally powerful package was "a breakthrough," as one of Brecht's partisans put it, "because morality is neither attacked nor negated, but simply suspended." It was funny too, a window into "a world where the line between tragedy and humor has vanished"—a world more like the real one than that of the convention-bound stage.[27]

But even with the rise of "objectivity," radical ideas flourished in Berlin throughout the mid-1920s. For example, while the city never became Sigmund Freud's base, by that point it had become the vital center of Freudian thinking. Karl Abraham had founded the Berlin Psychoanalytic Society in 1908, a grand name for a group with just five members. In the '20s, the society became the center of the most vigorous band of Freudians working anywhere in the world, even gaining members from Vienna, the analysts' Ur. It spawned an institute that developed the basic form of Freudian psychoanalytic training, including the principle that all would-be psychiatrists must undergo analysis themselves. The training program made Freudianism a worldwide phenomenon, attracting an international group of students who then brought the gospel according to Freud to Paris, London, New York and beyond.[28]

Freud's theories were controversial, of course. With his extraordinary claims for the power of sexual feeling, early childhood events and parental actions to dominate human emotions and behavior, Freud threatened passionately held notions of human nature. In the popular press, it was easy to see Freud as yet one more of those famous Jews out to challenge eternal verities, just like Berlin's own Albert Einstein. Freud relished the comparison. He told his son that "Jews all over the world boast of my name, pairing me with Einstein."[29] He was bragging a little, shining in the reflected light of Einstein's outsized reputation. But in popular culture, the claim was close to true, for the two men were often paired. They met in 1926 and formed a kind of friendship, mostly through a sporadic exchange of letters. Freud did feel an emotion, rare for him, in the relationship: hero worship, a kind of awe. He appeared to envy Einstein, calling him a "happy one," only to be checked, sharply. Einstein wrote back, "You, who have got into the skin of so many people, and indeed of humanity, have had no opportunity to get into mine"—nor ever would, as he said privately.[30]

Beyond this defense of his own privacy, Einstein remained as skeptical of psychoanalysis itself as he had been before the war when he met Freud's onetime disciple Jung in Zurich. Although he seems to have felt Freud had developed a genuinely important approach, the detailed architecture of his theories left him cold. On Freud's seventy-fifth birthday he wrote in his congratulatory note that he had been reading his works with a lady companion, and that he greatly enjoyed their "beauty and clarity," to which, he added, none but the great Schopenhauer could compare. But significantly, he twice refused to support Freud for a Nobel Prize in medicine. He could not, he said, convince himself of "the extent of truth in Freud's teachings." Much later, with his usual gift for double-edged compliments, Einstein told a friend that Freud had "a sharp vision; no illusion lulled him asleep except for an often exaggerated faith in his own ideas."[31]

Nonetheless, in Berlin itself, those ideas carried great force in their depiction of an unsuspected cause and cure for human misery. Works like G. W. Pabst's film *Secrets of a Soul,* released in 1926, told the public the news: there had been a breakthrough in the science of the mind that offered new hope to those in despair. The film's story was a complicated interweaving of its main character's crisis and his treatment, in what was seen almost as a documentary chronicling of the process of analysis. The film had the obligatory happy ending; the patient receives a sudden shock when he finally recognizes the nature of the subconscious forces that have been tormenting him, and at that moment is released from their power. But this simple-minded finale only strengthened the Freudian myth. There is a hidden country within the mind, such works proclaimed, unmapped continents of terrors and forgotten truths. Now, thanks to Freud (or so the popular version went), we can find our way there and home again.[32]

And for all its extraordinary influence, Freud's burgeoning empire was just one example of the torrent of creativity in postinflation Weimar Germany and its capital, Berlin. There was the eruption of Bauhaus-inspired architecture; the striking innovations of German design that produced everything from the now ubiquitous tubular metal chair to the stark, abstract lines that characterized the best Weimar interior design; a radical new photographic aesthetic, influenced (as was much else in Weimar culture) by work and ideas from Soviet Russia; continuing innovations in painting that ranged all over the map, from newly objective portraiture to the development of highly formalized abstraction; earnest, dedicated productions of workers' theater, alongside experiments that ranged from movable stages placed in elliptical theaters to the shocking innovation of theatrical lights visible to the audiences; all this and much, much more.[33] No cultural icons, no old warhorses of culture or belief were safe—and the result, predictably, was a continuous battle fought between partisans of the new and defenders of the old.

The sound of critical jousts rang across all the arts, but perhaps nowhere so violently as within the world of music. For most musical Berliners, even in the 1920s, "real music" meant the classics, especially the German giants who had dominated European composition in the nineteenth century. Yehudi Menuhin was a child prodigy during the Weimar years, making his Berlin debut at the age of thirteen. As he remembered it, Weimar Berlin "was still a bastion of the traditional world . . . Beethoven and Brahms were gods. Furtwängler and Walter were their vicars on earth."[34] But alongside them came men who organized themselves around the banner of New Music. Arnold Schönberg and his rival Igor Stravinsky were the unquestioned leaders of the international new music movement, and they brought in their train a generation of younger composers. Schönberg was one of the pioneers of atonal music, breaking with the traditions of harmony that had dominated Western music for centuries. In the early 1920s he went further, inventing the idea of the tone row, or twelve-tone music, just before his move to Berlin from Vienna in 1925. Twelve-tone compositions were built up from a series using all twelve notes of the chromatic scale, placed in any order the composer chose, which could then be manipulated to create a wide range of musical effects. The results could be astonishing, difficult, and uncompromisingly complex both on the page and to the ear. For Schönberg, the great virtue of his new style was the control it gave him—he loved the "unifying effect" of his tone rows. And if his audiences reacted with confusion or worse, that was their problem; as he wrote, grandly, "The laws of nature manifested in a man of genius are but the laws of the man of the future."[35]

There were those who violently disagreed. Thomas Mann spoke for many when he cast Schönberg's invention as devil-inspired in his novel *Doctor Faustus.* In the blunt exchanges within Berlin's musical world in the '20s a charge like this did not seem all that extreme—many endured worse. Schönberg's student Alban Berg premiered his opera *Wozzeck* in Berlin in 1925. The opera derived from Georg Buchner's play "Woyzeck" in which a private soldier is brutalized by his life in the army, tortured by his superiors, his doctor, his peers, and his mistress—a plot that was a distant echo of Berg's own military experience. He was a sickly man, a near invalid whose wartime service had alternated between the merely insanely boring and the genuinely dehumanizing. *Wozzeck* had a troubled birth—Schönberg warned Berg that the play was too rich emotionally to make good music, but the younger man persisted, completing the work by 1920. No one cared. Berg self-published and distributed copies of the score as widely as he could, to no effect. Finally, in 1924, one of Berlin's youngest and most daring conductors, Erich Kleiber, learned of the project, promised a performance by the prestigious State Opera, and after some delays, managed to deliver. The public finally got to hear the work on December 14, 1925—and the result was mayhem. Eyewitnesses reported that catcalls and boos threatened to drown out the music, defenders rose to quell the noise, and the two sides actually began to brawl. By the end of the performance, when Berg took his curtain call, "the riots increased, the bravos and boos, the wave of enthusiastic excitement and outraged hostility."[36] Music mattered. Berliners truly cared about what they heard.

What drove such passions was the belief that such new forms of expression took part in a battle for the soul of Berlin, of Germany. To its defenders, Berg's opera was a work of "strange perfection and uniqueness," and the composer himself displayed "evidence of genius."[37] Those on the other side of what Schönberg accurately termed the barricades put it very differently. Harsh sounds, strange sights, the assault on harmony, seemingly on beauty itself—all of this could be taken as an anarchist's bomb, yet one more assault on fundamental human values. One critic spat that *Wozzeck* was "a deliberate swindle. Fragments, rags, sobs, belches. Tormenting, ugly-sounding cackle." In response, Berg sought to defuse the most extravagant rhetoric on both sides, declaring that with *Wozzeck* "I simply wanted to compose good music."[38] Soft words did not turn away wrath. He found himself pilloried with language like that used to condemn mass murderers and the troublesome, culturally dangerous Jews (like his mentor, Schönberg). He was "a fountain poisoner of German music . . . a musical mountebank, a composer dangerous to the public welfare."[39]

This was heavy artillery indeed, even in the middle of what was becoming a true culture war. That something so apparently innocuous as an opera could be seen not merely as bad but as evil itself, suggests just how fragile Weimar's golden age actually was. The true believers saw only the excitement of the new, the fact that virtually every day something appeared that stimulated minds and emotions: a play, a picture, a poem in a new magazine, art that brought the unconscious to the light of a new day or that captured real life, music that shocked the ear—it did not matter what, for it was the overall effect that set the tone. The playwright Carl Zuckmayer, a true defender of the republic, expressed the general belief and the passionate hope: "Berlin tasted of the future, and that is why we gladly took the crap and the coldness."[40]

Chapter Nineteen

"I, AT ANY RATE, AM CONVINCED"

FROM THIS DISTANCE, THE BRAVE AND HOPEFUL ERUPTIONS OF WEIMAR'S artists are colored by the terrible vengeance that would be wrought against them. The nationalist poet Gottfried Benn stated the case against Weimar's avant-garde in plain language, couched as an ambiguous compliment. It was the Jews who were responsible, he said. Berlin's triumphs in art, science and business, he wrote, "stemmed for the most part from the talents of this sector of the population, its international connections, its sensitive restlessness and above all its absolute instinct for quality."[1] They had good taste, Benn reckoned, but they were restless—the wandering Jews—and excessively cosmopolitan. That was no isolated remark; even at the height of Weimar's creative explosion, to be Jewish was to be automatically suspect, always potentially the traitor. In this light, Berlin's art, the great achievements of Weimar, were too often the work of the kind of individuals who could poison the public well.

Benn's comments, insinuating, veiled threats, were indicative of a broader campaign. What went unnoticed by too many of those under attack was that garden-variety anti-Semitism, the sort that had flourished in Germany for fifty years, could provide cover for something much more pernicious. Hammer home a familiar notion of the Jews as both alien and evil, then paint the republic itself as a Trojan horse for treacherous Zion—and the outcome became a direct assault on the always shaky foundations of German democracy.

Compounding the danger was the weakness of democracy's defenders. One of the great tragedies of Weimar was that too many of those who flourished there valued the republic so little. Einstein himself was one of the honorable exceptions. Weimar's cultural ambitions did not move him much. He had little patience for modern music. Given that he felt that even Brahms had gone too far, there was little chance he would warm to the clash and bang of twentieth-century compositions. He showed no passion for Expressionist forms when he viewed Mendelsohn's Einstein Tower. He decorated his office with portrait prints of his scientist heroes—Faraday and Newton—which suggests how little modern artistic expression interested him. Kessler captured Einstein accurately in that description of a typical, bourgeois dinner party at the physicist's home, an evening saved from deadly ordinariness only by the "emanation of goodness and simplicity" of his hosts. Einstein, however radical he could be in science, politics and dress, was a surpassingly conventional man when it suited him.

Nonetheless, whatever he may have thought about Berlin's greatest extravagances during the 1920s, he did his part to defend the system that made Weimar's golden age possible. He had gone to Paris when Rathenau told him to. He served on a League of Nations committee, and had made a public stand to seek equal, fair treatment for Germans within international cultural institutions. He spoke out against the French and Belgian occupation of the Ruhr. From his early postwar journeys through to the end of the 1920s, he served as an informal cultural ambassador for the republic whenever he traveled beyond Germany's borders. Once, on failing to recruit Max Planck for one of his causes, he complained, "It is a difficult job to contribute in some way to the life of human beings in the world."[2] But he continued to try. He had done so from the earliest days of the formation of the republic, when he told students in Berlin that they owed real loyalty to the new form of German government: "Our common goal is democracy, the rule of the people," adding that "all true democrats must stand guard" to defend democracy equally "against tyrannies of the left and the right."[3]

This was what too many of Weimar's brightest lights would not do. Hermann Hesse, for example, complained that these times were shorn of value—"everything has died that was good and unique in us."[4] In response to this perceived crisis of meaning, Hesse seemed to argue in works like his 1927 novel *Steppenwolf* that randomly applied cruelty was a perfectly sound reaction, a paean to the irrational that could have come as naturally from the far right as from a clearly talented writer on the left side of the fight. George Grosz understood the basic dialectic: "My friends and I believed in a future of progress as if there were some preconceived international agreement on that score."[5] That meant he could deride the present state of Weimar at will. He had, he wrote, no faith in its promises, and its leaders inspired him still less. "Ebert, the former saddlemaker now president of the Republic, was occupied with having his mustache cut just so, so that he could look like the executive of a large corporation."[6] The brilliant satirist Kurt Tucholsky, genuinely and courageously determined to fight the right wing, still damned Weimar's democratic defenders time and again. His descriptions of the November revolutionaries who founded the republic were almost as scathing as anything Hitler wrote. Ebert was anathema to him too—"a functionary of mediocre talents . . . a mediocre bourgeois, the worst mixture that one can imagine: personally incorruptible and professionally dirty." For himself, Tucholsky wrote, he "belonged to those people who believe that the German spirit is poisoned almost beyond recovery, who do not believe in an improvement, who regard German democracy as a facade and a lie, and who, despite all assurances and optimistic touches, believe that an empty steel helmet is not as dangerous as a silk hat."[7]

With friends like these! Those in Germany who did the banal, bourgeois work of democratic civic life needed whatever support they could get. Those of the fashionable left in Berlin gave far less than they could have. When they did speak, too often it was to ridicule the ambitions of the Weimar state, that captive of bourgeois convention. Their scorn did not bring Weimar down—far from it. The republic faced bitter opposition from the start, and it was finally destroyed by the brutalities of the right. Even if every member of the cultural avant-garde had stood on the barricades in defense of the modest republican goals of a stable, bourgeois democracy, it is unlikely they would have made a decisive difference. And from their perspective, the avant-garde had plenty to complain about, especially all the accommodations the republican government had made with the old order, from the army to the state bureaucracy. But whatever the validity of the grievances expressed, the cultural left picked the wrong enemy much too often. The bitter mockery of the republican idea created a background hum of discontent, or even worse, mere contempt for the existing order. And there were those fully willing to take advantage of whatever opportunities presented themselves to transform that order catastrophically.

THE PREEMINENT SUCH OPPORTUNIST—bar one—came to Berlin to stay in November of 1926. He was then very young, just twenty-nine, short, emaciated, lame and limping, badly dressed. He loathed what he saw. Berlin was "a monster city of stone and asphalt," in which he recognized the same dark hands that Benn had indicted with his terrible, carefully worded praise. It was "those rootless international Jews" who, he said, spread their poison throughout the city.[8] The evidence was everywhere: even something so benign as a jazz band could move him to rage. "Such music was," Joseph Goebbels wrote, "Negrodom, the art of the subhuman . . . offal"—the product of that "Babylon of Sin" that was Berlin in the eyes of its enemies. It was "Nigger-Jew jazz,"[9] just one more example of the garbage that passed for culture in Weimar Germany.

It is almost impossible to overestimate the importance of Goebbels's arrival in Berlin. Handpicked by Hitler as Berlin's *Gauleiter*—the leader of the local branch of the National Socialist party, his tenure there was decisive. It is conceivable that without him, the Nazis would never have achieved the critical weight of force and fear in the streets of the capital that proved so useful in their drive for power. Goebbels was probably the brightest of the Nazi leadership; certainly he possessed the most overt intellectual pretensions. He had received a doctor of philosophy degree for a thesis on a minor Romantic playwright—and later, as a member of the Nazi inner circle, he would make sure that anyone unaware of his *Herr Doktor* status would get the message by signing his name "Dr. G."[10] Like Hitler, he was hardly an Aryan archetype. Clubfooted, he hobbled all his life. Early photographs show a slight, dark, unprepossessing man, speechifying from the back of an open car; only the unwavering harshness of his gaze seems impressive. Nonetheless, he turned out to be a master at creating useful chaos on the streets, and in manipulating the media into magnifying Nazi accomplishments after every brawl.

Most important, Goebbels was a true believer. That had not always been the case. He was not, at least at first, a hard-core anti-Semite, recalling one of his literature professors, a Jew, as a "charming and agreeable man."[11] His early involvement with right-wing politics took the form of undergraduate longing for a Germany reborn in the wake of its defeat, which he initially conceived in the vague and inchoate terms common in the broad current of ultranationalist politics. He was driven by the same emotions that had convinced Rathenau's murderers to strike an exemplary blow that could call Germany to its senses. He had heard of Hitler as one more player in antirepublican politics as early as 1921, shortly after he had completed his doctorate, but the name meant little then, and he drifted. A disastrously bad novel expressed his discontent and hinted at a solution: the discovery of the great leader who could rescue Germany from itself.

He met the man who he believed could fill that role in 1925. Hitler's impact was immediate and overwhelming. Goebbels wrote in his diary after reading Volume I of *Mein Kampf,* "Who is this man? Half plebian, half God!" Soon afterward he added, "This man has everything to be a king," and "the coming dictator . . . How I love him."[12] A moment of disillusion came when Goebbels suffered through a crude and bombastic two-hour Hitler speech at a party conference in February 1926. His hero was suddenly revealed to be "amazingly clumsy and uncertain," his political program "dreadful," and Goebbels himself felt "devastated." It was "one of the greatest disappointments of my life. I no longer fully believe in Hitler. That's the terrible thing: my inner support has been taken away."[13] But Hitler, a skilled party infighter, retrieved the situation. The February meeting had served his purposes, helping him consolidate his control of a party still prone to factions; and with that end now in hand, he turned to the cultivation of key subordinates, above all, the messiah-hungry Goebbels. At the climactic reconciliation meeting, Hitler spoke for three hours, and this time Goebbels was transported. "I love him," he wrote in his diary, and shortly thereafter, "I believe he has taken me to his heart like no one else. . . . Adolf Hitler, I love you. . . ."[14] Such loyalty commanded its reward. For Goebbels it was the critical Berlin assignment, the task on which the future of the Nazis as a national party turned.

At first, it seemed an impossible job. In 1926, the Berlin branch of the party was a hollow shell, a band of a few hundred at most. Goebbels moved energetically, setting up proper offices, stabilizing the local party's finances, and leading it on a series of publicity-gaining stunts that at first mostly involved taunting and brawling with the far more numerous Communists. He founded a newspaper, *Der Angriff—The Attack*. He began to pillory Berlin, its degenerate culture, its Jews, its democrats. He cultivated press attention, and was a master of the staged outrage that the mainstream newspapers would be forced to notice. In February 1927, three months after his arrival, he led a rally in the Wedding district of Berlin, famously a Communist stronghold. He surrounded the stage with SA men, the Brownshirts, anticipating the inevitable brawl with an armory that included chains, brass knuckles, clubs and crowbars. As Goebbels mounted the platform, a crowd of Communists rushed the speaker's stage. The battle spilled out onto the public streets and the Brownshirts, having sought and prepared for combat, had the edge. They lost thirteen of their own to injuries against eighty-five of their enemies.

The Berlin SA's first overt anti-Semitic action came the following month, with an organized campaign of beatings and public harassment of Jews and anyone who looked Jewish. Similar provocations continued throughout 1927 and 1928. Goebbels was careful to confine the bloody work to slum districts. To the middle class and the wealthy he presented the "respectable" face of Nazism. The movement, he proclaimed, "came . . . into Berlin with peaceful intentions." At the same time, he refined the anti-Jewish focus of the party, emphasizing the peculiar Jewish nature of the cancer on Berlin—disease vectors that ranged from the money-obsessed businessman to the corrosive, destructive intellectuals and professionals. It was fiction, but that hardly mattered to a man whose most famous aphorism was "Propaganda has nothing to do with the truth."[15]

Still, for all Goebbels's words and all the routine thuggery, the beer hall brawls, street fights, frightened Jews and smashed Communists, it had remained possible in the middle and late 1920s to view the Nazis in Berlin and in Germany on the whole as a mad and minor fringe. *Der*

Angriff lost money until the crash year of 1929, and its early circulation peaked at a risible two thousand. Although party membership grew, it did not break out of its core of the angry unemployed. Most important, political power appeared completely out of reach. The Social Democrat president, Ebert, died suddenly in 1925 and new presidential elections were called for the spring. Field Marshal Paul von Hindenburg was one of the candidates, the consensus choice of the right-wing parties. Hindenburg, with his adroit avoidance of responsibility for both Germany's defeat and the need to sign the Versailles Treaty, remained the nationalists' hero. The National Socialists put up their own candidate for the first time: not Hitler himself but Hindenburg's old co-conspirator, General Ludendorff. But Ludendorff could only muster 240,000 votes against Hindenburg's final total of 14.6 million. To save face, the Nazis felt compelled to dump their man before the runoff.

But Hindenburg was a deep disappointment, at least to the radical fringe of Germany's right. In the several years after he captured the presidency, he actually became a defender of the republic, cloaking it in his own impeccable patriotic credentials. Even Harry Kessler, absolutely no friend of the high command, came away from the new president's inauguration with the judgment that "with Hindenburg, it [the republic] becomes respectable, and so do its black-red-gold colors, which will now appear everywhere with him as his personal banner." There was work to be done, Kessler acknowledged, still wary, but "if the Republicans do not abandon their vigilance and unity, Hindenburg's election may yet turn out even quite useful for the Republic and peace."[16]

Certainly Albert Einstein, for all his commitment to the moderate left, reacted to Hindenburg's election with none of the despair he had felt after Rathenau's murder three years before. In the early spring of 1925, he and Elsa left for a three-month tour of South America, and so missed the furor of the campaign itself. The trip was primarily a vacation. He lectured at local scientific societies—the price to be paid for the invitations that brought him to Argentina, Uruguay and Brazil—and he spoke to local Jewish organizations, but mostly, he played the tourist. He was, as usual, amused by his reception. The German community in Buenos Aires was staunchly nationalist, and had previously denounced Einstein's antiwar stance as the work of a traitor. But now that he was actually on the scene, presented to Argentine society as a world-famous representative of German culture, the local expatriates embraced him. He was not fooled. "Strange people, these Germans," he wrote in his travel diary. "I am a foul-smelling flower to them, and yet they keep tucking me into their buttonholes."[17]

But aside from his round of receptions and talks, punctuated by the usual quota of questions Einstein found silly enough to make him strain to remain serious, he had the pleasure of being a highly honored guest without having much expected of him. He reported having a lovely time in Uruguay and its capital, Montevideo, and did his duty in Rio de Janeiro, appearing at both Jewish venues and the local German club. The embassies in each of the countries along the way reported back to Berlin that as on his earlier trips, Einstein had been a persuasive and valuable spokesman for Germany's ongoing attempt to rehabilitate itself within the circle of nations. But primarily, as far as he was concerned, the whole journey was merely "enjoyably exciting without any interest." The best part, he wrote, were the "few quiet weeks on the voyage."[18]

After his return in the late spring, the aftermath of the election made little impression on him. He took his usual summer trip to Switzerland, and he spent the entire month of August on the seashore near Kiel. What political energy he possessed went toward his internationalist causes. In 1924, having resumed his work with the League of Nations' International Committee on Intellectual Cooperation, he served as a German advocate at the League's headquarters that winter, pressing for full membership in the League for Germany. He found himself consistently frustrated in his efforts to create a committed, genuinely international community of intellectuals, and by 1925, he increasingly let this frustration show in public. He complained of the inability of his academic colleagues, even his beloved Max Planck, to rise above their nationalist blinders. "The epidemic that afflicts Europeans is an emotional condition," he wrote to Lorentz, then chairman of the International Committee.[19] Reason could not cure it, and it seemed to afflict the intelligentsia as much as or more than others. As he pointedly told a highly distinguished audience in Paris, the only conclusion to draw from the decisions to bar Germans from international cultural organizations was that "scientists and artists, at least in the countries with which I am familiar, are guided by narrow nationalism to a much greater extent than are men of affairs."[20]

Such backhanded praise for the moderation of public men, coming from someone with Einstein's sensitive antennae for political cant, confirms the more general impression. Given the dismal performance of the ultranationalist parties in the recent elections, even the most thoughtful observers could not get terribly excited over Hitler and the rest of the rabid right. By late 1925, the most violent ultranationalists seemed to have been pushed back into the rough underbrush at the fringes of German politics. Whatever shrill noise they might make was being drowned out by the hubbub of daily life in Hindenburg's stabilized republic. Einstein, at any rate, took no note of them. He was occupied instead with what was for him a far more pressing danger, the imminent, overwhelming threat of revolutionary change at the heart of what he held most dear. The breakthrough had finally come, as he had guessed and feared it might, and the problem of the quantum now revealed itself to be intimately intertwined with the fundamental nature of reality. There was a solution to that problem, one descended in substantial measure from Einstein's own labor. The only difficulty was that Einstein hated it.

EVEN WORSE, Einstein knew how much he was to blame for his predicament. He was, after all, one of the founders of quantum theory. More recently—up to the point of total revolution—he had continued to produce work that pushed the field ever closer to its decisive break with the view of reality that he held most dear. As late as 1924 and early 1925, he came up with two major new insights. Both of his ideas emerged from the work of other, younger physicists. In June of 1924, he received a letter and a manuscript from a then-unknown Indian researcher named Satyendranath Bose. Einstein's discovery of Bose is one of the few true Hollywood stories in science—think Lana Turner at Schwab's drugstore. Bose, then a professor at the University of Dacca, had published a few papers that gained him absolutely no recognition. The one he sent to Einstein, his sixth, had already been rejected by an English journal. Undeterred, Bose asked Einstein to read the new article, not mentioning the rejection, and asked his help to get it published in Germany. Einstein recognized its value immediately and shepherded it to the prestigious *Zeitschrift für Physik*.

He attached a comment of his own to Bose's work, declaring it "an important advance," and added tantalizingly that the methods Bose had developed led further still, "as I shall discuss elsewhere in more detail."[21] Bose himself had found a way to derive Max Planck's original discovery, the very first quantum law describing the structure of energy, that did not rely on assumptions from classical, nonquantum physics. That was part of what made the work so attractive to Einstein. In Bose's new formulation, Planck's original quantum breakthrough ceased to be a desperate measure, becoming instead the inevitable, correct reading of nature itself.

Bose's breakthrough turned on the seemingly abstruse matter of the statistical treatment of light quanta: how to count particles of light. He discovered that it was impossible to treat quanta as distinct, individual objects that could be counted one by one. Instead, the best that could be done was to count aggregates: cells—partitions—within a given space, each of which held some number of identical particles of light. The new counting method may have appeared to be a small and wholly technical step, but in fact, it contained a radical and ultimately fundamental claim about the nature of quantum reality. By dropping the old idea that each particle in the universe must at least conceptually be a unique, recognizable individual, Bose's results strongly suggested that in the quantum realm there are certain facts that cannot be known, such as the precise path through space of each individual quantum. And that, of course, contradicted one of the scientists' most deeply held articles of faith: that science explicitly describes the real world as it is.

Einstein pledged that faith as fervently as anyone, although his confidence had been shaken by his earlier realization that quantum processes seemed to ignore the rules of cause and effect. If such licentiousness truly held sway in the quantum realm, he told Born that same spring, "I would rather be a cobbler, or even an employee in a gaming-house, than a physicist."[22] Still, Bose's paper was simply too good to ignore—in fact, he grasped better than Bose himself just how powerful the ideas were. He swiftly extended the new counting method to apply to matter—ordinary gases made up of atoms and molecules, such as oxygen or hydrogen. Again, this seems like an incremental, purely technical step, but its importance came from the way it tied two pieces of the quantum world together, linking the understanding of light with that of matter, making the claim that for both there is a limit to what can be observed directly. Slowly, piece by piece, the quantum worldview was severing its connection to objective reality, the old classical world in which the sequence of causes and effects, event following event, could be traced in all its particulars. Einstein knew what he was doing; it troubled him. But the work led him on.

It was very good work too, good enough to have been the crowning achievement of most scientists' careers. Einstein used Bose-Einstein statistics to predict that at very low temperatures liquids would lose their viscosity, or stickiness, and flow without constraint in a state called superfluidity.[23] Superfluidity was observed in the laboratory in 1928, just four years later. He also predicted that at extremely low temperatures, matter could make the transition into a new form, one different from the ordinary states of solid, liquid, and gas. Until 1938 Einstein's colleagues doubted that this "Bose-Einstein condensate" was even a theoretical possibility, and it was not until 1995 that the stuff was actually created in a laboratory. Einstein, even in his second-tier output, was routinely ahead of his time.

His other and final original contribution to quantum physics also came in 1924, building on the work of a young French graduate student named Louis de Broglie. In a highly original piece of work, de Broglie asked whether matter—electrons—displayed wavelike properties, just as Einstein had originally asked if light waves behaved like particles. The answer in both instances was yes. De Broglie found an equation that linked both wavelike and particle-like behavior in the electron, a relationship that connected an electron's wavelength to its momentum. In other words, de Broglie showed that Einstein's wave-particle duality was ubiquitous, as true for chunks of hard matter as it was for ethereal oscillating rays of light. The notion seemed fanciful, at least to de Broglie's thesis advisor, Paul Langevin, who was "probably a bit astonished by my ideas," as de Broglie later wrote. Langevin asked de Broglie to give him a second copy of the thesis to send on to the master for judgment. When Einstein replied that the thesis was quite interesting, de Broglie's degree was guaranteed.[24]

Beyond this, Einstein added one last insight to the evolving quantum picture. He recognized that de Broglie's concept of matter waves and his own work on the Bose-Einstein statistics led to the same point. His quantized gases could also be seen to display wavelike behavior, a finding that in itself gave a strong boost to de Broglie's idea. But Einstein took the concept farther still, arguing in 1925 that the wave-particle duality was an inherent property of the quantum realm. He wrote that "it seems as if an undulatory [wave] field is associated with every motion process, just as the optical undulatory field is associated with the movement of light quanta."[25] Everything that moved—matter, light, energy, anything—all events that took place within the realm of the very small, Einstein said, present a double face to the world.

THESE EPISODES MARKED the end of Einstein's productive contributions to quantum theory. Matter waves were observed within the laboratory in 1927, and in 1929 de Broglie won the Nobel Prize for his prediction. But by then, the quantum mechanical revolution had absorbed these last insights into a comprehensive, new, and—to Einstein—ultimately unlovable conception of reality. The first breakthrough toward this had come in the spring of 1925 while he was still en route from South America. It emerged in the mind of a very young man recovering from a bout of hay fever on a remote island off the German North Sea coast. Werner Heisenberg was just twenty-five—younger even than Einstein had been in his miraculous year of 1905. Heisenberg was then working in Göttingen as a *Privatdozent,* the equivalent of postdoctoral student, under Einstein's close friend Max Born. That spring, he was wrestling with the problem of atomic spectra, searching for the rules that governed the color and energy of light emitted by atoms. Back in 1912, Niels Bohr had solved part of that problem for the spectrum of hydrogen by introducing the quantum idea to the atom. But like the other early quantum concepts—Planck's quantum of energy and Einstein's photon—Bohr's was an ad hoc response. It patched over one troubling issue, but it did not generalize. His results did not yield the broader rules or laws that could predict the spectra of any element but the very simplest.

Heisenberg had begun his search for that more general idea in a more or less conventional way. Bohr's solution included a picture or model of the atom: atoms came with a core, the nucleus, surrounded by an electron (or electrons) that could occupy one position in an ascending staircase of quantized, discrete orbits. This picture allowed him to visualize events within the atom. Each flash of spectral light, he argued, came when an electron "jumped" between orbits. Because this idea worked, at least well enough to account for the behavior of hydrogen, it seemed plausible to try to fill in that picture, to analyze this image of the atom until one found the underlying regularities that explained how electrons and their orbits should behave. Heisenberg had started down this road, but sometime in the spring of 1925, he remembered a diktat he attributed to Einstein: when wrestling with the atomic puzzle, "physicists must consider none but observable magnitudes." Put in plain language: pay attention only to what you can see or measure, and not to any idealized picture of what the inside of an atom "really" looks like.[26]

Taking that idea to heart, Heisenberg abandoned Bohr's model of the atom, orbits and all, and began to examine the numbers alone, the frequency and energies associated with each of the lines (or colors) within the hydrogen spectrum. For several weeks, he made no significant headway. Finally, as the spring blossoms opened, his hay fever grew intolerable, and he persuaded Born to give him two weeks off to spend on the pollen-free rocks of the island of Heligoland. There, completely undisturbed, his head and nose clear, he found himself able to focus with extraordinary concentration. It took him only a few days of isolation to develop what he called a "new mathematical scheme," a strange and unwieldy form of algebra that, among other oddities, included the property that quantities multiplied in one order do not produce the same answer as do the identical quantities multiplied in a different order. (In effect, Heisenberg's new math, if applied to ordinary numbers, would assert that two times three does not equal three times two. Physicists are not joking when they say that the mathematics of quantum phenomena is deep, difficult, and perplexing, even to the experts.) Odd though this may have seemed, the idea seemed to work, building the elements of a broad, fundamental description of the quantum structure of the atom.

Heisenberg put his theory to the test while still on Heligoland, checking to make sure that his new equations actually produced predictions that matched known results. "When the first terms seemed to accord with the energy principle," he wrote, "I became rather excited, and I began to make countless arithmetical errors. As a result it was almost three o'clock in the morning before the final result of my computations lay before me." He had found a piece of truth, and he knew it, to the point that he felt actually frightened. He wrote, "I had the feeling that, through the surface of atomic phenomena, I was looking at a strangely beautiful interior, and felt almost giddy at the thought that I now had to probe this wealth of mathematical structures nature had so generously spread out before me."[27] The epiphany came in the darkest hours of the night. Heisenberg was wholly alone. Only he had seen that sudden glimpse of Xanadu; for a brief time he would remain the one human being in all the world who knew of the paradise that lay within. He could not sleep. The hours passed. He waited until first light and then headed for the southern tip of the island. There was a rock there that leaned out over the sea. He climbed up, looked across the water, and watched the new day dawn.

At that moment, the modern science of the quantum world was born, a body of physical theory describing the behavior of the smallest structures of matter and energy. When Heisenberg returned to Göttingen, Born recognized his student's bizarre calculations as a form of complicated algebra that was well-known to professional mathematicians—and he also understood (as he told Einstein in mid-July) that the idea was "rather mystifying but . . . certainly true and profound."[28] Born joined with Heisenberg and another of his assistants, Pascual Jordan, to elaborate Heisenberg's basic scheme into a broadly usable theory of atomic structure, now called matrix mechanics. The young English physicist Paul Dirac soon developed a different and in some ways more general set of mathematical techniques that achieved the same end. The name of the theory would change once more to incorporate the idea's roots: the world of the very small, the microscopic behavior of both matter and energy, are described by the body of science we now know as quantum mechanics. By whatever name, these new ideas made no claims about what "truly" happened within the atom. Instead, Heisenberg insisted, all they did was make statements about what could be measured, statistical relations between sets of numbers. With that, the hints dropped by the old quantum theory were now proved true. At the level of quanta, conventional ideas about the nature of reality could not hold; abstractions, approximations and even absurdities took the place of observations of the thing itself, the world—the atom—as it exists. The only thing that made such strangeness palatable was that by early 1926 it was clear the new system could account for an increasingly large set of experimental results. However queer they may have seemed, quanta were no longer the bastard progeny of a desperate Planck. Rather, they formed the basis of a general, formal theory that accurately described events in nature. This was the physicist's grail, the answer to that "supremely important but unfortunately still essentially unanswered question" Albert Einstein had posed as long ago as 1911.[29]

At first, Einstein himself was fascinated with the new idea—appropriately skeptical, but at least hopeful, and sometimes positively enthusiastic. Heisenberg detailed his theory in a lecture at the Prussian Academy in the fall of 1925, and spoke with Einstein afterward. According to Heisenberg, Einstein's greatest concern was for the fate of objective reality. "If your theory is right," Heisenberg remembered Einstein telling him, "you will have to tell me sooner or later what the atom does as it passes from one stationary state to the next."[30] (Privately, to Ehrenfest, Einstein had become much less hopeful. Heisenberg had "laid a quantum egg," in which he refused to believe.)[31] But despite this initial hesitation, Einstein clearly recognized the power of the new idea, writing in early 1926 to Hedwig Born that "the Heisenberg-Born concepts leave us all breathless and have made a deep impression on all theoretically oriented people. Instead of a dull resignation, there is now a singular tension in us sluggish people."[32]

What bothered Einstein was the statistical nature of Heisenberg's work, with its insistence on considering only observed numbers and not the underlying mechanism. When an alternative appeared, he grabbed it. The apparent escape hatch appeared within another new theory, this one created by the Austrian physicist Erwin Schrödinger. Schrödinger, then thirty-eight, had been recognized as a man of great intelligence and ability, but he had never displayed true originality. He could critique and extend the ideas of others, but he had not yet come up with first-class work of his own. By now, even Schrödinger had begun to question whether he ever would.

But at Christmas 1925, he went on holiday to Arosa, a skiing village in the Swiss Alps, and in the midst of his holiday, he was struck by a truly novel idea, a concept that became the famous Schrödinger wave equation. Most significant, in the very first paper on his theory, Schrödinger was able to show that his wave equation could be solved to yield the same analysis of the hydrogen atom as that found in Heisenberg's matrix mechanics. The newer theory had the same seal of nature's approval as the original, and the advantage that it seemed to possess some quality of material reality that Heisenberg's concept did not. Schrödinger's waves were, as he and Einstein both thought, genuine natural phenomena, actual oscillating fields within the atom. To Einstein, this was a lifesaver: "a clear idea, and logical in its application,"[33] vastly preferable to the mathematical abstraction and formalism of Heisenberg's ideas.

It was much more than that. Paul Dirac made a famous statement that Schrödinger's wave function contained most of physics and all of chemistry—a claim that is, in essence, true. The wave function had the advantage of coming in a form physicists know how to use; it invokes a straightforward set of mathematics, not nearly as forbidding as Heisenberg's arcane tangle of matrices. As a consequence, it has served as the foundation for much of the enormous body of quantum mechanical research that followed. Given that quantum mechanics underlies so much of the technology that early-twenty-first-century humankind treasures (the microchip and most of the hardware behind the information revolution, for just one example), the wave equation is now wholly woven into the fabric of our experience.

But for all its power, the new theory was not what both Einstein and Schrödinger had longed for. Schrödinger's claim that his waves were real fields oscillating within the atom was simply wrong. In mid-1926, Max Born intervened. He argued that the waves that Schrödinger described had nothing to do with material reality at all. As Born interpreted them, Schrödinger's waves defined *probabilities*—the measure of the constantly changing likelihood that a particle occupied one quantum state or another. Schrödinger's work made it possible to calculate the odds that something might happen in the quantum world—that an electron might "jump" from one energy level to another, for instance. (Subsequently Schrödinger himself showed that his equation and Heisenberg's theory were actually mathematically equivalent ways of saying the same thing.)

Born's interpretation represented a fundamental break, a redefinition of the kind of knowledge a physicist could hope to gain about nature. Before quantum mechanics, it had been possible to think about the details of events—what happened before, during and after some occurrence. But with the new physics, as Born wrote in 1926, at the quantum level "one does not get the answer to the question, What is the state after collision? but only to the question, How probable is the collision?" That means, Born added, that "from the standpoint of our quantum mechanics, there is no quantity that causally fixes the effect of a collision in an individual event"[34]—or, in other words, there is no way to tell that a specific outcome, the path of a particle after a collision, was caused by any single specific crash. In the game of quantum billiards it is impossible to determine which interaction of stick or cue-ball set a given ball on its path across the table. One cannot even identify the path of a given ball until one has made an actual direct observation. In the old Newtonian world, or even in the realm of Einstein's relativistic physics, one could calculate and predict the path an object had to take through spacetime, given the appropriate knowledge of its initial trajectory and interactions. Not so in the quantum world. Rather, in this new, probabilistic view, the electron and quantum phenomena in general cease to be actual things located at specific points in space and time. Instead, they remain probabilities—some likelihood that they might be here, a different likelihood that they could be over there—with no way to tell for sure without actually looking for them. It was almost as if (or exactly as if, some have argued) quantum phenomena do not exist at all until observed.

From Einstein's perspective, worse was still to come. In March 1927, Heisenberg published his famous uncertainty principle. There, he showed that in the quantum realm there are certain pairs of properties for which the more you know about one, the less you can determine about the other. The better you are able to measure the speed of a particle, the less certain you can be of its position, and similarly for a number of other linked quantities. Richard Feynman put the situation in its plainest terms: "Physics *has* given up. *We do not know how to predict what would happen in a given circumstance,* and we believe now that it is impossible, that the only thing that can be predicted is the probability of different events."[35] (Italics in the original.) There is a genuine, absolute limit to human knowledge.

That was the final blow that Einstein had dreaded from the first days when he realized that quantum processes threatened causality. The quantum world defined itself by numbers, statistics, probabilities and chance. Einstein's initial response to Heisenberg, a stance of critical attention, now resolved into clear rejection. A few months after proclaiming himself breathless at the new developments, he wrote to Born that "quantum mechanics is certainly imposing. But an inner voice tells me that it is not yet the real thing. The theory says a lot, but does not really bring us any closer to the secret of the 'Old One.'" And after that, the crushing and flawed verdict in its earliest form: "I, at any rate, am convinced that *He* is not playing dice."[36] (Italics in the original.)

Born wrote much later that Einstein's judgment "came as a hard blow to me." What upset him most was that Einstein reached his conclusion "not for any definite reason," but in response to that "inner voice" against which there could be no appeal.[37] But through the middle of 1927, Born, Bohr and others held out hope that he could be brought around. The first good chance to do so would come in October, at the fifth Solvay Conference. All of the major figures in the development of the quantum idea were to attend: Planck, Einstein and Bohr, the founding fathers, and the entire younger generation, from Heisenberg, Schrödinger and Born to de Broglie, Dirac and the rest. The entire edifice of the theory to date would be on display. If that could not persuade Einstein, nothing could.

Nothing did. He was unmovable. He had come to the meeting not to engage the new mechanics but to try to bury it. He said little at the formal meetings, but matters were different out of session. One morning, he came to breakfast with a thought experiment that he believed exposed a logical flaw in the structure of quantum mechanics. "Pauli and Heisenberg, who were there," the physicist Otto Stern recalled, "did not pay much attention, [saying] *'Ach was, das stimmt schon, das stimmt schon.'*" ("Ah, well, it will be all right, it will be all right.")[38] But Niels Bohr took Einstein seriously, and spent the day seeking the flaw in his scenario. By dinnertime, Bohr had found the solution. Einstein retreated, only to repeat the process the next morning. Bohr worried, thought, and answered again.

That was the beginning of the debate between them that would continue for the rest of their lives. The argument ended in victory for Bohr. Einstein never found a logical flaw in quantum mechanics, nor did he prove that it could be superseded by a deeper theory that would restore the law of cause and effect. Bohr had what should have been the last word: hearing Einstein say too often that God does not play dice, Bohr finally shot back, "Who are you to tell God what to do?"[39]

He was Albert Einstein, convinced that he knew how God ought to have made the universe. If Bohr won in the eyes of the world, Einstein remained unpersuaded, at Solvay in 1927 and ever after. In a lecture at Oxford in 1933 he stated his credo: "I still believe in the possibility of a model of reality—that is to say, of a theory that represents things themselves and not merely the probability of their occurrence."[40] Near the end of his life, his faith wavered, but not his desire. In 1953, he wrote that his quest for an idea that would "provide the key to a more complete quantum theory" was based on "a modest hope, but certainly not a conviction." Two years later, in one of his last writings, he let his doubts show yet more clearly. "It appears dubious," he admitted, that a theory could be found that would provide a direct, causal explanation for atomic and quantum phenomena. "Most physicists will reply with a convinced 'No,' since they believe that the quantum problem has been solved in principle by other means. However that may be," he added, "Lessing's comforting word stays with us: the aspiration to truth is more precious than its assured possession."[41]

Many of his colleagues saw Einstein's willingness to keep chasing down a blind alley as a tragedy. He did not. As he wrote once to Born, rather cheerfully, "I am generally regarded as a sort of petrified object, rendered blind and deaf by the years. I find this role not too distasteful, as it corresponds very well with my temperament."[42] He was perfectly prepared to—and did—continue on his own, pursuing his dream of a unified theory that could supplant quantum mechanics. But even so, his three decades of opposition to a theory that he had done as much as almost anyone else to create, does beg the question. For a man who until 1925 had throughout his career showed an exceptional ability to hold radical, even contradictory, ideas in his mind, what made quantum mechanics so impenetrable? Einstein himself responded to the question in aesthetic terms. The point of the Oxford lecture of 1933 was to demand a picture of the world that depicted the actual stuff of nature—things themselves, as he put it, and not merely gambler's odds.

But though a sense of what was beautiful in science had always motivated Einstein, his rejection of quantum theory came at least in part for the simplest of reasons. He was growing old. In 1927, when his opposition to the new ideas hardened, he was forty-eight, ancient for a theoretical physicist. His own first breakthroughs had come when he was twenty-six; Bohr was twenty-seven when he completed his greatest work; Heisenberg was just twenty-four; Schrödinger had feared that he was over the hill at thirty-eight. That Einstein had managed to produce work at the highest level for twenty years, well into his forties, was almost unprecedented, a sustained output unmatched in the history of modern physics. (And the quality remained so high; a lesser man might have shared a Nobel Prize just for what he did to extend Bose's and de Broglie's thinking.) The mystery is not that Einstein's flexibility of mind eroded eventually but that it took so long.

Einstein himself was aware that his powers might not be equal to the new physics. In early 1927 he had agreed to prepare a report on quantum statistics—the field he had largely invented—for the coming Solvay Conference. But over the summer he begged off, saying that "I have come to the conclusion that I am not competent to give such a report. . . . The reason is that I have not been able to take such an intensive part in the modern development of the quantum theory as would have been necessary for this purpose." He admitted that part of his reluctance to speak was based on his disapproval of the probabilistic nature of the new theory. But he also acknowledged that he was the one with the problem: "I have on the whole too little receptive talent for fully following the stormy developments" that had seized hold of his science.[43] Later, he told an assistant that he could detect a real change due to age: he still came up with "as many new ideas as ever," he said to Ernst Straus, but he found "that it had become more difficult for him to decide which ones ought to be rejected and which he thought were worth pursuing."[44]

But whatever the changes forged by time, the issue was not merely talent or its ebb. Einstein's own history was at war with any effort he could make to come to terms with the new ideas. The very form of quantum mechanics—its probabilistic description of events—was in direct opposition to the assumptions and conclusions of his own most powerful discoveries, the special and general theory of relativity. Those theories were and are overwhelmingly successful. They are true to the limits of our ability to test them. Einstein, no longer in his truly freewheeling first youth, did not choose to leave their world behind.

Even so, he knew that such old allegiances carried their own risks. In that same lecture at Oxford in 1933 he spoke of Newton, and the fact that he had clung to certain ideas that he recognized might not be true. He did so, Einstein said, because "the enormous practical success of his theory may well have prevented him . . . from recognizing the fictitious character of the principles of his system."[45] It was terribly hard to abandon a good road, Einstein was telling his listeners, even for the great Isaac Newton. Unspoken, conceivably even unthought: it was also hard, too hard, even for the one scientist who ranks with Newton in the history of physics: the speaker that day, Einstein himself.

There is a photograph that was taken in 1911 at the first Solvay Conference. In the places of honor in the center sit the old men (and the one woman, Marie Curie), peering down or straight ahead, solid, heavy, unmovable. Einstein, the youngest present, stands to one side, far in the corner. He is staring off into space, as if thinking, seeing something no one else there could perceive. Sixteen years later, the official photograph from the Solvay Conference of 1927 captured Einstein again. It was a much more formal, staged picture, its three rows of physicists forming one of the most extraordinary collections of scientific talent ever assembled.

In the later picture, Einstein's position is unchallenged. He sits in the front row, dead center. Behind him, standing at the back, Heisenberg grins. Schrödinger looks directly at the camera, flirting, as he was known to do. Bohr is seated far off to the right, his head cocked as if listening to something, or chasing a stray thought. These are men in a high state of excitement, exhilaration. Einstein stares straight ahead, without expression. The people he values most in the world surround him. He holds himself apart. He is alone.

Chapter Twenty

"OUR NECESSARILY PRIMITIVE THINKING"

THERE HAVE BEEN PHYSICISTS LESS PRACTICAL THAN EINSTEIN. THE GREAT theorist Wolfgang Pauli was notoriously dangerous around actual experiments. Supposedly, just his presence in the same *town* could derange a delicately constructed observation. One researcher, a common tale went, was so frustrated by the failure of his elegantly complex apparatus that he cabled Pauli to ask if his malignant presence had somehow made its way to the researcher's city on a particular day. As the legend continued, a chagrined Pauli wired back that indeed, his train had made an unscheduled stop at the local train station. The halt had lasted for perhaps half an hour. It was enough. Pauli was death on experiments.

Einstein was in a much different class. His years at Switzerland's patent office had given him a deep appreciation of the intellectual complexity of sophisticated machinery. It had not been a job obviously suited to the man Einstein would become. He was, after all, expected to be diligent, reviewing patent applications eight hours a day, six days a week, seated on his government-issue chair. But while it is hard to imagine Einstein as a dutiful office drone, throughout his life he acknowledged that the work itself had been worth doing. Life at the patent office was, he told a friend, "uncommonly diverse, and there is much thinking to be done."[1] He still felt the same in the year before he died, declaring that his exposure to the hard facts of practical problems had sharpened his mind. "Working on the final formulation of technological patents was a veritable blessing for me," he wrote in a last autobiographical sketch. "It enforced many-sided thinking and also provided important stimuli to physical thought."[2]

Some scholars have gone farther still, suggesting that Einstein's remarkable gift for visual thinking had been honed by the countless hours of staring at patent drawings. There is something of a chicken-and-egg issue here. He was valued at the patent office precisely because he could swiftly pierce through to the physical principles that lay beneath the surface of technically complex inventions. This makes it hard to calculate the balance between his innate talent and any mental acuity sharpened at the patent office. Ultimately, to be sure, he became so much the otherworldly thinker that he never owned or learned to drive an automobile (even during all those years in car-bound New Jersey!)—but he certainly loved clever machines, and took great pleasure when he could design his own.

His career as an inventor began in his twenties, while he was still at the patent office. There, a collaboration with his friends Paul and Conrad Habicht produced a design of what Einstein called their *machinechen*—their little machine. The gadget in question was a precision voltmeter that could measure extremely small electrical potentials. The Habichts built the device, patented it, and even reached the point of manufacturing it on a small scale. It turned out to be more of a virtuoso display than a truly valuable invention, and was soon superseded by more stable and easy-to-manufacture instruments. Einstein remembered the episode fondly, though, telling Conrad Habicht years later that "it was wonderful, even though nothing useful came of it."[3]

As he rose higher and higher up the academic ladder, Einstein continued to indulge his taste for practical work. His 1915 attempt to perform very delicate experiments did not go well, of course, as noted earlier. That was when he fell into a familiar trap, recognizing only those observations that matched his expectations. But his wartime work on the Anschütz Company's gyrocompass was far more successful. By 1927, the device had advanced to the point where it was clearly superior to existing maritime compasses, and Anschütz began to make export sales. Einstein's role in the project was recognized in his royalty deal: he received 1 percent of the sales of each device and 3 percent of any license fees Anschütz's agents collected. Prudently, he had his share paid into a Dutch bank. (He had not forgotten the lessons of Germany's hyperinflation.) The sums involved amounted to real money for the time, several hundred dollars a year, and Einstein continued to collect them until 1938, by which time the Anschütz gyrocompass floated in the navies of all the major powers except Britain and the United States.

Even in the late 1920s, when the crisis in quantum mechanics loomed so threateningly over him, he continued to dabble in technology. In November 1927, for example, he and Szilard applied for the first of a series of patents on their famous refrigerator. Seemingly, almost any problem could intrigue him. After the refrigerator came the hearing aid. A singer friend of Einstein's—one of the women to whom he was linked during the late 1920s—was becoming hard of hearing, so Einstein set out to create a hearing aid for her. He enlisted the help of an industrial engineer named Rudolf Goldschmidt, and the two men received a patent for their invention on January 10, 1934. (By that time, of course, a German patent was of little use to either of them. Einstein's location was listed as "address unknown" and Goldschmidt would leave Germany for Britain that year.) But again, Einstein had had his fun. Just as in his days at the patent office, much of his practical research evoked some very pretty tinkering, stimulated by the kind of direct observation of a phenomenon in the real world that had spurred some of his best "serious" work. As he wrote to Goldschmidt in doggerel verse, "A bit of technique, now and then/Can also amuse thinkers. . . ."[4]

But his fun came to a halt in the spring of 1928, along with his deeper efforts to wrestle with the quantum theory. In March he traveled to the Swiss Alps for a brief holiday. He arrived at night, and walked uphill for several hundred yards in the cold and snow, carrying his suitcase himself. He collapsed as he reached his hotel. His old friend Heinrich Zangger came up from Zurich and found what Einstein called "his corpse" in frighteningly bad shape. The initial diagnosis was a heart attack, and while the episode turned out to be not that serious, it was the first in the series of circulatory and heart problems that would trouble him off and on for the rest of his life.

After Einstein recovered some strength, Zangger carefully packed his patient up for his journey back to Berlin. At home he remained seriously ill. As usual when sick, Einstein displayed no concern for the outcome—this time, he told Besso that "I came close to leaving for good; still, one shouldn't put that off indefinitely."[5] He had little faith in medicine in general. He told his doctor that "our necessarily primitive thinking must inevitably prove inadequate to something as complex as a living organism"[6]—a vote of no-confidence in medicine that he never saw much reason to change.

Even so, he found some silver linings. The first came early in the crisis in the person of Helen Dukas, a young woman who entered the Einstein household on April 13, 1928. She was hired to be his secretary, but rapidly took over the administration of the entire household, relieving an exhausted and fearful Elsa of the task. She became invaluable, protecting Einstein to the end of his life and beyond, when she acted both as his literary executor and the guardian of his memory.

The other great reward of illness came as he regained some of his vigor but remained sick enough to relish the convalescent's privileges. One early biographer caught him in the act: "He seemed to enjoy the atmosphere of the sickroom, since it permitted him to work undisturbed."[7] He had not given up his opposition to quantum mechanics since his failure to dent its progress at the 1927 Solvay Congress. Now, as his health permitted him to concentrate deeply once more, he was ready to try again.

AS IT HAD FROM THE START, the element of randomness goaded Einstein, repelled as he was by the corrosive role of probability and chance in quantum mechanics. In the summer of 1928, just strong enough to renew his assault upon the theory, he wrote to Ehrenfest that "I now believe less than ever in the essentially statistical nature of events." So, he went on, he had "decided to use what little energy is left me in accordance with my own predilection, regardless of the present bustle around me."[8]

Einstein's renewed attack on quantum mechanics proceeded on two separate fronts. On one side lay his continuing efforts to produce a unified field theory, work that predated the quantum mechanical revolution. At first he had turned to unification in an attempt to move beyond general relativity, to include both gravity and electromagnetism in a single mathematical scheme. But the pressure from the new quantum discoveries forced unification to do double duty: generalizing as before, but in a way that would tame quantum mechanics, incorporating it as a special case of a much richer theory that could eliminate the role of chance in the world.

That July he thought he had found it. From his sickroom he came up with a new body of mathematics, a variant of the geometry he had used in the creation of general relativity. Like his original unification proposal of three years before, the new work was a nearly impenetrable mare's nest of mathematical complexity. Though the idea looked promising (to him, at least), he found that he could not extract even very simple actual physics from his novel equations. Worse, the new mathematics actually undercut his earlier work. Its equations did not include critical elements of general relativity. This latest alleged unification could not account for the orbit of Mercury, the conservation of energy, even the bending of light. Einstein did not seem to care. All the stunning results that had once left him breathless were now to be abandoned. He was always bold, ready to cast aside even good work for the promise of better. But this reckless profligacy with what he himself had called his own greatest discovery demonstrated how eager he was to find some way to slay his Moby-Dick, the quantum theory. He persevered, working on into the fall, exploring the new mathematics in an effort to find some path that would link that formal, abstract structure to the behavior of real gravity and real electromagnetic phenomena in the real world. By late autumn, he had become hopeful enough to ready his first paper on the new theory for publication.

And then, somehow, the press found out about the whole farrago. On November 4, 1928, *The New York Times* announced the prospect of another shattering breakthrough in an article headlined "Einstein on Verge of Great Discovery; Resents Intrusion." Ten days later, the paper noted that he still wasn't talking about his novel ideas, stating that the physicist "will not count unlaid eggs." In January 1929, he finally published the new theory, a treatise six pages long, and *The New York Times* reported breathlessly that "the length of this work—written at the rate of half a page a year [sic!]—is considered prodigious when it is considered that the original presentation of his theory of relativity filled only three pages."[9] Arthur Eddington in England told Einstein that the tempest had reached the point where Selfridges, the famous posh department store in London's West End, posted the paper in its windows, all six pages of dense, unorthodox mathematical reasoning—and that crowds stopped to stare.

Despite such uncomprehending enthusiasm, and despite his own best efforts to extract valid physics from his equations, most of those actually competent to judge found that the new work made no sense. It was disconnected from the real world, unable to account for even the simplest phenomena it sought to explain. It was untestable, a claim about the world that did not yield predictions that could be proved accurate or false. It contradicted earlier, successful theories. It seemed like a kind of mock science. It looked like the real thing—it had all the elements that are supposed to be present in a scientific theory: an argument, a detailed line of mathematical reasoning, a conclusion. But at its core it was mere equation chopping. The work saddened and frustrated his colleagues. Pauli was the harshest, betting that Einstein would give up on the new theory within a year. He went public with his scorn, writing that Einstein's "never-failing inventiveness as well as his tenacious energy . . . guarantees us on the average one theory per annum." Worse, scathingly, he added that "it is psychologically interesting that for some time, [whatever is] the current theory is usually considered by its author to be the 'definitive solution.'"[10]

At first, Einstein answered Pauli with an aloof and needling dismissal. "Only a man who is certain that he is viewing the unity of natural forces from the correct viewpoint is entitled to write as you did,"[11] he told his gadfly, with the appropriate level of benign hauteur from the man who had once proposed to feel sorry for God if general relativity had proved false. Throughout 1929, he continued to believe that this latest version of unification would work out, declaring that "the latest results are so beautiful that I have every confidence" that they were the real thing.[12] Einstein never stinted praise, for his own ideas or those of others. (Perhaps the most elegant tribute he ever wrote was to his beloved adversary, Niels Bohr, when he termed Bohr's quantum account of the hydrogen spectrum "the highest sphere of musicality in the sphere of thought.")[13] At the time he composed them, he believed such accolades. When he thought he had hold of something good, he could stick to the task indefinitely. If his unified theory seemed beautiful to him, then perhaps that elegance was a sign that a deep kernel of truth lay within; and that meant he had the obligation to remain on the job until the work triumphed or collapsed.

As Pauli had predicted, the theory did fall apart. It took more than two years, not the one he had wagered, but Einstein finally admitted that his equations had no physical meaning. Einstein sent Pauli an almost graceful concession—"You were right after all, you rascal"[14]—and quietly moved on to the next in his lengthening list of unification theories, just as Pauli had said he would. Doing so, he dismissed any complaints about his persistent pursuit of what seemed a blind alley in elevated but unbudging language. "The theorist," he conceded, must approach "this Herculean task fully aware that his efforts may only be destined to prepare the death blow to his theory." What of it? "The theorist who undertakes such a labor should not be carped at as fanciful"—take that, Pauli! "On the contrary, he should be granted the right to give free reign to his fancy, for there is no other way to the goal." Einstein was not wasting his time, he said, no matter what others might think, for the physicist's labor was "no idle daydreaming, but a search for the logically simplest possibilities and their consequences." That was a divinity that he always acknowledged: the god of simplicity. Einstein was his prophet, and no matter how much the unbelievers might scoff, his was a faith that would not waver.

But while the ultimate goal of unification remained his chief ambition, throughout the late 1920s he also directly challenged what he continued to see as the evident absurdity of the quantum theory. Beginning with the Solvay Conference of 1927, he had tried to identify a contradiction within quantum mechanics that would undermine the entire enterprise. Einstein had argued then that quantum mechanics gave an inadequate description of a particular experiment that in classical physics could be analyzed in full, causal detail. Bohr had headed Einstein off by agreeing that his assertion was correct but that his conclusion was wrong: quantum mechanics did not fail by virtue of what it did not say. Instead, it succeeded *because* at each step, it defined precisely the limits of the accuracy of its predictions and descriptions. Such limits, Bohr said, were not merely technical difficulties. Rather, they were inherent properties of the world being studied—what are commonly called laws of nature.[15]

This was exactly what Einstein sought to deny, though he could not overcome Bohr then. But by 1930, when the two met at the sixth Solvay Conference, he had prepared a new challenge, one that attacked the core of Bohr's earlier argument, the validity of Heisenberg's uncertainty principle. He proposed a seemingly simple thought experiment, described in detail by Einstein's friend Abraham Pais.[16] First, Einstein said, imagine that a box is filled with light. Start by weighing the box, and then open a shutter at a particular time to allow a single photon to escape. Weigh the box again. You now know, Einstein triumphantly concluded, the energy of the photon (because of the relationship between energy and mass laid down in special relativity's famous $E = mc^2$) and you can determine the time of its departure from the system, both to any level of precision you require. But such precise knowledge violates the quantum mechanical uncertainty principle that says that energy and time are a complementary pair (just as velocity and position are). The more you know about the one, the less precise must be your knowledge of the other. If Einstein's thought experiment held, then the uncertainty principle did not apply in all cases, and that would destroy one of the central pillars on which the entire edifice of quantum mechanics rested. Einstein presented his scenario to Bohr, and said in effect, Your turn.

There are two photographs of Einstein and Bohr together that capture the complex ties of affection and dispute they shared. In one, the two physicists are seated, lounging, legs crossed, each evidently comfortable with the other. Einstein leans well back, one arm behind his head, one gesturing slightly, as if caught in the middle of a crucial point. Bohr's head cocks just slightly forward, ready to respond. These are men who know each other very well, easing their way through the familiar turns of a conversation that stretches over years. The urgency visible in Bohr's pose was real. The stakes between them were as high as they could get for men in their profession. Confronted with Einstein's new scenario in 1930, Bohr was desperately concerned. He spent the next several hours talking to all those he could buttonhole at the conference, one witness reported, "trying to persuade them that it could not be true, that it would be the end of physics if Einstein were right." That evening the two of them left the meeting together, "Einstein a majestic figure, walking quietly, with a somewhat ironical smile, and Bohr trotting near him, very excited."[17] A photograph survives that shows exactly that scene (though it may not have been taken that night): Einstein walks gaily, just ahead of Bohr. Bohr hurries to keep up, leaning into his stride, pushing forward, his head angled so that he can talk more directly into Einstein's ear. He is visibly agitated; there is something he has to say. Einstein listens and smiles, as one does who may have just captured a long-sought prize.

Bohr truly feared for physics that one night—but only for a few hours. By the next morning, as at the previous Solvay Conference three years before, he had found the mistake. Bohr took Einstein's simple sketch of an experiment, and mapped out in detail how to make each of the measurements he had called for. When he did, he was able to show that Einstein had ignored the effects of gravity on the measurements of time. When the photon escapes, the apparatus moves, because whatever scale one uses to weigh the box of light will shift with the loss of the weight of the photon. Einstein's theory of gravity described how measurements of time vary depending on where a clock sits in a gravitational field. Because the clock in the box moves within such a field, there is some mystery—some uncertainty—about the precise moment when the photon leaves the box. That slight imprecision emerged directly out of Einstein's own relativity theory. It was enough to set an inherent limit to the precision with which he could measure either the energy of his photon or the time of its passage in his thought experiment. The uncertainty principle held.

Einstein was right on one score, however. Quantum mechanics appeared absurd then and in some ways still does. Bohr once said, "Anyone who is not shocked by quantum theory has not understood it." Famous examples only emphasize its core of strangeness. Consider the cat in a thought experiment by Erwin Schrödinger. The cat is locked in a closed cage. The cage also contains a vial of poison, which can be released by a radioactive trigger, the decay of one atom of some radioactive substance. Schrödinger set up his imaginary experiment so that there was a 50 percent chance that the decay event, and hence the death of the cat, would take place in a given amount of time. At this point in the experiment, with the cage closed and the set amount of time still passing, Schrödinger asked the question: Can one say that the cat is either alive or dead?

On the macroscopic level of ordinary life, the answer is obvious. An observer may not be sure whether the cat is walking or a corpse, but it must be one or the other. But this experiment depends on the decay of one of billions of atoms in a chunk of radium or some other radioactive element, and that is a quantum event. Within quantum mechanics, such events remain probabilities until measured. Before making the observation, one cannot say whether the atom has decayed or not—and that means, absent taking a direct look, that the cat too remains a kind of quantum zombie, neither alive nor dead. Even more worrying, the cat exists in that quantum limbo up to the moment someone opens the cage. Then, according to quantum mechanics as interpreted by Born and Bohr, the act of looking inside actually changes the animal. In the jargon of the trade, observation collapses the cat's probability wave so that in an instant it becomes either living or dead. It took and takes a special flexibility of mind to accept that the very act of measurement actually alters what is being observed. The idea seemed ridiculous on its face, a scandal, and it was something that Einstein could not countenance without a fight.

But he was an honest man, above all when it came to physics. After Bohr knocked down this latest thought experiment, Einstein gave way somewhat: he ceased to seek or claim that there was an inherent inconsistency within quantum mechanics. He acknowledged the theory was real physics. He made the concession in the most gracious way possible by nominating Heisenberg and Schrödinger for the Nobel Prize. In his nomination letter he wrote, "I am convinced that this theory undoubtedly contains a part of the ultimate truth."[18] Still, he no more loved the theory then than he ever had. He continued to seek some way of expressing his doubts, and over a number of years developed what became known as the EPR paradox. The paradox was named for Einstein and two research assistants, Boris Podolsky and Nathan Rosen. It was another thought experiment aimed at demonstrating that the quantum theory had a logical flaw in it; but in the end it became clear that the argument simply illustrated the fact that quantum mechanics makes some very strange predictions. Ultimately, it was reasoning born of grief, an emotional appeal to a world that no longer existed. The EPR paradox boiled down to the simple assertion that quantum mechanics *felt* wrong, that it made Einstein unhappy. As he put it in the more controlled language required of scientific communication, "No reasonable definition of reality could be expected to permit" the excesses of modern quantum theory.[19]

That cry of outrage is what makes this seem so sad. It was not Einstein's insistence on traveling his own road—he did, as he said, have the right. If he had to endure a few bricks hurled at his results along the way, that went with the territory. (Think of Pauli as Ignatz, heaving his missiles at Einstein's blithe Krazy Kat.) But he felt genuine loss at the death of true, objective knowledge of the world. Between 1927 and 1930, he had struggled to preserve what he felt was essential if human beings were to grasp the order of the universe. No reasonable notion of reality should deny such a vision of the cosmos. Quantum mechanics did, and left Einstein behind, bereft.[20]

THE TUMULT IN THE SCIENCES had echoes in the broader sphere of culture, but for the most part the quantum crisis got lost in the ferment of late Weimar life. Radical assertions of the new, of old orders overturned and novel ideas that left behind those incapable of grasping them, occurred throughout Weimar intellectual life. Berlin was, as usual, the epicenter of those who championed such movements and those who saw the new as a betrayal of Germany. That strain between these warring urges for nostalgia and revolution could be seen perhaps most easily at the movies. By the late 1920s, German cinema had almost completely settled down from the exuberantly innovative extravanganzas of the Expressionist films of the early '20s, but the mid decade focus on social realism persisted. Still, even the best movies from this period found themselves caught between the incompatible versions of salvation that contended beneath the surface quiescence of the republic.

Even now, more than seventy years after its 1927 premiere, it remains an open question whether or not Fritz Lang's *Metropolis* counts as one of Weimar's best films. Lang set out to make a blockbuster, and he succeeded, spending to the point where the film almost bankrupted Germany's leading film studio, UFA. The outcome was certainly spectacular, with Lang's technically extraordinary depiction of its two-layered city: the extravagant, wealthy, future world above with its lofty towers and graceful air cars, inhabited by the blessed rich, resting on the shuttered misery below, where workers served giant machines in windowless caverns. But while the film was a visual triumph, gaining an international audience, contemporary observers noticed that his story had a fatal compromise at its heart. In the film, Freder, the son of the ruling capitalist, revolts against his father and joins the oppressed in the subterranean city. He finds himself drawn to a young woman, Maria, a saintly presence among the wretched workers. Maria counsels patience and love rather than revolution, and the evil father in the film, terrified by the power of the heart, creates a robot-Maria programmed to incite a rebellion that can then be crushed. The revolt happens, and as planned, threatens to destroy its own, but the true Maria and the prodigal son save the day. The film ends with the father, joined by Freder and the saint, shaking hands with the factory foreman in a symbolic reconciliation between owners and workers.

Whatever its politics, Lang's film certainly reveled in modernity. His lofty city was a vision, one inspired by New York that he distilled into a place of great beauty, of unbounded possibility. His depiction of the hell lurking beneath its towers may have seemed a piece of trenchant, leftist social criticism—until the film offered its prescription: do not emancipate those below. Rather, persuade them to acquiesce in their own oppression. To the critic Siegfried Kracauer, writing after Hitler's rise, the climax of *Metropolis* anticipated the essence of fascist triumph: the father, receiving the delegation of workers, "does not give up his power, but will expand it over a realm not yet annexed—the realm of the soul." As Kracauer pointed out, Lang's tycoon displayed the same tactical flexibility as that master of propaganda, Goebbels, who said that while "power based on guns may be a good thing, it is better, however, and more gratifying, to win a people's love and to keep it." Lang ultimately corroborated this reading of the film. He reported that Goebbels sent for him after the Nazis had seized power, telling him that "he and the Führer had seen my picture *Metropolis* in a small town, and Hitler had said at the time that he wanted me to make Nazi pictures."[21]

However, anecdotes like this highlight the problem of hindsight, the inescapable distortion of meaning that comes from knowing what comes next. That bias contorts any review of German life during the 1920s. Every event, every action, seems tinged with the fact of Hitler's rise, still in the future. But the reality of Berlin culture in the '20s, high and low, mass entertainment as well as the more targeted work of the avant-garde, was that almost any event, any production or display, could inspire extraordinary reactions, and all of them were or seemed to be equivalent. This was a time of extravagant enthusiasms; politics for many people became simply one of any number of passions in

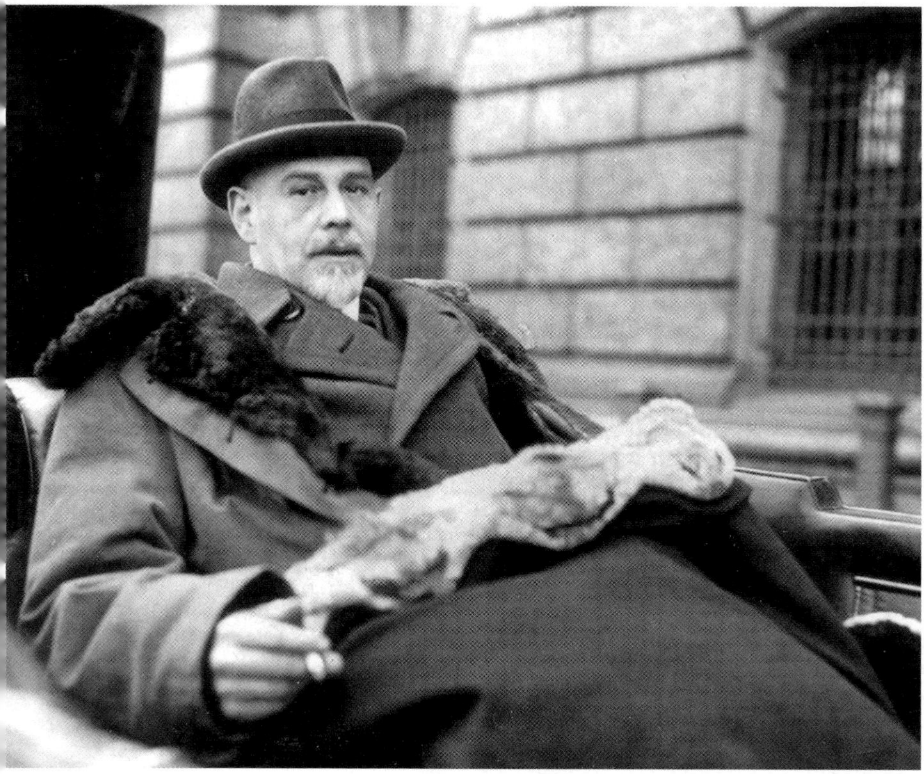

"Jesus im Frack": Jesus in tails. Foreign Minister Walther Rathenau shortly before his murder.

A soldier guards paper money during the hyperinflation.

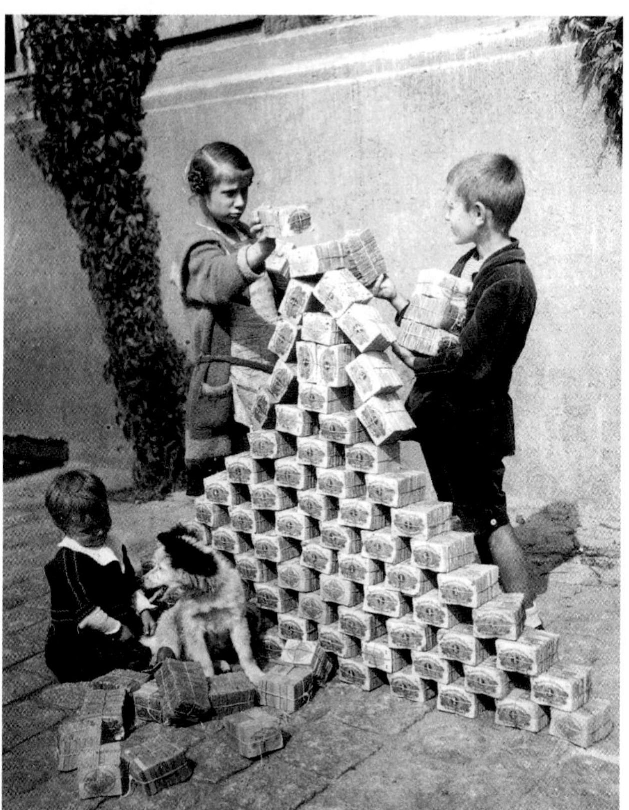

The hyperinflation of 1922—1923 always had an element of the surreal. Here children play with blocks of worthless paper money.

Hitler and General Erich von Ludendorff with the other Beer Hall Putsch defendants.

How the other half lived: slum conditions in postwar Berlin.

The divine Josephine Baker.

Anita Berber in her persona as an elegant siren.

Modern architecture comes to Berlin: Mies van der Rohe's memorial to Karl Liebknecht and Rosa Luxemburg.

In a patriotic tableau, the Haller Girls array themselves as the statuary atop the Brandenburg Gate.

Weimar Berlin's notorious El Dorado nightclub. Only one person in this image is biologically a woman.

Some postwar Wandervögel groups embraced a peculiar mixture of fantasy and nudism.

The body-beautiful side of Germany's nudist movement produced the young people Stephen Spender described as "dragon's teeth...poised at the heart of Europe."

Einstein in his turret study in the Berlin home he shared with Elsa.

Five Nobel laureates at one table in Berlin, 1928. From the left: Walther Nernst, Einstein, Max Planck, R. A. Millikan, and Max von Laue.

The Fifth Solvay Conference, Brussels, 1927. Einstein sits front row center. His beloved Hendrik Lorentz is at his right, with Curie next to him. Niels Bohr is in the second row, far right, with Max Born next to him. Werner Heisenberg stands third from the right and Erwin Schrödinger stands sixth from the right.

Niels Bohr and Albert Einstein in Brussels at the height of their dispute over quantum mechanics.

Joseph Goebbels stands just behind Hitler's left shoulder as the two pose with local party officials at a provincial rally in 1926.

National Socialist youth groups pursued the icon of the perfect Aryan.

Max Planck and Albert Einstein in 1929, receiving the first and second Planck medals.

Einstein, Charlie Chaplin, and Elsa Einstein at the opening of *City Lights* in 1931.

Einstein being inducted as the "Great Relative" of the Hopis; with Elsa on the Hopi reservation in New Mexico.

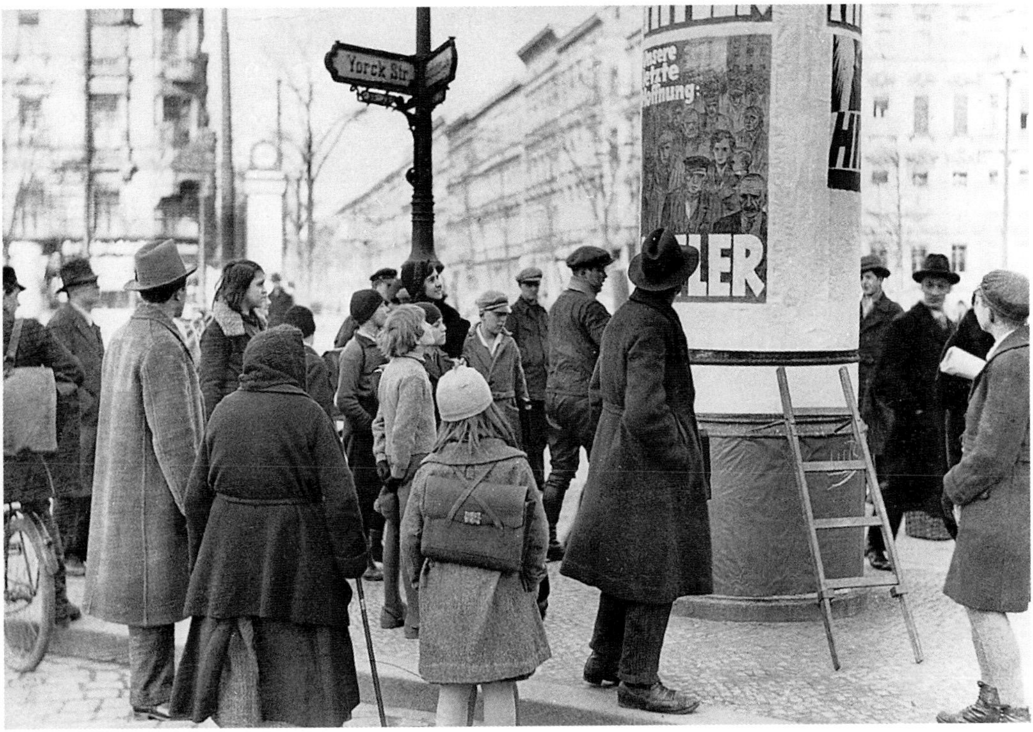

Berliners examine an election poster from 1932. It reads, "Hitler is our only hope."

Anti-Semitic cartoon celebrating Einstein's departure from Germany. The cartoon was seized as war booty after the Second World War.

Hitler and Reichspräsident Hindenburg on their way to a rally on May 1, 1933, the day before Hitler's government crushed Germany's independent labor movement.

Fighting the good fight: Einstein speaking at a rally in London in 1933 on behalf of refugees from Hitler's Germany. Ernest Rutherford sits behind him.

Albert Einstein in Berlin.

which one could lose oneself, and only one target among many for the ironist's wit.

For example, the Weimar cabaret revival that produced the Girl shows was also famous for its apparently political edge. But appearances deceived, as Peter Jelavich has documented in his history of Berlin cabaret. By the latter half of the 1920s, most mainstream acts increasingly avoided direct political polemics, and even the honorable exceptions had a de facto equal-time rule for its targets. One of the most famous comic sketches (and one of the few to be transcribed) captured the mood almost too well. Performed in 1929, the skit described how different newspapers would cover a catastrophe: a collision between a bicyclist and a dog. The liberal *Berliner Tageblatt,* ever cheerful, reported that "dog and bicyclist race along the Kurfürstendamm; they hurry—despite a little scratch here and there—toward the brilliant future of the German republic." The more dour though still liberal *Vossische Zeitung* opined that the juxtaposition of red blood on a black dog with white spots constituted an expression of right-wing politics with its evocation of the colors of the Imperial German flag. *Lokal Anzeiger,* the nationalist organ, declared that "a foreign bicyclist ran over a retired general's dog. Fifteen years ago the German people would have stood up as one body and swept the bicyclist away with ringing manly fury, but today our faithful dogs lie limply on the ground, shattered by the Treaty of Versailles." The Communist paper saw it differently: "On the Kurfürstendamm, that pompous boulevard of satiated capitalism on which the proletarian revolution will march against the imperialists in the very near future, a dog attacked a simple proletarian bicyclist!!!!! That's how it starts! First one dog attacks a single bicyclist, then all dogs unite against the Soviet Union!" And of course, bringing up the rear, there was the Nazi newspaper *Völkischer Beobachter:* "Once more one of our party comrades has been attacked from behind in the dark of night by a bow-legged, flat-footed dachshund. Bow-legged—that betrays the true race of these eastern Jewish pets, with their sagging ears and curls, who suck the marrow of our countrymen and steal the bones from under the noses of our German shepherds. Tomorrow our Führer Adolf Hitler will speak in the sports palace about this national affair. Party comrades should appear in simple battledress, with hand grenades and flame-throwers."[22]

This was, or rather appeared to be, biting political humor. But beneath its veneer of satire, it was so careful, ridiculing everyone to avoid exposing the fatuousness of any single political idea or stance. It was an easy joke, intentionally so, designed to extract a laugh without offending anyone more than anyone else. Such skits did have a target. They aimed not at individual parties or ideologies but at politics itself. They're all fools, the newspaper parody said, all of them slaves to windy rhetoric, each unable to perceive the simple truths of daily life. We, the performer and the audience—we are different. We can see; we can laugh. Better by far, the message implied, to go about one's business, to seek diversion as one may, to leave the political to those unfortunate, driven, blinkered buffoons.

And entertain themselves people did. Germany in the '20s was sports mad. Heroic endurance fliers, race drivers, boxers, runners, those who excelled at some physical feat would enjoy their moment in the newspapers and the popular imagination. A zeppelin flight to the North Pole became front-page news. The first rocket-powered race car, an Opel that could go from zero to sixty-five miles per hour in eight seconds, was victorious at the famous Berlin Avus speedway in 1928. Avus, with its screamingly dangerous north curve, at 44 degrees the sharpest in the world, was itself a prop to national pride. There were any number of boxing heroes, including the black fighter known as the Dixie Kid, but the headliner was certainly Max Schmeling, whose rise to the world heavyweight title he finally won in 1931 highlighted the sport's crossover appeal to every segment of Weimar society. The tabloids raved over their new warrior, while Bertolt Brecht lauded him in verse and George Grosz painted his portrait.

Berlin had no monopoly on this extravagant awe of athletic heroes; it appeared everywhere in Europe. But there was an enormous hunger in Berlin not only for heroes but for excitement that, to foreign and native observers alike, seemed unique. Almost every visitor commented on the city's peculiar fascination with six-day bicycle races in the 1920s. The competitions, held at the Sportpalast, involved two-man teams at least nominally cycling continuously for six days, with the victors chosen through a complex scoring system. Bizarrely, the races became must-see events, drawing everyone from the wealthy and the decadent to workingmen still smelling of the factories. Music roared as the cyclists struggled on and full houses leaned in toward the arena track, the appearance of cycling stars or local favorites evoking a tidal wave of cheers. The dramatist Georg Kaiser caught the almost addictive hold the sport possessed over its audiences in his play *From Morning to Midnight,* writing, "The frothing is least at the bottom, among the well-bred public. . . . One row higher the bodies sway and vibrate, the limbs begin to dance, a few cries are heard—your respectable middle class! Higher still, all veils are dropped. A wild fanatic shout, a bellowing nakedness, a gallery of passions."[23]

As the '20s wore on, the frenzy that Kaiser observed penetrated almost any imaginable activity. The pace and price of diversion seemed only to grow, consuming those who could not keep up. There was an exemplary death in 1927, an end to the sad, swift passage of one woman who came to symbolize the peril inherent in Berlin's cult of sensation. Anita Berber, the classically trained dancer who had caused the vice squad such anguish with her performances earlier in the decade, continued to command attention and envy. Through the mid-'20s she was the headliner at the notorious White Mouse Club, and offstage she was celebrated as a sexual athlete, standing out even amid Berlin's formidable competition. She was serially married, even more frequently linked to lovers both male and female, brassy, obscene, alternately cursing and flirting with her public as she passed in and out of the Sportpalast, surrounded by her bodyguards. She consumed hugely, ecumenically bingeing on alcohol, cocaine, morphine and heroin. She was young, and alluring, and a harpy—one witness remembered her tantrum up and down the Tiergartenstrasse when she was denied entrance to a masked ball in 1927. She left Berlin shortly after that display for a tour abroad, but her body was already collapsing under the load of drugs, drink, and exhaustion. She caught tuberculosis, but kept on performing until she finally collapsed in Baghdad, penniless. Her theater friends got up a collection and brought her back to Berlin, where she lingered briefly. She was twenty-nine when she died.

Her funeral was a carnival. Everyone came: "prominent film directors marched alongside the whores of Friedrichstrasse, young male hookers with hermaphrodites from the Eldorado . . . men in top hats next to the most famous transvestites in Berlin."[24] This was the Berlin of legend seeing one of its own off in proper style. With hindsight, it can be seen as a wake for Weimar itself, almost the last hurrah for a city that was as much a dream in the minds of those who loved its excesses as it was a real place deeply threatened by those who loved it not at all. The good life in Berlin was sustained on borrowed cash, the foreign loans that had poured into Germany once the hyperinflation ended. In good times, the loans could be rolled over when they came due, and so far, there had been no bad times to test the system. But Weimar's enemies were still present, waiting for their chance to strike. In early 1928, not long after Berber's funeral, Goebbels wrote of cabaret Berlin's "eternal repetition of corruption and decay . . . of inner emptiness and despair . . . sunk to the level of the most repulsive pseudoculture." This was foreign ground, Goebbels declared: "The German people is alien and superfluous here." But their day would come, he assured his readers: "Berlin West is the abscess on this gigantic city of diligence and industry. . . . This is not the true Berlin. . . . The other Berlin is lurking, ready to pounce." And at the last: "The day of judgment! It will be a day of freedom."[25]

Throughout the late 1920s, that sense of almost tribal conflict between wholly unconnected Germanys could be found in almost any corner of Berlin's life. The local love of association meant that an amazing range of activities took place in groups, which then provided obvious targets for political manipulation. The *Wandervögeln*—the youth groups—had flourished before the war. It was their members who supplied the volunteers who died in waves to become the "heroes of Langemarck" in the fall of 1914. When the movement revived in the 1920s, the initial mood as before was explicitly *völkisch,* not so much nationalist as romantically German. Typical activities centered around the woodland walk, the campfire, the inevitable guitars and traditional folk songs. The groups sought to celebrate youth, and even more, to preserve and extend the time in which one could feel young, without constraint. But though they had no political associations at first, the major parties soon recognized the value of creating an idealistic movement of young supporters. The Socialists had been the first to create a truly organized youth wing, but the other major parties quickly followed suit. The National Socialists organized their first Hitler Youth groups as early as 1922.

The influence of these partisan youth groups grew, especially on the right, until 1929, when one of the original *Wandervögel* idealists, Eberhard Köbel, known by his nickname "Tusk," tried to reinvigorate the original, antipolitical romance of the movement. He was an innovator, creating what was in essence a marketing campaign to capture young hearts and minds before partisan ideologues could grab them. He created flashy new uniforms, black flannel shirts for the boys, brought in new songs—traditional tunes from Russia and Finland—and even introduced something of the international style to the layout of his magazine. These moves worked for a time. But as always, the Nazis were there, fast learners who borrowed the surface trappings of Tusk's ideas, natty shirts and all.

While the competition for the next generation of soldiers (as Hitler saw it) was going on, this was just one of the dizzying array of cultural skirmishes contested over Weimar's last years. The nudist fad had survived the earlier attempts to crush it as a Jewish plague, but it continued to be a left/right battleground. In 1930, the French sculptor Aristide Maillol visited a Frankfurt swimming pool and reveled in the sight of the naked flesh. His friend and biographer, the ubiquitous Kessler, wrote that the seventy-year-old painter "kept drawing my attention to the beautiful bodies of the girls and the young men and boys," and Maillol said that if he lived in Frankfurt, he would come there every day to draw. Kessler told him that "this is indicative of only a part of a new vitality, a fresh outlook on life" risen since the war. "People want really to *live,*" he said, adding that "in many ways, especially in Germany, we are returning unconsciously and naturally, to the habits of the Greeks. Nudity, light, fresh air, sunshine, worship of living, bodily perfection, sensuousness without either false shame or prudishness."[26]

But what the usually acute Kessler ignored was that even the apparently apolitical passions of the body-beautiful movement had long since split on party lines. Adolf Koch, a nudist schoolteacher fired in a burst of anti-Semitic vitriol by the Berlin city council, ran the naturist club aligned with the Socialists, while the Nationalists had their own huge camp under the direction of a Dr. Fuchs. Such segregation would have been funny but for the nudist credos that lay behind such schisms—the contrast between Kessler's delight in life on one side, and an ideal of bodily perfection whose significance seems to have passed Kessler by. The English writer Stephen Spender sensed the danger. While he delighted in the nakedness that embraced him on his visit to Germany in 1929, he argued that all those nude, would-be Aryan gods had emerged from the despair left behind by the trenches, the hunger, the desolation of Germany during and just after the war. Germany's naked youth,

Spender wrote presciently, had "no money and no beliefs and an extraordinary anonymous beauty." They were overtly dangerous: "a breed of dragon's teeth waiting for its leader," poised at the heart of Europe.[27]

THAT PREMONITION WAS RARE in the summer of 1929. But the evidence that German society was divided and growing more so could be found almost anywhere one looked, down to the most trivial of public matters. There were few such incidents more trivial than one that snared Einstein himself, but the comic fiasco of his fiftieth birthday gift illuminated the growing political tension present in Berlin and throughout Germany.

The affair began innocently enough. A few weeks before the day itself, March 14, 1929, one of Einstein's friends approached the mayor of Berlin, Gustav Böss, with the suggestion that the city of Berlin could give Einstein a gift in honor of that significant birthday. The friend, Einstein's doctor, Janos Plesch, had a particular present in mind: a house on the water in the countryside near Berlin. Böss welcomed the idea, but prudently approached Einstein himself to see if the physicist would welcome such a proposal. Einstein, no fool, was happy to accept. He already spent as much time as he could in the houses of his friends along Berlin's lakes, and the prospect of being able to work, sail and relax as he pleased was an obvious delight.

For a moment, the matter seemed as good as done. Berlin's municipal government had recently bought what should have been the perfect property—a fine house set in a large estate that came complete with a river winding through the gardens. Unfortunately, when Elsa Einstein went to inspect the place, she found that someone already lived there. Böss had ignored or forgotten the fact that when the previous owners had sold the estate, they had retained the right to occupy their former house for five years. When the mayor heard of the problem, he told Einstein that he would force the previous owner to move out, but Einstein refused to benefit from someone else's eviction.

What followed swiftly turned into a farce. The erstwhile owners of the disputed property refused to give up a portion of the gardens to permit the city to build Einstein a house there. Berlin then offered him several other choices, each of which was unsuitable—one of them was near a noisy motorboat club; another could only be reached by water; and a third was merely a bug-infested building site cut off from the shore. Under pressure, the city made a new suggestion: Einstein could find his own site, the city would buy it and donate it to him, and he could then build his own house to his own specifications and at his own expense. Elsa Einstein had long since grown frustrated by the whole affair, and when she learned that they were now to pay for the house, her anger erupted. "Modest as he is, my husband even accepted this," she said. "The gift is getting smaller and smaller."[28]

Meanwhile, March 14 had come and gone. Overtly, it was an occasion for public celebration. Several newspapers published adulatory tributes—*Vossische Zeitung* announced that "Einstein stands close to Leonardo"; that he was "blessed with a laughing vitality"; that he was "a silent and lonely working scientific genius" who yet possessed "a strong loving interest in human beings." In sum, Einstein was "unique in our times . . . this very important homo universalis."[29] Most of the major press published similar tributes. One of them had also begun to report on Berlin's proposed gift to its great hero. As site after site proved untenable, the press picked up on that too. On April 18, *Vossische Zeitung* listed the series of attempted gifts and concluded that "it is therefore more than unclear if and when Einstein will receive his birthday present. It is more than clear, certainly, that the Berlin Senate once again proved its talent for extremely embarrassing performances."[30]

It only got worse. By the time that Einstein managed to find a suitable piece of land in the village of Caputh, near Potsdam, the gift had become thoroughly enmeshed in politics. Böss had passed the word to Einstein that the city would move quickly to buy the land in question, but when the Berlin city council tried to appropriate the funds necessary to do so, the Nationalist opposition to Böss's Social Democrats seized on the issue as a perfect vehicle to humiliate their rivals. They blocked the budget measure, demanding a secret debate. Their objection: Einstein was a prominent, pacifist Jew, only tenuously a German, annoyingly blunt in his political opinions. Why should he, of all great Berlin scientists, be singled out for an unprecedented civic gift?

With that, Einstein gave up. In May he told the council that he would not now accept any offer from the city. His letter was gently sarcastic. The *Berliner Tageblatt* reported that he had merely noted that "life was too short and the affair of this gift . . . had gone on too long" to tolerate.[31] In the end, he simply did it himself. He bought the property he had found in Caputh, had a very pleasant house built (which still stands), was given a sailboat, the *Tümmler,* and began to enjoy the life of the country gentleman. He genuinely loved the Caputh house, and Elsa did too, despite its unfortunate associations as the scene of some of her husband's trysts. Home movies from the period show Einstein reveling in the complete freedom from fashion he enjoyed there, walking around barefoot, his caps made from knotted handkerchiefs, eating outdoors, sailing. He and Elsa smile frequently for the camera and Elsa laughs out loud. Their guests are relaxed. The sun shines. These are happy memories, good times.

Caputh remained Einstein's haven for the rest of his time in Germany. He refused to install a telephone, and the distance from central Berlin was such that few intruders were willing to make the journey on the off chance the professor would see them. Those were fine times for him and for Berlin in that last good year. The economy seemed sound. The boom that had begun in 1924 after the end of the hyperinflation and the continuous flow of foreign loans was still rolling along. In 1928, Germany's industrial production finally matched that of 1913, and the following year it passed the rest of Europe to become the largest industrial economy on the Continent, second in the world only to the United States. Perhaps it was better simply to ignore politics, to avoid the messy, bitter contentiousness of the street, and to retreat instead into the comfort of private pleasures leavened with the excitement of spectacular, resolutely apolitical entertainment. After so many hardships over so many years, why not enjoy life?

Chapter Twenty-one

"WHILE WOLVES WAIT OUTSIDE"

THE WARM AND PLEASANT MONTHS OF THE SUMMER OF 1929 LULLED many in Berlin, not just Einstein, sailing happily in the *Tümmler.* There were some scattered signs of real trouble, though. A few people tried to sound a familiar warning. As early as 1920, in fact, long before Hitler had poked even an eyebrow above the swamp of Bavarian *völkish* wrangling, the cabaret poet and Dadaist Walter Mehring had written of the vicious confluence of new propaganda methods, nostalgic revanchism and anti-Semitism in a poem titled "Simultaneous Berlin" *(Berlin simultan),* performed by Rosa Valetti in her revue *Megalomania.* "An UFA film/Hails Kaiser Wil'm./Cathedrals wag reaction's flag,/With Swastikas and poison gas,/Monocles won't let hooked noses pass/On to the pogrom/In the hippodrome!"[1]

But Mehring was an exception, unrelenting in his readiness to twist the rhetorical knife into each and every instance of cruelty or hypocrisy. It was easier, and much more common, to lose oneself in the pleasures of the moment and the place. And so it was that 1929 saw Marlene Dietrich's breakthrough in the *Blue Angel.* As Lola, the nightclub singer with the infinite legs, she sang with disdainful hauteur, proclaiming the gospel of easy sex, love begun and ended with the same equanimity—and she became a smash, an icon for the uninvolved. This was a year of facile heroes. Hugo Eckener piloted his giant airship, the

Graf Zeppelin, on its flight around the world. The trip took him twenty-one days at an average speed of seventy miles per hour, and he carried with him a gorilla and a grand piano. Eckener came home in triumph to suggestions that he might be a perfect presidential candidate in the next elections. This was the year in which Weimar Berlin celebrated excess as a civic achievement—even a new swimming pool could attract accolades from so usually sober a journal as the *Vossische Zeitung.* It breathlessly reported that "the swimming hall is the most luxurious public pool ever built in the city." No expense had been spared: "The walls are covered with pure white ceramics, the shower rooms have been designed in different colors of blue and the entrance hall is a composition of green porcelain tiles and a snow-white marble floor." And it was a bargain, too: "The entrance fee of 3.50 marks is relatively cheap compared to the level of luxury" to be found there, although the reporter remembered himself long enough to note that most Berliners still could not afford such a tariff.[2]

In that last note lay the fracture, the point at which the whole facade blew apart. Even at the best of times, hardship and genuine poverty remained a constant in Berlin's enormous slums. Ironic contrasts were a commonplace even before the bubble burst. The movie *L'Argent, Geld, Geld, Geld—Gold, Gold, Gold*—became a hit that spring, at the same time that the papers were reporting that unemployment had risen during the winter, until more than 2.25 million Germans were out of work by early March. Mies van der Rohe lavished the German pavilion for the 1929 World's Fair in Berlin with expanses of marble and chrome-plated columns—all in a building destined to disappear within a few months. At the same time, the *Vossische Zeitung* announced that the age of Berlin suicides was dropping. The youngest yet to kill herself in the city had been found on April 19. She was a ten-year-old girl who strangled herself because, the paper reported, "she does not want to be a burden for her parents anymore, and had decided to make room for the new baby her mother was expecting."[3] Come May Day, the streets exploded in a spasm of violence, battles between workers' organizations and Nazis, that ended with 19 dead and 65,000 under arrest.

Tensions ratcheted up across the year in tandem with the economic hardships that lay beneath them. The numbers of homeless children in Berlin swelled. So did the citywide housing shortage. A bomb exploded at the Reichstag against the sporadic background of street skirmishes that marked Goebbels's ongoing campaign to irritate the Weimar body politic. Yet even so, from summer into fall, a precarious equilibrium persisted between the reality of poverty and the love of wealth so recently regained in Berlin. The event that destroyed that balance came late in October. On Tuesday, October 22, 1929, the New York Stock Exchange's Dow Jones Industrial Index had closed at 326. The Stock Exchange opened for business as usual the next morning, but a selloff of stocks became a rout as the hours passed. The selling continued in waves of panic for another five trading sessions, culminating on the disaster of Tuesday, October 29. At the closing bell the Dow Jones Index stood at 230—a 29 percent drop over the previous week. (The industrials index would eventually bottom out at 41 in 1932.) That one week, marked by iconic names like Black Friday and Black Tuesday, sounded the opening bell of the Great Depression, the worldwide economic collapse of the 1930s.

For all the misery to come, however, no one in Berlin seemed to notice what had happened at first. The private ostentation of Weimar's wealthy—including those who had turned the hyperinflation to their profit—persisted well after the crash. In December, Harry Kessler wrote in his diary of yet another dinner party with the fabulously rich. "Eight to ten people, intimate party, extreme luxury," he noted. "Four priceless masterpieces by Manet, Cezanne, van Gogh and Monet respectively. After the meal, thirty van Gogh letters, in an excessively ornate, ugly binding were handed round with cigarettes and coffee. Poor van Gogh!" It was all too much. "I saw red, and would gladly have instituted a pogrom. Not out of jealousy, but disgust at the falsification and degradation of intellectual and artistic values to mere baubles, 'luxurious' possessions."[4]

To a repelled and weary Kessler, there was no substance left. It was a diagnosis that could be leveled more broadly; the ostentation of the rich was a magnified example of the pathology that infected the wider culture as well. Snow white marble or an ape on a round-the-world flight made for good copy, but the sheer noise, the unfocused cheers for each well-publicized novelty, served to distract attention from the real warning signs. The evidence was there for anyone to see: that Berlin itself, Germany as a whole, tottered on the edge of a cliff.

* * *

BLACK FRIDAY WAS THE MOMENT that Hitler and Goebbels had been waiting for ever since the debacle of the presidential election in 1925, when Hindenburg had outpolled the Nazis' Ludendorff by a sixty-to-one margin. 1928 had been their nadir. In the Reichstag elections in May, Hitler's party won just 2.6 percent of the total vote, which translated into a mere twelve seats in the Reichstag. Though Goebbels was one of those elected, the party's results in his territory, Berlin itself, were even worse; the Nazis took just 1.5 percent of the vote in a city that remained a left-wing stronghold. Compared with the high-water marks of earlier years, especially the heady breakthrough time in 1924 when the far right had first burst into national attention, this was a debacle, a humiliation.

In Berlin itself, as in the nation, the party's response was to attack. The Goebbels strategy of maintaining a low-level violence married to a continuing drumbeat of propaganda had changed little since his first provocations in early 1927. But despite the election results, the party had been transformed. It was no longer a tiny splinter group within Berlin's radical right. At the national level, the Nazis' assaults on political opponents grew extraordinary virulent, extending to public calls for the assassination of men like Gustav Stresemann, who throughout the '20s, as foreign minister and then chancellor, had directed Germany's reentry into European political life, beginning with his controversial decision to stop the policy of passive resistance against the Franco-Belgian occupation of the Ruhr. In Berlin itself, this furious propaganda war was augmented by direct action, an organized campaign of violent crime intended to foster an ongoing sense of crisis. The Nazis may have been vote-poor, but Goebbels and his men set out to demonstrate that they had to be taken seriously as the face and fists of the antirepublican right.

Thus, while 1927 had been relatively quiet, with almost no newspaper mention of Nazi disturbances within the city itself, in 1928 Goebbels used the occasional outrage to refocus attention on his party, his men, and its leader. In March, he was convicted of breach of the peace and other crimes and sentenced to six weeks in jail, the police having earlier foiled an attempt by Berlin's Nazis to kidnap their leader from the courthouse. (Goebbels never actually served the time.) In May, a public brawl broke out when party members commanded by Goebbels started to batter several apparently randomly chosen people on the street. When the group of about twenty was finally subdued and arrested, they said that their target had been the Jewish synagogue at the end of the road. In September, Nazi party leaders trapped the Brazilian consul on the street and beat him to the ground, breaking several bones, apparently because he seemed to them to be Jewish. When they came to trial, they explained their actions by complaining that the consul had provoked them with a sarcastic remark as they passed by.

On the surface, this was a record of minor thuggery. Goebbels and his gang were clearly violent and dangerous, but the newspaper accounts leave the image of a fringe group trying to batter its way to prominence without much effect. Still, Goebbels kept up the pressure throughout early 1929. In January, four drunk Nazis clubbed down two Communist party supporters, leaving one man crippled for life. The *Vossische Zeitung* reported with concern that although the attackers were found guilty, they received sentences of only two weeks of prison and fines of fifty marks each. As noted earlier, Nazi leaders had enjoyed easy treatment in the courts ever since Hitler's high treason in the Beer Hall Putsch had earned him less than a year in a comfortable jail. But by late 1929 this immunity would extend to the rank and file who committed essentially ordinary crimes, barroom brawls and the like. Increasingly, the Nazi badge was becoming a license for whatever antisocial act they could dream up, and the Berlin party took full advantage of this free pass.

Another measure of growing Nazi party influence came with the scale of its actions. Twenty-man marches became a relic of the past. May Day 1929 prompted a major show of strength, and on the tenth anniversary of the signing of the Versailles Treaty in June, several hundred National Socialist students stepped up their campaign to destabilize and "cleanse" Berlin University of its Jews, socialists and other undesirables. Thousands more swept into widespread street battles in mid-October, carrying the fight to inner city neighborhoods where the Communists, heirs to Liebknecht's Spartacists, had built their power base. The goal was to provoke, threaten, and overawe both potential political allies on the nationalist right and enemies on the left.

Nonetheless, until Black Friday the Nazis seemed no more than a loud, brutal, vicious nuisance. They could do damage, but in Berlin they did so as minor players.

Then came the crash. Black Friday itself aroused no more comment on the right than it had in the mainstream press: *Völkischer Beobachter,* the Nazi newspaper, carried no mention of the stock market debacle. But as the consequences of America's crisis began to trigger an avalanche of economic distress in Germany, Hitler and his associates realized that this was their moment. On one level, the raw numbers tell the story. Unemployment in Germany had fallen as low as 6.2 percent in 1927. In official figures it ticked up to 6.3 percent in 1929, and then increased significantly in 1929, rising to 8.5 percent. Then came the crash and the numbers snowballed: within months nationwide jobless totals hit 14 percent. In Berlin itself, it was the same story. There had been 31,800 Berliners registered as unemployed in 1929. The numbers climbed throughout 1930, and into the next year, until by the fall of 1931, two years after the crash, 323,000 were listed as unemployed—a tenfold leap from before the stock market collapse. (There were, of course, tens of thousands more who slipped through the official tallies.) Berlin ultimately accounted for up to one in seven of the jobless in the entire country. The upshot of all this: almost from the moment of the crash, the city reeled. Only six years removed from the hyperinflation and little more than ten from the end of the war, the lives of ordinary working people were once again being rendered almost unlivable.

The government did little, in part because it had so little to do anything *with.* Ever since the end of the hyperinflation, Germany had used its access to foreign capital markets to secure short-term loans, most of them American, to sustain local and national government budgets along with much of the country's industrial economy. This was in part a policy of necessity—the experience of runaway inflation made many lenders reluctant to tie up cash in long-term deals. Nonetheless, what appeared to be easy money had been flowing into Germany from 1924 on. The danger it brought with it seems blindingly obvious in hindsight: in bad times, short-term loans can be called home, leaving the borrowers broke or, even worse, bankrupt. In the wake of Black Friday, American lenders made the predictable decision, calling in existing loans and refusing to make new ones. As the crisis deepened through

1930, so did Germany's cash crunch, which only became more dire as the rising tide of right-wing political violence spooked creditors further. In just two months in autumn 1930, foreign lenders called in 633 million marks of gold and foreign exchange.[5] German domestic production collapsed almost overnight; the Berlin city government faced a 400-million-mark debt and the prospect of default. Subway fares, water bills, any city-levied rates, all went up and local and regional government spending evaporated. Berlin's poor and infirm had nowhere to turn for help.

In consequence, once-respectable Berliners were forced into the slums and then into tent camps that sprang up in open tracts on the fringes of town. The camps were well organized. The tents lined "streets" that had names and signs. "Mayors" were elected, along with camp councils. It was a systematic, very German response to disaster, but it did not alleviate the hard truth. The men in the camps sat without purpose day after day, their anger festering.[6] Pawnshops prospered. A newspaper survey found that their most common clients were shopkeepers, followed by housewives.[7] Once again, the middle class had first to pledge and then to sell whatever was movable—furniture, silverware, ultimately their houses.

More threatening, as in the hyperinflation of 1922–1923, real hunger took hold. Horsemeat restaurants boomed and farmers near Berlin took to patrolling their land with rifles to dissuade potato foragers. Exhausted men too poor to afford a room rented beds by the hour in slum apartments; the children in such homes took what rest they could on the floor.[8] Those too weak to stand erect—and their numbers grew each year the crisis lasted—simply collapsed where they stood. In ever more famished Berlin, those hale enough to keep moving stepped over those who fell. It would have been impossible to imagine a more perfect opening for Goebbels and his master, Adolf Hitler.

Yet even with the crash and the exploitable economic misery that followed, the Nazis appeared unable to break through to power, blocked both by their own demonstrated incompetence in the few state and local offices they held and by the fact that they remained only one among several forces on the right. As spring approached in 1930 and economic conditions were worsening rather than improving, they seemed to have reached a limit to their own growth. To move forward, they needed a gift from their enemies.

That gift came in March. When the Social Democrats and the center parties failed to reach a compromise on a social welfare measure, the Socialist-led government fell, to be replaced by a center-right administration led by Chancellor Heinrich Brüning, leader of the moderately conservative Center party. Brüning tried to rule by decree, but was blocked by an alliance of convenience in the Reichstag that included the Nazis. In July the Reichstag was dissolved and Brüning called new elections for September 14, two years ahead of schedule. It was, as Hitler and Goebbels recognized, both an extraordinary opportunity for them and a colossal blunder on the part of the democratic parties.

The story of Hitler's rise repeats the same basic pattern. There was nothing inevitable about his triumph, not then and not even in the last days of the Weimar Republic, late in 1932 and early in 1933. Time and again decisions that were available to the people making them—real choices, not impossible ones—would have barred the door. But his enemies routinely underestimated Hitler. Brüning knew that there would be Nazi gains, but he expected them to be counterbalanced by victories on the center-right. It was just one of many such delusions. And Hitler was more than merely lucky. He was a profoundly effective party leader, magnetic and obsessive, a mesmerizing speaker, able to carry others along with him and inspire them to perform heroic labor on his behalf. The detailed story of the ultimate Nazi victory is beyond the scope of this book, but its essence lies in the utter failure of the democratic forces within Weimar either to assess his true strength accurately or to unite to bar his way.

Throughout, they had due warning. The election campaign of 1930 was a model of what would follow. Goebbels led the charge as the newly appointed director of party propaganda. His was by far the most dynamic and most powerfully organized effort of any of the parties. He leavened the usual diet of street fights and provocations—one thousand Nazis in uniform marching through the center of Berlin in July, bar brawls and the like—with an enormous grassroots effort across Germany. In the last month before the election, the Nazis held an astounding 34,000 political rallies. No one else came close. Hitler himself gave twenty major speeches in forty days.

Moreover, it was a newly impressive Hitler, who reached out to his largest audience yet. In his first official campaign speech in Berlin, he presented himself as the only leader capable of saving a desperate nation. He spoke at the Sportpalast to a packed house—Goebbels claimed that 100,000 people had tried in advance to get tickets to a venue that held just 16,000. The hall had been prepared meticulously, with special lighting and a beefed-up sound system able to project the Führer's words to the farthest corner of the arena. By then, Goebbels and his Berlin party team had mastered every nuance of the political rally. The crowd was admitted early, and was carefully primed through hours of waiting amid the noise, the banners, the stark black swastika floating on the forest of flags. The first hint of Hitler's approach came from the roar in the street. As he reached the stage, the audience went wild, jumping to its feet, cheering and shouting "*Heil* Hitler!" When at last he spoke, he played his listeners superbly, alternating his attacks with a dramatic vision of the future.

With a precise sense of what the moment required, Hitler proposed no concrete policies. As Gregor Strasser, an early rival to Hitler for Nazi party leadership, pointed out, the Nazis had no actual program. Rather, they had targets: the Jews, foreign powers, the Weimar Republic itself, any of whom—all of whom—were responsible for Germany's plight and the individual German's despair. To heal the nation, Hitler offered the simplest of visions. His Germany (echoing the kaiser's rhetoric from 1914) would know no divisions, no classes or warring factions. Rather, it would become "a community of people, which, beyond all difference, will rescue the common strength of the nation." He spoke of "the liberation of the entire people," to be completed only through allegiance to the "high ideal" of National Socialism—and to the heart of that movement, its Führer, the leader, he himself.[9]

The idea of the transcendent, heroic leader above and at odds with democratic processes is one that predated Hitler, of course. The right had always seen democracy not as the expression of the will of the people but as leaderless anarchy, mob rule, a plague to be eliminated at any cost. By contrast, the man on a white horse was a venerated figure to many Germans, a familiar one given the reverence that had been accorded heroic autocrats from Frederick the Great to Bismarck. Hitler himself seems to have picked up the idea of the aloof, ineffable, infallible Führer by observing how Italy's Benito Mussolini exploited the image of Il Duce to create an air of inevitability about his own rise to power in 1922. As early as 1923, a year before his farcical Beer Hall Putsch, Hitler was already speaking of the leader who comes as "a gift from heaven," for whom his supporters must "create the sword that this person will need. . . ."[10] He did not then see himself as that divine gift. That was to come a little later, with his propaganda victory in the treason trial that followed the putsch and then with the months of intoxicating self-absorption in prison writing *Mein Kampf.*

Hitler was able to persuade those closest to him of his ordained role well before the economy collapsed. Goebbels, of course, was an early and devout convert, and in an article written in 1928 he captured the essential creed of the Nazi true believer: "We are all convinced, so that our conviction can never be shaken, that he is the mouthpiece and the pathbreaker of the future. Therefore, we believe in him. Beyond his human form, we can see in this man the active grace of destiny, and we cling to his thought with all our hopes and bind ourselves to that creative power that drives him and all of us forward."[11]

Published in *Der Angriff,* this proclamation was aimed at the party faithful. But by the economic debacle of 1930, the idea of surrendering oneself to revealed authority had vastly broader appeal, as did the Nazi promise of revenge against all those who had brought Germany so low. Hitler was, in fact, extraordinarily cynical about the poor and their desires; the masses, he said behind closed doors, sought only bread and circuses.[12] Perhaps so; certainly, in the 1930 campaign he gave them the circus and the promise of bread. And they loved his act, his brilliant, mesmerizing portrayal of himself as Germany's savior.

The September election results were an earthquake for Germany. Most startling to establishment conservatives led by the chancellor, the KPD, the German Communist party, received 4.6 million votes, bringing it to third place in the national tally. The Communists had been a growing political presence in Berlin even before the crash, but the focus of their fury was not enemies on the right but their more hated rivals on the near left, the SPD. In 1928, on orders from Stalin's Comintern—the Communist International—the KPD launched a series of attacks on the Social Democrats, publishing newspaper broadsides that branded them fascists. This was a term of abuse imported from Benito Mussolini's Italy, and KPD-inspired theatrical groups portrayed the SPD either as the willing puppet of the arms industry or as counterrevolutionaires as hidebound and vicious as capitalism itself. As the third largest delegation in the Reichstag, they could now make mischief at the heart of the republic with unprecedented success, and they colluded with other extremist parties to disrupt the orderly functions of the legislature.

The identity of their most eager partner in this sabotage only seems unlikely. The other group with the most to win from the collapse of Weimar institutions had won an even greater triumph than the KPD. The National Socialists gained 6.4 million votes—ten times their total just two years before—and one hundred seven seats. They were now the second largest party in the Reichstag behind the SPD. When combined with the Communist delegation, that meant that the parties of the extremes now represented the plurality of the German electorate. The word *Nazi* no longer evoked images of the madhouse, as one commentator wrote. Suddenly the party was almost respectable.

It was also still short of its ultimate goal. Hitler and Chancellor Brüning met secretly after the election, but the outcome failed to achieve either man's aims. Brüning wanted Hitler to moderate his public language and agree to take on the role of a loyal opposition in parliament. Hitler wanted power. In an hour-long harangue he stunned the chancellor with his relentless use of the word "annihilate" in reference to all perceived enemies, foreign and domestic.[13] No agreement of any sort was possible. Thus untrammeled by any inconvenient parliamentary obligations, Hitler launched the Nazis on a new round of political organization and agitation. The party held almost twice as many rallies after the election as it had throughout the campaign—seventy thousand in the months immediately following the vote—and in an unholy alliance with the Communists, began to wage a series of staged street battles to emphasize the established order's inability to keep order. Hitler was clearly dangerous, clearly and openly seeking absolute rule, and clearly able to command the allegiance of a growing multitude.

But even with his sudden rise to the edge of power, he still seemed to many to be a temporary evil, to be overcome before long. Shortly after the September elections Thomas Mann gave a lecture that took the threat of Hitler's rise to power very seriously, yet, repeatedly interrupted by Nazi heckling, he could not resist expressing a kind of bemused contempt, dismissing Hitler as a figure of "politics in the grotesque style, with Salvation Army attractions, mass fits . . . and dervish-like repetition of monotonous slogans until everyone is foaming at the mouth."[14] Perhaps so, as Count Kessler had acknowledged in his very depressed diary entry on the day after the election. National Socialism, he wrote, was "a delirium of the dying German lower middle class." But madness or not, he added, "the poison of its disease may, however, bring down ruin on Germany and Europe for decades ahead."[15]

ALBERT EINSTEIN AGREED, but at first only up to a point. Hitler's sudden rush to prominence confirmed his historic distrust of the German body politic. At this time, though, he did not see Hitler or National Socialism as a lasting danger. He had nothing but contempt for the man himself. Asked in December of 1930 what to make of the new force in German politics, he answered, "I do not enjoy Herr Hitler's acquaintance. He is living on the empty stomach of Germany. As soon as economic conditions improve, he will no longer be important."[16] He did not feel that any action was needed to bring Hitler low. He reaffirmed to a Jewish news agency that the "momentarily desperate economic situation" and the chronic "childish disease of the Republic" were to blame for the Nazi success. "Solidarity of the Jews, I believe, is always called for," he wrote, "but any special reaction to the election results would be quite inappropriate."

Einstein should have been right—the evidence for the fragility of Hitler's support over the next two years makes for frustrating, bitter what-if history. But even if (like so many Germans) he underestimated Hitler, he did recognize the need to act to counter the more general pathology of which his rise was a symptom. So, throughout the end of the 1920s, anticipating the crisis to come, Einstein launched his last significant attempt to sway public sentiment within Germany. It would prove to be an even more hopeless crusade than his campaign against the quantum theory.

The specific spur that moved him to act was not Hitler but the threat of German rearmament, along with a resurgence of militarism across the European continent. Germany had been almost completely disarmed by the Versailles Treaty. Its army could total no more than one hundred thousand men; its forces were denied most heavy weapons; it could not build an air force; its warships had to meet strict tonnage and armament restrictions. But evasion of these terms had been the rule almost from the start. Some of the tricks used were more or less legitimate. Army maneuvers in 1921 practiced offensive tactics; combined operations using borrowed aircraft and motorized troops followed in 1923 and 1924. And again in 1924, army captain Heinz Guderian organized a series of exercises in which motorcycles, armored cars on loan from police forces, and armored troop carriers stood in for tanks in a rehearsal for mobile armored campaigns. Guderian, eventually a general, would put the lessons learned in these and subsequent exercises into practice in the blitzkrieg assault that defeated France in 1940.

Ultimately, these actions were misdemeanors, violations of the spirit of the Versailles Treaty that remained reasonably true to its letter. But at the same time, there was a series of moves that led the military into direct and more ominous defiance of the treaty. The manpower limits were evaded by using the police as an active reserve, producing a total of seventy thousand in excess of the hundred-thousand-man limit, arming them with automatic weapons and heavy machine guns, quartering them on military bases with retired army officers to command them. Much more significant were the sustained efforts to gain access to the full range of modern offensive military technology. The Krupp munitions firm continued to design forbidden weapons, to be built by its overseas subsidiaries. A nationwide network of private flying clubs provided the nucleus of pilots to serve in a restored air force. Submarine development took place in Cadiz, Spain, in factories under German control. Most threatening of all, secret negotiations with the Soviet Union sponsored by the army General Staff led to the establishment of a German arms industry there, a network of production facilities that churned out airplanes built from German designs, poison gas, and the shells needed for Krupp's illegal cannon.[17] By the end of the 1920s, the veneer of secrecy was wearing thin, while at the same time, pressure came from the right to drop the pretense and rearm openly.

This military ambition, coming barely a decade after the war that ought to have inoculated Germany against the contagion of battle lust, was intolerable to Einstein. In response, he advocated mass rejection of compulsory military service by young men throughout Europe, a campaign that had become a major pillar of pacifist politics after the war. His initial statements on draft resistance were general, almost vapid: "Every thoughtful, well-meaning and conscientious human being," he wrote in January 1928 in a letter to London's No More War movement, "should assume, in time of peace, the solemn and unconditional obligation not to participate in any war for any reason. . . ."[18] More pointedly, but still abstractly, he said in another message that "no one has the moral right to call himself a Christian or a Jew if he is prepared to commit murder upon the instruction of a given authority."[19]

He grew more insistent as time passed. In the spring of 1929, he wrote, again to London, "The people *themselves* [emphasis in the original] must take the initiative to see to it that they will never again be led to slaughter. To expect protection from their governments is folly."[20] He did not abandon his other causes—he broke with a group named the League against Imperialism and National Independence, resigning an honorary chairmanship in protest of the league's criticism of Jewish settlement in Palestine. But he continued to devote the bulk of the energy and time he was willing to commit to public life to the cause of military refusal. His was neither an ideological commitment nor a reasoned argument of principle. He told the editor of *Christian Century* in July of 1929, "My pacifism is an instinctive feeling, a feeling that possesses me; the thought of murdering another human being is abhorrent to me. My attitude is not the result of an intellectual theory but is caused by a deep antipathy to every kind of cruelty and hatred."[21]

Einstein continued to argue that same emotional case throughout the year, concluding an exchange with a Frenchman who feared for nations that disarmed unilaterally by restating his bedrock argument: killing innocent people and training people to kill were simply unacceptable under any circumstances. "As far as I am concerned," he concluded, "the welfare of humanity must take precedence over loyalty to one's own country—in fact, over anything and everything."[22] During the next several months of 1930, driven by the rise of militant nationalism across Europe, his level of urgency and passion grew. War had become an absolute anathema to him: "I would rather be torn limb from limb," he wrote, "than take part in such an ugly business."

Einstein's activism, unsurprisingly, made no significant impact on German opinion. But whatever his weakness as a practical politician, there is no question that he himself fully embraced the hope of preventing war through the conscientious, courageous acts of individual human beings. He was willing to put his clout and public capital on the line to do so. He wrote, he spoke, he joined. Even though he felt that the Nazi triumph in September of 1930 was a temporary phenomenon, a threat that would evaporate as times improved, the sudden upsurge in support of the most militarily ambitious elements in Germany increased his sense of urgency. In December 1930, he sounded the clarion call. "When those who are bound together by pacifist ideals hold a meeting," he said, "they are usually consorting with their own kind. They are like sheep huddled together while wolves wait outside." That was no longer good enough, far from it. Serious pacifists must take courage, organize internationally, raise funds to support draft resisters. They must spread the word, loudly, eagerly. If they did not, they would become twins to those who allowed themselves to be herded into the armies of the world. "They will remain sheep," he said, "pacifist sheep."[23]

YET FOR ALL OF EINSTEIN'S ANGER at what he saw as the threat of militarism, on a personal level 1930 remained a mostly ordinary year for him. His ability to earn hard currency by writing or speaking insulated him from the immediate pressure of the economic crisis. He was to change his mind about the threat that Hitler represented much faster than most Germans who shared his views, but at the moment, he felt little immediate and no personal danger. In any case, he had more pressing and immediate matters to deal with.

The summer of 1930 began much as usual for the Einstein family. They spent as much time as they could at Caputh, where, in July, Einstein renewed his acquaintance with the Indian pacifist and poet Rabindranath Tagore. The two men talked at length, first about causation, a topic about which they not only could not agree but could not even understand each other, and then more satisfactorily about music. To Tagore, Einstein seemed the ultimate disinterested man of ideas. He had "withdrawn himself from the world and its superficialities," Tagore wrote. "He is devoted to peace and the well-being of mankind." Tagore was not wrong, but as usual the iconic image was incomplete, especially that summer, when Einstein was forced to confront a crisis overwhelming his younger son, Eduard.

Einstein's relations with Eduard had always had been fraught. The boy, born in 1910, was just four years old when his parents separated. After the break in 1914, Einstein kept in touch with both of his sons by mail and saw them on visits to Switzerland, but his contacts with Eduard were complex from very early on. The boy was talented, perhaps even brilliant. He wrote well and in his teens corresponded with his father eagerly and ambitiously, discussing favorite ideas, writers and music.

Einstein's response to this outpouring was ambivalent. At this remove of time, it seems clear that Eduard was trying to find some path to engage his distant father. But while Einstein probably grasped this, and certainly replied encouragingly to many of the letters, the attempt to build an intellectual bridge between that father and that son was a risky venture from the start. Einstein could and did forget that he was talking with his child, not with a peer. Eduard complained of an impersonal tone to Einstein's letters, and this was to get worse, as when Einstein told Eduard that he thought some of his ideas were copied from other writers. That would have been a legitimate observation to make to an intellectual adversary, but teenagers with active minds echo their sources as a matter of course. Einstein was never much good at empathy, and as he had with Hans Albert at a similar age, he found himself unable to put himself in his son's place. Instead, he in effect dismissed what Eduard himself called his "rather rapturous letters," ones clearly aimed to capture his father's attention.[24]

Einstein had had his troubles with each of his boys at different times throughout the 1920s. He reacted furiously when Hans Albert became involved with, and then in 1927, aged twenty-three, married an older and—to Einstein—an unattractive woman. The old joke that one's children are the grandparents' revenge on their own offspring was surely true here. Einstein reacted to the news much as his mother had at his own engagement to Mileva, damning the union, swearing that Hans Albert's bride was a scheming woman preying on his son. When all else failed, he begged Hans Albert not to have children, as it would only make the inevitable divorce harder. It took years—well into the 1930s—before Einstein fully calmed down; the episode added one more layer to what was already a highly complicated weave of love and deep anger between the two. But in 1929, and especially in 1930, it was Eduard who inspired at first concern, then anguish.

In 1929, Eduard entered medical school in Zurich, intending to become a psychiatrist. He had venerated Freud for years, precociously, despite—or perhaps, as the master himself might say, because of—his father's ultimate scorn for the ideas and methods of psychoanalysis. But within the first few months of his medical training, Eduard fell into a deep depression, possibly triggered by an unhappy relationship with the obligatory older woman. He began to cut classes and avoid his friends, confining himself to his darkened rooms. Einstein gave Eduard sturdy, fatherly advice—find another girlfriend, get a job, just keep moving—all of which did no good. In the summer of 1930 Eduard began to write harshly and bitterly to his father, a series of what a family friend said were "incoherent letters in which the desire to affirm a weak personality through grand language alternated with outbursts of despair . . . pathetic, unhinged letters."[25]

Here was not just rebellion but madness—the real thing this time, schizophrenia. There was nothing Einstein feared more than such derangement, the destruction of the capacity to make sense of the world. He went to Zurich that summer to try to talk Eduard out of his collapse, but failed. According to Elsa, it was a terrible trauma: "This sorrow is eating Albert up. He finds it difficult to cope with it, more difficult than he would care to admit." By this time, Elsa knew her husband very well. Eduard's disaster, she said, struck Einstein to the heart. "He has always aimed at being invulnerable to everything that concerned him personally," she wrote. "He really is so, much more than any other man I know. But this has hit him very hard."[26]

Eduard never recovered. Mileva was able to care for him at home for a time, but in 1932, his condition worsened, and Einstein and Mileva sent him to the Burghölzli psychiatric hospital where Carl Jung had once trained. In later years Einstein paid to have Eduard seen by specialists elsewhere, in Zurich and Vienna. He fell prey to the pet treatments of the day for his intractable disorder. He was given electroshock therapy, which Hans Albert blamed for rendering his brother's condition irreversible. He even received a course of insulin shocks—the grotesque, almost medieval treatment in which doctors administered high doses of insulin in the hope that these would stun a diseased brain back into reason. Nothing worked. Eduard became bloated, overweight, increasingly withdrawn, incapable of handling even ordinary tasks. Although his mother brought him home as much as possible, Eduard was ultimately to remain at the Burghölzli until his death in 1965.

To Einstein, the cause of the debacle was obvious. Mileva, herself prone to depression, had a sister who was truly unhinged, and Einstein felt that there was nothing more to say on the subject. Both Mileva and his friends suggested on more than one occasion that Eduard might benefit if Einstein would either move to Zurich to spend more time with him or if he would invite the boy to Berlin to travel with him. Einstein refused. There was no point; there could be no cure. "Everything unfortunately indicates that grave heredity will have its decisive effect" on Eduard, he told Besso. "I have seen it coming, slowly but irresistibly, ever since Tedel's [Eduard's nickname] youth."[27] He visited his son occasionally. He made sure that money was never an issue in Eduard's care. But he made no move to bring himself closer to his son. "I have come to know the mutability of all human relations," he had written, years before. With that knowledge, he told one of his closest friends, he had "learned to isolate myself from heat and cold so that the temperature balance is fairly well assured."[28]

And so, after the summer's anguishing drama, Einstein returned to the normal round of his affairs. That year he had reemphasized his public allegiance to Germany's Jews. He agreed to play his violin in a benefit concert at the main synagogue in Berlin. The photograph of the event is the only known image of Einstein in a yarmulke. Again the contrast between his feelings for the individual and the mass is overt. Given his opinions of the ritual tradition of the Jews, his willingness to be seen in uniform, as it were, marks the depth of his connection to the idea of a Jewish community.

In the autumn, Einstein began to travel again. He had already made plans to visit the United States for the first time in a decade, agreeing to a visiting professorship at Caltech for the first few months of 1931. But before setting out on that long absence from Berlin, he made the short hop to Brussels for the Solvay Conference, and then went to London for three days. He had added the extra destination to be the guest of honor for a charity dinner to benefit Eastern European Jews. London society turned out in impressive numbers to fill the Savoy Hotel's ballroom. It was a vast, elegant crowd that met him, all dressed impeccably—even Einstein wore white tie and tails, looking quite comfortable in what he termed the "monkey comedy" of such affairs.

Baron Rothschild hosted the event. (Einstein laughed afterward, telling Chaim Weizmann that most people weren't sure whose hand to shake first, the peer's or the "Jewish saint's.")[29] George Bernard Shaw acted as master of ceremonies. Shaw had argued beforehand that Einstein ought to have the prime minister as MC, but he gave a bravura performance nonetheless. When Shaw rose to speak, he complained that he had to cover "Ptolemy and Aristotle, Kepler and Copernicus, Galileo and Newton, gravitation and relativity and modern astrophysics and Heaven knows what . . ." and then summed up the whole story in a paragraph: "Ptolemy made a universe which lasted for two thousand years. Newton made a universe which lasted for three hundred years. Einstein has made a universe, which I suppose you want me to say will never stop, but I don't know how long it will last."[30]

In the newsreel of the event Einstein can be seen laughing out loud at this, and the whole audience laughs with him. Shaw concluded by calling Einstein "the greatest of our contemporaries"—and who would argue with the claim? He apologized to Einstein for butchering his account of physics, and Einstein, laughing again, told him not to worry, that it wasn't his job to get that stuff right. And so it went at the Savoy on that pleasant, witty evening. In that grand room, the bedrock strength of what might be called western civilization seemed intact. Men and women of goodwill and wealth, taste and charity, joined together on behalf of struggling strangers. Poverty, misery, and anger might derange surprising numbers on the streets of Europe for a while—these were troubled days, without doubt. But here they all were, that bright, opulent crowd, come together so that their glow might push back the darkness one small step.

Einstein rose to respond to his accolades. He was a fine, compelling figure that night, his hair dramatic rather than merely unkempt, his formal clothes lending him a surprising aura of worldly authority. He thanked Shaw for his remarks "addressed to my mythical namesake, who makes life so difficult for me." He praised his hosts and his audience, especially the non-Jews among them, for their commitment to "uplifting human society and liberating the individual from degrading oppression." That job was still unfinished, certainly. But at that moment, in that hall, it seemed reasonable to believe that there was a community of like-minded people committed to the task. That should be enough, Einstein said. The Jews persist—by implication, in that context, humankind prospers—by "remaining faithful to the moral traditions that have enabled us to survive for thousands of years despite the fierce storms that have broken over our heads." He added one last thought, a remark spoken in hope and sincere belief. It reads now like an epitaph. "In the service of life," Einstein told the good and the great, "sacrifice becomes grace."[31]

Chapter Twenty-two

"WHO IS MARY PICKFORD?"

HOW MUCH DID HE STILL VALUE BERLIN? THAT WAS THE QUESTION Einstein confronted in earnest late in 1930, the first time since Rathenau's murder that he seriously weighed his choices. At first he did not propose leaving Berlin permanently, not yet; but he was beginning to welcome the idea of the occasional respite from the turmoil there. His extended visit to Caltech, to begin in January 1931, gave him a chance to test the waters beyond Germany. The journey across the Atlantic to New York, then down to the Panama Canal and back up again to Los Angeles, promised to be the one sure episode of peace and quiet in the coming year. But even when he simply sought to get out of town, Einstein could not avoid Berlin's tumult. The Nazis, so recently arrived at the edge of real power in Germany, required a constant supply of targets to fire up the troops, and Einstein, Germany's most famous Jew, fit the bill perfectly. Any pretext would do. So when he and his entourage—Elsa, his secretary Helen Dukas, and Walther Mayer, his "calculator" (mathematical assistant)—set off for America in a Belgian ship instead of a German one, the Nazi propaganda machine was ready and waiting. The choice of shipping line was purely practical. The German-flag alternative did not call at Los Angeles and the *Belgenland* did. Nonetheless, the *Völkisher Beobachter* attacked Einstein by name for the choice, implying the obvious: this Jewish interloper harbored anti-German sentiments that colored his every act, no matter how trivial.

Not that he had ever truly dropped off the German right's enemies list. Philipp Lenard and his coreligionists in the old antirelativity gang of the early 1920s had not allowed any of the evidence in support of relativity to distract them. They had been lying low, in deference to the fact that virtually every competent physicist defended relativity. But with the rise of the radical right at the tail end of the decade, the old campaign resumed. In 1929, a publishing house in Leipzig fired the first shot with a little book titled *One Hundred Authors against Einstein.* As before, Lenard was the most prominent member of the crew, his Nobel Prize casting an aura of respectability over the whole proceeding. The collection did include a few non-German authors—a Dr. Reuterdahl wrote from Minnesota on "Einsteinism: His Deceitful Conclusions and Frauds."[1] But most of the authors were German, and except for Lenard and one or two others, all were mediocrities at best. This time, unlike the antirelativity campaign of 1920, there was no real attempt to engage the scientific establishment; this was propaganda, aimed at the wider world. In itself, the volume had little impact but it was a warning. The bull's-eye painted on prominent Jews may have faded during the stabilized mid-1920s, but now, increasingly, the threat was back.

All this made leaving town in December that much more pleasant. Einstein could count on privacy for the voyage itself, though on learning about the *Belgenland*'s radio telephone, he worried that reporters might "call me up in the middle of the ocean to ask me how I slept the night before."[2] His arrival in New York evoked the usual stampede. The horde of correspondents seeking a word from him was so overwhelming that Einstein tried to wait them out in his cabin, but ultimately he gave in and appeared for a measured fifteen minutes. The questions rained down, laughable and impossible by turns—define the fourth dimension in a word; give a brief account of relativity (Einstein dodged that one by saying it would take him three days to do the job); could religion bring peace on earth? (It hadn't yet, he said, adding that "as to the future, I am not a prophet.")[3] One reporter felt a little pity, noting that he "looked like a man who would pay a high price to escape,"[4] while for the victim himself the experience was "worse than the most fantastic expectation. . . . The reporters asked exquisitely stupid questions, to which I replied with cheap jokes, which were enthusiastically received."[5]

The furor persisted throughout his five-day stay in New York. Dr. Harry Emerson Fosdick, pastor of the Riverside Church, had filled his sanctuary with images of the great through history, not just churchmen and saints but philosophers and scientists as well. Immanuel Kant was there, to Einstein's satisfaction. So were Darwin, Descartes, Beethoven, Emerson, Moses, John Bunyan—a truly catholic wall of honor. There was only one living person who made the cut: Einstein, of course. As the only one still breathing among the demigods, he realized that he would have to be "very careful for the rest of my life as to what I do and say."[6] But what truly perplexed him was his presence there at all. "I might have imagined that they could make a Jewish saint out of me, but I never thought I would become a Protestant one."[7]

The frenzy of celebrity that surrounded Einstein on this second American tour was, if anything, more intense than that which had greeted him in 1921. In the intervening decade, though, he had grown far more sophisticated in the tricks of turning the publicity to his own ends. In New York, he emphasized two causes, his perennial concerns: support for the Zionist program and, above all, his radical pacifism, aimed especially at Germany's increasingly militarized politics. The Zionist campaign had assumed renewed urgency ever since 1929, when a sudden explosion of Arab riots in Palestine aimed against Jewish communities spread from Jerusalem to Hebron, Safed, and beyond. At the time, Einstein had emphasized the need for Jewish settlers to forge a common cause with the Arab population already present there. He told Chaim Weizmann, "Should we be unable to find a way to honest cooperation and honest pacts with the Arabs, then we have learned absolutely nothing during our two thousand years of suffering and deserve all that will come to us."[8]

Einstein promised Weizmann that he would keep as quiet as he could about his concerns. Nonetheless, he still took some political stands, most significantly joining with a number of other signatories to ask the British High Commissioner to commute the death sentences brought against twenty-five Arabs convicted of murder in the uprising. (Twenty-two had their the sentences reduced, leaving only three, those convicted of multiple murders.) At the same time, the riots in Palestine had led the British to bar almost all further Jewish emigration into the territory. That effective closing of what the British continued to call the Jewish homeland was unacceptable, so much so that when he reached New York Einstein was prepared to make another of his very public displays of solidarity with Judaism and the Zionist movement. This time he overcame his antipathy to religious ritual to celebrate the Jewish festival of liberation, Chanukah, in an intimate gathering of fifteen thousand of his fellow Jews at Madison Square Garden.

But it was the threat of war that continued to take pride of place. Before Einstein landed in New York, he cabled ahead a kind of official greeting: "One idea only occupies my mind, or rather only one hope," he wrote, "that the forces that work under the surface in the country should come out into the open in order to more effectively fight against professional militarism, dangerous and strong as it is."[9] On arrival, he gave his famous 2 percent speech, calling on at least 2 percent of those eligible in each country to refuse military service. If they did, Einstein claimed, no government could put that many people in jail. Not even his old comrades-against-arms believed that. Romain Rolland, for one, wrote that there was little practical hope for that 2 percent solution. Given the deadliness of modern weapons, he argued, if only a few or even 10 percent of a country's fighting men evaded the draft, governments would still possess ample means to make war.

The speech received wide play despite such criticism, reaching Germany in excerpted form. There, the reaction was less than welcoming. Newspaper headlines castigating Einstein's "Unbelievable Publicity Methods" prompted official questions directed at Max Planck about his political inclinations.[10] Undeterred, Einstein continued to demonstrate his mastery of the media. Before he left Berlin, an American magazine had approached him "to write an article for an amount that would make an ordinary man dizzy." As he prepared to depart, more proposals came in, requests that he endorse one product after another. It was as if he were a prizefighter or a film star, Einstein said, and to be treated thus was an affront.[11] To his surprise and sorrow, it truly seemed as if companies "make these offers with no thought of insulting me," which meant, he concluded, "that this form of corruption is widespread."[12] But by the time he actually arrived in New York, he and Elsa had worked out a lucrative scheme of their own. He would grant all the requests for interviews, autographs, photo opportunities and the like that he could stand, while Elsa would collect a small fee from every person lining up to seize their slice of Einstein's celebrity. The money all went to charity—poor relief in Berlin and support for draft resisters internationally—and the total amounts involved were considerable. After the first day he reported that Elsa had already managed to pocket one thousand dollars for the cause, a measure of the extraordinary crush he faced each time he showed his face in public.

The ferocious gaze of public attention continued on their arrival in California. The *Belgenland* docked at San Diego to a scene straight out of bedlam. There were crowds at the dock, led by the usual phalanx of reporters, cameramen and the newsreel crews. This was the landfall where Einstein received his honor guard of cheerleaders, five hundred of them, chanting his name as he and Elsa strolled by. Viewed now in the scratchy black-and-white of the newsreels, the scene is surreal. Given his loathing for uniform and his deep belief that "the herd as such remains dull in thought and feeling," it beggars the imagination to guess Einstein's thoughts as he passed along the row of roaring girls.

There were those who did make their opinions known, and not just his enemies. Hedwig Born saw a newsreel account of Einstein's reception and wrote that she was "very amused to see and hear you . . . being presented with a floral float containing lovely sea-nymphs in San Diego, and that sort of thing." She did not quite approve. She expressed the hope that implies its opposite, writing, "However crazy such things look from the outside, I always have the feeling that the dear Lord knows very well what he is up to. . . ." She also tossed a barb at Einstein himself, subtly but in an allusion that could sting: "In the same way as Gretchen sensed the demon in Faust, so he makes people sense in you—well, just the Einstein." Mephisto and Einstein make for quite a juxtaposition, but Hedwig Born had never been shy about warning her friend of the perils of fame.

Not that Einstein could have avoided the limelight in Los Angeles, of all places. Though barely ten years into its reign as the American movie capital, Hollywood already knew how to respond to celebrity. The comedian Will Rogers, with his ironic gift, summed up the experience as well as Einstein himself could have, saying, "He came here for rest and seclusion. He ate with everybody, talked with everybody, posed for everybody that had any film left, attended every luncheon, every dinner, every movie opening, every marriage, and two thirds of the divorces."[13] The only difficulty was that "he made himself such a good fellow that nobody had the nerve to ask what his theory was."[14]

The movie industry, of course, lionized him. He and Elsa toured several of the studios, and they were frequent guests when new movies were screened. At one event, the lights came up as the film stopped in midscene. A young woman came down the aisle of the screening room and walked up to Einstein. She said, "My name is Mary Pickford. I am sorry to disturb you but I wanted so much to shake your hand." Einstein complied and made what was apparently adequate small talk for a few moments. Once she was safely out of earshot, he turned to Elsa and asked what would have been an impossible question for anyone else then in Hollywood: "Who is Mary Pickford?"[15] (Turnabout is fair play. The previous year, Harry Kessler and Aristide Maillol had gone to a luncheon to which Einstein had also been invited. Einstein arrived a little later than the others, and Kessler pointed him out to Maillol. The sculptor examined the newcomer with a professional eye. He turned back to Kessler and said, "A beautiful head. Is he a poet?")[16]

Also on this visit, Einstein spent a good deal of time with Upton Sinclair, one of the founders of the American tradition of investigative journalism. He much admired the writer's social activism, but he had not heard of Sinclair's abiding belief in the supernatural. That led to yet another scene of pure absurdity: Einstein, trapped one evening at Sinclair's house, taking part in what was almost certainly the only séance he ever attended. A witness left a description of the event: Everyone sat in a circle, with their hands placed on top of a table. Before the other world was invoked, Sinclair had warned his guests not to be frightened at any untoward event, noises or flying objects. The medium entered his trance and began to vocalize, a strange, nonverbal chain of utterances. The participants waited patiently. Nothing happened. Perhaps, Sinclair suggested, it was because there were unbelievers present.[17]

ALL OF THIS WAS, of course, secondary to Einstein's real purposes. Caltech had brought him to California on the first of what were supposed to be three annual visits. Each had its reasons for wooing and being wooed. For Caltech, by far the youngest and least established of America's major centers of scientific research, nabbing Einstein as a regular guest was a coup, a distant echo of the one achieved by Planck and Nernst for Berlin all those years before. And for Einstein, the benefits were the gratification of his usual desires. In part, he sought peace and quiet—the chance to do his work in an unfettered environment, in this case a pleasant cottage in Pasadena. And, just as Berlin had promised in 1914, Caltech offered him the company of men he could consider peers, including a surprising number of people working at the cutting edge of research Einstein himself had begun more than a decade before.

One such encounter had special poignancy, a meeting with Albert Michelson, whose experiments with Edward Morley on the speed of light through the ether—a substance that was supposed to be present everywhere, even in empty space—formed the background to Einstein's discovery of the special theory of relativity. Michelson was then seventy-eight years old and very ill (he died later that year). He and Einstein had a somewhat tense history. Michelson had believed deeply in the reality of the ether, and so for years after most other physicists had accepted Einstein's ideas without reservation, had kept hoping that special relativity might prove flawed.

But now, perhaps with some sympathy for physicists who found it difficult to embrace concepts they did not like, Einstein left such unpleasantness behind. In a speech at Caltech, he reminded the audience that Michelson had begun his work when Einstein was just three years old. Then, generously, he gave Michelson full credit for the outcome: "Without your work, this theory [special relativity] would today be scarcely more than an interesting speculation."[18] It was a kindly lie, of course. Michelson's work had been tangential to Einstein's own intellectual development, and the theory of relativity would have remained a fundamental idea in twentieth-century physics with or without the perplexing results of the Michelson-Morley experiments. But Einstein deeply admired passion in science, and Michelson, whatever blinders he may have worn, had struggled to push the limits of experimental technique for decades. Einstein had no hesitation in honoring such a veteran, even one who had fought for a time on the wrong side of an honorable campaign.

But after that graceful nod to the glorious past, Einstein turned to the real business at hand. As far as he was concerned, the most important new ideas to be found in Pasadena turned on discoveries made at the Carnegie Observatory's Mount Wilson facility, perched at the summit of a mountain looming just above Pasadena. Edwin Hubble had made the key observations, first, in 1924, confirming the existence of galaxies beyond the Milky Way, and then in 1929 demonstrating that those galaxies were receding from the earth in a systematic pattern. As discussed in Chapter Eight, Hubble had shown that the speed with which a galaxy retreated from the earth increased with distance; the farther away a galaxy was, the faster it was receding. The relationship was simple and unmistakable and is now known as Hubble's law. It has one clear interpretation. Hubble's plot of the distances to galaxies against the speed of their travel implies an expanding universe, accelerating out from the event that we now call the big bang.

Einstein had thought differently in 1917 when he proposed his stable universe, held in place by his invented "cosmological constant." But in California, he made the trek up Mount Wilson to see the the one-hundred-inch telescope there that Hubble had used for himself. More significant, he examined the red shift data, the measurements that revealed the fact that most galaxies were flying away from our own.[19] Hubble's conclusion was inescapable, obviously correct: such motion was incompatible with any conception of a stable universe. Einstein had simply got it wrong, and he knew it. His cosmological constant was, he said, "the greatest blunder of my life."[20]

Einstein acknowledged the error publicly. In 1931, in one of a series of lectures at Oxford University, he generously and accurately credited Aleksandr Friedmann and Georges Lemaître for their solutions for the equations of general relativity that had predicted that the universe had to be either expanding or contracting. And then he posed the logical problem. If the universe were expanding, as Hubble's results convincingly declared, what was it expanding *from*? He had no answer to give his audience, but as usual for Einstein, he had homed in on the crucial issue. How the universe began remains the motivating mystery behind modern big bang cosmology.

The remainder of his efforts in California did not even lead to interesting questions. He continued to work on what he saw as the flaws in quantum mechanics to no meaningful outcome, and in a later lecture at Oxford in 1933, he reported on his continuing efforts toward a unified field theory. Despite his failures of the previous years (and his embarrassing recantations before Wolfgang Pauli's unforgiving inquisition), he told his audience that he was chasing yet one more glimmer of a unification between gravity and electromagnetism. He admitted that the work was controversial. He acknowledged that no experimental or observational facts demanded it. He continued to pursue it, he said, because of its "mathematical simplicity and logical form." In time, he hoped "that experiments would follow the mathematical flag."[21] It was the same old story, more of what his colleagues had already condemned as equation chopping: his ongoing hunt for some body of mathematics that might just turn out to have some real-world physical meaning.

All this labor ended in frustration. What had been a guide in Einstein's youth became a snare as he aged. As a young man he had recognized that there was a contradiction between special relativity and Newton's gravity, and his belief in the ultimate consistency of scientific accounts of nature urged him on to seek a new idea free of such contradictions. What he sought in unification, though, had little to do with that kind of hunger for simplicity. Rather, the old Einstein now believed in the necessity of what he on his own had decided made sense. In his search for unification, he had to hope that his assumptions about how a well-brought-up universe should behave were correct. That they were not is a matter of record.

In Pasadena in early 1931, however, Einstein did not seem much troubled by his predicament. He had enjoyed himself greatly, for all the noise around him. He hadn't worked that hard, as he admitted or perhaps boasted to Max Born, telling his friend stuck in the midst of the German winter that "for the last five weeks we have been loafing in this paradise without, however, forgetting our friends."[22] It was an interlude. When real life called he was ready to return to Germany, no matter how little it resembled an earthly paradise. He wrote to Queen Elisabeth of Belgium that America was a country of "contrasts and surprises, where one in turns admires and shakes one's head." It was too much of a good thing, perhaps, too easy. At any rate, he wrote, "one feels that one is attached to the old Europe with its pains and hardships."[23] (Einstein had met the queen in 1929, when, while visiting a relative in Antwerp, he received an invitation to the palace. Elisabeth was an avid amateur musician, and a session of chamber music on that first visit led to a lasting friendship.)

At the same time, Einstein knew that the pain that Europe could inflict and endure was real, and that the hardships could be bitter indeed. On the eve of his departure from California he told reporters that his visit had made a profound impression on him. What struck him the most reads strangely today, almost a reversal of the usual clichés that contrast America and Europe. "To me, the U.S. revealed itself as . . . a new world of commanding interest," he said. "It is a world of confraternity, of cooperation, just as Europe is one of individualism."[24] Taken as political code, rather than amateur anthropology, Einstein's meaning becomes clearer. America and Americans then were recognizably nonbelligerent, uninterested in war or the aggrandizement of its military machine. Europe was an entirely different kind of place, and Germany, as Einstein knew, was especially subject to "the monstrously exaggerated spirit of nationalism that goes by the appealing but misused name of patriotism."

His journey across America and then back to Berlin continued to have its moments of comic relief. There was, for example, the famously photographed encounter he and his wife had with members of the Hopi Nation near the Grand Canyon. The Hopis awarded Einstein the title of Great Relative, and he posed with the Hopi delegation, beaming beneath his full-feathered headdress. But even the mob scene at the pier where the *Deutschland* waited (he traveled on a proper German ship this time), where he met with a crowd of pacifists who cheered him home by chanting slogans against war, could not erase Einstein's sense of danger. He had followed events back home during his travels, and the news of continuing economic collapse and resulting political chaos seemed more threatening at the moment of return than it had through his months away. During the voyage he wrote to his sister, Maja, that "everything in Germany is rocking, much worse than on this ship." He held out a bit of hope—"One cuts one's clothes according to one's cloth at the time." But his final thought must have seemed terribly weak, even to him: "For the moment, at least, the Republic still stands."[25]

JUST BARELY. The Berlin to which Einstein returned in March bore only a superficial resemblance to the renascent capital of the middle and late 1920s. The streets had been taken over by an ongoing, brutal, staged political drama. Official Berlin, the government under Chancellor Brüning, was held captive by the ebb and flow of futile, half-planned stratagems, bluffs and counterploys, while on the streets the slow-motion wreck of Germany continued, propelled by the utter misery that continued to spread throughout the city and the state.

The unemployment avalanche of 1930 only accelerated with each passing month. The newspapers reported every move in the numbers. Occasionally, a weekly figure would tend down a few thousand or so, and ever hopeful, the papers would announce the beginning of the end of the economic catastrophe. But the few good reports were merely blips. The true trend was clear for all to see. When Einstein left for America in December 1930, at the end of the first full year of economic crisis, there were 4.38 million Germans without jobs. One year later, as he set out for his second stint at Caltech, the number topped 5.6 million. Almost one in seven of Germany's army of the unemployed then lived in Berlin. Once out of work, they remained jobless. By 1933, many would have been without a job for five years. Behind such statistics was the obvious reality: every month, almost every day, life grew worse. The critical fact was not merely that there were Germans languishing in poverty—there had always been desperately poor people in Berlin and throughout the country. The real change in Germany and German politics came when once-tolerably well-off people were compelled to confront total impoverishment.

The evidence of erosion, of the collapse of any hint of good times, could come from almost anywhere. For a while, the cabarets remained open; people went to the movies when they could; they drank and danced. But beyond the occasional bitter joke from a cabaret master of ceremonies, most of the available diversions emphasized escape and the total futility of action. Bertolt Brecht had caught the mood early in his libretto for the opera *Mahagonny,* created with Kurt Weill. Nazi Brownshirts tried to break up the premiere of a work by two known leftists, but the last line of the last chorus was still audible: "We cannot help ourselves or you or anyone!"[26] It was true. The pleasures of life in Berlin began to melt away amid the larger collapse. In April 1932 Café Josty closed its doors. The *Vossische Zeitung* described the Josty as a second home for Berlin's leading intellectuals, boasting such figures as the novelist Alfred Döblin, the critic Siegfried Kracauer, and the director Max Reinhardt as regulars. The loss was more than a simple business failure. With it went a part of Berlin's self-image as Germany's arbiter of ideas. And in a very different context, bringing the crisis home in the most basic form imaginable, in January 1932 the newspapers had reported a catastrophic drop in Berlin's beer consumption. The average take at licensed bars dropped by 40 percent, and citywide consumption fell by 1.4 million liters from 1929 to 1931. The crisis grew so bad that in February, Berlin's pubs and bars went on general strike. For forty-eight hours one could not buy a drink in Germany's capital.

Even in Germany, beer might conceivably be considered a luxury. But as the number of Berliners on the dole rose, the amount of money available for each person in need dropped, until an unemployed worker simply could not hope to buy enough food to live. The *Vossische Zeitung* described the typical diet for a Berlin family on welfare. It matched the near-famine levels endured during the wartime blockade—a prescription for constant hunger and permanent malnutrition. Yet even now, witless foreign observers, blessed with hard currency and an ability to gloss over any unpleasantness, still saw Berlin as Europe's dynamic, wicked playground. Sex had become one of the last commodities Berlin had to offer otherwise closed foreign markets, and in the depths of the crisis, such witnesses as Harold Nicholson could write as late as 1932 that Berlin was "a girl in a pullover, not much powder on her face, Hölderlin in her pocket, thighs like those of Atalanta . . . and a breadth of view that charms one's repressions from their poison and shames one's correctitude." The city, still floating on its perfume of urban eroticism, "stimulates like arsenic, and then when one's nerves are ajingle she comes with her hot milk of human kindness. . . ."[27]

A closer look revealed the compulsion behind the fantasy of the freethinking flirt. In one of the more specialized travel books of the era, Willi Pröger wrote an ironic guide to Berlin's prostitute strolls. As he led his readers north up the Frankfurter Allee toward Alexanderplatz, he let himself be drawn in by a ten-year-old boy, a tout. The boy told Pröger that he'd got a live one, "a sister, what's not bad, I'm tellin ya . . . ace, cheap, but ain't no snap to it either." Pröger followed the boy four flights up to a tenement apartment that reeked of herring and cabbage. The "sister" turned out to be the boy's stepmother, a woman in her midthirties. "Good Lord, you have to live," she told Pröger. "I used to walk the streets . . . but the competition is too tough." Pröger paid the woman for her time, walked out, and ran into the boy again, tugging on another man's sleeve.[28]

A diligent reporter could probably have turned up stories like these almost any time during the 1920s, but individual disasters accumulated so swiftly in the early '30s as to color virtually every corner of daily life. Perhaps the most poignant single clue to Germany's collective emotional state came from a study of kindergarten-age children of the unemployed. The researcher, Ruth Weiland, found that "the children's play imitates adult life, and going to sign on for the dole plays a great part in it." Trivial incidents could become disasters. "The children are really terrified when they tear their clothes: 'Papa will beat me, we haven't got the money to buy anything new.'" Games depicted what the children knew: "The children play 'mothers and fathers': 'father' cooks the dinner because he has nothing else to do. . . . In children's games the father is always at home in a bad mood. A small boy wants to be 'father' because 'then I can scold everyone all the time.'"[29]

Hunger; anger; the belief, grounded in daily experience, that one's own life had become irrelevant, a burden—all this was, of course, fertile ground for the extremes in German politics, both the NSDAP, the Nazis, and the KDP, the Communists, both of whom continued in informal collaboration to riot and brawl, emphasizing the republic's weakness and inability to rule. The special appeal of both lay in their promise of the transformation of individual suffering into a triumph of the collective will. Some defenders of what had been Weimar culture recognized what was going on and tried to sound the alarm. The writer Ludwig Bauer warned against "the train of development . . . racing . . . straight into a new Middle Ages." Germany in the nineteenth century had declared faith in progress and had "lighted the torch of human rights." Most important, it had "discovered the individual as an end in himself" with "the state a necessary evil." (This was exactly what Einstein argued in virtually all of his anticonscription writings.) But the evident failure of the idea of progress visible throughout postcrash Germany damned the individual. "Today we are thirsting to be unburdened of our 'I.' [We] are born right into a uniform; we unburden ourselves of our soul and submit to the mass. Tolerance is replaced by fanaticism, a smile by inflexibility." All this was taking place in a new Middle Ages "that wants to believe, but in truth no longer can." Bauer answered his ultimate question, "Will it merely be an episode?" by concluding that even a brief epoch of barbarian rule "could, in haste, destroy more than more clever centuries have built."[30]

Bauer was a fatalist. His proposed remedy for what ailed Germany was to contemplate the Age of Enlightenment. There were others, however, who tried to act as if the culture of Weimar still mattered, that what was made, displayed and said could still move minds. The Bauhaus put on its international design exhibition in April 1931, still hoping that it could survive the rise of the Nazi party in its home city of Dessau. The Nazis, following their strategy of seizing power wherever and whenever they could, managed to gain control of Dessau's local government and promptly shut the Bauhaus down. In response, Mies van der Rohe led a move to Berlin, where the school would continue as a private institution, continuing to fight the good fight for modern design. Radical and communist-inspired drama troupes continued to play in Berlin, with key figures consciously trying to create art that would move the masses in the right direction. Even the establishment helped, with several of the mainstream theaters—never before hotbeds of radical thought—staging works by such left-wing playwrights as Carl Zuckmayer, Julius Hay and Ödön von Horváth throughout 1931 and 1932. Bertolt Brecht, in addition to his own work for the stage, published a children's book in 1931, *The Three Soldiers.* It told a bitter, unhappy tale that would, Brecht hoped, "provoke children to ask questions." George Grosz illustrated it with ghastly cartoon images of drawn, haggard, cold, wounded and thin soldiers to emphasize the bloody, unheroic side of war.

But such efforts, though undertaken with all the goodwill and determination in the world, were sideshows, spears against cannon fire in skirmishes of the early 1930s. The fate of *All Quiet on the Western Front (Im Westen Nichts Neue)* showed who was winning the battle for the popular mind. Erich Maria Remarque's now-classic novel of the pain and pointlessness of the German trench-soldier's existence at the end of the Great War was published very successfully in 1929. It was explicitly apolitical. Remarque wrote the book as "neither an indictment nor a confession," aiming simply to describe what had happened to an entire generation "destroyed by the war—even when they escaped the shells."[31] And it was a gripping story, achieving the writer's dream of critical success and popular sales.[32]

The book told of the fate of a group of ordinary soldiers, all of whom die, ground up by the relentless, inglorious, anonymous machinery of the war. Remarque drove home the inconsequence of their fate on the last page by killing Baümer, the novel's narrator, less than a month before the war ended on a day when, officially, it was "all quiet on the Western Front." The pathos was there, the sense of despair and sheer bloody waste, but throughout the book Remarque never once criticized the German army as an institution, nor did he condemn the German high command's handling of the war. Thus, his book could appeal to those large numbers of Germans who could respond to its plot and theme, but did not particularly wish to face yet another argument about who was to blame for Germany's debacle.

But even though he avoided any broad indictment, there was no mistaking what Remarque thought of war itself, war as a calling; and this was where the trouble started. The German version of *All Quiet on the Western Front* was released in late 1930. The first showing of the film passed without incident. But in the first week of December, Goebbels and about a hundred fifty party members bought tickets to the second screening. As soon as the lights dimmed and the film began, the Nazi claque began to work. They shouted anti-Semitic slogans, harassed the audience, and flung tomatoes at the screen. One more subtle thug released several mice into the crowd, while more conventional members of the gang threw stink bombs. The police came, the Nazis argued, and the theater was cleared without further incident.

But the tactic worked. Goebbels proclaimed that the antiwar message of the film was unpatriotic, and called a rally. Six thousand supporters showed up, and further protests brought Hitler himself to view and bless these defenders of German pride. Flashes of violence in the campaign against the film ratcheted up the pressure until the government chose to intervene. In the Reichstag, members complained that it was guilty of "representing the reality of war in a one-dimensional personal way" that could have "an unpredictable influence on students, teenagers and children faced with scenes of the World War."[33] In consequence, the censor banned the film throughout Germany. Goebbels's campaign had been a naked, blunt test of strength, and both he and his opponents drew the same conclusion from the results. He boasted that he had made official policy for the first time, while his enemies concluded that "with this decision, the Reichstag permitted the undemocratic and anti-constitutional forces to stab it in the back."[34]

Einstein, learning of this while still in California, agreed. He made a point of arranging a special screening of the film. He proclaimed it "a fine piece," and said that "the suppression . . . marks a diplomatic defeat for our government in the eyes of the whole world," and, he added, such censorship was a surrender to the mob in the street.[35]

Chapter Twenty-three

"A BIRD OF PASSAGE"

EINSTEIN'S PROTEST WENT UNHEEDED, AND GOEBBELS PRESSED HOME HIS victory through the years that followed. He was a virtuoso and the mob was his instrument. No one could match his skill in honing the outrages that would most emphasize the frailty, the incapacity, of democracy. Hitler continued to remain largely above the fray, while his aides stage-managed the steady campaign of street fighting, periodic brawls and rehearsed violence. By the 1930s, Hitler had refined his image. In public he was the visionary, the mesmerizing leader, a conjurer of visions of a greater Germany. He could use the riots and murders his followers provided him with to drive home his *Führerprinzip,* his claim that Germany could be saved only by his own unquestioned and transcendent genius for leadership. Absolute loyalty to the absolute authority of the Führer was all it would take—and he, uniquely above the rabble of Germany's failed democratic leaders, was prepared for the role.

To ready the ground for the Nazi rise to ultimate power, the party raised the level of violence witnessed by ordinary Germans with each passing month. An incident on June 10, 1932, was typical of the strategy. That afternoon, several hundred members of the Nazi SA and the newer SS private armies invaded the working-class district of Berlin-Wedding. The detachment split up; two platoons blocked the ends of a stretch of road while the main body marched along it, chanting anti-Semitic slogans and in a more or less random display of brutality attacking anyone luckless enough to be out and about. The Nazis beat up some thirty locals, including several old people and one pregnant woman, who was hospitalized in dire condition. When the police arrived, the Nazis barricaded themselves in several buildings and opened fire; it took six hours to clear the entire street.

It was a meticulously calibrated provocation, not quite an outright revolt, for the SA did not target the government directly, or exercise its tactics in neighborhoods of people rich or powerful enough to make their complaints stick in official quarters. But it lent credence to the perception that life for ordinary Germans was becoming more chaotic, more dangerous, ever more out of control. Malevolently and masterfully, Hitler was able to portray the Nazi creators of the violence as both admirable and the source of the ultimate solution to the chaos. In January 1932, he had told an audience of wealthy industrialists that "I know perfectly well, gentlemen, that when the National Socialists march through the streets and there is a sudden tumult and uproar, the *Bürger* . . . looks out and says 'they're disturbing my rest again.'" But, Hitler pleaded, "don't forget that it is also a sacrifice when hundreds of thousands of men of the SA and SS have to get into trucks every day to protect meetings and make marches." There was a way to ease the common man's disturbed sleep, Hitler promised: If only "the whole nation had the same faith in its calling as these hundreds of thousands, if the whole nation possessed this idealism, a quite different Germany would be standing before the world today."[1]

Come unto me, in other words, and the heavenly kingdom lies open before us. Hitler's speech contained the usual falsehoods—his private armies numbered far fewer than the hundreds of thousands claimed. But the proclaimed figure was impressive and helped to forge a reality out of the lie. That was his standard repertory. His force of personality, his ability to make incidents conform to his imagining of them, was a central pillar of his rise. To that he added an obsessive's persistence. The actual record of events in 1931 and 1932 includes several key turning points at which he could have been stopped altogether. That he was not turned on the failures of both his nominal allies and of his enemies.

Chief among Hitler's foes were, of course, the Communists of the

KPD. In the 1930 election the economic crisis had helped them to startling numbers at the polls just as it had boosted the National Socialists. Their leadership, however, was at once inept and ultimately self-destructive, as was evident in their making common cause with the Nazis to block any legislation that might improve Germany's dire economic condition. From their viewpoint, this shared objective—to destroy the democratic functioning of the republic—was meant to pave the way for a new, revolutionary regime. The KPD seems to have believed that it was in the vanguard of history, that all it needed to do was to create a crisis, any crisis, and power would flow to it. These calculations proved to be a ghastly echo of Liebknecht's fatal mistakes in 1919. The outcome was the same and for the same reason. In 1932, as at the end of the war, the radical left failed to count the guns arrayed against them. Their leader, Ernst Thälmann, would pay for that error with his death in the Buchenwald concentration camp.

But if the KPD conspired toward its own destruction, the direct route to power for Hitler lay through the destruction of the established center-right wing, the more or less legitimate government of the Weimar Republic itself. There, a series of would-be statesmen committed blunder after blunder. In 1930 and 1931, Chancellor Brüning demonstrated his stunning incompetence. He sought to shore up his position after his debacle in the election of 1930 by seeking some foreign-policy success, hoping to extract from France and Britain concessions on reparations payments demanded under the terms of the Versailles Treaty. These requests mutated into a proposal to create a customs with Austria. Such demands were calculated to please nationalist sentiments at home, but they were a red flag to Britain and especially to France, always aware of the threat of a resurgent Germany. The approach was rejected out of hand. Brüning was instructed to take his claims to the World Court, which ruled against him, and the resulting damage was irreversible. He looked weak at home, while his bluster on the international scene alienated all those who could have given him any kind of face-saving concession. Meanwhile, his government's neglect of the economic collapse earned him a fatal nickname. He was now known as "the hunger chancellor."

By early 1932, Brüning had run out of options, losing the support of the business community, the remnants of the parties representing the political center, and most important, of the army. The final blow came that spring, when, much too late, he tried to counteract the Nazi rise by banning the SA and the even more brutal SS. The army chief, General Kurt von Schleicher, orchestrated a calculated campaign of opposition and persuaded the president of the republic, Hindenburg, now aged and with his term of office running out, to abandon Brüning as chancellor. That was one key missed chance, for if the army had backed the ban, Hitler would have lost both the physical means to impose his will by force and the chance to appropriate the prestige of the military. Schleicher handpicked the new chancellor, the disastrous Franz von Papen. Papen was famously a mediocrity, an opportunistic conservative politican with good connections to both Germany's Catholic community and to its business elite. He supplied virtually all the remaining opportunities Hitler would need. Schleicher had intended to utilize Papen as a puppet, an aristocratic stalking horse for the army to use to overwhelm the upstart Hitler. Instead, he turned out to be "a smiling frivolous dilettante," in Harry Kessler's words, who "in six months . . . did more harm than any preceding chancellor had ever accomplished in so short a time."[2]

Papen's key delusion was that he could use the Nazis and then discard them at will. Hindenburg himself had banned public appearances by the SA and the SS, and Papen, to avoid a vote of no-confidence in the Reichstag, promised the Nazis that he would not only call new elections for the summer but as an extra bonus would lift the ban. The move amounted to an open invitation to murder. Within five weeks, in Prussia alone ninety-nine people lay dead and over one thousand were injured in fighting. Continual mayhem like this became a central motif in the three electoral campaigns that took place in the early months of 1932. First came the presidential elections in March and April, when for the first time Hitler ran for the highest office in Germany. In the runoff, he was pitted against the incumbent, Hindenburg, and the final vote had been far closer than anyone had expected. Hindenburg won, but his total of 19.4 million votes gave him a much smaller margin against the combined totals of 13.4 million for Hitler and 3.7 million for the Communist, Thälmann, than he had mustered in either of his previous victories. Next came the April elections for control of the state parliaments, which left the Nazis in commanding positions in most regions of the country. Finally, in the Reichstag elections in July, the Nazis used the fierce chaos they had fomented in the streets during the campaign to argue that only a truly strong man could save Germany—only Hitler. The tactic worked. The elections ended with the National Socialists holding 230 seats in the Reichstag, up from 107 in 1930. The Nazis were now the largest political party in the chamber.

Thus emboldened, Hitler went to Hindenburg and demanded the chancellorship for himself. But here he overplayed his hand. Hindenburg was deeply insulted that he should have been challenged for the presidency, flatly rejected the idea, and named Papen to the post. As Hitler biographer Ian Kershaw has pointed out, that should have been that. With Hindenburg's backing, Papen and Schleicher should have been able to bar Hitler indefinitely. But the Nazis and the Communists joined forces once again, determined to force a vote of no-confidence, so Papen dissolved the Reichstag and called for yet another election on November 6. This time the Nazis actually suffered a loss of support, doing well in Berlin but dropping two million votes and thirty-four seats in the Reichstag. Nonetheless, Hitler persisted in his demand for total authority, and Hindenburg, continuing to defend the republic, wrote to him that "a presidential cabinet led by you would develop necessarily into a party dictatorship with all its consequences for an extraordinary accentuation of the conflicts in the German people."[3]

Brave words by a man not usually remembered as a defender of pluralism. But he could not make them stick. By then, Schleicher and Papen had fallen out irretrievably. Despite Hindenburg's antipathy to him, Schleicher was able to force his way into the chancellorship. An angry Papen began to agitate for a return to power by joining forces with the Nazi party, and in early January 1933, Schleicher sought to defuse the threat by asking Hindenburg to dissolve the Reichstag and give him the right to rule Germany by decree, a move he himself had opposed when Papen had proposed it months before. Hindenburg turned him down flat. Schleicher could call new elections if he chose, but the president refused to allow his chancellor to rule as a dictator.

Meanwhile, Papen continued to meet with Hitler in an effort to forge a coalition between the Nazis and the conservative parties in the Reichstag, negotiations brokered by right-wing business leaders. Schleicher, faced with Hindenburg's virtually complete lack of confidence in him, resigned on January 28. Papen now agreed to serve as vice-chancellor in a new government in which Hitler would be chancellor. Hindenburg, under pressure from several sides, finally gave in.

Hitler had never won an election outright; by most measures, his support was dwindling; and those who had observed him at close quarters recognized, as Hindenburg had, that a Hitler government would almost certainly turn into a violent dictatorship. Nonetheless, just past noon on Monday, the 30th of January, 1933, he was sworn in as chancellor of the German Republic.

The Great Man theory of history has come in for much abuse over the years. Most famously, Tolstoy railed against it in *War and Peace,* in which he tried to demonstrate that Napoleon the man was an insignificant actor in the actual events that decided his disastrous Russian campaign. In kindred arguments, Hegel's idea of history and its Marxist heirs emphasized a logic to history, progress that was achieved by the clash of forces too large and impersonal for any one person to affect. Reworked, ideologically cleansed, extended and reanalyzed, such approaches are now ordinary tools for historians, and they are not entirely wrong, far from it. But at certain times and in particular places, there can be no doubt that the individual matters, that the life or death, the rise or fall, of a single person, reverberates through the experience of untold, unnamed millions.

In Germany in 1933 Adolf Hitler began to shape what would become the twentieth century's collective nightmare. There was nothing inevitable about his triumph—no forces of history, no ineluctable hand of progress. The ground had been prepared long since. The enemies of the German Republic, both left and right, attacked democratic institutions from the moment of their birth. Both probably did more than any other single force to prepare Germany for its man on horseback.[4] But from the spring of 1930 to January 1933, decisions made by a handful of known, identifiable individuals made a decisive difference. Hitler himself was the key actor: who he was and what he committed himself to provided the decisive push that led Germany in one direction and not another. Yet arrayed against him were several men who could have stopped him cold. Hindenburg was perhaps the most important, but there were others who had the chance. Theirs were genuine choices, not false options. But Hitler was both extraordinarily skilled politically and just plain lucky, particularly in the selection of those who stood in his way. He was routinely underestimated, especially at the last, for all that those who had observed him for years should have known better. When some who did worry raised the subject after the creation of the Hitler government, Papen put it most staggeringly in his comment: "We've captured him." It was perhaps the worst misjudgment on record.

The Tolstoyan argument holds this far. Larger forces than Hitler brought the Nazi party and its leader to the surface. There is little doubt that Germany was headed for the political rocks. But which particular breed of right-wing nationalism would triumph was crucial. One tired old man, a former conspirator in his own right, had learned this truth from hard personal experience. Two days after Hitler became chancellor, General Erich von Ludendorff sent Hindenburg a bitter telegram, telling his former commander that "you have delivered up our holy German Fatherland to one of the greatest demagogues of all time." Only misery could result. "I solemnly predict," Ludendorff wrote, "that this accursed man will cast our Reich into the abyss. . . . Future generations will damn you in your grave for what you have done."[5]

Albert Einstein had anticipated the possibility of this catastrophe for at least a year and a half. In the summer of 1931, he had already begun to prepare for life after Berlin. He drafted a letter to Max Planck that is one of the earliest indications that he recognized the Nazis as genuinely dangerous. "I feel impelled to call your attention to a matter which is closely related to the conditions of my employment," Einstein wrote. He reminded Planck that after the war he had accepted German citizenship in addition to Swiss, but in this new Germany "the events of recent days suggest that it is not advisable to maintain this situation." He asked Planck to arrange to have his citizenship revoked, and to see whether he could remain a member of the Prussian Academy, despite the renunciation. He declared that there was nothing to fear yet. He acknowledged his debt to "a country and an institution which have granted me enviable living and working conditions during the best years of my life." To date, he continued, he had rejected all offers from abroad, for he had not wished to leave the place where he had done his work, and he concluded by saying, "I hope I shall be able to maintain this attitude also in the future." It was a wish, but clearly not an expectation.[6]

He did not send the letter. He apparently decided that the crisis was not yet deep enough to require action. But the reasons that led him to draft it remained. Chief among them, he wrote, was his "certain need for personal independence." The deliberate polarization of German academic life, and, close to home, a running conflict at Berlin University in which Nazi-aligned students launched a series of attacks on left-leaning students and organizations, clearly put that autonomy at risk. The Nazis had in fact targeted all the major German universities, and Einstein had become the focus of controversy as he attempted to champion the handful of liberal outposts that remained. Even so, he calmed down, backing away from the open break contemplated in the unsent letter to Planck. But his sense of urgency remained, an awareness that Germany was in the midst of a fundamental transformation that would soon make life there untenable. In late 1931, just before leaving to take up his second visiting appointment at Caltech, he told his friend Philipp Frank that "I believe that the present unstable state of affairs in Germany will continue to hold for about ten years." Thus, he concluded, "it might be good to be in America."[7] On December 6, at sea en route to California he moved to epiphany. "I decided today that I shall essentially give up my Berlin position and shall be a bird of passage for the rest of my life," he wrote in his diary. The bonds of friendship and science that had held him in Berlin despite anti-Semitism, death threats, the murder of friends, mayhem on the streets and all the rest, could no longer stand the strain. "Gulls are still escorting the ship, forever on the wing," he continued. "They are my new colleagues, although, heaven knows, they are much more efficient than I."[8]

Still, even as that decision was germinating throughout 1931, Einstein kept trying to influence events. His primary cause continued to be draft resistance, and during the year he intervened on behalf of conscientious objectors in a number of criminal cases around the world. In 1930, he had submitted testimony to a Bulgarian court, declaring "the fight against war is legal in all those countries which have any claim to true civilization."[9] In April of 1931, he wrote to Tomás Masaryk, president of Czechoslovakia, to protest the prison sentence handed down to a pacifist there; Masaryk, unlike many targets of Einstein's protests, took the trouble to reply thoughtfully, in his own hand. September saw an appeal to Polish military courts in a draft-dodging case there, and throughout that year and the next he produced a stream of letters, statements and speeches that sounded variations on the familiar theme.

At the same time he had also responded to a series of what appeared to him to be more general miscarriages of justice, wherever they occurred. He joined an international protest in support of the Scottsboro Boys—eight black youths convicted of raping two women, despite one of the alleged victims retracting her testimony. And in one of the most depressing anticipations of subsequent events, back in February 1931, Einstein had openly indicted the government of Yugoslavia, under the Serbian king Alexander I, for its involvement in the assassination of Professor Milan Sufflay, a prominent Croatian intellectual. He and the novelist Heinrich Mann signed a protest letter circulated by the German League of Human Rights that accused Alexander of having supported the assault on Sufflay and a number of other political murders. (Documents released later that year served to confirm Einstein and Mann's charges, and Alexander himself was assassinated in October 1934. Ethnic conflict in the Balkans had not ended with the First World War, nor with the next round of violence—nor yet.)

But of all of Einstein's attempts to move public opinion, the most ambitious came in a public exchange of letters with Sigmund Freud during the summer of 1932. There, he set down his basic internationalist credo: "The quest of international security involves the unconditional surrender by every nation, in a certain measure, of its liberty of action—its sovereignty, that is to say—and it is clear beyond all doubt that no other road can lead to such security." He conceded that recent efforts to achieve such a surrender of national prerogatives had met with what he termed "ill success"—an understatement, especially in Germany in mid-1932. But why, he asked, should so many individual citizens within a nation succumb "to such wild enthusiasm" even at the cost of their own lives? Perhaps, he said, in a thought that hints at the influence of surrounding events, it is "because man has within him a lust for hatred and destruction." Yet even that grim conclusion triggered one more question, the one he wanted Freud to answer: "Is it possible to control man's mental evolution so as to make him proof against the psychosis of hate and destructiveness?" No one was immune. "I am thinking by no means only of the so-called uncultured masses," he wrote, possibly alluding to the daily mayhem in the streets of Berlin. Einstein could count. By 1932, a majority of German university professors and an even higher percentage of students were either outright Nazis or persuadable supporters of the *völkisch* right.

"Experience proves"—*his* experience, the accumulation of incidents witnessed and endured over eighteen years within Berlin's academic community—"that it is rather the so-called 'intelligentsia' that is the most apt to yield to these disastrous collective suggestions."[10]

Freud's response to Einstein was essentially gloomy. He produced a long and nuanced analysis of the multiple motives that could impel apparently civilized people to perform violent and destructive acts and concluded that he saw "no likelihood of our being able to suppress humanity's aggressive tendencies." At best, there might be some hope of channeling such aggression. Improving relations between man and man would help, Freud argued, though he recognized that the command to love one's neighbor as oneself was "a pious injunction, easy to announce, but hard to carry out." In the longer run, his real hope was that more and more people would turn away from war on rational grounds. They would turn to pacifism for two reasons: first, because fighting-age men would come to recognize that war "forces the individual into situations that shame his manhood, obliging him to murder fellow men against his will," and second, because war had simply become too overwhelmingly ghastly to sustain. "Wars, as now conducted," Freud wrote, "afford no scope for acts of heroism according to the old ideals, and given the high perfection of modern arms, war today would mean the sheer extermination of one of the combatants, if not of both."[11]

Einstein announced himself satisfied despite the fact that neither he nor Freud saw any real hope that pacifism might spread swiftly enough to prevent wars soon. Who knew, he wrote back, what effect their exchange might have, "what may grow from such seed?" There was of course no harvest, nothing gained from their best efforts. The correspondence was published under the title *Warum Krieg?—Why War?*—in 1933, long after it could have been of any use in Germany. No more than two thousand copies were printed, monuments to good intentions. By the time they appeared, Einstein was gone from Berlin.

THE END CAME ABRUPTLY, almost without fanfare. In February 1932, while he was still at Caltech, Abraham Flexner approached him. Flexner was an intellectual entrepreneur looking for recruits for his new Institute for Advanced Study in Princeton and his pitch aped the one, eighteen years earlier, when Planck and Nernst came to Zurich. The Germans then had dangled both unprecedented prestige and the promise of the greatest roster of scientific talent in the world to draw Einstein to Berlin. Now it was Flexner who sought the luster Einstein carried with him, and offered in exchange four bare walls in an embryonic institution in the wilds of New Jersey. Each offer was appropriate to its time. Einstein no longer needed or even valued company very much. Princeton's greatest virtue was that it was safely far away from Germany. Negotiations with Flexner over the terms of his professorship at the institute continued through the summer, with Einstein displaying a certain, possibly calculated, naïveté about money. Flexner asked Einstein what he wanted for a salary. Einstein answered that three thousand dollars would do. When Flexner hesitated, Einstein asked if he could survive on less. It is hard to believe that his modesty was merely a negotiating ploy, but the exchange apparently impressed Flexner enough to make sure the institute's offer was beyond reproach. They settled on a salary of ten thousand dollars, plus funds to cover Einstein's taxes and traveling expenses.[12] In return, Einstein committed himself to five months each year at the new institute.

Yet, despite his near-readiness to leave during the winter just past, he proved unwilling to cut the cord to Berlin openly through most of 1932. Princeton and the institute served as a bolt-hole, a refuge ready to hand if life in Germany became absolutely untenable. He announced his departure in stages, cushioning the blow to those who looked to him as one of the last bulwarks of reason to survive in Germany. Thus, in October 1932 he released the news that he had decided to spend five months a year in the U.S. for the next five years. But as he emphasized for *The New York Times,* "I am not abandoning Germany. . . . My permanent home will still be in Berlin."[13]

That was diplomacy, but little more. Privately Einstein concluded that nothing could save the worsening situation. That summer, he told friends visiting him in Caputh that a Nazi victory seemed inevitable. Someone asked him if a military coup might do the trick, but Einstein answered, "I am convinced that a military regime will not prevent the imminent National Socialist revolution. The military dictatorship will suppress the popular will and the people will seek protection against the Junkers and the officers in a right-radical revolution."[14] The issue was not whether but when. Close friends were already encouraging him to leave. The threat popped up, tragicomically, surprisingly close to home. The local baker in Caputh began to speak up against Einstein's "Jewish house." In late spring, he stopped walking alone. And as negotiations with Flexner stalled briefly, Antonina Vallentin warned Elsa that to "leave Einstein in Germany was to perpetrate a murder."[15]

The Nazi setbacks in the November elections produced a brief moment of hope. Several quite acute political observers, including Einstein's friend Kessler, thought that the Nazi losses marked the beginning of the end. But the moment evaporated, destroyed by Papen's vacuous incompetence and Hitler's relentless pursuit of power. Einstein had spoken at home and abroad against the collective surrender to unreason he saw around him. He had written, campaigned, served on committees, encouraged others, raised money when he could. But by late 1932, the end had clearly come.

From very early in his life, Einstein gave hints of a deep-seated streak of fatalism. It never prevented him from acting, from behaving as if what he sought to do could influence events. But the countervailing strain was always there, the perception that the apparently unique spark of any one human life must ultimately vanish into the vastness of the cosmos. The previous year, on shipboard bound for California, he experienced a storm at sea. He wrote in his travel diary that "the sea has a look of indescribable grandeur, especially when the sun falls on it. One feels as if one is dissolved and merged into nature. Even more than usual, one feels the insignificance of the individual and it makes one happy."[16]

Insignificant—and hence autonomous, free to do what one had to do. In the autumn of 1932, Einstein began to prepare for the third of his visits to Caltech. His departure for the United States was scheduled, as usual, for early December 1932. He was interrupted by a minor, comic public squabble. A group of self-styled patriotic American women had heard that the dangerous pacifist and communist (sic) Albert Einstein planned to threaten the security of the United States by yet another visit to Pasadena. They prepared a pamphlet and sent it on to the State Department, which forwarded the complaint to the embassy in Berlin. Questioned by a local consular official about his alleged radicalism, Einstein leaped gleefully to reply in the public glare of the newspapers. "Never before have I been so brusquely rejected by the fair sex, at least never by so many of its members at once," he wrote.

"How right they are, those vigilant, civic-minded ladies! Why open one's door to someone who devours hard-boiled capitalists with as much appetite and gusto as the Cretan Minotaur devoured luscious Greek maidens in days gone by; by one who is wicked enough to reject every kind of war . . ." except, Einstein acknowledged in his notorious gibe, "the inexorable war with one's own spouse!" It all made sense to him and so, O Americans, "Give ye therefore heed to your prudent and loyal womenfolk and remember that the Capitol of mighty Rome was once saved by the cackling of her faithful geese."[17]

The pleasing glow of that wicked thought faded quickly, though Einstein liked the joke well enough to include the statement in his first anthology of writings and aphorisms. The first week of December passed quietly. There were no changes either at the house at Caputh or the apartment in Berlin. Everything seemed routine. At least as late as November 20, Einstein was still making adjustments to his schedule in Berlin for the following spring.[18] To any observer, the Einsteins were merely traveling, not emigrating; they would return.

In April 1914, Einstein had come to Berlin a young man, taking his place as the first among equals in a city striving to become the unquestioned capital of European civilization. Berlin and Einstein had been an awkward fit from the start, an alliance of convenience, never one of mutual love. But the essential bargain had remained intact. Berlin would continue to aspire, and Einstein would remain, tangible emblem of the city's drive to excel. Now, in those last days in December 1932, Einstein knew no better than anyone else precisely how the political maneuvering in Berlin would finish. But on one level it did not matter. There was no possible outcome that would preserve the essence of that city to which he had for eighteen years been bound "by the closest human and scientific ties."[19]

In the end, he simply left the stage. He did not comment; he dropped no public hint. On December 12, Albert and Elsa Einstein set out from Berlin for the United States. A photograph taken at the entrance of the train station shows an ordinary travelers' tableau. Elsa looks a little worried, harried; she could be thinking about the luggage, or perhaps, more seriously, about her daughter Ilse, who was ailing. Einstein's face is unrevealing, almost grim. The rest of the party seeing them off stands in the wings, and the overall impression is of impatience, a desire to be done with photography and catch their train. There is no way to read the image, except with hindsight, as the end of an era.

Before they reached the train station, Einstein and Elsa had had to close up their house at Caputh. They must have made one last check, a final sweep through the cottage. They may have paused at the door to Einstein's study or on the porch, looking down the sweep of lawn to the lake, visible then through the leafless trees. There might have been a glance around the back of the house, a survey of windows shut and doors latched, and then in and out again, carrying their bags. One of them locked the door—probably Elsa, the master of all practical matters in the Einstein household. Finally, when nothing remained to be done, they walked away from the house. Einstein spoke. "Take a good look," he told Elsa. "You will never see it again."[20]

Chapter Twenty-four

"AS LONG AS I HAVE ANY CHOICE IN THE MATTER"

ON JANUARY 30, 1933, AS HITLER TOOK THE OATH AS CHANCELLOR OF A republic about to become a reich, Albert Einstein was safely out of reach in Pasadena. For the moment, there was little overt danger. Well treated by his American friends, he could be positively playful, even trying his hand at bicycling. The famous photograph of Einstein atop his two-wheeler was taken that February. He leans over, his front wheel a little askew. He seems a trifle unsteady but he grins hugely; life is pleasant in southern California. The week before Hitler took power, Einstein had given a nationally broadcast radio speech, funded by a German-American family foundation that had asked him to give a talk "helpful to American-German relations." Einstein confined himself to warning against the use of scare tactics in labeling one's opponents, which he said happened in both Germany and the United States. It was a mild speech—an anodyne—words that sought to do no harm.

Even after Hitler consolidated his hold, Einstein restrained himself for a while. Early in February, he even wrote to the Prussian Academy to discuss salary matters, fully as if he intended to resume work in Berlin later that year. But any illusions he may have had shattered almost immediately thereafter. On February 27, the Reichstag in Berlin caught fire. A supposed Communist allegedly committed the crime, a young Dutch man, who, as Harry Kessler noted in his diary, had ostensibly been suborned by Communists to do the dirty deed while also in contact with Socialist deputies. Most impressive, that single arsonist was supposed to have placed flammable stores at thirty locations throughout the building and to have lit them all "without either his presence, his activity, or his bestowal of this enormous quantity of material being observed by anyone." Then, so it was said, the arsonist ran headlong into the police, "having carefully taken off all his clothes except his trousers and depositing them in the Reichstag so as to ensure that no sort of mistake could fail to result in his identification."[1]

In response to such overwhelming evidence of a Communist conspiracy, Hindenburg signed a presidential decree that suspended political and civil rights, transferring extraordinary emergency power to Hitler. The crackdown on the left began immediately, with the SA and the SS competing to arrest and brutalize any perceived threat to the reich. The implications for known partisans of the republic were obvious. By coincidence, the same day that the Reichstag burned, Einstein wrote to his quondam mistress, Margarethe Lebach, the woman whose Wednesday visits to the Caputh house had so vexed Elsa, and told her that "I dare not enter Germany because of Hitler."[2] He canceled a forthcoming lecture at the Prussian Academy, and the day before he left Pasadena, bound eventually for Belgium, he launched his first public attack against Germany's new regime. "As long as I have any choice in the matter, I shall live only in a country where civil liberty, tolerance and equality of all citizens before the law prevail." He defined his terms: "Civil liberty implies freedom to express one's political convictions, in speech and in writing; tolerance implies respect for the convictions of others, whatever they may be." The completion of the syllogism was simple—"These conditions do not exist in Germany at the present time"—and would not, Einstein implied, as long as the current regime remained in power.[3]

Hitler's government reacted swiftly and bitterly to his charges. The *Völkischer Beobachter* published a series of attacks on him, and more mainstream papers followed suit. One headline read "Good News of Einstein—He Is Not Coming Back!" over an article condemning "this puffed-up bit of vanity [who] dared to sit in judgment on Germany without knowing what is going on here—matters that forever must remain incomprehensible to a man who was never a German in our eyes and who declares himself to be a Jew and nothing but a Jew."[4] A list that surfaced some months later reprinted Einstein's photograph in a collection of enemies of Nazi Germany, over the caption "Not Yet Hanged."[5] Over the course of the spring, events in Germany left no doubt that he was an important target for the new regime. The press reported that the Caputh house was searched on March 20, allegedly because of charges that a cache of weapons was hidden there. The report was a hoax, but in April the government froze Einstein's bank accounts. Police raided his Berlin apartment repeatedly in a quest for compromising papers, though again the invaders came up empty-handed, because his stepdaughter Margot had already sent the most significant documents off to the French Embassy, from whence they were eventually shipped on to Einstein by diplomatic pouch.

Word of such harassment did not touch him very deeply. He condemned the reported invasion of his Caputh house as one among many of "the arbitrary acts of violence now taking place throughout Germany," and then turned the joke on the Nazis. "My summer house has often in the past been honored by the presence of guests," he wrote. "They were always welcome. No one had any reason to break in."[6] The sharpest blows came not from the Nazis themselves but from those who had once formed his chief reason for being in Berlin, his fellow members of the Prussian Academy. While still at sea on the way to Belgium, Einstein drafted his letter of resignation from the Academy, and on arrival he gave it to the German legation in Brussels along with his renunciation of German citizenship. In his letter, he emphasized the old ties. "Throughout nineteen years the Academy provided me with the opportunity to devote myself to scientific work," he acknowledged. "I realize the great measure of gratitude I owe to it." More than that, he added, "It is also with great reluctance that I leave its circle because of the stimulation and the beautiful personal relations which, during that long period of my membership, I enjoyed." Still, inevitably, the political reality trumped all: "Dependence on the Prussian government entailed by my position is something that under the present circumstances I feel to be intolerable."[7]

The subsequent exchange of letters between Einstein and the Academy revealed the depth to which the rot had spread. Hitler called the last election he would permit in Germany on March 5, to select a new Reichstag. The elections did not produce the out-and-out triumph for the Nazis that he had sought, but the party made substantial gains, and with its conservative coalition partners commanded an absolute parliamentary majority. On March 23, that majority transferred all legislative powers to their leader, now virtually unchallenged as dictator of Germany. Within the week, Hitler's government ordered the Prussian Academy to begin the process of expelling Einstein from its midst. His resignation caught the government by surprise. Enraged that he had quit before he could be fired, the minister in charge demanded a proclamation from the Academy condemning its erstwhile hero. Timed to coincide with the first of Nazi Germany's official sanctions against its Jews, a boycott against Germany's Jewish-owned businesses scheduled for April 1, the press release declared that "we have no reason to regret Einstein's resignation. The Academy is aghast at his foreign agitation."[8] Einstein's old friend Max von Laue was horrified at the idea that the Academy might issue such a document, and he spoke against it at an extraordinary meeting on April 6. None of the fourteen members present supported him. Even Haber, the converted Jew and Einstein's close friend, voted with the majority.

Haber's action was bad, but he would perform better soon. Max Planck disgraced himself. Einstein had written to Planck to refute privately the charge that he had spread rumors against Germany, telling him that he spoke now only to combat what was clearly a Nazi "war of extermination against my Jewish brethren."[9] Planck answered Einstein in a letter that identified Jewishness and National Socialism as "ideologies that cannot co-exist." He deplored both and emphasized his loyalty to Germany, no matter who was in charge.[10] Each man assured the other of his lasting regard and friendship, and Einstein always felt something akin to love for the older man. But Planck's public statement on Einstein's resignation from the Academy illustrated the mental gymnastics he had mastered so quickly in Hitler's new Germany. He praised Einstein as a physicist without equal since the days of Kepler and Newton, but, he concluded, his exile was his own fault: "It is . . . greatly to be regretted," he said at the Academy meeting that day, "that Mr. Einstein through his political behavior himself rendered his continued membership in the Academy impossible."[11] Einstein's politics were to blame, not those of a German government that had chosen to destroy him.

Planck's declaration was as clear a signal as Einstein needed of the state of affairs in Berlin. Planck had always ranked with the best of Germany's intellectuals, an honest, generous friend and an uncompromising scientist. But just as he had thrilled to the call of war in 1914, in 1933 he could not resist the siren lure of loyalty to the state, even one run by Hitler. Apart from his condemnation of Einstein, a measure of his blind devotion to the idea of the German state came with his willingness to acquiesce in statements he knew to be false. As was to be expected, Einstein's old nemesis Philipp Lenard resurfaced with the Nazi seizure of power. As the head of a new, properly National Socialist physics institute, Lenard announced that "it is unworthy of a German to be an intellectual follower of a Jew. Natural science, properly so called, is of completely Aryan origin, and Germans must today also find their own way into the unknown. *Heil* Hitler."[12] Planck passed over such travesties in silence, apparently unwilling or unable to oppose what National Socialist Germany demanded of its citizens. His devotion to authority—to the idea of Germany, no matter what was done in the name of Germany—rendered him impotent in the face of power. He became a kind of moral imbecile: not evil in himself, not at all, but still incapable of acknowledging evil's presence at the heart of his beloved state.

Einstein never condemned his old friend and mentor. Ultimately he seems to have concluded that Planck was more tragic than bad, just a man who could not find a way to oppose the unacceptable. Planck suffered for his sins. He lost both of his sons to the demands of two successive German empires. One had died in combat during the First World War. Hitler cost him his other boy, strangled in 1945 on suspicion of involvement in the bungled assassination attempt on the Führer the previous year. In the end, Einstein forgave him all his political failings, choosing to focus instead on the hero of his youth. "The standard of our ideal search for truth," Einstein wrote in his obituary notice, "a bond forever uniting scientists in all times and all places, was embodied with rare completeness in Max Planck."[13] It wasn't true, but Planck had befriended Einstein very early. He had nothing as charitable to say for almost every other German who stayed behind.

THE CLASH WITH HIS FORMER COLLEAGUES confirmed Einstein in his conviction that Nazi rule and civilized existence in Germany could not coexist. A few days after his exchange with Planck, Einstein wrote to

Born (who also emigrated) that "you know, I think, that I have never had a particularly favorable opinion of the Germans (morally and politically speaking). But I confess that the degree of their brutality and cowardice came as something of a surprise to me."[14] The behavior of the intellectuals struck him as appalling. The Nazis, he wrote, were "moving in a direction that will become increasingly destructive," while "the lack of courage on the part of the intellectual classes has been catastrophic."[15]

The auto-da-fé of May 10, 1933, when twenty thousand volumes culled from Berlin's academic libraries and bookstores went up in a bonfire presided over by Goebbels himself, showed what university life had become within three months of the Nazi takeover. The "racial cleansing" of the civil service and the educational system had begun the month before, when the Aryan clause of the new Nazi civil service law was passed. Under its terms, Jewish government workers and university staff were to be dismissed, with their places taken by loyal servants of the German Reich. And these first months of the Nazi regime were only a hint of what was to come. The political repression, the torture, the trial runs for what became Germany's concentration camp state—all these began to take shape within weeks of the Nazi triumph.

The book burning was itself an augury of what was to happen throughout German cultural life. All the arts suffered their purges. Nazi paramilitaries raided the Bauhaus in April, and the school shut down shortly thereafter. Twentieth-century music vanished from the repertory, to be replaced by safe German warhorses composed by Beethoven, Brahms, and, of course, Wagner. American jazz became anathema, irrevocably tainted by its association with black musicians. Suspect works of art began to vanish from museum walls, and in 1937 the "Degenerate Art" exhibit in Munich and Berlin attracted 2 million visitors, most of whom came to scoff at the foul and polluted trash that had passed for masterpieces in the 1920s—works by artists like Klee, Dix, Grosz, Beckmann, and many others. Goebbels actually had a taste for such works, but that failed art student Adolf Hitler overruled his deputy; and in 1939 another convenient fire destroyed several thousand of the best works of Germany's modern artists. In early 1933, just after Hitler had become chancellor, a sympathetic journalist could already gloat that "a miracle has taken place. . . . They claimed they were the German *Geist,* German culture, the German past and future." That unnamed "they"—the men and women who had created Weimar culture—had ruled so long, and whatever they favored became omnipresent, unavoidable, "whether it was cheese or relativity . . . patent medicine or human rights, democracy or Bolshevism . . . rotten Negro music or dancing in the nude"—Weimar Berlin in a capsule. But there was reason to rejoice for one great truth had emerged: "They are no longer here." That much was true. Those who could, those clear-headed enough to comprehend what was actually happening, had run for safety as quickly as they could, fleeing a Berlin that was unequivocally no longer theirs.

From the very first weeks of the exodus Einstein set himself the task of helping the new refugees, especially those in the sciences—particularly the young ones for whom, he told Born, his heart ached. Not everyone received the same consideration, however. Fritz Haber was at loose ends in Europe. There was some honor in his plight. According to the earliest versions of the Aryanization laws, as a former soldier in the Great War, Haber was entitled to keep his job despite his Jewish origins. He resigned anyway, because he was unwilling to fire those under him in his institute who had no such immunity. Planck, to his credit, took the risk of interceding with Hitler personally on Haber's behalf, but the encounter ended in complete failure. Suddenly out of work, and because of Planck's intervention now in the Führer's direct line of sight, Haber stumbled into exile. He escaped to Switzerland, but planned to move on. Now, long after his conversion of convenience, Haber, that once and future Jew, accepted a position at the Hebrew University in Jerusalem. Whatever impulse to sympathy Einstein might have felt, this was a target too good to resist. "I am delighted to learn," he wrote, "that your love for the blond beast has somewhat cooled." He was almost gloating: "Who would have thought that my dear Haber would turn up here as the champion of the Jewish and indeed the Palestinian cause."[16]

While Haber must have seemed simply too tempting a target for Einstein to avoid, given all those years in which Haber had tried to convert his friend to the cause, there was an edge of cruelty here. Einstein did not empathize in the slightest with Haber's misery, for, after all, as he reminded him, "I never had any respect or sympathy" for the Germany that Haber had so desperately sought to embrace. But Haber was truly bereft. He never reached Palestine; in January 1934, he collapsed and died in Basel. He thus became in some sense one of the new reich's early victims. The official cause of death went into the records as cardiac arrest. It seems reasonable to take that as a medical description of a broken heart.

BY THEN EINSTEIN WAS ALREADY disentangling himself not just from Germany but from Europe as well. Throughout the spring and summer of 1933 he divided his time between Belgium and England. Working with Leo Szilard, his fellow refrigerator inventor, he helped create what became the Academic Assistance Council, a body that helped resettle the extraordinary outpouring of German intellectual talent throughout the 1930s. They had to deal with a wave of refugees that included scientists like Born, Schrödinger, Lise Meitner; artists, among them George Grosz, Max Beckmann, Kandinsky; musicians: Schönberg, Weill, and the pianist Artur Schnabel; Mies van der Rohe and other leaders of the Bauhaus architects; philosophers like Ernst Cassirer and theater people like Brecht and Lotte Lenya; writers—the Mann brothers, of course; and so many more, from every discipline. Einstein did what he could to help. Throughout the summer of 1933, he sounded his warning about Hitler wherever he could. In September he visited Winston Churchill, then languishing in political exile; but while Churchill did not require much persuasion to view Hitler as a menace, he had no influence to bring to bear.

Later that month, Einstein's frustration became more obvious. "I cannot understand the passive response of the whole civilized world to this modern barbarism," he told one interviewer. "Does the world not see that Hitler is aiming at war?"[17] Finally, on October 3, Einstein rose before ten thousand listeners at the Royal Albert Hall at a rally to aid Germany's political refugees. Security was tight, for the police had received a tip about an assassination threat, but Einstein was determined to appear, intent on pleading his cause one more time. He moderated his language, deferring slightly to German sensibilities. "It cannot be my task to sit in judgment over the conduct of a nation which for many years counted me among its citizens," he said. "It is perhaps futile even to try to evaluate its policies at a time when it is so necessary to act." By implication: Nazi ambitions for Germany would not collapse of their own weight. Rather, Einstein said, "leading statesmen" of Western

Europe would have to unite to forestall a repetition of the unchecked slide into catastrophe of the summer of 1914, almost twenty years before.

That speech contained hints of the tectonic shift that had overtaken Einstein's core political passion. By the time he spoke, he was no longer a pacifist, at least not in the pure form of that faith. In September he had announced his change of heart in a letter to a Belgian war resister published in *The New York Times.* "Until quite recently, we in Europe could assume that personal war resistance constituted an effective attack on militarism," he began. But circumstances alter cases, and now, "in the heart of Europe lies a power, Germany, that is obviously pushing towards war with all available means." Imagine, he asked his correspondent, what the consequences would be for Belgium if Germany occupied it again, how much worse off it would be than it had been in the last war. For Einstein, even deeply held principles had to bend to the pressure of an overwhelming threat. "I should not, in the present circumstances, refuse military service," he concluded. "Rather I should enter such service cheerfully in the belief that I would thereby be helping to save European civilization."[18]

Einstein's opposition to war in the abstract had not altered, nor had his desire to reduce the likelihood of war in the future. But from 1933 onward he tried to persuade anyone he could that Hitler was beyond the politics of passive resistance. The most important difference between Einstein and the great majority of those who tried to anticipate what the new German ruler might do next was that Einstein took Hitler at his word. Nazi Germany would never be defeated by moral suasion or the power of positive thinking.

The culmination of Einstein's commitment to defeat Hitler by whatever means necessary came in 1939 and 1940, when he sent his two letters to President Roosevelt about the possibility of the United States building an atomic bomb. In late 1938, Otto Hahn and Friedrich Strassman, two scientists still working in Berlin, were wrestling with some novel results from a series of experiments in which they bombarded uranium with a newly discovered subatomic particle, the neutron. Lise Meitner, Hahn's former collaborator, and her nephew Otto Frisch, both exiles from Hitler's Germany, met at Christmas in the Swedish village of Kungälv and together they identified the process the Berliners had observed: neutrons striking uranium atoms had sparked nuclear fission, the violent destruction of atomic nuclei in which both energy and more neutrons are released. The result was published several months before wartime secrecy would have rung the curtain down. Every competent physicist who heard the news realized that the fact that each fission event could release more neutrons created the possibility of a chain reaction in which the new neutrons would split more atoms in an escalating cascade. The next step was obvious even to the newspapers. As early as the spring of 1939, *The Washington Post* reported that nuclear fission could lead to weapons powerful enough to destroy everything over two square miles of ground.

Einstein had not paid much attention to the subject in the first months after the fission experiments became public knowledge. During the summer of 1939, however, Leo Szilard came to visit him at his vacation house on Long Island, accompanied by his fellow physicists Eugene Wigner and Edward Teller. The three émigré Hungarians laid out the principle of the chain reaction, and then told Einstein of the interest the Germans were already showing in the use of uranium as a weapon. That was enough to persuade him to sign the first letter, in which he urged the president to consider the possibility of creating atomic weapons. Roosevelt replied in mid-October, saying that he had set up a committee to investigate Einstein's suggestions. Nothing much happened—no surprise, given the initial committee budget of six thousand dollars for its first year of operation—so Szilard got Einstein to try again. In March 1940, he sent a second letter to Roosevelt, urging him to give greater impetus to the effort because, he wrote, "Since the outbreak of the war, interest in uranium has intensified in Germany. I have now learned that research there is carried out in great secrecy."[19]

Not much came of this letter either. Despite his attempt at presidential lobbying, and contrary to the often-repeated fable that he was somehow the creator of the atom bomb, Einstein had next to nothing to do with the invention of nuclear weapons. The American government did not begin to investigate military applications of atomic physics until October 1941. Even then, Einstein took no role at all in what became the Manhattan Project. The significance of his letters to Roosevelt was not the results they failed to achieve but what they reveal about Einstein's own political evolution. Until 1932, he had argued as fervently as he could that no civilized man should permit the state to order him to kill. By 1939, absolutely committed to the idea that the Western democracies faced a fight for the survival of civilization, he committed the full weight of his influence to the creation of weapons of unprecedented power and frightfulness.

In the end, the use of America's bombs deeply saddened him. On hearing of the attack on Hiroshima he is reported to have said, "*Oy weh*"—"Woe is me."[20] He later said that "had I known that the Germans would not succeed in producing an atomic bomb, I would not have lifted a finger."[21] During the war, he began to propose a new set of pacifist goals, emphasizing the need of supranational security and the international control of nuclear weapons. After it ended, he became one of the founding forces in the scientists' antinuclear movement. The last public act of Einstein's life was to add his name to a manifesto drafted by Bertrand Russell that called for global nuclear disarmament. But he never wavered in the basic argument he had made in the summer of 1933. Hitler was a deadly poison. He had to be neutralized. No greater goals could be contemplated until Hitler and Germany had been utterly defeated. Once he reached that conclusion, he followed it through to its ultimate destination: the bomb itself.

HAD THE BOMB LANDED on Germany rather than Japan, it is conceivable that Einstein might not have felt much regret. He never forgave the Germans for the Holocaust. He blamed all of them, or almost all. There was nothing to do with such people, Einstein concluded, but to make sure they never again attained real power, for they would simply kill again. "The crime of the Germans is truly the most abominable ever to be recorded in the history of the so-called civilized nations," he wrote in 1949 to Otto Hahn, the atom splitter and one of few among his old Berlin colleagues with whom he still cared to communicate. Hahn had hoped that Einstein might rejoin a German scientific society as part of the postwar reconciliation, but Einstein would have no further contact with a nation that had "massacred my Jewish brothers in Europe." And to make sure that Hahn understood who stood among the guilty, he added that "the conduct of the German intellectuals—seen as a group—was no better than the common mob."[22]

After the war, he welcomed the state of Israel as the necessary refuge of last resort needed to defend his fellow Jews from that mob. He supported its creation wholeheartedly, though he deplored the war that broke out immediately between the surrounding Arab states and the new nation. When Chaim Weizmann died in 1952, Prime Minister David Ben Gurion offered Einstein the honor of succeeding his old Zionist sparring partner as president of Israel. To the relief of both, Einstein declined. He was a model diplomat in public, writing that it saddened him to refuse "because my relationship to the Jewish people has become my strongest human bond, ever since I became fully aware of our precarious situation among the nations of the world." But privately he had no desire to find himself in a position where he might have to argue publicly against the decisions of the Israeli government. At the far end of the Mediterranean, Ben-Gurion was equally happy he would not have Einstein to confront. "Tell me what to do if he says yes," he said to an aide. "If he accepts, we are in for trouble."[23]

THERE HAD BEEN, of course, no real chance that Ben-Gurion would be so discomfited. Einstein had long since lost any urge he might have had to dazzle the wide world. Up until the early 1930s, of course, matters stood otherwise. Over the years of his greatest fame he had become a cosmopolitan. Any notion that Einstein was an uncompromising social rebel falls at the sight of a photograph from 1931 that shows him at dinner, gorgeous in white tie and tails, gesturing vigorously among companions that included Ramsay MacDonald, then prime minister of Great Britain, along with a German cabinet minister and a grandee of the soon-to-be-notorious I. G. Farben chemical company. By then, he had perfected his public persona, part wise man, part court jester, sneaking home truths in between jokes. Between 1921 and 1933, he had taken his show on the road, incessantly traveling the globe as both informal ambassador and tourist. But when he finally came to rest in Princeton in November 1933, he suddenly became almost completely unmovable. He never returned to Europe, and left the United States only once, spending a weekend in Bermuda in 1935. He became an American citizen in 1940, and in keeping with his preferred daily style, he appeared at his induction ceremony presentably enough in a dark suit, a tie, acceptable shoes—but no socks.

Still, Einstein in his American years was no recluse—far from it. Princeton had amused him from the start. Soon after he arrived he wrote to his friend Queen Elisabeth of Belgium that it was a "quaint ceremonious village of puny demigods on stilts."[24] But if local pretensions chafed, he remained accessible to anyone who wished to speak with him about science, although some of his later contacts with Niels Bohr in particular were tense, as he began to avoid confrontations over quantum mechanics that he could not win. He lectured occasionally, devoting most of his energy to his own work, almost exclusively unification problems and philosophical challenges to quantum theory. (He did, however, make a few minor contributions to the development of general relativity in his American years.)

He complained early in his Princeton days that he was too old to find many friends there, but his circle grew around him, populated both by some newly met and some from his Berlin days who had escaped in time. He sailed on a local lake in his boat *Tinnef*—"cheaply made"—a successor to the much-loved *Tümmler* in Caputh, long since seized and sold by the German authorities as an asset of an enemy alien. (Gabriella Oppenheim-Errara, who had known Einstein since the first Solvay Conference in 1911, recalled the hazards of shipping out in a vessel that had Einstein for a skipper. She was aboard *Tinnif* one day when he capsized the boat. Her two most distinct memories were of Einstein carefully keeping his pipe above water as he paddled, and of the shock aboard the boat that came to rescue them when its crew recognized whom they were pulling out of the water).[25] And as suggested by the recent, somewhat overblown revelations of Einstein's relationship with a woman who may have been a Russian spy, he still enjoyed the company of women. (The lover in question, a Russian émigré named Margarita Konenkova, was listed by a Russian intelligence officer as one of his agents. The full list included a wide range of alleged spies, even Niels Bohr, which has led to the suspicion that the entire file was fake, a real-life version of Graham Greene's *Our Man in Havana*.)

But though he rarely ventured far from Princeton, Einstein remained very much in the public eye. The newspapers would occasionally report on the "progress" of a new, definitive physical theory, but when he did seek out the media and a mass audience, it was always to serve one of his causes. From the anti-Hitler efforts of the 1930s to his Zionism and his antinuclear campaigns of his last years, Einstein proved willing throughout his time in America to campaign to the point of exhaustion. Shortly before he was to enter the hospital in his final illness, he was drafting a radio address for the upcoming eighth anniversary of the founding of Israel. What would have been his last public speech was a warning, issued by a man who had been there and seen it happen. "Political passions," he wrote, but never got to say, "once they have been fanned into flame, exact their victims."[26]

But even if Einstein was hardly a hermit throughout his twenty-two years in the United States, there is no doubt that his life had narrowed sharply compared with his Berlin days. He lived within walking distance of his office, though he did most of his work in the second-floor study of the house he bought in 1935 at 112 Mercer Street.[27] He did not drive; he never flew. Elsa and Helen Dukas settled in with him at Mercer Street, along with his younger stepdaughter, Margot. Her sister, Ilse, had fallen ill with cancer in Paris in 1934, and Elsa traveled back to Europe that May to help care for her daughter. Einstein remained in place, already unwilling to resume anything resembling his wanderings of the decade before. Ilse died that summer, aged thirty-seven. Elsa declined soon after, as parents often do when their children break the normal sequence by dying before them. She was diagnosed in 1935 with kidney and circulatory problems, and her condition deteriorated over the winter. Einstein's reaction surprised her. "He wanders about like a lost soul," she told her friend Vallentin. "I never thought he loved me so much, and that comforts me."[28]

Her death in 1936 confirmed Einstein in his increasing commitment to solitude. It was almost as if once Elsa was gone, he could give up the pretense of paying attention to anything that he did not care to engage. "I am settling down splendidly here," he told Born. "I hibernate like a bear in its cave and really feel more at home than ever before in all my varied existence." He credited the loss of Elsa for this result: "This bearishness has been accentuated still further by the death of my mate, who was more attached to human beings than I."[29] To Max Born, Einstein's seeming indifference to Elsa's death was consistent with lifelong attitudes. Assessing Einstein, he wrote that "for all his kindness, sociability, and love of humanity, he was nevertheless totally detached from his environment and the human beings included in it."[30] This was true—and that sense of remove from his surroundings only grew over the next decades.

In 1937, Hans Albert Einstein and his family emigrated to the United States; he visited his father on arriving in New York but the two men never became close. Hans Albert ultimately became a respected professor of engineering at the University of California, Berkeley. Einstein's sister, Maja, left Italy in 1939 to join her brother in the house on Mercer Street. The war years passed extremely quietly. Einstein had a consulting contract with the U.S. Navy to offer some advice on ballistics, but in fact he had little connection with the war effort. Mileva Maric-Einstein died in Zurich in 1948, lonely and miserable. Einstein's younger son, Eduard, passed the war years in his asylum, and died there in 1965. Einstein never saw him again after leaving Europe. Maja suffered a stroke shortly after the war, and became bedridden. She died in 1951, and Einstein mourned her loss as he had no other since his mother's death three decades before. He consoled himself in his usual manner. He told Margot how he did it: "Look deep, deep into nature, and then you will understand everything better."[31]

Einstein had already received his own warning. In 1948, exploratory surgery had found an aneurysm, a swelling and weakening in his abdominal aorta. Nothing could be done about it—arterial surgery was then an extremely risky procedure—and for the time being the aneurysm seemed stable. In 1950, however, it began to enlarge perceptibly. That year, Einstein made out his will, specifying his desire for the minimum of funeral arrangements. He told a student he would have no headstone, no marker, nothing that could become "a place of pilgrimage, where pilgrims would come to view the bones of a saint."[32] He was otherwise untroubled. "To one bent on age, death will come as a release," he told a friend two months before the end, though "instinctively one does everything possible to delay this last fulfillment. Thus is the game which nature plays with us." He was not immune from the impulse, he said, but "I have grown old myself and have come to regard death like an old debt, at long last to be discharged."[33]

On March 14, 1955, Einstein turned seventy-six. A few days before he had written Belgium's queen Elisabeth and had made one small attempt to amend the record. "I must confess that the exaggerated esteem in which my lifework is held makes me very ill at ease. I feel compelled to think of myself as an involuntary swindler. If one attempts to do anything about this, one succeeds only in making matters worse."[34] On April 13, he began to feel severe chest pains and had to stop working on the birthday address for the State of Israel. Two days later he was taken to the hospital. As suspected, the wall of the aneurysm had begun to fail. Einstein refused both morphine for his pain and the offer of emergency surgery. "I want to go when *I* want," Dukas reported him as saying. "It is tasteless to prolong life artificially; I have done my share, it is time to go." He would rather choose than be chosen, preferring to endow his passing with the virtue he loved best in science. If it were time to die, he said, "I will do it elegantly."[35]

On Sunday, April 17, he felt a little better. He asked to see the Israel speech along with his latest version of unification theory. He scribbled a few calculations, confronting the grand problem that held him even then. Just a few years before, in an autobiographical sketch he called "something like my own obituary," he had tried to explain why he had chosen the life he had led. From the beginning he had sensed that "out yonder there was this huge world . . . [which] exists independently of us human beings, and which stands before us like a great, eternal riddle." A riddle; a mystery; a grand, vast unknown—but crucially, one that was "at least partially accessible to our inspection and thinking." The old Einstein, already ill, still remembered that for the very young Einstein, "the contemplation of this world beckoned like a liberation."[36]

Shortly after midnight in the early morning of April 18, Einstein's sleep became disturbed. He said a few words. The night nurse strained to hear, but he spoke in German and she could not make out what he was trying to say. He settled back into silence. Just past 1:00 A.M. the aneurysm burst, and Albert Einstein died. His body was cremated.[37] A dozen friends met at the crematorium, and someone spoke a few words. His ashes were scattered. All those who knew where are themselves now dead.

NOTES

Abbreviations: AE = Albert Einstein
CPAE = *The Collected Papers of Albert Einstein*
KJD = *The Weimar Republic Sourcebook,* edited by Anton Kaes, Martin Jay, and Edward Dimendberg

Prologue: THE ADORATION

[1]German professors were employees of state or national governments, with compensation regulated by the same rules that governed other civil service jobs. Einstein also received the regular academy stipend of nine hundred marks per year. See *CPAE,* vol. V, doc. 485.
[2]The story of the flowers was reported by Einstein's biographer and friend Carl Seelig and has been reprinted widely.
[3]Carl Seelig, *Albert Einstein,* p. 148.
[4]AE to Max Planck, 17 July 1931, unsent, cited in Otto Nathan and Heinz Norden, *Einstein on Peace,* 1963, pp. 155–56.
[5]AE to Elsa Löwenthal (Einstein), after 22 November 1913, *CPAE,* vol. V, doc. 486.
[6]Irwin Cobb, *Paths of Glory,* pp. 176–77. Cobb's informant spoke in early August 1914.
[7]Jeffrey Allen Johnson, *The Kaiser's Chemists,* p. 114.
[8]Johnson, op. cit., pp. 119–20. See also the discussion of Einstein's Jewish background in Switzerland at the time of his appointment as an associate professor at the University of Zurich in 1909, cited in Albrecht Fölsing, *Albert Einstein,* p. 250.
[9]Fritz Haber et al., 1913, in *CPAE,* vol. V, doc. 445.

Chapter One: "SUSPICION AGAINST EVERY KIND OF AUTHORITY"

[1]Maja Einstein-Winteler, in *CPAE,* vol. I, introductory document.
[2]Pauline Einstein to Fanny Einstein, 1 August 1886, *CPAE,* vol. I, doc. 2.
[3]Maja Einstein-Winteler, *CPAE,* vol. I, introductory document.
[4]AE, "Autobiographical Notes" in Paul Schilpp, ed., *Albert Einstein: Philosopher-Scientist,* p. 5.
[5]AE in Paul Schilpp, ed., *Albert Einstein: Philosopher-Scientist,* pp. 3–5.
[6]AE in Schilpp, ed., *Albert Einstein: Philosopher-Scientist,* p. 5.
[7]Maja Einstein-Winteler, *CPAE,* vol. I., introductory document.
[8]Maja Einstein-Winteler, *CPAE,* vol. I, introductory document.
[9]Fritz Stern, *Dreams and Delusions,* p. 33.
[10]*CPAE,* vol. I, doc. 66.
[11]*CPAE,* vol. I, doc. 91.

[12]Maja Einstein-Winteler, *CPAE,* vol. I, introduction.
[13]Ibid.
[14]AE, "Autobiographical Notes" in Schilpp, ed., *Albert Einstein: Philosopher-Scientist,* p. 9.
[15]AE, *Autobiographische Skizze,* 1954, p. 9 (German edition), published in Seelig, *Albert Einstein: Dunkel Zeit Helle Zeit,* and available on the World Wide Web at: http://philoscience. unibe.ch/archiv/lehre/winter99/einstein/ 2_Dez.html.
[16]Seelig, *Albert Einstein,* p. 21.
[17]AE, "Matura Exam (B) French: *Mes Projets d'Avenir,*" 18 September 1896, *CPAE,* vol. I, doc. 22.
[18]AE in Schilpp, ed., *Albert Einstein: Philosopher-Scientist,* pp. 15–17.
[19]AE to Mileva Maric, 16 February 1898, *CPAE,* vol. I, doc. 39.
[20]AE in Schilpp, ed., *Albert Einstein: Philosopher-Scientist,* p. 17.
[21]Seelig, *Albert Einstein,* p. 48.
[22]AE in Schilpp, ed., *Albert Einstein: Philosopher-Scientist,* p. 17.
[23]Antonina Vallentin, *The Drama of Albert Einstein,* p. 11.
[24]AE to Pauline Winteler, May 1897, in *CPAE,* vol. I, doc. 34.
[25]AE to Mileva Maric, August 1899, *CPAE,* vol. I, doc. 50.
[26]AE to Mileva Maric, 1 August 1900, Jürgen Renn and Robert Schulmann, eds., *The Love Letters,* doc. 15.
[27]AE to Mileva Maric, 9 August 1900, 1992, in Renn and Schulmann, eds., *The Love Letters,* doc. 17.
[28]AE to Mileva Maric, 20 August 1900, 1992, in Renn and Schulmann, *The Love Letters,* doc. 19.
[29]Ibid.
[30]AE to Mileva Maric, 4 February 1902, 1992, in Renn and Schulmann, *The Love Letters,* doc. 49.
[31]Robert Schulmann, the editor of the Einstein papers who has pursued Lieserl's story with the greatest determination, has been unable to find any records of her birth, her naming, or her death in any of the likely registries. Her fate thus remains a mystery, but Schulmann believes she died before the age of five.
[32]AE to Mileva Maric, 4 April 1901, *CPAE,* vol. I, doc. 96.
[33]AE to Heinrich Zangger, summer 1912, *CPAE,* vol. V, doc. 406. The Polytechnic had been renamed since Einstein's school days there. It is now known as Eidgenössiche Technische Hochschule—the Federal Technical University—from which the usual abbreviation ETH is derived.
[34]Hermann Einstein to Wilhelm Ostwald, 13 April 1901, *CPAE,* vol. I, doc. 99.
[35]Einstein to Cecile Grossmann, Einstein Archives.
[36]Abraham Pais, *Subtle Is the Lord,* p. 47.
[37]AE to Mileva Maric, 28 December 1901; *CPAE,* vol. I, doc. 131.
[38]AE to Carl Seelig, 5 May 1952, cited in Abraham Pais, *Subtle Is the Lord,* p. 47.
[39]AE, *CPAE,* vol. II, doc. 23; see also editor's note, p. 253.
[40]AE, *CPAE,* vol. II, doc. 23.
[41]See Desanka Trbuhovic-Gjuric, cited in Abraham Pais, *Einstein Lived Here,* pp. 14–16. See also Highfield and Carter, *The Private Lives of Albert Einstein,* pp. 108–117.
[42]AE to Mileva Maric, 27 March 1901, *CPAE,* vol. I, doc. 94.
[43]Max Planck had advance notice of the breakthrough. He was on the *Annelen* editorial board, and his approval cleared it for publication.
[44]Fölsing, *Albert Einstein,* pp. 201–203.
[45]AE to Johann Jakob Laub, 19 May 1909, *CPAE,* vol. V, doc. 161.
[46]Mileva Maric to Helene Savić, published in Roger Highfield and Paul Carter, *The Private Lives of Albert Einstein,* p. 128.
[47]AE in Schilpp, ed., *Albert Einstein: Philosopher-Scientist,* 1949, pp. 4 and 5.
[48]See *CPAE,* vol. V, docs. 154 and 166.

[49]AE to Heinrich Zangger, 15 November 1911; *CPAE,* vol. II, doc. 305; AE, *Ideas and Opinions,* p. 73.
[50]Mileva Maric to AE, 4 October 1911, *CPAE,* vol. V, doc. 290.
[51]AE to Mileva Maric, 28 October 1911, *CPAE,* vol. V, doc. 300.
[52]See Highfield and Carter, *The Private Lives of Albert Einstein,* pp. 145–46.
[53]AE to Elsa Einstein, 30 April 1912, in *CPAE,* vol. V, doc. 389.
[54]AE to Elsa Einstein, 10 October 1913, *CPAE,* vol. V, doc. 476.
[55]AE to Elsa Einstein, December 1913, *CPAE,* vol. V, docs. 489 and 497.
[56]AE to Elsa Einstein, 2 December 1913, *CPAE,* vol. V, doc. 488.
[57]AE to Mileva Maric, 10 August 1899, *CPAE,* vol. I, doc. 52.
[58]Mileva Maric to AE, 3 May 1901, *CPAE,* vol. I, doc. 104.
[59]AE to Mileva Maric, 18 July 1914, *CPAE,* vol. VIII, doc. 22.
[60]AE to Mileva Maric, 18 July 1914, *CPAE,* vol. VIII, doc. 23.
[61]G. J. Whitrow, ed., *Einstein: The Man and His Achievement,* p. 20.
[62]AE to Mileva Maric, 18 August 1914, in *CPAE,* vol. VIII, doc. 33.
[63]AE to Elsa Einstein, 30 July 1914, *CPAE,* vol. VIII, doc. 29.
[64]AE to Elsa Einstein, 30 July 1914, *CPAE,* vol. VIII, doc. 30.
[65]He would ship most of his furniture to Maric before the end of the year, and move in to a smaller apartment nearer the middle of town. Elsa's apartment was still a short walk away.

Chapter Two: "CONSISTENCY AND SIMPLICITY"

[1]AE to Adolf Hurwitz, 4 May 1914, in *CPAE,* vol. VIII, doc. 6.
[2]AE to Paul Ehrenfest, before 10 April 1914, *CPAE,* vol. VIII, doc. 2.
[3]AE to Adolf Hurwitz, 4 May 1914, *CPAE,* vol. VIII, doc. 6.
[4]Pais, *Subtle Is the Lord,* citing a letter to Pais by E. G. Straus in 1979.
[5]AE to Ernest Freundlich, around 20 January 1914, *CPAE,* vol. V, doc. 506.
[6]Robert Lawson in *Nature,* vol. 175, 28 May 1955, pp. 926–27, cited in Ronald Clark, *Einstein,* p. 200. See also Fölsing, *Albert Einstein,* p. 319.
[7]Maxwell's equations yield a specific, fixed velocity for the electromagnetic wave (of which light is a particular form). Experiment confirmed that this velocity remains fixed for any pair of observers moving uniformly relative to each other. But as Newton developed his mechanics, the speed of light should be no more a constant than any other velocity; hence the conflict.
[8]The best experimental test of the unchanging speed of light came with a series of experiments by the Americans Albert A. Michelson and Edward W. Morley, using exceptionally precise measuring techniques developed by Michelson. Einstein himself either did not know of the Michelson-Morley work or had passed over it without much attention. For a detailed discussion on what Einstein knew and when he knew it, see especially Pais's *Subtle Is the Lord,* Chapter Six, which includes a technical as well as a historical account.
[9]*CPAE,* vol. V, doc. 27, p. 20.
[10]Joseph Sauter in Max Flückiger, *Albert Einstein in Berlin;* also cited in Fölsing, *Albert Einstein,* p. 177.
[11]*CPAE,* vol. II, doc. 23, p. 141.
[12]Recent work has uncovered what seem to be superluminal—faster than light—effects. One experiment produced pulses of light that in one interpretation are moving up to three hundred times the speed of light as fixed by Maxwell and Einstein. The conditions in which such superluminal pulses are produced are, however, so constructed as not to violate special relativity. Even though individual pulses are or appear to be moving faster than what is supposed to be an absolute speed limit, they can carry no information, which meets the requirements of Einstein's theory.
[13]$E = mc^2$ is not, however, "the equation for the atomic bomb." The equation does provide

the formula to calculate the energy released in a nuclear explosion. But it contains nothing about the underlying reactions that convert mass to energy.

[14]There are several good accounts of the development and logical structure of special relativity. Einstein's own account from 1916, in *Relativity,* contains a well-written explanation of the special theory, bound with a slightly less clear analysis of the general theory that followed in 1915. Max Born's *Einstein's Theory of Relativity,* originally published in 1924, is a more technical version, but it is still quite a readable and expanded account of relativity, giving a much broader picture of the background of physics against which relativity emerged. David Bohm's hard-to-find but excellent *The Special Theory of Relativity* is somewhat mathematical in its approach but is absolutely worth the effort.

[15]See AE, *Ideas and Opinions,* p. 230, and the letter to Carl Seelig cited in Fölsing, *Albert Einstein,* p. 219. For a broader discussion of the origins of relativity, see Gerald Holton's excellent *Thematic Origins of Scientific Thought.*

[16]Einstein in various places gives his account of the intellectual genesis of general relativity as a problem, which differs somewhat from that given above. See *Relativity* (Einstein, A., 1962), pp. 59–62, and also "Autobiographical Notes," in Schilpp, ed., *Albert Einstein: Philosopher-Scientist,* especially pp. 63–81.

[17]AE and Leopold Infeld, *The Evolution of Physics,* p. 213.

[18]AE to Michele Besso, c. 10 March 1914, *CPAE,* vol. V, doc. 514.

[19]Reply by Max Planck to Einstein's Inaugural Address in proceedings of the Prussian Academy, vol. 2, pp. 742–44.

Chapter Three: "THIS 'GREAT EPOCH' "

[1]This account has been drawn mostly from Martin Gilbert's *The First World War,* pp. 15–17.

[2]*Die Post,* 11 March 1914, quoted in Dieter Glatzer and Ruth Glatzer, *Berliner Leben,* vol. I, p. 500.

[3]Ibid., p. 512.

[4]T. Wolff, in *Das Vorspiel,* vol. 1, quoted in Glatzer and Glatzer, *Berliner Leben,* p. 506.

[5]Glatzer and Glatzer, *Berliner Leben,* p. 517.

[6]See Gordon Craig, *Germany 1866–1945,* p. 175.

[7]Otto Bismarck to then–Prince Wilhelm (later Kaiser Wilhelm II) in 1887, cited in Craig, *Germany 1866–1945,* p. 172.

[8]Glatzer and Glatzer, *Berliner Leben,* p. 499.

[9]See Robert Massie, *Dreadnought,* p. 107.

[10]Alexandra Richie, *Faust's Metropolis,* p. 256.

[11]Massie, *Dreadnought,* 1991, p. 472.

[12]See Gordon Craig, *The Politics of the Prussian Army,* p. 296. Widenmann told the British admiral Jellico that Germany sought a 2:3 ratio of capital ships. Given Britain's imperial commitments, this meant that Germany sought parity or better in home waters.

[13]Ibid., p. 298.

[14]Donald Kagan, *On the Origins of War,* p. 209. There is an enormous number of sources about the prelude to war. The chapter on World War I in Kagan's book is a masterful summary of the events and balance of forces that led to the European conflict. Eric Hobsbawm's *The Age of Empire* provides a magisterial background, written from a Marxist perspective. A good, if iconoclastic, introduction to Great Power politics comes in Paul Kennedy's *The Rise and Fall of the Great Powers,* especially Chapters Four and Five. His notes and bibliography provide a good starting point for a deeper investigation of the subject. Robert Massie's *Dreadnought* details the astounding pace and consequences of the naval race between the two powers. The intensive examination of the particular German responsibility for the war was pioneered by Fritz Fischer, with his work *Griff nach der Weltmacht* in 1961. For an introduction to Fischer's work and his response to the first round of critics,

see *World Power or Decline.* James Joll's *The Origins of the First World War* (second edition) provides one of the best one-volume summaries of the forces that led to war (and is rather critical of Fischer's argument). Finally, Gordon Craig's *The Politics of the Prussian Army* is a masterful account of military thinking in Germany from unification through the Hitler years.

[15]Peter Gay, *Weimar Germany,* p. 11.

[16]*Vossische Zeitung,* 19 September 1914.

[17]AE, "The World as I See It," originally published in 1930; reprinted in *Ideas and Opinions,* p. 10.

[18]AE to Paul Ehrenfest, 19 August 1914, *CPAE,* vol. VIII, doc. 34.

[19]AE, "The World as I See It," in *Ideas and Opinions,* p. 10.

[20]Johnson, *The Kaiser's Chemists,* pp. 85–86.

[21]AE to Heinrich Zangger, 17 May, 1915, *CPAE,* vol. VIII, doc. 40.

[22]Einstein Archives doc. 19–406, cited in Alice Calaprice, *The Quotable Einstein,* p. 76.

[23]Max Planck in *Deutsche Hochschulstimmen,* no. 33, 1914, cited in Fölsing, *Albert Einstein,* p. 344.

[24]Quoted in Gilbert, *The First World War,* p. 36. The incident was recorded in Hugh Gibson's memoir, *A Journal from Our Legation in Belgium.*

[25]Gilbert, *The First World War,* p. 43.

[26]*Vossische Zeitung,* 4 October 1914, p. 7.

[27]Georg Friedrich Nicolai, *Die Biologies des Kriegs,* p. 13.

[28]Cited in Gilbert, *The First World War,* p. 32.

[29]AE in the Albert Einstein Archives, document 13–115, cited in Hans Groener and Giuseppi Castagnetti, "Albert Einstein as a pacifist and democrat during the First World War."

[30]From the 16 September 1915 diary entry by Romain Rolland, written after his meeting with Einstein. The entire entry is reprinted in Clark, *Einstein: The Life and Times,* pp. 232–36.

[31]From Rolland's diary, published as *Journal des annees de guerre, 1914–1919,* Paris, 1952, quoted in Nathan and Norden, *Einstein on Peace,* p. 15.

[32]AE to Paul Ehrenfest, December 1914, *CPAE,* vol. VIII, doc. 39.

Chapter Four: "ALL THE LOATHSOME NONSENSE"

[1]Friedrich von Bernhardi, quoted in Dominic Hibberd, *The First World War,* pp. 9–10.

[2]Ibid., p. 21.

[3]Bronsart von Schellendorf quoted in Hibberd, *The First World War,* p. 12.

[4]AE to Romain Rolland, 22 August 1917, *CPAE,* vol. VIII, doc. 374.

[5]Quoted in Gordon Martel, ed., *Modern Germany Reconsidered,* p. 104.

[6]Heinrich von Treitschke, *History of Germany in the Nineteenth Century,* p 273.

[7]Treitschke quoted in David Blackbourn and Geoff Eley, *The Peculiarities of German History.*

[8]From one of Treitschke's lectures at Berlin University, cited in Gordon Craig, *Germany 1866–1945,* p. 49.

[9]The western Allies shared Einstein's view that Treitschke was dangerous and significant. Both his *History* and his influential two-volume *Politics* were translated and published in Britain and America during the war.

[10]Treitschke, *Politics,* vol. II, pp. 598–99.

[11]Treitschke, *Politics,* I, p. 33.

[12]Treitschke, *Politics,* I, pp. 231–32.

[13]Cited in Kagan, *On the Origins of War,* p. 134.

[14]David Lloyd George's memoirs, quoted in Hibberd, *The First World War,* p. 33.

[15]*The Times* (of London), 5 August 1914, quoted in Hibberd, *The First World War,* p. 35.

[16]A. L. Smith, quoted in Daniel Pick, *War Machine,* p. 149.

[17]Ramsay Muir, quoted in Pick, *War Machine,* p. 154.
[18]Gustave Le Bon, *The Psychology of the Great War,* p. 63.
[19]See Bernd Ulrich's essay in the collection produced by Berliner Geschichtswerkstatt, *August 1914, Ein Volk zieht in den Krieg,* pp. 232–41. Volunteers were given a very short training course—two to three weeks. Torture and sexual abuse were apparently common enough to invoke official instructions to officers about the handling of untrained recruits as early as 22 August 1914. The shock of battle for such poorly trained soldiers was such that army mental wards were as crowded, Ulrich reports, as the front line hospitals.
[20]Hans Peter Hanssen, *Diary of a Dying Empire,* p. 13ff.
[21]Adolf Hitler, from *Mein Kampf,* Munich, 1939, p. 173, quoted in Werner Maser, *Hitler's Letters and Notes,* p. 41.
[22]Thomas Mann quoted in Peter Gay, *Weimar Germany,* p. 348.
[23]Rainer Maria Rilke, quoted in Gay, *Weimar Germany,* p. 348.
[24]Thomas Mann, quoted in Peter Gay, *Freud,* p. 348.
[25]*Vossische Zeitung,* 2 August 1914, "Mobilization—Speech of the Emperor."
[26]*Vorwärts,* 8 August 1914, quoted in Ray Rosdale's essay in Berliner Geschichtswerkstatt, *August 1914, Ein Volk zieht in den Krieg,* p. 284.
[27]A. F. Wedd, *German Students' War Letters,* p. 1. Letter dated 4 August 1914.
[28]Wedd, op. cit., pp. 2–3. Letter dated 7 August 1914.
[29]Wedd, op. cit. Letter dated 7 September 1914.
[30]For a compelling analysis of both prewar and wartime military thinking and execution, see B. H. Liddell Hart's classic *Strategy,* pp. 151–204. The Schlieffen plan and its fate are discussed in detail on pp. 153–58. For a more institutional analysis of the plan, see Craig's *The Politics of the Prussian Army,* pp. 273–300. See also Kagan, *On the Origins of War,* p. 128. Kagan also cites A. J. P. Taylor's analysis of this issue, while taking issue with some of Taylor's broader arguments.
[31]Hitler to Joseph Popp, 2 December 1914, in Maser, *Hitler's Letters and Notes,* 1974, pp. 50–57.
[32]Hitler to Ernst Hepp, 5 February 1914, in Maser, op. cit., pp. 68–90.
[33]Rudolf Binding, *A Fatalist at War,* p. 31.

Chapter Five: "UNNECESSARY ERUDITION"

[1]*Kölnische Zeitung,* cited in Gilbert, *The First World War,* p. 157.
[2]Rathenau, in the *Berliner Tageblatt,* 31 July 1914, cited in Gilbert, op. cit., p. 28.
[3]Rathenau to Hermann Stehr, 11 August 1914. Hartmut Pogge von Strandmann, ed., *Walther Rathenau: Notes and Diaries 1907–1922,* p. 189.
[4]Einstein to Heinrich Zangger, 6 December 1917, *CPAE,* vol. VIII, doc. 403.
[5]AE to Heinrich Zangger, 17 May 1915; *CPAE,* vol. VIII, doc. 84.
[6]AE to Heinrich Zangger, April 1915; *CPAE,* vol. VIII, doc. 73.
[7]AE, *The Origins of the General Theory of Relativity.*
[8]The first quote is from a manuscript now owned by the J. Pierpont Morgan Library in New York City, and the second from notes taken at a lecture Einstein gave in Kyoto in 1922. Both are cited in Pais, *Subtle Is the Lord,* pp. 178–79.
[9]AE, *Ideas and Opinions,* p. 290.
[10]Martin Klein, private communication, 1995.
[11]AE's 1922 Kyoto talk, cited in Pais, *Subtle Is the Lord,* p. 179.
[12]Kip Thorne, *Black Holes and Time Warps,* p. 552.
[13]Astronauts in earth orbit are in fact experiencing the falling elevator. Such space travelers are in fact falling toward earth; they do not crash into the earth because the energy and trajectory imparted to them on liftoff places them in orbit rather than on a ballistic (up-and-down) track.

[14]Thorne, *Black Holes and Time Warps,* p. 80. See also pp. 96–99 for an excellent account of the equivalence principle.
[15]Newton also explored this, in an argument derived from his assumption that light was made of particles whose motions could be affected by gravity.
[16]Red shifts occur within the electromagnetic spectrum—the range of all the wavelengths of light. The term *red shift* comes from the fact that spectral lines observed from luminous sources—stars or galaxies—that are moving away from us are observed to be "shifted" to longer wavelengths, the red end of the visible spectrum. It is the direction that counts, whether or not the light is in the visible range. The magnitude of the shift corresponds to a given velocity for a source moving away from an observer—or in the case of gravitational red shifts, for a given mass for the source.
[17]Pais, *Subtle Is the Lord,* p. 183.
[18]Max Born, cited in Fölsing, *Albert Einstein,* p. 243.
[19]Reported by Carl Seelig and reprinted in Fölsing, *Albert Einstein,* p. 245.
[20]Hermann Minkowski, lecture given at the physics and mathematics section of the Naturforscher meeting held in Cologne, 21 September, 1908, republished in Minkowski's collection, *Raum und Zeit.*
[21]The Pythagorean approach actually applies to "space-like" measurements in spacetime. Including time does add significant mathematical complications.
[22]For a good treatment of Minkowski's spacetime idea, see the first few pages of the second chapter of Thorne's *Black Holes and Time Warps,* beginning on p. 87. He uses an example from *Spacetime Physics* by Edward Taylor and John Wheeler, which is a somewhat more technical introductory work.
[23]In fact, this *is* a simplification. Time intervals or distances in Minkowski's spacetime are measured with imaginary numbers, those multiplied by the $\sqrt{-1}$, "i".
[24]From the Solvay Conference Proceedings, 1911.
[25]AE to Michele Besso, 26 December 1911; *CPAE,* vol. 5, doc. 331.

Chapter Six: "MY GRANDEST DREAMS HAVE COME TRUE"

[1]Friedrich Adler to Victor Adler, 19 June 1908, cited in Fölsing, *Albert Einstein,* p. 247.
[2]See Dennis Overbye, *Einstein in Love,* p. 197.
[3]Emil Fischer to AE, 1 October 1910, *CPAE,* vol. 5, doc. 230.
[4]AE to H. Zangger, 7 April 1911, *CPAE,* vol. 5, doc. 263.
[5]AE to M. Besso, 13 May 1911, *CPAE,* vol. 5, doc. 267.
[6]Dmitri Marianoff, cited in Highfield, R. and Carter, P., *The Private Lives of Albert Einstein.* 1993, p. 137.
[7]Max Brod, cited in Highfield, R. and Carter, P., *The Private Lives of Albert Einstein.* 1993, p. 138.
[8]Philipp Frank, *Einstein: His Life and Times,* 1947, p. 85.
[9]AE to Hedwig Born, 8 September 1916, in Max Born, *The Einstein-Born Letters,* p. 4.
[10]AE, *CPAE,* vol. III, doc. 23.
[11]Einstein did not simply settle for pictures. For the bending of light, he calculated how much a mass the size of the sun would divert a ray of starlight just scraping past its edge. He came up with a figure, .83 of an arc second, the same value that Newton's theory generates. The number was wrong, as we shall see, but Einstein believed it for the next four years.
[12]Richard Feynman, in the final lecture reprinted in *Six Not-So-Easy Pieces,* presents one of the best and most straightforward discussions of the ideas discussed here. See pp. 131–36. See also Kip Thorne's note on gravitational time dilation, in *Black Holes and Time Warps,* pp. 102–103, for a subtle discussion of the same material.
[13]A test of the gravitational dilation of time that is an exact replica of the rocket ship thought experiment was performed using two atomic clocks placed in the basement and on

the top floor of Harvard's applied physics building. As expected, the clocks ran at the rates predicted by Einstein's final gravitation equations.

[14]Linear functions are easy, at least in principle. The essential property of a linear differential equation is that proportional changes in the input variables produce proportional changes in the solutions. A classic example is the equation for an oscillating spring. For a perfect spring, unaffected by friction or air resistance, the equation that describes its behavior when pulled from its resting equilibrium state says that the mass of the spring times its acceleration is exactly equal to the restoring force of the spring, the tug of the coil itself that pulls the mass back to its equilibrium position. (The equation reads $m \times d^2x/dt^2 = -kx$, where m is the mass of the spring, $d^2 \times /dt^2$ is the acceleration term, k is a constant describing the spring's resistance, and x is the distance the spring is pulled or displaced.)

This equation is *linear.* Displace the spring by x distance, let go and the mass experiences an acceleration proportional to (linear with) the displacement x. Solving this equation one obtains perfect sinusoidal motion, the steady back-and-forth oscillation of the spring. Displace it by 2x, and the solution is the same—perfect sinusoidal oscillation, again. The only difference is that; the sine wave traced out by the spring bouncing over time will have twice the amplitude, twice the height from top to bottom, of the previous solution. The solution has changed in precise proportion to the change in inputs.

By contrast, nonlinear equations have feedbacks buried in their terms that prevent this clean proportionality. For example, a spring's resistance to being tugged—the term "k" in the equation above—can vary depending on how far it is displaced from rest, how big the "x" term becomes. k now depends on x. Doubling x yields a new value for k; and that difference would be enough to throw off the clean, perfect up-and-down oscillation of the spring. Every change in x produces a feedback that affects the value of k, and thus alters the behavior of the system in ways that distinguish it, increasingly as x grows larger, from the behavior of truly linear oscillation.

[15]AE to Michele Besso, 26 March 1912, *CPAE,* vol. V, doc. 377.

[16]AE to Heinrich Zangger, after 5 June 1912, *CPAE,* vol. V, doc. 406.

[17]AE Kyoto talk, cited in Pais, *Subtle Is the Lord,* 1981, p. 212. The Einstein scholar John Stachel first pointed out the significance of the rotating disk in the development of Einstein's thought.

[18]There are in fact several non-Euclidean geometries, and Riemann's was not the first. See Robert Osserman's *Poetry of the Universe.*

[19]Cited in Pais, *Subtle Is the Lord,* p. 212.

[20]AE to Ludwig Hopf, 16 August 1912, *CPAE,* vol. V, doc. 416.

[21]AE to Arnold Sommerfeld, 29 October 1912, *CPAE,* vol. V, doc. 421.

[22]AE to Paul Ehrenfest, 7 November 1913, *CPAE,* vol. V, doc. 481.

[23]AE to Hendrik Lorentz, 14 August 1913, *CPAE,* vol. V, doc. 467.

[24]AE to Heinrich Zangger, 10 March 1914, *CPAE,* vol. V, doc. 513.

[25]AE from the proceedings of the Prussian Academy; cited in Fölsing, *Albert Einstein,* p. 372.

[26]AE to Ehrenfest, 17 January 1916, *CPAE,* vol. VIII, doc. 182.

[27]AE to Arnold Sommerfeld, 9 December 1915, *CPAE,* vol. VIII, doc. 161.

[28]AE to Michele Besso, 10 December 1915, *CPAE,* vol. VIII, doc. 162.

Chapter Seven: "IS THE OLD JEHOVAH STILL ALIVE?"

[1]AE to Berliner Goethebund, as cited in Fölsing, *Albert Einstein,* p. 368.

[2]AE, "My Opinion on the War," *CPAE,* vol. VI, doc. 20.

[3]P. Wiglin, *Berlin im Glanze,* Köln, 1954, in Glatzer and Glatzer, *Berliner Leben,* p. 119.

[4]From the show *Woranwir denken—Bilder aus Grosser Zeit,* quoted in Glatzer and Glatzer, op. cit., p. 102.

[5]*Vorwärts,* 13 May 1915, in Glatzer and Glatzer, op. cit., p. 142.
[6]Ibid.
[7]In Tim Cross, *The Lost Voices of World War I,* p. 46.
[8]Robert Graves, *Goodbye to All That,* pp. 110–11.
[9]Johnson, *The Kaiser's Chemists,* p. 190.
[10]The account of this first gas attack is drawn from Martin Gilbert's *The First World War,* pp. 144–45.
[11]Gilbert, *The First World War,* p. 144.
[12]John Singer Sargent's monumental painting is located in the Imperial War Museum in London.
[13]Gilbert, *The First World War,* p. 199.
[14]Ibid.
[15]Graves, *Goodbye to All That,* p. 145.
[16]Liddell Hart, *Strategy,* p. 162.
[17]Quoted in Fritz Fischer, *Germany's Aims in the First World War,* p. 109.
[18]Ibid., p. 111.
[19]Bethmann-Hollweg, 18 May 1915, quoted in Fischer, op. cit., pp. 195 and 199.
[20]Romain Rolland, quoted in Ronald Clark, *Einstein: The Life and Times,* p. 236.
[21]AE, *Ideas and Opinions,* p. 3.
[22]AE to Paul Ehrenfest, 3 June 1917, *CPAE,* vol. VIII, doc. 350.
[23]AE in *Ideas and Opinions,* p. 9.
[24]AE to Michele Besso, 13 May 1917, *CPAE,* vol. VIII, doc. 339.

Chapter Eight: "I HAVE BECOME FAR MORE TOLERANT"

[1]AE to David Hilbert, 30 May 1916, *CPAE,* vol. VIII, doc. 223.
[2]AE to Michele Besso, 14 May 1916, *CPAE,* vol. VIII, doc. 219.
[3]For a discussion in detail about these strange cosmological beasts, see Thorne's *Black Holes and Time Warps,* subtitled accurately *Einstein's Outrageous Legacy.*
[4]The evidence for gravitational waves comes from the analysis of the behavior of a binary star system, PSR1913+6. In that system an object—possibly an ordinary star, possibly an object as exotic as a neutron star—is orbiting around and spiraling in toward a pulsar. Pulsars are themselves neutron stars that are rotating rapidly—the remnants of supernovae explosions and their associated stellar collapses. Because the two objects are in accelerated motion relative to each other, Einstein's theory predicts that they should generate gravity waves—and that those waves should have a measurable impact on the orbital period of the stars. Detailed observations of the visible companion showed the effect to be $1.04^{+}/-.13$ times the predicted value—which in astronomical terms is dead on the money.
[5]AE, "Cosmological Considerations in the General Theory of Relativity," first published in 1917, reprinted in *CPAE,* vol. VI, doc. 43.
[6]Osserman, *The Poetry of the Universe,* pp. 89–90.
[7]AE, *CPAE,* vol. VI, doc. 43.
[8]In a letter to Willem de Sitter in April 1917 *(CPAE,* vol. VIII, doc. 325), Einstein declared that he did not want to "devote all that much time to our difference of opinion, which is only a difference in creed, so to speak. . . . We should see the possibilities without wishing. . . . Conviction is a good mainspring, but a bad judge!" De Sitter responded politely but firmly, stating in a letter (*CPAE,* vol. VIII, doc. 327) that "the main point in our difference in creed is that you have a specific belief and I am a skeptic."
[9]For a very good and up-to-date report on the state of modern cosmology, see Timothy Ferris's *The Whole Shebang.*
[10]AE, "Elementary Theory of Water Waves and of Flight," *CPAE,* vol. VI, doc. 39.
[11]See Overbye, *Einstein in Love,* p. 308.

[12]AE, "On the Quantum Theory of Radiation," *CPAE,* vol. VI, doc. 38.
[13]Pais, *Subtle Is the Lord,* p. 182.

Chapter Nine: "SLAVERY MADE TO APPEAR CIVILIZED"

[1]AE to Michele Besso, 9 March 1917, *CPAE,* vol. VIII, doc. 306.
[2]Asta Nielsen, cited in Glatzer and Glatzer, *Berliner Leben,* pp. 265–66.
[3]Hermann Böhlaus Nachfolger, *Dokument aus geheimen Archiven. Berichte des Berliner Polizeipräsidenen zur Stimmung und Lage der Bevolkering in Berlin,* published as *Veröffentlichungen des Staatsarchivs Potsdam, band* 22, pp. 209, 213, and 215.
[4]AE to Michele Besso, 9 March 1917, *CPAE,* vol. VIII, doc. 306, and to Heinrich Zangger, before 11 August 1918, *CPAE,* vol. VIII, doc. 597.
[5]AE to Hedwig Born, quoted in Calaprice, *The Quotable Einstein,* p. 31.
[6]AE to Michele Besso and Anna Besso-Winteler, 1 August 1917, *CPAE,* vol. VIII, doc. 367, and AE to Michele Besso, 15 August 1917, *CPAE,* vol. VIII, doc. 371.
[7]AE to Heinrich Zangger, after 10 March 1917, *CPAE,* vol. VIII, doc. 310.
[8]AE to Heinrich Zangger, 6 December 1917, *CPAE,* vol. VIII, doc. 403. Einstein had told Besso of the move in September, in similarly casual terms.
[9]AE to Mileva Maric, 15 September 1914, *CPAE,* vol. VIII, doc. 36.
[10]AE to Heinrich Zangger, 10 April 1915, *CPAE,* vol. VIII, doc. 73.
[11]AE to Mileva Maric, *CPAE,* vol. VIII, doc. 187.
[12]AE to Mileva Maric, *CPAE,* vol. VIII, doc. 200.
[13]AE to Michele Besso, 14 July 1916, *CPAE,* vol. VIII, doc. 233.
[14]Michele Besso to AE, 17 July 1916, *CPAE,* vol. VIII, doc. 237.
[15]AE to Michele Besso, 9 March 1917, *CPAE,* vol. VIII, doc. 306.
[16]AE to Michele Besso, 21 July 1916, *CPAE,* vol. VIII, doc. 238. Einstein was aiming at the wrong target here. Anna Besso-Winteler, Michele's wife, had added a postscript to an earlier letter from Besso. Einstein failed to notice the change in correspondents, and so burst out at his old friend.
[17]AE to Elsa Einstein, 23 March 1913, *CPAE,* vol. V, doc. 434, and July 1913, *CPAE,* vol. V, doc. 454.
[18]See Highfield and Carter, *The Private Lives of Albert Einstein,* p. 148.
[19]AE to Elsa Einstein, 2 December 1913, *CPAE,* vol. V, doc. 488.
[20]AE to Elsa Einstein, 30 July 1914, *CPAE,* vol. VIII, doc. 30.
[21]AE to Elsa Einstein, 3 August 1914, *CPAE,* vol. VIII, doc. 31.
[22]AE to Elsa Einstein, after 3 August 1914, *CPAE,* vol. VIII, doc. 32.
[23]AE to Michele Besso, 12 February 1915, *CPAE,* vol. VIII, doc. 56.
[24]AE in various interviews, cited in Calaprice, *The Quotable Einstein,* pp. 206–207.
[25]AE to Anna Besso-Winteler, after 4 March 1918, *CPAE,* vol. VIII, doc. 474.
[26]Anna Besso-Winteler to AE, after 4 March 1918, *CPAE,* vol. VIII, doc. 475.
[27]Mileva Maric to AE, after 6 February 1918, *CPAE,* vol. VIII, doc. 457.
[28]The one concern was that Nobel Prizes are not given posthumously, and Einstein could have died before the Nobel committee got around to what was already perceived as an overdue award. So in an amendment to the agreement, Einstein deposited forty thousand marks' worth of securities to Maric's benefit, that amount to be deducted from the prize money, when and if it materialized.
[29]See Overbye, *Einstein in Love,* p. 275.
[30]Ilse Einstein to Georg Nicolai, 22 May 1918, *CPAE,* vol. VIII, doc. 545.
[31]AE to Vero and Bice Besso, 21 March 1955, in *Albert Einstein and Michele Besso: Correspondence,* p. 538.
[32]AE to Heinrich Zangger, before 11 August 1918, *CPAE,* vol. VIII, doc. 597.

Chapter Ten: "A NEGATION OF SUPERSTITION"

[1]AE to Michele Besso, 9 March 1917, *CPAE,* vol. VIII, doc. 306.
[2]George Grosz to Otto Schmalhausen, quoted in Frank Whitford, *The Berlin of George Grosz,* p. 7. The painting in question is titled *Widmung an Oskar Panizza*—"Dedicated to Oskar Panizza," and can be seen at the Staatsgalerie Stuttgart. *Metropolis 1916–1917* is held by the Fundacion Collecion Thyssen-Bornemisza in Madrid, and the Museum of Modern Art in New York owns *Metropolis 1917.*
[3]Leon Wolff, *In Flanders Fields,* p. 253.
[4]Both cited in Alistair Horne, *The Price of Glory,* p. 22.
[5]Henry Williamson, cited in Paul Fussell, *The Great War and Modern Memory,* p. 29.
[6]Following a calculation suggested by Martin Gilbert, the total Allied loss of over 5 million killed in the war works out to approximately 3,200 dead every day. In other words, the British toll on the first day of the Somme battle was matched every seven days or so, week in and week out, for four years. See Gilbert, *The First World War,* p. 541.
[7]For a detailed account of the battle for Verdun, see Horne's *The Price of Glory.*
[8]Count Brockdorff-Rantzau, cited in Richie, *Faust's Metropolis,* p. 289.
[9]See Edmund Wilson's *To the Finland Station,* for an elegant study in intellectual history that culminates in Lenin's journey.
[10]Eduard Bernstein, in his work *Die deutsche Revolution,* cited in Richie, *Faust's Metropolis,* p. 290.
[11]See Whitford, *The Berlin of George Grosz,* pp. 72–73.
[12]Cited in Richie, *Faust's Metropolis,* p. 279.
[13]Cited in Stephen Magill's essay "Defense and Introspection: German Jewry, 1914," in David Bronson, *Jews and Germans from 1860 to 1933,* p. 214.
[14]Rolf Vogel, *Ein Stück von uns, 1813–1976: Deutsch Juden in deutschen Armeen,* p. 72.
[15]Ernst Lissauer, excerpt from *Hassgesang gegen England,* in A. P. Wavell, *Other Men's Flowers,* p. 376.
[16]Ibid.
[17]See Vogel, *Ein Stück von uns, 1813–1976: Deutsch Juden in deutschen Armeen,* pp. 73–75 for a good example in an article from the Jewish newspaper *Im deutschen Reich* from September of 1914.
[18]Cited in Stephen Magill's essay in Bronson, *Jews and Germans from 1860 to 1933,* p. 220.
[19]The death toll army-wide was about one in six; the ratio among Jews of about one in eight. The disparity was explained in the analyses made after the war by the exceptionally low number of Jewish officers. Before the war, there were almost no such officers, and the rate of field promotion for Jews lagged far behind that for non-Jews. That had a direct impact on death rates, given that field-promoted officers led front-line formations. The casualty rate was correspondingly extraordinary.
[20]Vogel, *Ein Stück von uns, 1813–1976: Deutsch Juden in deutschen Armeen,* pp. 96–98.
[21]Both quotes from a collection of letters from Jewish soldiers killed during the war, published in Germany in 1935 in an attempt to counter Nazi propaganda about Jewish cowardice.
[22]Julius Marx, *Kriegstagebuch eines Juden,* p. 21.
[23]Ibid., p. 32.
[24]Vogel, *Ein Stück von uns, 1813–1976: Deutsch Juden in deutschen Armeen,* pp. 67–68.
[25]Marx, *Kriegstagebuch eines Juden,* p. 128.
[26]Ibid., 1964, p. 161.
[27]*Jahrbuch für jüdische Geschichte und Literatur* for the year 1918 (Jewish calendar 5677), reviewing 1917, p. 5.
[28]Ibid.
[29]Cited in H.-J. Bieber, in Bronson, *Jews and Germans from 1860 to 1933,* p. 52.

[30]AE to Heinrich Zangger, 24 August 1911, *CPAE,* vol. V, doc. 279.
[31]AE to Paul Ehrenfest, 25 April 1912, *CPAE* vol. V, doc. 384.
[32]This encounter was rather elliptically described in Frank, *Einstein: His Life and Times,* p. 242, and is expanded upon in Fölsing, *Albert Einstein,* p. 490.
[33]AE to Robert Eisler, 21 January 1925, in Fölsing, *Albert Einstein,* p. 491.
[34]For a specimen of such awkward apologies see the letter to Georg Nicolai in early March 1917, *CPAE,* vol. VIII, doc. 304.
[35]AE, *Ideas and Opinions,* p. 184.
[36]AE, *Ideas and Opinions,* p. 171.
[37]AE, "My Opinion on the War," *CPAE,* vol. VI, doc. 20.
[38]AE, "Why do they hate the Jews?" in *Ideas and Opinions,* p. 195.
[39]Micah, Chapter Six, Verse Eight, translation in *Tanakh,* JPS, Philadelphia, 1985, p. 1041. In the King James magnificent if idiosyncratic version, it reads "He hath shewed thee, O man, what *is* good; and what doth the Lord require of thee, but to do justly, and to love mercy, and to walk humbly with thy God?"
[40]AE to Edgar Mayer, 2 January 1915, *CPAE,* vol. VIII, doc. 44.

Chapter Eleven: "I PREFER TO STRING ALONG WITH MY COUNTRYMAN, JESUS CHRIST"

[1]AE to David Hilbert, before 27 April 1918, *CPAE,* vol. VIII, doc. 521.
[2]AE to K. C. Scheneider, 24 February 1918, *CPAE,* vol. VIII, doc. 471.
[3]Richie, *Faust's Metropolis,* p. 291.
[4]D. Lloyd George to the Supreme War Council on 12 November 1917, cited in Gilbert, *The First World War,* p. 377.
[5]Winston Churchill, private correspondence, cited in Gilbert, *The First World War,* p. 389.
[6]Winston Churchill in the *London Pictorial* for 12 January 1919, cited in William Seaver Woods, *Colossal Blunders of the War,* p. 98.
[7]Woods, *Colossal Blunders of the War,* p. 98.
[8]Erich v. Ludendorff, quoted in Hans Gatzke, *Germany's Drive to the West,* pp. 250–51.
[9]Kaiser Wilhelm II on 23 March 1918, in Gilbert, *The First World War,* p. 407.
[10]Ernst Jünger, *The Storm of Steel,* p. 260.
[11]For a comprehensive battlefield history of the last two years of the war, see Rod Paschall's *The Defeat of Imperial Germany.* Paschall provides a good analysis of the March campaign.
[12]Rudolf Binding, *A Fatalist at War,* pp. 206–207.
[13]Ibid., pp. 209–10.
[14]Ibid., p. 221.
[15]Hitler was recommended for his medal by the regimental adjutant, Captain Hugo Gutmann, a Jew.
[16]Quoted in Gilbert, *The First World War,* p. 444.
[17]*Vossische Zeitung,* 26 August 1918.
[18]Cited in Gatzke, *Germany's Drive to the West,* p. 285.
[19]AE to Romain Rolland, 22 August 1917, *CPAE,* vol. VIII, doc. 374.
[20]See Richie, *Faust's Metropolis,* pp. 284–87, for a description of Berlin's self-delusion in the last stages of the war.
[21]Quoted in Richie, *Faust's Metropolis,* p. 287.
[22]Price's death is documented in Gilbert, p. 501. There is still some dispute about the total casualties in the war. The best figures for Germany show that its armies lost 2,037,000 killed, 4,300,000 wounded, and 974,977 missing or captured. A total of about 9,500,000 from all nations died in the war.

Chapter Twelve: "Some Kind of High-Placed Red"

[1]John J. Pershing, quoted in Gilbert, *The First World War,* p. 503.
[2]Gilbert, *The First World War,* p. 483.
[3]Georg Bucher, *In the Line 1914–1918,* p. 309.
[4]Quoted in Gilbert, *The First World War,* p. 490.
[5]Arthur Rosenberg, *Imperial Germany,* p. 255. Rosenberg was a historian assigned by the Reichstag to the committee that from 1925–1928 studied the causes of the German collapse. He helped write the report intended to debunk the legend of the stab in the back.
[6]Rosenberg, *Imperial Germany,* pp. 250–51.
[7]Quoted in Richie, *Faust's Metropolis,* p. 318.
[8]Hitler, *Mein Kampf,* p. 199.
[9]Ibid., pp. 204–205.
[10]Walter Gropius, quoted in Richie, *Faust's Metropolis,* p. 295.
[11]Hitler, *Mein Kampf,* p. 206.
[12]See Hitler's speech of 8 September 1922 for an early instance of this usage, and the link between the events of 1918 and the Jews. Adolf Hitler, *My New Order,* pp. 45–46.
[13]Hanssen, *Diary of a Dying Empire,* p. 364.
[14]AE to Paul and Maja Winteler-Einstein, 11 November 1918, *CPAE,* vol. VIII, doc. 652.
[15]As remembered by Max Born in Born, *The Einstein-Born Letters,* p. 150.
[16]*Vossische Zeitung,* 22 December 1918.
[17]AE to Michele Besso, 4 December 1918, *CPAE,* vol. VIII, doc. 663.
[18]AE to Paul Ehrenfest, 6 December 1918, *CPAE,* vol. VIII, doc. 664.
[19]AE to Svante Arrhenius, 14 November 1918, *CPAE,* vol. VIII, doc. 654.
[20]AE to Michele Besso, 4 December 1918, *CPAE,* vol. VIII, doc. 663.
[21]AE to Paul and Maja Winteler-Einstein, 11 November 1918, *CPAE,* vol. VIII, doc. 652.
[22]AE to Hans Albert and Eduard Einstein, 10 December 1918, *CPAE,* vol. VIII, doc. 667.
[23]AE to Michele Besso, 4 December 1918, *CPAE,* vol. VIII, doc. 663.
[24]Quoted in Otto Friedrich, *Before the Deluge,* p. 32.
[25]Kessler, *The Diaries of a Cosmopolitan,* p. 42.
[26]Ibid., p. 54.
[27]Ibid., p. 57.
[28]Ibid., p. 57.
[29]Jacob Burkhardt, *The Civilization of the Renaissance in Italy,* p. 32.
[30]A. Iger, quoted in Richie, *Faust's Metropolis,* p. 306.
[31]See Gordon Craig, *Germany 1866–1945,* pp. 415–24 for a masterful dissection of the combination of blind hope and temerity that dogged the Weimar constitution's drafters.
[32]Käthe Kollwitz, quoted in Friedrich, *Before the Deluge,* p. 52.
[33]Quoted in Richie, *Faust's Metropolis,* p. 308.
[34]Quoted in Anton Gill, *A Dance Between Flames,* p. 31.
[35]Kessler, *The Diaries of a Cosmopolitan,* p. 63.

Chapter Thirteen: "A STATE OF MIND . . . AKIN TO THAT OF A . . . LOVER"

[1]Frank, *Einstein: His Life and Times,* p. 124.
[2]Ibid., p. 125.
[3]Elsa Einstein to H. Stuck and wife, 1929, cited in Fölsing, *Albert Einstein,* p. 429.
[4]AE quoted in Frank, *Einstein: His Life and Times,* p. 126.
[5]Kessler, *The Diaries of a Cosmopolitan,* 1971, p. 155.
[6]Review of Eddington's *Report on the Relativity Theory of Gravitation,* quoted in A. Vibert Douglas, *The Life of Arthur Stanley Eddington,* p. 39.

[7]A second of an arc is 1/60 of one minute of arc, which is 1/60 of a degree, which is 1/360 of a circle. So the predicted effect was a deviation of 1.7/1,296,000 of a circle, or more plainly, not very much.
[8]From Haig's Special Order of the Day for April 11; quoted in Gilbert, *The First World War,* p. 414.
[9]Eddington and Dyson's statements as cited in Douglas, *The Life of Arthur Stanley Eddington,* pp. 93–94.
[10]AE in *The Times* of London, 28 November 1919, reprinted in AE, *Ideas and Opinions,* pp. 227–28, under the title "What Is the Theory of Relativity?"
[11]AE to Arthur Eddington, 15 December 1919, in Douglas, *The Life of Arthur Stanley Eddington,* 1957, p. 41.
[12]Douglas, *The Life of Arthur Stanley Eddington,* p. 40.
[13]Reanalysis of the 1919 plates has shown that Eddington and his colleagues underestimated the size of their error bars. That does not make the conclusions wrong (as in fact, they are not) but does suggest that Eddington perhaps should have voiced less confidence in his results than he did.
[14]Gabriella Oppenheim-Errara, private conversation with the author in 1995.
[15]Alfred North Whitehead quoted in Douglas, *The Life of Arthur Stanley Eddington,* p. 43.
[16]Pais, *Subtle Is the Lord,* p. 305.
[17]Douglas, *The Life of Arthur Stanley Eddington,* p. 44.
[18]AE to a student, September 1919, cited in Calaprice, *The Quotable Einstein,* 1996, p. 168.
[19]AE, *Ideas and Opinions,* p. 227.

Chapter Fourteen: "ST. FRANCIS EINSTEIN"

[1]*The New York Times,* 9 November 1919. I have contemplated this headline for more than a decade, and still have no idea how to calculate someone's agogity quotient.
[2]*The New York Times,* 11 November 1919.
[3]*The New York Times* editorial, 7 December 1919.
[4]AE in *The Times* of London, 28 November 1919, reprinted in *Ideas and Opinions,* p. 232.
[5]AE to Heinrich Zangger, December 1919, quoted in Calaprice, *The Quotable Einstein,* p. 6.
[6]See Abraham Pais's invaluable review "Einstein and the Press" in Pais, *Einstein Lived Here,* pp. 173–74.
[7]See this scene in newsreel footage broadcast on *Einstein Revealed,* broadcast on PBS's *NOVA* series in October 1996.
[8]Describing his impressions of America for a Berlin newspaper, Einstein actually offered two objections to Prohibition. First, he noted that laws that cannot be enforced erode a government's authority. He also argued that the bar or the public house was a civic institution: the place in which people could meet and discuss current affairs.
[9]AE, *Ideas and Opinions,* p. 6.
[10]Pais, *Einstein Lived Here,* p. 151.
[11]Calaprice, *The Quotable Einstein,* p. 199.
[12]Ibid., p. 189.
[13]From the *Nieuwe Rotterdamische Courant,* 4 July 1921, reprinted in Calaprice, *The Quotable Einstein,* p. 7.
[14]Max Born, *Die Relativitattheorie Einsteins,* 1920.
[15]Born, *The Einstein-Born Letters,* p. 42.
[16]Hedwig Born to AE, 7 October 1920, in Born, *The Einstein-Born Letters,* p. 38.
[17]Max Born to AE, 13 October 1920, in Born, *The Einstein-Born Letters,* p. 40.
[18]*The New York Times,* 8 July 1921.
[19]*The New York Times,* 12 July 1921.

[20]*Vossische Zeitung,* 10 July 1921.
[21]Pais, *Eistein Lived Here,* p. 185.
[22]AE, *Ideas and Opinions,* pp. 15–16.
[23]AE in Calaprice, *The Quotable Einstein,* p. 6.
[24]AE to Heinrich Zangger, 7 November 1911, *CPAE,* vol. V, doc. 303.
[25]A mob even threw stones at Curie's windows at one point and press commentary displayed both an anti-Semitic and antiforeign streak. Curie and Langevin were also blackmail targets. See Susan Quinn's account of the fray in Chapter Fourteen of her biography *Marie Curie,* pp. 295–331.
[26]AE to Elsa Einstein, c. 11 August 1913, *CPAE,* vol. V, doc. 465.
[27]AE and Infeld, *The Evolution of Physics.,* 1966, p. xvi.
[28]See Pais, *Einstein Lived Here,* pp. 148–150 and Pais, *Subtle Is the Lord,* p. 311.
[29]AE in the *Nieuwe Rotterdamische Courant,* 4 July 1921, discussed in Pais, *Einstein Lived Here,* p. 149.
[30]William Carlos Williams, "St. Francis Einstein of the Daffodils," originally published in 1921, reprinted in Alan J. Friedman and Carol Donley, *Einstein as Myth and Muse,* pp. 195–98.
[31]See Richie, *Faust's Metropolis,* pp. 310–11.
[32]Cited in Gay, *Weimar Germany,* p. 97.
[33]Ibid., p. 97.
[34]L. Mies van der Rohe, "Architecture and the Will of the Age," 1924, reprinted in *KJD,* 1994, pp. 438–39.
[35]Walter Gropius, in W. Gropius and P. Schultze-Naumburg, "Who Is Right? Traditional Architecture or Building in New Forms," 1926, reprinted in *KJD,* 1994, p. 440.
[36]Erich Mendelsohn, "Why This Architecture?" *KJD,* 1994, pp. 451–52.
[37]Cited in Richie, *Faust's Metropolis,* p. 312.
[38]Walter Gropius, 1919, "Program of the Staatliches Bauhaus in Weimar," reprinted in *KJD,* 1994, p. 435.
[39]November Group Circular, 13 December 1918, in *KJD,* 1994, p. 435.
[40]Max Beckmann, "Creative Credo," 1920, republished in *KJD,* 1994, pp. 487–88.
[41]M. Raynal, writing in *Modern Painting,* Skira edition, cited in Alan J. Friedman and Carol C. Donley, *Einstein as Myth and Muse,* p. 22.
[42]Kurt Tucholsky reviewing *The Cabinet of Dr. Caligari* for *Die Weltbüne,* 13 March 1920; quoted in Friedrich, *Before the Deluge,* p. 68. See also Siegfried Kracauer's landmark, and still influential, account of Weimar cinema, *From Caligari to Hitler.*
[43]See Bärbel Schrader and Jürgen Schebera, *The Golden Twenties,* pp. 90–92.
[44]Carl Zuckmayer, from his memoirs cited in Ronald Taylor, *Literature and Society in Germany 1918–1945,* p. 16.

Chapter Fifteen: "GROW[ING] ANGRY WITH MY FELLOW MEN"

[1]The Treaty of Versailles, reprinted in part in *KJD,* 1994, p. 8.
[2]Cited in Craig, *The Politics of the Prussian Army,* p. 367.
[3]Kessler, *The Diaries of a Cosmopolitan,* p. 102, diary entries dated 17 June 1919 and 22 June 1919.
[4]See Craig, *The Politics of the Prussian Army,* pp. 369–70.
[5]Kessler, *The Diaries of a Cosmopolitan,* p. 103, entry dated 23 June 1919.
[6]Paul v. Hindenburg, 18 November 1919, cited in *KJD,* 1994, p. 16.
[7]Hitler, *My New Order,* p. 15.
[8]Ibid., p. 46.
[9]Cited in Geoffrey Barraclough, *The Origins of Modern Germany,* p. 445.
[10]AE to Max Born, 4 June 1919, in Born, *The Einstein-Born Letters,* p. 10.

[11]AE to Max Born, 9 December 1919, in Born, *The Einstein-Born Letters,* p. 19.
[12]AE to Max Born, 27 January 1919, in Born, *The Einstein-Born Letters,* p. 22.
[13]AE to Mileva Maric, early August 1899, *CPAE,* vol. I, doc. 50.
[14]AE to Paul Winteler (Maja's husband) in 1919 cited in Pais, *Subtle Is the Lord,* p. 302.
[15]AE to Heinrich Zangger, early March 1920, excerpted in Calaprice, *The Quotable Einstein,* p. 57.
[16]AE to Hedwig Born, 18 April 1920, in Born, *The Einstein-Born Letters,* p. 29.
[17]AE to Max and Hedwig Born, 3 March 1920, in Born, *The Einstein-Born Letters,* p. 26.
[18]AE to A. Stodola, 31 March 1920, excerpted in Fölsing, *Albert Einstein,* p. 460.
[19]Hitler, *My New Order,* p. 60.
[20]Adolf Bartels, in *KJD,* 1994, p. 124.
[21]AE, *Ideas and Opinions,* p. 226.
[22]Lorentz could not abandon fully the nineteenth-century concept of the ether, the medium through which light waves were thought to vibrate. Out of love for a man he deeply venerated, Einstein used the obsolete term in a lecture he gave in October 1920 in Leyden, Lorentz's home city.
[23]First published in *Naturwissenshaften,* vol. I, 1913, cited in Fölsing, *Albert Einstein,* p. 461.
[24]AE in *Berliner Tageblatt,* 27 August 1920, cited in Pais, *Einstein Lived Here,* p. 153.
[25]AE to Max and Hedwig Born, 9 September 1920, in Born, *The Einstein-Born Letters,* p. 35.
[26]Philipp Lenard, cited in Fölsing, *Albert Einstein,* p. 467.
[27]Philipp Lenard, preface to the second edition of a pamphlet titled *On Ether and Primal Ether,* cited in Fölsing, *Albert Einstein,* p. 523.
[28]Arnold Sommerfeld to Hendrik Lorentz, 26 December 1907, microfilm reel 4 in the Lorentz papers, at the American Institute of Physics, unearthed by Albrecht Fölsing, and published in his *Albert Einstein,* p. 203.
[29]Hitler, *Mein Kampf,* p. 303.
[30]*Vossische Zeitung,* 30 September 1920.
[31]AE quoted in Fölsing, *Albert Einstein,* p. 463.
[32]AE to K. Haenisch, 8 September 1920, cited in Frank, *Einstein: His Life and Times,* p. 169.
[33]AE to Paul Ehrenfest, September 1919, cited in Banesh Hoffman and Helen Dukas, *Albert Einstein: Creator and Rebel,* 1975, p. 138.
[34]Description in Shimon Attie, Michael Bernstein, and Erwin Leiser, *Die Schrift an der Wand,* p. 13.
[35]See Lucy Dawidowicz, *The War Against the Jews,* pp. 7–9.
[36]Hitler, *Mein Kampf,* p. 56.
[37]Ibid., pp. 57–58.
[38]For an excellent, succinct account of the origins of modern anti-Semitism in the German-speaking countries see Peter Pulzer's 1988 edition of *The Rise of Political Anti-Semitism in Germany and Austria.* Other sources include *Rehearsal for Destruction* by Paul Massing, and Jacob Katz's *From Prejudice to Destruction,* which provides an account of anti-Semitism across the wider sweep of history than the two works mentioned above. *Esau's Tears* by Albert Lindeman provides an excellent overview of anti-Semitism throughout Europe. He concentrates on the modern period, from the 1870s forward, but has two good chapters that provide the premodern background. Dawidowicz's *The War Against the Jews* is excellent, chilling history. Daniel Goldhagen's *Hitler's Willing Executioners* remains controversial, but is an essential entry into the nexus of historical and moral judgment that the Holocaust requires each of us to consider.
[39]Cited in Pulzer, *The Rise of Political Anti-Semitism in Germany and Austria,* p. 48.
[40]Published on 1 August 1881; cited in Pulzer, *The Rise of Political Anti-Semitism in Germany and Austria,* p. 64.
[41]Hitler in Munich in October 1922, in Hitler, *My New Order,* p. 37.
[42]For a terribly sad account of the history of the *Protocols,* see Binjamin Segel, *A Lie and a*

Libel. Written in 1926, Segel's book reads like a narrative of a train wreck in progress. He already senses the danger represented by the forgery, and hopes, without much faith, that by speaking out against it, he and those of like mind might prevent the already unfolding disaster.

[43]Julius H. Schoeps and Ludger Heid, eds., *Juden in Deutschland von der Aufklärung bis zuyr Gegenwart,* p. 245.

[44]Quoted in Frank, *Einstein: His Life and Times,* p. 150.

[45]Erwin Leiser in Attie, *Die Schrift an der Wand,* p. 14.

[46]From AE's travel diary for 3 February 1923, Einstein archive document 29–129, quoted in Calaprice, *The Quotable Einstein,* p. 95.

[47]AE, quoted in Banesh Hoffman, "Einstein and Zionism," in Peter C. Aichelburg and Roman U. Sexl, eds., *Albert Einstein,* p. 174.

[48]AE to the National Labor Committee for Palestine, 17 April 1938, in Calaprice, *The Quotable Einstein,* pp. 98–99.

[49]Martin Buber, *On Zion,* p. xvii.

[50]AE to Maurice Solovine, 16 March 1921, in AE, *Letters to Solovine,* p. 45.

[51]Quoted in Pais, *Subtle Is the Lord,* p. 315.

[52]Einstein had the same reaction a few months later when French scientists reported results inconsistent with general relativity. Einstein noted that their instruments were not precise enough to decide the question, and that he was confident that in a few years the outcome consistent with the general theory would be found—as it was.

[53]AE, cited in Banesh Hoffman, "Einstein and Zionism" in Aichelburg and Sexl, *Albert Einstein,* p. 173.

[54]AE to Maurice Solovine, 16 March 1921, in AE, *Letters to Solovine,* p. 45.

[55]AE, *Ideas and Opinions,* p. 246.

[56]AE to Marie Curie in Seelig, *Albert Einstein: A Documentary Biography,* p. 176.

[57]AE to Paul Langevin, in Fölsing, *Albert Einstein,* p. 516.

[58]AE to Paul Langevin, cited in Vallentin, *The Drama of Albert Einstein,* 1954, p. 106.

[59]AE to Maurice Solovine, 20 April 1922, in AE, *Letters to Solovine,* p. 55.

[60]Quoted in Ronald Clark, *Einstein,* p. 357.

[61]Ibid., p. 357.

Chapter Sixteen: "THAT BUSINESS ABOUT CAUSALITY"

[1]Harry Kessler, *Walther Rathenau,* p. 357. This account follows Kessler's description of the event, which was in turn taken verbatim from the *Vossische Zeitung,* for 25 June 1922.

[2]Walther Rathenau to AE, 10–11 May 1917, *CPAE,* vol. VIII, doc. 337.

[3]AE to Pauline Einstein, 8 October 1918, *CPAE,* vol. VIII, doc. 631.

[4]See E. J. Gumbel's report "Four Years of Political Murder" published in 1924 and reprinted in *KJD,* pp. 100–104.

[5]K. Blumenfeld, reprinted in Annegret Ehrmann, Rachel Livné-Freudenthal, Julius H. Shoeps, and Monika Richarz, eds., *Juden in Berlin 1671–1945, Ein Lesebuch,* pp. 236–37. Blumenfeld's memoirs were published separately as *Erlebte Judenfrage,* Stuttgart, 1962.

[6]AE in *Neue Rundschau,* 1922.

[7]Walther Rathenau, quoted in Friedrich, *Before the Deluge,* 1972, p. 113.

[8]Walther Rathenau, cited in Pogge von Strandmann, *Walther Rathenau,* pp. 98–99.

[9]AE in Nathan and Norden, *Einstein on Peace,* p. 52.

[10]Kessler, *The Diaries of a Cosmopolitan,* pp. 338–39.

[11]Kessler, *Walther Rathenau,* p. 254.

[12]Ibid., p. 289.

[13]K. Blumenfeld, reprinted in Ehrmann, Livné-Freudenthal, Schoeps, and Richarz, *Juden in Berlin 1671–1945, Ein Lesebuch,* p. 237.

[14]Kessler, *Walther Rathenau,* pp. 358–59.
[15]AE, in *Neue Rundschau,* 1922.
[16]E. J. Gumbel, in *KJD,* 1994, p. 102.
[17]See Richie, *Faust's Metropolis,* p. 319.
[18]AE to Maurice Solovine, 16 July 1922, in AE, *Letters to Solovine,* p. 57.
[19]AE to Max Planck, 6 July 1922, in Nathan and Norden, *Einstein on Peace,* p. 54.
[20]German embassy cable to Berlin, 3 January 1923, cited in Fölsing, *Albert Einstein,* p. 527.
[21]AE to Maurice Solovine, Pentecost 1923 (sic), in AE, *Letters to Solovine,* p. 59.
[22]Ibid.
[23]Pais, *Subtle Is the Lord,* p. 503.
[24]Special relativity and general relativity join the quantum theory of light as Nobel-worthy. Einstein's work on Brownian motion and on the reality and sizes of atoms and molecules was also extremely significant, and might have earned the Nobel committee's notice on its own if it had not been overshadowed by all the rest of his output.
[25]Christopher Aurivillius to AE, 10 November 1922, cited in Pais, *Subtle Is the Lord,* p. 503.
[26]*Quanta* is the Latin plural of the word *quantum*—a survivor in both formal diction and common use.
[27]Pais, *Subtle Is the Lord,* p. 511.
[28]AE to Otto Stern, cited in Calaprice, *The Quotable Einstein,* p. 182.
[29]AE to Mileva Maric, 28 May 1901, *CPAE,* vol. I, doc. 111.
[30]Quoted in Frank, *Einstein: His Life and Times,* pp. 71–72.
[31]Cited in Pais, *Subtle Is the Lord,* p. 370.
[32]AE in Schlipp, *Albert Einstein: Philosopher-Scientist,* p. 45.
[33]AE, *CPAE,* vol. II, doc. 14.
[34]AE to Conrad Habicht, 18 or 25 May 1905, *CPAE,* vol. V, doc. 27.
[35]AE cited in Pais, *Subtle Is the Lord,* p. 383.
[36]AE to Wilhelm Wien, 17 May 1912, *CPAE,* vol. V, doc. 395.
[37]AE to Heinrich Zangger, 12 May 1912, *CPAE,* vol. V, doc. 398.
[38]AE in *CPAE,* vol. II, doc. 56.
[39]AE in *CPAE,* vol. II, doc. 60.
[40]AE and Infeld, *The Evolution of Physics,* p. 263.
[41]AE to Michele Besso, 29 July 1918, *CPAE,* vol. VIII, doc. 591.
[42]AE in conversation to Valentine Bargmann, cited in Calaprice, *The Quotable Einstein,* p. 169.
[43]AE to Max Born, 27 January 1920, in Born, *The Einstein-Born Letters,* p. 21.
[44]AE in the *Berliner Tageblatt,* 20 April 1924, cited in Pais, *Subtle Is the Lord,* p. 414.
[45]AE and Infeld, *The Evolution of Physics,* p. 243.
[46]See Brian Greene, *The Elegant Universe,* pp. 186–98.
[47]AE to Theodor Kaluza, 5 May 1919, cited in Pais, *Subtle Is the Lord,* p. 330.
[48]AE to Paul Ehrenfest, 18 August 1925 and 20 September 1925, cited in Pais, *Subtle Is the Lord,* p. 344. Einstein was right in that harsh judgment, though Albrecht Fölsing has pointed out that the 1925 paper contained, subtly disguised, a prediction of the existence of antimatter. Neither Einstein nor anyone else noticed that implication of the work, and antimatter was ultimately independently proposed by the British physicist Paul Dirac in 1930 and was discovered as a consequence of Dirac's work in 1932 through cosmic ray observations.
[49]AE, quoted by Maurice Solovine in AE, *Letters to Solovine,* pp. 7–8.
[50]AE to Maurice Solovine, 25 November 1948, in AE, *Letters to Solovine,* p. 107.
[51]AE to Maurice Solovine, 28 March 1949, AE, *Letters to Solovine,* p. 111.
[52]AE to Maurice Solovine, 27 February 1955, AE, *Letters to Solovine,* p. 157.
[53]Cited in Calaprice, *The Quotable Einstein,* p. 16.
[54]Kessler, *Diaries of a Cosmopolitan,* p. 233.

Chapter Seventeen: "A REICH GERMAN"

[1]Max Born to AE, 21 October 1921, in Born, *The Einstein-Born Letters,* p. 57.
[2]These statistics come from the German official records of the event, reprinted on page 5 of Gerald Feldman's exceptional account of the German inflation, *The Great Disorder.*
[3]See Feldman's analysis of the cost and benefits of the inflation to Germany in the last chapter of *The Great Disorder.*
[4]Feldman, *The Great Disorder,* p. 598.
[5]Feldman, *The Great Disorder,* p. 528.
[6]Franz Baum, 23 February 1923, in a speech reprinted in Fritz K. Ringer, *German Inflation of 1923,* p. 118.
[7]Friedrich Kroner, in *KJD,* 1994, pp. 63–64.
[8]Feldman, *The Great Disorder,* p. 838.
[9]Konrad Heiden, excerpted in Ringer, *German Inflation of 1923,* p. 167.
[10]Hitler, from various speeches in 1923, cited by Konrad Heiden in Ringer, *German Inflation of 1923,* p. 175.
[11]Wolf von Eckhardt and Sander L. Gilman, *Bertolt Brecht's Berlin,* p. 131.
[12]Eckhardt and Gilman, *Bertolt Brecht's Berlin,* pp. 131–32.
[13]Gill, *A Dance Between Flames,* 1993, p. 197.
[14]E. J. Gumbel, "Four Years of Political Murder" reprinted in *KJD,* 1993, pp. 102–103.
[15]George Antheil quoted in John Willet, *Art and Politics in the Weimar Period,* p. 160.
[16]See Frank, *Einstein: His Life and Times,* pp. 203–204.
[17]See Clark, *Einstein,* pp. 373–74.
[18]AE in *Die Friedenswarte,* June 1923, in Nathan and Norden, *Einstein on Peace,* p. 62.
[19]AE to Hendrik Lorentz, 15 July 1923, in Nathan and Norden, *Einstein on Peace,* p. 63.
[20]AE to the Prussian Academy, February 1924. The entire story is covered in detail in Pais, *Einstein Lived Here,* pp. 66–67.
[21]Einstein was writing to George Murray, an English scientist and one of his colleagues on his League of Nations committee. See Pais, *Subtle Is the Lord,* pp. 316–17.
[22]AE in *Judische Rundschau,* 1925, cited in Pais, *Einstein Lived Here,* p. 163.
[23]AE to Michele Besso, 24 May 1924, in *Albert Einstein–Michele Besso: Correspondence,* pp. 201–202.

Chapter Eighteen: "A SINGULAR TENSION"

[1]Ilse Einstein to Georg Nicolai, 22 May 1918, *CPAE,* vol. VIII, doc. 545.
[2]Pais, *Subtle Is the Lord,* p. 320. Pais never revealed Neumann's name, which was brought to light by Highfield and Carter in *The Private Life of Albert Einstein.*
[3]Dmitri Marianoff, with Palma Wayne, *Einstein,* pp. 188–89.
[4]Vallentin, *The Drama of Albert Einstein,* pp. 143–44.
[5]Ibid., pp. 141–42.
[6]Marianoff and Wayne, *Einstein,* p. 186.
[7]Ibid., p. 129.
[8]Vallentin, *The Drama of Albert Einstein,* p. 143.
[9]Herta Waldow, in Friedrich Herneck, *Einstein Privat,* p. 124.
[10]Kessler, *The Diaries of a Cosmopolitan,* p. 280.
[11]Ibid., p. 281.
[12]Ibid., 1971, p. 282.
[13]Ibid., pp. 284–85.
[14]Peter Jelavich, *Berlin Cabaret,* p. 164.
[15]Christopher Isherwood, quoted and discussed by John J. White, "Sexual Mecca, Nazi

Metropolis, City of Doom," in Dexter Glass, Dieter Rösler, and John J. White, *Berlin,* pp. 125–28.
[16]Ibid., p. 134.
[17]Walter Benjamin and Gustav Landauer, quoted in Richie, *Faust's Metropolis,* pp. 354 and 355. Benjamin's comment comes from an article written with Bernhard Reich, "Revue Oder Theater," *Querschnitt,* 1925.
[18]Lang's original title for the project was *The Murderer Among Us.* His studio executives wavered, as they thought from the title that it was to be an indictment of Nazism. Though Lang later did say that was his intention, he told the studio that he was trying to make a thriller about the Dusseldorf murderer—and the funding appeared—along with the new title.
[19]Cited in Maria Tatar, *Lustmord,* p. 43.
[20]Robert Musil wrote perhaps the most elegant and acid description of this queasy embrace between the mass murderer and his public in the first part of his enormous novel *The Man Without Qualities.* In the Moosbrugger chapter, Musil introduces his killer, who appeared better than ordinary, full of "good-hearted strength and the wish to do right." The difficulty with that impression was that "Moosebrugger had killed a street-woman, a prostitute of the lowest type, in a horrifying manner. The reporters had described in detail a throat-wound extending from the larynx to the back of the neck, as well as the two stab wounds in the breast, which had pierced the heart, the two others on the left side of the back and the cutting off of the breasts, which could almost be detached from the body. They had expressed their abhorrence of it, but they did not leave off until they had counted thirty-five stabs in the abdomen and described the long slash from the navel to the sacra, which continued up the back in a multitude of smaller slashes, while the throat showed the marks of throttling."
[21]Kessler, *The Diaries of a Cosmopolitan,* p. 187.
[22]The story was retold in Gill, *A Dance Between Flames,* p. 176, and derives from M. Kay Flavall's biography *George Grosz* (Yale University Press, 1988).
[23]The translation of the term *Sachlichkeit* is complex, and "objectivity" covers only part of the German sense. See Willet's discussion of the issue on p. 112 of *Art and Politics in the Weimar Republic.*
[24]Siegfried Kracauer, *From Caligari to Hitler,* p. 165.
[25]Cited in Gay, *Weimar Germany,* p. 129.
[26]Alfred Kerr, critic for the *Berliner Tageblatt,* cited in W. v. Eckhardt and S. L. Gilman, *Bertolt Brecht's Berlin,* 1993, p. 88.
[27]Brecht supporter Herbert Ihering, cited in Eckhardt and Gilman, *Bertolt Brecht's Berlin,* p. 88.
[28]I have drawn on Peter Gay's *Freud* for this brief synopsis of Berlin's psychoanalytic history. See especially pp. 180–82 and 460–64 for more detail.
[29]Quoted in Gay, *Freud,* p. 455.
[30]AE to Sigmund Freud, 22 March 1929, cited in Fölsing, *Albert Einstein,* p. 609.
[31]AE to A. Bacharach, 25 July 1949, cited in Pais, *Einstein Lived Here,* p. 190.
[32]See Kracauer, *From Caligari to Hitler,* pp. 170–72.
[33]For a broader description of the accomplishments of German art in the 1920s, see Willet's *Art and Politics in the Weimar Period.* For a view of the same story written from the East German perspective, see Schrader and Scheberer's *The "Golden" Twenties.*
[34]Yehudi Menuhin, interviewed by Otto Friedrich in Friedrich, *Before the Deluge,* p. 175. Wilhelm Furtwängler conducted the Berlin Philharmonic and Bruno Walter both guest-conducted that orchestra and directed the municipal opera.
[35]Arnold Schönberg, writing in his *Manual of Harmony,* cited by Friedrich, *Before the Deluge,* p. 178.
[36]Hans Heinsheimer, quoted in Friedrich, *Before the Deluge,* p. 183.
[37]H. H. Stuckenschmidt, quoted in Friedrich, *Before the Deluge,* p. 183.

[38]Alban Berg, in *KJD,* p. 583.
[39]Paul Zschorlich, critic for the *Deutsche Zeitung,* quoted in Friedrich, *Before the Deluge,* p. 183.
[40]Carl Zuckmayer in *Als Wars ein Stuck von mir,* 1966, quoted in Gay, *Weimar Germany,* p. 132.

Chapter Nineteen: "I, AT ANY RATE, AM CONVINCED"

[1]Gottfried Benn, quoted in Gay, *Weimar Germany,* p. 132.
[2]Nathan and Norden, *Einstein on Peace,* 1963, p. 73.
[3]Ibid., p. 25.
[4]Cited in Craig, *Germany: 1866–1945,* p. 482.
[5]George Grosz, *A Little Yes and a Big No,* 1946, p. 163.
[6]Ibid., pp. 165–66.
[7]Cited in Craig, *Germany: 1866–1945,* pp. 485–86.
[8]Joseph Goebbels, diary entry cited in Friedrich, *Before the Deluge,* p. 190.
[9]Joseph Goebbels, cited in Michael M. Kater, *Different Drummers: Jazz in the Culture of Nazi Germany,* p. 23.
[10]See Richie, *Faust's Metropolis,* p. 381.
[11]Ibid., p. 380.
[12]Joseph Goebbels, *Die Tagebücher von Joseph Goebbels [The Diary of Joseph Goebbels]* cited in Ian Kershaw, *Hitler: 1889–1936: Hubris,* p. 276. The entries were from 14 October, 6 November, and 23 November 1925.
[13]Ibid., p. 275.
[14]Ibid., p. 277.
[15]The account of Goebbels's early work in Berlin draws on Richie's treatment of the subject in *Faust's Metropolis,* pp. 379–90.
[16]Kessler, *The Diaries of a Cosmopolitan,* p. 267.
[17]In Nathan and Norden, *Einstein on Peace,* p. 74.
[18]AE to Michele Besso, 5 June 1925, in *Albert Einstein–Michele Besso: Correspondence,* p. 204.
[19]AE to Hendrik Lorentz, 9 January 1925, cited in Nathan and Norden, *Einstein on Peace,* p. 73.
[20]AE in a speech at the founding of the Institute for Intellectual Cooperation, 16 January 1926, cited in Nathan and Norden, *Einstein on Peace,* p. 77.
[21]Quoted in Pais, *Subtle Is the Lord,* p. 423.
[22]AE to Max Born, 29 April 1924, in Born, *The Einstein-Born Letters,* p. 82.
[23]Bose-Einstein condensates were first observed by a team from the National Institute of Standards and Technology and the University of Colorado. See "Very Cold Indeed: Nanokelvin Physics of Bose-Einstein Condensation," by one of the codiscoverers of the condensate in the July-August 1996 issue of the *Journal of Research of the National Institute of Standards and Technology (J. Res. Natl. Inst. Stand. Technology* 101, 419, 1996).
[24]Louis de Broglie's recollection and this entire anecdote were relayed by de Broglie to Abraham Pais and can be found in his *Subtle Is the Lord,* pp. 437–38.
[25]AE in a paper titled "The Quantum Theory of Single-Atom Ideal Gases," published in the proceedings of the Prussian Academy of Sciences in 1925.
[26]Werner Heisenberg, *Physics and Beyond,* p. 60. This collection of loosely linked memoirs/essays has to be taken with some grains of salt. Heisenberg included lengthy quotations from conversations that took place forty years and more before the book was published, and many of the quotations have something of Heisenberg's own diction. Also, it should be remembered that he published this long after he made the decision to remain in Germany to lead research into military uses of atomic physics. After the war Heisenberg struggled to rehabilitate himself among his colleagues, a task made obviously more difficult as the

revelation of the depth of Nazi brutality became clear in 1945 and after. His account of himself in those years may not be false, but it cannot be seen to be the whole truth, either.
[27]Ibid., p. 61.
[28]Max Born to AE, 15 July 1925, in Born, *The Einstein-Born Letters,* p. 84.
[29]From the Solvay Conference proceedings, 1911.
[30]Heisenberg, *Physics and Beyond,* p. 68.
[31]AE to Paul Ehrenfest, 30 September 1925, cited in Fölsing, *Albert Einstein,* p. 566.
[32]AE to Hedwig Born, 7 March 1926, in Born, *The Einstein-Born Letters,* p. 88.
[33]AE to Paul Ehrenfest, 12 April 1926, cited in Fölsing, *Albert Einstein,* 1997, p. 582.
[34]Max Born, cited in Pais, *Subtle Is the Lord,* 1982, p. 442.
[35]Richard Feynman, *Six Easy Pieces,* p. 135.
[36]AE to Max Born, 4 December 1926, in Born, *The Einstein-Born Letters,* p. 91.
[37]Born, *The Einstein-Born Letters,* p. 91.
[38]Otto Stern, cited in Pais, *Subtle Is the Lord,* p. 445.
[39]Abraham Pais, private communication, repeated in the *NOVA* program *Einstein Revealed,* broadcast on PBS in October 1996.
[40]AE, *Ideas and Opinions,* p. 276.
[41]AE, cited in Pais, *Subtle Is the Lord,* p. 468.
[42]AE to Max Born, 12 April 1949, in Born, *The Einstein-Born Letters,* p. 181.
[43]AE to Hendrik Lorentz, 27 June 1927, cited in Pais, *Subtle Is the Lord,* p. 431.
[44]E. Straus, "Memoir," in French, *Einstein: A Centenary Volume,* p. 32.
[45]AE, 1933, cited in Pais, *Einstein Lived Here,* p. 56.

Chapter Twenty: "OUR NECESSARILY PRIMITIVE THINKING"

[1]AE to Hans Wohlwend, 15 August–3 October 1902, *CPAE,* vol. V, doc. 2.
[2]AE in *Autobiographische Skizze* reprinted in *Einstein: Dunkel Zeit Helle Zeit* and available on the World Wide Web at: *http://philoscience.unibe.ch/archiv/lehre/winter99/einstein/2 Dez.html.* A similar thought is expressed in Peter Bucky, *The Private Albert Einstein,* p. 28.
[3]AE to Conrad Habicht, 15 August 1948, cited in Pais, *Subtle Is the Lord,* p. 484.
[4]In German: *Ein biszchen Technic dann und wann/Auch Grübler amusieren kann. . . .* The story of the Goldschmidt collaboration was unearthed by Abraham Pais. See Pais, *Subtle Is the Lord,* pp. 490–91.
[5]AE to M. Besso, 5 January 1929, in Speziali, ed., *Albert Einstein–Michele Besso: Correspondence,* pp. 240–41.
[6]Cited in Fölsing, *Albert Einstein,* p. 601.
[7]Anton Reiser, cited in Pais, *Subtle Is the Lord,* p. 317.
[8]AE to Paul Ehrenfest, 28 August 1928, cited in Fölsing, 1997, p. 603.
[9]All cited in Abraham Pais's survey of Einstein's press coverage, published in Pais, *Einstein Lived Here,* pp. 178–79.
[10]Wolfgang Pauli, 1932, cited in Pais, *Subtle Is the Lord,* p. 347.
[11]AE to Wolfgang Pauli, 24 December 1929, cited in Fölsing, *Albert Einstein,* p. 607.
[12]AE to Paul Ehrenfest, 24 September 1929, cited in Fölsing, *Albert Einstein,* p. 606.
[13]AE in Schilpp, *Albert Einstein: Philosopher-Scientist,* p. 47.
[14]AE to Wolfgang Pauli, 22 January 1932, cited in Pais, *Subtle Is the Lord,* p. 347.
[15]My account of this and the following Einstein objections to quantum mechanics are derived from Abraham Pais's dissection of them in *Subtle Is the Lord,* pp. 445–48.
[16]Pais, *Subtle Is the Lord,* pp. 445–448.
[17]Léon Rosenfeld, cited in Pais, *Subtle Is the Lord,* p. 446.
[18]AE to the Nobel Prize committee in September 1931, cited in Pais, *Subtle Is the Lord,* p. 448.

[19]AE, B. Podolsky, and N. Rosen, *Phys. Rev.* 47, 1931, cited in Pais, *Subtle Is the Lord,* p. 456.
[20]For a summary of the reaction of younger, less constrained physicists' responses to Einstein's stance, see J. R. Oppenheimer's memoir, in French, *Einstein: A Centenary Volume,* pp. 44–49.
[21]Kracauer, *From Caligari to Hitler,* pp. 162–64. The Lang quote appeared first in an article published in the *New York World Telegram,* 11 June 1941.
[22]K. Robitschek, *"Zeitungsparodie"* published in *5 Jahre Kabarett der Komiker* 5, quoted and discussed in Jelavich, *Berlin Cabaret,* pp. 199–201.
[23]Cited in Friedrich, *Before the Deluge,* p. 241.
[24]See the description of Berber's funeral in both Richie, *Faust's Metropolis,* pp. 360–61 and in Gill, *Dancing Between Flames,* p. 109.
[25]Joseph Goebbels, "Around the *Gedächtniskirche,*" *Der Angriff* (13 January 1928), in *KJD,* pp. 560–62.
[26]Kessler, *The Diaries of a Cosmopolitan,* pp. 390 and 395.
[27]See Richie, *Faust's Metropolis,* p. 375, and Eckhardt and Gilman, *Bertolt Brecht's Berlin,* pp. 131–32.
[28]Interview of Einstein's architect, Konrad Wachsmann, by Michael Grüning, in Grüning's *Ein Haus für Albert Einstein.*
[29]Balthazar Reiser, "Einstein as a Private Person" in the *Vossische Zeitung,* 13 March 1929.
[30]*Vossische Zeitung,* 18 April 1929.
[31]Cited in Fölsing, *Albert Einstein,* p. 611.

Chapter Twenty-one: "WHILE WOLVES WAIT OUTSIDE"

[1]W. Mehring, from "Berlin Simultan," original published in *Das Politische Cabaret: Chansons Songs Couplets,* Dresden, 1920, pp. 44–46, quoted and discussed in Jelavich, *Berlin Cabaret,* pp. 149–50. The translation captures the rhythm and almost physical punch of Mehring's style pretty well—but the German says it better:

Im Ufafilm
Hoch Kaiser Wil'm
Die Reaktion flaggt schon am Dom,
Mit Hakenkreuz und Blaukreuzgas,
Monokel kontra Hakennas'
Auf zum Pogrom
Beim Hippodrom!

[2]*Vossische Zeitung,* 10 November 1929.
[3]*Vossische Zeitung,* 20 April 1929.
[4]Kessler, *The Diaries of a Cosmopolitan,* p. 374.
[5]Gill, *Dancing Between Flames,* p. 224.
[6]Friedrich, *Before the Deluge,* p. 302.
[7]Friedrich, *Before the Deluge,* p. 301.
[8]See the anecdote recalled by Karma Rauhut quoted in Richie, *Faust's Metropolis,* p. 391.
[9]For a description of the Sportpalast speech see Richie, *Faust's Metropolis,* pp. 395–96. For an analysis of Hitler's speeches and campaign tactics in 1930, see Kershaw, *Hitler: 1889–1938: Hubris,* pp. 329–33.
[10]From a speech on 4 May 1923, quoted in Kershaw, *Hitler: 1889–1938: Hubris,* p. 184.
[11]Joseph Goebbels in *Der Angriff,* November 1928, cited in Craig, *Germany: 1866–1945,* p. 545.
[12]See Kershaw, *Hitler: 1889–1938: Hubris,* p. 327, for an account of one of Hitler's arguments with a member of the party who took seriously the Socialist half of the National Socialist name.

[13]Ibid., p. 339.
[14]Ibid., p. 336.
[15]Kessler, *The Diaries of a Cosmopolitan,* pp. 396–97.
[16]AE, December 1930, cited in Dennis Brian, *Einstein,* p. 204.
[17]See Craig, *The Politics of the Prussian Army,* pp. 397–415 for a review of German defiance of the Versailles Treaty.
[18]Nathan and Norden, *Einstein on Peace,* p. 91.
[19]Ibid., p. 92.
[20]Ibid., p. 96.
[21]Ibid., p. 98.
[22]Ibid., pp. 100–101.
[23]Ibid., p. 118.
[24]This account is based on Highfield and Carter's analysis in *The Private Lives of Albert Einstein,* pp. 229–42.
[25]Vallentin, *The Drama of Albert Einstein,* 1954, p. 196.
[26]Ibid., pp. 196–97.
[27]Cited in Fölsing, *Albert Einstein,* pp. 672–73. Tedel was a family nickname for Eduard.
[28]AE to Heinrich Zangger, 10 March 1917, *CPAE,* vol. VIII, doc. 309.
[29]See Fölsing, *Albert Einstein,* p. 630.
[30]George Bernard Shaw, seen in newsreel footage broadcast in the *NOVA* program *Einstein Revealed.*
[31]Albert Einstein cited in Brian, *Einstein,* p. 201.

Chapter Twenty-two: "WHO IS MARY PICKFORD?"

[1]See Clark, *Albert Einstein,* p. 508.
[2]AE in *The New York Times,* 30 December 1930, cited in Pais, *Einstein Lived Here,* p. 182.
[3]See Brian, *Einstein,* pp. 203–204.
[4]Cited in Pais, *Einstein Lived Here,* p. 182.
[5]Einstein's travel journal for 11 December 1930, cited in Fölsing, *Albert Einstein,* pp. 633–34.
[6]AE in *The New York Times,* cited in Brian, *Einstein,* p. 205.
[7]AE cited in Vallentin, *The Drama of Albert Einstein,* p. 193.
[8]AE to Chaim Weizmann, 25 November 1929, quoted in Calaprice, *The Quotable Einstein,* p. 95.
[9]Vallentin, *The Drama of Albert Einstein,* pp. 191–92.
[10]See Fölsing, *Albert Einstein,* p. 635.
[11]Pais, *Einstein Lived Here,* p. 181.
[12]AE cited in Brian, *Einstein,* p. 202.
[13]Pais, *Einstein Lived Here,* p. 184.
[14]Ibid., p. 184.
[15]Ibid., p. 185.
[16]*"Oui, une belle tête; c'est un poète?"* See Kessler, *The Diaries of a Cosmopolitan,* p. 396.
[17]See Brian, *Einstein,* for a fuller account of the session. He derives his description of the event from an interview with Helen Dukas, who was present.
[18]AE, 15 January 1931, quoted in Brian, *Einstein,* p. 211.
[19]The significance of red shifts and their opposites, blue shifts, in this context turns on what is known as the Doppler effect. Doppler had studied sound, but a similar phenomenon affects light. The motion of a light source alters the wavelength or color of the light involved. If an object is moving away from earth, observers here will see all of the light that comes off that object as being stretched, moved to longer or redder wavelengths. The blue shift works the same way in reverse: motion toward earth compresses the wavelength and

hence the color of the light we detect here. The signal seems bluer than it would if its source were stationary relative to the earth. Red and blue shifts are actually detected by looking for spectral patterns within the light emitted by an object. Because we know exactly what the spectral pattern that the element hydrogen, for example, forms here on earth, it is possible to look for that same pattern in light from a star or a galaxy, measure very precisely how far that pattern has been displaced in the red or the blue direction, and from that calculate how fast an object is heading toward or away from us.

[20]A comment reported by George Gamow in his memoir, *My World Line,* cited in Clark, *Albert Einstein,* p. 270.

[21]AE quoted in Brian, *Einstein,* p. 219.

[22]AE to Max Born, 5 February 1931, in Born, *The Einstein-Born Letters,* p. 108.

[23]AE to Queen Elisabeth of Belgium, 9 February 1931, cited in Fölsing, *Albert Einstein,* p. 640.

[24]AE quoted in *The New York Times,* 15 March 1931, cited in Pais, *Einstein Lived Here,* p. 185.

[25]AE to Maja Winteler-Einstein, March 1931, cited in Fölsing, *Albert Einstein,* p. 642.

[26]Friedrich, *Before the Deluge,* p. 329.

[27]Harold Nicholson, "The Charms of Berlin," in *Der Queerschnitt* 9, no. 5, 1932, reprinted in *KJD,* 1994, pp. 425–26.

[28]Willi Pröger, *Stätten der Berliner Prostitution,* Auffenberg Verlagsgesellschaft, Berlin, 1930, excerpt reprinted in *KJD,* 1994, p. 736.

[29]Ruth Weiland, *Die Kinderder Arbeitslosen,* Eberswalde-Berlin, 1933, pp. 23–24, cited in Detlev Peukert's article, "The Lost Generation," in Richard J. Evans and Dick Geary, eds., *The German Unemployed: Experiences and Consequences of Mass Unemployment from the Weimar Republic to the Third Reich.*

[30]L. Bauer, *"Mittelalter, 1932"* in *Das Tagebuch* 13, no. 1, 2 January 1932, pp. 10–13, reprinted in *KJD,* 1994, pp. 384–86.

[31]Erich Maria Remarque, cited in Willet, *Art and Politics in the Weimar Period,* p. 193.

[32]Deservedly so. *All Quiet on the Western Front* is one of the must-read novels of the century; it is both a powerful work of art and an important historical document.

[33]*Vossische Zeitung,* 10 December 1930.

[34]Ibid.

[35]AE in Nathan and Norden, *Einstein on Peace,* p. 120.

Chapter Twenty-three: "A BIRD OF PASSAGE"

[1]Hitler, speaking to the Industry Club of Düsseldorf, January 1932, cited in Craig, *Germany: 1866–1945,* p. 556.

[2]Kessler, *The Diaries of a Cosmopolitan,* p. 437.

[3]Paul v. Hindenburg, cited in Kershaw, *Hitler: 1889–1938: Hubris,* pp. 394–95.

[4]Kershaw makes this argument, but he follows here a long line of other thinkers, all of whom seem correct to me.

[5]Cited in Kershaw, *Hitler: 1889–1938: Hubris,* p. 427.

[6]AE to Planck, 17 July 1931, unsent, cited in Nathan and Norden, *Einstein on Peace,* pp. 155–56.

[7]Cited in Pais, *Einstein Lived Here,* p. 187.

[8]AE, diary entry 6 December 1931, cited in Nathan and Norden, *Einstein on Peace,* p. 155.

[9]AE to the president of a court in Sofia, Bulgaria, 20 February 1931, cited in Nathan and Norden, *Einstein on Peace,* p. 128.

[10]AE to Sigmund Freud, 30 July 1932, reprinted in Nathan and Norden, *Einstein on Peace,* pp. 188–91.

[11]Sigmund Freud to AE, September 1932, reprinted in Nathan and Norden, *Einstein on Peace,* pp. 191–202.

[12]Ultimately, that number was raised even higher, so that Einstein's salary would be equal to that of the mathematician Oswald Veblen. Both men were hired at $15,000, with identical retirement benefits for themselves and their spouses.
[13]AE in *The New York Times,* 16 October 1932, cited in Brian, *Einstein,* p. 237.
[14]AE, as recalled by Philipp Frank in Frank, *Einstein: His Life and Times,* p. 226.
[15]Vallentin, *The Drama of Albert Einstein,* p. 203.
[16]AE, December 1931, cited in Brian, *Einstein,* p. 223.
[17]AE, first collected in *Mein Weltbild,* 1934, translated and republished numerous times since, including Nathan and Norden, *Einstein on Peace,* p. 207.
[18]See his letter to Maurice Solovine, 20 November 1932, in AE, *Letters to Solovine,* pp. 78–79.
[19]Frank, *Einstein: His Life and Times,* p. 226.
[20]Ibid.

Chapter Twenty-four: "AS LONG AS I HAVE ANY CHOICE IN THE MATTER"

[1]Kessler, *Diaries of a Cosmopolitan,* p. 448.
[2]AE to Margarethe Lebach, 27 February 1933, reprinted in Nathan and Norden, *Einstein on Peace,* pp. 210–11.
[3]Reprinted in Nathan and Norden, *Einstein on Peace,* p. 211.
[4]*Berliner Lokalanzeiger,* 17 March 1933, cited in Fölsing, *Albert Einstein,* 1997, p. 661, and Brian, *Einstein,* p. 244.
[5]Vallentin, *The Drama of Albert Einstein,* p. 228.
[6]AE after 20 March 1933, reprinted in Nathan and Norden, *Einstein on Peace,* p. 213.
[7]AE to the Prussian Academy, 28 March 1933, reprinted in Fölsing, *Albert Einstein,* p. 661.
[8]Reprinted in Frank, *Einstein: His Life and Times,* p. 234.
[9]AE to Max Planck, 6 April 1933, quoted in Fölsing, *Albert Einstein,* p. 664.
[10]Max Planck to Albert Einstein, 31 March 1933, quoted in Fölsing, *Albert Einstein,* p. 664.
[11]Max Planck, 11 May 1933, quoted in Fölsing, *Albert Einstein,* p. 665.
[12]Philipp Lenard, quoted in Frank, *Einstein: His Life and Times,* p. 232.
[13]AE, *Ideas and Opinions,* p. 78.
[14]AE to Max Born in Born, *The Einstein-Born Letters,* p. 114.
[15]AE to Paul Ehrenfest, 14 April 1933, reprinted in Nathan and Norden, *Einstein on Peace,* p. 219.
[16]AE to Fritz Haber, 8 August 1933, cited in Fölsing, *Albert Einstein,* 1997, p. 668.
[17]*New York World Telegram,* 19 September 1933, cited in Pais, *Einstein Lived Here,* p. 194.
[18]AE in *The New York Times,* 10 September 1933, reprinted in Pais, *Einstein Lived Here,* p. 194.
[19]AE to Franklin Delano Roosevelt, 7 March 1940, in Pais, *Einstein Lived Here,* p. 218.
[20]Pais, *Einstein Lived Here,* p. 219.
[21]Ibid.
[22]From a letter to Otto Hahn, 28 January 1949, and one to Arnold Sommerfeld, 14 December 1946. Einstein counted both men as among the few Germans he recognized as civilized, along with Planck and Max von Laue. Both letters were excerpted in Calaprice, *The Quotable Einstein,* p. 86.
[23]See Fölsing, *Albert Einstein,* pp. 734–35; see also Pais, *Einstein Lived Here,* p. 225.
[24]AE to Queen Elisabeth of Belgium, 20 November 1933, cited in Pais, *Einstein Lived Here,* p. 200.
[25]Gabriella Oppenheim-Errara, private communication with the author.
[26]The entire statement is reprinted in Nathan and Norden, *Einstein on Peace,* pp. 640–41.
[27]Einstein resorted to an unusual stratagem to buy his American home. A friend of his,

knowing that his assets were frozen by the German government, suggested that he sell one of his handwritten original manuscripts. The J. P. Morgan Library in New York City agreed to buy one of his general relativity papers from 1912 for the price of a house. See Pais, *Einstein Lived Here,* p. 199.

[28]Vallentin, *The Drama of Albert Einstein,* p. 240.

[29]AE to Max Born, undated, in Born, *The Einstein-Born Letters,* p. 128.

[30]Born, *The Einstein-Born Letters,* p. 130.

[31]Calaprice, *The Quotable Einstein,* p. 32.

[32]Quoted in Fölsing, *Albert Einstein,* p. 739.

[33]AE to an unnamed friend, 5 February 1955, in Nathan and Norden, *Einstein on Peace,* p. 616.

[34]AE to Elisabeth, Queen Mother of Belgium, 11 March 1955, in Nathan and Norden, *Einstein on Peace,* p. 619.

[35]H. Dukas to A. Pais, 30 April 1955, quoted in Pais, *Subtle Is the Lord,* p. 477.

[36]AE "Autobiographical Notes" in Schilpp, *Albert Einstein: Philosopher-Scientist,* p. 5.

[37]In a macabre side show, Einstein's brain was removed at autopsy, weighed, found to display no extraordinary features on a gross examination, and stored in a jar filled with preservative. It is currently in the possession of a doctor in St. Louis, Missouri.

BIBLIOGRAPHY

Aichelburg, Peter C., and Roman U. Sexl, eds. *Albert Einstein.* Braunschweig: Friedr. Vieweg & Sohn, 1979.

Akademie der Wissenschaften der DDR. *Albert Einstein in Berlin* (with introduction by Hans-Jürgen Treder). Berlin (East): Akademie Verlag, 1979.

Ascheim, Steven. *Brothers and Strangers.* Madison: University of Wisconsin Press, 1982.

Attie, Shimon. *Die Schrift an der Wand.* Heidelberg: Edition Braus, 1993.

Bach, H. I. *The German Jew.* Oxford: Littman Library/Oxford University Press, 1984.

Barron, Stephanie, ed. *German Expressionism 1915–1925.* Los Angeles: Los Angeles County Museum of Art, 1988.

Berliner Geschichtswerkstatt, ed. *August 1914: Ein Volk zieht in den Krieg* (August 1914: A People Marches into War). Berlin, 1989.

Bernstein, Jeremy. *Albert Einstein and the Frontiers of Physics.* New York: Oxford University Press, 1996.

Bessel, Richard. *Germany After the First World War.* Oxford: Oxford University Press, 1993.

Binding, Rudolf. *A Fatalist at War.* Boston: Houghton Mifflin Company, 1929.

Blackbourn, David, and Geoff Eley. *The Peculiarities of German History.* Oxford: Oxford University Press, 1983.

Bodanis, David. *$E = mc^2$.* New York: Walker & Company, 2000.

Bohm, David. *The Special Theory of Relativity.* Reading, Mass.: Addison Wesley, 1965.

———. *Causality and Chance in Modern Physics.* Philadelphia: University of Pennsylvania Press, 1987.

Born, Max. *Einstein's Theory of Relativity.* New York: Dover Publications, Inc., 1962.

———. *The Einstein-Born Letters.* New York: Walker & Company, 1971.

Brian, Denis. *Einstein.* New York: John Wiley & Sons, Inc., 1996.

Bronner, Stephen Eric, and Douglas Kellner. *Passion and Rebellion.* New York: Universe Books, 1983.

Bronson, David. *Jews and Germans from 1860 to 1933.* Heidelberg: Carl Winter Universtätsverlag, 1979.

Buber, Martin. *On Zion.* London: T. & T. Clark, Ltd., 1985.

Bucher, Georg. *In the Line 1914–1918.* London: Jonathan Cape, 1932.

Bucky, Peter. *The Private Albert Einstein.* Kansas City: Andrews & McMeel, 1992.

Burkhardt, Jacob. *The Civilization of the Renaissance in Italy.* London: Penguin Books, 1990.

Calaprice, Alice. *The Quotable Einstein.* Princeton: Princeton University Press, 1996.

Carnegie Endowment for International Peace, Division of International Law. *Official German Documents Relating to the World War.* New York: Oxford University Press, 1923.

Carr, Edward Hallett. *The Twenty Years Crisis, 1919–1939.* New York: Harper & Row, 1964.

Cassidy, David. *Einstein and Our World.* Atlantic Highlands, New Jersey: Humanities Press, 1995.

Christianson, Gale. *Edwin Hubble.* New York: Farrar, Straus & Giroux, 1995.

Clark, Ronald. *Einstein: The Life and Times.* New York: Avon Books, 1972.

Cobb, Irvin S. *The Red Glutton: With the German Army at the Front.* London: Hodder & Stoughton, 1916.

Craig, Gordon. *The Politics of the Prussian Army.* Oxford: Oxford University Press, 1955 and 1964.

———. *Germany: 1866–1945.* Oxford: Oxford University Press, 1978.

———. *The Germans.* New York: Meridian (Penguin), 1983.

Cross, Tim. *The Lost Voices of World War I.* London: Bloomsbury Publishing Company, 1988.

Davidowicz, Lucy S. *The War Against the Jews.* New York: Bantam Books, 1986.

De Broglie, Louis, Louis Armand, and Pierre-Henri Simon, et al. *Einstein.* New York: Peebles Press International, 1979.

Douglas, A. Vibert. *The Life of Arthur Stanley Eddington.* London: Thomas Nelson & Sons, Ltd., 1971.

Drake, Stillman. *Galileo at Work.* New York: Dover Publications, Inc., 1978.

Dukas, Helen, and Banesh Hoffman. *Albert Einstein: The Human Side.* Princeton: Princeton University Press, 1979.

Eckhardt, Wolf Von, and Sander L. Gilman. *Bertolt Brecht's Berlin.* Lincoln: University of Nebraska Press, 1993.

Ehrmann, Annegret, Rachel Livné-Freudenthal, Julius H. Schoeps, and Monika Richarz, eds. *Juden in Berlin 1671–1945, Ein Lesebuch.* Berlin: Nicolai, 1988.

Eildermann, Wilhelm. *Jugend im Ersten Weltkrieg.* Berlin: Dietz, 1972.

Einstein, Albert. *The Collected Papers of Albert Einstein,* Vols. I–VIII. Princeton: Princeton University Press, 1987 et seq.

———. *Ideas and Opinions.* New York: Crown Publishers, Inc., 1954 and 1982.

———. "Kyoto Address." *Physics Today,* August 1982.
———. *Letters to Solovine.* New York: Citadel Press, 1993.
———. *The Origins of the General Theory of Relativity.* Glasgow: Jackson, Wylie, 1933.
———. *The Principle of Relativity.* New York: Dover Publications, Inc., 1952.
———. *Relativity.* New York: Crown Publishers, Inc., 1961.
——— and Michele Besso. *Correspondence, 1903–1955,* Pierre Speziale, ed. Paris: Hermann editeurs, 1972.
———. *The Einstein-Besso Working Manuscript.* History and reproduction of sample pages, published as a Christie's catalogue. New York: Christie's, 1996.
——— and Leopold Infeld. *The Evolution of Physics.* New York: Touchstone, 1966.
Eksteins, Modris. *Rites of Spring.* Boston: Houghton Mifflin Company, 1989.
Epstein, Lewis Carroll. *Relativity Visualized.* San Francisco: Insight Press, 1988.
Evans, Richard J., and Dick Geary, eds. *The German Unemployed: Experiences and Consequences of Mass Unemployment from the Weimar Republic to the Third Reich.* New York: St. Martin's Press, 1987.
Falkenheyn, General Erich von. *The German General Staff and Its Decisions, 1914–1916.* New York: Dodd, Mead & Company, 1920.
Feldman, Gerald. *The Great Disorder.* Oxford: Oxford University Press, 1993.
Ferris, Timothy. *The Whole Shebang.* New York: Simon & Schuster, 1997.
Feynman, Richard. *The Character of Physical Laws.* New York: The Modern Library, 1994.
———. *Six Easy Pieces.* Reading, Mass.: Addison Wesley, 1995.
———. *Five Not-So-Easy Pieces.* Reading, Mass.: Addison Wesley, 1997.
Fischer, Fritz. *Germany's Aims in the First World War.* New York: W. W. Norton & Company, 1967.
———. *World Power or Decline.* New York: W. W. Norton & Company, 1975.
Flückiger, Max. *Albert Einstein in Bern.* Bern: P. Haupt, 1972.
Fölsing, Albrecht. *Albert Einstein.* New York: Viking, 1997.
Frank, Philipp. *Einstein: His Life and Times.* New York: Alfred A. Knopf, 1947.
French, A. P. *Einstein: A Centenary Volume.* Cambridge: Harvard University Press, 1979.
Friedman, Alan J., and Carol C. Donley. *Einstein as Myth and Muse.* Cambridge: Cambridge University Press, 1985.
Friedrich, Otto. *Before the Deluge.* New York: Harper & Row, 1972.
Fussell, Paul. *The Great War and Modern Memory.* Oxford: Oxford University Press, 1975.
Galison, Peter. *How Experiments End.* Chicago: University of Chicago Press, 1987.
Gatzke, Hans W. *Germany's Drive to the West.* Baltimore: The Johns Hopkins University Press, 1966.
Gay, Peter. *Weimar Culture.* New York: Harper & Row, 1968.
———. *Freud.* New York: W. W. Norton and Company, 1988.

Geroch, Robert. *General Relativity from A to B.* Chicago: University of Chicago Press, 1978.

Gilbert, Martin. *The First World War.* New York: Henry Holt & Company, 1994.

Gill, Anton. *A Dance Between Flames.* London: Abacus, 1995.

Glass, Dexter, Dieter Rösler, and John J. White. *Berlin.* Dorstadt: Erich Schmidt Verlag, 1988.

Glatzer, Dieter, and Ruth Glatzer. *Berliner Leben,* 2 Vols. Berlin: Rütten & Loening, 1986.

Goener, Hans, and Giuseppi Castagnetti. "Albert Einstein as a pacifist and democrat during the First World War." Preprint 35, Max-Planck Institut Für Wissenschaftsgeschichte, Berlin, 1996.

Goldsmith, Maurice, Alan Mackay, and James Woudhuysen. *Einstein: The First Hundred Years.* Oxford: Pergamon Press, 1980.

Goodstein, David L., and Judith R. Goodstein. *Feynman's Lost Lecture.* New York: W. W. Norton & Company, 1996.

Grab, Walter. *Juden in der Deutschen Wissenschaft.* Tel Aviv: Universität Tel Aviv, 1986.

Graves, Robert. *Goodbye to All That.* Providence, R.I.: Berghahn Books, 1995.

Greene, Brian. *The Elegant Universe.* New York: W. W. Norton & Company, 1999.

Gribbin, John. *In Search of Schrödinger's Cat.* New York: Bantam Books, 1984.

——— and Michael White. *Einstein.* New York: Simon & Schuster, 1993.

Grosz, George. *A Little Yes and a Big No: The Autobiography of George Grosz,* translated by Lola Sachs Dorin. New York: The Dial Press, 1946.

Grundmann, Siegfried. *Einsteins Akte.* Berlin: Springer-Verlag, 1998.

Grüning, Michael. *Ein Haus für Albert Einstein.* Berlin: Verlag der Nation, 1990.

Hamann, Brigitte. *Hitler's Vienna.* Oxford: Oxford University Press, 1998.

Hannak, Dr. J. *Emanuel Lasker* (Foreword by Albert Einstein). New York: Dover Publications, 1991.

Hanssen, Hans Peter. *Diary of a Dying Empire.* Bloomington: Indiana University Press, 1955.

Hedin, Sven. *With the German Armies in the West.* London: John Lane, The Bodley Head, 1915.

Heisenberg, Werner. *Physics and Beyond.* New York: Harper & Row, 1971.

Herneck, Friedrich. *Einstein Privat.* Berlin: Buchverlag der Morgen, 1978.

Hibberd, Dominic. *The First World War.* London: Macmillan Education, Ltd., 1990.

Hiden, John. *Republican and Fascist Germany.* London: Longman, 1996.

Highfield, Roger, and Paul Carter. *The Private Lives of Albert Einstein.* London: Faber & Faber Ltd., 1993.

Hillgruber, Andreas. *Germany and the Two World Wars.* Cambridge: Harvard University Press, 1981.

Hitler, Adolf. *Mein Kampf.* Boston: Houghton Mifflin Company, 1943.

———. *My New Order.* New York: Reynal & Hitchcock, 1941.

Hobsbawm, Eric. *The Age of Empire.* New York: Vintage Books, 1989.

Hoffmann, Banesh, with Helen Dukas. *Albert Einstein: Creator and Rebel.* New York: The Viking Press, 1972.

Holton, Gerald. *Thematic Origins of Scientific Thought* (Revised Edition). Cambridge: Harvard University Press, 1988.

———. *Einstein, History and Other Passions.* Woodbury, New York: American Institute of Physics Press, 1995.

——— and Yehuda Elkana. *Albert Einstein.* Princeton: Princeton University Press, 1982.

Horne, Alastair. *The Price of Glory.* London: Penguin Books, 1993.

Howard, Don, and John Stachel, eds. *Einstein: The Formative Years, 1879–1909.* Cambridge, Mass.: Birkhauser Boston, 2000.

Howard, Michael. *The Lessons of History.* New Haven: Yale University Press, 1991.

Isherwood, Christopher. *Down There on a Visit.* New York: Simon & Schuster, 1962.

Jahrbuch für jüdische Geschichte und Literatur for the year 1918 (Jewish calendar 5677); published by A. Katz, Berlin.

Jammer, Max. *Einstein and Religion.* Princeton: Princeton University Press, 1999.

Jelavich, Peter. *Berlin Cabaret.* Cambridge: Harvard University Press, 1993.

Johnson, Jeffrey Allen. *The Kaiser's Chemists.* Chapel Hill: The University of North Carolina Press, 1990.

Joll, James. *The Origins of the First World War,* Second Edition. London: Longman, 1992.

Jünger, Ernst. *The Storm of Steel.* London: Constable and Company, Ltd., 1994.

Kagan, Donald. *On the Origins of War.* New York: Doubleday, 1995.

Kater, Michael M. *Different Drummers: Jazz in the Culture of Nazi Germany.* Oxford: Oxford University Press, 1992.

Katz, Jacob. *From Prejudice to Destruction.* Cambridge: Harvard University Press, 1980.

Keegan, John. *The Face of Battle.* London: Penguin Books, 1978.

———. *The Mask of Command.* London: Penguin Books, 1987.

Kennedy, Paul. *The Rise and Fall of the Great Powers.* New York: Random House, 1987.

Kern, Stephen. *The Culture of Time and Space.* Cambridge: Harvard University Press, 1983.

Kershaw, Ian. *Hitler: 1889–1938: Hubris.* New York: W. W. Norton & Company, 1998.

Kessler, Count Harry. *The Diaries of a Cosmopolitan,* translated and edited by Charles Kessler. London: Weidenfeld and Nicolson, 1971.

———. *Walther Rathenau.* New York: Harcourt Brace & Company, 1930.

Koch, H. W., ed. *The Origins of the First World War* (Second Edition). London: Macmillan Publishers, Ltd., 1984.

Kracauer, Siegfried. *From Caligari to Hitler.* Princeton: Princeton University Press, 1947.

Ladd, Brian. *The Ghosts of Berlin.* Chicago: University of Chicago Press, 1997.

Laffin, John. *Letters from the Front 1914–1918.* London: J. M. Dent & Sons, Ltd., 1973.

Langevin, Paul, and Maurice de Broglie, eds. *Proceedings of the First Solvay Conference.* Paris: Gauthier-Villars, 1912.

Le Bon, Gustave. *The Psychology of the Great War.* New York: The Macmillan Company, 1916.

Levenson, Jon. *Sinai and Zion.* New York: HarperCollins, 1985.

Liddell Hart, B. H. *Strategy* (Second Revised Edition). New York: Meridian, 1991.

Lindemann, Albert S. *Esau's Tears.* Cambridge: Cambridge University Press, 1997.

Lukacs, John. *The Hitler of History.* New York: Alfred A. Knopf, 1997.

MacDonogh, Giles. *Berlin.* New York: St. Martin's Press, 1997.

MacLeish, Archibald. *Poems:1924–1933.* Boston: Houghton Mifflin Company, 1933.

Manuel, Frank E. *A Portrait of Isaac Newton.* Cambridge, Mass.: Da Capo Press, 1968.

Marianoff, Dmitri, with Wayne Palma. *Einstein.* Garden City, New York: Doubleday Doran and Co., 1944.

Martel, Gordon, ed. *Modern Germany Reconsidered.* London and New York: Routledge, 1992.

Marx, Julius. *Kriegstagebuch eines Juden,* (Second Edition). Frankfurt/Main: Ner-Tamid-Verlag, 1964.

Maser, Werner. *Hitler's Letters and Notes.* New York: Harper & Row, 1974.

Massie, Robert K. *Dreadnought.* New York: Ballantine Books, 1991.

Massing, Paul W. *From Prejudice to Destruction.* New York: Harper & Brothers, 1949.

McDonogh, Giles. *Berlin.* New York: St. Martin's Press, 1997.

Miller, Arthur I. *Albert Einstein's Special Theory of Relativity.* Reading, Mass.: Addison-Wesley, 1981.

Minkowski, Hermann. *Raum und Zeit.* Leipzig: B. G. Taubner, 1909.

Moore, Walter. *Schrödinger.* Cambridge: Cambridge University Press, 1989.

Morris, Jan. *Fisher's Face.* New York: Viking, 1995.

Mosse, George, L. *Germans and Jews.* New York: Grosset & Dunlap, 1971.

Moszkowski, Alexander. *Einstein the Searcher.* London: Methuen & Co., Ltd., 1921.

Müller-Meiningen, Ernst. *Who Are the Huns?* New York: G. E. Stechert and Co., 1915.

Musil, Robert. *The Man Without Qualities.* New York: Capricorn Books, 1965.

Nathan, Otto, and Heinz Norden. *Einstein on Peace.* London: Methuen, 1963.

Nicolai, Georg Friedrich. *Die Biologies des Krieges.* Zurich: Art Institut Orell Füssli, 1919.

Niewyk, Donald. *The Jews in Weimar Germany.* Baton Rouge: Louisiana State University Press, 1980.

Overbye, Dennis. *Einstein in Love.* New York: Viking, 2000.

Pais, Abraham. *Subtle Is the Lord.* Oxford: Oxford University Press, 1982.

———. *Einstein Lived Here.* Oxford: Oxford University Press, 1994.

Paret, Peter. *The Berlin Secession.* Cambridge: Belknap Press of Harvard University Press, 1980.

Parkinson, Robert. *Tormented Warrior.* London: Hodder & Stoughton, 1978.

Paschall, Rod. *The Defeat of Imperial Germany.* New York: Da Capo Press, 1994.

Pick, Daniel. *War Machine.* New Haven: Yale University Press, 1993.

Pogge von Strandmann, Hartmut. *Walther Rathenau: Notes and Diaries 1907–1922.* Oxford: Clarendon Press, 1985.

Pulzer, Peter. *The Rise of Political Anti-Semitism in Germany and Austria.* London: Peter Halban Publishers, Ltd., 1988.

———. *Jews and the German State.* Oxford: Blackwell Publishers, 1992.

Pyenson, Lewis. *The Young Einstein.* Bristol: Adam Hilger, Ltd., 1985.

Quinn, Susan. *Marie Curie.* Reading, Mass.: Addison Wesley, 1995.

Read, Anthony, and David Fisher. *Berlin.* London: Pimlico, 1988.

Reiser, Anton. *Albert Einstein.* New York: A. and C. Boni, 1930.

Renn, Jürgen, and Robert Schulmann. *Albert Einstein/Mileva Maric: The Love Letters.* Princeton: Princeton University Press, 1992.

Rhodes, Richard. *The Making of the Atomic Bomb.* New York: Simon & Schuster, 1988.

Richie, Alexandra. *Faust's Metropolis.* New York: Carroll & Graf, 1998.

Ringer, Fritz K. *German Inflation of 1923.* Oxford: Oxford University Press, 1969.

Rosenberg, Arthur. *Imperial Germany.* Boston: Beacon Press, 1964.

Rother, Rainer. *Die letzten Tage der Menschheit Bilder des Ersten Weltkrieges.* Berlin: Deutsches Historischen Museums, 1994. (Catalogue of the exhibit of June 10–August 28, 1994.)

Rowley, Eric E. *Hyperinflation in Germany.* Aldershot: Scolar Press, 1994.

Rübel, Eduard. *Eduard Einstein.* Bern and Stuttgart: Verlag Paul Haupt, 1986.

Ryan, Dennis P. *Einstein and the Humanities.* New York: Greenwood Press, 1987.

Sassoon, Siegfried. *The Complete Memoirs of George Sherston.* London: Faber & Faber, 1937.

Schilpp, Paul Arthur, ed. *Albert Einstein: Philosopher-Scientist,* (Third Edition). La Salle, Indiana: Open Court, 1970.

Schoeps, Julius H., and Ludger Heid, eds. *Juden in Deutschland von der Aufklärung bis zuyr Gegenwart.* Munich: Piper Verlag, 1994.

Scholem, Gershom. *On Jews and Judaism in Crisis.* New York: Schocken Books, 1976.

Schrader, Bärbel, and Jürgen Schebera. *The Golden Twenties.* New Haven: Yale University Press, 1988.

Schuster, Peter-Klaus. *George Grosz: Berlin–New York*. National Galerie, Berlin 1994. (Catalogue of the exhibit at the Neue Nationalgalerie, Berlin, December 21, 1994–April 17, 1995.)

Schwartz, Joseph, and Michael McGuinness. *Einstein for Beginners.* New York: Pantheon Books, 1979.

Seelig, Carl. *Albert Einstein: A Documentary Biography,* translated by Mervyn Savill. London: Staples Press, Ltd., 1956.

Segel, Binjamin. *A Lie and a Libel*. Lincoln: University of Nebraska Press, 1995.

Stern, Fritz. *Dreams and Delusions.* New York: Alfred A. Knopf, 1987.

———. *Einstein's German World*. Princeton: Princeton University Press, 1999.

Tatar, Maria. *Lustmord*. Princeton: Princeton University Press, 1995.

Taylor, A. J. P. *The Struggle for Mastery in Europe.* Oxford: Oxford University Press, 1957.

Taylor, Edward, and John Wheeler. *Spacetime Physics.* San Francisco: W. H. Freeman and Company, 1963.

Taylor, Ronald. *Literature and Society in Germany 1918–1945*. Totawa, New Jersey: Barnes & Noble Books, 1980.

Thorne, Kip. *Black Holes and Time Warps.* New York: W. W. Norton & Company, 1994.

Traverso, Enzo. *The Jews and Germany,* translated by Daniel Weissbort. Lincoln: University of Nebraska Press, 1995.

Treitschke, Heinrich von. *Politics.* New York: The Macmillan Company, 1916.

———. *Origins of Prussianism*. New York: Howard Fertig, 1969.

———. *History of Germany in the Nineteenth Century,* edited and with an introduction by Gordon Craig. Chicago: Chicago University Press, 1975.

Tuchman, Barbara. *The Guns of August*. New York: Dell Publishing, 1962.

———. *The Proud Tower.* New York: The Macmillan Company, 1966.

Vallentin, Antonina. *The Drama of Albert Einstein*. Garden City, N.Y.: Doubleday & Co., 1954.

Vogel, Rolf. *Ein Stück von uns: Deutsch Juden in deutschen Armeen, 1813–1976*. Mainz: v. Hase und Koehler, 1977.

Wasserman, Jakob. *Mein Weg als Deutscher und Jude.* Berlin: Berlin Nishen, 1987.

Wavell, A. P. *Other Men's Flowers.* London: Pimlico, 1992.

Wedd, A. F. *German Students' War Letters,* translated by Dr. Philip Witkop. London: Methuen, 1929.

Weinstein, Joan. *The End of Expressionism*. Chicago: The University of Chicago Press, 1990.

Whalen, Robert Weldon. *Bitter Wounds.* Ithaca: Cornell University Press, 1984.

Whitehead, Alfred North. *Science in the Modern World*. New York: The Macmillan Company, 1925.

Whitford, Frank. *The Berlin of George Grosz*. New Haven: Yale University Press, 1997.

Whitrow, G. J., ed. *Einstein: The Man and His Achievement*. New York: Dover Publications, 1967.

Willet, John. *Art and Politics in the Weimar Period*. New York: Da Capo Press, 1996.

Wilson, Edmund. *To the Finland Station*. New York: The Noonday Press/Farrar, Straus & Giroux, 1972.

Wohl, Robert. *The Generation of 1914*. Cambridge: Harvard University Press, 1979.

Wolff, Leon. *In Flanders Fields.* New York: The Viking Press, 1958.

Woods, William Seaver. *Colossal Blunders of the War.* New York: The Macmillan Company, 1930.

Woolf, Harry, ed. *Some Strangeness in the Proportion*. Reading, Mass.: Addison Wesley, 1980.

Zackheim, Michele. *Einstein's Daughter.* New York: Riverhead Books, 1999.

Zechlin, Egmont. *Die deutsche Politik und die Juden im ersten Weltkrieg.* Göttingen: Vandenhoeck & Ruprecht, 1969.

PHOTO ACKNOWLEDGMENTS

Insert One

1. Einstein with Hans Albert: Albert Einstein™ Licensed by The Hebrew University of Jerusalem, Represented by The Roger Richman Agency, Inc., www.albert-einstein.net.
2. Mileva Maric in 1899: Schweizeriche Landesbibliothek.
3. Prewar Berlin street scene: Foto: Landesarchiv Berlin.
4. Berlin train station: Foto: Landesarchiv Berlin.
5. First Solvay Conference: Photograhie Benjamin Couprie, Institut International de Physique Solvay, courtesy AIP Emilio Segrè Visual Archives.
6. Einstein and Fritz Haber: courtesy AIP Emilio Segrè Visual Archives.
7. Hitler in the crowd in Munich in 1914: Bayarische Staats Bibliothek.
8. Kaiser Wilhelm II: Ullsteinbild.
9. Woman pinning flower on recruit: Ullsteinbild.
10. First casualty lists: Ullsteinbild.
11. Circus elephants hauling coal: Ullsteinbild.
12: Edith Cavell propaganda poster: Robert Hunt Library.
13. Painting of German soldiers charging: Bildarchiv Preussicher Kulturbesitz.
14. Hitler and two other dispatch messengers: Ullsteinbild.
15. Hindenberg statue: Ullsteinbild.
16. Model trench: Robert Hunt Library.
17. Destroyed German trench: Trustees of the Imperial War Museum, London, Q 4255.
18. Passchendaele battlefield: Imperial War Museum, London, CO 2264.
19. Gas attack victims: Trustees of the Imperial War Museum, London, reference number: Q 11586.
20. Spartacists firing behind newsprint rolls: Ullsteinbild.
21. Karl Liebknecht's corpse: Ullsteinbild.
22. Einstein with Elsa Einstein in 1921: Library of Congress, courtesy AIP Emilio Segrè Visual Archives.
23. Einstein letter to George Ellery Hale: Observatories of the Carnegie Institutio of Washington/Huntington Library.
24. Eclipse of 1922: photo © UC Regents Lick Observatory, courtesy of the Mary Lea Shane Archives of the Lick, Observatory, University of California, Santa Cruz.
25. *Berliner Illustrirte Zeitung* Einstein cover: Ullsteinbild.
26. Erich Mendelsohn's Einstein Tower: Bildarchiv Preussicher Kulturbesitz.
27. Einstein on parade in New York: Brown Brothers, Sterling, PA.
28. Einstein and Elsa Einstein in Japan: Albert Einstein™ Licensed by The Hebrew

University of Jerusalem, Represented by The Roger Richman Agency, Inc., www.albert-einstein.net.

29. Harry Kessler portrait by Edvard Munch: Bildarchiv Preussicher Kulturbesitz.
30. Einstein lecturing in Paris: Albert Einstein™ Licensed by The Hebrew University of Jerusalem, Represented by The Roger Richman Agency, Inc., *www.albert-einstein.net.*

Insert Two:

31. Walther Rathenau: Ullsteinbild.
32. Soldier guarding paper money: Ullsteinbild.
33. Children playing with paper money blocks: Ullsteinbild.
34. Hitler, Ludendorff and Beer Hall Putsch defendents: Bayarische Staats Bibliothek.
35. Two children in a slum room: AKG London.
36. Josephine Baker: Ullsteinbild.
37. Anita Berber: Ullsteinbild.
38. Mies van der Rohe's Liebknecht/Luxemburg memorial: Ullsteinbild.
39. Haller Girls: Bildarchiv Preussicher Kulturbesitz.
40. El Dorado nightclub: Bildarchiv Preussicher Kulturbesitz.
41. Wandervögel group: Bildarchiv Preussicher Kulturbesitz.
42. Nudist fitness club: Foto: Landesarchiv Berlin.
43. Einstein seated in his turret study: Bildarchiv Preussicher Kulturbesitz.
44. Fifth Solvay Conference: Photographie Benjamin Couprie, Institut International de Physique Solvay, courtesy AIP Emilio Segrè Visual Archives.
45. Einstein with four Nobel laureates: Physicalische-Technische Bundesanstalt, courtesy AIP Emilio Segrè Visual Archives.
46. Einstein and Niels Bohr: Photograph by Paul Ehrenfest, courtesy AIP Emilio Segrè Visual Archives.
47. Adolf Hitler and Joseph Goebbels in front of a crowd of supporters: United States Holocaust Memorial Museum.
48. National Socialist youth group: Foto: Landesarchiv Berlin.
49. Max Planck and Einstein receiving Planck medals: AIP Emilio Segrè Visual Archives, Fritz Reiche Collection.
50. Charlie Chaplin, Einstein and Elsa Einstein: Ullsteinbild.
51. Einstein in feather headdress with Elsa and Hopis: Photo by El Tovar\Studio, courtesy Museum of New Mexico, negative number 38193.
52. Hitler campaign poster: Bildarchiv Preussicher Kulturbesitz.
53. Anti-Semitic cartoon: Library of Congress, courtesy AIP Emilio Segrè Visual Archives.
54. Hitler and Hindenburg in car: AKG London.
55. Einstein addressing a rally in London: Brown Brothers, Sterling, PA.
56. Albert Einstein portrait: AIP Emilio Segrè Visual Archives.

ACKNOWLEDGMENTS

This book has had an unusually long gestation: nine years in all. In that time it and I have benefited from the aid of people who gave enormously generously of their time and brains. First among them is my editor, Ann Harris, who is a writer's dream. Her meticulous, thoughtful and elegant work became an advanced course in the craft of writing. Along the way, she has made the book far better than it otherwise would have been, while remaining gentle, kind, and implacably firm.

My agents have also been invaluable. Sallie Gouverneur was one of this project's earliest partisans; Doe Coover has managed the business of producing a book efficiently and smoothly. Abby Zidle, Ann's assistant at Bantam, has been a model of cheerful efficiency.

This book could not have been begun without the aid of my two research assistants. In Berlin, Hania Siebenpfeiffer read for me the German originals of thousands of pages of newspapers, documents, and other historical sources. In Boston, Thomas Bahr guided me through letters and primary documents, particularly those concerned with German experience during the First World War.

I cannot begin to adequately express my thanks to the scholars who have helped me make sense of both Einstein and Berlin. Robert Schulmann and Martin Klein, both editors with the Einstein Papers Project, gave me invaluable early help. Harvard's Gerald Holton also gave me early encouragement and advice. Abraham Pais was doubly generous, both for the guidance he provided and his exceptional, technical Einstein biography, *Subtle Is the Lord*. He died in 2000 and he is missed. I have had very useful conversations over several years with Matthew

Strassler of the University of Washington. Clifford Will of Washington University in St. Louis, Michael Salamon of NASA's Office of Space Sciences, Joshua Ehrlich of the University of Washington, and Daniel Kennefick of Caltech and the Einstein Papers Project all read portions of the manuscript. The errors that remain are all mine. Ze'ev Rosencranz, curator of the Einstein Archive at the Hebrew University in Jerusalem, and his assistant, Chaya Becker, have both been helpful in guiding me through the thicket of Einstein's literary estate.

The work of several writers was of very great help. Kip Thorne's *Black Holes and Time Warps* is an excellent introduction to Einstein's science and is a notable example of how to communicate complicated physics in plain language. Albrecht Fölsing's biography *Albert Einstein* is the best comprehensive portrait that takes Einstein from birth to death. Pais's books provide the best technical guide to Einstein's ideas, all placed within historical context. Alexandra Ritchie's *Faust's Metropolis* is a labor of love and great scholarship, a well-written account of the history of Berlin from its founding to the present. It is hard to choose among Gordon Craig's body of work, but I especially valued *The Politics of the Prussian Army.* Read attentively, this book has implications for the role of the military in civil life that extend far beyond the borders of Germany.

I must also thank several of my colleagues who worked with me on the television biography *Einstein Revealed,* broadcast on PBS's *NOVA* series. Paula Apsell, *NOVA*'s executive producer, helped me hone my grasp of the shape of Einstein's life and work, as did her colleague John Lynch, then editor of the Horizon strand on the BBC. My producing partner Peter Jones and the program editors Stephanie Munroe and Alex Anthony put in more labor on the project than any of us like to recall; their efforts remained invaluable as I worked on this book and tried to make sense of my subject.

Friends and family had the hardest task of all, keeping me sane and on track while providing critical encouragement and argument at every stage of the project. My thanks (in no particular order) go to Gary Taubes, Rob Whittlesey, Noel Buckner, Daniel and Helen Levensen, Ruth Anna Putnam, Lucinda Montefiore, Paul Levenson, David and Juliet Sebag-Montefiore, Diane Asadorian, Michael Franco and Isabel Pinto-Franco, Kelly Roney, Geoffrey Gestetner, Stephen

Glick, Joseph Girton, Merry White, Ben-Zion Gold, Emily and Max Levenson, Simon Sebag-Montefiore, Laurie Monahan, Sean Vickery, Eleanor Powers, Theo Theoharis, and Robert and Ann Seidman.

Special mention, though, to those who put up with the most. My siblings, Richard, Irene, and Leo, and their spouses, Jan, George, and Katherine, have listened to me rave about the man and his city for almost a decade, and have never once begged for mercy. I am especially thankful that they only very rarely asked how the book was going. My mother, who died while I was in the middle of this project, displayed throughout her illness all the reserves of courage, humor, and clarity of purpose that I can only hope I will display if called upon. Her pride and pleasure in all my work is one of my happiest memories. My young son Henry, a late arrival on the scene, has provided more joy than I dreamed possible, along with the necessary moments of comic relief to cut any apparent writing disaster down to size.

Finally, I cannot tally the debt I owe my wife, Katha Seidman. She has been everything from a very attentive critic to the rock on which I leaned whenever the task seemed just too hard. This book would not exist without her.

INDEX